GREAT ATHLETES
BOXING & SOCCER

GREAT ATHLETES
BOXING & SOCCER

Edited by
The Editors of Salem Press

Special Consultant
Rafer Johnson

SALEM PRESS
Pasadena, California Hackensack, New Jersey

Editor in Chief: Dawn P. Dawson
Editorial Director: Christina J. Moose   *Photo Editor:* Cynthia Breslin Beres
Managing Editor: R. Kent Rasmussen   *Acquisitions Editor:* Mark Rehn
Manuscript Editor: Christopher Rager   *Page Design and Layout:* James Hutson
Research Supervisor: Jeffry Jensen   *Additional Layout:* Frank Montaño and Mary Overell
Production Editor: Andrea Miller   *Editorial Assistant:* Brett Weisberg

Cover photos: Jeff Mitchell/Reuters/Landov; Adam Davy/PA Photos/Landov

Copyright © 1992, 1994, 2002, 2010, by Salem Press

All rights in this book are reserved. No part of this work may be used or reproduced in any manner whatsoever or transmitted in any form or by any means, electronic or mechanical, including photocopy, recording, or any information storage and retrieval system, without written permission from the copyright owner except in the case of brief quotations embodied in critical articles and reviews or in the copying of images deemed to be freely licensed or in the public domain. For information, address the publisher, Salem Press, P.O. Box 50062, Pasadena, California 91115.

∞ The paper used in these volumes conforms to the American National Standard for Permanence of Paper for Printed Library Materials, Z39.48-1992 (R1997).

Library of Congress Cataloging-in-Publication Data

Great athletes / edited by The Editors of Salem Press ; special consultant Rafer Johnson.
    p. cm.
    Includes bibliographical references and index.
    ISBN 978-1-58765-473-2 (set : alk. paper) — ISBN 978-1-58765-481-7 (boxing, soccer : alk. paper)
1. Athletes—Biography—Dictionaries. I. Johnson, Rafer, 1935-   II. Salem Press.
    GV697.A1G68 2009
    796.0922—dc22
    [B]

2009021905

First Printing

PRINTED IN THE UNITED STATES OF AMERICA

Contents

Publisher's Note vii
Introduction xi
Contributors xvii

Boxing

Laila Ali 3
Muhammad Ali 6
Alexis Arguello 10
Henry Armstrong 13
Max Baer 16
Riddick Bowe 19
Julio César Chávez 22
Billy Conn 26
Oscar De La Hoya 29
Jack Dempsey 33
Roberto Durán 36
Eddie Eagan 40
George Foreman 42
Bob Foster 45
Joe Frazier 48
Rocky Graziano 51
Marvin Hagler 53
Thomas Hearns 56
Larry Holmes 59
Evander Holyfield 62
Bernard Hopkins 66
Jack Johnson 69
Roy Jones, Jr. 72
Stanley Ketchel 75
Vitali and Vladimir Klitschko 78
Jake LaMotta 81
Sam Langford 84
Benny Leonard 86
Sugar Ray Leonard 88
Lennox Lewis 91
Sonny Liston 94
Joe Louis 96
Rocky Marciano 99
Christy Martin 102
Floyd Mayweather, Jr. 105
Archie Moore 108
Shane Mosley 111
Manny Pacquiao 114
László Papp 117
Floyd Patterson 119
Willie Pep 122
Sugar Ray Robinson 124
Sandy Saddler 127
Félix Savón 129
Max Schmeling 132
Earnie Shavers 135
Teófilo Stevenson 137
Dick Tiger 140
Félix Trinidad 143
Gene Tunney 146
Mike Tyson 149

Soccer

Freddy Adu 155
Michelle Akers 157
Roberto Baggio 160
Alan Ball 162
Gordon Banks 165
Franz Beckenbauer 167
David Beckham 170
George Best 173
Danny Blanchflower 175
Billy Bremner 178
Fabio Cannavaro 180
Eric Cantona 182
Roberto Carlos 184
Bobby Charlton 186
Jack Charlton 189
Brandi Chastain 191
Johan Cruyff 194
Landon Donovan 197
Eusébio 199
Julie Foudy 201
Garrincha 203
Steven Gerrard 205
Johnny Giles 208
Mia Hamm 210
April Heinrichs 213
Thierry Henry 215
Geoff Hurst 217
Pat Jennings 219
Cobi Jones 221
Kevin Keegan 224

Alexi Lalas	227
Denis Law	229
Kristine Lilly	231
Gary Lineker	234
Diego Maradona	237
Marta	240
Stanley Matthews	242
Bobby Moore	244
Gerd Müller	247
Michael Owen	249
Cindy Parlow	252
Pelé	254
Michel Platini	257
Ferenc Puskás	260
Tab Ramos	262
Alf Ramsey	265
Rivaldo	268
Romário	271
Ronaldinho	273
Ronaldo	275
Kyle Rote, Jr.	278
Karl-Heinz Rummenigge	280
Hugo Sánchez	282
Briana Scurry	285
Peter Shilton	288
Sissi	290
Alfredo di Stefano	293
Sun Wen	295
Marco van Basten	297
Abby Wambach	299
Billy Wright	301
Eric Wynalda	303
Lev Yashin	305
Zinedine Zidane	307
Steve Zungul	310
Bibliography	315
Boxing and Soccer Resources on the World Wide Web	318
Glossary	321
Boxers Time Line	328
Soccer Players Time Line	330
International Boxing Hall of Fame	335
Ring Magazine Eighty Best Fighters	337
Ring Magazine Fighters of the Year	338
ESPN Fifty Greatest Boxers of All Time	339
Multidivision Boxing Champions	342
International Football Hall of Champions	345
The FIFA 100	346
World Soccer Magazine 100 Greatest Twentieth Century Players	348
FIFA World Players of the Year	350
World Soccer Magazine World Players of the Year	351
Name Index	355
Country Index	356
Boxers by Weight Divisions	358
Soccer Position Index	360

Publisher's Note

Great Athletes: Boxing and Soccer is part of Salem Press's greatly expanded and redesigned *Great Athletes* series, which also includes self-contained volumes on baseball, basketball, football, golf and tennis, Olympic sports, and racing and individual sports. The full 13-volume series presents articles on the lives, sports careers, and unique achievements of 1,470 outstanding competitors and champions in the world of sports. These athletes—many of whom have achieved world renown—represent more than 75 different nations and territories and more than 80 different sports. Their stories are told in succinct, 1,000-word-long profiles accessible in tone and style to readers in grades 7 and up.

The 13 *Great Athletes* volumes, which include a cumulative index volume, are built on the work of three earlier Salem Press publications designed for middle and high school readers—the 20 slender volumes of *The Twentieth Century: Great Athletes* (1992), their 3-volume supplement (1994), and the 8 stouter volumes of *Great Athletes, Revised* (2002). This new 13-volume edition retains articles on every athlete covered in those earlier editions and adds more than 415 entirely new articles—a 40 percent increase—to bring the overall total to 1,470 articles.

The present volume increases the numbers of articles on boxers from 36 to 51 and those on soccer players from 42 to 65, for a combined increase of nearly 50 percent. The content of other articles has been reviewed and updated as necessary, with many articles substantially revised, expanded, or replaced, and the bibliographical citations for virtually all articles have been updated. Information in every article is current up to the beginning of Spring, 2009.

Criteria for Inclusion

In selecting new names to add to *Great Athletes: Boxing and Soccer*, first consideration was given to athletes whose extraordinary achievements have made their names household words in North America. These include such famous boxers as Jake LaMotta (the subject of the 1980 film *Raging Bull*) and Sonny Liston, and such international soccer stars as England's David Beckham, Brazil's Ronaldinho, and France's Zinedine Zidane. Consideration was next given to athletes who during the early twenty-first century appeared destined for future greatness, such as boxers Laila Ali, daughter of the legendary Muhammad Ali, and the Philippines' Manny Pacquiao, and such promising young soccer players as Americans Freddy Adu and Donovan Landon and Brazil's female sensation Marta.

Organization

Each article covers the life and career of a single athlete. Articles are arranged alphabetically by name within separate sections on boxers and soccer players. Every article is accompanied by at least one boxed table, summarizing the career statistics, honors and awards, records, and other milestones that set apart each great athlete. Most articles are also accompanied by photographs of their subjects. Every article also lists up-to-date bibliographical notes under the heading "Additional Sources." These sections list from three to five readily available books and articles containing information pertinent to the athlete and sport covered in the article. Appendixes at the end of the volume contain additional sources in published books and Web sites.

Averaging three pages in length, each article is written in clear language and presented in a uniform, easily readable format. All articles are divided into four subheaded sections that cover the athlete's life and achievements chronologically.

- *Early Life* presents such basic biographical information as vital dates, parentage, siblings, and early education. It also sketches the social milieu in which the athlete grew up and discusses other formative experiences.

- *The Road to Excellence* picks up where the athlete's earliest serious involvement in sports began. This section describes experiences and influences that shaped the subject's athletic prowess and propelled the athlete toward boxing or soccer greatness. These sections also often discuss obstacles—such as poverty, discrimination, and physical disabilities—that many great athletes have had to overcome.

- *The Emerging Champion* traces the subject's advance from the threshold of sports stardom to higher levels of achievement. This section explains the characteristics and circumstances that combined to make the athlete among the best in the world in boxing or soccer.

- *Continuing the Story* tracks the athlete's subsequent career, examining how the athlete may have set new goals and had achievements that inspired others. This section also offers insights into the athlete's life away from sports. Readers will also learn about the innovations and contributions that athletes have made to their sports and, in many cases, to society at large.

- *Summary* recapitulates the subject's story, paying special attention to honors that the subject has won and to the human qualities that have made the athlete special in the world of sports.

Appendixes

At the back of this volume, readers will find 15 appendixes, most of which are entirely new to this edition. The appendixes are arranged under these three headings:

- *Resources* contains a bibliography of recently published books on boxing and soccer and a detailed, categorized listing of sites on the World Wide Web that provide boxing and soccer information. The section also has a Glossary defining most of the specialized boxing and soccer terms used in essays and two Time Lines that list all the boxers and soccer players covered in essays in order of their birth dates.

- *All-Time Great Boxers* has 2 lists of all-time great boxers, a list of International Boxing Hall of Fame members, a list of *Ring* magazine's fighters of the year, and a list of multidivision boxing champions.

- *All-Time Great Soccer Players* contains a list of International Football Hall of Champions members, 2 lists of all-time greats, and 2 player-of-the-year lists.

The *Cumulative Indexes* volume, which accompanies the full *Great Athletes* series, includes every appendix found in this and other volumes on specific sports, *plus* additional appendixes containing information that pertains to all sports. These appendixes include a general bibliography, a comprehensive Web site list, a Time Line integrating the names of all 1,470 athletes in *Great Athletes*, 2 lists of the greatest athletes of the twentieth century, 3 multisport halls of fame, and 10 different athlete-of-the-year awards.

Indexes

Following the Appendixes in *Great Athletes: Boxing and Soccer*, readers will find indexes listing boxers and soccer players by their names and countries and additional indexes listing boxers by their weight divisions and soccer players by their positions. The last two indexes are completely new to this edition of *Great Athletes*. Because some athletes have competed in more than one sport, readers may wish also to consult the *Cumulative Indexes* volume. Its sport, country, and name indexes list all the athletes covered in the full *Great Athletes* series.

Acknowledgments

Once again, Salem Press takes great pleasure in thanking the 383 scholars and experts who wrote and updated the articles making *Great Athletes* possible. Their names can be found at the ends of the articles they have written and in the list of contributors that follows the "Introduction." We also take immense pleasure in again thanking our special consultant, Rafer Johnson, for bringing his unique insights to this project. As an Olympic champion and world record-holder in track and field's demanding decathlon, he has experienced an extraordinarily broad range of physical and mental challenges at the highest levels of competition. Moreover, he has a lifetime of experience working with, and closely observing, athletes at every level—from five-year-old soccer players to Olympic and professional champions. He truly understands what constitutes athletic greatness and what is required to achieve it. For this reason, readers will not want to overlook his "Introduction."

Publisher's Note

Acronyms Used in Articles

Salem's general practice is to use acronyms only after they have been explained within each essay. Because of the frequency with which many terms appear in *Great Athletes: Boxing and Soccer*, that practice is partly suspended for the acronyms listed below:

ESPN Entertainment and Sports Programming Network
FIFA International Federation of Association Football
IBF International Boxing Federation
MLS Major League Soccer
NASL North American Soccer League
WBA World Boxing Association
WBC World Boxing Council
WBF World Boxing Federation
WBO World Boxing Organization

Introduction

Five decades after reaching my own pinnacle of success in sports, I still get a thrill watching other athletes perform. I have competed with and against some of the greatest athletes in the world, watched others up close and from a distance, and read about still others. I admire the accomplishments of all of them, for I know something of what it takes to achieve greatness in sports, and I especially admire those who inspire others.

This revised edition of *Great Athletes* provides a wonderful opportunity for young readers to learn about the finest athletes of the modern era of sports. Reading the stories of the men and women in these pages carries me back to my own youth, when I first began playing games and became interested in sports heroes. Almost all sports interested me, but I gravitated to baseball, basketball, football, and track and field. Eventually, I dedicated most of my young adult years to track and field's decathlon, which I loved because its ten events allowed me to use many different skills.

Throughout those years, one thing remained constant: I wanted to *win*. To do that meant being the best that I could be. I wondered what I could learn from the lives of great athletes. From an early age I enjoyed reading about sports champions and wondered how they did as well as they did. What traits and talents did the greatest of them have? I gradually came to understand that the essence of greatness in sports lies in competition. In fact, the very word *athlete* itself goes back to a Greek word for "competitor." Being competitive is the single most important attribute any athlete can have, but other traits are important, too. Readers may gain insights into the athletes covered in these volumes by considering the ten events of the decathlon as symbols of ten traits that contribute to athletic greatness. All champions have at least a few of these traits; truly great champions have most of them.

Speed and Quickness

Decathlon events are spread over two days, with five events staged on each day. The first event is always the 100-meter dash—one of the most glamorous events in track and field. Men and women—such as Usain Bolt and Florence Griffith-Joyner—who capture its world records are considered the fastest humans on earth. In a race that lasts only a few seconds, speed is everything, and there is no room for mistakes.

Appropriately, speed is the first of the three standards of athletic excellence expressed in the Olympic motto, *Citius, altius, fortius* (faster, higher, stronger). Its importance in racing sports such as cycling, rowing, running, speed skating, swimming, and the triathlon is obvious: Athletes who reach the finish line soonest win; those who arrive later lose. Speed is also important in every sport that requires moving around a lot, such as baseball, basketball, boxing, football, handball, soccer, tennis, volleyball, water polo, and virtually all the events of track and field. The best athletes in these sports are usually fast.

Athletes who lack speed generally make up for it in other kinds of quickness. For example, while running speed has helped make some football quarterbacks—such as Vince Young—great, some quarterbacks who are slow afoot have achieved greatness with other forms of quickness. Joe Namath is an example. Although he was embarrassingly slow on his feet, he read opposing teams' defenses so fast that he could make lightning-quick decisions and release his passes faster than almost any other quarterback who played the game.

As important as speed is, there are a few sports in which it means little. Billiards, bowling, and golf, for example, all permit competitors to take considerable time responding to opponents' moves. Even so, speed can be important where one may least expect it. For example, major chess competitions are clocked, and making moves too slowly can cost players games.

Courage

The decathlon's second event, the long jump, represents one of the purest contests in sports: Competitors simply run up to a mark and jump as far as they can. Each jumper gets several tries, and only the best marks matter. While it sounds simple, it involves critical little things that can go wrong and ruin one's chance of winning. When the great Jesse Owens jumped in the 1936 Olympics in Berlin, for example, he missed his takeoff mark so many times that he risked disqualification. What saved him was the encouragement of a rival German jumper, who advised him to start his jump from well behind the regular takeoff mark. It takes courage to overcome the fear of making mistakes and concentrate on jumping. It also takes courage to overcome the fear of injury.

A great athlete may have abundant courage but rarely need to call upon it. However, most truly great athletes eventually face moments when they would fail if their courage abandoned them. In fact, courage is often what separates being good from being great. True courage should not be confused with the absence of fear, for it is the ability to overcome fear, including the very natural fears of injury and pain. A wonderful example is gymnast Kerri Strug's amazing spirit in the 1996 Olympics. Ignoring the pain of torn ligaments and a serious ankle sprain, she helped the U.S. women win a team gold medal by performing her final vault at great personal risk.

Some sports challenge athletes with real and persistent threats of serious injuries and even death. Among the most dangerous are alpine skiing, auto racing, boxing, football, horse racing, mountaineering, and rodeo—all of which have killed and disabled many fine athletes. No one can achieve greatness in such sports without exceptional courage.

Consider also the courage required to step up to bat against a baseball pitcher who throws hardballs mere inches away from your head at speeds of more than ninety miles an hour. Or, imagine preparing to dive from atop a 10-meter platform, resting only on your toes, with your heels projecting over the edge, knowing that your head will pass within inches of the rock-hard edge of the platform. Greg Louganis once cut his head open on such a dive. After he had his scalp stitched up, he returned to continue diving into a pool of water colored pink by his own blood. He won the competition.

Another kind of courage is needed to perform in the face of adversity that may have nothing to do with sport itself. The best known example of that kind of courage is the immortal Jackie Robinson, who broke the color line in baseball in 1947. As the first African American player in the modern major leagues, Jackie faced criticism, verbal harassment, and even physical abuse almost everywhere he played. He not only persevered but also had a career that would have been regarded as exceptional even if his color had never been an issue.

Strength

The shot put, the decathlon's third event, requires many special traits, but the most obvious is strength. The metal ball male shot putters heave weighs 16 pounds—more than an average bowling ball. Agility, balance, and speed are all important to the event, but together they can accomplish nothing without great strength. Strength is also the third standard expressed in the Olympic motto, *Citius, altius, fortius.*

Strength is especially valuable in sports that put competitors in direct physical contact with each other—sports such as basketball, boxing, football, and wrestling. Whenever athletes push and pull against each other, the stronger generally prevail. Strength is also crucial in sports requiring lifting, pulling, pushing, paddling, or propelling objects, or controlling vehicles or animals. Such sports include auto racing, baseball and softball, bodybuilding and weightlifting, canoeing and kayaking, golf, horse racing, rowing, and all track and field throwing events.

One sport in which the role of strength has never been underestimated is wrestling. One of the most impressive demonstrations of strength in the sport occurred at the 2000 Olympic Games at Sydney when Rulon Gardner, in a performance of a lifetime, defeated former Olympic champion Aleksandr Karelin in the super-heavyweight class of Greco-Roman wrestling.

Visualization

Visualization is the ability to see what one needs to do before actually doing it. Perhaps no sport better exemplifies its importance than the high jump—the decathlon's fourth event. In contrast to the long jump and throwing events—in which competitors strive to maximize distance in every effort, the high jump (like the pole vault) sets a bar at a fixed height that competitors must clear. Before jumping, they take time to study the bar and visualize what they must do to clear it. If the bar is set at 7 feet, a jump of 6 feet 11¾ inches fails; a jump of 8 feet succeeds, but counts only for 7 feet. To conserve strength for later jumps, jumpers must carefully calculate how much effort to exert at each height, and to do this, they must be able to visualize.

Great baseball and softball batters also visualize well. Before pitches even reach the plate, batters see the balls coming and visualize their bats hitting them. Likewise, great golfers see their balls landing on the greens before they even swing. Soccer players, such as Ronaldo, see the balls going into the goal before they even kick them. Billiard players, such as Jeanette Lee, see all the balls moving on the table before they even touch the cue balls. Bowlers, like Lisa Wagner, see the pins tumbling down before they release their balls.

Visualization is especially important to shooters, such as Lones Wigger, and archers, such as Denise Parker and Jay Barrs, who know exactly what their targets look like, as well as the spots from where they will fire, before they even take aim. In contrast to most other sports, they can practice in conditions almost identical to those in which they compete. However, the athletes against whom they compete have the same advantage, so the edge usually goes to those who visualize better.

Players in games such as basketball, hockey, soccer, and water polo fire upon fixed targets from constantly changing positions—often in the face of opponents doing everything they can to make them miss. Nevertheless, visualization is important to them as well. In basketball, players are said to be in a "groove," or a "zone," when they visualize shots so well they seem unable to miss. Kobe Bryant and Lisa Leslie are among the greatest visualizers in their sport, just as Babe Ruth, Hank Aaron, and Albert Pujols have been great at visualizing home runs in baseball. In tennis, I always admired Arthur Ashe's knack for planning matches in his mind, then systematically dismantling his opponents.

At another level, boxer Muhammad Ali was great at visualizing his entire future. Big, strong, and quick and able to move with the best of them, he had it all. I had the great pleasure of touring college campuses with him after we both won gold medals at the Rome Olympics in 1960. Muhammad (then known as Cassius Clay) had visualized his Olympic victory before it happened, and when I first knew him he was already reciting poetry and predicting what the future held for him. He saw it all in advance and called every move—something he became famous for later, when he taunted opponents by predicting the rounds in which he would knock them out.

Determination and Resilience

The final event of the first day of decathlon competition is the 400-meter run. Almost exactly a quarter mile, this race stands at the point that divides sprints from middle-distances. Should runners go all out, as in a sprint, or pace themselves, as middle-distance runners do? Coming as it does, as the last event of the exhausting first day of decathlon competition, the 400-meter race tests the mettle of decathletes by extracting one last great effort from them before they can rest up for the next day's grueling events. How they choose to run the race has to do with how determined they are to win the entire decathlon.

Every great athlete who wants to be a champion must have the determination to do whatever it takes to achieve that goal. Even so, determination alone is not enough. This was proven dramatically when basketball's Michael Jordan—whom journalists later voted the greatest athlete of the twentieth century—quit basketball in 1994 to fulfill his lifelong dream to play professional baseball. Despite working hard, he spent a frustrating season and a half in the minor leagues and merely proved two things: that determination alone cannot guarantee success, and that baseball is a more difficult sport than many people had realized.

Resilience, an extension of determination, is the ability to overcome adversity, or apparently hopeless situations, and to bounce back from outright defeat. Some might argue that no one can be greater than an athlete who never loses; however, athletes who continually win are never required to change what they do or do any soul searching. By contrast, athletes who lose must examine themselves closely and consider making changes. I have always felt that true greatness in sports is exemplified by the ability to come back from defeat, as heavyweight boxer Floyd Patterson did after losing his world title to Ingemar Johansson in a humiliating 3-round knockout in 1959. Only those athletes who face adversity and defeat can prove they have resilience.

Among athletes who have impressed me the most with their determination and resilience is speed skater Eric Heiden, who was not only the first American to win world speed-skating championships, but the first speed skater ever to win all five events in the Winter Olympics. Another amazingly determined athlete is Jim Abbott, who refused to allow the fact that he was born with only one hand stop him from becoming a Major League Baseball pitcher—one who even pitched a no-hit game. Who could not admire Bo Jackson? An all-star in both professional football and Major League Baseball, he suffered what appeared to be a career-ending football injury. After undergoing hip-joint replacement surgery, he defied all logic by returning to play several more seasons of baseball. Cyclist Lance Armstrong also falls into this category. He won multiple Tour de France championships after recovering from cancer.

Execution

Day two of the decathlon opens with the technically challenging 110-meter high hurdles. A brutally demanding event, it requires speed, leaping ability, and perfect timing. In short, it is an event that requires careful execution—the ability to perform precisely when it matters. Sports differ greatly in the precision of execution they demand. Getting off great throws in the discus, shot put, and javelin, for example, requires superb execution, but the direction in which the objects go is not critical. By contrast, archers, shooters, and golfers must hit precise targets. Some sports not only demand that execution be precise but also that it be repeated. A baseball pitcher who throws two perfect strikes fails if the opposing batter hits the third pitch over the fence. Likewise, a quarterback who leads his team down the field with five consecutive perfect passes fails if his next pass is intercepted.

Consider the differences between the kind of execution demanded by diving and pole vaulting. Divers lose points if their toes are not straight the moment they enter the water. By contrast, pole vaulters can land any way they want, so long as they clear the bar. Moreover, a diver gets only one chance on each dive, while pole vaulters get three chances at each height they attempt—and they can even skip certain heights to save energy for later jumps at greater heights. On the other hand, a diver who executes a dive badly will merely get a poor score, while a pole vaulter who misses too many jumps will get no score at all—which is exactly what happened to decathlete Dan O'Brien in the 1992 U.S. Olympic Trials. Although Dan was the world's top decathlete at that time, his failure to clear a height in the pole vault kept him off the Olympic team. (To his credit, he came back to win a gold medal in 1996.)

Figure skating and gymnastics are other sports that measure execution with a microscope. In gymnastics, the standard of perfection is a score of ten—which was first achieved in the Olympics by Nadia Comăneci in 1976. However, scores in those sports are not based on objective measures but on the evaluations of judges, whose own standards can and do change. By contrast, archery, shooting, and bowling are unusual in being sports that offer objective standards of perfection. In bowling, that standard is the 300 points awarded to players who bowl all strikes.

Among all athletes noted for their execution, one in particular stands out in my estimation: golf's Tiger Woods. After Tiger had played professionally for only a few years, he established himself as one of the greatest golfers ever. He has beaten the best that golf has had to offer by record margins in major competitions, and wherever he plays, he is the favorite to win. Most impressive is his seeming ability to do whatever he needs to win, regardless of the situation. Few athletes in any sport, or in any era, have come close to matching Tiger's versatile and consistent execution.

Focus

After the high hurdles, the decathlon's discus event is a comparative relief. Nevertheless, it presents its own special demands, one of which is focus—the ability to maintain uninterrupted concentration. Like shot putters, discus throwers work within a tiny circle, within which they must concentrate all their attention and all their energy into throwing the heavy disk as far as they can.

Not surprisingly, one of the greatest discus throwers in history, Al Oerter, was also one of the greatest examples of focus in sports. His four gold medals between 1956 and 1968 made him the first track and field athlete in Olympic history to win any event four times in a row. In addition to beating out the best discus throwers in the world four consecutive times, he improved his own performance at each Olympiad and even won with a serious rib injury in 1964. Eight years after retiring from competition, he returned at age forty to throw the discus farther than ever and earn a spot as an alternate on the 1980 U.S. Olympic team.

Important in all sports, focus is especially important in those in which a single lapse in concentration may result in instant defeat. In boxing, a knockout can suddenly end a bout. Focus may be even more crucial in wrestling. Wrestlers grapple each other continuously, probing for openings that will allow them to pin their opponents. Few sports match wrestling in nonstop intensity; a single split-second lapse on the part of a wrestler can spell disaster. Great wrestlers, such as Cael Sanderson and Aleksandr Karelin, must therefore rank among the most focused athletes in history.

Balance and Coordination

Of all the decathlon events, the most difficult to perform is the pole vault. Think of what it entails: Holding long skinny poles, vaulters run at full speed down a narrow path toward a pit; then, without breaking stride, push the tips of their poles into a tiny slot, propel their bodies upward, and use the poles to flip themselves over bars more than two or three times their height above the ground, finally to drop down on the opposite side. Success in the pole vault demands many traits, but the most important are balance and coordination. Vaulters use their hands, feet, and bodies, all at the same time, and do everything at breakneck speed, with almost no margin for error. There are no uncoordinated champion pole vaulters.

Despite its difficulty, pole vaulting is an event in which some decathletes have performed especially well—perhaps because they, as a group, have versatile skills. I have long taken pride in the fact that my close friend, college teammate, and Olympic rival, C. K. Yang, once set a world record in the pole vault during a decathlon. C. K.'s record was all the more impressive because he achieved it midway through the second day of an intense competition. Imagine what balance and coordination he must have had to propel his body over the record-breaking height after having subjected it to the wear and tear of seven other events.

I cannot think of any athlete, in any sport, who demonstrated more versatility in coordination and balance than Michael Jordan, who could seemingly score from any spot on the floor, at any time, and under any conditions. Not only did he always have his offensive game together, he was also one of the greatest defensive players in the game. Moreover, his mere presence brought balance to his entire team.

Preparation

The ninth event of the decathlon is the javelin—a throwing event that goes back to ancient times. A more difficult event than it may appear to be, it requires more than its share of special preparation. This may be why we rarely see athletes who compete in both the javelin and other events, though the versatile Babe Didrikson Zaharias was an exception.

Along with determination—to which it is closely allied—preparation is a vital trait of great athletes, especially in modern competition. It is no longer possible for even the greatest natural athletes to win against top competition without extensive preparation, which means practice, training for strength and stamina, proper diet and rest, and studying opponents diligently. Football players, especially quarterbacks and defensive backs, spend hours before every game studying films of opponents.

I was fortunate to grow up with an athlete who exemplifies preparation: my younger brother, Jimmy Johnson, who would become defensive back for the San Francisco 49ers for seventeen years and later be elected to the Pro Football Hall of Fame. Every week, Jimmy had to face a completely different set of pass receivers, but he was always ready because he studied their moves and trained himself to run backward fast enough to keep offenses in front of him so he could see every move they made. Coach Tom Landry of the Dallas Cowboys once told me that he always had the Cowboys attack on the side opposite from Jimmy.

Another exceptionally well prepared athlete was Magic Johnson, the great Lakers basketball guard, who played every position on the floor in more than one game. During his rookie season he had one of the greatest performances in playoff history during the NBA Finals. When a health problem prevented the Lakers' great center, Kareem Abdul-Jabbar, from playing in the sixth game against Philadelphia, Magic stunned everyone by filling in for him at center and scoring 44 points. He went on to become one of the great point guards in basketball history because he always knew where every player on the court should be at every moment.

Stamina

If there is one event that most decathletes dread, it is the grueling 1,500-meter race that concludes the two-day competition. While C. K. Yang once set a world-record in the pole vault during a decathlon, no decathlete has ever come close to anything even resembling a world-class mark in the 1,500 meters. On the other hand, it is probable that no world-class middle-distance runner has ever run a 1,500-meter race immediately after competing in nine other events. To win a decathlon, the trick is not to come in first in this final race, but simply to survive it. For decathletes, it is not so much a race as a test of stamina.

When I competed in the decathlon in the Rome Olympics of 1960, I had to go head-to-head against my friend C. K. Yang through nine events, all the while knowing that the gold medal would be decided in the last event—the 1,500 meters. C. K. was one of the toughest and most durable athletes I have ever known, and I realized I could not beat him in that race. However, after the javelin, I led by enough points so that all I had to do was stay close to him. I managed to do it and win the gold medal, but running that race was not an experience I would care to repeat.

Stamina is not really a skill, but a measure of the strength to withstand or overcome exhaustion. Rare is the sport that does not demand some stamina. Stamina can be measured in a single performance—such as a long-distance race—in a tournament, or in the course of a long season.

The classic models of stamina are marathon runners, whose 26-plus-mile race keeps them moving continuously for more than two hours. Soccer is one of the most demanding of stamina among team sports. Its players move almost constantly and may run as far as 5 miles in a 90-minute game that allows few substitutions. Basketball players run nearly as much as soccer players, but their games are shorter and allow more substitutions and rest periods. However, the sport can be even more tiring than soccer because its teams play more frequently and play more games overall. Baseball players provide yet another contrast. They spend a great deal of time during their games sitting on the bench, and when they are on the field, players other than the pitcher and catcher rarely need to exert themselves more than a few seconds at a time. However, their season has the most games of all, and their constant travel is draining. All these sports and others demand great stamina from their players, and their greatest players are usually those who hold up the best.

To most people, chess seems like a physically undemanding game. However, its greatest players must be in top physical condition to withstand the unrelenting mental pressure of tournament and match competitions, which can last for weeks. Bobby Fisher, one of the game's greatest—and most eccentric—champions, exercised heavily when he competed in order to stay in shape. Even sprinters who spend only 10 or 11 seconds on the track in each race, need stamina. In order to reach the finals of major competitions, they must endure the physical and mental strains of several days of preliminary heats.

In reducing what makes athletes great to just ten traits, I realize that I have oversimplified things, but that matters little, as my purpose here is merely to introduce readers to what makes the athletes in these volumes great. Within these pages you will find stories exemplifying many other traits, and that is good, as among the things that make athletes endlessly fascinating are their diversity and complexity.

Rafer Johnson

Contributors

Randy L. Abbott
University of Evansville

Tony Abbott
Trumbull, Connecticut

Michael Adams
City College of New York Graduate Center

Patrick Adcock
Henderson State University

Amy Adelstein
Toluca Lake, California

Richard Adler
University of Michigan, Dearborn

Paul C. Alexander II
Southern Illinois University

Elizabeth Jeanne Alford
Southern Illinois University, Carbondale

Eleanor B. Amico
Whitewater, Wisconsin

Ronald L. Ammons
University of Findlay

Earl Andresen
University of Texas, Arlington

David L. Andrews
University of Illinois, Urbana-Champaign

Frank Ardolino
University of Hawaii

Vikki M. Armstrong
Fayetteville State University

Bryan Aubrey
Maharishi International University

Patti Auer
United States Gymnastics Federation

Philip Bader
Pasadena, California

Sylvia P. Baeza
Applied Ballet Theater

Amanda J. Bahr-Evola
Southern Illinois University, Edwardsville

Alan Bairner
Loughborough University

JoAnn Balingit
University of Delaware

Susan J. Bandy
United States International University

Jessie F. Banks
University of Southern Colorado

Linda Bannister
Loyola Marymount University

C. Robert Barnett
Marshall University

David Barratt
Montreat College

Maryanne Barsotti
Warren, Michigan

Bijan Bayne
Association for Professional Basketball Research

Barbara C. Beattie
Sarasota, Florida

Suzanne M. Beaudet
University of Maine, Presque Isle

Joseph Beerman
Borough of Manhattan Community College, CUNY

Keith J. Bell
Western Carolina University

Stephen T. Bell
Independent Scholar

Alvin K. Benson
Utah Valley University

Chuck Berg
University of Kansas

S. Carol Berg
College of St. Benedict

Milton Berman
University of Rochester

Terry D. Bilhartz
Sam Houston State University

Cynthia A. Bily
Adrian College

Nicholas Birns
New School University

Joe Blankenbaker
Georgia Southern University

Carol Blassingame
Texas A&M University

Elaine M. Blinde
Southern Illinois University, Carbondale

Harold R. Blythe, Jr.
Eastern Kentucky University

Jo-Ellen Lipman Boon
Independent Scholar

Trevor D. Bopp
Texas A&M University

Stephen Borelli
USA Today

John Boyd
Appalachian State University

Great Athletes: Boxing and Soccer

Marlene Bradford
Texas A&M University

Michael R. Bradley
Motlow College

Carmi Brandis
Fort Collins, Colorado

Kevin L. Brennan
Ouachita Baptist University

Matt Brillinger
Carleton University

John A. Britton
Francis Marion University

Norbert Brockman
St. Mary's University of San Antonio

Howard Bromberg
University of Michigan Law School

Valerie Brooke
Riverside Community College

Dana D. Brooks
West Virginia University

Alan Brown
Livingston University

Valerie Brown
Northwest Kansas Educational Service Center

Thomas W. Buchanan
Ancilla Domini College

Fred Buchstein
John Carroll University

David Buehrer
Valdosta State University

Cathy M. Buell
San Jose State University

Michael H. Burchett
Limestone College

Edmund J. Campion
University of Tennessee, Knoxville

Peter Carino
Indiana State University

Lewis H. Carlson
Western Michigan University

Russell N. Carney
Missouri State University

Bob Carroll
Professional Football Researchers Association

Culley C. Carson
University of North Carolina

Craig Causer
Pompton Lakes, New Jersey

David Chapman
North American Society of Sports Historians

Paul J. Chara, Jr.
Northwestern College

Frederick B. Chary
Indiana University Northwest

Jerry E. Clark
Creighton University

Rhonda L. Clements
Hofstra University

Douglas Clouatre
MidPlains Community College

Kathryn A. Cochran
University of Kansas

Susan Coleman
West Texas A&M University

Caroline Collins
Quincy University

Brett Conway
Namseoul University

Carol Cooper
University of Northern Iowa

Richard Hauer Costa
Texas A&M University

Michael Coulter
Grove City College

David A. Crain
South Dakota State University

Louise Crain
South Dakota State University

Scott A. G. M. Crawford
Eastern Illinois University

Lee B. Croft
Arizona State University

Ronald L. Crosbie
Marshall University

Thomas S. Cross
Texas A&M University

Brian Culp
Indiana University

Michael D. Cummings, Jr.
Madonna University

Joanna Davenport
Auburn University

Kathy Davis
North Carolina State University

Mary Virginia Davis
California State University, Sacramento

Buck Dawson
International Swimming Hall of Fame

Dawn P. Dawson
Pasadena, California

Margaret Debicki
Los Angeles, California

Bill Delaney
San Diego, California

Paul Dellinger
Wytheville, Virginia

Andy DeRoche
Front Range Community College

James I. Deutsch
Smithsonian Institution

Contributors

Joseph Dewey
University of Pittsburgh, Johnstown

M. Casey Diana
Arizona State University

Randy J. Dietz
South Carolina State University

Jonathan E. Dinneen
VeriSign, Inc.

Marcia B. Dinneen
Bridgewater State College

Dennis M. Docheff
Whitworth College

Cecilia Donohue
Madonna University

Pamela D. Doughty
Texas A&M University

Thomas Drucker
University of Wisconsin, Whitewater

Jill Dupont
University of Chicago

William G. Durick
Blue Valley School District

W. P. Edelstein
Los Angeles, California

Bruce L. Edwards
Bowling Green State University

William U. Eiland
University of Georgia

Henry A. Eisenhart
University of Oklahoma

Kenneth Ellingwood
Los Angeles, California

Julie Elliott
Indiana University South Bend

Mark R. Ellis
University of Nebraska, Kearney

Robert P. Ellis
Northboro, Massachusetts

Don Emmons
Glendale News-Press

Robert T. Epling
North American Society of Sports Historians

Thomas L. Erskine
Salisbury University

Steven G. Estes
California State University, Fullerton

Don Evans
The College of New Jersey

Jack Ewing
Boise, Idaho

Kevin Eyster
Madonna University

Norman B. Ferris
Middle Tennessee State University

John W. Fiero
University of Southwestern Louisiana

Paul Finkelman
Brooklyn Law School

Paul Finnicum
Arkansas State University

Jane Brodsky Fitzpatrick
Graduate Center, City University of New York

Michael J. Fratzke
Indiana Wesleyan University

Tom Frazier
Cumberland College

A. Bruce Frederick
International Gymnastics Hall of Fame and Museum

Daniel J. Fuller
Kent State University

Jean C. Fulton
Maharishi International University

Carter Gaddis
Tampa Tribune

Thomas R. Garrett
Society for American Baseball Research

Jan Giel
Drexel University

Daniel R. Gilbert
Moravian College

Duane A. Gill
Mississippi State University

Vincent F. A. Golphin
The Writing Company

Bruce Gordon
Auburn University, Montgomery

Margaret Bozenna Goscilo
University of Pittsburgh

John Gould
Independent Scholar

Karen Gould
Austin, Texas

Lewis L. Gould
University of Texas, Austin

Larry Gragg
University of Missouri, Rolla

Lloyd J. Graybar
Eastern Kentucky University

Wanda Green
University of Northern Iowa

William C. Griffin
Appalachian State University

Irwin Halfond
McKendree College

Jan Hall
Columbus, Ohio

Roger D. Hardaway
Northwestern Oklahoma State University

William Harper
Purdue University

xix

Great Athletes: Boxing and Soccer

Robert Harrison
University of Arkansas Community College

P. Graham Hatcher
Shelton State Community College

Karen Hayslett-McCall
University of Texas, Dallas

Leslie Heaphy
Kent State University, Stark

Bernadette Zbicki Heiney
Lock Haven University of Pennsylvania

Timothy C. Hemmis
Edinboro University of Pennsylvania

Steve Hewitt
University of Birmingham

Carol L. Higy
Methodist College

Randall W. Hines
Susquehanna University

Joseph W. Hinton
Portland, Oregon

Arthur D. Hlavaty
Yonkers, New York

Carl W. Hoagstrom
Ohio Northern University

William H. Hoffman
Fort Meyers, Florida

Kimberley M. Holloway
King College

John R. Holmes
Franciscan University of Steubenville

Joseph Horrigan
Pro Football Hall of Fame

William L. Howard
Chicago State University

Shane L. Hudson
Texas A&M University

Mary Hurd
East Tennessee State University

Raymond Pierre Hylton
Virginia Union University

Shirley Ito
Amateur Athletic Foundation of Los Angeles

Frederick Ivor-Campbell
North American Society of Sports Historians

Shakuntala Jayaswal
University of New Haven

Doresa A. Jennings
Shorter College

Albert C. Jensen
Central Florida Community College

Jeffry Jensen
Altadena, California

Bruce E. Johansen
University of Nebraska, Omaha

Lloyd Johnson
Campbell University

Mary Johnson
University of South Florida

Alexander Jordan
Boston University

David Kasserman
Rowan University

Robert B. Kebric
University of Louisville

Rodney D. Keller
Ricks College

Barbara J. Kelly
University of Delaware

Kimberley H. Kidd
*East Tennessee State University
King College*

Leigh Husband Kimmel
Indianapolis, Indiana

Tom Kinder
Bridgewater College

Joe King
Alameda Journal

Jane Kirkpatrick
Auburn University, Montgomery

Paul M. Klenowski
Thiel College

Darlene A. Kluka
University of Alabama, Birmingham

Lynne Klyse
California State University, Sacramento

Bill Knight
Western Illinois University

Francis M. Kozub
College at Brockport, State University of New York

Lynn C. Kronzek
University of Judaism

Shawn Ladda
Manhattan College

P. Huston Ladner
University of Mississippi

Philip E. Lampe
University of the Incarnate Word

Tom Lansford
University of Southern Mississippi

Eugene Larson
Los Angeles Pierce College

Rustin Larson
Maharishi International University

Kevin R. Lasley
Eastern Illinois University

Mary Lou LeCompte
University of Texas, Austin

Denyse Lemaire
Rowan University

Contributors

Victor Lindsey
East Central University

Alar Lipping
Northern Kentucky University

Janet Long
Pasadena, California

M. Philip Lucas
Cornell College

Leonard K. Lucenko
Montclair State College

R. C. Lutz
Madison Advisors

Robert McClenaghan
Pasadena, California

Arthur F. McClure
Central Missouri State University

Roxanne McDonald
New London, New Hampshire

Alan McDougall
University of Guelph

Mary McElroy
Kansas State University

Thomas D. McGrath
Baylor University

Marcia J. Mackey
Central Michigan University

Michelle C. K. McKowen
New York, New York

John McNamara
Beltsville, Maryland

Joe McPherson
East Tennessee State University

Paul Madden
Hardin Simmons University

Mark J. Madigan
University of Vermont

Philip Magnier
Maharishi International University

H. R. Mahood
Memphis State University

Barry Mann
Atlanta, Georgia

Nancy Farm Mannikko
Centers for Disease Control & Prevention

Robert R. Mathisen
Western Baptist College

Russell Medbery
Colby-Sawyer College

Joella H. Mehrhof
Emporia State University

Julia M. Meyers
Duquesne University

Ken Millen-Penn
Fairmont State College

Glenn A. Miller
Texas A&M University

Lauren Mitchell
St. Louis, Missouri

Christian H. Moe
Southern Illinois University, Carbondale

Mario Morelli
Western Illinois University

Caitlin Moriarity
Brisbane, California

Elizabeth C. E. Morrish
State University of New York, Oneonta

Todd Moye
Atlanta, Georgia

Tinker D. Murray
Southwest Texas State University

Alex Mwakikoti
University of Texas, Arlington

Alice Myers
Bard College at Simon's Rock

Michael V. Namorato
University of Mississippi

Jerome L. Neapolitan
Tennessee Technological University

Alicia Neumann
San Francisco, California

Caryn E. Neumann
Miami University of Ohio, Middletown

Mark A. Newman
University of Virginia

Betsy L. Nichols
Reynoldsburg, Ohio

James W. Oberly
University of Wisconsin, Eau Claire

George O'Brien
Georgetown University

Wendy Cobb Orrison
Washington and Lee University

Sheril A. Palermo
Cupertino, California

R. K. L. Panjabi
Memorial University of Newfoundland

Robert J. Paradowski
Rochester Institute of Technology

Thomas R. Park
Florida State University

Robert Passaro
Tucson, Arizona

Cheryl Pawlowski
University of Northern Colorado

Leslie A. Pearl
San Diego, California

Judy C. Peel
University of North Carolina, Wilmington

Martha E. Pemberton
Galesville, Wisconsin

Great Athletes: Boxing and Soccer

William E. Pemberton
University of Wisconsin, La Crosse

Lori A. Petersen
Minot, North Dakota

Nis Petersen
Jersey City State College

Douglas A. Phillips
Sierra Vista, Arizona

Debra L. Picker
Long Beach, California

Betty L. Plummer
Dillard University

Bill Plummer III
Amateur Softball Association of America

Michael Polley
Columbia College

Francis Poole
University of Delaware

Jon R. Poole
Virginia Polytechnic Institute and State University

David L. Porter
William Penn University

John G. Powell
Greenville, South Carolina

Victoria Price
Lamar University

Maureen J. Puffer-Rothenberg
Valdosta State University

Christopher Rager
San Dimas, California

Steven J. Ramold
Eastern Michigan University

C. Mervyn Rasmussen
Renton, Washington

John David Rausch, Jr.
West Texas A&M University

Abe C. Ravitz
California State University, Dominguez Hills

Nancy Raymond
International Gymnast Magazine

Shirley H. M. Reekie
San Jose State University

Christel Reges
Grand Valley State University

Victoria Reynolds
Mandeville High School

Betty Richardson
Southern Illinois University, Edwardsville

Alice C. Richer
Spaulding Rehabilitation Center

David R. Rider
Bloomsburg University

Robert B. Ridinger
Northern Illinois University

Edward A. Riedinger
Ohio State University Libraries

Edward J. Rielly
Saint Joseph's College of Maine

Jan Rintala
Northern Illinois University

Thurman W. Robins
Texas Southern University

Vicki K. Robinson
State University of New York, Farmingdale

Mark Rogers
University of Chicago

Wynn Rogers
San Dimas, California

Carl F. Rothfuss
Central Michigan University

William B. Roy
United States Air Force Academy

A. K. Ruffin
George Washington University

Todd Runestad
American Ski Association

J. Edmund Rush
Boise, Idaho

Michael Salmon
Amateur Athletic Foundation of Los Angeles

Rebecca J. Sankner
Southern Illinois University, Carbondale

Timothy M. Sawicki
Canisius College

Ronald C. Sawyer
State University of New York, Binghamton

Ann M. Scanlon
State University of New York, College at Cortland

Daniel C. Scavone
University of Southern Indiana

Elizabeth D. Schafer
Loachapoka, Alabama

Lamia Nuseibeh Scherzinger
Indiana University

Walter R. Schneider
Central Michigan University

J. Christopher Schnell
Southeast Missouri State University

Kathleen Schongar
The May School

Stephen Schwartz
Buffalo State College

Deborah Service
Los Angeles, California

Chrissa Shamberger
Ohio State University

Contributors

Tom Shieber
Mt. Wilson, California

Theodore Shields
Surfside Beach, South Carolina

Peter W. Shoun
East Tennessee State University

R. Baird Shuman
University of Illinois, Urbana-Champaign

Thomas J. Sienkewicz
Monmouth College

Richard Slapsys
University of Massachusetts, Lowell

Elizabeth Ferry Slocum
Pasadena, California

John Slocum
Pasadena, California

Gary Scott Smith
Grove City College

Harold L. Smith
University of Houston, Victoria

Ira Smolensky
Monmouth College

A. J. Sobczak
Santa Barbara, California

Ray Sobczak
Salem, Wisconsin

Mark Stanbrough
Emporia State University

Alison Stankrauff
Indiana University South Bend

Michael Stellefson
Texas A&M University

Glenn Ellen Starr Stilling
Appalachian State University

Gerald H. Strauss
Bloomsburg University

Deborah Stroman
University of North Carolina

James Sullivan
California State University, Los Angeles

Cynthia J. W. Svoboda
Bridgewater State College

William R. Swanson
South Carolina State College

J. K. Sweeney
South Dakota State University

Charles A. Sweet, Jr.
Eastern Kentucky University

Glenn L. Swygart
Tennessee Temple University

James Tackach
Roger Williams University

Felicia Friendly Thomas
California State Polytechnic University, Pomona

Jennifer L. Titanski
Lock Haven University of Pennsylvania

Evelyn Toft
Fort Hays State University

Alecia C. Townsend Beckie
New York, New York

Anh Tran
Wichita State University

Marcella Bush Trevino
Texas A&M University, Kingsville

Kathleen Tritschler
Guilford College

Brad Tufts
Bucknell University

Karen M. Turner
Temple University

Sara Vidar
Los Angeles, California

Hal J. Walker
University of Connecticut

Spencer Weber Waller
Loyola University Chicago

Annita Marie Ward
Salem-Teikyo University

Shawncey Webb
Taylor University

Chuck Weis
American Canoe Association

Michael J. Welch
Guilford College

Paula D. Welch
University of Florida

Allen Wells
Bowdoin College

Winifred Whelan
St. Bonaventure University

Nan White
Maharishi International University

Nicholas White
Maharishi International University

Rita S. Wiggs
Methodist College

Ryan K. Williams
University of Illinois, Springfield

Brook Wilson
Independent Scholar

John Wilson
Wheaton, Illinois

Rusty Wilson
Ohio State University

Wayne Wilson
Amateur Athletic Foundation of Los Angeles

John D. Windhausen
St. Anselm College

Michael Witkoski
University of South Carolina

Philip Wong
Pasadena, California

Greg Woo
Independent Scholar

Sheri Woodburn
Cupertino, California

Jerry Jaye Wright
Pennsylvania State University, Altoona

Scott Wright
University of St. Thomas

Lisa A. Wroble
Redford Township District Library

Frank Wu
University of Wisconsin, Madison

Brooke K. Zibel
University of North Texas

Boxing

Laila Ali

Born: December 31, 1977
Miami Beach, Florida
Also known as: She Bee Stingin'

Early Life

Laila Ali was born the second daughter of boxer Muhammad Ali and his third wife Veronica Porsche. She became the most famous of Ali's nine children. As a child, Laila was not close to her father but lived with her mother and older sister. Laila's teen years were difficult; she displayed a defiance that got her in trouble with the law, primarily for street fighting. She was arrested for shoplifting and spent three months in a juvenile detention center. She graduated from college in Santa Monica and worked at a nail salon before deciding to follow her father's career path. Laila, at about 170 pounds and 5 feet 10 inches, was classified as a super middleweight.

The Road to Excellence

Despite her father's warnings regarding the potential for injury as a boxer, Laila proceeded with her plans. On October 8, 1999, at the Turning Stone Casino Convention Center in Verona, New York, Laila made her debut as a fighter against another unknown, April Fowler. The bout drew a crowd of more than three thousand and attracted media from all over the world. Laila won her second fight by a technical knockout (TKO), with 3 seconds remaining in the final round, on November 10, 1999, in West Virginia. Her opponent was Shadina Pennybaker. Laila was not as smooth and deadly as her father had been, but she carried a similar swagger, taunting Pennybaker.

On December 10, 1999, Laila knocked Nicolyn Armstrong flat on her back, scoring a TKO. On March 7, 2000, in Windsor, Ontario, Canada, in a fight that lasted only 70 seconds, Laila gained her fourth win by knocking out Crystal Arcand in the first round. Some spectators commented on Laila's power and quickness. On April 8, 2000, Laila got her first big scare as a fighter when she was knocked down in the second round of a fight with Karen Bill. Laila got up and counterattacked strongly, but she was still getting pummeled at the end of the round. After Laila delivered a number of punches in the third round, the referee stopped the fight in Laila's favor. The crowd booed, many feeling the fight had been stopped too soon.

The Emerging Champion

After her fight with Bill, Laila remembered her father's warnings and heeded her trainer, who told

Laila Ali displaying her championship belt after a fight in 2007. (AFP/Getty Images)

3

her not to turn her head away from punches. He also said she should not move away from contact. Instead, he advised, she should move in and take a beating: "People want to see women fight," he told her. Laila realized that her career was in danger and that she had to be more aggressive if she wanted to be a successful fighter.

Laila's sixth win was in China on April 22, 2000. She battered Kristina King, gaining a TKO 3 seconds into the fourth round. King was not able to handle Laila's combinations and struggled from the start. In the third round, Laila knocked out King's mouthpiece and bloodied her opponent.

After taking a break from fighting to get married, Laila won a unanimous decision over Kendra Lenhart on October 20, 2000. On March 2, 2001, Laila improved her pro record to 9-0 when she knocked out Christine Robinson with powerful right-handed punches and a left uppercut.

Continuing the Story

During the 1970's, Muhammad Ali fought a series of epic heavyweight bouts with the hard-punching Joe Frazier. On June 8, 2001, Laila fought a so-called "grudge match" against Frazier's daughter Jacqui Frazier-Lyde. The bout attracted attention not only because the combatants renewed a family rivalry, but also because Frazier-Lyde, a Philadelphia lawyer, had taken up boxing specifically to fight Laila. Both women deemed the match to be beneficial financially and an important public relations event for women's boxing. However, some in the sporting world thought that Laila and Frazier-Lyde would sully their famous fathers' reputations. In fact, the two women engaged in an exciting bout that Laila won in the eighth round.

In 2002, Laila became the International Boxing Association female middleweight champion. That September, the Women's Boxing Archive Network named Laila fighter of the month. In late 2002, in Las Vegas, Nevada, Laila defended her title and added the Women's International Boxing Association (WIBA) and International Women's Boxing Federation (IWBF) belts with an eighth-round knockout win over Valerie Mahfood. On June 21, 2003, Laila defended her title in a rematch with Mahfood, knocking her out in 6 rounds. On September 24, 2004, she captured the IWBF light-heavyweight title; on February 11, 2005, she beat Cassandra Geiggar in 10 rounds. In June of that year, Laila bested Erin Toughill to remain undefeated and won the World Boxing Council (WBC)

Boxing Record

Date	Location	Loser	Result
Oct. 8, 1999	Verona, N.Y.	April Fowler	1st-round knockout
Nov. 10, 1999	Chester, W.Va.	Shadina Pennybaker	4th-round technical knockout
Dec. 10, 1999	Detroit, Mich.	Nicolyn Armstrong	2d-round technical knockout
Mar. 7, 2000	Windsor, Ont.	Crystal Arcand	1st-round knockout
Apr. 8, 2000	Detroit, Mich.	Karen Bill	3d-round technical knockout
Apr. 22, 2000	Guangzhou, China	Kristina King	4th-round technical knockout
June 15, 2000	Universal City, Calif.	Marjorie Jones	1st-round technical knockout
Oct. 20, 2000	Auburn Hills, Mich.	Kendra Lenhart	6th-round unanimous decision
Mar. 2, 2001	Verona, N.Y.	Christine Robinson	5th-round technical knockout
June 8, 2001	Verona, N.Y.	Jacqui Frazier-Lyde	8th-round medical decision
June 7, 2002	Southaven, Miss.	Shirvelle Williams	6th-round unanimous decision
Aug. 17, 2002	Las Vegas, Nev.	Suzette Taylor	2d-round technical knockout
Nov. 8, 2002	Las Vegas, Nev.	Valerie Mahfood	8th-round technical knockout
Feb. 14, 2003	Louisville, Ky.	Mary Ann Almager	4th-round technical knockout
June 21, 2003	Los Angeles, Calif.	Valerie Mahfood	6th-round technical knockout
Aug. 23, 2003	Biloxi, Miss.	Christy Martin	4th-round knockout
July 3, 2004	Louisville, Ky.	Monica Nunez	9th-round technical knockout
July 17, 2004	Bowie, Md.	Nikki Eplion	3d-round technical knockout
Sept. 24, 2004	Atlanta, Ga.	Gwendolyn O'Neil	3d-round knockout
Feb. 11, 2005	Atlanta, Ga.	Cassandra Geiggar	8th-round technical knockout
June 11, 2005	Washington, D.C.	Erin Toughill	3d-round technical knockout
Dec. 17, 2005	Berlin, Germany	Asa Sandell	5th-round technical knockout
Nov. 11, 2006	New York, N.Y.	Shelley Burton	4th-round technical knockout
Feb. 3, 2007	Johannesburg, South Africa	Gwendolyn O'Neil	1st-round technical knockout

title in addition to defending her WIBA crown. Sportswriters called the Laila's bout with Toughill one of the most violent female-to-female fights in history.

On December 17, 2005, Laila defeated Åsa Sandell by TKO in the fifth round, marking her twenty-second win. Then, in 2006, she defeated Shelley Burton by a fourth-round TKO. On February 3, 2007, in Johannesburg, South Africa, Laila fought her last fight, retaining her WBC and WIBA super-middleweight world titles when she knocked out Gwendolyn O'Neil after 56 seconds.

Summary

In the past, women's boxing had been demeaned by male boxers, including Muhammad Ali, who once said that women were not meant to be punched in the face and breasts. Since boxing involves hard physical labor and mental toughness, boxers must be in top physical condition. Laila Ali successfully disproved the many people who thought women did not have the mental and physical endurance to be boxers.

Julia M. Meyers

Additional Sources

Ali, Laila, and David Ritz. *Reach! Finding Strength, Spirit, and Personal Power.* New York: Hyperion, 2002.

Horn, Geoffrey M. *Laila Ali.* Milwaukee, Wis.: Gareth Stevens, 2005.

Sekules, Kate. *The Boxer's Heart: How I Fell in Love with the Ring.* New York: Villard, 2000.

Ungs, Tim. *Muhammad Ali and Laila Ali.* New York: Rosen, 2005.

Muhammad Ali

Born: January 17, 1942
   Louisville, Kentucky
Also known as: Cassius Marcellus Clay, Jr. (full given name); Cassius Clay; Louisville Lip; the Greatest

Early Life

Cassius Marcellus Clay, Jr., was born on January 17, 1942, in Louisville, Kentucky. He was the eldest son of Cassius Marcellus Clay, Sr., and Odessa Clay. His father made a living as a sign painter. At the age of twelve, Cassius was given his first bicycle by his father. When the bike was stolen from him after only two days, Cassius looked for a police officer to report what had happened. The officer he came upon was Joe Martin, who was in charge of the amateur boxing program in Louisville. Martin convinced Cassius that he should learn how to box so that he could defend himself against the larger boys who probably stole his bicycle.

Soon, Cassius was completely dedicated to boxing. Cassius went to Louisville's Central High School, but boxing took precedence over school. Cassius's parents had made a stable home environment for him, and they wanted what was best for their son. They soon learned that Cassius wanted to pursue a boxing career and that he excelled at the sport.

The Road to Excellence

At the age of sixteen, Cassius won Louisville's Golden Gloves light-heavyweight title. He had grown to 170 pounds and stood 6 feet tall. In 1960, Cassius graduated from Central High School. A year earlier, he had won the National Golden Gloves and the Amateur Athletic Union (AAU) titles in the light-heavyweight division. After graduation from high school, Cassius was on his way to even greater victories. In 1960, he won the AAU title again and represented the United States in the Rome Olympics. By this stage of his amateur career, Cassius had developed a brash way of expressing himself. He could be loud and very outspoken. At Rome, Cassius defeated Zbigniew Pietrzykowski to win the gold medal. This victory marked Cassius's fortieth consecutive win. Cassius let it be known that he wanted to turn professional so that he could make a large amount of money.

Cassius came back home to Louisville as a hero. A group of local business people formed a syndicate to sponsor him. In the agreement between the syndicate and Cassius, which was in force for six years, Cassius received a ten-thousand-dollar bonus, training expenses, and guarantees, which varied over the length of the contract. The syndicate received half of all Cassius's earnings for the six-year period. On October 29, 1960, Cassius entered the ring at Louisville's Freedom Hall as a professional fighter. He won a six-round decision and collected two thousand dollars. After this fight, Angelo Dundee was hired as Cassius's trainer. Dundee's accomplished professional skills benefited Cassius throughout his career. Likewise, Cassius soon befriended a rising boxing broadcaster, Howard Cosell. The playful verbal sparring between Cassius and Cosell helped publicize both the boxer and the broadcaster throughout their careers.

The great Muhammad Ali. (Library of Congress)

Recognized World Heavyweight Championships

Date	Location	Loser	Result
Feb. 25, 1964	Miami Beach, Fla.	Sonny Liston	7th-round technical knockout
May 25, 1965	Lewiston, Maine	Sonny Liston	1st-round knockout
Nov. 22, 1965	Las Vegas, Nev.	Floyd Patterson	12th-round technical knockout
Mar. 29, 1966	Toronto, Canada	George Chuvalo	15th-round unanimous decision
May 21, 1966	London, England	Henry Cooper	6th-round technical knockout
Aug. 6, 1966	London, England	Brian London	3d-round knockout
Sept. 10, 1966	Frankfurt, West Germany	Karl Mildenberger	12th-round technical knockout
Nov. 14, 1966	Houston, Tex.	Cleveland Williams	3d-round technical knockout
Feb. 6, 1967	Houston, Tex.	Ernie Terrell	15th-round unanimous decision
Mar. 22, 1967	New York, N.Y.	Zora Folley	7th-round knockout
Mar. 8, 1971	New York, N.Y.	Muhammad Ali (Joe Frazier, winner)	15th-round unanimous decision
Oct. 30, 1974	Kinshasa, Zaire	George Foreman	8th-round knockout
Mar. 24, 1975	Cleveland, Ohio	Chuck Wepner	15th-round technical knockout
May 16, 1975	Las Vegas, Nev.	Ron Lyle	11th-round technical knockout
June 1, 1975	Kuala Lumpur, Malaysia	Joe Bugner	15th-round unanimous decision
Oct. 1, 1975	Manila, Philippines	Joe Frazier	15th-round technical knockout
Feb. 20, 1976	San Juan, Puerto Rico	Jean Pierre Coopman	5th-round knockout
Apr. 30, 1976	Landover, Md.	Jimmy Young	15th-round unanimous decision
May 24, 1976	Munich, West Germany	Richard Dunn	5th-round technical knockout
Sept. 28, 1976	New York, N.Y.	Ken Norton	15th-round unanimous decision
May 16, 1977	Landover, Md.	Alfredo Evangelista	15th-round unanimous decision
Sept. 29, 1977	New York, N.Y.	Earnie Shavers	15th-round unanimous decision
Feb. 15, 1978	Las Vegas, Nev.	Muhammad Ali (Leon Spinks, winner)	15th-round split decision
Sept. 15, 1978	New Orleans, La.	Leon Spinks	15th-round unanimous decision
Oct. 2, 1980	Las Vegas, Nev.	Muhammad Ali (Larry Holmes, winner)	11th-round technical knockout

The Emerging Champion

Always colorful, Cassius decided that before each fight he should announce in which round he would win. Reportedly, he got this idea from watching a wrestler by the name of "Gorgeous" George Wagner. His predictions often came true. His showmanship started to bring in larger and larger audiences. Cassius thrived on the crowds. He became known as the "Louisville Lip" because of his controversial comments. Some experts took issue with his pronouncements and believed that he was more talk than talent.

Cassius grew to 6 feet 3 inches and 220 pounds. Even at this size, he had surprising foot speed in the ring. After nineteen professional fights, he was still undefeated; fifteen of his victories were by knockout. Cassius finally got his chance to fight the heavyweight champion, Sonny Liston, on February 25, 1964. Cassius was as brash as ever before the fight. Liston had a reputation as a ferocious brawler, and few experts gave the twenty-two-year-old challenger much of a chance. Drew Brown, Cassius's assistant trainer, advised him to "float like a butterfly, sting like a bee." Cassius proved that a graceful and quick boxer could beat a brawny puncher. With a seventh-round technical knockout, Cassius became the champion and shouted to the world "I am the king." Over the next three years, he defended his title nine times. His remarkable skills as a boxer had proved every bit equal to his outsized personality.

Continuing the Story

On the day after defeating Liston in 1964, Cassius announced that he was becoming a member of the Nation of Islam (Black Muslims) and changing his name to Muhammad Ali. The boxing world was shocked by his statement, even though Cassius had met with Malcolm X and Elijah Muhammad on a number of occasions. Many fans and critics alike were confused and angered by his action. There were even some who felt that Muhammad was not sincere, and that his conversion was merely another prank.

The greatest challenge to Muhammad's beliefs came in 1966, when the U.S. military draft classified him 1-A. Muhammad requested exemption from military duty on the grounds of his Muslim beliefs, but the Justice Department refused to honor his request and ordered him to be inducted. Muhammad refused to go. He was almost immediately stripped of his heavyweight title, and on June

Statistics

Bouts, 61
Knockouts, 37
Bouts won by decision, 19
Knockouts by opponents, 1
Bouts lost by decision, 4

Honors, Awards, and Records

1959-60		National Golden Gloves light heavyweight champion
		National Amateur Athletic Union light heavyweight champion
1960		Gold medal, U.S. Olympic Boxing
		Kentucky Golden Gloves light heavyweight titleholder (six titles overall)
		Tournament of Champions light heavyweight titleholder
1963, 1972, 1974-75, 1978		*Ring* magazine Merit Award (1972 co-recipient)
1965, 1974-75		Edward J. Neil Trophy (1975 corecipient)
1971, 1978		Only boxer in history to recapture the world heavyweight title twice
1974		Associated Press Male Athlete of the Year
		Sports Illustrated Sportsman of the Year
		Hickok Belt
1975		Inducted into Black Athletes Hall of Fame
1983		Inducted into U.S. Olympic Hall of Fame
1987		*Ring* magazine greatest heavyweight champion in boxing history
		Inducted into *Ring* magazine Boxing Hall of Fame
1990		Inducted into International Boxing Hall of Fame
1996		Lit the torch at the Atlanta Olympic Games
1997		Arthur Ashe Courage Award
1998		Amnesty International Lifetime Achievement Award
		United Nations Messenger of Peace citation
1999		BBC Sports Personality of the Century Award
		Kentucky Athlete of the Century by the Kentucky Athletic Hall of Fame
2000		Library of Congress Living Legend Award
2005		Presidential Medal of Freedom
		Otto Hahn Peace Medal in Gold from the United Nations Association of Germany (DGVN)
2006		Boxing Writers Association of America Pat Putnam Perseverance Award
2007		Honorary doctorate of humanities from Princeton University

20, 1967, Muhammad was convicted of evading the draft. He was fined ten thousand dollars and sentenced to five years in prison.

Muhammad did not step into the ring again until after the United States Supreme Court reversed the conviction in June of 1970. Muhammad fought for eleven more years until his retirement after losing to Trevor Berbick on December 11, 1981. In those eleven years, Muhammad regained his title and lost it several times. He had three memorable fights with Joe Frazier, about which fight fans continue to talk.

Muhammad was the most controversial and well-known sports figure in the world. People either loved him or hated him. The third Ali-Frazier fight, which took place on October 1, 1975, in Manila, the Philippines, was considered by many fight experts as the greatest in the history of the sport. The fight came to be known as "the Thrilla in Manila." In 1975, Muhammad's autobiography came out and was titled *The Greatest: My Own Story*.

In the years after Muhammad's retirement from professional boxing, and in spite of the debilitating effects of Parkinson's disease, a neurological disorder that is characterized by tremors and slowness of speech and movement, Muhammad retained the dignity of a true champion. He made frequent public appearances in support of charitable causes. In 1996, he lit the Olympic cauldron in Atlanta to mark the opening of the Olympic Summer Games. An international television audience watched Muhammad's poignant appearance, which had been kept a secret. With his debilitating condition on display for the whole world to see, Muhammad exhibited the attributes of a still-courageous fighter. This time, he was battling a disease and was determined that he would not be stopped. In 1998, he was appointed the United Nations Messenger of Peace. In 2002, he visited war-torn Afghanistan on a United Nations mission. In September, 2003, he met with the Buddhist leader, the Dalai Lama, demonstrating Muhammad's religious openness.

By all accounts, Muhammad showed true nobility in his battle against Parkinson's disease, in his maturing beliefs, and in his humanitarian efforts. He converted to mainstream Sunni Islam and publicly regretted shunning Malcolm X at the command of others. He required of himself an abundance of good deeds to atone for any mistakes of his past. For example, he said that he considered signing autographs an act of religious kindness. He hugged and kissed small children when possible, often delighting them with magic tricks.

Summary

Muhammad Ali was named the greatest heavyweight champion in the history of boxing by *Ring* magazine. *Sports Illustrated* selected him as the athlete of the twentieth century. Besides his role as a great fighter, Muhammad was a colorful and outspoken public figure who stood up for his beliefs. Muhammad was larger than life and played a major role in the social revolution that transpired during the 1960's. With his speed, power, and incredible footwork, he was an awesome boxer. He was one of the greatest heavyweight champions in history and one of the great symbolic figures of his time. As a champion, he often courted controversy. In his physically debilitating older years, he became a symbol of graciousness, and an international figure of faith.

Jeffry Jensen, updated by Howard Bromberg

Additional Sources

Ali, Muhammad, and Hana Yasmeen Ali. *The Soul of a Butterfly: Reflections on Life's Journey.* New York: Simon & Schuster, 2004.

Ali, Muhammad, and Richard Durham. *The Greatest: My Own Story.* New York: Random House, 1975.

Edward, Audrey, and Gary Wahl. *The Picture Life of Muhammad Ali.* New York: Avon Books, 1978.

Kindred, Dave. *Sound and Fury: Two Powerful Lives, One Fateful Friendship.* New York: Free Press, 2006.

Mullan, Harry. *The Ultimate Encyclopedia of Boxing: The Definitive Illustrated Guide to World Boxing.* Edison, N.J.: Chartwell Books, 1996.

Myers, Walter Dean. *The Greatest: Muhammad Ali.* New York: Scholastic Press, 2001.

Alexis Arguello

Born: April 19, 1952
   Managua, Nicaragua
Died: July 1, 2009
   Managua, Nicaragua

Early Life
The life of Alexis Arguello seemed destined to play out in his beloved Nicaragua. Alexis was born on April 19, 1952, in the capital city of Managua; he and his brothers and sisters were likely to spend their lives much as their parents had. Working at an early age was something expected of everyone in the family. Alexis's father, with a wife and nine children to support, earned a meager income making shoes. The family's home was in one of the poorest and most crime-infested areas in the city. When he was fourteen, Alexis had to leave school to work full time.

Alexis's interest in boxing began when his oldest sister married a fighter. Boxing was popular throughout Nicaragua. To help support his family, Alexis became a professional boxer, utilizing the orthodox stance of right-handers. By the time he reached twenty years old, he had won 27 of 29 bouts in his home country. Alexis's life, by the standards in his country, had improved dramatically. While still a teenager, he married. One night, his home, along with much of the city, was destroyed by a devastating earthquake. More than two thousand people died; however, Alexis, his wife, and their six-month-old infant survived unhurt.

The Road to Excellence
Alexis had his first professional bout when he was only sixteen years old. Seven years passed before he fought outside his home country for the first time. Alexis traveled to Panama, a Central American country south of Nicaragua. While there, he contended for his first world championship. He lost in this attempt, but at only twenty-two years of age, he was still learning.

Alexis returned to Nicaragua to combat tougher opposition. He knew he could not achieve his goal of winning a world championship without meeting and learning from world-class fighters. He compiled four victories after his title loss. By November of 1974, he was ready for his second world-title opportunity and his first trip to the United States.

At 122 pounds, Alexis was a slender 5 feet 10 inches with a 72-inch reach. The tall, thin frame gave no outward indication of the power he carried in both hands. Because of his many knockout victories, he was given the nickname "the Explosive Thin Man."

The Emerging Champion
The acclaimed boxer Ruben Olivares soon found that Alexis packed a powerful punch. On the night of November 23, 1974, Olivares's loyal Mexican fans had much about which to cheer during the first 12 rounds of the fight. However, coming from far behind, Alexis scored a sensational knockout in the thirteenth round and became the World Boxing Association featherweight champion. At the 126-pound weight limit, he defended the title four times over the next two years. Alexis became a national hero in his native Nicaragua.

At that time in Nicaragua, the Somoza political dynasty was ending. In 1979, the politically leftist Sandinista rebels took over the country and implemented some communist policies, one of which was to confiscate property from the wealthy citizens. Alexis's bank accounts and property in Managua, worth more than $300,000, were taken from

Statistics

Bouts, 90
Knockouts, 65
Bouts won by decision, 17
Knockouts by opponents, 4
Bouts lost by decision, 4

Honors and Awards

1992   Inducted into International Boxing Hall of Fame

Milestones

Captured recognized world titles at three weight classifications

Recognized World Featherweight Championships

Date	Location	Loser	Result
Feb. 16, 1974	Panama City, Panama	Alexis Arguello (Ernesto Marcel, winner)	15th-round decision
Nov. 23, 1974	Inglewood, Calif.	Ruben Olivares	13th-round knockout
Mar. 15, 1975	Caracas, Venezuela	Leonel Hernandez	8th-round technical knockout
May 31, 1975	Granada, Nicaragua	Rigoberto Riasco	2d-round technical knockout
Oct. 12, 1975	Tokyo, Japan	Royal Kobayashi	5th-round knockout
June 19, 1976	Inglewood, Calif.	Salvador Torres	3d-round knockout

Recognized World Junior Lightweight Championships

Date	Location	Loser	Result
Jan. 28, 1978	Bayamon, Puerto Rico	Alfredo Escalera	13th-round technical knockout
Apr. 19, 1978	Inglewood, Calif.	Rey Tam	5th-round technical knockout
June 3, 1978	San Juan, Puerto Rico	Diego Alcala	1st-round knockout
Nov. 10, 1978	Las Vegas, Nev.	Arturo Leon	15th-round decision
Feb. 4, 1979	Rimini, Italy	Alfredo Escalera	13th-round knockout
July 8, 1979	New York, N.Y.	Rafael Limon	11th-round technical knockout
Nov. 16, 1979	Inglewood, Calif.	Bobby Chacon	7th-round technical knockout
Jan. 20, 1980	Tucson, Ariz.	Ruben Castillo	11th-round technical knockout
Apr. 27, 1980	San Juan, Puerto Rico	Rolando Navarrete	5th-round technical knockout

Recognized World Lightweight Championships

Date	Location	Loser	Result
June 20, 1981	London, England	Jim Watt	15th-round unanimous decision
Oct. 3, 1981	Atlantic City, N.J.	Ray Mancini	14th-round technical knockout
Nov. 21, 1981	Las Vegas, Nev.	Robert Elizondo	7th-round knockout
Feb. 13, 1982	Beaumont, Tex.	Bubba Busceme	6th-round technical knockout
May 22, 1982	Las Vegas, Nev.	Andrew Ganigan	5th-round knockout

Recognized World Junior Welterweight Championships

Date	Location	Loser	Result
Nov. 12, 1982	Miami, Fla.	Alexis Arguello (Aaron Pryor, winner)	14th-round technical knockout
Sept. 9, 1983	Las Vegas, Nev.	Alexis Arguello (Aaron Pryor, winner)	10th-round knockout

him, and he was left virtually penniless. Alexis fled Nicaragua, and the Sandinistas tried to erase his name from press, radio, and television, fearing he could become a high-profile symbol of hope to the opposition Contras.

Alexis moved to Florida and applied for U.S. citizenship. As a devout Catholic, he could not live under a communist regime. He also wanted his sons to receive a better education than he had as a young boy in his homeland. By 1977, Alexis's weight could no longer be kept down to the featherweight limit. He voluntarily gave up his championship and tried for the World Boxing Council (WBC) junior-lightweight title. On January 28, 1978, Alfredo Escalera, fighting in his native Puerto Rico, lost to Alexis by a technical knockout in the thirteenth round.

Fighting at 130 pounds, Alexis was much stronger. During the next thirty months, he successfully defended his title eight times, with seven of the victories coming by knockout. Fans in Central America, Europe, and the United States came to see this deadly puncher and clever boxer.

As 1980 came to a close, Alexis, the twenty-eight-year-old champion, realized he could no longer keep his weight under 130 pounds. For a second time, he gave up his title to pursue a championship in another weight division. He wanted to join the elite group of boxers that have held three world titles. On June 20, 1981, he traveled to London, England, to fight the WBC lightweight champion Jim Watt, who hailed from Scotland. The coveted title changed hands as Alexis won a unanimous decision.

Continuing the Story

At the 135-pound limit and approaching his thirtieth birthday, Alexis remained as busy as ever. He became a popular champion because many of his victories were seen on television. A young fighter from Ohio named Ray "Boom Boom" Mancini was also becoming a television favorite. On October 3,

1981, the two fighters met in a classic match. Both men gave a maximum effort; however, in the fourteenth round, the experience and power of Alexis outweighed Mancini's courage. The referee stopped the fight to save Mancini from excessive injury. A year after fighting Alexis, Mancini wrote an article about him. He said, "Arguello is a man to be respected. . . . I watch him. Study him. Admire him." These were unusual words from a defeated fighter about the man who beat him.

After three championships, Alexis tried for an amazing fourth world title. This time, he fought at 140 pounds. In 1982, Alexis was thirty years old, an advanced age for a fighter. To become juniorwelterweight champion, he had to defeat Aaron Pryor. Known as "the Hawk," Pryor had an aggressive style. For 14 rounds both men fought evenly, but the youth and power of Pryor was too much for Alexis. The referee stopped the bout in favor of Pryor.

Less than one year later, Alexis made one more attempt at defeating Pryor. The passing of one year had only slowed the proud Nicaraguan more. This time a series of powerful punches put him down and out. Alexis later described the loss as the most disappointing of his career since he desperately wanted a fourth title.

Meanwhile, in 1983, in Nicaragua, Alexis's brother died while fighting the Sandinistas. Filled with rage, Alexis abandoned boxing to return home secretly to fight for the Contras in the Nicaraguan mountains.

In 1985, after two years in retirement, Alexis returned to the ring and defeated Pat Jefferson by a fifth-round knockout. A year later, he fought Billy Williams; in the match, he struggled during the first 3 rounds but came back in the fourth to win by technical knockout. Alexis fought two more times, winning a tenth-round decision against Jorge Palomares and losing by decision in a 10-round match against Scott Walker. At the age of forty-two, hall-of-famer Alexis retired from the ring once again.

Retirement was not easy for Alexis. He developed a worsening cocaine and alcohol habit. He blamed his situation on both disillusionment with the Nicaraguan government, which stole American money destined for Nicaraguans, and depression about the end of his boxing career. Having returned to live in Managua, Alexis contemplated suicide when his drug problem became public knowledge. For months, he refused offers of help. However, a drug- and alcohol-fueled argument with his longtime girlfriend finally brought him to his senses. Ashamed that he had choked the mother of two of his seven children, Alexis spent ten weeks in a rehabilitation center to address his addictions to drugs, alcohol, and women.

In 2004, Alexis entered politics and became the vice mayor of Managua. In November, 2008, backed by the Sandinista Party, Alexis was elected mayor of Managua, beating Eduardo Montealegre, the conservative candidate of the Liberal Alliance Party. Less than one year later, Alexis's amazing comeback came to a sudden and shocking end. On July 1, 2009, he was found shot to death in his home.

Summary

Alexis Arguello is remembered as a boxer who won 82 out of 90 professional bouts, scored an amazing 65 knockouts, and gained three world championships. He was inducted into the International Boxing Hall of Fame in 1992. From the humblest of beginnings, he gained wealth and fame. During his fighting days and in his retirement, Alexis was an ambassador of goodwill for boxing.

Bruce Gordon, updated by Caryn E. Neumann

Additional Sources

Heller, Peter. *In This Corner . . . ! Forty-two World Champions Tell Their Stories.* New York: Da Capo Press, 1994.

Mercante, Arthur, and Phil Guarnieri. *Inside the Ropes.* Ithaca, N.Y.: McBooks Press, 2006.

Mullan, Harry, and Bob Mee. *The Ultimate Encyclopedia of Boxing.* London: Carlton, 2007.

Roberts, James, and Alexander Skutt. *The Boxing Register: International Boxing Hall of Fame Official record Book.* Ithaca, N.Y.: McBooks Press, 2006.

Schulman, Arlene. *The Prize Fighters: An Intimate Look at Champions and Contenders.* London: Virgin, 1995.

Henry Armstrong

Born: December 12, 1912
Columbus, Mississippi
Died: October 24, 1988
Los Angeles, California
Also known as: Henry Jackson, Jr. (birth name)

Early Life
Henry Jackson, Jr., was born on December 12, 1912, in Columbus, Mississippi. His parents were sharecroppers who decided to try their luck in urban life a few years after Henry's birth. They moved to St. Louis, Missouri, where Henry grew up and attended high school. Henry's family wanted him to go to college and become a minister. Although a quick learner in school, Henry did not like this plan. He managed to withstand the pressure from his mother and his maternal grandmother to embark upon a ministerial career. He was drawn to another profession.

Although Henry was never in serious trouble as a teenager, he was not slow to use his fists. As he saw it, he frequently had to prove his toughness to neighborhood bullies, who were tempted to pick on him because of his small size. Henry had a fierce will to win, and his determination and quickness almost always enabled him to finish on top.

The Road to Excellence
These youthful escapades gave Henry a career path. He decided to become a boxer and won a number of local fights in St. Louis. A crucial step in his progress occurred during a visit to a St. Louis boxing gymnasium. Here he encountered Harry Armstrong, a retired fighter who worked as a trainer. Armstrong's chief protégé was Eddie Foster, a young boxer of Henry's age. The self-confident Henry accepted Armstrong's challenge to box Foster. Much to Armstrong's surprise, and in spite of his lack of training, Henry quickly dispatched Foster.

Armstrong, recognizing an outstanding prospect, took Henry under his wing and smoothed out his brawling style. Henry depended on Harry Armstrong's training and management throughout his career. He was so attached to his adviser that he adopted "Armstrong" as his own last name.

Henry's style was unique. He rushed at his opponent and rained blows on him incessantly. He was willing to absorb his foe's counterpunches in order to land his own blows, which were of devastating effectiveness. Although a skilled fighter would parry many of Henry's punches, Henry's speed ensured that many got through to their target. He was able to maintain his fast and furious pace throughout a full match, and few boxers proved able to go the distance with him.

Henry Armstrong, who was the world champion in the featherweight, lightweight, and welterweight divisions. (Courtesy of Amateur Athletic Foundation of Los Angeles)

The Emerging Champion

During the late 1920's, the road to success for African Americans in professional sports was a hard one. In spite of his obvious ability, Henry did not immediately find sponsors with the necessary financial backing. In order to reach California, a center for amateur boxing, he "rode the rails" as a hobo. After arriving in California, Henry spent most of his time in Los Angeles, where he enjoyed a successful career as an amateur. He turned professional in 1931.

Henry was a crowd-pleasing favorite, and his perpetual-motion attacks won him a wide following. He still found it difficult to attract attention from major promoters, however, and he feared his career might languish before he was awarded fights against topflight opposition. Oddly enough, he secured a fortunate break after a controversial loss.

In a match with the Filipino boxer Baby Arizmendi, Henry thought he had won. The decision, before an audience of Arizmendi supporters, went against him, and a rematch was quickly arranged. This time Henry threw himself into his attack and defeated Arizmendi, whom he later named as the best of all of his opponents at absorbing punishment.

Henry's convincing victory attracted the attention of New York boxing promoters, and Henry soon showed the boxing public that he was of championship caliber. On October 29, 1937, he was matched with Peter Sarron, the featherweight champion. Sarron was an aggressive boxer and, like Henry, aimed at a quick knockout. Henry refused to be put on the defensive and mounted an assault of his own. Sarron succumbed in the sixth round; he had never before been knocked out.

Recognized World Featherweight Championship

Date	Location	Loser	Result
Oct. 29, 1937	New York, N.Y.	Peter Sarron	6th-round knockout

Recognized World Lightweight Championships

| Aug. 17, 1938 | New York, N.Y. | Lou Ambers | 15th-round decision |
| Aug. 22, 1939 | New York, N.Y. | Henry Armstrong (Lou Ambers, winner) | 15th-round decision |

Recognized World Welterweight Championships

May 31, 1938	Long Island City, N.Y.	Barney Ross	15th-round decision
Nov. 25, 1938	New York, N.Y.	Ceferino Garcia	15th-round decision
Jan. 10, 1939	Los Angeles, Calif.	Baby Arizmendi	10th-round decision
Mar. 4, 1939	Havana, Cuba	Bobby Pacho	4th-round knockout
Mar. 16, 1939	St. Louis, Mo.	Lew Feldman	1st-round knockout
Mar. 31, 1939	New York, N.Y.	Davey Day	12th-round knockout
May 25, 1939	London, England	Ernie Roderick	15th-round decision
Oct. 9, 1939	Des Moines, Iowa	Al Manfredo	4th-round knockout
Oct. 13, 1939	Minneapolis, Minn.	Howard Scott	2d-round knockout
Oct. 20, 1939	Seattle, Wash.	Ritchie Fontaine	3d-round knockout
Oct. 24, 1939	Los Angeles, Calif.	Jimmy Garrison	10th-round decision
Oct. 30, 1939	Denver, Colo.	Bobby Pacho	4th-round knockout
Dec. 11, 1939	Cleveland, Ohio	Jimmy Garrison	7th-round knockout
Jan. 4, 1940	St. Louis, Mo.	Joe Ghnouly	5th-round knockout
Jan. 24, 1940	New York, N.Y.	Pedro Montanez	9th-round knockout
Apr. 26, 1940	Boston, Mass.	Paul Junior	7th-round knockout
May 24, 1940	Boston, Mass.	Ralph Zanelli	5th-round knockout
June 21, 1940	Portland, Maine	Paul Junior	3d-round knockout
Sept. 23, 1940	Washington, D.C.	Phil Furr	4th-round knockout
Oct. 4, 1940	New York, N.Y.	Henry Armstrong (Fritzie Zivic, winner)	15th-round decision
Jan. 17, 1941	New York, N.Y.	Henry Armstrong (Fritzie Zivic, winner)	12th-round knockout

Recognized World Middleweight Championship

| Mar. 1, 1940 | Los Angeles, Calif. | Ceferino Garcia | 10th-round draw |

Continuing the Story

Henry had become a world champion. He was not yet content and decided to go after the welterweight title, held by Barney Ross. A match between the two champions was held on May 31, 1938. Ross was one of the fiercest fighters of the 1930's, but he was past his prime when he confronted Henry. As always, Henry attacked his opponent, and Ross proved unable to halt his eager foe. Nevertheless, Ross impressed Henry by refusing to be knocked down. He finished the fight on his feet, even though the beating Henry inflicted required a trip to the hospital afterward.

Henry held two world titles. He decided to try for another, and in August, 1938, fought Lou Ambers for the lightweight title. Ambers was a slugger who never backed down, but even he was unable to stop Henry. After a close match, Henry emerged with his third world title.

Henry's amazing feats in the ring took a heavy toll on him. His whirlwind attacks, combined with the brutal punishment he took in his efforts to destroy his opponents, wore him out. By the end of the 1930's, he was no longer at his peak, and by 1945, he had lost all of his titles. He suffered a particularly bad loss to Fritzie Zivic. After an early assault that almost put Zivic away, Henry tired badly. Zivic opened cuts over Henry's eyes and almost blinded him. Henry required eye surgery after the bout and soon thereafter announced his retirement.

After his boxing career, the high-living champion executed a complete about-face. He became a minister and devoted his energies to helping underprivileged youths. He developed a series of health problems and died in poverty in 1988, in Los Angeles, California.

Summary

Henry Armstrong's fighting ability became evident in many youthful escapades. Much more than a street brawler, he became a serious amateur boxer under the tutelage of veteran Harry Armstrong. His aggressive, nonstop style made him one of the major fighters of the 1930's, and he held three world championships simultaneously.

Bill Delaney

Statistics

Bouts, 174
Knockouts, 98
Bouts won by decision, 47
Knockouts by opponents, 2
Bouts lost by decision, 17
Bouts lost by fouls, 1
Draws, 9

Records

First professional boxer to hold recognized world titles at three weight classifications simultaneously

Honors and Awards

1937	*Ring* magazine Merit Award
1938	Citizens Savings Southern California Athlete of the Year
1940	Edward J. Neil Trophy
1954	Inducted into *Ring* magazine Boxing Hall of Fame
1975	Inducted into Black Athletes Hall of Fame
1990	Inducted into International Boxing Hall of Fame

Additional Sources

Armstrong, Henry. *Gloves, Glory, and God: An Autobiography.* Westwood, N.J.: Revell, 1956.

Blewett, Bert. *The A to Z of World Boxing: An Authoritative and Entertaining Compendium of the Fight Game from Its Origins to the Present Day.* Parkwest, N.Y.: Robson Books, 2002.

McGuigan, Barry. "Sorry, but Ali Would Not Be in My Top Five." *The Daily Mirror,* September 21, 2002, p. 69.

Sugar, Bert Randolph. *Boxing's Greatest Fighters.* Guilford, Conn.: Lyons Press, 2006.

Max Baer

Born: February 11, 1909
  Omaha, Nebraska
Died: November 21, 1959
  Hollywood, California
Also known as: Maximilian Adelbert Baer (full name); Livermore Larupper; Madcap Maxie

Early Life
Maximilian Adelbert Baer was the son of an Omaha butcher. Max's family soon left Omaha and eventually wound up in Livermore, California. Max attended high school only one year, quitting to work in his father's butcher shop. He developed great stamina and strength through the arduous labor he engaged in; he later admitted his famous right-hand punch developed from swinging the butcher's cleaver. By age eighteen, Max stood 6 feet tall and weighed 190 pounds. As a teenager, Max discovered that he had unusual strength and ability in fights. He also found fighting to be enjoyable and decided to try it professionally. He moved to Oakland, California, a leading area for boxing on the West Coast.

The Road to Excellence
After he moved to Oakland, Max quickly established himself as a promising local fighter. He did not win all his bouts: in 1930, a veteran heavyweight Les Kennedy won a decision against him in Los Angeles. Nevertheless, he compiled an impressive record and was able to defeat a number of more experienced opponents. The manner in which Max was able to accomplish this helped to account for his popularity. He did not know much boxing technique but made up for this deficiency with his fast and furious assaults. He came at his opponent again and again, slugging away until he battered his hapless foe unconscious. Most of his fights ended by knockout.

In 1930, Max's fighting strategy led to a sad outcome in his match with Frankie Campbell. Max attacked in his usual fashion and knocked Campbell out in the fifth round. Campbell never regained consciousness, and his death strongly affected Max. For a while he considered giving up boxing. Through the help of Ancil Hoffman, a promoter who took Max under his wing, Max was able to overcome the emotional shock of killing a man. On December 19, 1930, he made his New York debut against Ernie Schaaf in Madison Square Garden. Schaaf had superior ring knowledge and was able to win more points than

Max Baer, who captured the heavyweight championship in 1934. (Courtesy of Amateur Athletic Foundation of Los Angeles)

Statistics

Bouts, 83
Knockouts, 52
Bouts won by decision, 18
Knockouts by opponents, 3
Bouts lost by decision, 8
Bouts lost by fouls, 2

Honors and Awards

1933 Citizens Savings Northern California Athlete of the Year
1968 Inducted into *Ring* magazine Boxing Hall of Fame
1969 NCAA Performing Arts Salute

his young rival in a ten-round decision. The New York boxing audience, however, found Max's aggressive style and obvious talent impressive, and his career was well on its way.

The Emerging Champion

Max so far had proven to be an outstanding fighter but by no means one of the world's best. In 1931, Tommy Loughran, probably the smartest heavyweight of the early 1930's, easily won a decision against him. Max showed great determination, however, and came back from his losses resolved to do better. Under Hoffman's instruction, he developed into a skilled boxer as well as a lethal puncher. He continued to win most of his matches and became recognized as one of the best heavyweights in the country. On August 31, 1932, he avenged his loss to Schaaf in a bout in Chicago. The way in which the fight ended was vintage Max. In the ninth round, Max charged at Schaaf with a series of devastating punches. Schaaf collapsed unconscious, and, although he was saved by the bell, he was still unconscious when the next round began.

Max's career took a giant step forward in his victory over Max Schmeling on June 8, 1933. Schmeling had been world heavyweight champion and was a leading contender to regain his title. At first, Max Baer's characteristic charges had little effect on the former champion, who, in his methodical way, seemed on the road to an easy win. Max once more showed his determination to let nothing stop him. He began a counterattack against Schmeling, and by the eleventh round Max's opponent was helpless.

Winning the heavyweight title was something of an anticlimax. The champion, the gigantic Italian Primo Carnera, knew little about boxing and had become champion under odd circumstances. On June 14, 1934, in Long Island, New York, Max became world heavyweight champion by defeating Carnera. Before the fight was stopped, he had knocked Carnera down twelve times.

Continuing the Story

A problem had developed in Max's rise to the top, and this was to prove his undoing. He did not like to train. Instead, he preferred going to parties and drinking with his friends. He especially liked to associate with actors and knew many Hollywood personalities. Although his fun-loving personality helped him to become popular, it was hardly the best course of action for a successful boxer. He defended his title against James J. Braddock in Madison Square Garden on June 13, 1935, and was easily defeated. This was one of the biggest upsets in boxing history. Although Braddock had achieved a good record in his long career, he was not regarded as an extraordinary fighter. Max did not take him seriously and failed to train as much as he should have. He paid a heavy price: the loss of his title, which he never regained.

Max began training as he should have for the fight with Braddock, and a match with Joe Louis was scheduled for Yankee Stadium in September, 1935. Unfortunately for Max, his opponent was one of the greatest boxers of all time, and Louis showed himself the superior fighter with little difficulty, knocking Max out in four rounds. Max did not give up. Under the guidance of the ever-present Hoffman, he toured England. Although he lost to Tommy Farr, the English champion, Max decisively defeated Farr in a rematch held in the

Recognized World Heavyweight Championships

Date	Location	Loser	Result
June 14, 1934	Long Island City, N.Y.	Primo Carnera	11th-round technical knockout
June 13, 1935	Long Island City, N.Y.	Max Baer (James J. Braddock, winner)	15th-round unanimous decision

United States. Max's comeback seemed on its way when he scored a victory over Tony Galento, one of the roughest fighters of the period. Boxing is a sport marked by rapid reversals of fortune, however, and the comeback came to a quick end. In 1941, after two losses to Lou Nova, Max announced his permanent retirement from boxing.

During World War II, he served as a physical fitness instructor in the U.S. Army. After the war, he moved to Hollywood and made a number of movies. He died on November 21, 1959, after suffering a heart attack. In 2005, Craig Bierko portrayed Max in Ron Howard's movie *Cinderella Man*, based on the life of Braddock and centered on the fight between Braddock and Max.

Summary

Although Max Baer was not the greatest boxer of the 1930's, his ring power and tenacious attitude won him a world's title. He electrified his many fans with his fierce attacks and amused them with his party-going. Although he sometimes neglected his training, his natural talent and power made him a standout.

Bill Delaney

Additional Sources

Hudson, David L., and Mike Fitzgerald. *Boxing's Most Wanted: The Top Ten Book of Champs, Chumps, and Punch-Drunk Palookas.* Washington, D.C.: Brassey's, 2004.

Mee, Bob. *Boxing: Heroes and Champions.* Edison, N.J.: Chartwell Books, 1997.

Schaap, Jeremy. *Cinderella Man: James J. Braddock, Max Baer, and the Greatest Upset in Boxing History.* Boston: Houghton Mifflin, 2005.

Sugar, Bert Randolph. *Boxing's Greatest Fighters.* Guilford, Conn.: Lyons Press, 2006.

Riddick Bowe

Born: August 10, 1967
   Brooklyn, New York
Also known as: Riddick Lamont Bowe (full name)

Early Life
Riddick Lamont Bowe was born August 10, 1967, in the Brownsville section of Brooklyn, New York, to Dorothy Bowe, a factory worker. Riddick never knew his father. Riddick, the future heavyweight champion of the world, was born into an environment of poverty, crime, and drugs. His mother struggled to provide for him and his dozen siblings, and she did her best to keep her children out of trouble in one of the worst districts of New York's metropolitan area. Riddick always tried to follow his mother's example. She worked hard to support her family and stayed away from trouble. Riddick knew that he had to find a way out of his destructive surroundings.

The Road to Excellence
Riddick decided that boxing was the way to escape the evils of the ghetto. Before he turned twenty-one years old, he had become one of the most accomplished amateur heavyweights in boxing history. In 1984, he knocked out opponent James Smith in just 4 seconds to win his first New York Golden Gloves championship. In 1985, he lost to Donald Stephens in the Golden Gloves championship bout but won the 1987 and 1988 super-heavyweight bouts for a total of three Golden Gloves championships. Riddick was also a Junior Olympic National Champion in 1985 and 1986.

In 1988, he was chosen for the U.S. Olympic team for the Seoul Games. He won the silver medal in the super-heavyweight division, losing only to Great Britain's Lennox Lewis, who later become a major rival of Riddick when both fighters turned professional.

Despite his performance in the Olympics, professional boxing experts were wary of Riddick. Many believed he did not fight up to his capabilities in the Olympics, and they wondered if he would develop the desire and dedication necessary to become a champion. Even as a young boxer, Riddick was unable to control his weight, chiefly because of his love of fast-food hamburgers.

However, the experts did not know Riddick's entire story. Not long before the Olympics, Riddick had had surgery on his right hand to repair an injured tendon. During the Games, moreover, he was fighting on an injured ankle. Subsequent X-rays revealed that Riddick had a stress fracture, which affected his ability to move in the ring. He was having

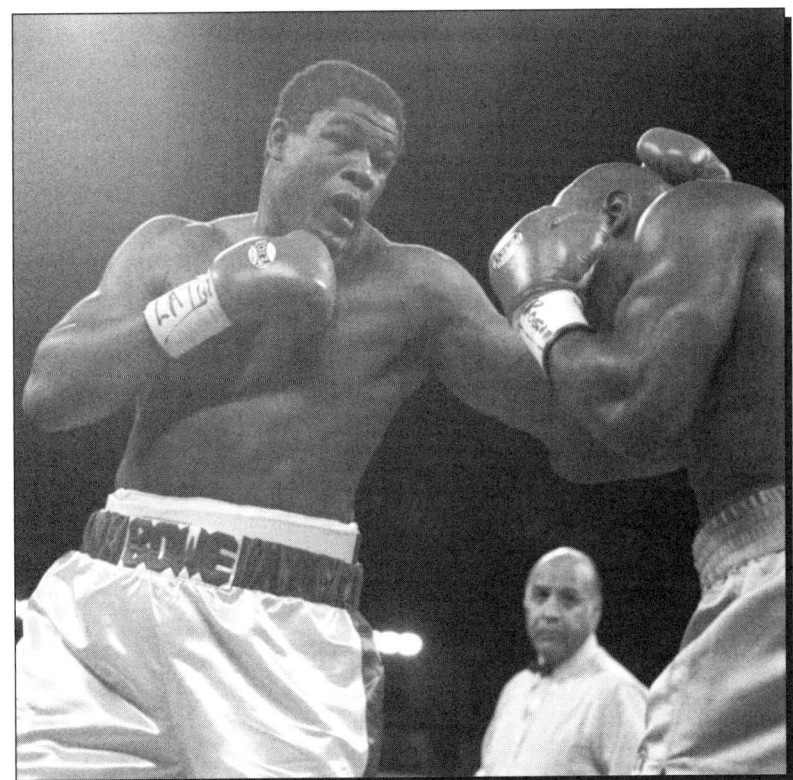

Riddick Bowe connecting with a left-handed punch against Evander Holyfield in 1995. (Al Bello/Getty Images)

Recognized World Heavyweight Championships

Date	Location	Loser	Result
Nov. 13, 1992	Las Vegas, Nev.	Evander Holyfield	12th-round decision
Feb. 6, 1993	New York, N.Y.	Michael Dokes	1st-round technical knockout
May 22, 1993	Washington, D.C.	Jesse Ferguson	2d-round technical knockout
Nov. 6, 1993	Las Vegas, Nev.	Riddick Bowe (Evander Holyfield, winner)	12th-round decision
Mar. 11, 1995	Las Vegas, Nev.	Herbie Hide	6th-round knockout
Nov. 4, 1995	Las Vegas, Nev.	Evander Holyfield	8th-round knockout
July 11, 1996	New York, N.Y.	Andrew Golota	7th-round winner by disqualification
Dec. 14, 1996	Atlantic City, N.J.	Andrew Golota	9th-round winner by disqualification

some personal problems as well. He had both a sister and a brother die during one five-month period before the Games, and his losses affected his mental preparation for his fights.

The Emerging Champion

At 6 feet 5 inches and about 240 pounds, Riddick had the size and strength to become a great heavyweight. However, his fortitude was questioned. No one in the boxing world wanted to take a chance on him. Eventually, Rock Newman, a young boxing promoter, intrigued by Riddick's Olympic performance, offered to manage him. Together, they became one of the most successful boxer-manager duos of the early 1990's. Eddie Futch, a legendary trainer, agreed to work with Riddick. Almost immediately, Riddick started paying dividends for his manager. On March 6, 1989, in his first professional bout Riddick knocked out Lionel Butler, an aggressive and experienced fighter, in the second round.

Riddick quickly emerged as one of the top contenders for the heavyweight title, winning his first 25 fights as a professional. Along the way, he defeated some of the top names in the heavyweight division at the time, including Tyrell Biggs and Tony Tubbs.

Riddick offered a unique combination. He was a powerful puncher and was quick afoot as well, having patterned himself after his idol, Muhammad Ali. Soon, Riddick earned a shot at the heavyweight title. He and Newman had set a target date of September, 1992, for their chance to fight for the heavyweight title, and they were not far off.

Continuing the Story

On November 13, 1992, Riddick got his chance to fight for the heavyweight title against veteran Evander Holyfield. Riddick took advantage of his opportunity: The fighter that nobody wanted just four years earlier easily gained the decision over Holyfield and became the heavyweight champion of the world.

By this time, Riddick had become rich enough to take care of his family. He had moved his wife and children away from Brooklyn into a huge home in suburban Maryland. Not long after, he bought a nearby house for his mother. Riddick was in tremendous demand as a spokesperson, and he took great care to make sure that he served as a responsible champion. He often spoke to youth and school groups, preaching about the values of positive thinking and the evils of drugs and crime. During his reign as heavyweight champion, he even had an audience with the pope in Rome.

After beating Holyfield, he won two more fights, defending his title each time. In Las Vegas, Nevada, in November, 1993, almost one year to the day that he took the title from Holyfield, Riddick battled Holyfield again. This time, Holyfield, stung by Riddick's victory in the first fight, came back and reclaimed his title with a majority decision after a tough battle. Riddick appeared overweight and poorly prepared for the bout. This fight became infamous for a bizarre stunt in which a parachutist

Statistics

Bouts, 45
Knockouts, 33
Bouts won by decision, 10
Bouts lost by decision, 1
No contest, 1

Honors and Awards

1988   Silver medal, U.S. Olympic Boxing

dropped into the open-air arena, landed near Riddick's corner, and was beaten by Riddick's cornermen before referee Mills Lane restored order. Riddick was undeterred by the loss, and he vowed to come back, much as Ali had done earlier. At the age of twenty-six, Riddick was determined to remain one of the world's best heavyweights.

In August, 1994, Riddick narrowly avoided a disqualification when referee Arthur Mercante, Jr., declared a no contest in the fourth round of a fight against Buster Mathis, Jr. Riddick had knocked out Mathis by hitting him illegally when he was down. Three months later, Riddick won a 12-round decision against Larry Donald, after throwing a punch at Donald in the preceding press conference.

Riddick was in position to claim the World Boxing Organization (WBO) heavyweight title. He faced Herbie Hide for the belt and knocked him down six times before knocking him out in the sixth round. In July, 1995, Riddick retained his WBO title in a match against Jorge Luis Gonzalez. However, his greatest challenge came in November, when he faced Holyfield for the third time in his career. Holyfield had the early momentum, knocking Riddick down. By the eighth round, however, Holyfield was tiring, and Riddick knocked him out.

Riddick fought two more matches, both against notoriously dirty fighter Andrew Golota and both won by disqualification. In each fight, Golota seemed to have the upper hand against a slower and less powerful Riddick. However, repeated low blows by Golota in each bout forced the disqualifications. The first fight also featured a riot in which one of Riddick's supporters struck Golota with a two-way radio, causing a cut that required eleven stitches.

With his life outside the ring beginning to unravel because of domestic problems and growing health concerns, Riddick retired from boxing in 1996. The following year, Riddick tried to fulfill a lifelong dream by enlisting in the Marines but lasted only eleven days in boot camp before quitting. In 1998, Riddick was charged with interstate domestic violence in the abduction of his estranged wife and children. During the trial, Riddick blamed the incident on pugilistic dementia, or brain damage sustained from boxing. The defense did not stop Riddick from ultimately serving seventeen months in prison for the crime.

Released in 2004, he tried to resume his boxing career. He knocked out Marcus Rhode in the second round of a fight and earned a split decision over Billy Zumbrun in 2005. Riddick did not box after 2005; his record stood at 42-1-1. In 2006, he declared bankruptcy. The following year, he pursued a career in mixed martial arts.

Summary

Riddick Bowe was one of the best heavyweight boxers of his time. His power and speed catapulted him to the top of his profession at a young age. Though his reign as boxing's heavyweight champion was brief, he was one of the greatest of his era and the first boxer to knock out Evander Holyfield.

John McNamara, updated by Caryn E. Neumann

Additional Sources

Baker, H. Eugene, III, and Kenneth M. Jennings. "Limitation in 'Realistic Recruiting' and Subsequent Socialization Efforts: The Case of Riddick Bowe and the U.S. Marine Corps." *Public Personnel Management* 29, no. 3 (September 22, 2000): 369-386.

Finger, David E. *Rocky Lives! Heavyweight Boxing Upsets of the 1990's.* Dulles, Va.: Brassey's, 2005.

Hoffer, Richard. "Blood Brothers." *Sports Illustrated* 98, no. 15 (April 14, 2003): 68.

Mullan, Harry, and Bob Mee. *The Ultimate Encyclopedia of Boxing.* London: Carlton, 2007.

Schulman, Arlene. *The Prize Fighters: An Intimate Look at Champions and Contenders.* New York: Lyons and Burford, 1994.

Stout, Glenn, and Bud Collins. *The Best American Sports Writing 2001.* Boston: Houghton Mifflin, 2001.

Julio César Chávez

Born: July 12, 1962
Ciudad Obregón, Mexico
Also known as: Julio César Chávez González (full name); J. C.

Early Life

Julio César Chávez was born on July 12, 1962, to Rodolfo and Isabel Chávez. Rodolfo, a railroad engineer, and Isabel, a homemaker, had four boys and five girls. The family had little money and lived in an abandoned railroad car. In Obregón, often referred to as the drug capital of Mexico, Julio grew up with the perpetual threat of violence. Early on, he began to feel a responsibility to care for and protect his family. He often took odd jobs—shining shoes, washing cars, and selling newspapers—to make extra money for the family.

As a boy, Julio enjoyed playing soccer and baseball, but his brothers, Rodolfo and Rafael, were involved with boxing. Former boxer Juan Antonio López, who had once been ranked fifth in the world as a super bantamweight, recognized Julio's boxing skills and persuaded him to begin training at a small gym in the suburb of Colonia Ejidal. Julio saw this as an opportunity to provide real financial security for his family.

The Road to Excellence

At the age of sixteen, Julio began training daily, going to fights on weekends, and building his boxing skills. Motivated by the need to provide a good life for his family, he was determined and self-assured in the ring. He fought his first amateur bout at sixteen. With an orthodox style, he won fourteen fights and lost only his last fight at a Mexico City tournament before becoming a professional boxer. During his time in the amateur ranks, Julio learned to deliver devastating blows to the body, a skill that was the key to his subsequent professional ability to dismantle an opponent. Supporters such as Augustin de Valdez promoted him within the boxing community and worked to ensure the continued growth of his career.

Julio's first professional fight, on February 5, 1980, ended in a win by knockout against Andres Felix. In the four years that followed, Julio had a fight almost every month. He added forty-two more victories to his record, thirty-five of them by knockout. Gradually, he faced greater opponents as his career progressed and the boxing world began to take notice of him.

Finally, after four years with no losses, Julio got his first title shot. On September 13, 1984, Julio fought Mario Martinez for the World Boxing Council (WBC) super-featherweight title. In his

Julio César Chávez after winning a WBC super-lightweight fight. (Jeff Haynes/AFP/Getty Images)

first televised bout, Julio won by knockout in the eighth round and became the WBC super-featherweight champion.

The Emerging Champion

Over the next three years, Julio used his combination of punching power and boxing strategy to defend his WBC title nine times. Promoted exclusively by Don King, he was able to appear against a steady stream of top-ranked fighters while preparing to pursue more titles at higher weight divisions.

On November 21, 1987, Julio fought Edwin Rosario for the World Boxing Association (WBA) lightweight title. Julio came into the fight with a record of 44-0. Angered by insults that the Puerto Rican Rosario had directed at the Mexican people, Julio viciously attacked him. Using double and triple hook shots to the body, Julio gradually wore his opponent down in his usual fashion. Near the end of the eleventh round, he won by technical knockout (TKO) and added a second world title to his record.

On October 29, 1988, Julio unified the WBA and the WBC lightweight titles against José Luis Ramírez. Ahead on points, Julio was declared the winner when the fight was called as the result of a bad cut on Ramírez's head. Although some observers said that Julio was not at his best in the fight, his powerful combinations of punches had him well ahead when the fight was stopped.

Moving up in weight class, Julio next pursued the WBC super-lightweight title. Julio had already defeated Roger Mayweather with a second round TKO in a defense of his WBC super-featherweight title. Julio was pitted against Mayweather to secure another title. Fighting on May 13, 1989, Julio earned his fourth championship belt by wearing down Mayweather with persistent punches to the body. Mayweather was felled with a TKO in the tenth round.

Julio's next fight earned *Ring* magazine's designation as the best boxing match of 1990. Going for his fifth championship, the International Boxing Federation junior-welterweight title, against Meldrick Taylor, Julio experienced one of the most controversial moments of his career. Throughout the fight, Taylor had been ahead of Julio, bewildering him several times with combinations. By the twelfth and final round, both fighters were exhausted and Taylor was ahead on the scorecards. Julio delivered

Statistics

Bouts, 115
Knockouts, 86
Bouts won by decision, 21
Bouts lost by decision, 2
Bouts lost by knockout, 4
Draws, 2

Honors and Awards

1987 Boxing Writers of America Fighter of the Year
1990 *Ring* magazine Fighter of the Year
1992 World Boxing Council Fighter of the Year

several punches that staggered Taylor before sending him to the canvas with one quarter of a minute remaining in the fight. Taylor staggered to his feet. However, the referee judged that Taylor was not in command of his senses and ended the fight with only 2 seconds to go. Julio won by a TKO.

Continuing the Story

Julio defended his WBC junior-welterweight title against such competitors as Lonnie Smith and Héctor Camacho. Against Camacho, for the first time, Julio fought as a main event on pay-per-view television. The much-anticipated fight proved long and difficult as Camacho ran or held while Julio tried to punch him. Julio finally earned the victory on points. He went on to face and defeat such fighters as Greg Haugen, retaining his title.

Controversy arose on September 10, 1993, when Julio fought a close battle with Pernell Whitaker that ended in a draw. Many observers argued that Whitaker had clearly won the fight and that Julio only retained his title because of his ties to controversial promoter King. On January 29, 1994, Julio lost his WBC junior-welterweight crown to Frankie Randall in a 12-round split decision. Julio dominated the fourth through seventh rounds, as well as the ninth and the tenth, on two of the judges' scorecards. Julio was penalized for low blows in the seventh and eleventh round, ultimately losing to Randall on points. The defeat was Julio's first in ninety-one fights. A rematch was scheduled almost as soon as the fighters left the ring. In May of 1994, in the rematch with Randall, Julio regained his title with an eighth-round technical decision when the fight was stopped because of a head butt.

In 1994, Julio defended his junior-welterweight

title two more times with victories against Taylor and Tony Lopez, both by TKO. The thirty-two-year-old Julio was approaching an astounding one hundred victories.

In 1995, Julio won close decisions against Giovanni Parisi and David Kamau to retain his title in the junior-welterweight division. In 1996, however, he faced the undefeated Oscar De La Hoya, whose youth and power were too much for the aging champion. De La Hoya won the fight by a fourth-round TKO. Julio and De La Hoya met again in 1998. After fighting Miguel Angel Gonzalez to a twelfth-round draw, Julio moved up one weight class to challenge De La Hoya for the WBC light-

Recognized World Super Featherweight Championships

Date	Loser	Result
Sept. 13, 1984	Mario Martinez	8th-round knockout
Apr. 19, 1985	Ruben Castillo	6th-round knockout
July 7, 1985	Roger Mayweather	2d-round knockout
Sept. 21, 1985	Dwight Pratchett	12th-round decision
May 15, 1986	Faustino Barrios	5th-round technical knockout
June 13, 1986	Refugio Rojas	7th-round knockout
Aug. 3, 1986	Rocky Lockridge	12th-round decision
Dec. 12, 1986	Juan La Porte	12th-round decision
Apr. 18, 1987	Tomás Da Cruz	3d-round technical knockout
Aug. 21, 1987	Danilo Cabrera	12th-round decision

Recognized World Lightweight Championships

Date	Loser	Result
Nov. 21, 1987	Edwin Rosario	11th-round technical knockout
Apr. 16, 1988	Rodolfo Aguilar	6th-round technical knockout
Oct. 29, 1988	José Luis Ramírez	11th-round decision

Recognized World Super Lightweight Championships

Date	Loser	Result
May 13, 1989	Roger Mayweather	10th-round knockout
Nov. 18, 1989	Sammy Fuentes	10th-round technical knockout
Dec. 16, 1989	Alberto Cortes	3d-round knockout

Recognized World Junior Welterweight Championships

Date	Loser	Result
Mar. 17, 1990	Meldrick Taylor	12th-round technical knockout
Dec. 8, 1990	Kyung-Duk Ahn	3d-round technical knockout
Mar. 18, 1991	John Duplessis	4th-round technical knockout
Sept. 14, 1991	Lonnie Smith	12th-round decision
Apr. 10, 1992	Angel Hernandez	6th-round technical knockout
Aug. 1, 1992	Frank Mitchell	4th-round technical knockout
Sept. 12, 1992	Héctor Camacho	12th-round decision
Feb. 20, 1993	Greg Haugen	5th-round technical knockout
May 8, 1993	Terrence Ali	6th-round technical knockout
Sept. 10, 1993	(Pernell Whitaker, opponent)	12th-round draw
Dec. 18, 1993	Andy Holligan	5th-round technical knockout
Jan. 29, 1994	Julio César Chávez (Frankie Randall, winner)	12th-round decision
May 7, 1994	Frankie Randall	8th-round decision
Sept. 17, 1994	Meldrick Taylor	8th-round technical knockout
Dec. 10, 1994	Tony Lopez	10th-round technical knockout
Apr. 8, 1995	Giovanni Parisi	12th-round decision
Sept. 16, 1995	David Kamau	12th-round decision
June 7, 1996	Julio César Chávez (Oscar De La Hoya, winner)	4th-round technical knockout
Mar. 7, 1998	Miguel Angel Gonzalez	12th-round draw
July 29, 2000	Julio César Chávez (Kostya Tszyu, winner)	6th-round technical knockout

Recognized World Welterweight Championship

Date	Loser	Result
Sept. 18, 1998	Julio César Chávez (Oscar De La Hoya, winner)	8th-round technical knockout

welterweight title on September 18. Again, he lost by TKO, this time in the eighth round.

Julio returned to title contention in 2000, facing Kostya Tszyu for the WBC junior-welterweight title. In a lopsided affair, the thirty-eight-year-old Julio was no match for Tszyu, suffering only his second knockdown in his career and a sixth-round TKO. The fight was Julio's last chance for a title. He had only one fight in the next three years, a second round TKO of Willy Wise.

Like many boxers, Julio had trouble putting down the gloves. He retired three times before unretiring for the last time in 2005 to embark on an "Adios Tour" that served as a showcase for him in areas with large Latino populations. Julio needed the money. Despite earning about $50 million during his career, he was broke. Part of the money went to feed a drug habit. Julio retired again in January, 2006, on the heels of a loss. He completed drug rehabilitation in 2007. In retirement, Julio watched the boxing careers of his sons, Julio, Jr., and Omar.

Summary

Julio César Chávez is considered by many to be the greatest fighter of his era. Idolized among boxing fans in the United States and Mexico, Julio enjoyed remarkable longevity in boxing. His career record of 107-6-2, with 86 knockouts and six world titles in three weight divisions, stands as testimony to the power of his fists and the strength of his chin. Though fans and analysts alike have criticized him for refusing to retire earlier, his presence in the ring always drew genuine support, and his achievements rank him among boxing's best fighters.

Margaret Debicki, updated by Caryn E. Neumann

Additional Sources

Creamer, Matthew. "Chávez, Julio César." *Current Biography* 60, no. 4 (April, 1999): 11-14.

Dumas, Andy. *Fit to Fight: Get in the Best Shape of Your Life with the Workouts of Professional Boxers.* New York: Skyhorse, 2008.

Mullan, Harry. *The Ultimate Encyclopedia of Boxing: The Definitive Illustrated Guide to World Boxing.* Edison, N.J.: Chartwell Books, 1996.

Schulman, Arlene. *The Prize Fighters: An Intimate Look at Champions and Contenders.* New York: Lyons and Burford, 1994.

Sugar, Bert Randolph. *Boxing's Greatest Fighters.* Guilford, Conn.: Lyons Press, 2006.

Billy Conn

Born: October 8, 1917
Pittsburgh, Pennsylvania
Died: May 29, 1993
Pittsburgh, Pennsylvania
Also known as: William David Conn, Jr. (full name); the Pittsburgh Kid

Early Life
William David Conn, Jr., was born on October 8, 1917, in Pittsburgh, Pennsylvania. His parents were William David Conn, a steam fitter at a Westinghouse plant, and Margaret Conn. At the age of thirteen, Billy began to take boxing lessons from Johnny Ray, a former boxer who ran a nondescript gym for fighters in East Liberty, a working-class neighborhood of Pittsburgh. In exchange for the lessons, Billy swept up and did other jobs around the gym.

Ray saw that Billy had the potential to become a professional boxer, and he began to tutor Billy carefully. As Billy grew older, he spent hours each day working out and sparring at the gym. He also watched many fights while at Ray's side. Never a good student, Billy dropped out of the parochial school he had been attending to concentrate on becoming a professional boxer. This seemed to make sense to Billy and his parents, given the depressed economic conditions of the 1930's. Billy made his professional debut at Fairmont, West Virginia, in January, 1935; Billy's share of the $2.50 purse was fifty cents.

The Road to Excellence
Billy fought more than three dozen times in 1935 and 1936, rarely traveling more than two hundred miles from Pittsburgh for a match. He lost six of his first fourteen professional fights, but he continued to work hard and developed an accurate jab, a great left hook, and a decent right cross. Realizing that Billy did not have a knockout punch, Ray especially wanted Billy to work on his combination punching and footwork.

Only six months after his professional debut, Billy began a twenty-seven-bout undefeated streak that stretched from August, 1935, to August, 1937. As Billy matured physically, he moved up from the lightweight to welterweight and then to the middleweight ranks, often fighting men four or five years older. On December 28, 1936, Billy beat Fritzie Zivic, who later won the welterweight crown; in 1937, he took on such quality middleweights as Teddy Yarosz, Young Corbett, and Solly Krieger, all three of whom made *Ring* magazine's list of top-ten middleweights in either 1937 or 1938. Billy lost to Corbett and Krieger the first time he fought them, but he beat each man in a rematch.

Except for one match each year in San Francisco, Billy continued to fight in Pittsburgh in 1937

Billy Conn, who was the light-heavyweight champion in the 1930's. (Courtesy of Amateur Athletic Foundation of Los Angeles)

Statistics

Bouts, 75
Knockouts, 14
Bouts won by decision, 49
Bouts lost by knockout, 2
Bouts lost by decision, 9
Draws, 1

Honors and Awards

1939 Edward J. Neil Trophy
1965 *Ring* magazine Boxing Hall of Fame
1990 International Boxing Hall of Fame

and 1938. His success against such opponents as Krieger, a popular New Yorker, attracted the attention of the prominent New York promoter Mike Jacobs, who booked Billy for a fight on January 6, 1939, in the famous Madison Square Garden. There, Billy beat Fred Apostoli, recognized as the middleweight titleholder by the New York State Athletic Commission, in a thrilling nontitle bout before nearly eleven thousand fans. Only five weeks later, in what he regarded as his hardest fight ever, Billy won an even more exciting fifteen-rounder against Apostoli.

The Emerging Champion

Jacobs took a liking to Billy and believed that he could become an attraction at the box office. To sharpen Billy's image, Jacobs saw that the young fighter dressed well and met the right people, including show-business celebrities. Nicknamed the "Pittsburgh Kid," Billy did not let his growing prominence distract him from his mission of becoming champion. On July 13, 1939, Billy, who had outgrown the middleweight class, claimed the light-heavyweight title in a fight with Melio Bettina.

After defeating Bettina in a rematch, Billy defended his title in two memorable fights against top challenger Gus Lesnevich. Billy gained decisions over Lesnevich in a fifteen-round fight in New York on November 17, 1939, and in another fifteen-round battle in Detroit on June 5, 1940.

Billy, who was named fighter of the year in 1940, then stepped up to the heavyweight class, boxing's most publicized division and the only one where big money—perhaps $100,000 for a title match—could be earned. Ray and Jacobs both wanted to see Billy challenge the heavyweight champion, Joe Louis, who had held the title since 1937 and who so dominated the division that one writer referred to Louis's victims as members of the "Bum-of-the-Month Club." Fan interest in the heavyweights was declining, and Billy could revive it by challenging Louis, thought Ray and Jacobs.

Broad-shouldered and just more than 6 feet in height, Billy rarely weighed as much as 175 pounds, the light-heavyweight limit, but for heavyweight fights his weight was usually announced as close to 180 pounds. Before he could fight Louis, Billy had to vacate his own light-heavyweight title. After beating rated heavyweights Lee Savold and Bob Pastor, he outclassed four consecutive opponents early in 1941. He met Louis for the title on June 18, 1941, at the Polo Grounds, a baseball park in New York City that could seat more than fifty thousand spectators.

Earlier in his career, Billy had sometimes been careless about his conditioning, but he had since learned to keep in good shape. Billy rarely won by a knockout, but he consistently went the distance to win his fights on points. He had never been knocked out. Although he was the underdog against Louis, several experts believed that Billy

Recognized World Light Heavyweight Championships

Date	Location	Loser	Result
July 13, 1939	New York, N.Y.	Melio Bettina	15th-round decision
Sept. 25, 1939	Pittsburgh, Pa.	Melio Bettina	15th-round decision
Nov. 17, 1939	New York, N.Y.	Gus Lesnevich	15th-round decision
June 5, 1940	Detroit, Mich.	Gus Lesnevich	15th-round decision

Recognized World Heavyweight Championships

Date	Location	Loser	Result
June 18, 1941	New York, N.Y.	Billy Conn (Joe Louis, winner)	13th-round knockout
June 19, 1946	New York, N.Y.	Billy Conn (Joe Louis, winner)	8th-round knockout

could outpoint the bigger, stronger Louis if he fought intelligently and took advantage of his nimble feet and remarkably quick hands.

The Polo Grounds was jammed for the contest, and for twelve rounds, Billy gave spectators and millions of radio listeners all the excitement they could want, taking seven rounds on points. Billy's cornermen told him to keep using his hit-and-run tactics and combination punching, but Billy, who had been dominating the fight since the eighth round and had nearly knocked the champion down in the twelfth, thought that Louis was weakening. Billy abandoned the tactics that had been working to try for a knockout. Billy's decision was a mistake, for Louis, who had won more than 80 percent of his fights by knockout, staggered him with several hard blows. Billy went down for the count just before the end of the thirteenth round. In tears as reporters interviewed him after the fight, he said, "I lost my head and a million bucks."

To fans, however, Billy's near-upset of the champion enhanced his popularity. His curly hair and "toothpaste ad grin" made him perfect for Hollywood and earned him a contract soon after the Louis fight to star with actress Jean Parker in *The Pittsburgh Kid*, a 1941 film about boxing in which he played himself.

Many assumed Billy and Louis would soon fight again, and fan and media anticipation of a rematch was high. In December, 1941, however, the United States entered World War II, and both Billy and Louis enlisted in the armed forces. On February 13, 1942, he took a twelve-round decision from Tony Zale, the "Man of Steel," in Billy's last fight before entering the Army.

Continuing the Story

In the service, Billy visited hospitals for military personnel and led a group of boxers who fought exhibition matches to entertain the troops. In June, 1944, he led his group of boxers to England and around European battlefronts. While in Italy, Billy and some army companions helped to rescue an American pilot from a flaming plane that had crashed near them. He later toured military bases in France with several popular entertainers headed by film star Bob Hope.

In 1945, both Louis and Billy were discharged from the U.S. Army. Billy resumed training and fought two exhibitions before fighting Louis for the heavyweight title in New York's Yankee Stadium on June 19, 1946. In their first battle, Billy had given fight fans much more than they had expected, but in the second, he gave them less. Neither man had recaptured his 1941 form, but at one time in his Army service, Billy had put on close to 25 pounds. For the fight with Louis, Billy could slim down only to 182 pounds, nearly 10 pounds above his normal prewar fighting weight. He could not regain the speed and timing that had been essential to his success. Billy realized this and tried to stay away from the champion; some disappointed fans in the capacity crowd booed. Louis knocked Billy out in the eighth round.

Billy no longer had the desire and the reflexes that had made him a great boxer. He did not fight at all in 1947, and had only a handful of bouts in 1948. After an exhibition match with Louis in December, 1948, he retired with a career record of sixty-three wins, eleven defeats, and one draw.

Billy, who had invested his earnings wisely, lived comfortably in Pittsburgh after his retirement, occasionally appearing as a referee at a boxing or wrestling match and, for a while, taking a job as a greeter at a Las Vegas casino. He was named to *Ring* magazine's Boxing Hall of Fame in 1965. In 1993, he died in Pittsburgh at the age of seventy-five.

Summary

Billy Conn is remembered more for his 1941 loss to Joe Louis than for the dozens of victories he earned in the ring with his deft footwork and quick hands. Win, lose, or draw, the "Pittsburgh Kid" was a popular fighter who dazzled the boxing world with his brash but appealing personality and prowess in the ring. Long after he retired, Billy was still considered one of boxing's immortals.

Lloyd J. Graybar

Additional Sources

Blewett, Bert. *The A to Z of World Boxing*. London: Robson Books, 1996.

Kennedy, Paul F. *Billy Conn: The Pittsburgh Kid*. Bloomington, Ind.: AuthorHouse, 2007.

Mullan, Harry, and Bob Mee. *The Ultimate Encyclopedia of Boxing*. London: Carlton, 2007.

O'Toole, Andrew. *Sweet William: The Life of Billy Conn*. Urbana: University of Illinois Press, 2007.

Sugar, Bert Randolph. *Boxing's Greatest Fighters*. Guilford, Conn.: Lyons Press, 2006.

Oscar De La Hoya

Born: February 4, 1973
Los Angeles, California
Also known as: Golden Boy

Early Life

Oscar De la Hoya was born on February 4, 1973, in East Los Angeles, California, to Joel De La Hoya, a shipping and receiving clerk, and Cecilia Gonzalez De La Hoya. Boxing was a part of several generations of Oscar's large and close-knit Mexican American family. Before moving to the United States, Oscar's grandfather, Vincente De La Hoya, had been an amateur featherweight boxer in Durango, Mexico, and Oscar's father had been a professional boxer in Los Angeles in his youth.

Oscar's first experience in the ring was at the age of six, when his father entered him in pee-wee boxing tournaments at the neighborhood Resurrection Boys Club. In his debut fight, Oscar knocked out his opponent in the first round. Boxing shielded Oscar from the tensions of a notoriously dangerous city. The pressures of gangs, drugs, and crime were widespread in East Los Angeles. Once, Oscar was mugged by gang members as he walked home from his girlfriend's house. Frequently, he could hear the sounds of gunshots echoing just a few blocks away. Unlike some of his peers who became caught up in this violent street life, Oscar went directly to the Resurrection Gym on South Lorena Street every day after school.

The Road to Excellence

The long hours spent sparring in the ring paid off quickly for Oscar. His trainer during these first years was Al Stankie, a former Los Angeles police officer. Stankie had guided another boxer from East Los Angeles, Paul Gonzalez, to an Olympic gold medal in 1984.

In 1988, at the age of fifteen, Oscar won his first national championship, the 119-pound Junior Olympic title. His skill was widely recognized, especially his confident way of moving and punching with a powerful left hook in an orthodox style. Many people called the 5-foot 11-inch lightweight a "natural" at the sport. They marveled at his rapid development inside the ring and noticed his likable spirit outside it. In 1989, he earned the national Golden Gloves 125-pound title. One year later, he won the 125-pound division of the United States Boxing Championships.

In 1990, Oscar, as the youngest participant at the Goodwill Games in Seattle, Washington, won his first gold medal. He also returned home knowing for the first time that his mother was terminally ill. The day

Oscar De La Hoya (left) cocking his right hand against Floyd Mayweather in a 2007 fight. (Barry Sweet/Landov)

Recognized Junior Lightweight Championships

Date	Location	Loser	Result
Mar. 5, 1994	Los Angeles, Calif.	Jimmi Bredahl	10th-round technical knockout
May 27, 1994	Las Vegas, Nev.	Giorgio Campanella	3d-round technical knockout

Recognized Lightweight Championships

Date	Location	Loser	Result
July 29, 1994	Las Vegas, Nev.	Jorge Paez	2d-round knockout
Nov. 18, 1994	Las Vegas, Nev.	Carl Griffith	3d-round knockout
Dec. 10, 1994	Los Angeles, Calif.	John Avila	9th-round technical knockout
Feb. 18, 1995	Las Vegas, Nev.	John-John Molina	12th-round decision
May 6, 1995	Las Vegas, Nev.	Rafael Ruelas	2d-round technical knockout
Sept. 9, 1995	Las Vegas, Nev.	Genaro Hernandez	6th-round technical knockout
Dec. 15, 1995	New York, N.Y.	Jesse James Leija	2d-round technical knockout

Recognized Light Welterweight Championships

Date	Location	Loser	Result
June 7, 1996	Las Vegas, Nev.	Julio César Chávez	4th-round technical knockout
Jan. 18, 1997	Las Vegas, Nev.	Miguel Angel Gonzalez	12th-round decision

Recognized Welterweight Championships

Date	Location	Loser	Result
Apr. 12, 1997	Las Vegas, Nev.	Pernell Whitaker	12th-round decision
June 14, 1997	San Antonio, Tex.	David Kamau	2d-round knockout
Sept. 13, 1997	Las Vegas, Nev.	Héctor Camacho	12th-round decision
Dec. 6, 1997	Atlantic City, N.J.	Wilfredo Rivera	8th-round technical knockout
June 13, 1998	El Paso, Tex.	Patrick Charpentier	3d-round technical knockout
Sept. 18, 1998	Las Vegas, Nev.	Julio César Chávez	8th-round technical knockout
Feb. 13, 1999	Las Vegas, Nev.	Ike Quartey	12th-round decision
May 22, 1999	Las Vegas, Nev.	Oba Carr	11th-round technical knockout
Sept. 18, 1999	Las Vegas, Nev.	Oscar De La Hoya (Félix Trinidad, winner)	12th-round decision
Feb. 26, 2000	New York, N.Y.	Derrel Coley	7th-round knockout
June 17, 2000	Los Angeles, Calif.	Oscar De La Hoya (Shane Mosely, winner)	12th-round decision

Recognized Super Welterweight Championships

Date	Location	Loser	Result
June 23, 2001	Las Vegas, Nev.	Javier Catillejo	12th-round decision
May 5, 2006	Las Vegas, Nev.	Ricard Mayorga	6th-round technical knockout
May 5, 2007	Las Vegas, Nev.	Oscar De La Hoya (Floyd Mayweather, Jr., winner)	12th-round split decision

Recognized Super Welterweight/Light Middleweight Championships

Date	Location	Loser	Result
Sept. 14, 2002	Las Vegas, Nev.	Fernando Vargas	11th-round technical knockout
May 3, 2003	Las Vegas, Nev.	Luis Ramon	7th-round technical knockout
Sept. 13, 2003	Las Vegas, Nev.	Oscar De La Hoya (Shane Mosley, winner)	12th-round decision

Recognized Middleweight Championships

Date	Location	Loser	Result
June 5, 2004	Las Vegas, Nev.	Felix Sturm	12th-round decision
Sept. 18, 2004	Las Vegas, Nev.	Oscar De La Hoya (Bernard Hopkins, winner)	9th-round knockout

after the Goodwill Games ended, the De La Hoya family told Oscar that his mother had breast cancer. Until then, he was unaware that she had been receiving radiation therapy for many months. The news was devastating for Oscar, who thought of his mother as his best friend. When she died at the age of thirty-nine in October, 1990, the young champion vowed to win her the highest honor, a gold medal, at the Olympic Games in Barcelona, Spain.

The next year brought other changes in Oscar's life. He graduated from Garfield High School, where he had been a good student and had particularly enjoyed classes in art and architecture. He also switched coaches, replacing Stankie with Robert Alcazar. Frequent victories followed at home and abroad, including gold medals at the 1991 U.S. Olympic Sports Festival and the 1991 U.S. amateur boxing tournament. USA Boxing voted Oscar the 1991 boxer of the year.

In the fall of 1991, Oscar suffered his first defeat in four years. After 36 consecutive victories in international competition, Oscar lost to Marco Rudolph of Germany at the World Amateur Boxing Championships in Sydney, Australia. Initially, the loss confused Oscar, who had grown accustomed to winning. Before long, however, he realized that the experience had helped him to rediscover his determination for the sport. With renewed enthusiasm, Oscar prepared for his greatest challenge yet: the 1992 Summer Olympic Games.

The Emerging Champion
Making the U.S. Olympic boxing team was easy for Oscar. Tryouts in Massachusetts and Arizona earned him a place among other American amateur athletes bound for Barcelona. Once he was there, however, the thrill of Olympic competition was diminished by judging that sometimes seemed unfair to Oscar and his coaches. Still, Oscar steadily advanced from one round to the next in the 132-pound class.

In his first match, Oscar knocked out Adison Silva of Brazil. He then outpointed Moses Odion of Nigeria and Dimitrov Tontchev of Bulgaria to advance to the semifinals. In that round, South Korean boxer Hong Sung-Sik proved to be a difficult opponent. His wrestling style distracted Oscar, but the young American won by a single point.

This narrow triumph was critical. Because of it, Oscar advanced to a gold-medal bout against the only boxer to defeat him since childhood: Marco Rudolph of Germany. On August 8, he avenged the loss in Australia by beating Rudolph. By a convincing score of 7-2, Oscar fulfilled his promise to his mother and won the U.S. team's only gold medal in boxing of the 1992 Games.

While Oscar was sad that his mother could not share his triumph, he had many reasons for happiness after winning the Olympic gold. As an amateur, Oscar had achieved an astonishing record: 225 wins and only 5 losses, with 153 knockouts. Because of this record, Oscar signed one of the richest deals in boxing history, a $1 million contract with New York managers Bob Mittleman and Steve Nelson. The package included cash, cars, and a new house for his family in Montebello, California. Oscar also signed contracts with a promoter and an agent, who handled endorsement deals.

Continuing the Story
Oscar's professional debut occurred on November 23, 1992, at the Great Western Forum in Los Angeles. Wearing a black sombrero and carrying both American and Mexican flags as he walked into the ring, East Los Angeles's "Golden Boy" knocked out competitor Lamar Williams after only 1 minute and 42 seconds. More than ever, observers said that Oscar was destined for stardom. After 11 consecutive wins—10 by knockout—in less than a year, Oscar met Jimmi Bredahl for the World Boxing Organization (WBO) junior-lightweight title. In the tenth round, Oscar scored a technical knockout (TKO) to capture his first professional championship. In 1994, he moved up to the lightweight division and knocked out Jorge Paez in 2 rounds for the WBO's vacant lightweight title.

On May 6, 1995, Oscar added the International Boxing Federation (IBF) lightweight title to his collection by scoring a second-round TKO against Rafael Ruelas. In that year, he was also named *Ring* magazine's fighter of the year. By April of 1996, Oscar had abandoned his lightweight titles as he moved up in weight to the light-welterweight division. He faced the aging but still dangerous Julio César Chávez on June 7, overpowering him with a fourth-round TKO.

In 1997, Oscar moved up in weight again, this

Statistics

Bouts, 45
Knockouts, 30
Bouts won by decision, 9
Losses, 6

Honors and Awards

1991-92	USA Boxing Boxer of the Year
1992	Gold medal, U.S. Olympic Boxing
1995	*Ring* magazine Fighter of the Year
	Edward J. Neil Trophy
2001	WBC 1990's Boxer of the Decade
2007	WBO 2000's Fighter of the Decade

time to face Pernell "Sweet Pea" Whitaker for the World Boxing Council (WBC) welterweight title. In a close fight, which many thought Whitaker should have won, Oscar took a twelfth-round decision and began a lengthy reign at the top of the welterweight division. Oscar's dominance ended controversially on September 18, 1999, when he suffered his first loss in a close decision to Félix Trinidad. Oscar seemed to have the fight under control as it entered the final rounds, but his failure to seal the victory convincingly and Trinidad's aggressive approach near the end swayed the judges in Trinidad's favor.

After defeating Derrel Coley to win the IBF welterweight title on February 26, 2000, Oscar faced the undefeated "Sugar" Shane Mosely on June 17 in Los Angeles. In a much anticipated bout, both fighters electrified the crowd with their speed and power. Mosely won by split decision after landing 45 of 88 punches in the final round, handing Oscar his second loss in three fights. Oscar lost to Mosely a second time in a controversial decision, with many viewers giving the bout to Oscar.

Although Oscar announced his intention to retire if he lost to the same man twice, he returned to the ring after his loss to Mosely. He still did not have a trademark style of boxing, probably the result of working with many different trainers.

On June 5, 2004, Oscar won the WBO middleweight title with a unanimous decision against defending champion Felix Sturm. However, he did not hold the title for long. On September 18, Oscar fought middleweight champion Bernard Hopkins in a title unification bout. Hopkins stopped Oscar in the ninth round. On May 5, 2006, Oscar returned from a twenty-month layoff to defeat Ricardo Mayorga in 6 rounds, winning the WBC super-welterweight title.

On May 5, 2007, Oscar battled Floyd Mayweather, Jr., in a much-anticipated 12-round bout that set records for pay-per-view purchases and revenue generated in the state of Nevada. Oscar lost by a split decision. On May 3, 2008, Oscar prepared for a rematch against Mayweather by defeating Steve Forbes with a dominating performance. However, Mayweather suddenly retired in June. Oscar intended to retire at the end of 2008, after a final fight.

Summary

Oscar De La Hoya overcame the obstacles of a childhood in East Los Angeles and his mother's death to win the only gold medal in boxing for the United States at the 1992 Olympics. His quick rise to the forefront of the sport led him to be called the pride of East Los Angeles and the Golden Boy.

While many boxers struggle to find a life outside of the ring, Oscar had more success than most. In 2000, Oscar recorded a pop music album that was nominated for a Grammy Award. In December, 2001, he formed a boxing promotion company, Golden Boy Promotions. In 2004, he joined with the Mervyn's department store to launch the Oscar De La Hoya Collection of casual clothing and accessories for men. Meanwhile, Oscar married Puerto Rican singer Millie Corretjer in October, 2001. The couple has a son and daughter. A charismatic and handsome man with superb ring skills, he became one of boxing's most celebrated figures.

Alecia C. Townsend Beckie,
updated by Caryn E. Neumann

Additional Sources

De La Hoya, Oscar, and Steve Springer. *American Son: My Story.* New York: Harper Entertainment, 2008.

Kawakami, Tim. *Golden Boy: The Fame, Money, and Mystery of Oscar De La Hoya.* Kansas City, Kans.: Andrews McMeel, 1999.

Mullan, Harry. *The Ultimate Encyclopedia of Boxing: The Definitive Illustrated Guide to World Boxing.* Edison, N.J.: Chartwell Books, 1996.

Saracano, Jon. *Twelve Rounds with Oscar De La Hoya: An Illustrated Tribute to Boxing's Brightest Star.* Dallas, Tex.: Beckett, 1998.

Schulman, Arlene. *The Prize Fighters: An Intimate Look at Champions and Contenders.* New York: Lyons and Burford, 1994.

Jack Dempsey

Born: June 24, 1895
 Manassa, Colorado
Died: May 31, 1983
 New York, New York
Also known as: William Harrison Dempsey (birth name); the Manassa Mauler

Early Life
William Harrison Dempsey was born June 24, 1895, in Manassa, Colorado, the town that is the origin of his nickname, "The Manassa Mauler." He adopted the name "Jack" in his teens. His parents were sharecroppers, and he was one of eleven children. The family moved to Utah during Jack's early youth, but their fortunes did not improve.

Jack had little formal education, never getting beyond the eighth grade. He held a number of jobs, all of which involved heavy physical labor. He was variously a fruit picker, a lumberjack, and a miner. At this stage of his life, his future prospects appeared dim. He spent much of his spare time in pool halls and bars and appeared to be no more than a local slacker.

The Road to Excellence
One fact made Jack stand out from other young men of his limited social background: his fierce determination to succeed. He liked to fight and was good at it; therefore, he decided to put all his effort into becoming a topflight boxer. Jack adopted a rigorous program of training. In addition to the usual sparring and running, he soaked his hands, face, and upper body in brine to toughen them. He also did exercises to strengthen his jaw muscles.

Jack's determination and training paid off. After turning professional in 1915, he began to win all his bouts, almost always by knockout. Starting from a crouch, he carried the fight to the opponent with relentless punching. Although thoroughly acquainted with ring technique, he was much more a slugger than a boxer. Jack's relentless aggression placed him at risk of tiring, but this problem rarely arose. Jack was an incredibly hard puncher, ranking, according to most authorities, among the most devastating of all time. Few opponents could withstand one of Jack's assaults.

At the end of 1916, the young fighter faced a challenge. He had proved himself against all local competition. His next step was to national recognition.

Jack Dempsey, who was one of the most popular athletes of the Roaring Twenties and scored 51 knockouts in a fourteen-year career. (Library of Congress)

The Emerging Champion

In 1917, Jack Kearns, a boxing expert, became Jack's manager. Kearns was a master of publicity and promotion.

Kearns matched Jack against a number of prominent fighters. Jack continued to knock out almost all his opponents. The combination of Jack's ability and Kearns's promotion secured Jack a national reputation. Only one setback marred his rise to the top. For the first time in his career, he was knocked out in a match by "Fireman" Jim Flynn, a veteran heavyweight who was often underestimated because he appeared to be fat and out of shape.

Jack did not let this defeat interfere with his progress. By 1919, he was clearly the leading contender for the heavyweight title, and a match between Jack and the champion, Jess Willard, was held on July 4.

Jack was tall and muscular, standing 6 feet and weighing 190 pounds. Willard towered 6 inches over him and outweighed him by 70 pounds, but Willard's size and strength did him little good. Jack demolished Willard, knocking him out in four brutal rounds. As a result of the beating, the left side of Willard's face was permanently caved in.

Jack's slashing style made him a popular champion, and he successfully defended the title five times from 1919 to 1926. He easily defeated the French champion, Georges Carpentier, in a match held in Jersey City, New Jersey, in 1921, the first million-dollar gate in boxing history.

Jack's 1923 match against the "Wild Bull of the Pampas," Argentine boxer Luis Firpo, proved much more exciting. The fight lasted only 3 minutes and 57 seconds. Firpo's style was an exaggerated version of Jack's: He floored Jack in the first round and, at the round's close, hit him so hard that Jack was knocked out of the ring. Showing his iron determination, Jack retaliated in the second round by knocking out his wild-swinging opponent.

Statistics

Bouts, 78
Knockouts, 49
Bouts won by decision, 12
Bouts won by fouls, 1
Knockouts by opponents, 1
Bouts lost by decision, 5
Draws, 10

Honors and Awards

1923	Citizens Savings Southern California Athlete of the Year
1938	Edward J. Neil Trophy
1954	Inducted into *Ring* magazine Boxing Hall of Fame
1957	Walker Memorial Award
1990	Inducted into International Boxing Hall of Fame

Continuing the Story

By 1926, Jack had passed his peak as a fighter. He signed for a match against Gene Tunney, whose approach to boxing differed strikingly from Jack's. Tunney lacked Jack's killer instinct and power but made up for this with a careful study of boxing technique. In their fight, held in September, 1926, in Philadelphia, Tunney avoided Jack's charges, scoring heavily with jabs. Jack had not trained very hard for the bout. Tunney's steady pressure wore him down, and by the end of the tenth round, the match was over. Tunney was awarded the world's title by unanimous decision.

As one might anticipate, Jack was not finished. He trained hard to regain his title, and the rematch in 1927, in Chicago, made boxing history. Tunney repeated his tactics of the preceding year and by the seventh round had established a comfortable lead. Jack then charged at Tunney and battered

Recognized World Heavyweight Championships

Date	Location	Loser	Result
July 4, 1919	Toledo, Ohio	Jess Willard	4th-round technical knockout
Sept. 6, 1920	Benton Harbor, Mich.	Billy Miske	3d-round knockout
Dec. 14, 1920	New York, N.Y.	Bill Brennan	12th-round knockout
July 2, 1921	Jersey City, N.J.	Georges Carpentier	4th-round knockout
July 4, 1923	Shelby, Mont.	Tommy Givvons	15th-round referee's decision
Sept. 14, 1923	New York, N.Y.	Luis Firpo	2d-round knockout
Sept. 23, 1926	Philadelphia, Pa.	Jack Dempsey (Gene Tunney, winner)	10th-round unanimous decision
Sept. 22, 1927	Chicago, Ill.	Jack Dempsey (Gene Tunney, winner)	10th-round unanimous decision

him to the canvas with a series of seven punches. Instead of retreating to a neutral corner, as the rules of boxing mandated, Jack stood over his dazed foe.

The length of time that elapsed before Jack moved away and the referee began his count is uncertain, but Tunney gained at least 3 or 4 crucial seconds. He beat the ten count, lasted out the round, and came back strongly in the remaining few rounds to win the fight.

Jack made a few attempts at a comeback but eventually recognized that his time in the ring had passed. After his retirement, he enjoyed a long career as a successful businessman and restaurant owner. He died in New York City in 1983.

Summary

Jack Dempsey's aggressiveness and punching power made him one of the greatest of all heavyweight boxers. His was successful not only because of natural talent but also because of hard work and study. Strong and fast boxers are not unusual, but few, if any, have equaled Jack in his desire to win and willingness to sacrifice to attain his goals.

Bill Delaney

Additional Sources

Cavanaugh, Jack, and Gene Tunney. *Tunney: Boxing's Brainiest Champ and His Upset of the Great Jack Dempsey.* New York: Random House, 2006.

Dempsey, Jack, and Frank G. Menke. *How to Fight Tough.* Boulder, Colo.: Paladin Press, 2002.

Howard, Robert E., and Earle Bergey. *Jack Dempsey's Fight Magazine: May 1934.* Silver Spring, Md.: Adventure House, 2005.

Kahn, Roger. *A Flame of Pure Fire: Jack Dempsey and the Roaring Twenties.* San Diego, Calif.: Harcourt Brace Jovanovich, 2000.

Platt, Jim, and James Buckley. *Sports Immortals: Stories of Inspiration and Achievement.* Chicago: Triumph Books, 2002.

Roberto Durán

Born: June 16, 1951
 Guararé, Panama
Also known as: Roberto Carlos Durán (full name); El Cholo; Hands of Stone; Manos de Piedra

Early Life
Roberto Carlos Durán was born on June 16, 1951, in Guararé, Panama, a short distance from the Panama Canal Zone. Roberto was the third of nine children of Clara Samaniego, a domestic, and Margarito Durán, a cook serving in the United States Army, who left the family and moved to the United States when Roberto was three. Roberto did not see his father again until he was twenty-three years old.

Roberto Durán in a 1983 fight. (Al Messerschmidt/WireImage/Getty Images)

Roberto grew up on the streets with little guidance. He helped his mother and his brothers and sisters by working and entertaining in bars as a youth. Growing up, Roberto had to defend himself against tough neighborhood children. He often got into fights when others tried to take away the tips he earned at work.

The Road to Excellence
When Roberto was twelve years old, he walked into a boxing gymnasium. Sammy Medina, a former boxing champion of Panama, was impressed by Roberto's fighting abilities and became Roberto's first boxing manager and trainer. Roberto fought sixteen amateur fights, winning thirteen, before he turned professional.

Many young boxers do not have the money to pay for the expenses connected with training for fights. Managers and trainers have to be paid, and money is needed for the gymnasiums where fighters work out. Fortunately for Roberto, a wealthy Panamanian, Carlos Eleta, helped the young boxer. "Papa," as Roberto affectionately called Eleta, had met Roberto years before under difficult circumstances. He had caught the tough boy stealing coconuts on his estate. Instead of calling the police or punishing him, Eleta brought him into his home and gave him breakfast. When Roberto needed a sponsor, Eleta remembered him and helped him out financially.

Eleta never signed a contract with Roberto as many managers do. Eleta, a millionaire, never took any of Roberto's money. Instead, he invested Roberto's earnings so that Roberto would not squander his money like many boxers do who experience success at a young age. Eleta also tried to keep the rough youngster out of trouble, counseling him to stay out of nightclubs.

The Emerging Champion
Eleta, recognizing Roberto's raw potential, wisely found him an excellent trainer, Ray Arcel, who had trained nineteen boxing champions. On June 26, 1972, in Madison Square Garden in New York City, the twenty-one-year-old Roberto heeded Arcel's

counsel and defeated lightweight champion Ken Buchanan of Scotland for the title.

Over the next six years, Roberto defended his lightweight title twelve times, knocking out almost every challenger. The 5-foot 7-inch, 135-pound slugger earned his nickname, "Manos de Piedra" (hands of stone) by pounding his opponents relentlessly to the body and the head. Roberto was a vicious fighter who knew only one strategy, to keep pressing forward and never step back. He absorbed a tremendous number of punches with his street-fighting style, but he always gave more than he received in these encounters.

Despite Eleta's advice, when Roberto was not defending his title he lived like a playboy, frequenting bars and night clubs in Panama City. He loved to eat steaks, drink whiskey, and dance to salsa music. A national hero in Panama, Roberto was treated like royalty wherever he went.

In 1979, Roberto gave up his lightweight crown to move up to a higher weight class, the welterweight division. He made that move for several reasons: He had defeated nearly all the lightweight contenders, and he was having trouble keeping his weight to the 137-pound lightweight maximum because of his penchant for high living. In fact, according to Roberto, his weight was the toughest opponent he faced during his career; he struggled constantly to meet the requirements of his weight division. In addition, he wanted to earn more money by fighting well-known welterweights like Carlos Palomino and Sugar Ray Leonard.

Recognized World Lightweight Championships

Date	Location	Loser	Result
June 26, 1972	New York, N.Y.	Ken Buchanan	13th-round technical knockout
Jan. 20, 1973	Panama City, Panama	Jimmy Robertson	5th-round knockout
June 2, 1973	Panama City, Panama	Hector Thompson	8th-round technical knockout
Sept. 8, 1973	Panama City, Panama	Ishimatsu Suzuki	10th-round technical knockout
Mar. 16, 1974	Panama City, Panama	Esteban De Jesus	11th-round technical knockout
Dec. 21, 1974	San Juan, Puerto Rico	Masataka Takayama	1st-round technical knockout
Mar. 2, 1975	Panama City, Panama	Ray Lampkin	14th-round technical knockout
Dec. 14, 1975	San Juan, Puerto Rico	Leoncio Ortiz	15th-round knockout
May 22, 1976	Philadelphia, Pa.	Lou Bizzarro	14th-round knockout
Oct. 15, 1976	Miami, Fla.	Alvaro Rojas	1st-round knockout
Jan. 29, 1977	Miami, Fla.	Vilomar Fernandez	13th-round knockout
Sept. 17, 1977	Philadelphia, Pa.	Edwin Viruet	15th-round decision
Jan. 21, 1978	Las Vegas, Nev.	Esteban De Jesus	12th-round knockout

Recognized World Welterweight Championships

Date	Location	Loser	Result
June 20, 1980	Montreal, Canada	Sugar Ray Leonard	15th-round decision
Nov. 20, 1980	Los Angeles, Calif.	Roberto Durán (Sugar Ray Leonard, winner)	8th-round knockout

Recognized World Junior Middleweight Championships

Date	Location	Loser	Result
Jan. 20, 1982	Las Vegas, Nev.	Roberto Durán (Wilfredo Benitez, winner)	15th-round decision
June 16, 1983	New York, N.Y.	Davey Moore	8th-round knockout
June 15, 1984	Las Vegas, Nev.	Roberto Durán (Thomas Hearns, winner)	2d-round knockout

Recognized World Middleweight Championships

Date	Location	Loser	Result
Nov. 10, 1983	Las Vegas, Nev.	Roberto Durán (Marvin Hagler, winner)	15th-round decision
Feb. 24, 1989	Atlantic City, N.J.	Iran Barkley	12th-round decision

Recognized World Super Middleweight Championships

Date	Location	Loser	Result
Dec. 7, 1989	Las Vegas, Nev.	Roberto Durán (Sugar Ray Leonard, winner)	12th-round decision
Aug. 28, 1998	Las Vegas, Nev.	Roberto Durán (William Joppy, winner)	3d-round technical knockout
June 16, 2000	Panama City, Panama	Pat Lawlor	12th-round decision
July 14, 2001	Denver, Colo.	Roberto Durán (Héctor Camacho, winner)	12th-round decision

Continuing the Story

In 1979, Roberto defeated Palomino easily, and then fought Leonard in Olympic Stadium, Montreal, Canada, for the welterweight title on June 20, 1980. Leonard was undefeated and was the classic boxer, jabbing, feinting, and moving constantly. Roberto was the quintessential brawler. In a classic confrontation, Roberto won a hard-fought 15-round decision as Leonard abandoned his usual style to slug it out with the Panamanian. Leonard learned from his mistake and avenged his defeat later that year in a rematch. Meanwhile, Roberto was honored in Panama for his victory, and the day he returned to Panama was declared a national holiday.

Leonard's victory in the late-1980 rematch was Roberto's worst defeat. He was out of shape for the fight, and Leonard shrewdly elected to box and not brawl. Leonard, recognizing that Roberto could not hurt him, taunted the Panamanian mercilessly throughout the fight. In the eighth round, Roberto simply stopped fighting, telling the referee, "no más, no más," ("no more, no more"). Roberto later claimed he had stomach cramps from gorging himself before the fight on steak, eggs, french fries, and fried chicken. From that point on, despite all his accomplishments, Roberto was labeled a quitter—in Panama and around the world—the worst thing that a fighter, especially a proud man like Roberto, could be called. He wanted revenge.

To make matters worse for Roberto, Leonard refused to give him a rematch for a long time. Roberto kept busy and won the junior-middleweight title in 1983 by defeating Davey Moore. His skills were diminished, however, after years of battering in the ring. He lost a 15-round title bout against Marvin Hagler and was knocked out by Thomas Hearns. Roberto claimed that what he really wanted was to fight Leonard and avenge the "no más" episode. Though he knew he was not in the prime of his career, Roberto, as he told Pat Putnam in *Sports Illustrated* in 1988, "was born to fight. I do not know what else to do." Roberto also had a problem with the Internal Revenue Service, which claimed that he had not paid $2 million in taxes on his earnings. Roberto had to keep fighting to pay off his debts.

Finally, on December 7, 1989, Roberto got his rematch with Leonard for the world super-middleweight title. Roberto had to wait nine years for his second chance. By this time, both fighters were diminished in their abilities. Leonard boxed and threw a few punches that did little damage, but he was too fast and elusive for Roberto. Leonard won an easy victory, but this time Roberto fought nobly to the end and did not quit, redeeming his reputation even in defeat.

Long after contemporaries like Leonard and Hagler retired from the ring, Roberto remained, despite his age and decreasing ability. Following his rematch with Leonard in 1989, Roberto fought only three title bouts, losing two by decision and the third by knockout in the third round against William Joppy in 1998. Roberto's performance against Joppy was so bad that the Nevada Boxing Commission suspended his license. Shortly after, he announced his retirement, but he was not long in returning to the ring.

In 1999, in Buenos Aires, Argentina, Roberto lost a decision to Omar Gonzalez. He won a decision against Pat Lawler in Panama City. Both fights were unsanctioned. Roberto's license was reinstated in August of 2000, and Roberto returned to the United States to face P. J. Gossen in Yakima, Washington. Looking well-trained and trim, the forty-nine-year-old Roberto won an easy tenth-round decision and vowed to box well into his fifth decade in the sport. In October 2001, Roberto suffered a broken nose, eight broken ribs, and a punctured lung in a serious car accident in Buenos Aires. A few months later, he announced that he had

Statistics

Bouts, 119

Knockouts, 70

Bouts won by decision, 33

Knockouts by opponent, 4

Bouts lost by decision, 12

Milestones

Captured recognized world titles at four weight classifications

Honors and Awards

2002	Named by *Ring* magazine the fifth-greatest fighter of previous 80 years
2006	Inducted into World Boxing Hall of Fame
2007	Inducted into International Boxing Hall of Fame

officially retired from competitive boxing. In 2002, *Ring* magazine named him the fifth greatest fighter of the previous eighty years.

Summary

Some athletes choose to retire when they are at the peak of their careers. Others, swayed by the promise of lucrative offers, extend their careers too long. Roberto Durán remains one of only a few boxers to compete in five different decades. Perhaps he boxed too long, but he had many accomplishments throughout his career. After he retired, he began working as a boxing promoter in Panama, where he lives with his family.

Roberto continued to fight after more than ninety prize fights and four world championship belts. A legend in his time, Roberto ranks as one of the greatest boxers of the twentieth century. Known for his endurance, toughness, and tenacity, he was also a master of technique. Those who faced him in the ring praised his elusive quickness and his jab. Roberto will be remembered for his competitive spirit and his ability to give and take the heavy punches.

Allen Wells, updated by Caroline Collins

Additional Sources

Brogan, Wrigley. *The Last Round: Roberto Durán's Final Victory*. San Francisco: Ink & Lens, 2006.

Giudice, Christian. *Hands of Stone: The Life and Legend of Roberto Durán*. Wrea Green, Lancashire, England: Milo Books, 2006.

Hoffer, Richard. "Lost in Translation." *Sports Illustrated* 103, no. 2 (July 11, 2005): 126-129.

Kimball, George. *Leonard, Hagler, Hearns, Durán, and the Last Great Era of Boxing*. Ithaca, N.Y.: McBooks Press, 2008.

Mullan, Harry, and Bob Mee. *The Ultimate Encyclopedia of Boxing*. London: Carlton, 2007.

Schulman, Arlene. *The Prize Fighters: An Intimate Look at Champions and Contenders*. New York: Lyons and Burford, 1994.

Sugar, Bert Randolph. *Boxing's Greatest Fighters*. Guilford, Conn.: Lyons Press, 2006.

Eddie Eagan

Born: April 26, 1897
Denver, Colorado
Died: June 14, 1967
Rye, New York
Also known as: Edward Patrick Francis Eagan (full name)
Other major sport: Bobsledding

Early Life
Edward Patrick Francis Eagan was born on April 26, 1897, in Denver, Colorado. Edward, who was called Eddie, was the son of John and Clara Eagan. His father was killed in a railroad accident when Eddie was just one year old. Eddie's mother raised him and his four brothers. She spoke five languages and supported her children by teaching German and French. Eddie became interested in boxing while in high school. The family had moved to Longmont, Colorado, a cattle town. Eddie's boxing coach, Abe Tobin, encouraged him to continue his education instead of seeking a career as a professional boxer.

The Road to Excellence
Eddie won a number of amateur boxing matches in tough competition in mining towns throughout Colorado. After his boxing tour, he enrolled at the University of Denver and spent one year there. He won the Western Amateur Middleweight title while a student. Eddie decided to enlist in the United States Army and was commissioned as an artillery lieutenant. After he was discharged, he entered Yale University in New Haven, Connecticut. During his first year at Yale, he entered the 1919 Amateur Athletic Union boxing championships. He fought seven bouts in two days. Eddie lost a close decision in the light heavyweight class; however, he returned later that evening and won the heavyweight title.

Later in 1919, Eddie competed in the Inter-Allied Games in Paris, France, and won the middleweight championship. In 1920, Eddie tried out for the U.S. Olympic boxing team. He represented the United States at the 1920 Antwerp Olympics in the light heavyweight division. He defeated boxers from South Africa, Great Britain, and Norway to win the gold medal.

Eddie returned to the United States and graduated from Yale University. He enrolled in law school at Harvard University, but he dropped out to try out for the 1924 Olympic Games. He made the U.S. Olympic team again and sailed to Paris, but he was eliminated in the first round of the heavyweight division.

The Emerging Champion
Apparently, Eddie had been influenced by Coach Tobin's encouragement to pursue an education rather than a professional boxing career. He was awarded a Rhodes scholarship and continued his studies at Oxford University in England. He competed on Oxford's boxing team and participated in several exhibitions with the American heavyweight champion Jack Dempsey. After completing his studies at Oxford, Eddie toured the world, competing in numerous boxing matches. When Eddie returned to the United States, he helped Gene Tunney train for a rematch with Dempsey. Tunney had become the new heavyweight champion.

In 1932, Eddie tried out for the U.S. Olympic bobsled team. The 1932 Olympic Winter Games were held in Lake Placid, New York. Eddie made the four-person bobsled team. The finals of the four-person bobsled were delayed because of a severe winter storm. Despite poor weather conditions, a crowd of twenty thousand arrived for the competition and were disappointed when just two of the four runs could be completed. The snow was so deep that sleds slowed down and poor times were recorded. The competition had to be postponed until the following day.

The Olympic Games were actually over when the two bobsled heats were made up. Billy Fiske was

---

Honors, Awards, and Milestones

1919	Amateur Athletic Union heavyweight champion
	Inter-Allied Games middleweight champion
1920	Gold medal, U.S. Olympic light heavyweight boxing
1932	Gold medal, U.S. Olympic four-person bobsled
1983	Inducted into U.S. Olympic Hall of Fame

the pilot of the team, Eddie was the number-two man, and Clifford Gray was the third man. Jay O'Brien was the brakeman. Very few people turned out in the bitter cold to view the last two runs. Eddie's team had the best time for each of the first three runs and the best overall time and claimed the Olympic championship. Eddie and his teammates were each presented with a gold medal. Eddie became the first Olympic athlete to win gold medals in both the Winter and Summer Olympic Games. He distinguished himself as a true competitor in two sports at the international level.

In 1932, Eddie entered private law practice. He served as assistant attorney for five years. He joined the Army Air Force when World War II began. He was chief of special services in the Air Transport Command and visited nearly every part of the world where American planes were based. He retired from the Army as a lieutenant colonel.

Continuing the Story

When Eddie returned to civilian life in 1945, he was appointed head of the New York State Athletic Commission, which governed boxing. Because of his boxing background, Eddie was well suited for the job. Eddie served as head of the commission for six years. He made a major contribution by developing a scoring system for boxing that became the basis of the modern system. He also required strict physical examinations of boxers before and after their bouts. In 1956, President Dwight D. Eisenhower appointed Eddie chairperson of the People-to-People Sports Committee. Eddie also served as director of the sports program at the 1964 New York World's Fair. He headed the Boys' Athletic League of New York for two years.

Eddie's involvement in sports organizations gave him many opportunities to express his belief that sports serve as a "common denominator" of all people. He viewed sports activities as a way to bring people of different backgrounds together. Eddie died of a heart attack on June 14, 1967, at Roosevelt Hospital in New York. He was survived by his wife, son, and daughter.

Summary

Eddie Eagan's athletic ability and his educational background served him well. His interest in reading about a Yale University student introduced him to the school, and his involvement in boxing and bobsledding led him to international competition in the Olympic Games. He was the first athlete to win gold medals in both the Winter and Summer Olympic Games.

Paula D. Welch

Additional Sources

Blewett, Bert. *The A to Z of World Boxing: An Authoritative and Entertaining Compendium of the Fight Game from Its Origins to the Present Day.* Parkwest, N.Y.: Robson Books, 2002.

Conner, Floyd. *The Olympics' Most Wanted: The Top Ten Book of Gold Medal Gaffes, Improbable Triumphs, and Other Oddities.* London: Brassey's, 2002.

Herzog, Brad. "Modeled on a Myth." *Sports Illustrated* 87, no. 26 (December 29, 1997): 6-7.

Wallechinsky, David, and Jaime Loucky. *The Complete Book of the Olympics: 2008 Edition.* London: Aurum Press, 2008.

_____. *The Complete Book of the Winter Olympics.* Wilmington, Del.: Sport Media, 2005.

George Foreman

Born: January 10, 1949
Marshall, Texas
Also known as: George Edward Foreman (full name)

Early Life

George Foreman was born in Marshall, Texas, on January 10, 1949. He was the fifth of seven children born to Nancy and J. F. Foreman. George had a rough childhood. His family lived in the "Fifth Ward" slums of Houston, Texas, and his father left the family when George was fourteen. George was the only athletic child of the family—he had strength, energy, and agility. His athleticism was a mixed blessing during his childhood. Because he was one of the bigger and stronger boys, he did not shy away from fights or trouble. George grew up as a street brawler. In spite of difficulties, George still remained close to his family, especially his mother. He often found trouble, but to avoid upsetting his mother, he shunned serious crime.

The Road to Excellence

George played some organized high school sports, but sports alone could not keep him in school. He dropped out and found a job as a forest conservation worker with the Job Corps. Although he was employed, he still found trouble. He nearly lost his job several times. Then he met Nick "Doc" Broadus, a boxing instructor who taught George how to box and put him on a strict training routine. The athletic discipline appealed to George, and he began to excel. In January, 1967, George scored a knockout in his first official amateur bout. Within two years of his boxing debut, George fought his way to the 1968 Amateur Athletic Union national heavyweight championship. That victory qualified him for the U.S. Olympic team. In 1968, at the nineteenth Olympiad in Mexico City, George defeated a Soviet fighter to win the gold medal.

George became famous for two reasons that day. Besides winning the gold medal, he won the hearts of many Americans as he circled the ring after his victory waving a small American flag. His brave symbol of patriotism was a stark contrast to the antiestablishment actions of many young people during the late 1960's. George became a professional boxer after the 1968 Olympiad. In a furious schedule of fights, he defeated thirty-six opponents in just thirty-six months. Steadily working through the ranks of heavyweight contenders, George was soon in the ring with Joe Frazier, the reigning heavyweight champion.

George Foreman staring down an opponent. (Focus on Sport/Getty Images)

Recognized World Heavyweight Championships

Date	Location	Loser	Result
Jan. 22, 1973	Kingston, Jamaica	Joe Frazier	2d-round technical knockout
Sept. 1, 1973	Tokyo, Japan	Jose (King) Roman	1st-round knockout
Mar. 26, 1974	Caracas, Venezuela	Ken Norton	2d-round technical knockout
Oct. 30, 1974	Kinshasa, Zaire	George Foreman (Muhammad Ali, winner)	8th-round knockout
Apr. 28, 1991	Atlantic City, N.J.	George Foreman (Evander Holyfield, winner)	12th-round decision
June 7, 1993	Las Vegas, Nev.	George Foreman (Tommy Morrison, winner)	12th-round decision
Nov. 5, 1994	Las Vegas, Nev.	Michael Moorer	10th-round knockout
Apr. 22, 1995	Las Vegas, Nev.	Axel Schulz	12th-round decision
Nov. 2, 1996	Atlantic City, N.J.	Lou Savarese	12th-round decision
Nov. 22, 1997	Atlantic City, N.J.	George Foreman (Shannon Briggs, winner)	12th-round decision

The Emerging Champion

Going into the championship fight, George was a three-to-one underdog. Frazier was also undefeated and had been champion for three years. However, the young challenger was undaunted and shocked the sports world with an amazing victory. The fight took place on January 22, 1973, in Kingston, Jamaica, and lasted only two rounds. George, at 6 feet 4 inches and 218 pounds, knocked down the champion three times in the first round and three times in the second round. The referee stopped the fight 2 minutes and 35 seconds into the second round, and George was the new heavyweight champion of the world.

George was a dignified champion but reigned for only twenty-one months. He defended his title twice successfully but then lost it in a famous fight against Muhammad Ali in October, 1974, in Zaire, Africa. George was favored to win, but Ali used his famous "rope-a-dope" strategy to tire the champ. In the eighth round, Ali knocked out George to regain the heavyweight crown. George fought six more bouts, finally losing to Jimmy Young in March, 1977. Following that defeat, George retired and moved to Houston, Texas, where he built a small church and became a preacher. George was through with boxing, or so he thought.

Continuing the Story

George lived a peaceful life for ten years after his retirement. He served as pastor for his small congregation and spent much of his time working on his ranch. He also dedicated time and money to charity work, helping young boys. However, the champion inside of George grew restless. In 1987, George decided to make a boxing comeback at the age of thirty-nine. Many sports fans had forgotten the name George, but he quickly revived the memory of boxing enthusiasts with impressive victories.

As a young fighter, George was known for his awesome power and vicious ring assaults. Although he displayed poise outside the ring, he was not known for humor or joviality. With his comeback, a different George emerged. Still a powerful puncher, George had maintained much of his former ring presence. A purely offensive fighter, he charged his opponents and smothered them with mighty blows. Outside the ring, however, he was more a preacher than a puncher. He became gentle and jovial, often joking about his age and weight—he had gained nearly 60 pounds since his championship days.

By 1991, George's comeback dream was a reality. He fought twenty-four bouts, knocking out twenty-three of his opponents. His skeptics became believers, and George soon rose to the rank of the number-one contender. Determined to regain the heavyweight crown, George fought champion Evander Holyfield on April 28, 1991. Holyfield, twenty-eight years old and a former light-heavyweight boxer, had youth and speed on his side. In a tremendous bout termed "the Battle of the Ages," George went the twelve-round distance only to lose in a close decision.

Although George did not regain the title, he won the hearts of fans worldwide with his courageous stand. He inspired middle-aged athletes and showed the world that great performances are as much a result of a positive attitude as they are of a youthful body. George continued to fight until 1997, winning the WBO world heavyweight title in 1994 against Michael Moorer with a knockout in the tenth round. He successfully defended his title until November 22, 1997, when he fell to Shannon Briggs in a hotly disputed twelfth-round decision

Statistics

Bouts, 81
Knockouts, 68
Bouts won by decision, 8
Knockouts by opponents, 1
Bouts lost by decision, 4

Milestones

Knocked out 68 of 81 opponents, or 84 percent—one of the highest knockout percentages in professional heavyweight boxing history

Honors and Awards

1968	National Amateur Athletic Union heavyweight champion
	Gold medal, U.S. Olympic Boxing
1973	Edward J. Neil Trophy
1973-74	Freedom Foundation Award
1973, 1976	*Ring* magazine Merit Award
1990	Inducted into U.S. Olympic Hall of Fame
1994	Edward J. Neil Trophy
2003	Inducted into International Boxing Hall of Fame

that resulted in an investigation of possible corruption among promoters and New Jersey boxing commissioner Larry Hazzard.

Though no longer in the ring, George appeared frequently as a boxing commentator for HBO. He formally retired shortly after the Briggs fight but later discussed the possibility of returning to the ring. In 2003, he was inducted into the International Boxing Hall of Fame. In retirement, George had a successful career as an entrepreneur. His George Foreman Grill became a popular product.

Summary

George Foreman had two boxing careers. Both periods were successful and exciting. As a younger man, George was known as a savage brawler whose power took him to the top of the heavyweight world in a few short years. As an older man, George's image was different, although his power was still fearsome. The toughest part about George was his fighting spirit. He had a boxing career that spanned more than twenty years.

William B. Roy

Additional Sources

Brunt, Stephen. *Facing Ali: The Opposition Weighs In.* Guilford, Conn.: Lyons Press, 2004.

Finger, David E. *Rocky Lives! Heavyweight Boxing Upsets of the 1990's.* Dulles, Va.: Potomac, 2006.

Foreman, George, and Ken Abraham. *God in My Corner.* Nashville, Tenn.: Thomas Nelson, 2007.

Hill, E. D. *Going Places: How America's Best and Brightest Got Started down the Road of Life.* New York: ReganBooks, 2005.

Mullan, Harry, and Bob Mee. *The Ultimate Encyclopedia of Boxing.* London: Carlton, 2007.

Ohebsion, Rodney, and Thomas Mesenbring Field. *Athletes That Inspire Us: The Remarkable True Life Stories of Twenty Unique Athletes.* Los Angeles: Immediex, 2005.

Sugar, Bert Randolph. *Boxing's Greatest Fighters.* Guilford, Conn.: Lyons Press, 2006.

Bob Foster

Born: December 15, 1938
Albuquerque, New Mexico
Also known as: Robert Lloyd Foster (full name)

Early Life
Robert Lloyd Foster was born on December 15, 1938, in Albuquerque, New Mexico. Bob came from a working-class family. As a young man he enjoyed and excelled at many sports, but not until he reached junior high school did he became interested in boxing. In a playground fight, Bob shattered a classmate's jaw with a punch of ferocious power. Despite getting into trouble with the school authorities, for the first time, Bob was aware of the frightening strength he possessed within his wiry frame. From that moment on, Bob realized he had a talent for boxing.

The Road to Excellence
Bob was a star athlete at high school, especially in football. His play was so outstanding that the University of New Mexico offered him a football scholarship. Bob declined the offer, preferring to join the United States Air Force. In the Air Force, Bob's amateur boxing career took off. He became a noted boxer, and the more success he achieved, the more time he was given to train for his chosen sport. During his career in the service, Bob won four all-Air Force light-heavyweight titles and one all-service title. Boxing agents and promoters were awaiting Bob's military discharge eagerly, and his early professional career lived up to the promise he showed as an amateur. In March, 1961, Duke Williams was Bob's first professional opponent. Bob easily disposed of Williams in two rounds.

In his first year in professional boxing, Bob won all of his seven contests. His managers wanted to nurture him slowly in order to get the best out of his immense talent.

This prudence did not continue, and between 1962 and 1965, Bob was forced into some extremely unsuitable, but financially lucrative, contests. He was pitted against a string of heavyweights, all of whom out-powered him. Despite standing 6 feet 3½ inches, Bob was a natural light heavyweight and simply could not survive in the ring against heavier fighters. Bob's final indignity came when the heavyweight Zora Folley beat him in 1965. Realizing he had talent, but disheartened because of his career's poor management, Bob decided to give up boxing. At the age of twenty-seven, Bob found himself working in a Pennsylvania munitions factory.

The Emerging Champion
A promising career had taken a seemingly irreversible plunge. Luckily for Bob, boxing manager Morris Salow had been struck by his potential. Salow lo-

Bob Foster, who held the World Boxing Council's light-heavyweight title from 1968 to 1974. (Courtesy of Amateur Athletic Foundation of Los Angeles)

Recognized World Light Heavyweight Championships

Date	Location	Loser	Result
May 24, 1968	New York, N.Y.	Dick Tiger	4th-round knockout
Jan. 22, 1969	New York, N.Y.	Frank DePaula	1st-round knockout
May 24, 1969	West Springfield, Mass.	Andy Kendall	4th-round knockout
Apr. 4, 1970	Missoula, Mont.	Roger Rouse	4th-round knockout
June 27, 1970	Baltimore, Md.	Mark Tessman	10th-round knockout
Mar. 2, 1971	Scranton, Pa.	Hal Carroll	4th-round knockout
Apr. 24, 1971	Tampa, Fla.	Ray Anderson	15th-round decision
Oct. 29, 1971	Scranton, Pa.	Tommy Hicks	8th-round knockout
Dec. 16, 1971	Oklahoma City, Okla.	Brian Kelly	3d-round knockout
Apr. 7, 1972	Miami Beach, Fla.	Vicente Rondon	2d-round knockout
June 27, 1972	Las Vegas, Nev.	Mike Quarry	4th-round knockout
Sept. 26, 1972	London, England	Chris Finnegan	14th-round knockout
Aug. 21, 1973	Albuquerque, N. Mex.	Pierre Fourie	15th-round decision
Dec. 1, 1973	Johannesburg, South Africa	Pierre Fourie	15th-round decision
June 17, 1974	Albuquerque, N. Mex.	(Jorge Ahumada, opponent)	15th-round draw

Recognized World Heavyweight Championship

Date	Location	Loser	Result
Nov. 18, 1970	Detroit, Mich.	Bob Foster (Joe Frazier, winner)	2d-round knockout

cated Bob and bought his professional contract from his previous manager. Understandably, Bob was less than enthusiastic about picking up his professional career. Salow promised him the type of guidance and management he had previously lacked, and in 1966, Bob decided to give boxing another chance.

Bob's return to the ring in December, 1966, was an immediate success. His defeat of Leroy Green was followed by seven consecutive victories in 1967. These wins helped Bob to regain his confidence and reminded the boxing world that he was still a light heavyweight with which to be reckoned. Salow guided Bob to a world title bout against the champion Dick Tiger, who was heavily favored. In order not to let the opportunity pass, Bob trained diligently. On May 24, 1968, he entered the ring in peak physical condition. More important, Bob was hungry for victory; he desperately desired to become world titleholder in order to forget the frustrations of his early professional career. Bob's tremendous punching power, vicious left hook, and huge reach belied his apparent frailty and gave him a great advantage over his opponent. Tiger succumbed to a fourth-round knockout, and, at the age of twenty-nine, Bob became the light-heavyweight champion of the world.

Continuing the Story

As light-heavyweight champion, Bob dominated the division like few boxers have before or since. During his six-year reign, he made fourteen successful title defenses against the best light heavyweights in world boxing. In all his bouts, Bob demonstrated the power, reach, and boxing know-how that made him virtually impossible to beat. After twenty consecutive victories, once again, Bob was lured into a lucrative fight against a heavyweight. In November, 1970, Bob faced the undefeated heavyweight champion Joe Frazier. As before, Bob simply could not survive against a heavier, more

Statistics

Bouts, 65
Knockouts, 46
Bouts won by decision, 10
Knockouts by opponents, 6
Bouts lost by decision, 2
Draws, 1

Milestones

All-Air Force light heavyweight champion (four titles overall)
All-Service light heavyweight champion

Honors and Awards

1959	Silver medal, U.S. Pan-American Games
1968	Edward J. Neil Trophy
1983	Inducted into *Ring* magazine Boxing Hall of Fame
1990	Inducted into International Boxing Hall of Fame

powerful opponent, and was stopped in the second round.

Back in more familiar territory, Bob continued to head the light-heavyweight division. In April of 1972, he humiliated Vicente Rondon, the World Boxing Association champion, by knocking him out in the second round. That was followed by an epic victory against the gallant English champion, Chris Finnegan. Soon afterward, Bob again challenged for the heavyweight title, this time against Muhammad Ali. The outcome was entirely predictable, as Bob was stopped in eight rounds, having hit the canvas seven times.

Following the defeat by Ali, Bob's career went into decline. He won two closely fought battles against the South African Pierre Fourie, and then, in June, 1974, he barely managed to retain his title after drawing with Jorge Ahumada. At the age of thirty-six, Bob realized his reign as world champion was drawing to an end. Contractual disputes with boxing's governing bodies also encouraged him to quit the sport. Bob announced his retirement in September, 1974.

Despite a moderately successful comeback between 1975 and 1978, Bob's future lay elsewhere. He had been a sergeant in the Bernalillo, New Mexico, Sheriff's Department for a number of years and planned to follow a career in law enforcement. In 1990, he was inducted into the International Boxing Hall of Fame.

Summary

Bob Foster was one of the greatest light-heavyweight boxers of all time—he was never beaten by a light heavyweight as an amateur or as a professional. Bob could have easily drifted out of boxing for good after the disappointments of his early professional career. Luckily, Bob was enticed back to the ring and made the most of his second chance.

David L. Andrews

Additional Sources

Mullan, Harry, and Bob Mee. *The Ultimate Encyclopedia of Boxing*. London: Carlton, 2007.

Sugar, Bert Randolph. *Boxing's Greatest Fighters*. Guilford, Conn.: Lyons Press, 2006.

Joe Frazier

Born: January 12, 1944
Beaufort, South Carolina
Also known as: Joseph William Frazier (full name); Smokin' Joe

Early Life
Joseph William Frazier was born on January 12, 1944, in Beaufort, South Carolina. Raised in poverty on his father's small hog and vegetable farm, Joe was the seventh son in a family of thirteen. His father taught him how to work on the farm, and at the age of nine he was driving a tractor and toiling in the fields. Sometimes Joe would get into street fights, which he always won. He did not believe that any other boy could beat him. He watched boxing matches on television and dreamed of becoming a boxing great like his hero, Joe Louis. Taking his mother's advice, Joe dropped out of school during the tenth grade and traveled north to Philadelphia. In Philadelphia, he worked in a slaughterhouse and also began working out at the Police Athletic Club gymnasium.

Joe Frazier. (Courtesy of Amateur Athletic Foundation of Los Angeles)

The Road to Excellence
Joe came under the influence of Yancey "Yank" Durham, who persuaded him to take up amateur boxing and supervised his training. Durham was convinced that Joe could win a gold medal and convinced him that the goal was worth the hard work. He pointed out that boxers such as Cassius Clay (later known as Muhammad Ali) had gone from Olympic medals to world championships, and if Joe could follow in their footsteps, he would never have to worry about money again. Joe respected Durham and took his advice. Durham helped him to lose weight and steered him to success as an amateur boxer. Fighting in the heavyweight division at about his ideal weight of 205 pounds, Joe won thirty-five out of thirty-seven bouts as an amateur. The highlight of his early career occurred when he won a gold medal for the United States in the 1964 Olympic Games, held in Tokyo, Japan. He achieved this in spite of a broken left hand, an injury he suffered in an earlier bout.

The Emerging Champion
In 1965, Joe turned professional and won his first fight by a knockout in the first round. He recorded nineteen wins in less than two and one-half years. Only two of these fights went the full distance of ten rounds. Joe's aggressive boxing style was summed up by his own comment, "I'm comin' out smoking." This remark earned him the nickname "Smokin' Joe."

Joe did not possess the ideal physique for a heavyweight. At 5 feet 11½ inches, he was comparatively short, and much of his weight was concentrated in his legs. The latter, however, gave him almost unlimited endurance. This quality, allied with his ferocious punching power in both fists, made Joe an awesome fighter. His massive strength made up for any deficiencies in skill or technique. During a fight, he kept coming forward, relentlessly putting pressure on his opponent, both fists pounding hard. He knew how to hit and then slip away from a counterattack.

In 1967, the World Boxing Association (WBA) stripped the reigning world heavyweight champion, Muhammad Ali, of his title for refusing to serve in the U.S. military. The following year, Joe defeated Buster Mathis to win the New York State Athletic Commission's version of the world heavyweight crown. After defending his title four times, Joe was named fighter of the year by the Boxing Writers Association in 1969. The following year, Joe further advanced his claim as the true heavyweight champion. He won the WBA heavyweight title, beating Jimmy Ellis at Madison Square Garden, in New York City. Ellis was knocked down twice in the fourth round and could not make it for the start of the fifth. Although Joe was the champion, he still had to prove himself against the great Muhammad Ali.

Continuing the Story

In 1970, the ban on Ali was lifted. In March, 1971, at Madison Square Garden, Joe faced Ali in the showdown for which boxing fans had been waiting, billed as the "fight of the century," the most highly publicized match in boxing history. An estimated 300 million people watched the fight on television, and Joe's share of the purse was reputed to be $2.5 million. Ali had never been beaten, but Joe dominated the fight. He knocked Ali down in the fifteenth round with a terrific left hook, and when the final bell sounded, Joe knew he had become the undisputed heavyweight champion of the world.

In 1972, Joe defended his title twice, easily knocking out his opponent on each occasion. That marked the peak of his career; he looked unbeat-

Statistics

Bouts, 37
Knockouts, 27
Bouts won by decision, 5
Knockouts by opponents, 3
Bouts lost by decision, 1
Draws, 1

Honors and Awards

1962-64	Golden Gloves Champion
1964	Gold medal, U.S. Olympic Boxing
1967, 1970-71	*Ring* magazine Merit Award
1969	Boxing Writers Association Fighter of the Year
1969, 1971, 1975	Edward J. Neil Trophy (1975 co-recipient)
1975	Inducted into Black Athletes Hall of Fame
1980	Inducted into *Ring* magazine Boxing Hall of Fame
1987	*Ring* magazine's tenth greatest heavyweight boxer of all time
1989	Inducted into U.S. Olympic Hall of Fame
1990	Inducted into International Boxing Hall of Fame

Recognized World Heavyweight Championships

Date	Location	Loser	Result
Mar. 4, 1968	New York, N.Y.	Buster Mathis	11th-round technical knockout
June 24, 1968	New York, N.Y.	Manuel Ramos	2d-round technical knockout
Dec. 10, 1968	Philadelphia, Pa.	Oscar Bonavena	15th-round unanimous decision
Apr. 22, 1969	Houston, Tex.	Dave Zyglewicz	1st-round knockout
May 23, 1969	New York, N.Y.	Jerry Quarry	8th-round technical knockout
Feb. 16, 1970	New York, N.Y.	Jimmy Ellis	5th-round technical knockout
Nov. 18, 1970	Detroit, Mich.	Bob Foster	2d-round knockout
Mar. 8, 1971	New York, N.Y.	Muhammad Ali	15th-round unanimous decision
Jan. 15, 1972	New Orleans, La.	Terry Daniels	4th-round technical knockout
May 26, 1972	Omaha, Nebr.	Ron Stander	5th-round technical knockout
Jan. 22, 1973	Kingston, Jamaica	Joe Frazier (George Foreman, winner)	2d-round technical knockout
Oct. 1, 1975	Manila, Philippines	Joe Frazier (Muhammad Ali, winner)	15th-round technical knockout

able. In Kingston, Jamaica, in January, 1973, he suffered a blow from which he never fully recovered. He was a heavy favorite to beat George Foreman, but he was no match for his challenger. Foreman knocked him down six times in two rounds before the referee stopped the fight. The loss was Joe's first as a professional.

The following year, Joe lost a nontitle rematch with Ali. In October, 1975, he faced Ali yet again, after Ali had regained the heavyweight crown by defeating George Foreman. The third Frazier-Ali fight, in Manila, the Philippines, dubbed the "thrilla in Manila," resulted in a win for Ali.

In 1976, after suffering another defeat, at the hands of George Foreman, in the fifth round of a fight in Uniondale, New York, Joe retired from the ring. For a brief period, he made appearances as a nightclub singer with a group called the Knockouts. In 1980, Joe was inducted into *Ring* magazine's Boxing Hall of Fame. He made a brief comeback in 1981, but only managed to draw a fight with a mediocre opponent, Jumbo Cummings. After his retirement from professional boxing, Joe trained fighters out of his Philadelphia gym.

Summary

In his time, Joe Frazier possessed one of the highest knockout ratios in the history of modern boxing. Twenty-seven of his thirty-two victories came from knockouts. He is frequently compared to Rocky Marciano, a great heavyweight champion of the 1950's. In 1987, *Ring* magazine named Joe the tenth greatest heavyweight of all time. He was inducted into the International Boxing Hall of Fame in 1990.

Bryan Aubrey

Additional Sources

Frazier, Joe, and Phil Berger. *Smokin' Joe: The Autobiography of a Heavyweight Champion of the World, Smokin' Joe Frazier.* New York: Macmillan USA, 1996.

Fussman, Cal. "Joe Frazier, Fifty-nine." *Esquire* 141, no. 1 (January, 2004): 90-91.

Kram, Mark. *Ghosts of Manila: The Fateful Blood Feud Between Muhammad Ali and Joe Frazier.* New York: Perennial Currents, 2002.

Mullan, Harry, and Bob Mee. *The Ultimate Encyclopedia of Boxing.* London: Carlton, 2007.

Rocky Graziano

Born: January 1, 1919
New York, New York
Died: May 22, 1990
New York, New York
Also known as: Thomas Rocco Barbella (birth name)

Rocky Graziano. (Hulton Archive/Getty Images)

Early Life
Rocky Graziano was born Thomas Rocco Barbella on January 1, 1919. He grew up during the Great Depression in New York City's lower East Side, a slum where poverty and violence were a fact of life. His authoritarian and tyrannical father, Joseph Barbella, was an alcoholic former boxer who never held a steady job. His battered mother provided most of the family's meager income by doing washing and ironing for more fortunate neighbors. Like many of the boys in his neighborhood, Rocky was drawn into petty crime, drugs, and alcohol. In an interview in 1971, Rocky said he had been a juvenile delinquent during his youth. In and out of jail in the 1930's, he turned to professional boxing to earn money in the early 1940's.

The Road to Excellence
Rocky entered the ring in 1942. Although he had few boxing skills, he was a ferocious street fighter, a skill necessary for survival in the environment in which he grew up. His boxing career was curtailed, however, when the United States Army drafted him several months later. Rocky did not adapt well to military life, quickly getting into trouble for striking an officer. Fearful of the punishment he might receive, Rocky went AWOL (Absent Without Leave). To support himself as a fugitive, he resumed his boxing career. In order to avoid apprehension by the military police, he changed his name to Graziano. Eventually, the authorities found him. He was court-martialed and, after confinement in a military prison, was dishonorably discharged. In later years, Rocky called his problems with the Army his greatest regret in life.

In 1943, Rocky won sixteen of eighteen fights largely because of strength and tenacity—he lacked true boxing skills. Criminal figures permeated boxing in New York City at the time, so Rocky was little removed from the life of crime and delinquency he was trying to escape. In 1971, Rocky said that it was during this period that he decided to change the direction of his life. He resolved to use his boxing career to escape the poverty and criminality of his youth, and to give up narcotics and alcohol.

The Emerging Champion
Rocky began to train diligently and to learn boxing skills to augment his natural ability and the rage inside him. By 1946, he had scored impressive nontitle knockouts over several highly regarded boxers, including two against welterweight champion Freddie Cochrane and one against future welterweight champion Marty Servo. Those victories were enough to earn Rocky a bout for the middleweight championship of the world against titleholder Tony Zale, at Madison Square Garden on September 27, 1946. The fight was remembered by boxing experts as one of the most savage middleweight championship fights of all time. Rocky

seemed to be winning before Zale suddenly rallied in the sixth round and knocked out the challenger.

Pleased by the sellout crowd the first Zale-Graziano fight had attracted, fight promoters rematched the two men. Zale and Rocky met in Chicago on July 16, 1947. The second fight was almost an instant replay of the first, but with the roles reversed. Zale seemed to be beating Rocky easily until the sixth round, when Rocky suddenly rallied and knocked out his opponent. The poor Italian child from a New York slum, the juvenile delinquent who had received a dishonorable discharge, was the middleweight boxing champion of the world.

Statistics

Bouts, 83
Knockouts, 52
Bouts won by decision, 14
Bouts won by fouls, 1
Knockouts by opponents, 3
Bouts lost by decision, 7
Draws, 6

Honors and Awards

1971	Inducted into *Ring* magazine Boxing Hall of Fame
1991	Inducted into International Boxing Hall of Fame

Continuing the Story

Rocky's reign as world champion lasted less than one year. Rematched with Zale in Newark, New Jersey, on June 10, 1948, he lost by knockout in the third round. Rocky continued boxing for the next three years after his second loss to Zale, defeating all twenty-one opponents he faced, seventeen by knockout. This string of victories finally earned him another chance at the middleweight championship, then held by Sugar Ray Robinson.

On April 16, 1952, Rocky met Robinson in Chicago. Rocky started strong, even knocking down the champion in the second round. In the third round, however, Robinson knocked out his challenger. Rocky had one more fight after his unsuccessful bid for the championship, losing a decision to Chuck Davey on September 17, 1952. After the Davey fight, he retired from boxing. During his career, Rocky compiled a record of 67 wins (52 by knockout), 10 losses, and 6 draws.

After retiring, Rocky wrote a best-selling autobiography entitled *Somebody Up There Likes Me* (1955). Made into a successful motion picture starring Paul Newman, the book launched Rocky into a successful show business career. For the next twenty-five years, he appeared frequently in motion pictures and on television, especially on variety and game shows. He became a popular speaker on the celebrity circuit and made substantial sums of money as a spokesperson for many products in television commercials. He also operated a successful restaurant in New York City, which was frequented by the boxing crowd. In 1985, Rocky retired from most of his activities. He died in his home in New York City on May 22, 1990.

Summary

Rocky Graziano story is a classic example of how athletics can save someone from a life of poverty and probable crime. His most important legacy was to demonstrate that every individual can choose the sort of life they will pursue: to become part of society's problems or part of the solution to those problems.

Paul Madden

Additional Sources

Graziano, Rocky, and Rowland Barber. *Somebody Up There Likes Me: The Story of My Life Until Today.* New York: Simon & Schuster, 1955.

Graziano, Rocky, and Ralph Corsel. *Somebody down Here Likes Me, Too.* New York: Stein & Day, 1981.

Mullan, Harry, and Bob Mee. *The Ultimate Encyclopedia of Boxing.* London: Carlton, 2007.

Sugar, Bert Randolph. *Boxing's Greatest Fighters.* Guilford, Conn.: Lyons Press, 2006.

Recognized World Middleweight Championships

Date	Location	Loser	Result
Sept. 27, 1946	New York, N.Y.	Rocky Graziano (Tony Zale, winner)	6th-round knockout
July 16, 1947	Chicago, Ill.	Tony Zale	6th-round knockout
June 10, 1948	Newark, N.J.	Rocky Graziano (Tony Zale, winner)	3d-round knockout
Apr. 16, 1952	Chicago, Ill.	Rocky Graziano (Sugar Ray Robinson, winner)	3d-round knockout

Marvin Hagler

Born: May 23, 1954
Newark, New Jersey
Also known as: Marvin Nathaniel Hagler (full name); Marvelous Marvin Hagler

Early Life
Marvin Nathaniel Hagler was born on May 23, 1954, in Newark, New Jersey. His difficult childhood was the ideal training ground for an aspiring young fighter. When Marvin was very young his father abandoned his mother and her six children to welfare. Without a father to guide him, Marvin spent much of his time in the streets of Newark. Like many boys from underprivileged backgrounds, Marvin grew up believing that his only way out was to imitate famous sports figures such as Floyd Patterson or Walt Frazier. His mother cultivated his fighting skills by refusing to let him in the house if he was beaten in a street fight. He received his first formal training in boxing at the age of twelve, when an elderly social worker put gloves on him and paired him off with the other street children. Marvin's initiation into the harsh realities of the adult world came at an early age. He quit school at the age of fourteen and went to work at a toy factory to supplement his mother's income as a housekeeper. During the race riots of 1967 and 1969, Marvin and his brothers and sisters were forced to huddle under their beds on several occasions to keep from getting hit by gunfire.

The Road to Excellence
Marvin's fortunes changed dramatically when his mother moved to Brockton, Massachusetts, in 1970. There he first met Goody and Pat Petronelli, who ran a gymnasium for young boxers. Because these were the first white men who had ever been nice to him, he vowed to work hard to justify the faith that they had in him. An unwed father at the age of sixteen, Marvin worked all day as a construction worker, then spent his evenings training in the gymnasium.

The Petronellis did not know Marvin's full potential until 1973. During the national Amateur Athletic Union finals, he won the outstanding fighter award in a tournament that included Aaron Pryor and Sugar Ray Leonard. His first professional match two weeks later marked the beginning of his long, frustrating climb in the middleweight division. Marvin's stubborn loyalty to the Petronellis held back his career. He could have had a title fight much sooner than he did, but he refused to sign up with a big promoter. Consequently, it would be six and one-half years before he was given a title fight. In 1979, Marvin's determination and patience finally paid off when he fought Vito Antuofermo for the crown. However, the fight ended in a draw. The following year, Marvin gained the middle-

Marvin Hagler delivering a blow to Willis Warren in a 1978 fight. (AP/Wide World Photos)

Recognized World Middleweight Championships

Date	Location	Loser	Result
Nov. 30, 1979	Las Vegas, Nev.	(Vito Antuofermo, opponent)	15th-round draw
Sept. 27, 1980	London, England	Alan Minter	3d-round knockout
Jan. 17, 1981	Boston, Mass.	Fulgencio Obelmejias	8th-round knockout
June 13, 1981	Boston, Mass.	Vito Antuofermo	5th-round knockout
Oct. 3, 1981	Rosemont, Ill.	Mustafa Hamsho	11th-round knockout
Mar. 7, 1982	Atlantic City, N.J.	William Lee	1st-round knockout
Oct. 30, 1982	San Remo, Italy	Fulgencio Obelmejias	5th-round knockout
Feb. 11, 1983	Worcester, Mass.	Tony Sibson	6th-round knockout
May 27, 1983	Providence, R.I.	Wilford Scypion	4th-round knockout
Nov. 10, 1983	Las Vegas, Nev.	Roberto Duran	15th-round decision
Mar. 30, 1984	Las Vegas, Nev.	Juan Roldan	10th-round knockout
Oct. 19, 1984	New York, N.Y.	Mustafa Hamsho	3d-round knockout
Apr. 15, 1985	Las Vegas, Nev.	Thomas Hearns	3d-round technical knockout
Mar. 10, 1986	Las Vegas, Nev.	John Mugabi	11th-round knockout
Apr. 6, 1987	Las Vegas, Nev.	Marvin Hagler (Sugar Ray Leonard, winner)	12th-round decision

weight title with his three-round pounding of England's Alan Minter.

The Emerging Champion

After returning from England, Marvin began to think of himself as a true champion. The ovation that he received from a crowd of ten thousand at Brockton's City Hall Square showed that he had come a long way since he had first arrived in town as a Newark ghetto child eleven years before. In 1982, flushed with victory, Marvin had his name legally changed to "Marvelous Marvin Hagler."

Marvelous Marvin's name change was justified a few months later when he scored a first-round knockout against Bill "Caveman" Lee. In 1983, he continued to live up to his new name with his crushing defeats of Tony Sibson in six rounds and Wilford Scypion in four rounds. In November, 1983, Marvin's reputation was diminished somewhat by his lackluster fifteen-round fight with Roberto Durán, which Marvin won by a decision. Marvin's disappointing performance in the Durán fight actually had a positive effect on him while he trained for his most formidable opponent up to this time: Thomas Hearns. Marvin began a rigorous training regimen that included running a minimum of six miles every morning and enduring one and one-half-hour, nearly nonstop workouts seven days a week. As a result of his determination, Marvin shocked boxing fans in 1985, by scoring a third-round technical knockout against Hearns, just as Marvin had predicted. This surprise victory was the pinnacle of Marvin's career.

Continuing the Story

While preparing for his last major title defense, against Sugar Ray Leonard, Marvin felt that he was fighting against more than just a man. Marvin resented the fact that the world seemed to be more impressed with Sugar Ray's pleasant personality and easy manner than it was with his own relentless approach to the sport. On April 6, 1987, in a controversial split decision, Marvin lost his middleweight championship to Sugar Ray.

The title meant everything to Marvin. After losing it, he became bitter and frustrated, blaming his loss on unfair judging. After the fight, his old se-

Statistics

Bouts, 67

Knockouts, 52

Bouts won by decision, 9

Bouts won by fouls, 1

Bouts lost by decision, 3

Draws, 2

Honors and Awards

1973	National Amateur Athletic Union middleweight champion
	National Amateur Athletic Union Finals Outstanding Fighter
1983, 1985	*Ring* magazine Merit Award (1985 co-recipient)
1993	Inducted into International Boxing Hall of Fame

cure world began to fall apart. In 1988, he retired from boxing to begin a second career as a film star. He also went into business as the owner of a novelty and sportswear store. Even though he had started a new life, the specter of defeat continued to haunt him, and it was reported that he began abusing drugs and alcohol, charges that Marvin repeatedly denied. In 1990, Marvin ended his seven-year marriage to his wife, Bertha. He then moved to Milan, Italy, to focus on his acting career.

Marvin was a throwback to the middleweight champions of yesteryear. Like Rocky Graziano, he rose to the top of the boxing world, not through glamour or glitz, but through patience and drive. Between 1973 and 1978, he worked his way up to the top of the middleweight division the hard way: as an independent. After winning the unified World Boxing Council-World Boxing Association crown from Alan Minter, he successfully defended it twelve times over the next six and one-half years. During that time, he proved to be a fearsome puncher who ended eleven of his title defenses in knockouts.

Summary

Before age finally took its toll, Marvelous Marvin Hagler was one of the greatest middleweight boxers of all time. Because he believed that his ability was never fully appreciated by either the fans or the promoters, he pushed himself relentlessly during his career in an effort to make the world take notice. Even though he eventually lost the championship, Marvin is still considered a champion.

Alan Brown

Additional Sources

McIlvanney, Hugh. *The Hardest Game: McIlvanney on Boxing.* Chicago: Contemporary Books, 2001.

Mullan, Harry, and Bob Mee. *Boxing: The Complete Illustrated Guide.* London: Carlton, 2002.

_____. *The Ultimate Encyclopedia of Boxing.* London: Carlton, 2007.

Platt, Jim, and James Buckley. *Sports Immortals: Stories of Inspiration and Achievement.* Chicago: Triumph Books, 2002.

Sugar, Bert Randolph. *Boxing's Greatest Fighters.* Guilford, Conn.: Lyons Press, 2006.

Thomas Hearns

Born: October 18, 1958
Memphis, Tennessee
Also known as: Hit Man Hearns

Early Life

Thomas Hearns was born on October 18, 1958, in Memphis, Tennessee. He grew up in poverty with his mother, Lois, two siblings, and six half siblings. When he was five, the family moved to Detroit, Michigan. Thomas had a tough upbringing. The family lived on the city's East Side, the scene of violent race riots in 1968, when Thomas was ten years old. A shy boy, Thomas became interested in boxing at the age of eight when he watched matches on television. His mother tried to discourage him but found that Thomas was not interested in anything except boxing. When he was ten, he started taking boxing lessons at King Solomon's Gymnasium, near his home. A year later he switched to the Kronk Recreation Center, on the other side of town.

The Road to Excellence

As a youngster, Thomas seemed an unlikely candidate for future boxing stardom. When he was eleven, he weighed only 55 pounds, and his natural boxing ability was not great. What enabled Thomas to stand out eventually was his fierce determination and fearlessness. He never missed a day's training and worked exceptionally hard at his craft. When it seemed Thomas might have a future in boxing, he dropped out of his twelfth-grade high school class so that he could become a full-time member of the Kronk amateur boxing team. His coach and mentor was Emanuel Steward, without whom he probably would not have become a boxing champion. Steward, who developed the boxing program at Kronk, insisted on strict discipline, spartan training conditions, and tough sparring practice.

Thomas lost two of his first six fights as an amateur but then showed rapid improvement. In 1976, when he was eighteen, he contended for a place on the U.S. Olympic team, but his defeat in the finals of the Amateur Athletic Union's (AAU's) 132-pound competition ended his chances. That was one of the biggest disappointments of his career. His mother and Steward—who had become almost like a father to Thomas—persuaded Thomas that his boxing prospects were still bright. The following year, Thomas proved them right by winning the 1977 National AAU title and the National Golden Gloves welterweight championship. In November, 1977, he turned professional with Steward as his manager.

The Emerging Champion

Thomas was an immediate success as a professional. He won his first twenty-eight fights, including twenty-six by a knockout. Most of the bouts lasted only three or four rounds. Thomas's opponents had no answer to his speed, his long reach, and his fearsome right fist. His devastating punching power earned him the nickname "Hit Man."

Thomas's initial string of victories gained him a shot at the World Boxing Association (WBA) welterweight championship, in August, 1980, in his hometown of Detroit. The reigning champion, José Cuevas, had successfully defended his title

---

Statistics

Bouts, 67
Knockouts, 48
Bouts won by decision, 13
Knockouts by opponents, 4
Bouts lost by decision, 1
Draws, 1

Records

Has held world titles in five weight classifications—the most of any professional boxer (record shared with Sugar Ray Leonard)

Honors and Awards

1977	National Amateur Athletic Union light welterweight champion
	National Golden Gloves welterweight champion
1980, 1984	*Ring* magazine Merit Award

Recognized World Welterweight Championships

Date	Location	Loser	Result
Aug. 2, 1980	Detroit, Mich.	José Cuevas	2d-round knockout
Dec. 6, 1980	Detroit, Mich.	Luis Primera	6th-round knockout
Apr. 25, 1981	Phoenix, Ariz.	Randy Shields	13th-round knockout
June 25, 1981	Houston, Tex.	Pablo Baez	4th-round knockout
Sept. 16, 1981	Las Vegas, Nev.	Thomas Hearns (Sugar Ray Leonard, winner)	14th-round knockout

Recognized World Junior Middleweight Championships

Date	Location	Loser	Result
Dec. 3, 1982	New Orleans, La.	Wilfred Benitez	15th-round decision
Feb. 11, 1984	Detroit, Mich.	Luigi Minchillo	12th-round decision
June 15, 1984	Las Vegas, Nev.	Roberto Durán	2d-round knockout
Sept. 15, 1984	Saginaw, Mich.	Fred Hutchings	3d-round knockout
June 23, 1986	Las Vegas, Nev.	Mark Medal	8th-round technical knockout

Recognized World Middleweight Championships

Date	Location	Loser	Result
Apr. 15, 1985	Las Vegas, Nev.	Thomas Hearns (Marvin Hagler, winner)	3d-round technical knockout
Oct. 29, 1987	Las Vegas, Nev.	Juan Roldan	4th-round knockout
June 6, 1988	Las Vegas, Nev.	Thomas Hearns (Iran Barkley, winner)	3d-round technical knockout

Recognized World Super Middleweight Championship

Date	Location	Loser	Result
June 12, 1989	Las Vegas, Nev.	(Sugar Ray Leonard, opponent)	12th-round draw

Recognized World Light Heavyweight Championships

Date	Location	Loser	Result
Mar. 7, 1987	Detroit, Mich.	Dennis Andries	10th-round technical knockout
June 3, 1991	Las Vegas, Nev.	Virgil Hill	12th-round unanimous decision
Mar. 20, 1992	Las Vegas, Nev.	Thomas Hearns (Iran Barkley, winner)	12th-round unanimous decision

eleven times and had never been knocked down. He was no match for Thomas, who was in his most aggressive form. Thomas was in complete control of the fight from the opening bell. When the battered Cuevas took a count of six in the second round, his manager threw in the towel and the fight was stopped.

After three successful defenses of his title—none of which went the distance—Thomas faced boxing superstar Sugar Ray Leonard in September, 1981, in Las Vegas. At stake were the combined WBA and World Boxing Council (WBC) welterweight titles. Thomas was in control for most of the fight and was well ahead on points at the end of the twelfth round. Leonard made a late comeback, aggressively winning the thirteenth round and pinning Thomas on the ropes in the middle of the fourteenth. Thomas was knocked out in the fourteenth round, his first defeat as a professional. He had become a rich man, however, earning more than five million dollars from this one fight.

Not a man to be easily discouraged, Thomas was soon back to his winning ways. The following year, he moved up to the super welterweight—or junior middleweight—division. In December, 1982, he fought the WBC champion, Wilfred Benitez, in New Orleans. The two fighters had contrasting styles. Benitez was a skilled craftsman, whereas Thomas was known as a big hitter. On this occasion, however, Thomas surprised everyone by his astute tactics. In spite of suffering an injury to his right hand in the eighth round, he managed to outmaneuver his opponent throughout the fight. After fifteen rounds, Thomas was declared the winner by a decision.

Continuing the Story

Thomas was at the peak of his career. In 1984, he successfully defended his WBC junior middleweight title three times, winning on points against Luigi Minchillo of Italy and knocking out Roberto Durán of Panama and Fred Hutchings of the United States.

In 1985, however, Thomas suffered a setback

when he took on Marvin Hagler for the undisputed world middleweight crown. The match between two of the deadliest fighters in the world was brief and ferocious. Savage punches were traded almost from the first bell, with neither fighter holding anything back. Thomas lost by a technical knockout in the third round. He remained the junior middleweight champion, however.

Thomas reacted to his loss with typical determination and grit. Moving up to the light heavyweight division, in 1987, he won the WBC title from Dennis Andries of England. In this fight, Thomas showed that he had lost none of his lethal power and will to win.

In 1989, Thomas had another showdown with Sugar Ray Leonard for the super middleweight title. These two veteran warriors put on a stirring battle. Twice Thomas knocked Leonard down, but Leonard held on and the match was declared a draw, which meant that Leonard retained his title. Leonard later conceded, however, that Thomas ought to have been declared the winner.

Thomas continued to fight throughout the 1990's, defeating Virgil Hill for the WBA light heavyweight title in 1991 and losing the title a year later to Iran Barkley in a twelfth-round decision. After several bouts with outmatched opponents, Thomas defeated Nate Miller by decision in 1999 for the IBO cruiserweight title, his seventh title in six weight classes. At the age of forty-one, Thomas faced the former cruiserweight champ Uriah Grant in what was billed as the final fight of his career. After the third round, however, Thomas retired from the match because of an ankle injury sustained during the second round. Thomas returned to the ring in 2005, defeating John Long. In February of the following year, he scored a tenth-round technical knockout against Shannon Landberg. This was the sixty-first victory of his career.

Summary

With titles in weight classes ranging from 147 to 190 pounds, Thomas Hearns proved to be a durable and versatile champion. Even in his losses to Leonard and Hagler, he was impressive, and he maintained his remarkable punching power throughout his long career, justifying his nickname, "Hit Man."

Bryan Aubrey

Additional Sources

Mullan, Harry, and Bob Mee. *The Ultimate Encyclopedia of Boxing.* London: Carlton, 2007.

Myler, Thomas. *The Sweet Science Goes Sour: How Scandal Brought Boxing to Its Knees.* Vancouver, B.C.: Greystone Books, 2006.

O'Keefe, John. "Thomas Hearns, Boxer." *Sports Illustrated* 96, no. 20 (May 13, 2002): 14.

Larry Holmes

Born: November 3, 1949
Cuthbert, Georgia
Also known as: Easton Assassin

Early Life
Larry Holmes, born on November 3, 1949, spent the first few years of his life with his eleven brothers and sisters in the small southwest Georgia town of Cuthbert. Life was not easy for his mother, Flossie, so she took the family to Easton, Pennsylvania. During Larry's early years of school and well into his teenage years, he was continually in trouble. His mother could not keep track of him, and he was often involved in street fights. Some positive direction came to his life when he joined the Easton Police Athletic League, where he learned both to control his anger and to take part in supervised boxing matches. He hoped boxing would bring some success because he dropped out of school in the seventh grade.

The Road to Excellence
After a series of low-paying jobs that included washing cars, pouring steel, and making artillery shells, he decided to become a professional fighter. At twenty-three years of age, Larry was rather old to become a fighter. He had twenty-five amateur bouts and lost only three. Larry won two regional amateur heavyweight titles during this time. In 1973, as a professional, Larry won a four-round decision but made only sixty-three dollars. From age twenty-three to twenty-eight, he fought only twenty-six times. Larry earned extra money by acting as a sparring partner for the heavyweight champion, Muhammad Ali.

The life of a sparring partner is not glamorous. For Larry, it helped him to learn his trade against the best fighter of the 1960's. Slowly, he gained respect by winning each time he fought. He soon became so capable that many top-rated fighters refused to box him. In 1978, he fought Ernie Shavers, who was believed to be the hardest puncher in the past forty years. Larry—never knocked down during the fight—won a unanimous decision. There was no more avoiding Larry. At the start of 1978, the heavyweight championship was split between two ruling groups. The World Boxing Association (WBA) recognized Leon Spinks as a champion. The World Boxing Council (WBC) decided to match Ken Norton, who had beaten Muhammad Ali in 1973, against Larry to determine its world champion.

Challenger Larry Holmes (right) lands a blow to Ken Norton during their title fight in 1978. (AP/Wide World Photos)

The Emerging Champion
On June 9, 1978, Larry and Norton met in Las Vegas, Nevada. After fourteen close, hard-fought rounds, they touched gloves to start the fifteenth and final round. This was a memorable round. First, Norton took the lead, throwing and landing hard blows. On the verge of losing, Larry came

Recognized World Heavyweight Championships

Date	Location	Loser	Result
June 9, 1978	Las Vegas, Nev.	Ken Norton	15th-round split decision
Nov. 10, 1978	Las Vegas, Nev.	Alfredo Evangelista	7th-round knockout
Mar. 23, 1979	Las Vegas, Nev.	Osvaldo Ocasio	7th-round technical knockout
June 22, 1979	New York, N.Y.	Mike Weaver	12th-round technical knockout
Sept. 28, 1979	Las Vegas, Nev.	Ernie Shavers	11th-round technical knockout
Feb. 3, 1980	Las Vegas, Nev.	Lorenzo Zano	6th-round technical knockout
Mar. 31, 1980	Las Vegas, Nev.	Leroy Jones	8th-round technical knockout
July 7, 1980	Minneapolis, Minn.	Scott Le Doux	7th-round technical knockout
Oct. 2, 1980	Las Vegas, Nev.	Muhammad Ali	11th-round technical knockout
Apr. 11, 1981	Las Vegas, Nev.	Trevor Berbick	15th-round unanimous decision
June 12, 1981	Detroit, Mich.	Leon Spinks	3d-round technical knockout
Nov. 6, 1981	Pittsburgh, Pa.	Renaldo Snipes	11th-round technical knockout
June 11, 1982	Las Vegas, Nev.	Gerry Cooney	13th-round technical knockout
Nov. 26, 1982	Houston, Tex.	Randall Cobb	15th-round unanimous decision
Mar. 27, 1983	Scranton, Pa.	Lucien Rodriguez	12th-round unanimous decision
May 20, 1983	Las Vegas, Nev.	Tim Witherspoon	12th-round unanimous decision
Sept. 10, 1983	Atlantic City, N.J.	Scott Frank	5th-round technical knockout
Nov. 25, 1983	Las Vegas, Nev.	Marvin Frazier	1st-round technical knockout
Nov. 9, 1984	Las Vegas, Nev.	Bonecrusher Smith	12th-round technical knockout
Mar. 15, 1985	Las Vegas, Nev.	David Bey	10th-round technical knockout
May 20, 1985	Las Vegas, Nev.	Carl Williams	15th-round unanimous decision
Sept. 21, 1985	Las Vegas, Nev.	Larry Holmes (Michael Spinks, winner)	15th-round unanimous decision
Apr. 19, 1986	Las Vegas, Nev.	Larry Holmes (Michael Spinks, winner)	15th-round split decision
Jan. 22, 1988	Atlantic City, N.J.	Larry Holmes (Mike Tyson, winner)	4th-round technical knockout
June 19, 1991	Las Vegas, Nev.	Larry Holmes (Evander Holyfield, winner)	12th-round unanimous decision
Apr. 8, 1995	Las Vegas, Nev.	Larry Holmes (Oliver McCall, winner)	12th-round unanimous decision

roaring back. At the final bell, Larry had done enough to win the WBC world championship.

As WBC champion, Larry was busy. During the next five years, he defended his championship two to four times each year. A year after defeating Norton, he met the feared Ernie Shavers for the second time. Once again he came out on top, but this time Shavers was saved by the referee in the eleventh round. In 1979, Muhammad Ali retired after regaining the WBA version of the title from Leon Spinks. Larry became recognized by most boxing experts as the true world champion. Because Larry became champion following the legendary Ali, he had problems gaining the public's respect. No matter how well he fought, he was compared with Ali.

From 1978 to late 1980, there were few outstanding contenders. Larry fought both the best ones available and a few others who were not highly ranked. In 1980, Ali decided to make a comeback. On October 2, 1980, the former sparring partners, Larry and Ali, fought. The fans rooted for the old champion, but the years had taken their toll. Larry was in command from the start. A tiring Ali was driven to the ropes in the tenth round. It would have been easy for Larry to knock out the former champion. He held back and did not throw his heaviest punches. Between the tenth and eleventh rounds, Ali retired. Larry was the undisputed champion of the world.

People who loved the defeated Ali found it difficult to forgive Larry for ending Ali's career. However, Larry was gracious in victory. "There can be only one Ali," he remarked. Larry greatly enjoyed

Statistics

Bouts, 75
Knockouts, 44
Bouts won by decision, 25
Knockouts by opponents, 1
Bouts lost by decision, 5

Honors and Awards

1982	*Ring* magazine Merit Award
2002	Ranked 27th in *Ring* magazine's best fighters of previous 80 years
2008	Inducted into International Boxing Hall of Fame

his reign as the undisputed world heavyweight champion. It brought him wealth far greater than any other boxer in history up to that time. Of equal importance to the "Easton Assassin," as he was nicknamed, was the image he conveyed to children. He once wrote, "This title means everything to me. I want children to be able to look at me and say, 'I want to be just like Larry Holmes when I grow up.'"

After eighteen months and three more title defenses, Larry finally fought another highly ranked opponent. The often inactive Gerry Cooney was a fan favorite and a great puncher. At thirty-two years of age, many thought Larry was too old to fight at the championship level. Larry fought a brave Cooney, who lasted thirteen rounds, but in the end, Larry was victorious.

Continuing the Story

By 1985, Larry had fought forty-eight times without a single defeat. The great heavyweight champion of the 1950's, Rocky Marciano, had retired undefeated with forty-nine victories. Larry wanted to equal and surpass that record before retiring. For his forty-ninth bout, he selected the light heavyweight champion, Michael Spinks. He believed in the old saying, "A good big man will defeat a good little man." In more than ninety years of heavyweight history, no light heavyweight champion had ever defeated a heavyweight champion. History was made on September 21, 1985, as Michael Spinks won a disputed decision. No longer could Larry retire undefeated. Seven months later, Larry tried to regain his championship. Once again a close decision went against him. After thirteen years of boxing and at thirty-six years of age, he announced his retirement.

In 1988, Larry returned to the ring against the dreaded Mike Tyson. Few people gave the old champion much of a chance, and youth was served. After three even rounds, Tyson caught Larry along the ropes and knocked him out—the only time Larry has ever been knocked out. In retirement, Larry lived in his hometown of Easton, Pennsylvania. Unlike many former fighters, he was careful with the money he earned. He had learned the value of preparing for his future with his wife and two children. He purchased a large restaurant and motel and invested in numerous local businesses.

Larry did not stay out of the ring for long. He fought five bouts in 1991, winning three by knockout and two by decision, on his way to a world title bout with Evander Holyfield in 1992. The aging champion could not overpower the younger Holyfield, and Larry lost a twelfth-round unanimous decision. In the next two years, Larry put together an impressive string of wins, though against decidedly lesser talents, and once again fought for a heavyweight title in 1995 against Oliver McCall. Though still a potent threat in the ring, Larry was unable to match speed and accuracy with his younger opponent and lost a twelfth-round decision.

Following the McCall fight, Larry began a series of retirements and comebacks, though never straying far from the ring. In 1998, the much-anticipated bout between Larry and George Foreman was set for the following year but was first postponed and then canceled after Foreman's retirement. Instead, in June of 1999, Larry fought James "Bonecrusher" Smith and scored an eighth-round knockout.

Although Larry has retired numerous times, he always watched for an opportunity to return for a big fight, insisting that he still had the skill to compete with younger fighters. Even into his fifties, he lobbied for a marquee fight with the likes of Tyson, Holyfield, or Foreman. In 2008, he was inducted into the International Boxing Hall of Fame.

Summary

The greatness of Larry Holmes is sometimes overlooked because his championship followed that of Muhammad Ali. He was less outgoing than Ali, and his ring style was not as flashy. Larry, however, was excellent as both a boxer and a puncher. As the years pass and records are compared, Larry will gain greater recognition. Winning forty-eight straight bouts over twelve years is a feat few boxers have equaled.

Bruce Gordon

Additional Sources

Dahlberg, Tim. *Fight Town: Las Vegas, the Boxing Capital of the World*. Las Vegas, Nev.: Stephens Press, 2007.

Holmes, Larry, and Phil Berger. *Larry Holmes: Against the Odds*. London: Robson, 1999.

Mullan, Harry, and Bob Mee. *The Ultimate Encyclopedia of Boxing*. London: Carlton, 2007.

Sugar, Bert Randolph. *Boxing's Greatest Fighters*. Guilford, Conn.: Lyons Press, 2006.

Evander Holyfield

Born: October 19, 1962
Atmore, Alabama
Also known as: The Real Deal

Early Life

Evander Holyfield was born on October 19, 1962, in Atmore, Alabama. Soon after he was born, his mother moved the family to Atlanta, Georgia, where Evander grew up. Evander had his first fight at the age of nine, when he weighed only 65 pounds. During the early part of his high school career, he preferred football to boxing. However, although he made the football team, he was relatively small and spent most of his time on the bench. By then he had become more interested in boxing. Evander listened as his mother taught him discipline and the values of hard work.

The Road to Excellence

Carter Morgan, the boxing coach at the Warren Memorial Boys' Club, noted Evander's natural talent and encouraged him to continue. Morgan died when Evander was sixteen, and Evander felt a deep sense of loss. After a short while, however, he resumed training under the guidance of Ted Morgan.

After graduating from high school, Evander worked at an airport, fueling planes. After watching the 1980 U.S. Olympic boxing trials, held in Atlanta, Evander decided to become an Olympic boxer. He began to train hard to achieve this ambition.

The Emerging Champion

In 1983, Evander won the National Sports Festival boxing title. This victory made him a leading contender for a place on the U.S. Olympic team in the light-heavyweight division. In the Olympic trials, Evander came close to elimination, but he recovered and won his place on the team in the final qualifying bout.

At the 1984 Olympic Games in Los Angeles, California, Evander won three bouts to reach the semifinals. Then, however, disaster struck for Evander. Near the end of the second round of his fight with Kevin Barry of New Zealand, the referee called for a break. Evander did not hear the call and knocked Barry out. Evander was then disqualified. In the

Evander Holyfield punches George Foreman during their championship match in 1991. (AP/Wide World Photos)

Recognized World Cruiserweight Championships

Date	Location	Loser	Result
July 12, 1986	Atlanta, Ga.	Dwight Qawi	15th-round decision
Feb. 14, 1987	Reno, Nev.	Henry Tillman	7th-round technical knockout
May 15, 1987	Las Vegas, Nev.	Rickey Parkey	3d-round technical knockout
Aug. 16, 1987	St. Tropez, France	Ossie Ocasio	11th-round technical knockout
Dec. 5, 1987	Atlantic City, N.J.	Dwight Qawi	4th-round technical knockout
Apr. 9, 1988	Las Vegas, Nev.	Carlos DeLeon	8th-round technical knockout

Recognized World Heavyweight Championships

Date	Location	Loser	Result
Oct. 25, 1990	Las Vegas, Nev.	Buster Douglas	3d-round knockout
Apr. 19, 1991	Atlantic City, N.J.	George Foreman	12th-round decision
Nov. 23, 1991	Atlanta, Ga.	Bert Cooper	7th-round technical knockout
June 19, 1992	Las Vegas, Nev.	Larry Holmes	12th-round decision
Nov. 13, 1992	Las Vegas, Nev.	Evander Holyfield (Riddick Bowe, winner)	12th-round decision
Nov. 6, 1993	Las Vegas, Nev.	Riddick Bowe	12th-round decision
Apr. 22, 1994	Las Vegas, Nev.	Evander Holyfield (Michael Moorer, winner)	12th-round decision
Nov. 9, 1996	Las Vegas, Nev.	Mike Tyson	11th-round knockout
June 28, 1997	Las Vegas, Nev.	Mike Tyson	3d-round disqualification
Nov. 8, 1997	Las Vegas, Nev.	Michael Moorer	8th-round knockout
Sept. 19, 1998	Atlanta, Ga.	Vaughn Bean	12th-round decision
Mar. 13, 1999	New York, N.Y.	Lennox Lewis	12th-round draw
Nov. 13, 1999	Las Vegas, Nev.	Evander Holyfield (Lennox Lewis, winner)	12th-round decision
Aug. 12, 2000	Las Vegas, Nev.	John Ruiz	12th-round decision
Mar. 3, 2001	Las Vegas, Nev.	Evander Holyfield (John Ruiz, winner)	12th-round decision
Dec. 12, 2001	Mashantucket, Conn.	John Ruiz, opponent	Draw
Dec. 14, 2002	Atlantic City, N.J.	Evander Holyfield (Chris Byrd, winner)	12th-round decision
Nov. 13, 2004	New York, N.Y.	Evander Holyfield (Larry Donald, winner)	12th-round decision
Nov. 10, 2006	San Antonio, Tex.	Fres Oquendo	12th-round decision
Oct. 13, 2007	Moscow, Russia	Evander Holyfield (Sultan Ibragimov, winner)	12th-round decision
Dec. 20, 2008	Zurich, Switzerland	Evander Holyfield (Nikolay Valuev, winner)	12th-round decision

controversy that followed, Evander won widespread respect for the dignified way he accepted the decision.

With a 160-40 record as an amateur, Evander decided to turn professional in November, 1984. After five fights as a light-heavyweight, he moved up to the cruiserweight division, just below the heavyweight category.

In 1986, Evander beat Dwight Mohammad Qawi to win the World Boxing Association (WBA) and International Boxing Federation (IBF) cruiserweight titles. Two years later, he won recognition from the World Boxing Council (WBC) as cruiserweight champion. Then Evander embarked on the biggest challenge of his career: He decided to move up to the heavyweight division to challenge Mike Tyson for the world title. During the next two years, Evander showed the determination and patience that were his hallmarks. Concentrating on weight training and aerobic exercise, he went through an intensive conditioning program, eager to defy the skeptics who said he was not a true heavyweight.

Continuing the Story

After two easy wins as a heavyweight, Evander had a tough battle against Michael Dokes. The referee stopped the fight in the tenth round, with Evander the victor. The victory made Evander the leading contender for the heavyweight title, then held by the seemingly invincible Tyson. However, in February, 1990, Buster Douglas defeated Tyson unexpectedly. Eight months later, Evander challenged Douglas for the world title. Evander won easily, knocking Douglas out in the third round with a straight right to the chin.

Evander successfully defended his title three times. In April, 1991, he defeated forty-two-year-old former heavyweight champion George Foreman on points, earning at least $20 million in the process. In June, 1992, Evander beat former champion Larry Holmes on points.

Statistics

Bouts, 54
Knockouts, 27
Bouts won by decision, 15
Bouts lost by decision, 7
Draws, 2

Honors and Awards

1984 Bronze medal, U.S. Olympic Boxing
1990 Boxing Writers Association of America Fighter of the Year

In November, 1992, after twenty-eight victories, Evander finally lost, to a younger and heavier Riddick Bowe. During two years as champion, Evander had amassed a fortune of $80 million, making him the wealthiest boxer alive. He had also distinguished himself by his modest, courteous demeanor, making him a fine role model for youngsters in a sport that had few such figures.

After losing his title, Evander announced his retirement. However, in January, 1993, he decided to return to the ring. In November, he regained the heavyweight title from Bowe with a twelve-round majority decision, becoming only the third fighter to win the title a second time. In April, 1994, Evander lost a narrow majority decision to Michael Moorer. He was looking ahead to a possible rematch when doctors who were treating him after the fight noticed that he was showing signs of heart trouble. Several days later, specialists confirmed that he was suffering from a congenital heart defect that made it impossible for his heart to expand properly during extreme physical exertion. Doctors advised Evander to retire.

Like many champions before him, Evander eventually returned to the ring. He fought twice in 1995, defeating Ray Mercer by decision and losing by technical knockout (TKO) to Bowe in the eighth round. In 1996, however, Evander reclaimed his WBA heavyweight title from Tyson in one of the most anticipated and exciting heavyweight championship fights in boxing history. Evander scored a TKO in the eleventh round to become the first three-time heavyweight champ since Muhammad Ali.

In June, 1997, Evander faced Tyson again. As their first meeting was one of the most exciting fights, their rematch was one of the most bizarre. Thirty-three seconds into the second round, a desperate Tyson bit Evander on the left ear. In the third round, Tyson made another lunge, this time biting off a piece of Evander's right ear and spitting it onto the mat. The referee ended the bout by disqualifying Tyson, and Evander retained his title.

In 1999, Evander and Lennox Lewis met to unify the heavyweight titles, and the result was controversial. Having predicted a third-round knockout, Evander struggled throughout the fight. At the final bell, the judges scored the bout a draw, eliciting displeasure from the sellout crowd. Final punch statistics, however, showed Lewis leading in all categories.

In November, 1999, Evander and Lewis fought again, and this time the decision was unanimous. After twelve hard-fought rounds, Evander lost a unanimous decision to Lewis, who showed much greater strength and speed. After his disappointment in the Lewis rematch, Evander set a goal to retire as the undisputed heavyweight champion. He won an unprecedented fourth heavyweight title against John Ruiz in August, 2000.

In March, 2001, Evander and Ruiz fought again. Ruiz won a 12-round decision. The third Evander-Ruiz fight came in December, 2001. Despite Evander's hopes, Ruiz maintained his title as the fight was called a draw.

By 2002, Evander started fighting again, defeating Hasim Rahman. In December, he lost to the IBF heavyweight champion Chris Byrd. Evander continued to struggle, as he lost to James Toney in October, 2003, and Larry Donald in November, 2004.

By 2005, officials began to question Evander's boxing abilities. The New York State Athletic Commission refused to license Evander to fight in New York because of health issues. Nonetheless, in August, 2006, Evander won his fight with Jerry Bettis in two rounds. In November, 2006, he defeated Fres Oquendo. In 2007, Evander won two more fights. However, given another chance to win the heavyweight title, he lost to champion Sultan Ibraginmov.

For Evander, life outside the ring was lucrative. He appeared on a number of television series and did commercials. His personal life, though, was not so happy. He went through a number of divorces, had his $10-million mansion foreclosed, and was even accused of using steroids. Over his career,

Evander grossed more than $248 million. Nonetheless, he had money problems, paying child support for thirteen children.

Summary

Although Evander Holyfield was not a natural heavyweight, he used a combination of skill and intensive conditioning to become a heavy champion multiple times. During his reign as champion, he brought a rare dignity to the sport.

Bryan Aubrey and Michael V. Namorato

Additional Sources

Holyfield, Evander, and Lee Gruenfeld. *Becoming Holyfield: A Fighter's Journey*. New York: Atria Books, 2008.

Holyfield, Evander, and Bernard Holyfield. *Holyfield: The Humble Warrior*. Nashville, Tenn.: T. Nelson, 1996.

Kirkpatrick, Rob. *Evander Holyfield: Heavyweight Champion*. New York: PowerKids Press, 2000.

Schultz, Jeff. "Difficult Times for Evander Holyfield." *Atlanta Journal-Constitution*, June 6, 2008.

Bernard Hopkins

Born: January 15, 1965
Philadelphia, Pennsylvania
Also known as: The Executioner

Early Life
Bernard Hopkins was born in Philadelphia, Pennsylvania, on January 15, 1965. Early on, he became a street tough. Self-described as a "thug," Bernard was sentenced to eighteen years in prison for "strong-arm robbery" in 1982. From 1984 to until his early release in 1988, Bernard was housed in Graterford State Penitentiary, where he earned a high school diploma, converted to Islam, and discovered boxing. While in prison, he was a four-time national penitentiary middleweight champion.

The Road to Excellence
On October 11, 1988, Bernard had his first professional bout: a four-round loss by decision to Clinton Mitchell, the only time he lost a nontitle fight. Soon after, Bernard went to Augie's Gym in Philadelphia and joined trainer Bouie Fischer, who helped guide Bernard to world championships. On February 22, 1990, Bernard had his second fight, this time as a middleweight, and won a four-round decision over Greg Paige. On December 4, 1992, he beat Wayne Powell to win the United States Boxing Association middleweight title.

In May, 1993, Bernard fought Roy Jones for the vacant International Boxing Federation (IBF) middleweight championship. Although competitive, Bernard lost the fight, the last time Bernard was defeated for twelve years. After wins over Roy Ritchie, Wendall Hall, Melvin Wynn, and Lupe Aquino, Bernard was matched against Segundo Mercado in Quito, Ecuador, for the IBF belt Jones had vacated. Although knocked to the canvas twice in the early rounds, Bernard fought hard at the end and earned a draw in Mercado's hometown. The IBF ordered a rematch.

The Emerging Champion
On April 29, 1995, Bernard won the IBF middleweight title when he knocked out Mercado in the seventh round in Landover, Maryland. Bernard held this title for twelve years and defended it twenty times, a middleweight record. In his second title defense, he knocked out undefeated Joe Lipsey in the third round, ending the challenger's career. On January 27, 1996, Bernard stopped Steve Frank in 19 seconds, the fastest knockout in a middleweight title fight.

By the end of 2000, he had defended his title twelve times against premier fighters, such as former light-middleweight and middleweight champion John David Jackson, later light-heavyweight champion Glen Johnson, former welterweight and light-middleweight champion Simon Brown, and hard-punching Antwun Echols. In his second fight with Echols, Bernard made a notable choice. He was thrown to the canvas, injuring his left shoulder and, thus, had the option to

Bernard Hopkins delivering a hard left hand to Antonio Tarver's head in a 2006 heavyweight title fight. (Al Bello/Getty Images)

win by disqualification. However, he decided to continue fighting and knocked out Echols in the tenth round. This act earned Bernard the reputation as an old-school fighter who refused to take the easy path. Bernard was also gaining the reputation as a disciplined fighter out of the ring, always staying within a few pounds of the middleweight limit and studying fights of the classic boxing stylists like Jersey Joe Walcott, Archie Moore, and Ezzard Charles. Bernard was considered the best middleweight in the world.

In 2001, Bernard had his best year. Promoter Don King arranged "the Middleweight Championship Series" among the junior-middleweight champion Félix Trinidad, World Boxing Council middleweight champion Keith Holmes, World Boxing Association middleweight champion William Joppy, and Bernard, who held the IBF belt. Trinidad was a heavy favorite, especially after he knocked out Joppy in 5 rounds in May. After Bernard defeated Holmes in April, 2001, he fought Trinidad in Madison Square Garden on September 29, 2001. This fight was delayed two weeks because of the terrorist attacks of September 11. In an upset, Bernard dominated Trinidad, knocking him out in the twelfth round. Bernard won the middleweight tournament and the accompanying Sugar Ray Robinson trophy and was considered by many the best boxer in the world. Bernard was voted the 2001 fighter of the year by *Ring* magazine, the so-called "Bible of boxing."

Statistics

Bouts, 54
Knockouts, 32
Bouts won by decision, 17
Bouts lost by decision, 5

Continuing the Story

After the middleweight tournament, Bernard defended his title six more times. On February 2, 2002, he beat former junior-middleweight champion Carl Daniels in 10 rounds. He won a decision against Joppy on Dec 13, 2003. On September 18, 2004, in Las Vegas, Nevada, he had the biggest victory of his career when he knocked out five-division champion Oscar De La Hoya in the ninth round. After the fight, De La Hoya named Bernard the president of the East Coast chapter of De La

Recognized World Middleweight Championships

Date	Location	Loser	Result
Apr. 29, 1995	Landover, Md.	Segundo Mercado	7th-round technical knockout
Jan. 27, 1996	Phoenix, Ariz.	Steve Frank	1st-round technical knockout
Mar. 16, 1996	Las Vegas, Nev.	Joe Lipsey	4th-round knockout
July 16, 1996	Atlantic City, N.J.	William Bo James	11th-round technical knockout
Apr. 19, 1997	Shreveport, La.	John David Jackson	7th-round technical knockout
July 20, 1997	Indio, Calif.	Glen Johnson	11th-round technical knockout
Nov. 18, 1997	Upper Marlboro, Md.	Andrew Council	12th-round unanimous decision
Jan. 31, 1998	Atlantic City, N.J.	Simon Brown	6th-round technical knockout
Feb. 6, 1999	Washington, D.C.	Robert Allen	7th-round technical knockout
Dec. 12, 1999	Miami, Fla.	Antwun Echols	12th-round unanimous decision
May 13, 2000	Indianapolis, Ind.	Syd Vanderpool	12th-round unanimous decision
Dec. 1, 2000	Las Vegas, Nev.	Antwun Echols	10th-round technical knockout
Apr. 4, 2001	New York, N.Y.	Keith Holmes	12th-round unanimous decision
Sept. 29, 2001	New York, N.Y.	Félix Trinidad	12th-round technical knockout
Feb. 2, 2002	Reading, Pa.	Carl Daniels	10th-round technical knockout
Mar. 3, 2003	Philadelphia, Pa.	Morrade Hakkar	8th-round technical knockout
Dec. 13, 2003	Atlantic City, N.J.	William Joppy	12th-round unanimous decision
June 6, 2004	Las Vegas, Nev.	Robert Allen	12th-round unanimous decision
Sept. 18, 2004	Las Vegas, Nev.	Oscar De La Hoya	9th-round knockout
Feb. 19, 2005	Los Angeles, Calif.	Howard Eastman	12th-round unanimous decision
July 17, 2005	Las Vegas, Nev.	Bernard Hopkins (Jermain Taylor, winner)	12th-round split decision
Dec. 3, 2005	Las Vegas, Nev.	Bernard Hopkins (Jermain Taylor, winner)	12th-round unanimous decision

Recognized World Light Heavyweight Championship

Date	Location	Loser	Result
June 10, 2006	Atlantic City, N.J.	Antonio Tarver	12th-round unanimous decision

Hoya's Golden Boy Promotions, one of boxing's top promotional companies.

After defeating Howard Eastman for his twentieth title defense, Bernard fought young, Olympic bronze-medal-winner Jermain Taylor. On July 16, 2005, Bernard gave up the early rounds but surged at the end only to lose a split-decision to Taylor. Less than five months later, they had a rematch, and Taylor again won a close unanimous decision. Both results were controversial wins for Taylor; many believed Bernard deserved the victories.

After announcing his retirement, Bernard fought again, this time against light-heavyweight champion Antonio Tarver. Given Bernard's age, forty-one, and Tarver's weight of 175 pounds, many felt Bernard did not have a chance. However, like the Trinidad fight before, Bernard dominated, winning a unanimous decision and the title. Later, he defended his title against junior-middleweight champion Ronald "Winky" Wright. In 2008, in Las Vegas, he lost his title to Joe Calzaghe.

Summary

Bernard Hopkins was significant for many reasons. He showed that commitment to boxing can save someone from a life of crime. He also showed how discipline and a work ethic can lead to success in the ring. He and Nigerian Dick Tiger are the only two fighters to jump from the middleweight division and win the light-heavyweight title, something the great Sugar Ray Robinson failed to do. His twenty defenses of the middleweight title were more than any other middleweight.

Brett Conway

Additional Sources

Hauser, Thomas. *Chaos, Courage, Corruption, and Glory: A Year in Boxing.* Toronto: Sport Classic Books, 2005.

_____. *I Don't Believe It, but It's True: A Year in Boxing.* Toronto: Sport Classic Books, 2006.

Sugar, Bert Randolph. *Boxing's Greatest Fighters.* Guilford, Conn.: Lyons Press, 2006.

Jack Johnson

Born: March 31, 1878
   Galveston, Texas
Died: June 10, 1946
   Raleigh, North Carolina
Also known as: John Arthur Johnson (full name); Galveston Giant

Early Life
John Arthur "Jack" Johnson was born on March 31, 1878, in Galveston, Texas. Although life was hard for African Americans living in this southern town, Jack's father Henry Johnson, a former slave, and his mother, Tiny Johnson, provided all six of their children with a basic education. Henry, who was disabled, worked as a porter and janitor and owned his small home. Jack finished about six years of school, more than most southern African American children. He held odd jobs to help with family expenses while he was in school, and when he left school, he worked as a day laborer in and around Galveston.

The Road to Excellence
As Jack worked as a day laborer around southern Texas, he soon found that he was physically superior to other young men and that he could make money by prizefighting. Fighting for money was illegal in Texas but was widely practiced in private clubs. Jack's boxing career was shaped by the racial conditions of his time. American racism and segregation was prevalent as he entered manhood. His first experience in organized boxing was in "battles royal," in which white people paid African Americans to fight under sideshow conditions, such as fighting blindfolded. Jack excelled and began to fight regularly in local private clubs. The official record lists him as fighting five times in 1897 and 1898.

In these years he improved his boxing skills. In 1899, after defeating all of the best local fighters, he went to Chicago, where he acted as sparring partner to major fighters. He was poorly paid and fed, and he lost his first big fight to a good African American fighter named Klondike Haynes. Jack went back to Galveston. Jack is listed as fighting twelve times in 1900 and 1901. His major bout was with Joe Choynski, a legendary Jewish fighter. Choynski was past his prime but still had his reputation and enough skill to defeat Jack. They were both jailed for breaking the prizefighting law. Jack put his jail time to good use by sparring with Choynski.

The Emerging Champion
In 1901, Jack, at the age of twenty-three, moved to California. In 1901 and 1902, he increasingly impressed the boxing world even when he lost. He was 180 pounds at that time and would be heavier

Jack Johnson, who faced racial discrimination throughout his heavyweight boxing career. (Courtesy of Amateur Athletic Foundation of Los Angeles)

Statistics

Bouts, 112
Knockouts, 45
Bouts won by decision, 29
Bouts won by fouls, 4
Knockouts by opponents, 5
Bouts lost by decision, 2
Bouts lost by fouls, 1
Draws, 12
No decisions, 14

Honors and Awards

1954	Inducted into *Ring* magazine Boxing Hall of Fame
1975	Inducted into Black Athletes Hall of Fame
1990	Inducted into International Boxing Hall of Fame

in his prime. He fought gracefully, standing straight, with his weight over his back foot. He was a smart fighter who used his unequaled speed to become a master of defensive fighting. Racial morés of the time forced African American fighters into more defensive boxing styles than whites.

In 1902, Jack defeated Jack Jeffries, brother of champion James J. Jeffries. This fight brought Jack to the forefront of the heavyweights. He lost no fights in 1902 and 1903, and in the latter year, he defeated Denver Ed Martin for the black heavyweight championship. Jack ran into another racial barrier. Most Americans did not want top white heavyweights to fight African Americans. The best white boxers would not give him a match. In 1905, James J. Jeffries retired as champion, and Jack maintained steady pressure on his successors to give him a shot at the title. Finally, in Australia, on December 26, 1908, heavyweight champion Tommy Burns fought Jack for the title. Jack dominated the fight and knocked Burns out in the fourteenth round.

Promoters rushed to put forward a "great white hope" to take back the title, but Jack pounded the white challengers. Finally, in 1910, James J. Jeffries came out of retirement to fight Jack. Most whites expected Jeffries to win, even though he was obviously old and out of shape. They fought in Reno, Nevada, on July 4, 1910. Jack dominated the fight, and the Jeffries corner stopped the fight in the fifteenth round. Many African Americans were killed in racial conflicts after the fight because whites feared that Jack's victory would encourage black insubordination.

Any African American champion would have faced problems in 1910, but Jack generated special fears in white society. He was a complex man who intended to live his life as a free individual, without concerns for public opinion. He led a "sporting" life, spending lavishly on himself and on women. In 1911, he married the first of a series of white women. Hatred for him among whites intensified. Most areas of the United States banned boxing, and Congress passed a law, seemingly aimed at Jack, forbidding the interstate shipment of fight films. He was convicted of violating the Mann Act, a law aimed at suppressing prostitution, although his real crime was flouting the racial morés of his time.

Rather than go to prison, Jack fled to Europe and fought several times there. Meanwhile, the search went on for a new white boxing champion. Jess Willard emerged from the pack. Jack, thirty-seven years

Recognized World Heavyweight Championships

Date	Location	Loser	Result
Dec. 26, 1908	Sydney, Australia	Tommy Burns	14th-round technical knockout
Mar. 10, 1909	Vancouver, Canada	Victor McLagler	6th-round no decision
May 19, 1909	Philadelphia, Pa.	"Philadelphia Jack" O'Brien	6th-round no decision
June 30, 1909	Pittsburgh, Pa.	Tony Ross	6th-round no decision
Sept. 9, 1909	San Francisco, Calif.	Al Kaufman	10th-round no decision
Oct. 16, 1909	Colma, Calif.	Stanley Ketchel	12th-round knockout
July 4, 1910	Reno, Nev.	James J. Jeffries	15th-round knockout
July 4, 1912	Las Vegas, Nev.	Jim Flynn	9th-round technical knockout
Dec. 19, 1913	Paris, France	(Jim Johnson, opponent)	10th-round draw
June 27, 1914	Paris, France	Frank Moran	20th-round referee's decision
Apr. 5, 1915	Havana, Cuba	Jack Johnson (Jess Willard, winner)	26th-round knockout

old and poorly trained, fought Willard on April 5, 1915, in Havana, Cuba. Jack tired under the hot sun and was knocked out in the twenty-sixth round.

Continuing the Story
Jack returned to Europe, where he fought some matches and exhibitions and worked in the entertainment world. Finally, in 1920, he returned to the United States and served his prison sentence. When he was released in 1921, he was nearly forty-two years old and had lost his speed. Jack Dempsey, then heavyweight champion, refused to fight him. Jack fought a few more fights, but mainly earned money through boxing exhibitions and in entertainment. He appeared in the ring until 1945, when he was sixty-seven years old. On June 10, 1946, he was killed in an automobile accident in Raleigh, North Carolina.

Jack faced racial harassment and barriers that seemed incredible to a later generation. The cost to him was great, but he faced racism with unfailing courage and dignity. His career helped destroy the color line in boxing. As the years passed, people began to recognize that he had been one of the greatest boxers in history.

Summary
Jack Johnson overcame great handicaps to become the first African American world heavyweight champion. He lived life as a free man who refused to bend to society's racial rules. He was the predecessor of Jackie Robinson and other African American athletes who stood up to the racial segregation in American society.

William E. Pemberton

Additional Sources
Bennett, Lerone, Jr. "Jack Johnson and the Great White Hope." *Ebony* 60, no. 3 (January, 2005): 110-114.

Hietala, Thomas R. *The Fight of the Century: Jack Johnson, Joe Louis, and the Struggle for Racial Equality.* Armonk, N.Y.: M. E. Sharpe, 2004.

Kent, Graeme. *The Great White Hopes: The Quest to Defeat Jack Johnson.* Stroud, Gloucestershire, England: Sutton, 2006.

Ward, Geoffrey C. *Unforgivable Blackness: The Rise and Fall of Jack Johnson.* New York: Vintage Books, 2006.

Roy Jones, Jr.

Born: January 16, 1969
Pensacola, Florida
Also known as: Roy Jones, Jr. (full name); Junior

Early Life

Roy Jones, Jr., was born in Pensacola, Florida, on January 16, 1969. From childhood, he loved sports and the outdoors. After school and on weekends he joined friends in basketball games, his favorite sport at that time, or fished with his father.

Vietnam veteran "Big" Roy Jones, Sr., ran an amateur boxing program for local youths. Through his tutelage, "Little" Roy was introduced to boxing. Big Roy was merciless in teaching his son, whipping him with whatever was handy to make him angry enough to fight. Roy, Jr., trained hard and, by the age of ten was winning bouts against older and heavier opponents. In 1984, he won the U.S. Junior Olympics in the 119-pound weight division. Roy graduated from Washington High in 1987. After high school, he took courses at Pensacola Junior College.

The Road to Excellence

In 1986, at 139 pounds, Roy won the National Golden Gloves Competition and followed that with a similar victory in the 156-pound class the next year. As an amateur, Roy sported a career record of 121-13.

At the 1988 Olympics in Seoul, South Korea, fighting as a light middleweight, Roy dominated opponents throughout the competition and never lost a round on his way to the final bout. In the gold medal match, he overwhelmed South Korean Park Si-hun. However, after the final bell, officials ruled Park the victor. Roy had to settle for the silver medal. He also received the Val Barker Cup as the Olympics' outstanding boxer.

After the Olympics, an official investigation, finally concluded in 1997, revealed that the judges of the Jones-Park match had accepted favors from the Korean hosts in return for decisions benefiting Korean boxers. The judges were eventually suspended. Though Roy appealed to be awarded the Olympic gold medal, the International Olympic Committee took no action. However, the incident was a key element in the establishment of a new and fairer scoring system for Olympic boxing matches.

The Emerging Champion

Roy turned professional in 1989. During that first year, he tallied three impressive wins. Roy quickly established himself as the brightest new star in boxing. The following year, he added six more knockout victories to his record. He compiled a 15-0 record, all by knockout. In 1993, he defeated Bernard Hopkins by a unanimous decision to become the International Boxing Federation (IBF) middleweight champion. He defended his title the following year in a bout with Thomas Tate.

In 1994, Roy captured the super-middleweight title with a twelfth-round decision over defending champion James Toney. The following year, he defended his super-middleweight title with a first-round knockout of top contender Antoine Byrd. Roy's third defense came against former Canadian champion Eric Lucas. He defended his title for a fifth time in October, 1996, with a second-round knockout of Bryant Brannon.

However, Roy was not content with only one title. In November, 1996, he fought three-time world champion Mike McCallum and became the World Boxing Council (WBC) champion in a twelve-round decision. In doing so, he became a member of an exclusive club: world champion in three different weight divisions.

Continuing the Story

In March 1997, Roy lost the WBC title to Montell Griffin when he was disqualified. In the seventh

Statistics

Bouts, 57
Knockouts, 38
Bouts won by decision, 14
Bouts lost by decision, 2
Bouts lost by knockout, 2
Bouts lost by disqualification, 1

round, Roy knocked Griffin down. In the ninth, Griffin hit the canvas again. Roy kept punching Griffin when he was down, which led to Roy's disqualification and cost him the title. In August of the same year, Roy regained the title with a first-round knockout of Griffin.

The following year, though Roy was knocked down for the first time in his career, he defended his WBC title and won the World Boxing Association (WBA) title from Lou Del Valle by unanimous decision. In 1999, he again won the IBF championship, making him the simultaneous WBC, WBA, and IBF champion, a rare occurrence that earned him the title of best pound-for-pound boxer in the world.

In 2000, Roy won a 12-round decision against David Telesco to retain the light-heavyweight world title. He defended his championship with a TKO against Richard Hall. After scoring a couple of knockouts in 2002, Roy gained weight to try for a heavyweight championship in 2003. Though outweighed by more than 30 pounds, he defeated John Ruiz in 12 rounds to capture the WBA heavyweight title, becoming the first former middleweight champion in 106 years to capture a heavyweight title. Afterward, Roy decided the light-heavyweight division was more to his liking and vacated the heavyweight title without defending it.

Roy won back the light-heavyweight crown, beat-

Recognized World Middleweight Championships

Date	Location	Loser	Result
May 22, 1993	Washington D.C.	Bernard Hopkins	12th-round unanimous decision
May 27, 1994	Las Vegas, Nev.	Thomas Tate	2d-round knockout

Recognized World Super-Middleweight Championships

Dec. 5, 1992	Atlantic City, N.J.	Percy Harris	4th-round knockout
Nov. 18, 1994	Las Vegas, Nev.	James Toney	12th-round unanimous decision
Mar. 18, 1995	Pensacola, Fla.	Antoine Byrd	1st-round technical knockout
June 24, 1995	Atlantic City, N.J.	Vinny Pazienza	6th-round technical knockout
Sept. 30, 1995	Pensacola, Fla.	Tony Thornton	2d-round technical knockout
June 15, 1996	Jacksonville, Fla.	Eric Lucas	11th-round knockout
Oct. 4, 1996	New York, N.Y.	Bryant Brannon	2d-round knockout

Recognized World Light-Heavyweight Championships

Nov. 22, 1996	Tampa, Fla.	Mike McCallum	12th-round unanimous decision
Mar. 21, 1997	Atlantic City, N.J.	Roy Jones, Jr. (Montell Griffin, winner)	9th-round disqualification
Aug. 21, 1997	Ledyard, Conn.	Montell Griffin	1st-round knockout
July 18, 1998	New York, N.Y.	Lou Del Valle	12-round unanimous decision
Nov. 14, 1998	Mashantucket, Conn.	Otis Grant	10th-round technical knockout
Jan. 9, 1999	Pensacola, Fla.	Rick Frazier	2d-round knockout
June 5, 1999	Biloxi, Miss.	Reggie Johnson	12th-round unanimous decision
Jan. 15, 2000	New York, N.Y.	David Telesco	12th-round unanimous decision
May 13, 2000	Indianapolis, Ind.	Richard Hall	11th-round technical knockout
Sept. 9, 2000	New Orleans, La.	Eric Harding	10th-round technical knockout
Feb. 24, 2001	Tampa, Fla.	Derrick Harmon	10th-round technical knockout
July 28, 2001	Los Angeles, Calif.	Julio Gonzalez	12th-round unanimous decision
Feb. 2, 2002	Miami, Fla.	Glenn Kelly	7th-round technical knockout
Sept. 7, 2002	Portland, Oreg.	Clinton Woods	6th-round technical knockout
Nov. 8, 2003	Las Vegas, Nev.	Antonio Tarver	12th-round split decision
May 15, 2004	Las Vegas, Nev.	Roy Jones, Jr. (Antonio Tarver, winner)	2d-round technical knockout
Sept. 25, 2004	Memphis, Tenn.	Roy Jones, Jr. (Glen Johnson, winner)	9th-round knockout
Oct. 1, 2005	Tampa, Fla.	Roy Jones, Jr. (Antonio Tarver, winner)	12th-round unanimous decision
July 29, 2006	Boise, Idaho	Prince Badi Ajamu	12th-round unanimous decision
July 14, 2007	Biloxi, Miss.	Anthony Hanshaw	12th-round unanimous decision
Nov. 8, 2008	New York, N.Y.	Roy Jones, Jr. (Joe Calzaghe, winner)	12th-round unanimous decision

Recognized World Heavyweight Championship

March 1, 2003	Las Vegas, Nev.	John Ruiz	12th-round unanimous decision

ing Antonio Tarver by majority decision. In 2004, Roy was knocked out for the first time in his career. Later that year, attempting to win the IBF light-heavyweight title, Roy was caught by a punch from champion Glen Johnson and knocked out for the second consecutive time.

After sitting out more than a year to train and serve as an analyst on HBO, Roy lost again to Tarver by a decision. In 2006, he began his comeback by outpointing Prince Badi Ajamu. In mid-2007, he beat Anthony Hanshaw in a unanimous decision to capture the International Boxing Congress (IBC) light-heavyweight belt. Early in 2008, he fought five-time world champion Félix Trinidad and won a unanimous victory. This set him up for the *Ring* magazine light-heavyweight championship against Joe Calzaghe, a Welsh fighter of Italian heritage with an unbeaten record.

The two men faced off in November, 2008, in Madison Square Garden in New York. Though Roy scored a first-round knockdown, Calzaghe held the upper hand throughout the fight, opening a cut over Roy's eye and winning a unanimous decision. Roy, at thirty-nine and with a professional record of 52-5, had lost four of his last seven fights and contemplated retiring.

Summary

A talented amateur who won a silver medal in boxing at the 1988 Olympics, Roy Jones, Jr., achieved extraordinary success as a professional, compiling a 52-5 record with 38 knockouts. Considered one of the best pound-for-pound fighters ever, Roy held championship belts in four different weight classes. He was the first former welterweight champion in more than a century to win a heavyweight title.

Don Evans, updated by Jack Ewing

Additional Sources

Boddy, Kasia. *Boxing: A Cultural History.* London: Reaktion Books, 2008.

Freeman, Mike. "Jones Has Belts but No Challengers." *The New York Times*, May 15, 2000.

Lidz, Franz. "Boxing's Best Takes the Big Stage." *Sports Illustrated*, January 24, 2000.

Sugar, Bert Randolph. *Boxing's Greatest Fighters.* Guilford, Conn.: Lyons Press, 2006.

Todd, Gary. *Workouts from Boxing's Greatest Champs: Get in Shape with Muhammad Ali, Fernando Vargas, Roy Jones, Jr., and Other Legends.* Berkeley, Calif.: Ulysses Press, 2004.

Stanley Ketchel

Born: September 14, 1886
Grand Rapids, Michigan
Died: October 15, 1910
Springfield, Missouri
Also known as: Stanisław Kiecal (birth name); the Michigan Assassin; the Michigan Marvel

Early Life
Stanley Ketchel was born Stanisław Kiecal on September 14, 1886. His father, Thomas, of Polish heritage, was born in Russia and immigrated to the United States. He married Julia, a Polish American woman. They farmed in Grand Rapids, Michigan.

Stanley Ketchel. (Library of Congress)

Stanley grew strong by performing daily chores. However, the monotonous nature of life on a farm was not for him. At the age of twelve, he ran away from home, heading west. For several years, Stanley joined a group of miners traveling from boomtown to boomtown. He worked at odd jobs. His body became lean and hard. He became expert with a pistol and learned to use his fists in the turbulent environment of the mining camps. By the age of seventeen, Stanley had settled in Butte, Montana. There, he worked regularly as a saloon bouncer. However, he made more money as a boxer. At night, Stanley was house champion at a local casino. For $20 in weekly wages, he took on all challengers.

The Road to Excellence
Within a year, Stanley had fought in about 250 amateur boxing matches. Though he had no formal training, Stanley gained valuable experience with each fight. He also developed a winning tactic. At the opening bell, he rushed out of his corner to throw a flurry of hard punches with both hands. His attack never abated from round to round. His brawling style bewildered opponents with a constant barrage of leather. Stanley piled up knockout victories and earned the nickname the "Michigan Assassin."

Stanley turned professional in 1904. In his debut, he knocked out "Kid" Tracy in the first round. During his first year as a professional, Stanley was 13-2, with 12 knockouts. By the end of 1905, his record was 31-2, with 29 knockouts. In his first 41 bouts, Stanley fought exclusively in Montana. He ran his record to 36-2, with 3 no decisions. Then he joined the larger, more important boxing market of California. There, Stanley achieved everlasting fame.

The Emerging Champion
The 5-foot 9-inch Stanley was at his prime fighting weight of 142 pounds. A middleweight, he scored knockouts in his first 3

Recognized World Welterweight Championship

Date	Location	Loser	Result
Sept. 2, 1907	Colma, Calif.	Joe Thomas	32d-round knockout

Recognized World Middleweight Championships

Date	Location	Loser	Result
Dec. 12, 1907	San Francisco, Calif.	Joe Thomas	20th-round decision
Feb. 22, 1908	Colma, Calif.	Mike "Twin" Sullivan	1st-round knockout
May 9, 1908	Colma, Calif.	Jack "Twin" Sullivan	20th-round knockout
June 4, 1908	Milwaukee, Wis.	Billy Papke	10th-round decision
July 31, 1908	San Francisco, Calif.	Hugo Kelly	3d-round knockout
Aug. 18, 1908	San Francisco, Calif.	Joe Thomas	2d-round technical knockout
Sept. 7, 1908	Vernon, Calif.	Stanley Ketchel (Billy Papke, winner)	12th-round technical knockout
Nov. 26, 1908	Colma, Calif.	Billy Papke	11th-round knockout
July 5, 1909	Colma, Calif.	Billy Papke	20th-round decision

Recognized World Heavyweight Championship

Date	Location	Loser	Result
Oct. 16, 1909	Colma, Calif.	Stanley Ketchel (Jack Johnson, winner)	12th-round knockout

bouts in California and won 6 straight fights. Early in 1908, he knocked out Mike "Twin" Sullivan, a middleweight-championship contender. In May of that year, he knocked out highly ranked Jack "Twin" Sullivan in 20 rounds. At the age of twenty-one, Stanley was declared world middleweight champion.

In 1908, Stanley defended his championship three times. He knocked out Billy Papke, Hugo Kelly, and Joe Thomas. In a rematch with Papke in September, 1908, the challenger won on a technical knockout in 12 rounds. Two months later, Stanley knocked out Papke to become the first middleweight to regain the championship.

As reigning champion in 1909, Stanley fought in a series of exhibition bouts in Michigan, Pennsylvania, and New York. A fearless scrapper, he took on light-heavyweight champion "Philadelphia Jack" O'Brien and knocked him out in 3 rounds. After another successful title defense, Stanley challenged world heavyweight champion Jack Johnson. The charismatic African American accepted the challenge. The boxing match, filmed for posterity, took place in Colma, California, on October 16, 1909. Though bulked up to 160 pounds, Stanley was small compared to the 6-foot, 209-pound Johnson. Stanley, while bloodied, gave a good account of himself. In the twelfth round, he sent Johnson to the canvas with a hard blow to the head. The champion got to his feet and delivered a crushing right hand just as Stanley charged. Johnson knocked out several of Stanley's teeth, and the challenger fell unconscious. Stanley was out cold for ten minutes.

Statistics

Bouts, 64
Knockouts, 48
Bouts won by decision, 5
Draws, 6
Knockouts by opponents, 2
Bouts lost by decision, 3

Honors, Awards, and Milestones

1907-09	Middleweight champion
1954	Inducted into *Ring* magazine Boxing Hall of Fame
1990	Inducted into International Boxing Hall of Fame
2000	One of the twenty greatest boxers of the twentieth century (*Ring* magazine)
2003	Ranked sixth greatest puncher ever (*Ring* magazine)
2005	Ranked as third greatest middleweight by the International Boxing Research Organization

Continuing the Story

Stanley recovered from the loss to Johnson. He continued to fight exhibitions and nontitle bouts. His last match was on June 10, 1910. That day, he knocked out Jim Smith in New York City, in 5 rounds. The victory boosted his official record to

53 wins—48 by knockout. Stanley talked wistfully about fighting Johnson again.

R. P. Dickerson, a friend and sportsman, invited Stanley to train for upcoming fights at his ranch in the Ozarks. At the Conway, Missouri, property Stanley grew fond of the countryside. He decided to give up boxing after one more fight. Afterward, he would return to his roots and take up farming. He became engaged to a local woman named Jewell. However, Stanley's life took an unexpected and shocking turn. On the morning of October 15, 1910, a farmhand named Walter Kurtz shot Stanley with a rifle. Mortally wounded, Stanley was rushed by train to a hospital in Springfield, Missouri, where he died at the age of twenty-four. Days later, most citizens of Grand Rapids, Michigan, attended his funeral.

At his trial, Kurtz was revealed to be Walter Dipley, a U.S. Navy deserter. Dipley claimed Stanley had assaulted his wife, Goldie, the ranch cook. Dipley said he had shot the pistol-packing boxer in self-defense. However, evidence revealed that Goldie was not Dipley's wife. There was no proof of assault, either. Furthermore, Stanley was shot in the back. The jury convicted Dipley and Goldie Smith of first-degree murder. Goldie's conviction was later overturned, though she served time for robbery. Dipley spent twenty-three years in prison for killing the "Michigan Assassin" and died in 1956.

Summary

A fierce competitor, Stanley Ketchel is perennially ranked among the all-time best middleweight boxers. Sports historians rate him one of the hardest punchers ever. Stanley was enshrined into the *Ring* magazine Boxing Hall of Fame in 1953. The International Boxing Hall of Fame inducted him in 1990.

Jack Ewing

Additional Sources

Blake, James Carlos. *The Killings of Stanley Ketchel: A Novel.* New York: William Morrow, 2005.

Kent, Graeme. *The Great White Hopes: The Quest to Defeat Jack Johnson.* London: Sutton, 2007.

Nash, Jay Robert. *World Encyclopedia of Twentieth Century Murder.* New York: Marlowe, 1992.

Roberts, James, and Alexander Skutt. *The Boxing Register: International Boxing Hall of Fame Official record Book.* 4th rev. ed. Ithaca, N.Y.: McBooks Press, 2006.

Silverman, Jeff, ed. *The Greatest Boxing Stories Ever Told: Thirty-six Incredible Tales from the Ring.* Guilford, Conn.: Globe Pequot Press, 2004.

Vitali and Vladimir Klitschko

Vitali Klitschko
Born: July 19, 1971
Belovodsk, Soviet Union
(now in Kyrgyzstan)
Also known as: Vitali Vladimirovich Klitschko (full name); Dr. Ironfist

Vladimir Klitschko
Born: March 25, 1976
Semipalatinsk, Soviet Union
(now in Kazakhstan)
Also known as: Vladimir Vladimirovich Klitschko (full name); Wladimir Klitschko; Dr. Steelhammer

Early Lives

Brothers Vitali Vladimirovich Klitschko and Vladimir Vladimirovich Klitschko were both born during the 1970's, but in different parts of the Soviet Union: Vitali in Kyrgyzstan and Vladimir in Kazakhstan. This was because their father, Russian air force colonel Vladimir Rodionovich Klitschko, and their mother, Nadezhda Ulyanova Klitschko, a teacher, moved frequently to various military postings. The family eventually settled in the Ukraine. There, during the decade of the 1980's, both the Klitschko brothers discovered the sport that made them famous: boxing.

The Road to Excellence

Vitali, the elder of the two boys, took up boxing at the age of thirteen. He started as a kickboxer. He had excellent agility despite his massive, well-proportioned size—he eventually reached more than 6 feet 7 inches in height—and became quite successful. Vitali reigned as kickboxing world champion six times, twice as an amateur and four times as a professional. Only after his domination of kickboxing, when he looked for new worlds to conquer, did Vitali turn to boxing at the age of twenty-four.

Vitali (left) and Vladimir Klitschko pose after the former's fight with Samuel Peter in 2008. (Tobias Schwarz/Reuters/Landov)

Vladimir Klitschko's Recognized Heavyweight Championships

Year	Location	Loser	Result
Feb. 14, 1998	Stuttgart, Germany	Marcus McIntyre	3d-round knockout
July 17, 1999	Düsseldorf, Germany	Joseph Chingangu	5th-round technical knockout
Sept. 25, 1999	Cologne, Germany	Axel Schulz	8th-round technical knockout
Dec. 4, 1999	Hanover, Germany	Lajos Eros	2d-round knockout
Mar. 18, 2000	Hamburg, Germany	Paea Wolfgramm	1st-round knockout
Oct. 14, 2000	Cologne, Germany	Chris Byrd	12th-round unanimous decision
Mar. 24, 2001	Munich, Germany	Derrick Jefferson	2d-round technical knockout
Aug. 4, 2001	Las Vegas, Nev.	Charles Shufford	6th-round technical knockout
Mar. 16, 2002	Stuttgart, Germany	Francois Botha	8th-round technical knockout
June 29, 2002	Atlantic City, N.J.	Ray Mercer	6th-round technical knockout
Dec. 7, 2002	Las Vegas, Nev.	Jameel McCline	10th-round technical knockout
Mar. 8, 2003	Hanover, Germany	Vladimir Klitschko (Corrie Sanders, winner)	2d-round technical knockout
Aug. 30, 2003	Munich, Germany	Fabio Eduardo Moli	1st-round knockout
Dec. 20, 2003	Kiel, Germany	Danell Nicholson	4th-round technical knockout
Apr. 10, 2004	Las Vegas, Nev.	Lamon Brewster	5th-round technical knockout
Sept. 24, 2005	Atlantic City, N.J.	Samuel Peter	12th-round unanimous decision
Apr. 22, 2006	Mannheim, Germany	Chris Byrd	7th-round technical knockout
Nov. 11, 2006	New York, N.Y.	Calvin Brock	7th-round technical knockout
Mar. 10, 2007	Mannheim, Germany	Ray Austin	2d-round technical knockout
July 7, 2007	Cologne, Germany	Lamon Brewster	6th-round referee's technical decision
Feb. 23, 2008	New York, N.Y.	Sultan Ibragimov	12th-round unanimous decision
July 12, 2008	Hamburg, Germany	Tony Thompson	11th-round knockout
Dec. 13, 2008	Mannheim, Germany	Hasim Ratiman	7th-round technical knockout

He was an immediate success, winning the super-heavyweight championship at the 1995 World Military Games. Later that year, he won the silver medal at the World Amateur Boxing Championships. In short order, Vitali earned 195 amateur wins, 80 of which came by knockout. He won the Ukrainian heavyweight championship three times, and he lost only 15 matches during his amateur days.

Meanwhile, Vladimir, who grew to be just as imposing as his brother at more than 6 feet 6 inches, began to box at the age of fourteen. Within three years, he captured the junior European heavyweight championship in his age division. In 1995, he won the gold medal at the military championships. As an amateur, he ruled as five-time Ukrainian boxing champion and took second place as a super heavyweight at the 1996 European Amateur Boxing Championships. Vladimir capped his amateur career when he won the gold medal in the super-heavyweight division at the 1996 Summer Olympic Games in Atlanta, Georgia.

The Emerging Champions

Both Klitschko brothers turned professional in 1996. In that same year, Vitali and Vladimir each graduated from the Ukraine's Pereyaslav-Khmelnitsky State Pedagogical Institute and were admitted into the postgraduate program of Kiev University. Vitali also married in 1996, to former athlete and model Natalia Egorova, and the couple later had three children: Egor-Daniel, Elizabeth-Victoria, and Max.

To improve their chances of success inside and outside the boxing ring, the brothers moved from Ukraine to Germany, where they signed with the promotional firm of Universum. Articulate, personable, able to speak several languages, and superb athletes, Vitali and Vladimir were shaped into popular European celebrities even as they experienced success in the sporting world.

Vitali began his professional boxing career in fine fashion. He won his first twenty-four fights either by knockout or technical knockout (TKO). In 1999, he captured the European Boxing Union (EBU) heavyweight championship. The same year, he gained the World Boxing Organization (WBO) title, part of the fragmented world heavyweight championship, by knocking out Herbie Hide of England. In 2000, after two title defenses, Vitali lost the championship to Chris Byrd and suffered a shoulder injury during the bout. In 2003, he fought Lennox Lewis in a World Boxing Congress (WBC) title match, in which Vitali was cut severely and lost by TKO. Vitali demanded a rematch, but Lewis retired, vacating the WBC title.

Like Vitali, Vladimir started strong as a professional, with a knockout over his opponent in his

Vitali Klitschko's Recognized Heavyweight Championships

Date	Location	Loser	Result
Oct. 24, 1998	Hamburg, Germany	Mario Schiesser	2d-round technical knockout
Dec. 5, 1998	Kiev, Ukraine	Francesco Spinelli	1st-round technical knockout
Feb. 20, 1999	Hamburg, Germany	Ismael Youla	2d-round technical knockout
June 26, 1999	London, England	Herbie Hide	2d-round knockout
Oct. 9, 1999	Oberhausen, Germany	Ed Mahone	3d-round technical knockout
Dec. 11, 1999	Hamburg, Germany	Obed Sullivan	9th-round technical knockout
Apr. 1, 2000	Berlin, Germany	Vitali Klitschko (Chris Byrd, winner)	9th-round referee's technical decision
Nov. 25, 2000	Hanover, Germany	Timo Hoffmann	12th-round unanimous decision
Jan. 27, 2001	Munich, Germany	Orlin Norris	1st-round knockout
Dec. 8, 2001	Oberhausen, Germany	Ross Puritty	11th-round technical knockout
Nov. 23, 2002	Dortmund, Germany	Larry Donald	10th-round technical knockout
June 21, 2003	Los Angeles, Calif.	Vitali Klitschko (Lennox Lewis, winner)	6th-round technical knockout
Dec. 6, 2003	New York, N.Y.	Kirk Johnson	2d-round technical knockout
Apr. 24, 2004	Los Angeles, Calif.	Corrie Sanders	8th-round technical knockout
Dec. 11, 2004	Las Vegas, Nev.	Danny Williams	8th-round technical knockout
Oct. 11, 2008	Berlin, Germany	Samuel Peter	9th-round referee's technical decision

first fight. He earned the EBU heavyweight championship in 1999 and took the WBO title in 2000. Vladimir successfully defended his championship belt five times before losing the title in 2003 on a TKO to South African Corrie Sanders. In 2004, he fought for the vacated WBO title but ran out of energy in the later rounds and lost.

Continuing the Story

In 2000, Vitali received his doctoral degree in sports science from Kiev University. The following year, Vladimir received his doctoral degree from the same institution in the same discipline. In 2004, the brothers moved from Germany to Southern California to continue their boxing careers.

In April, 2004, Vitali beat Sanders to earn the WBC heavyweight boxing title. He defended the title before back and knee injuries forced him to retire in 2005, though the WBC allowed him the chance to later return to regain the championship. He did so in October, 2008, beating Samuel Peter to reclaim the WBC belt. As of 2008, Vitali remained the WBC heavyweight champion and had a 92 percent knockout rate, the highest of any heavyweight champion in history.

Meanwhile, Vladimir did even better than his brother. In 2006, he beat Byrd to win both International Boxing Organization (IBO) and International Boxing Federation (IBF) heavyweight championships. He also captured the WBO title in early 2008, outpointing champion Sultan Ibragimov. In December, 2008, he fought American Hasim Rahman.

The Klitschko brothers returned to the Ukraine, where Vitali twice ran unsuccessfully for mayor of Kiev. The Klitschkos started a collection of men's sportswear through designer Hugo Boss. Both were active in charitable causes involving education and children and worked for the United Nations Educational, Scientific and Cultural Organization (UNESCO), which funds projects around the world. Both brothers also enjoyed chess.

Summary

The first siblings in history to hold world heavyweight boxing championships at the same time, Vitali and Vladimir Klitschko did not fit the traditional mold of pugilists as slow-witted brutes. Intelligent, well spoken in a variety of languages, and highly educated, Vitali and Vladimir each exhibited a combination of speed and power that produced a knockout rate unmatched in the annals of boxing.

Jack Ewing

Additional Sources

Fitzgerald, Mike, and David L. Hudson. *Boxing's Most Wanted: The Top Ten Book of Champs, Chumps, and Punch-Drunk Palookas.* Dulles, Va.: Potomac Books, 2003.

Hauser, Thomas. *The View from Ringside: Inside the Tumultuous World of Boxing.* Toronto: SportClassic Books, 2004.

Mullan, Harry. *Boxing: The Complete Illustrated Guide.* London: Carlton Books, 2003.

Roberts, James, and Alexander Skutt. *The Boxing Register: International Boxing Hall of Fame Official record Book.* Ithaca, N.Y.: McBooks Press, 2006.

Jake LaMotta

Born: July 10, 1921
New York, New York
Also known as: Giacobe LaMotta (full name); Bronx Bull; Raging Bull

Early Life

Giacobe "Jake" LaMotta was the oldest of five children born to Giussepe and Elizabeth LaMotta. Jake's father, a Sicilian immigrant, had settled on the lower East Side of Manhattan, where he met and married Elizabeth, a second-generation Italian American. Jake was born there, but the family eventually moved to the Bronx. Jake dropped out of high school early, and after several brushes with legal authorities, he was arrested for attempted burglary of a jewelry store. At the age of fifteen, he was sentenced to three years at the State Reform School in Coxsackie, New York. There, the prison chaplain helped Jake channel his aggression into boxing. He developed some boxing skills and a determination to seek a career as a pugilist. After his release, he started boxing competitively, and after winning all forty of his amateur matches, he turned professional at the age of nineteen.

The Road to Excellence

Jake began his professional career as a light heavyweight, winning his first fifteen fights. After two years, his professional record was 28-6, and he shifted to the middleweight class. The quality of his opponents improved, highlighted by an October, 1942, bout with Sugar Ray Robinson. The undefeated Robinson won a unanimous 10-round decision. Four months later, however, Jake gave Robinson his first defeat and first knockdown. Robinson barely averted an eighth-round knockout when a punch sent him through the ropes and down for a count of nine before the bell rang.

Next, Jake defeated Jimmy Reeves in a rematch, and over a six-month period in 1943, he won three of four fights with former welterweight champion Fritzie Zivic. The boxing press took notice of Jake's impressive victories and came to regard him as the "uncrowned" middleweight champion. Despite Jake's success, a championship fight eluded him because, in his judgment, he refused to cooperate with the mobsters in control of boxing.

Jake's brother Joseph arranged for Jake to fight Billy Fox on November 14, 1947, in Madison Square Garden. Fox won by a technical knockout in the fourth round, when referee Frank Fullam called the fight because of Jake's injuries. Since

Jake LaMotta (right) fighting Dick Wagner in Detroit in 1952. (Popperfoto/Getty Images)

Statistics

Bouts, 106
Knockouts, 30
Bouts won by decision, 53
Knockouts by opponents, 4
Bouts lost by decision, 15
Draws, 4

Jake had made little effort to defend himself from Fox's punches, suspicions were raised that the fight had been fixed. The New York State Boxing Commission investigated the fight, and despite his denial of a fix, Jake was suspended for seven months. Later, during the June, 1960, Subcommittee on Antitrust and Monopoly of the Senate Judiciary Committee hearings on professional boxing, Jake admitted that this fight had been fixed. He testified that a $100,000 bribe was received but insisted the reason he complied was the guarantee of a championship fight.

The Emerging Champion

Jake resumed boxing in mid-1948, winning all but one of his fights, a loss to Canadian Laurent Dauthuille. Finally, on June 16, 1949, in Detroit, Michigan, Jake got his opportunity for a world middleweight championship in a title match against Marcel Cerdan, the renowned French boxer from Casablanca, Morocco. Cerdan injured his shoulder early in the fight and surrendered after the ninth round, giving Jake the victory by technical knockout.

A scheduled rematch had to be canceled when Cerdan's plane crashed in the Azores islands, killing all aboard. In 1950, Jake successfully defended the middleweight crown against Italian champion Tiberio Mitri in July and in a rematch with Dauthuille in September. The latter, a fifteen-round, bruising fight, was designated by *Ring* magazine as the 1950 fight of the year. On February 2, 1951, Jake met Robinson for the sixth time in a middleweight championship fight in Chicago. The fight, often called "the St. Valentine's Day Massacre," was stopped in the thirteenth round because of damage Robinson had inflicted on Jake. That marked the end of Jake's reign as world middleweight champion.

Continuing the Story

Jake continued his boxing career for several more years, moving to the light-heavyweight division. He defeated several leading light middleweights, and by the end of 1951, he was ranked as one of the top-ten light heavyweights by *Ring* magazine. Jake's 1952 loss to Danny Nardico included a seventh-round knockdown, the first and only one in Jake's career. After a layoff of fourteen months, Jake fought three more times. He won two but lost his last fight, to Billy Kilgore on March 14, 1954. After this loss, Jake retired from boxing.

Jake, his wife Vicki, and their three children moved to Miami Beach, where he opened a nightclub. He had difficulty adjusting to life outside of the boxing ring, and his heavy drinking and frequent womanizing led to a marital breakup. Vicki, who married Jake ten years earlier while still a teenager, was the second of six wives; all of the marriages ended in divorce.

Jake's personal troubles continued. His self-described "lowest of lows" was his arrest and conviction of aiding and abetting prostitution of a fourteen-year-old girl. His already tarnished reputation sustained further damage from his testimony during the Senate subcommittee investigation of professional boxing that he accepted a bribe to lose the Fox fight. Personal, financial, and employment problems followed. He returned to New York and eventually got speaking engagements and acting jobs. His biggest break came when his 1970 autobiography *Raging Bull* was made into a movie by the same name. The 1980 film, directed by Martin Scorsese, starred Robert De Niro as Jake, a role which earned him the Academy Award for Best Actor.

Recognized World Middleweight Championships

Date	Location	Loser	Result
June 16, 1949	Detroit, Mich.	Marcel Cerdan	10th-round technical knockout
July 12, 1950	New York, N.Y.	Tiberio Mitri	15th-round unanimous decision
Sept. 13, 1950	Detroit, Mich.	Laurent Dauthuille	15th-round knockout
Feb. 2, 1951	Chicago, Ill.	Jake LaMotta (Sugar Ray Robinson, winner)	13th-round technical knockout

Summary

Jake LaMotta was proud of his career record of 83 wins—30 by knockouts—and 19 losses, but he especially savored the fact that he was never knocked out. Best remembered are his six bouts with Sugar Ray Robinson, whom Jake regarded as the greatest boxer. Jake was elected to the World Boxing Hall of Fame in 1986. Despite open acknowledgement of serious misconduct, his several rehabilitations and his resistance to mob influence during his boxing career drew him some favor. *The New York Times* movie critic Vincent Canby observed in his review of *Raging Bull* that, in the end, there is a deep mystery about Jake, about what propelled him through his tumultuous and remarkable life.

Mario Morelli

Additional Sources

Anderson, Chris, Sharon McGee, and Jake LaMotta. *Raging Bull II*. Secaucus, N.J.: Lyle Stuart, 1986.

Hauser, Thomas, and Stephen Brunt. *The Italian Stallions: Heroes of Boxing's Glory Days*. Toronto: Sport Media, 2003.

LaMotta, Jake, Joseph Carter, and Peter Savage. *Raging Bull*. Englewood Cliffs, N.J.: Prentice Hall, 1970.

Sam Langford

Born: March 4, 1883
Weymouth Falls, Nova Scotia, Canada
Died: January 12, 1956
Cambridge, Massachusetts
Also known as: Sam E. Langford (full name); the Boston Terror; the Boston Tar Baby

Early Life
Sam E. Langford was born in Weymouth Falls, Nova Scotia, Canada, on March 4, 1883. His great-grandfather, an escaped slave, was said to have arrived in Nova Scotia from New Jersey in 1793. Sam's father worked as a sailor, farmer, lumberjack, and dockworker in the Weymouth area. Like all of the men of the Langford family, he was known for his physical strength and love of fighting. Because of abuse suffered at the hands of his father, Sam left home at an early age and for several years traveled around, surviving by whatever work he could find. He eventually arrived in Boston, Massachusetts, where he secured a job as a janitor at the Lennox Athletic Club operated by Joe Woodson, a local fight manager. There, his decision to become a boxer was made.

The Road to Excellence
Having learned his craft by sparring with the fighters training at Woodson's gym, Sam, in 1902, embarked on a brief amateur career. He won the local amateur featherweight title that same year and shortly thereafter, turned professional. Within a relatively short period of time, he had grown into a welterweight at 147 pounds.

Since boxing at this time was largely unregulated, boxers frequently fought outside of their primary weight class. One of Sam's most significant early victories occurred in December of 1903, when he scored a 15-round decision over the great lightweight champion Joe Gans. Even more important was a closely contested loss to later heavyweight champion Jack Johnson in 1906. Although maintaining a clear height and weight advantage over Sam, Johnson never gave him a chance to fight for the heavyweight title after winning it in 1908.

The Emerging Champion
Over the twenty-four years of his professional boxing career, Sam had an amazing number of fights, although not unprecedented for the time period. He fought more than three hundred times. He averaged one fight a month during much of his career, although in some years, he fought at a much higher rate. In 1920, for example, he fought twenty-three times. Inevitably, he fought some of the same opponents more than once. In fact, Sam fought many of the best fighters of his day numerous times. Among these were heavyweights Harry Wills, whom he fought twenty-three times; Sam McVey, fifteen times; and Joe Jeanette, fourteen

Canadian Sam Langford, who won two hundred fights in his career. (Library of Congress)

times. At 5 feet 7 inches in height and weighing between 165 and 180 pounds in his prime, Sam was at a distinct size disadvantage against these individuals, but he fought them all on even terms. He also engaged in bouts with several lighter weight boxing greats of the time period, including welterweight champion Joe Walcott, with whom he gained a draw in 1904; middleweight champion Stanley Ketchel, with whom he fought to a sixth-round no decision in 1910; and later middleweight champion Tiger Flowers, whom he knocked out in the second round in 1922.

After his draw with Walcott for the welterweight title in 1904, Sam did not fight for a championship again until late in his career. During his reign as heavyweight champion, from 1908 to 1915, Johnson refused to fight him. Then, after Johnson lost the title, for more than twenty years, no African American was given a chance to fight for the heavyweight championship because of racial prejudice resulting from Johnson's success against white fighters and his flamboyant lifestyle as champion. Finally, in 1923, at the age of forty, Sam fought for and won the Mexican heavyweight title, which he defended several times the same year.

Continuing the Story

In 1917, in a fight with Fred Fulton, Sam severely injured his left eye; in his 1922 bout with Flowers his right eye was injured as well. He fought the remainder of his career barely able to see. He often described the experience of fighting in this condition, stating that, in his fight for the Mexican title, he simply felt around until he knew his opponent was close to him and then threw the punch that scored the knockout. In 1924 and again during his retirement, he underwent eye surgeries, none of which were completely successful.

During his career Sam earned a good deal of money. There are newspaper accounts of him returning to his hometown surrounded by a large entourage of sparring partners and assistants. In the end, however, he ended up blind, without money, and living in a run-down apartment in Harlem. During his retirement he was hospitalized at least

Statistics

Bouts, 314
Knockouts, 130
Bouts won by decision, 70
Bouts lost, 47
Draws and no decisions, 67

Honors and Awards

1955   Inducted into *Ring* magazine Boxing Hall of Fame

twice for injuries suffered when hit by vehicles while attempting to cross streets. In 1944, a newspaper article written about him brought knowledge of his plight to the public, and a trust fund was set up in his behalf. He spent his last years living with his daughter in Cambridge, Massachusetts. Sam died on January 12, 1956, at the age of seventy-two.

Summary

Sam Langford is considered one of the top boxers in the history of the sport who never won or even fought for— other than the 1904 welterweight title bout—a world championship. In large part, this was because of the racial prejudice of the time, especially in regard to the heavyweight division. As evidence of his greatness, in 1955, Sam became the first nonchampion to be elected to the *Ring* magazine Boxing Hall of Fame. The famous boxing writer Nat Fleischer ranked Sam in seventh place on his 1958 list of the all-time best heavyweights, despite his small size and that he never fought for the world title.

Scott Wright

Additional Sources

Fleischer, Nat. *Fifty Years at Ringside.* New York: Greenwood Press, 1969.

Myler, Patrick. *A Century of Boxing Greats: Inside the Ring with the Hundred Best Fighters.* London: Robson Books, 1999.

Smith, Kevin. *Boston's Boxing Heritage: Prizefighting from 1882 to 1955.* Charleston, S.C.: Arcadia, 2002.

Benny Leonard

Born: April 7, 1896
New York, New York
Died: April 18, 1947
New York, New York
Also known as: Benjamin Leiner (birth name); the Ghetto Wizard

Early Life
Benny Leonard was born Benjamin Leiner in New York, New York, on April 7, 1896. He grew up on the lower East Side of the city, a rough area where children had to know how to fight to survive. Ethnic background was a major factor during the early twentieth century, and Benny, who was Jewish, had to be ready to do battle against youths of Italian and Irish descent. This fighting experience, combined with the poverty of inner-city life, caused many young boys of Benny's generation and situation to dream of a career in the boxing ring. Benny and his two brothers frequented a local gym known as the Silver Heel Club where their uncle, who was a member, taught them basic boxing skills. In his mid-teens, Benny determined to become a professional fighter.

The Road to Excellence
Because boxing had not been legalized in New York when Benny began in the profession, his first fights were in private clubs. The payment for these bouts, which went only to the winner, was a couple of dollars at most. None of Benny's early fights are listed on his professional record. However, by 1912, at the age of sixteen, and using the last name Leonard so that his mother would not know what he was doing, Benny's fights began to be recorded.

During the next two years Benny had close to fifty fights, chiefly as a lightweight. By early 1914, his growing reputation as a boxing prospect brought him to the attention of well-known boxing manager Billy Gibson. In June of 1914, Benny signed a contract with Gibson, who remained his manager until the final stages of his career. Under the guidance of Gibson and his assistant, George Engel, Benny improved rapidly in both boxing technique and punching power. In 1915, he began a series of bouts that included matchups with and victories over many of the best lightweights of the era.

The Emerging Champion
The lightweight champion at the time was Freddie Welsh (Frederick Hall Thomas) of Wales. Welsh had won the world title in 1914 and defended it numerous times. Benny had fought Welsh in two "no-decision" bouts, so named because decisions were not allowed in boxing matches in New York at that time. The two had fought on fairly even terms in their first two fights. In the eyes of most at ringside, Benny got the better of the champion in the second bout. The title, however, could not change hands except by knockout. On May 28, 1917, in the third bout between the two fighters, Benny knocked Welsh out in the ninth round to gain the championship.

Benny Leonard. (Hulton Archive/Getty Images)

Statistics

Bouts, 217
Knockouts, 70
Bouts won by decision, 113
Knockouts by opponents, 4
Bouts lost by decision, 15
Draws, 15

Honors and Awards

1979	Inducted into International Jewish Sports Hall of Fame
1980	Inducted into World Boxing Hall of Fame
1990	Inducted into International Boxing Hall of Fame
1996	Inducted into National Jewish Sports Hall of Fame

Benny held the title for the next eight years, until his first retirement from the ring in 1925. Among the great fighters against whom he boxed were featherweight champion Johnny Kilbane and lightweight and welterweight contender Lew Tendler. In July, 1922, in the first of his two fights with Tendler, Benny used his wits as well as his boxing skills to gain victory. Benny, badly hurt in the eighth round, engaged Tendler in a conversation while in a clench, which gained him the precious seconds needed to clear his head and continue the fight. His only defeat during this eight-year span was a loss by disqualification in a fight for the world welterweight championship against Jack Britton.

Continuing the Story

After his retirement in 1925, Benny remained out of the ring for six years. In 1931, however, after losing most of his savings in the stock market crash two years earlier, he attempted a comeback. Well past his prime, he was still able to win nineteen consecutive fights before he was finally knocked out by later welterweight champion Jimmy McLarnin in 1932. Following the loss to McLarnin, Benny retired for good. He served in the U.S. Merchant Marine during World War II and continued to remain active in boxing, working as a referee. On April 17, 1947, he died suddenly of a heart attack while refereeing a bout in New York City.

Summary

Benny Leonard has consistently been ranked as one of the greatest lightweight boxers of all time. Nat Fleischer, the famous boxing writer and founder of *Ring* magazine, ranked him second behind the great African American champion Joe Gans, who fought during the early years of the century. A more recent ranking of lightweights in *Ring* placed him second behind Roberto Durán of Panama, who held the title in the 1970's. Among Benny's distinctive characteristics was his famous slicked-back hair, which, despite its length and pompadour style, seldom got mussed in the ring.

Scott Wright

Additional Sources

Bodner, Allen. *When Boxing Was a Jewish Sport*. Westport, Conn.: Praeger, 1997.

Fleischer, Nat. *Leonard the Magnificent: Life Story of the Man Who Made Himself King of the Lightweights*. Whitefish, Mont.: Kessinger, 2007.

Fleischer, Nat, and Sam Andre. *An Illustrated History of Boxing*. 6th ed. New York: Citadel Press, 2001.

Schulberg, Budd. *Sparring with Hemingway: And Other Legends of the Fight Game*. Chicago: Ivan R. Dee, 1995.

Suster, Gerald. *Lightning Strikes: The Lives and Times of Boxing's Lightweight Heroes*. London: Robson Books, 1994.

Recognized World Lightweight Championships

Date	Location	Loser	Result
May 28, 1917	New York, N.Y.	Freddie Welsh	9th-round technical knockout
Sept. 21, 1917	New York, N.Y.	Leo Johnson	1st-round technical knockout
Sept. 23, 1918	Newark, N.J.	Ted "Kid" Lewis	Draw, 8th-round newspaper decision
Nov. 26, 1920	New York, N.Y.	Joe Welling	14th-round technical knockout
Jan. 14, 1921	New York, N.Y.	Richie Mitchell	6th-round technical knockout
Feb. 10, 1922	New York, N.Y.	Rocky Kansas	15th-round unanimous decision
June 26, 1922	Bronx, N.Y.	Benny Leonard (Jack Britton, winner)	13th-round disqualification
July 4, 1922	Michigan City, Ind.	Rocky Kansas	8th-round technical knockout
July 27, 1922	Jersey City, N.J.	Lew Tendler	12th-round newspaper decision
July 24, 1923	Bronx, N.Y.	Lew Tendler	15th-round unanimous decision

Sugar Ray Leonard

Born: May 17, 1956
Wilmington, North Carolina
Also known as: Ray Charles Leonard (full name)

Early Life

Ray Charles Leonard was born in Wilmington, North Carolina, on May 17, 1956, the fifth of seven children born to Cicero and Getha Leonard. Leonard grew up in Wilmington; Washington, D.C.; and Palmer Park, Maryland, a lower-middle-class suburb of Baltimore. Although his father and grandfather had been amateur boxers, as a boy Ray had no desire to follow in their footsteps. He preferred basketball. His mother wanted her quiet and shy son to become a singer and had named him after rhythm and blues singer Ray Charles. Ray began to realize his talent when his older brother Roger introduced him to boxing.

The Road to Excellence

Encouraged by his brother and his school friend Derrik Holmes, Ray began attending the Palmer Park Recreation Center in 1971. The facilities for boxing were poor; boundary lines had to be taped on the basketball court to create a makeshift ring.

Dave Jacobs, a volunteer boxing coach, saw that Ray had natural talent, even though at first young Ray knew nothing at all about boxing. Ray was a quick learner, and after three or four months in the gymnasium, Jacobs predicted he would be a world champion if he continued to work hard.

After only one year of training, Ray was successful in regional tournaments. In 1972, he won the National Golden Gloves 132-pound title and reached the quarterfinals of the national Amateur Athletic Union (AAU) tournament in the same year. Although he was only sixteen, he almost made the 1972 U.S. Olympic team, losing in the semifinals of the Eastern Olympic trials in Cincinnati.

In 1974, Ray became discouraged and considered quitting. He was confused about his future and did not want to follow the discipline of training. Janks Morton, who was assistant trainer at Palmer Park, persuaded him to continue. Morton became Ray's closest adviser. He and Jacobs felt it was their responsibility to instill in their young fighters a sense of good conduct both inside and outside the ring. The walls of the gymnasium were covered with maxims such as "Do unto others as you would have them do unto you" and "Don't forget the bridge you cross. You may have to cross it again."

Put back on the right track by Morton, Ray won the light-welterweight gold medal at the Pan-American Games in 1975. The stage was set for his greatest triumph as an amateur.

The Emerging Champion

Ray had set his heart on winning a gold medal at the Olympic Games in Montreal in 1976. His

Sugar Ray Leonard fighting Thomas Hearns in a 1981 title bout. (AP/Wide World Photos)

Recognized World Welterweight Championships

Date	Location	Loser	Result
Nov. 30, 1979	Las Vegas, Nev.	Wilfred Benitez	15th-round knockout
Mar. 31, 1980	Landover, Md.	Dave Green	4th-round knockout
June 20, 1980	Montreal, Canada	Sugar Ray Leonard (Roberto Durán, winner)	15th-round decision
Nov. 25, 1980	New Orleans, La.	Roberto Durán	8th-round knockout
Mar. 28, 1981	Syracuse, N.Y.	Larry Bonds	10th-round knockout
Sept. 16, 1981	Las Vegas, Nev.	Thomas Hearns	14th-round knockout
Feb. 15, 1982	Reno, Nev.	Bruce Finch	3d-round knockout

Recognized World Junior Middleweight Championships

Date	Location	Loser	Result
June 25, 1981	Houston, Tex.	Ayub Kalule	9th-round knockout
Feb. 9, 1991	New York, N.Y.	Sugar Ray Leonard (Terry Norris, winner)	12th-round decision

Recognized World Middleweight Championship

Date	Location	Loser	Result
Apr. 6, 1987	Las Vegas, Nev.	Marvin Hagler	12th-round decision

Recognized World Super Middleweight Championships

Date	Location	Loser	Result
Nov. 7, 1988	Las Vegas, Nev.	Donny LaLonde	9th-round technical knockout
June 12, 1989	Las Vegas, Nev.	(Thomas Hearns, opponent)	12th-round draw
Dec. 7, 1989	Las Vegas, Nev.	Roberto Durán	12th-round unanimous decision

Recognized World Light Heavyweight Championship

Date	Location	Loser	Result
Nov. 7, 1988	Las Vegas, Nev.	Donny LaLonde	9th-round technical knockout

dream came true when he won the final bout by a decision over Andrés Aldama of Cuba. Millions watched the fight on television, and afterward Ray became a national celebrity.

What made Ray so lethal in the ring was his artistry. He was not a brutal slugger but a skilled boxer. His speed and clever footwork and handwork enabled him to land left hooks or jabs and right uppercuts and crosses before moving out of the range of his opponent.

As an amateur, Ray won all but 5 of his 150 fights, 75 of them by knockouts. However, he had no desire to turn professional. He planned to retire from boxing and attend college. He changed his mind because his parents were in poor health; he decided that as a professional boxer he would be able to support them financially. He resolved to prove he was the best in the world.

Angelo Dundee, Muhammad Ali's former manager, was hired as Ray's training supervisor. Ray's professional career got off to a spectacular start. In 1977 and 1978, he won all seventeen of his fights. He was hailed as the most exciting fighter since Ali. Eight more victories followed from January to September, 1979. Many of Ray's bouts were televised, and in two and a half years, he had earned between $2.5 million and $3 million.

In November, 1979, Ray challenged Wilfred Benitez for the World Boxing Council (WBC) welterweight championship. He won on a technical knockout (TKO), 6 seconds from the end of the fifteenth and last round.

Continuing the Story

After only one successful defense, Ray lost his title in June, 1980, to the tough Panamanian fighter Roberto Durán, after fifteen brutal rounds. Ray had made the mistake of trying to beat Durán using Durán's style, not his own. He had allowed himself to be lured into a brawl in which his superior boxing skill did not count for much. In the rematch in November, 1980, Ray outboxed Durán, leaving Durán frustrated and unable to press home his attacks. Durán quit in the eighth round.

In September, 1981, Ray won the World Boxing Association (WBA) welterweight title after a TKO against Tommy Hearns. In 1982, Ray experienced a setback; he sustained an injury to his right eye in training, diagnosed as a detached retina. After undergoing surgery, Ray announced his retirement from boxing in November, 1982.

Ray surprised everyone a year later by announcing his return to the ring. After one successful fight in 1984, he said he was quitting boxing for good. In 1987, Ray staged yet another comeback, this time with remarkable results. He had not boxed for three years and had only one fight in the previous five. He had eye surgery twice. However, he wanted to prove himself against Marvin Hagler, the most formidable middleweight of the day. In a controversial match, Ray gained the verdict over Hagler on a split decision.

Ray had become the WBC middleweight titleholder. In 1989, he narrowly held on to his title by a draw with his old rival, Thomas Hearns; he then won a unanimous decision over another old foe, Roberto Durán.

Ray made two final appearances in the ring, first, in 1991, against Terry Norris for the junior middleweight title. He lost in a twelfth-round decision. He returned six years later to face Héctor "Macho" Camacho, who knocked him out in the fifth round. Ray's bout with Camacho was his last.

Summary

Professional boxing can be a brutal sport, but Sugar Ray Leonard brought to boxing a level of skill, speed, and precision that few fighters in the history of the sport have attained. As one of the most popular fighters of recent times, Ray also was admired not only for his skill but for his courteous and modest manner out of the ring. Ray was elected to the International Boxing Hall of Fame in January of 1997.

Bryan Aubrey

Statistics

Bouts, 39
Knockouts, 25
Bouts won by decision, 11
Bouts lost by decision, 2
Draws, 1

Records

Has held recognized world championship titles in five weight classifications—the most of any professional boxer (record shared with Thomas Hearns)

Honors and Awards

1972	National Golden Gloves 132-pound champion
1973-74	National Golden Gloves light welterweight champion
1974-75	National Amateur Athletic Union light welterweight champion
1975	Gold medal, U.S. Pan-American Games
1976	Gold medal, U.S. Olympic Boxing
1979, 1981	*Ring* magazine Merit Award (1981 co-recipient)
1981	*Sports Illustrated* Sportsman of the Year
1985	Inducted into U.S. Olympic Hall of Fame
1997	Inducted into International Boxing Hall of Fame

Additional Sources

Kilmeade, Brian. *It's How You Play the Game: The Powerful Sports Moments That Taught Lasting Values to America's Finest.* New York: HarperCollins, 2007.

Mullan, Harry, and Bob Mee. *The Ultimate Encyclopedia of Boxing.* London: Carlton, 2007.

Myler, Thomas. *The Sweet Science Goes Sour: How Scandal Brought Boxing to Its Knees.* Vancouver, B.C.: Greystone Books, 2006.

Raz, Tahl. "Sugar Ray Leonard's Toughest Fight." *Inc.* 25, no. 6 (June, 2003): 103-110.

Sugar, Bert Randolph. *Boxing's Greatest Fighters.* Guilford, Conn.: Lyons Press, 2006.

Lennox Lewis

Born: September 2, 1965
London, England

Also known as: Lennox Claudius Lewis (full name); the Lion

Early Life

Lennox Claudius Lewis was born in 1965, in London's East End, to Violet Lewis, a single mother of Jamaican descent. His mother worked as a nursing auxiliary. His father, Carlton Brooks, was a Jamaican factory worker in England. At the age of four, Lennox lived with an aunt while his mother worked abroad. Large for his age, he grew up rebellious in a tough, working-class neighborhood.

Lennox's mother, when financially stronger, brought her twelve-year-old son to Kitchener, Ontario, Canada. There, Lennox flourished under his mother's care and eventually became a strongly competitive, star high school athlete in football, basketball, and track. Characteristically combating taunts with his fists, he channeled aggression into boxing. In the Kitchener police headquarters gym, Lennox learned fundamentals from former amateur boxer and gym owner Arnie Boehm, who became his coach and father figure. Lennox immediately liked boxing, later commenting: "It was ego against ego . . . the one-on-one is what appealed to me."

The Road to Excellence

In his first official amateur bout, Lennox scored a second-round knockout; he remained undefeated for three years. He was Ontario Golden Gloves champion by the time he was fifteen years old. In 1980, he ran out of opposition in his 165-pound weight class. However, he defeated a twenty-two-year-old, former Canadian-amateur-middleweight champion before losing to another twenty-two-year-old boxer about to turn professional.

When he was seventeen years old, Lennox won his first major international title, the World Junior Championship, to become Canada's under-twenty male athlete of the year. He then captured five consecutive all-Canadian super-heavyweight titles. Representing Canada at the 1984 Olympic Games in Los Angeles, California, Lennox lost to American Tyrell Biggs.

However, at the 1988 Olympic Games in Seoul, South Korea, Lennox defeated Riddick Bowe in the second round to win the gold medal. He was determined to turn professional. Before the 1988 Olympics, he had 104 contests with 95 wins. A big man with the mobility of a middleweight, Lennox, "the Lion," learned from his losses and invariably defeated opponents who had previously beaten him.

In 1989, Lennox's new manager, Frank

Lennox Lewis retaining his belt after a fight with Mike Tyson in 2002. (AP/Wide World Photos)

Maloney, brought him to England and helped him attain a favorable contract from the financier-controlled Levitt Group. There, Lennox was considered the long-sought hero who could become the first British world heavyweight titleholder since Bob Fitzsimmons in 1897. To some, he was also deemed a Canadian carpetbagger. However, in 1989, detractors were quieted when he won his first professional fight by a second-round knockout.

In 1990, after a string of 12 victories, including 5 knockouts, Lennox won his first title as an Englishman, the European Belt, by beating France's Jean-Maurice Chanet by a sixth-round technical knockout. His second title, the British heavyweight belt, was won in 1991, by defeating Gary Mason.

In 1992, after six more successful fights, he vanquished Canadian fighter Donovan "Razor" Ruddock by a second-round knockout and became the leading contender for the World Boxing Council (WBC) heavyweight title, then held by Bowe. Lennox continued to compile ring victories, often knocking down opponents with a powerful right. Although detractors faulted him as an overcautious underachiever, supporters applauded him as "the great Brit hope" and a gentlemanly boxer.

The Emerging Champion

Because of the collapse of the Levitt Group, accountant Panos Eliades became Lennox's new co-promoter. In December, 1992, Lennox won the WBC heavyweight title by default when Bowe refused to meet him in a mandatory title defense match. To improve his WBC image, Lennox negotiated with an American promotion company for a 1993 title defense against American Tony Tucker, winning a 12-round decision.

Two victories in 1993 and 1994 did not quell accusations of empty wins. Since most top heavyweights did not actively challenge him, Lennox had trouble setting up fights. Proposed fights never materialized against Bowe and titleholder Evander Holyfield. Lennox wanted to fight a top opponent and unite the World Boxing Association (WBA) and International Boxing Federation (IBF) heavyweight titles with his WBC title. In September, 1994, in an upset, Lennox lost his WBC belt after suffering a knockout loss to Oliver McCall.

Replacing trainer Pepe Correa with McCall's trainer, Emmanuel Steward, who taught him more effective combinations and a stronger jab, Lennox started his campaign to recapture the WBC title. Becoming more aggressive and focused, he defeated three rivals in 1995. In 1996, Lennox had a respected 12-round win against former heavyweight champion Ray Mercer. However, choice opponents were exceptionally few. In a lackluster 1997 rematch with McCall, Lennox regained the WBC belt. Four more successful title defenses in 1997 and 1998 gained scant admiration.

Recognized World Heavyweight Championships

Date	Location	Loser	Result
May 8, 1993	Las Vegas, Nev.	Tony Tucker	12-round unanimous decision
Oct. 1, 1993	Cardiff, Wales	Frank Bruno	7th-round technical knockout
May 6, 1994	Atlantic City, N.J.	Phil Jackson	8th-round technical knockout
Sept. 24, 1994	London, England	Lennox Lewis (Oliver McCall, winner)	2d-round technical knockout
Oct. 7, 1995	Atlantic City, N.J.	Tommy Morrison	6th-round technical knockout
Feb. 7, 1997	Las Vegas, Nev.	Oliver McCall	5th-round technical knockout
July 12, 1997	Lake Tahoe, Nev.	Henry Akinwande	5th-round win by disqualification
Oct. 4, 1997	Atlantic City, N.J.	Andrew Golota	1st-round knockout
Mar. 28, 1998	Atlantic City, N.J.	Shannon Briggs	5th-round technical knockout
Sept. 26, 1998	Uncasville, Conn.	Zeljko Mavrovic	12th-round unanimous decision
Mar. 13, 1999	New York, N.Y.	Evander Holyfield	12th-round draw
Nov. 13, 1999	Las Vegas, Nev.	Evander Holyfield	12th-round unanimous decision
Apr. 29, 2000	New York, N.Y.	Michael Grant	2d-round knockout
July 15, 2000	London, England	Frans Botha	2d-round technical knockout
Nov. 11, 2000	Las Vegas, Nev.	David Tua	12th-round unanimous decision
Apr. 22, 2001	Brakpan, South Africa	Lennox Lewis (Hasim Rahman, winner)	5th-round knockout
Nov. 17, 2001	Las Vegas, Nev.	Hasim Rahman	4th-round knockout
June 6, 2002	Memphis, Tenn.	Mike Tyson	8th-round knockout
June 21, 2003	Los Angeles, Calif.	Vitali Klitschko	6th-round technical knockout

Continuing the Story

In March, 1999, Lennox's goal of unifying titles seemed closer when he faced Holyfield in a bout in which Lennox landed 348 punches to Holyfield's 130. Despite the disparity, the judges ruled the fight a draw, a controversial decision widely criticized as unfair. In a November, 1999, rematch Lennox reacted by winning a unanimous decision over Holyfield. He left the ring with the WBC and WBA titles and later regained the IBF belt withheld over a sanctioning-fee dispute.

Lennox forfeited his WBA crown when he fought American Michael Grant in April, 2000, rather than the WBA's top contender, whom he had to face by November, 2000, to regain the crown. Winning the Grant fight by a second-round knockout, on July 15, 2000, in London, Lennox successfully defended his WBC and IBF titles against South African Frans Botha with another second-round knockout. He concluded the year by defeating the Samoan heavyweight David Tua in a Las Vegas, Nevada, bout that went the 12-round distance.

In early 2001, Lennox hoped to parlay his 36-1-1 record into a high-stakes bout with former champion Mike Tyson. However, in April, in South Africa, an unexpected knockout by American boxer Hasim Rahman derailed his plans and cost him both the WBC and IBF heavyweight titles. On November 17, 2001, Lennox avenged his loss to Rahman with a knockout in the fourth round and regained the titles. In 2002, in Memphis, Tennessee, Lennox scored an eighth-round knockout over Tyson. Lennox's final fight came against Vitali Klitschko. The Ukrainian heavyweight was ahead on all the scorecards before the bout was stopped in the sixth round because of several nasty cuts over the challenger's left eye.

On February 6, 2004, Lennox announced his retirement from boxing, walking away from a lucrative rematch against Klitschko that would have earned him millions of dollars. Boxers are notorious for having difficulty leaving the sport; many make repeated retirements. Lennox vowed that he would never fight again, saying that he wanted to be like former middleweight champion Marvin Hagler, who had retired only once. With his retirement, Lennox became the first heavyweight in fifty years to leave boxing as champion.

Lennox settled in Miami, Florida, and focused on his family and his acting career. He appeared in several television shows and movies, including *Ocean's Eleven* (2001) and *Johnny Was* (2006).

Statistics

Bouts, 44	Knockouts by opponents, 2
Knockouts, 32	Bouts lost by decision, 0
Bouts won by decision, 6	Draws, 1
Other wins, 3	

Summary

At 6 feet 5 inches and 245 pounds with an 82-inch reach, Lennox Lewis left boxing as one of the world's top heavyweights, with a record of 41-2-1 and 32 knockouts. By defeating the greatest boxers of his era and unifying the heavyweight division, he accomplished everything that he had set out to do. With his skills, dignity, and intelligence, Lennox was a credit to the sport and deservedly won many fans and supporters. His departure left the sport without a dominant champion.

Christian H. Moe, updated by Caryn E. Neumann

Additional Sources

Evans, Gavin. *Kings of the Ring: The History of Heavyweight Boxing.* London: Weidenfeld & Nicolson, 2005.

Hoffer, Richard. "Redefining Moment." *Sports Illustrated* 91, no. 19 (November 15, 1999): 54-57.

Lewis, Lennox, with Joe Steeples. *Lennox Lewis: The Autobiography of the WBC Heavyweight Champion of the World.* London: Faber and Faber, 1993.

McIlvanney, Hugh. *The Hardest Game: McIlvanney on Boxing.* New York: Contemporary Books, 2001.

Nack, William. "The Great Brit Hope." *Sports Illustrated* 78, no. 4 (February 1, 1993): 38-42.

Sonny Liston

Born: May 8, 1932 or January, 1929
Sand Slough, Johnson Township,
St. Francis County, Arkansas
Died: December 30, 1970 (body found on
January 5, 1971)
Las Vegas, Nevada
Also known as: Charles L. Liston (full name); the Big Bear; Black Bear; the Bear

Early Life
Charles "Sonny" Liston was born in Sand Slough, Johnson Township, St. Francis County, Arkansas, to a sharecropper. He was the twelfth of either thirteen or as many as twenty-five children. The exact date of his birth is in dispute. Some say he was born May 8, 1932. However, others have reported January, 1929, as his birth date. As a young teenager, he left Arkansas and went to St. Louis, Missouri, to join relatives there. He soon got into trouble with the law: He was arrested twenty times, convicted of robbery, and sentenced to three concurrent five-year terms. In 1952, he was released after he befriended a Roman Catholic priest who introduced him to boxing and recommended him for parole.

The Road to Excellence
After prison, Sonny began a professional boxing career. He won the 1953 Chicago Golden Gloves Championships and, on September 2, 1953, in St. Louis, he had his first professional bout, a first-round knockout of Don Smith. He won all his fights until he met a boxer named Marty Marshall. In this fight, Sonny's jaw was broken, and he lost a decision. In 1955, Marshall and Sonny had a rematch. This time, Sonny knocked out Marshall in 6 rounds. Sonny's rise through the heavyweight ranks continued until 1956, when he assaulted a police officer and earned a six-month prison sentence. Consequently, he was banned from boxing for all of 1957.

In 1958, he won eight matches. In 1959, he defeated contenders Mike DeJohn in 6 rounds, Cleveland Williams in 3 rounds, and Nino Valdez in 3 rounds, making everyone in boxing realize he might be the next heavyweight champion. In 1960, he continued to beat up the heavyweight contenders. He defeated Williams in 2 rounds, Roy Harris in 1 round, and Zora Folley in 3 rounds. The only fighter to avoid a knockout was Eddie Machen, whom Liston beat in 12 rounds. However, Floyd Patterson, and especially his manager, Gus D'Amato, refused to give Sonny a shot at the heavyweight title. Sonny was able to get fights against top heavyweights thanks to his management, headed by gangster Blinky Palmero. Unfortunately for Sonny, the presence of that same management prevented a shot at Patterson's title.

The Emerging Champion
Finally, in September, 1962, Sonny got his shot at the heavyweight title thanks to Patterson's veto of his manager's protests. The fight was supposed to be held in New York City, but denied a license, the fight was relocated to Chicago. This fight tran-

Sonny Liston (right) connecting with a right cross against Floyd Patterson in a 1962 title fight. (AP/Wide World Photos)

> **Statistics**
>
> Bouts, 54
> Knockouts, 39
> Bouts won by decision, 11
> Knockouts by opponents, 3
> Bouts lost by decision, 1

scended the boxing ring. The first person to hear of the fight from Patterson was President John F. Kennedy. Many luminaries of the literary establishment, such as Norman Mailer and James Baldwin, attended the bout at ringside, feeling that this bout echoed the rising Civil Rights movement, a battle between the so-called "good negro" and "bad negro"; Sonny was cast as the latter. Patterson was a decent heavyweight champion, winning the title at a younger age than anyone else had and becoming the first fighter to regain that title. However, Sonny, with his power and size, was too much for the champion. Sonny knocked Patterson out in the first round, becoming the first person to win the heavyweight title at such an early stage of a fight. They had a rematch on July 22, 1963, in Las Vegas, Nevada. Sonny stopped Patterson in the first round again. He seemed indestructible.

Continuing the Story

Sonny's defeat of Patterson in Las Vegas was his only defense of the title. In February, 1964, Sonny met the young heavyweight Cassius Clay, later known as Muhammad Ali. A heavy favorite to win the bout, Sonny could not cope with Clay's movement, jab, and speed. After 6 rounds, he resigned his championship to Clay, claiming an injured shoulder. After a delay, because Clay—now Ali—was injured, they fought again, this time in Lewiston, Maine. With Sonny's mob connections and Ali's recent conversion to the Nation of Islam, considered a hate group at the time, few cared for either fighter. In one of the most controversial championship bouts, Sonny was knocked out in the first round from an Ali right hand later known as "the phantom punch." To spectators the punch did not seem to pack knockout power. Given his criminal career, his ties to the mob, and his two strange losses to Ali, Sonny, despite winning all but one of his remaining bouts, never got another shot at the heavyweight title.

After fifteen wins in a row, Sonny was knocked out by Leotis Martin. His last bout was in June, 1970, a knockout of Chuck Wepner, a fighter later to gain fame as the real-life model for the movie character Rocky Balboa. On January 5, 1971, Sonny was found dead in his Las Vegas home of an apparent heroin overdose. However, many have questioned the cause of death, arguing that he was killed by the mob.

Summary

Sonny Liston was a lightning rod of controversy, becoming heavyweight champion—a crown once worn by respected titlists Jack Dempsey, Joe Louis, and Rocky Marciano—despite a criminal past and questionable acts in the ring, especially in his two losses to Ali. Nonetheless, some consider him one of the best heavyweights ever. He had a great left hook, but his left jab and right hands were just as powerful. He was technically solid. Sonny is also remembered for his influence on former heavyweight champion Mike Tyson, who identified with Sonny more than with any other champion. After his death, Sonny became a cult hero, the subject of novels, songs, and biographies. In 1991, he was elected to the International Boxing Hall of Fame in Canastota, New York.

Brett Conway

Additional Sources

Remnick, David. *King of the World: Muhammad Ali and the Rise of an American Hero.* New York: Random House, 1998.

Sugar, Bert Randolph. *Boxing's Greatest Fighters.* Guilford, Conn.: Lyons Press, 2006.

Tosches, Nick. *The Devil and Sonny Liston.* Boston: Little, Brown, 2000.

Title Fights

Year	Location	Loser	Result
Sept. 25, 1962	Chicago, Ill.	Floyd Patterson	1st-round knockout
July 22, 1963	Las Vegas, Nev.	Floyd Patterson	1st-round knockout
Feb. 24, 1964	Miami Beach, Fla.	Sonny Liston (Cassius Clay (Muhammad Ali), winner)	7th-round referee technical decision
May 25, 1965	Lewiston, Maine	Sonny Liston (Muhammad Ali, winner)	1st-round knockout
Dec. 6, 1969	Las Vegas, Nev.	Sonny Liston (Leotis Martin, winner)	9th-round knockout

Joe Louis

Born: May 13, 1914
Near Lafayette, Alabama
Died: April 12, 1981
Las Vegas, Nevada
Also known as: Joseph Louis Barrow (birth name); the Brown Bomber

Early Life
Joe Louis was born Joseph Louis Barrow on May 13, 1914, about six miles outside the small village of Lafayette, Alabama. The town is located in the Buckalew Mountains, a hilly area of red clay soil that was difficult for the farmers to work.

Joe was the seventh of eight children born to Lillie and Munroe Barrow. His family, like most farm families in the Buckalew Mountains, was poor. They lived in an unpainted, windowless shack that had no electricity. The Barrow children seldom wore shoes, and kerosene lamps lit the small home. Joe worked hard for his family by washing floors and doing other chores around the house and in the fields. Although he got into several rock fights as a child, there were few indications of the boxer he would become.

The Road to Excellence
Like many other southern African American families who went north in search of a better life during the 1920's, Joe's family moved to Detroit in 1926. There, Joe gradually took an interest in boxing when he began taking part in friendly fights among the boys who lived on Catherine Street. He quickly earned recognition as the best fighter in the neighborhood.

At the Brewster Recreation Center, a local athletic club, Joe, sixteen, gained serious training in boxing. Fearing his mother would not approve of his interest in boxing, Joe dropped his last name and became known as Joe Louis. At about the same time, Joe quit school and began to work full time at a nearby factory while continuing to box on the weekends. In 1932, he fought his first amateur bout against former Olympian Johnny Miler. The more experienced Miler quickly defeated Joe, knocking him down seven times in two rounds.

Joe's mother encouraged him to continue fighting, while his stepfather urged him to get a job at the Ford Motor Company. Joe took his stepfather's advice and stayed away from the ring for seven months. In mid-1933, Joe went back to boxing and later reached the light heavyweight finals of the Amateur Athletic Union (AAU) championships, where he lost in three rounds.

Joe's third and final amateur defeat—out of fifty-four fights—marked a turning point in his boxing career. John Roxborough, a leading businessman in Detroit's African American community, was impressed enough with Joe's skill to lend his financial support to the promising boxer. Roxborough also hired Jack Blackburn, a former professional boxer, to train Joe. Blackburn taught Joe

Joe Louis. (Library of Congress)

Recognized World Heavyweight Championships

Date	Location	Loser	Result
June 22, 1937	Chicago, Ill.	James J. Braddock	8th-round knockout
Aug. 30, 1937	New York, N.Y.	Tommy Farr	15th-round unanimous decision
Feb. 23, 1938	New York, N.Y.	Nathan Mann	3d-round knockout
Apr. 1, 1938	Chicago, Ill.	Harry Thomas	5th-round knockout
June 22, 1938	New York, N.Y.	Max Schmeling	1st-round knockout
Jan. 25, 1939	New York, N.Y.	John Henry Lewis	1st-round knockout
Apr. 17, 1939	Los Angeles, Calif.	Jack Roper	1st-round knockout
June 28, 1939	New York, N.Y.	Tony Galento	4th-round technical knockout
Sept. 20, 1939	Detroit, Mich.	Bob Pastor	11th-round knockout
Feb. 9, 1940	New York, N.Y.	Arturo Godoy	15th-round split decision
Mar. 29, 1940	New York, N.Y.	Johnny Paychek	2d-round knockout
June 20, 1940	New York, N.Y.	Arturo Godoy	8th-round technical knockout
Dec. 16, 1940	Boston, Mass.	Al McCoy	6th-round technical knockout
Jan. 31, 1941	New York, N.Y.	Red Burman	5th-round knockout
Feb. 17, 1941	Philadelphia, Pa.	Gus Dorazio	2d-round knockout
Mar. 21, 1941	Detroit, Mich.	Abe Simon	13th-round technical knockout
Apr. 8, 1941	St. Louis, Mo.	Tony Musto	9th-round technical knockout
May 23, 1941	Washington, D.C.	Buddy Baer	7th-round disqualification
June 18, 1941	New York, N.Y.	Billy Conn	13th-round knockout
Sept. 29, 1941	New York, N.Y.	Lou Nova	6th-round technical knockout
Jan. 9, 1942	New York, N.Y.	Buddy Baer	1st-round knockout
Mar. 27, 1942	New York, N.Y.	Abe Simon	6th-round knockout
June 9, 1946	New York, N.Y.	Billy Conn	8th-round knockout
Sept. 18, 1946	New York, N.Y.	Tami Mauriello	1st-round knockout
Dec. 5, 1947	New York, N.Y.	Jersey Joe Walcott	15th-round split decision
June 25, 1948	New York, N.Y.	Jersey Joe Walcott	11th-round knockout
Sept. 27, 1950	New York, N.Y.	Joe Louis (Ezzard Charles, winner)	15th-round unanimous decision

balance in the ring, showed him how to throw punches with both hands, and discussed strategy and conditioning with the young fighter.

The Emerging Champion

Blackburn's coaching paid off, as Joe won his first twenty-two fights in the heavyweight division after turning professional in 1934. Eighteen of these victories came when Joe knocked his opponent out with powerful punches from both hands, and it was this strength that captured the imagination of fight fans around the country. In 1935, he won the Associated Press male athlete of the year award.

In 1936, Joe's suffered his first professional defeat at the hands of a German fighter named Max Schmeling. Although some began to doubt Joe's ability after this bout, he dedicated himself to training and studying under the direction of Blackburn. His hard work earned him the heavyweight championship in 1937 and another fight with Schmeling in 1938. Joe defeated Schmeling this time, and people began to speak of him as one of the best boxers ever.

Between 1937 and 1948, Joe defended his title twenty-five times without a loss, more than any other champion. Joe's willingness to defend his title so many times, his skill inside the ring, and his respectable conduct outside the arena brought to boxing a dignity that the sport had been missing since the 1920's.

Joe gave other African American men and women a sense of pride and dignity in a nation that treated African Americans unfairly, if not harshly. Despite his great success, Joe never lost contact with the ordinary man and woman in the neighborhood, so that his success was in some ways shared by African Americans of lesser fame. They saw their struggles in everyday life as similar to those that Joe faced in the ring against an opponent.

Continuing the Story

Joe's popularity with white America came mainly from his service in the U.S. Army during World War II. Joe continued to defend his title while carrying out his military duties, and he won praise for donating much of his prize money to the Navy Re-

Statistics

Bouts, 66
Knockouts, 49
Bouts won by decision, 13
Bouts won by fouls, 1
Knockouts by opponents, 2
Bouts lost by decision, 1

Records

Successfully defended his world boxing title for almost twelve years—the longest of any world heavyweight champion

Honors and Awards

	1934	National Amateur Athletic Union light heavyweight champion
	1935	Associated Press Male Athlete of the Year
1936, 1938-39, 1941		*Ring* magazine Merit Award
	1940	Schomberg Collection of the New York Public Library and the Association for the Study of Negro Life and History Award for Improving Race Relations
	1941	Edward J. Neil Trophy
	1944	Legion of Merit Award
	1954	Inducted into *Ring* magazine Boxing Hall of Fame
	1967	Walker Memorial Award
	1990	Inducted into International Boxing Hall of Fame

lief Society to help the war effort. His actions won the respect of people the world over. Many Americans saw Joe as an example of the love of country that every citizen should possess, and as time passed, Joe became a national hero. His strength in the ring was seen as an example of America's strength as a nation, and songs and posters celebrated his patriotism.

Joe continued to box after the war was over, but, as with any athlete, age eroded his skills. Joe had been a great boxer because his hands were quicker and stronger than those of his opponents. Although he was still powerful, his quickness diminished. In 1950, he lost his heavyweight crown to Ezzard Charles in a unanimous decision. His last, nontitle fight, which ended in only his third loss as a professional, was against Rocky Marciano on October 26, 1951.

Despite the purses he had earned in the ring, Joe spent much of his life after boxing with little or no money because most of his business plans failed. He had also been generous with friends and charities throughout his life, donating heavily to educational causes. Joe spent most of his retired life golfing and working at Caesars Palace in Las Vegas, where he died on April 12, 1981.

Summary

Joe Louis's brilliance in the ring, and his generosity outside it, gave to African Americans, white Americans, and boxing a sense of dignity during a difficult time in American history. Joe is still regarded as one of the best boxers, and one of the most popular athletes, in American history.

Jill Dupont

Additional Sources

Erenberg, Lewis A. *The Greatest Fight of Our Generation: Louis Versus Schmeling.* New York: Oxford University Press, 2006.

Hietala, Thomas R. *The Fight of the Century: Jack Johnson, Joe Louis, and the Struggle for Racial Equality.* Armonk, N.Y.: M. E. Sharpe, 2004.

McRae, Donald. *Heroes Without a Country: America's Betrayal of Joe Louis and Jesse Owens.* New York: Ecco, 2002.

Margolick, David. *Beyond Glory: Max Schmeling Versus Joe Louis and a World on the Brink.* London: Bloomsbury, 2006.

Monninger, Joseph. *Two Ton: One Fight, One Night—Tony Galento Versus Joe Louis.* Hanover, N.H.: Steerforth Press, 2006.

Myler, Patrick. *Ring of Hate: Joe Louis Versus Max Schmeling—The Fight of the Century.* New York: Arcade, 2006.

Rocky Marciano

Born: September 1, 1923
 Brockton, Massachusetts
Died: August 31, 1969
 near Newton, Iowa
Also known as: Rocco Francis Marchegiano (birth name); Brockton Blockbuster; Rock from Brockton

Early Life

Rocky Marciano, born Rocco Francis Marchegiano on September 1, 1923, in Brockton, Massachusetts, was the oldest of six children born to Pierino and Pasqualena Marchegiano. His parents, both Italian immigrants, lived with his maternal grandfather in Brockton, Massachusetts, throughout most of Rocky's adolescence.

Rocky's father, a World War I veteran who had been seriously wounded at the battle of Château Thierry, worked in a shoe factory in Brockton most of his adult life. The shoe factory job paid only a modest wage. The poverty in which the Marchegiano family lived was deepened by the Great Depression, but Rocky's father always managed to keep food on the table. Rocky's fear of spending his life in a job similar to his father's made him determined to excel at sports in order to escape the Italian-Jewish-Irish ghetto in which he grew up.

The Road to Excellence

Rocky and his small circle of friends all dreamed of becoming professional baseball players. The boys spent most of their spare time playing sandlot games in a park near Rocky's home. Rocky was a good hitter but was painfully slow and had only an average throwing arm. None of the group was interested in schoolwork, and most dropped out before finishing high school. Rocky left school at the age of sixteen and took a series of jobs doing manual labor in order to help his father support the family. He continued to spend many hours every week during seasons of good weather playing baseball with his friends. Although never a bully, Rocky established himself as the best street fighter in the neighborhood, but he never considered a career in boxing.

In March, 1943, Rocky was drafted by the U.S. Army. Assigned to a supply unit in England, he did not see combat action during World War II. After the surrender of Germany in May, 1945, Rocky was sent back to the United States and stationed at Fort Lewis, Washington. He quickly learned that successful participation in sports would exempt him from routine duties. In addition to playing baseball, he began to box for the Fort Lewis team.

In the spring of 1946, an overweight Rocky Marciano arrived at his parents' home in Brockton on leave. Needing money, Rocky convinced his maternal uncle to contact a fight promoter to help him compete in local prizefighting. Rocky was inexperienced and not in peak physical condition; he consequently lost the fight, for which he received thirty dollars. In later years, he related that he learned a valuable lesson from this first fight: to

Rocky Marciano punching Jersey Joe Walcott. (Library of Congress)

Recognized World Heavyweight Championships

Date	Location	Loser	Result
Sept. 23, 1952	Philadelphia, Pa.	Jersey Joe Walcott	13th-round knockout
May 15, 1953	Chicago, Ill.	Jersey Joe Walcott	1st-round knockout
Sept. 24, 1953	New York, N.Y.	Roland LaStarza	11th-round technical knockout
June 17, 1954	New York, N.Y.	Ezzard Charles	15th-round unanimous decision
Sept. 17, 1954	New York, N.Y.	Ezzard Charles	8th-round knockout
May 16, 1955	San Francisco, Calif.	Don Cockell	9th-round technical knockout
Sept. 21, 1955	New York, N.Y.	Archie Moore	9th-round knockout

properly prepare for a fight. Before all his fights for the rest of his career, he trained his body mercilessly. However inauspiciously, Rocky had launched his career in professional boxing.

The Emerging Champion

After his discharge from the U.S. Army, Rocky embarked on a career as a boxer, despite his mother's almost hysterical objections. He entered a local Amateur Athletic Union tournament, for which he trained hard. Although he scored two first-round knockouts, he lost in the final bout primarily because he had dislocated one of his knuckles during the second knockout.

Rocky entered several more amateur tournaments, during which he demonstrated devastating punching power, clumsiness, and inexperience. He ended his amateur career the next year with an unimpressive 8-4 record. During the spring of 1948, he secured a manager, changed his name to Marciano, and began to train hard and to fight regularly. In 1948, Rocky had eleven fights, winning all of them by knockout within the first three rounds. In 1949, he added thirteen more victories, eleven by knockout, and became a featured fighter at Madison Square Garden in New York.

By 1950, Rocky was receiving large purses for his fights and was rated by many as a top contender for the heavyweight championship. During that year, he married Barbara Cousins, with whom he had one daughter, Mary Anne. Over the next two and one-half years, he scored seventeen more victories, including a knockout over the legendary Joe Louis. On September 23, 1952, he finally got his chance at the world championship and responded by knocking out Jersey Joe Walcott in the thirteenth round of a brutal fight. The poor Italian child from a Brockton slum was heavyweight champion of the world.

Continuing the Story

During the next three years, Rocky defended his championship six times. He won five of those fights by knockout and won the other in a fifteen-round decision over Ezzard Charles. In April, 1956, he retired with a record of 49-0 as the only undefeated heavyweight champion in the history of boxing. Rocky intended, according to his friends, to spend his time in retirement with his family, making up for neglecting them during his boxing days. Instead, Rocky spent most of his time after retirement traveling.

Always fearful of descending again into the poverty in which he grew up, Rocky spent most of his time from 1956 to 1969 as a professional celebrity. He was in great demand for personal appearances at clubs and on television. He often made three or four of those appearances a week, in widely separate parts of the world. He also made movies and

Statistics

Bouts, 49

Knockouts, 43

Bouts won by decision, 6

Losses, 0

Records

First undefeated world heavyweight champion in professional boxing history

Honors and Awards

1952	Edward J. Neil Trophy
	Hickok Belt
1952, 1954-55	*Ring* magazine Merit Award
1959	Inducted into *Ring* magazine Boxing Hall of Fame
1990	Inducted into International Boxing Hall of Fame

pursued many business ventures. Rocky never trusted banks and hid most of the money he made from these endeavors in various places around the country. Very little of the money he hid was found after his death. On August 31, 1969, the plane carrying Rocky to a personal appearance in Des Moines crashed near Newton, Iowa, killing everyone aboard.

Summary

Rocky Marciano achieved the pinnacle of boxing success despite his relatively small size for a heavyweight—5 feet 10 inches, 185 pounds—because of the same attributes that mark most sports champions. He had an indomitable will to win, a heightened self-confidence, and trained perhaps harder than any other fighter in the history of the sport, subordinating everything to his goal. In 1971, in a computer simulation of a boxing tournament involving all the heavyweight champions, Rocky was the projected winner.

Paul Madden

Additional Sources

Carnes, Mark C. *Invisible Giants: Fifty Americans Who Shaped the Nation but Missed the History Books.* New York: Oxford University Press, 2002.

Orr, Frank, and George Tracz. *The Dominators: The Remarkable Athletes Who Changed Their Sport Forever.* Toronto: Warwick, 2004.

Skehan, Everett M. *Undefeated: The Life and Times of Rocky Marciano.* Cambridge, Mass.: Rounder, 2005.

Sullivan, Russell. *Rocky Marciano: The Rock of His Times.* Urbana: University of Illinois Press, 2005.

Varveris, Michael N. *Rocky Marciano: The Thirteenth Candle—The True Story of an American Legend.* Youngstown, Ohio: Ariana, 2000.

Christy Martin

Born: June 12, 1968
 Bluefield, West Virginia
Also known as: Christy Renea Salters (birth name); the Coal Miner's Daughter

Early Life

An athletic young woman, Christy Salters played basketball at Concord University in Athens, West Virginia. She entered a Tough Woman competition on a dare and discovered a love for boxing. In 1991, she earned a degree in education and then, with the support of her mother Joyce, began to seriously pursue a boxing career. At a gym in Bristol, Tennessee, Christy met trainer Jim Martin. He initially planned to have a male boxer break Christy's ribs in a bout to dissuade her from boxing. However, Martin became impressed with Christy's talent and dedication. He became her trainer, her manager, and, eventually, her husband.

Christy Martin in 2001. (John Gichigi/Getty Images)

The Road to Excellence

Christy never had any interest in making a statement as a woman boxer or for women's boxing. She simply fought for the love of the sport. A junior welterweight standing 5 feet 4½ inches, she began her professional career on September 9, 1989, with a 5-round draw against Angela Buchanan of Australia. In a rematch three weeks later, in Durham, North Carolina, Christy knocked out Buchanan in the second round. By 1993, the Martins had moved to Orlando, Florida. When Christy, promoted as the "Coal Miner's Daughter," defeated Texas police officer Melinda Robinson at Miami Jai-Alai, famed boxing promoter Don King took note. King signed Christy in October, 1993. Christy fought many of her subsequent fights on the undercards of fights featuring heavyweight champion Mike Tyson, also a fighter in King's stable. The publicity aided her rise.

Christy typically sparred with men. Of the three women with whom she sparred, she broke the jaws of two and the nose of the third. Despite some pressure to fight a man in an official bout, Christy refused to do so because of the risk of injury. By the end of 1993, Christy had a record of 21 wins and 2 losses against women. Many of her victories were knockouts of fighters making their professional debuts, revealing the lack of depth in women's boxing.

The Emerging Champion

In her first two fights of 1994, Christy earned first-round technical knockouts. She then earned a controversial draw with Mexican lightweight champion Laura Serrano in a fight at the MGM Grand Hotel in Las Vegas, Nevada, on May 7, 1994. Many observers felt that Serrano had won the fight. Nevertheless, the fight helped make Christy the "face" of women's boxing. The next year, she only fought three times but knocked out all three opponents in early rounds. On February 10, 1996, in a fight televised by the cable network Showtime, Christy knocked out for-

Boxing Record

Date	Location	Loser	Result
Sept. 9, 1989	Bristol, Tenn.	N/A	Draw
Sept. 30, 1989	Durham, N.C.	Angela Buchanan	2d-round knockout
Oct. 21, 1989	Bristol, Tenn.	Tammy Jones	1st-round technical knockout
Nov. 4, 1989	Bristol, Tenn.	Christy Martin (Andrea DeShong, winner)	5th-round points
Apr. 21, 1990	Bristol, Tenn.	Andrea DeShong	5th-round points
Sept. 22, 1990	Johnson City, Tenn.	Jamie Whitcomb	6th-round points
Oct. 27, 1990	Bristol, Tenn.	Lisa Holpp	1st-round technical knockout
Jan. 12, 1991	Bristol, Tenn.	Jamie Whitcomb	5th-round unanimous decision
Feb. 25, 1991	Bristol, Tenn.	Suzanne Riccio	5th-round points
Mar. 16, 1991	Chattanooga, Tenn.	Pat Watts	1st-round technical knockout
May 25, 1991	Tennessee	Rhonda Hefflin	1st-round knockout
Sept. 10, 1991	West Virginia	Shannon Davenport	2d-round technical knockout
Jan. 11, 1992	Grundy, Va.	Rose Noble	1st-round technical knockout
Jan. 25, 1992	Daytona Beach, Fla.	Jackie Thomas	3d-round technical knockout
May 30, 1992	Daytona Beach, Fla.	Stacey Prestage	8th-round points
Sept. 5, 1992	Daytona Beach, Fla.	Tracy Gordon	1st-round technical knockout
Nov. 14, 1992	Greenville, S.C.	Angela Buchanan	1st-round technical knockout
Jan. 29, 1993	Columbia, S.C.	Susie Hughes	1st-round technical knockout
May 28, 1993	Punta Gorda, Fla.	Deborah Cruickshank	1st-round knockout
Aug. 27, 1993	Punta Gorda, Fla.	Rebecca Kirkland	1st-round technical knockout
Oct. 10, 1993	Auburn Hills, Mich.	Beverly Szymanski	3d-round knockout
Jan. 29, 1994	Las Vegas, Nev.	Susie Melton	1st-round technical knockout
Mar. 4, 1994	Las Vegas, Nev.	Sonja Donlevy	1st-round technical knockout
May 7, 1994	Las Vegas, Nev.	N/A	Draw
Sept. 12, 1994	Las Vegas, Nev.	Chris Kreuz	4th-round technical knockout
Apr. 1, 1995	Las Vegas, Nev.	Beverly Szymanski	4th-round technical knockout
Aug. 12, 1995	Las Vegas, Nev.	Angela Buchanan	2d-round technical knockout
Dec. 16, 1995	Philadelphia, Pa.	Erica Schmidlin	1st-round technical knockout
Jan. 13, 1996	Miami, Fla.	Melinda Robinson	6th-round unanimous decision
Feb. 10, 1996	Las Vegas, Nev.	Sue Chase	Technical knockout
Feb. 24, 1996	Richmond, Va.	Del Pettis	1st-round technical knockout
Mar. 16, 1996	Las Vegas, Nev.	Deirdre Gogarty	6th-round unanimous decision
Sept. 7, 1996	Las Vegas, Nev.	Melinda Robinson	4th-round knockout
Nov. 9, 1996	Las Vegas, Nev.	Bethany Payne	1st-round technical knockout
June 28, 1997	Las Vegas, Nev.	Andrea DeShong	7th-round technical knockout
Aug. 23, 1997	New York, N.Y.	Isra Girgrah	8th-round unanimous decision
Dec. 5, 1997	Pompano Beach, Fla.	Marcela Eliana Acuña	10th-round unanimous decision
Aug. 29, 1998	Las Vegas, Nev.	Cheryl Nance	9th-round technical knockout
Sept. 19, 1998	Atlanta, Ga.	Christine Robinson	5th-round technical knockout
Dec. 18, 1998	Fort Lauderdale, Fla.	Christy Martin (Sumya Anani, winner)	10th-round medical decision
Apr. 24, 1999	Washington, D.C.	Jovette Jackson	1st-round technical knockout
Oct. 2, 1999	Las Vegas, Nev.	Daniella Somers	5th-round technical knockout
Mar. 3, 2000	Las Vegas, Nev.	Belinda Laracuente	8th-round medical decision
Aug. 12, 2000	Las Vegas, Nev.	Dianna Lewis	10th-round unanimous decision
Dec. 2, 2000	Las Vegas, Nev.	Sabrina Hall	1st-round knockout
Mar. 3, 2001	Las Vegas, Nev.	Jeanne Martinez	10th-round unanimous decision
May 12, 2001	New York, N.Y.	Kathy Collins	10th-round medical decision
Nov. 17, 2001	Las Vegas, Nev.	Lisa Holewyne	10th-round unanimous decision
Dec. 6, 2002	Pontiac, Mich.	Mia St. John	10th-round unanimous decision
Aug. 8, 2003	Biloxi, Miss.	Christy Martin (Laila Ali, winner)	4th-round knockout
Apr. 30, 2005	Lula, Miss.	Lana Alexander	2d-round knockout
Sept. 16, 2005	Albuquerque, N.Mex.	Christy Martin (Holly Holm, winner)	10th-round unanimous decision
Oct. 6, 2006	Worley, Idaho	Christy Martin (Angelica Martinez, winner)	10th-round split decision
June 2, 2007	Lake Charles, La.	Amy Yuratovac	6th-round unanimous decision
July 18, 2008	Houston, Tex.	N/A	Draw

Statistics

Bouts, 55	Knockouts by opponents, 1
Knockouts, 31	Bouts lost by decision, 4
Bouts won by decision, 16	Draws, 3

mer Ohio state kickboxing champion Sue Chase.

A televised fight with Irish featherweight Deirdre Gogarty made Christy into a star. On March 16, 1996, Gogarty badly bloodied Christy before losing in a 6-round decision on the undercard of a Mike Tyson-Frank Bruno heavyweight title fight. The women's fight proved far more exciting than the men's battle. The fight, seen in an estimated 30 million homes and in more than one hundred countries, made Christy into a media sensation. The World Boxing Council (WBC) subsequently recognized Christy as its nominal women's lightweight champion of the world. The WBC did not offer women's title belts for open competition. Christy concluded 1996 with 2 more knockouts.

In 1997, King removed Christy from a card in Nashville, Tennessee, on the grounds that she had been cut in training. Christy denied that she had been hurt. The incident received criticism from the press as a publicity stunt. Christy had several more public clashes with King. However, in a fight that he arranged against Andrea De Shong on June 28, 1997, Christy reportedly earned $150,000, then a record purse for women's boxing.

Continuing the Story

Despite Christy's success, women's boxing remained stigmatized. Mexico City authorities put a stop to a proposed March, 1998, fight between Christy and Belgium's Daniella Somers by citing a 1947 law forbidding women to fight professionally. Christy won her next few bouts, all of which were fought in the United States. She stepped away from the ring until 2002.

Christy had once talked about fighting to earn enough money to purchase a house and then walking away from the sport. Like many boxers, she found it difficult to leave. On December 6, 2002, Christy ended a thirteen-month layoff with a unanimous 10-round decision over Mia St. John at the Silverdome in Pontiac, Michigan, before fewer than 500 fans.

By this time, several daughters of boxing greats had entered boxing, including Muhammad Ali's daughter Laila. Ali knocked out Christy on August 23, 2003, in Biloxi, Mississippi. However, Christy earned $250,000. Her record dropped to 45 wins, 3 losses, 2 draws, with 31 knockouts. Ali, as physically and verbally gifted as her father, subsequently replaced Christy as the leading figure in women's boxing.

Summary

Women boxers fight against the common beliefs that it is unnatural for a woman to be athletic, strong, and aggressive in a violent sport historically dominated by men. Boxing has always had some female competitors. In the eighteenth century, barefisted women bit, scratched, and pulled the hair of their opponents. By the nineteenth century, scantily clad women fought in saloons, brothels, and on the vaudeville circuit for the amusement of males. With her skills and professionalism, Christy Martin gave credibility to women's boxing. She rekindled interest in the sport, prompting other young women to pursue boxing careers. However, Christy also steadfastly refused to be an advocate for women's boxing. She stated that she was promoting Christy and not women's sports. She sought other business opportunities for herself and not the advancement of women's boxing.

Caryn E. Neumann

Additional Sources

Montoya, Delilah, María Teresa Márquez, and C. Ondine Chavoya. *Women Boxers: The New Warriors.* Houston, Tex.: Arte Público Press, 2006.

"On the Move: Pro Boxing's Latest Sensation Is a Two-Fisted Coal Miner's Daughter Named Christy Martin." *People Weekly,* June 24, 1996.

Woolum, Janet. *Outstanding Women Athletes: Who They Are and How They Influenced Sports in America.* 2d ed. Phoenix, Ariz.: Oryx Press, 1998.

Floyd Mayweather, Jr.

Born: February 24, 1977
Grand Rapids, Michigan
Also known as: Floyd Joy Sinclair (birthname); Pretty Boy; Money May; Floyd Joy Mayweather, Jr. (full name)

Early Life
Floyd Mayweather, Jr., was born Floyd Joy Sinclair into an accomplished boxing family on February 24, 1977, in Grand Rapids, Michigan. Floyd's father Floyd Mayweather, Sr., was a respected former welterweight boxer, his uncle Jeff Mayweather was a former International Boxing Organization (IBO) featherweight champion, and his uncle Roger Mayweather was a former world champion in two divisions. With the superb training that was available from his family, Floyd was predestined to become an accomplished boxer.

The Road to Excellence
Before he was twenty years old, Floyd proved he belonged in boxing. Floyd won the Golden Gloves Championship three times, while accumulating a record of 84 wins and 6 losses as an amateur. In 1993, 1994, and 1996, Floyd won the Golden Gloves Championship at 103 pounds, 112 pounds, and 125 pounds, respectively. Floyd's success in these amateur tournaments was mainly because of the shoulder roll defense taught to him by his father and his uncle Roger. This defensive style allowed Floyd to roll his body with the rhythm of his opponent's body, which prevented him from receiving costly face cuts. Thus, he earned the nickname of "Pretty Boy."

Despite his Golden Gloves Championship success, Floyd was unsuccessful at the 1996 Summer Olympics in Atlanta, Georgia. He won the first three rounds of the tournament easily, but his luck ended in the semifinals, when he suffered a controversial loss to Serafim Todorov of Bulgaria. Those who believed the decision was wrong included the U.S. boxing team, the referee of the fight—who raised Floyd's hand after the judges had released their decision—and many observers. This controversial loss did not hamper Floyd's rise to greatness. Two months after the Olympics, on October

Floyd Mayweather, Jr., pounding Oscar De La Hoya during their WBC super-welterweight title fight in 2007. (Gabriel Bouys/AFP/Getty Images)

11, 1996, Floyd won his first professional boxing match, knocking out Roberto Apodaca in the second round.

The Emerging Champion
By 1998, Floyd, had earned the World Boxing Council (WBC) junior-lightweight belt. He had accomplished this by defeating Genaro Hernandez in 8 rounds. This victory led *Ring* magazine to name Floyd the 1998 fighter of the year. In 2000, Floyd fired his father because of various legal troubles and rehired his uncle Roger to be his trainer. Under his uncle's tutelage, Floyd was able to defeat Diego Corrales on January 20, 2001. Before the fight, both Floyd and Corrales boasted that they had never been knocked down nor defeated in professional action; however, Floyd dominated the fight. This earned him the moniker of best pound-for-pound fighter in boxing.

Floyd solidified his status over the next six years by constantly fighting and winning championships in higher weight classes. In 2002, he earned the WBC and *Ring* belts in the lightweight division by defeating José Luis Castillo on consecutive occasions. Floyd fought only three more fights in the lightweight division and then moved to the light welterweight division in 2004. Once again, Floyd won a championship belt, beating Arturo Gatti on June 25, 2005, in Atlantic City, New Jersey. Floyd won the WBC light-welterweight belt in such dominating fashion that Gatti's corner had to stop the fight in the sixth round.

Continuing the Story
In 2005, Floyd moved up weight classes once again, to the welterweight division. He was just as dominant as a welterweight and won the International Boxing Federation (IBF) and IBO belts by unanimous decision by defeating Zab Judah. During the fight, Judah threw unsportsmanlike punches at

Recognized World Super-Featherweight Championships

Date	Location	Loser	Result
Oct. 3, 1998	Las Vegas, Nev.	Genaro Hernandez	8th-round referee technical decision
Dec. 19, 1998	Miami, Fla.	Angel Manfredy	2d-round technical knockout
Feb. 17, 1999	Grand Rapids, Mich.	Carlos Alberto Ramon Rios	12th-round unanimous decision
Sept. 11, 1999	Las Vegas, Nev.	Carlos Gerena	7th-round technical knockout
May 22, 1999	Las Vegas, Nev.	Justin Juuko	9th-round knockout
Mar. 18, 2000	Las Vegas, Nev.	Gregorio Vargas	12th-round unanimous decision
Jan. 20, 2001	Las Vegas, Nev.	Diego Corrales	10th-round technical knockout
May 26, 2001	Grand Rapids, Mich.	Carlos Hernandez	12th-round unanimous decision
Nov. 10, 2001	San Francisco, Calif.	Jesus Chavez	9th-round technical knockout

Recognized World Lightweight Championships

Date	Location	Loser	Result
Apr. 20, 2002	Las Vegas, Nev.	Jose Luis Castillo	12th-round unanimous decision
Dec. 7, 2002	Las Vegas, Nev.	Jose Luis Castillo	12th-round unanimous decision
Apr. 19, 2003	Fresno, Calif.	Victoriano Sosa	12th-round unanimous decision

Recognized World Light-Welterweight Championships

Date	Location	Loser	Result
May 22, 2004	Atlantic City, N.J.	DeMarcus Corley	12th-round unanimous decision
Jan. 22, 2005	Miami, Fla.	Henry Bruseles	8th-round technical knockout
June 25, 2005	Atlantic City, N.J.	Arturo Gatti	6th-round technical knockout
Nov. 4, 2006	Las Vegas, Nev.	Carlos Manuel Baldomir	12th-round unanimous decision

Recognized World Welterweight Championships

Date	Location	Loser	Result
Apr. 8, 2006	Las Vegas, Nev.	Zab Judah	12th-round unanimous decision
Dec. 8, 2007	Las Vegas, Nev.	Ricky Hatton	10th-round technical knockout

Recognized World Light-Middleweight Championship

Date	Location	Loser	Result
May 5, 2007	Las Vegas, Nev.	Oscar De La Hoya	12th-round split decision

Statistics

Bouts, 39
Knockouts, 25
Bouts won by decision, 14
Knockouts by opponents, 0
Bouts lost by decision, 0

Floyd; Floyd's uncle Roger charged Judah in response. For their actions, Judah and Roger earned one-year suspensions. Floyd relinquished the IBF title on June 20, 2006.

Floyd wanted to challenge the "The Golden Boy" Oscar De La Hoya. On November 4, 2006, Floyd defeated Carlos Baldomir for the WBC and *Ring* titles by unanimous decision and earned $8 million. Thus, in 2007, De La Hoya finally accepted Floyd's challenge. De La Hoya placed his WBC junior-middleweight belt on the line against Floyd, who gladly jumped up to the higher weight class and faced De La Hoya in what many claimed was the best matchup of the generation. Floyd won the "superfight" on May 5, 2007, by split decision. The fight set the record for pay-per-view purchases with 2.4 million households watching. Floyd earned more than $25 million from the fight and immediately retired. He stayed in retirement until he defeated Ricky Hatton on December 8, 2007, in what turned out to be his last fight. On June 6, 2008, he officially retired from boxing with a 39-0 record.

Summary

Floyd Mayweather, Jr., was born into a boxing family. His pedigree and training helped him became one of the greatest fighters of his generation. For a man that was only thirty-one years old at the time of his retirement, Floyd will be remembered for his rapid rise to the top and his pugilistic domination.

Paul C. Alexander II

Additional Sources

Bechtel, Mark, and Kostya Kennedy. "The Questions with Floyd Mayweather." *Sports Illustrated* 106, no. 21 (May 21, 2007).

Beech, Mark. "The Year of Magical Living." *Sports Illustrated* 107, no. 23 (December 10, 2007).

Hoffer, Richard. "Golden Boy Versus Pretty Boy." *Sports Illustrated* 106, no. 19 (May 7, 2007).

Jones, Chris. "The Game." *Esquire* 148, no. 3 (September, 2007).

Sugar, Bert Randolph. *Boxing's Greatest Fighters*. Guilford, Conn.: Lyons Press, 2006.

Archie Moore

Born: December 13, 1913 (or 1916)
   Benoit, Mississippi
Died: December 9, 1998
   San Diego, California
Also known as: Archibald Lee Wright (birth name); the Old Mongoose

Early Life
Archibald Lee Wright was born on December 13, in either 1913 or 1916, depending upon whether one believes the testimony of his mother or of Archie himself. Archie was born into a poor family who lived in Benoit, Mississippi. His father made a little money working on a local farm, but, throughout Archie's early childhood, the family struggled to make ends meet. When Archie was still young, his parents separated and, along with his older sister, he moved to St. Louis, Missouri, where he was raised by his aunt, from whom he acquired the surname Moore. While attending Lincoln High School in St. Louis, Archie became involved in petty crime. He eventually ended up in reform school.

The Road to Excellence
Archie's early experiences with authority changed his entire outlook on life. After spending nearly two years at reform school, he returned to the outside world determined to succeed. During the Great Depression of the early 1930's, jobs were extremely scarce. As a result, Archie decided to join the Civilian Conservation Corps (CCC).

Archie was an eager seventeen-year-old, and he worked hard on numerous CCC projects. All the hard physical labor paid off; Archie became fit and strong. While working with the CCC, Archie first became involved with boxing. He had a few amateur contests, all of which he won. Archie saw that boxing offered him a real chance of doing something positive with his life. Consequently, he put all his energy into becoming a prizefighter.

In 1935, following a successful amateur career, Archie had his first professional bout, an impressive two-round victory over "Piano Man" Jones. Initially fighting as a middleweight, Archie rapidly discovered that his natural fighting weight was as a light heavyweight. Archie developed his professional boxing skills in fights in the St. Louis area, where he was extremely successful, winning all but four of his forty-eight contests up to 1938.

In 1938, Archie moved to the West Coast in order to further his career. As he became better known, Archie was nicknamed the "Old Mongoose," because of his canny defensive style and explosive punching power. Despite continued success in the ring, Archie was prevented persistently from getting a shot at the world light-heavyweight title. He was even forced to go to Australia to fight when he was refused important bouts in the United States.

Archie often became disillusioned with his managers, who consistently failed to arrange title fights

Archie Moore on the eve of a bout with Yolande Pompey in London in 1956. (Monty Fresco/Hulton Archive/Getty Images)

for him. As a result, he frequently changed managers. This lack of continuity among his entourage was another reason why, although he was the number-one contender throughout the 1940's, Archie had to wait until 1952 for a shot at the world light-heavyweight crown.

The Emerging Champion
On December 17, 1952, in St. Louis, Archie fought for the world title against the champion, Joey Maxim. Even this long-overdue contest came about only because Archie agreed to receive a paltry $800 for the fight, with Maxim securing $100,000. Despite his advancing years, Archie outpointed Maxim. At last, and at the age of thirty-nine, Archie was light-heavyweight champion of the world.

Although Archie was a popular champion, few expected him to retain his title for any length of time. Most people believed the Old Mongoose was simply too old. Archie, however, was not going to give up the title easily, after it had taken him nearly seventeen years to win it. Archie's extended boxing apprenticeship had developed him into a skillful strategist, which, in conjunction with his devastating punching power, enabled him to dominate his weight division for more than ten years.

Archie's first two defenses of the world title were against Maxim, the former champion. Both bouts ended in points victories for Archie. Between 1954 and 1961, Archie went undefeated in eight title defenses and won numerous nontitle bouts. Archie so dominated the light-heavyweight division that he, unsuccessfully and perhaps misguidedly, challenged for the heavyweight title, first against Rocky Marciano in 1955, then against Floyd Patterson in 1956.

One of Archie's most memorable fights was his titanic struggle against the Canadian Yvon Durelle in December, 1958. Archie was floored three times in the fourth round, and both fighters hit the canvas four times before Archie finally knocked out Durelle in the eleventh round. The rematch, eight months later, was anticlimactic, with Archie winning easily in three rounds.

Continuing the Story
Archie's last title defense came in June, 1961, when he defeated the Italian Giulio Rinaldi. Archie never lost the light-heavyweight title in the ring. Only inactivity cost him his crown, when in February, 1962, the New York state and European boxing commissions stripped him of the title. At that time, he was the oldest world boxing champion of all time.

Archie retired after a third-round knockout over a wrestler, Mike DiBiase, in March, 1963. In 1960, Archie starred in the film *The Adventures of Huckleberry Finn*, and after his retirement from boxing, he decided to do more film and television work. He also worked with youth and amateur boxers and trained and advised George Foreman during his career. The Old Mongoose must have been especially helpful during Foreman's comeback, for more than any other boxer, Archie Moore was adept at using an old head to defeat a younger opponent.

Recognized World Light Heavyweight Championships

Date	Location	Loser	Result
Dec. 17, 1952	St. Louis, Mo.	Joey Maxim	15th-round win by decision
June 24, 1953	Ogden, Utah	Joey Maxim	15th-round win by decision
Jan. 27, 1954	Miami, Fla.	Joey Maxim	15th-round win by decision
Aug. 11, 1954	New York, N.Y.	Harold Johnson	14th-round technical knockout
June 22, 1955	New York, N.Y.	Carl (Bobo) Olson	3d-round knockout
June 5, 1956	London, England	Yolande Pompey	10th-round technical knockout
Sept. 20, 1957	Los Angeles, Calif.	Tony Anthony	7th-round technical knockout
Dec. 10, 1958	Montreal, Canada	Yvon Durelle	11th-round knockout
Aug. 12, 1959	Montreal, Canada	Yvon Durelle	3d-round knockout
June 10, 1961	New York, N.Y.	Giulio Rinaldi	15th-round win by decision

Recognized World Heavyweight Championships

Date	Location	Loser	Result
Sept. 21, 1955	New York, N.Y.	Archie Moore (Rocky Marciano, winner)	9th-round knockout
Nov. 30, 1956	Chicago, Ill.	Archie Moore (Floyd Patterson, winner)	5th-round knockout

Statistics

Bouts, 215
Knockouts, 129
Bouts won by decision, 54
Knockouts by opponents, 7
Bouts lost by decision, 13
Bouts lost by fouls, 2
Draws, 9
No contests, 1

Records

Scored 129 knockouts as a professional, 145 overall—both current world records

At 48 years, 51 days of age, the oldest professional boxer ever to hold any world title

Honors and Awards

1958	Edward J. Neil Trophy
1966	Inducted into *Ring* magazine Boxing Hall of Fame
1987	Rocky Marciano Memorial Award
1990	Inducted into International Boxing Hall of Fame

Summary

Archie Moore went astray early in his life but had the strength of character to bounce back. He discovered his talent for boxing and became determined to use his physical skills and mental ability to be the best boxer he could possibly be. Despite numerous setbacks in his career, Archie eventually triumphed and became one of the greatest professional boxing champions ever.

David L. Andrews

Additional Sources

Douroux, Marilyn G. *Archie Moore—the Ole Mongoose: The Authorized Biography of Archie Moore, Undefeated Light Heavyweight Champion of the World.* Boston: Branden, 1991.

Fitzgerald, Mike, Jake La Motta, Bert Randolph Sugar, and Pete Ehrmann. *The Ageless Warrior: The Life of Boxing Legend Archie Moore.* Champaign, Ill.: Sports, 2004.

Moore, Archie. *The Archie Moore Story.* London: Nicholas Kaye, 1960.

Moore, Archie, and Leonard B. Pearl. *Any Boy Can: The Archie Moore Story.* Englewood Cliffs, N.J.: Prentice-Hall, 1971.

Shane Mosley

Born: September 7, 1971
Lynwood, California
Also known as: Sugar

Early Life
Shane Mosley was born to Jack and Clemmie Mosley and was the youngest of three children. He was an active child who rode his Big Wheel at day care while all the other children took naps. His father, who later served as his trainer and was himself once an amateur fighter, introduced Shane to boxing. When he was only eight years old, Shane went with his father to the local gym and attended karate class. His earliest swings at the heavy bag were karate kicks, not punches. When Shane attended Pomona High School he ran cross-country, played in a local basketball league, trained three to five hours each day after school in the gym, and had at least one boxing match per week. As a professional, Shane fought Oscar De La Hoya twice and won by decision on both occasions. However, he first fought De La Hoya when De La Hoya was eleven and Shane was twelve.

The Road to Excellence
Shane was a three-time national amateur boxing champion. As an amateur, he had a record of 230-12. In 1989, he won both the junior-lightweight title at the U.S. championships and the lightweight title at the junior world championships. He was the 1992 U.S. amateur champion in the junior-welterweight division and a member of the 1992 Olympic team. In February, 1993, Shane made his professional debut, a five-round rout of California state champion Greg Puente. Each of Shane's seven bouts in 1993 ended in a knockout. Eight of his nine victories in 1994 ended in a knockout. The pattern continued over the next few years. Despite Shane's overwhelming early success, a 23-0 record with 22 knockouts, few noticed the talented young fighter until August, 1997, when he stepped into the ring against International Boxing Federation (IBF) lightweight champion Philip Holiday. Shane bested Holiday over twelve rounds, capturing the IBF title. By the end of 1998, Shane had defended his title five times, each victory ending in a knockout. The Boxing Writers Association of America named Shane fighter of the year.

The Emerging Champion
Displaying a quick left jab and a solid right hand, Shane looked beyond his weight class to the welterweight division, knowing the talent at that level was superior to the competition in the lightweight division. Shane's first big fight as a welterweight was against his old Los Angeles junior Golden Gloves rival, De La Hoya. Heavily favored over Shane, De La Hoya was an established champion and an Olympic gold medalist. Despite his record going into the bout, 34-0 with 32 knockouts, Shane remained the underdog against De La Hoya, a fan favorite known

Shane Mosley being lifted after his victory against Fernando Vargas in 2006. (Steve Marcus/Reuters/Landov)

as the "Golden Boy." In what many experts ranked the best fight of 2000, Shane and De La Hoya boxed a full 12 rounds. Shane won a split decision, instant name recognition, and $4.5 million. De La Hoya received $12 million. Shane defended his welterweight title three times against unknown fighters. In 2000, the World Boxing Hall of Fame named Shane fighter of the year, but his real test at the welterweight division came against former Olympic boxer Vernon Forrest, who had defeated Shane at the Olympic trials. On January, 2002, at Madison Square Garden in New York, New York, Shane entered his fight against Forrest with a record of 38-0 with 35 knockouts. A head butt from Forrest opened a cut on Shane's forehead, and Forrest knocked the champion to the mat twice, taking his welterweight title and his undefeated record. Seven months later, at Conseco Fieldhouse in Indianapolis, Indiana, Shane and Forrest met again. Just as De La Hoya had no answer for Shane, Shane had no answer for Forrest. Shane lost his second consecutive unanimous 12-round decision to Forrest.

Continuing the Story

After a no contest against Raul Marquez in February, Shane's rematch against De La Hoya took place in September, 2003, at the MGM Grand in Las Vegas, Nevada. In the much-anticipated rematch, Shane won a unanimous 12-round decision, acquiring both the World Boxing Association and the World Boxing Council (WBC) junior-middleweight titles. Shane became one of the few fighters in boxing history to have won a title in three or more divisions. In March, 2004, he brought his middleweight titles to a unification bout against IBF champion Ronald "Winky" Wright. Shane lost a 12-round unanimous decision to Wright. The rematch, at Las Vegas's Mandalay Bay Resort and Casino, was another victory for Wright, who won a decision over twelve rounds. However, many observers of the bout thought Shane had fought well enough to win the rematch.

Shortly after losing to Wright for a second time, Shane replaced his father as his trainer, hiring Joe Goossen and then John David Jackson. In September, 2005, Shane won a unanimous 10-round decision over previously unbeaten Jose Luis Cruz, then scored a technical knockout in his first fight against Fernando Vargas in late February, 2006. In July of that year, Shane reinforced his superiority over Vargas, defeating him again by a technical knockout in six rounds. Dropping back to the welterweight division, Shane, at thirty-five, won the interim WBC welterweight title in a 12-round unanimous decision over Luis Collazo. Seeking a fight against another welterweight titleholder, Shane

Title Fights

Date	Location	Loser	Result
Aug. 2, 1997	Uncasville, Conn.	Philip Holiday	12th-round unanimous decision
Nov. 25, 1997	El Paso, Tex.	Manuel Gomez	11th-round knockout
Feb. 6, 1998	Uncasville, Conn.	Demetrio Ceballos	8th-round technical knockout
May 9, 1998	Atlantic City, N.J.	John John Molina	8th-round technical knockout
June 27, 1998	Philadelphia, Pa.	Wilfredo Ruiz	5th-round knockout
Sept. 22, 1998	New York, N.Y.	Eduardo Bartolome Morales	5th-round technical knockout
Nov. 14, 1998	Mashantucket, Conn.	Jesse James Leija	9th-round technical knockout
Jan. 9, 1999	Pensacola, Fla.	Golden Johnson	7th-round knockout
Apr. 17, 1999	Indio, Calif.	John Brown	8th-round technical knockout
June 17, 2000	Los Angeles, Calif.	Oscar De La Hoya	12th-round split decision
Nov. 4, 2000	New York, N.Y.	Antonio Diaz	6th-round technical knockout
Mar. 10, 2001	Las Vegas, Nev.	Shannan Taylor	6th-round technical knockout
July 21, 2001	Las Vegas, Nev.	Adrian Stone	3d-round knockout
Jan. 26, 2002	New York, N.Y.	Shane Mosley (Vernon Forrest, winner)	12th-round unanimous decision
July 20, 2002	Indianapolis, Ind.	Shane Mosley (Vernon Forrest, winner)	12th-round unanimous decision
Sept. 13, 2003	Las Vegas, Nev.	Oscar De La Hoya	12th-round unanimous decision
Mar. 13, 2004	Las Vegas, Nev.	Shane Mosley (Ronald Wright, winner)	12th-round unanimous decision
Nov. 20, 2004	Las Vegas, Nev.	Shane Mosley (Ronald Wright, winner)	12th-round medical decision
Feb. 25, 2006	Las Vegas, Nev.	Fernando Vargas	10th-round technical knockout
Feb. 10, 2007	Las Vegas, Nev.	Luis Collazo	12th-round unanimous decision
Nov. 10, 2007	New York, N.Y.	Shane Mosley (Miguel Angel Cotto, winner)	12th-round unanimous decision
Sept. 27, 2008	Carson, Calif.	Ricardo Mayorga	12th-round knockout

turned to WBC champion Miguel Cotto, who was undefeated in 30 fights and had 25 knockouts. Before 18,000 fans at Madison Square Garden, Cotto won a 12-round unanimous decision.

Summary

One of the few fighters to win a title in three different divisions, Shane Mosley was a dominant fighter throughout the 1990's and the 2000's. A champion as both an amateur and a professional, Shane was the only fighter to defeat De La Hoya twice in professional bouts.

Randy L. Abbott

Additional Sources

Hoffer, Richard. "Conspiracy Theory: Oscar De La Hoya Lost His Rematch with Shane Mosley, Then Made Wild Charges About It." *Sports Illustrated* 99, no. 11 (2003): 46.

Spousta, Tom. "Mosley and De La Hoya Renew a Boyhood Rivalry." *The New York Times*, June 15, 2000, p. D7.

Wong, Edward. "At Thirty, Shane Mosley Seeks Stardom Beyond the Ring." *The New York Times*, January 25, 2002, p. D1.

Manny Pacquiao

Born: December 17, 1978
Kibawe Bukidnon, Mindanao, Philippines
Also known as: Emmanuel Dapidran Pacquiao; Pac-Man; the Destroyer; the Mexican Assassin; People's Champ

Early life

Manny Pacquiao, born in the Philippines on December 17, 1978, became a professional boxer in the light-flyweight division at the age of sixteen. On January 1, 1995, he earned his first victory with a 4-round decision over Ting Ignacio. He won his next ten fights before he was knocked out in the third round in a fight against Rustico Torrecampo. After this loss, he won eight straight and then fought for the Oriental and Pacific Boxing Federation flyweight championship, knocking out Chokchai Chokwiwat in the fifth round. He won his next three fights, including first-round knockouts against Tanompdej Singwangcha, in the only defense of his title, and Shin Terao in Japan, his first fight outside the Philippines.

The Road to Excellence

In December, 1998, Manny went to Thailand and knocked out Chatchai Sasakul in the eighth round to capture the World Boxing Council (WBC) flyweight title. He defended the title on April 24, 1999, knocking out Gabriel Mira in 4 rounds, but lost the title on September 17, 1999, in Thailand, in a third-round knockout by Medgoen Singsurat.

Manny left the flyweight division and jumped over the super flyweight and bantamweight divisions. He premiered as a super bantamweight on December 18, 1999, beating Reynante Jamili in Manila, Philippines, for the WBC international title. Manny defended this title five times before going to the United States. He fought the highly regarded Lehlo Ledwaba at the MGM Grand Hotel in Las Vegas, Nevada, knocking him out in the sixth round on June 23, 2001, procuring Ledwaba's International Boxing Federation (IBF) super-bantamweight title. He tried to unify the super-bantamweight titles when he faced World Boxing Organization (WBO) champion Agapito Sanchez in San Francisco, California. The fight became a technical draw after 6 rounds when halted because of a cut on one of Manny's eyes. By November, 2003, Manny had defended his IBF title four times.

The Emerging Champion

Next, he fought *Ring* magazine featherweight champion Marco Antonio Barrera, a fighter who had earned that title by beating undefeated Naseem Hamed. Because of a glut of sanctioning organizations—WBC, WBO, WBA, IBF, and others—many of which had

Manny Pacquiao (right) boxing against Marco Antonio Barrera in 2007. (Ethan Miller/Getty Images)

disreputable reputations, *Ring* magazine, the so-called bible of boxing, created its own titlists. Manny was ranked the number-one super bantamweight when he took on Barrera, a featherweight, considered one of the best pound-for-pound fighters in the world. In an upset, Manny dominated Barrera, winning via eleventh-round knockout in San Antonio, Texas. Six months later, Manny fought Juan Manuel Marquez, the WBA and IBF featherweight champion, to a controversial draw. Manny knocked Marquez down three times in the first round, but Marquez counterpunched effectively. Afterward, one of the judges admitted to scoring the first round incorrectly, a mistake that cost Manny the decision.

In March, 2005, Manny took on Erik Morales, a fighter known for his bitter three-fight rivalry with Barrera. Manny lost the decision, but he won the next two fights between the boxers by knockout: in the tenth round in January, 2006, and in the third round in November, 2006. In October, 2007, Manny fought Barrera again and won a unanimous decision. After these bouts, Manny was ranked in the top three of most "pound-for-pound" lists. On March 15, 2008, in a rematch against Marquez, Manny won the WBC super-featherweight title via a split decision after knocking down the Mexican fighter in the third round. On June 28, 2008, Manny won a title in his fifth weight class by beating lightweight champion David Diaz.

Recognized World Flyweight Championships

Date	Location	Loser	Result
Dec. 4, 1998	Bangkok, Thailand	Chatchai Sasakul	8th-round technical knockout
Feb. 20, 1999	Kidapawan City, Philippines	Todd Makelin	3d-round technical knockout
Apr. 24, 1999	Quezon City, Philippines	Gabriel Mira	4th-round knockout
Sept. 17, 1999	Nakhon Si Thammarat, Thailand	Manny Pacquiao (Medgoen Singsurat, winner)	3d-round knockout

Recognized World Super-Bantamweight Championships

Date	Location	Loser	Result
Dec. 18, 1999	Manila, Philippines	Reynante Jamili	2d-round technical knockout
Mar. 4, 2000	Manila, Philippines	Arnel Barotillo	4th-round knockout
June 28, 2000	Manila, Philippines	Seung-Kon Chae	1st-round technical knockout
Oct. 14, 2000	Antipolo City, Philippines	Nedal Hussein	10th-round technical knockout
Feb. 24, 2001	Manila, Philippines	Tetsutora Senrima	5th-round technical knockout
Apr. 28, 2001	Kidapawan City, Philippines	Wethya Sakmuangklang	6th-round technical knockout
June 23, 2001	Las Vegas, Nev.	Lehlohonolo Ledwaba	6th-round technical knockout
Nov. 10, 2001	San Francisco, Calif.	Agapito Sanchez	6th-round draw
June 8, 2002	Memphis, Tenn.	Jorge Eliecer Julio	2d-round technical knockout
Oct. 26, 2002	Davao City, Philippines	Fahprakorb Rakkiatgym	1st-round knockout
July 26, 2003	Los Angeles, Calif.	Emmanuel Lucero	3d-round technical knockout

Recognized World Featherweight Championship

Date	Location	Loser	Result
May 8, 2004	Las Vegas, Nev.	Juan Manuel Marquez	12th-round draw

Recognized World Super-Featherweight Championships

Date	Location	Loser	Result
Mar. 19, 2005	Las Vegas, Nev.	Manny Pacquiao (Erik Morales, winner)	12th-round unanimous decision
Sept. 10, 2005	Los Angeles, Calif.	Héctor Velázquez	6th-round technical knockout
Jan. 21, 2006	Las Vegas, Nev.	Erik Morales	10th-round technical knockout
July 2, 2006	Manila, Philippines	Oscar Larios	12th-round unanimous decision
Nov. 18, 2006	Las Vegas, Nev.	Erik Morales	3d-round knockout
Apr. 14, 2007	San Antonio, Tex.	Jorge Solís	8th-round knockout
Oct. 6, 2007	Las Vegas, Nev.	Marco Antonio Barrera	12th-round unanimous decision
Mar. 15, 2008	Las Vegas, Nev.	Juan Manuel Márquez	12th-round split decision

Recognized World Lightweight Championship

Date	Location	Loser	Result
June 28, 2008	Las Vegas, Nev.	David Diaz	9th-round technical knockout

Statistics

Bouts, 52
Knockouts, 35
Bouts won by decision, 12
Knockouts by opponents, 2
Bouts lost by decision, 1

Honors and Awards

2002-06	Philippine Sportswriters Association sportsman of the year
2006	*Ring* magazine fighter of the year
	Boxing Writers Association of America fighter of the year
2007	WBC emeritus champion
2008	University Athletic Association of the Philippines sports excellence award
	Named the "people's champ" by the Philippines' house of representatives

Continuing the Story

In the Philippines, Manny transcended sport: He became a pop icon. Manny appeared in action movies, recorded music, and ran for political office. Before his first rematch with Morales, he entered the ring to his own song, "This Fight Is for You," a song recounting his struggles in the ring. When he won the rematch, the song became a popular hit in the Philippines. On June 21, 2006, *Pacquiao: The Movie* was released in the Philippines. On July 24, 2006, President Gloria Arroyo mentioned him in her state of the union address, calling him a national hero. In 2007, Manny lost in his bid to become a member of the Philippines' congress. In September, 2006, Manny signed a promotional contract with Golden Boy Promotions headed by Oscar De La Hoya. However, he decided to stay with the Bob Arum-led promotional company Top Rank. Litigation with Golden Boy Promotions followed, delaying the long awaited rematch with Marquez, a Golden Boy Promotions fighter. Despite this distraction, Manny was named the fighter of the year for 2006 by *Ring* magazine for his wins over Morales and Oscar Larios.

Summary

Like Muhammad Ali during the 1970's, Manny Pacquiao transcended the sports pages, especially in his home country of the Philippines. Manny proved that the best boxers in the world do not necessarily come from the United States. In the 2000's, many fighters from Asia and Eastern Europe came to the United States and had success. However, few reached the superstar status enjoyed by Manny.

Brett Conway

Additional Sources

Collins, Nigel. "Who Walked Away from Pacquiao-Barrera II the Winner?" In *The Ring: The 2008 Boxing Almanac and Book of Facts.* Ambler, Pa.: London, 2008.

Lerner, Ted. "At Home with Manny Pacquiao: Get to Know the Pac-Man You Never Knew Before." *Ring*, August, 2008, 48-54.

Santoliquito, Joseph. "The Pacquiao-Marquez Feud: All We Can Do Is Pray for a Third Fight." *Ring*, July, 2008, 30-36.

László Papp

Born: March 25, 1926
Budapest, Hungary
Died: October 16, 2003
Budapest, Hungary

Early Life
László Papp was born in Budapest, Hungary, on March 25, 1926. His parents were Imre and Erzsebet Burgus Papp. His father was a car driver who worked for a big factory. He died when László was only eleven. As a young boy, László helped his mother run the family grocery business.

At elementary school, László's first love was soccer. After he finished his schooling he started work as a mechanic in a factory and began boxing at the factory's boxing club in 1943. In 1944, he was forced to leave Hungary and narrowly escaped having to become a soldier in the German army.

The Road to Excellence
As a result of his boxing performances at the 1948 Olympic Games in London, László established an international reputation as a premier athlete. László, a fighter who led with his left hand, won the middleweight title. However, another Hungarian athlete, fencer Ilona Elek, received more recognition on her return to her homeland. Her 1948 gold medal was a celebrated follow-up to the gold medal she received twelve years before at the 1936 Berlin Olympics.

The Emerging Champion
At the 1952 Helsinki Olympics, Hungarian journalists filed reports on the successes of the Hungarian female swimmers, who achieved gold medals in four of the seven swimming and diving competitions, and on the return of László, fighting as a light middleweight. He easily made it to the finals, where he defeated Theunis Van Schalkwyk of South Africa with a third-round knockout.

Four years later, at the 1956 Melbourne Olympics, the sporting events were overshadowed by Cold War political events. On November 4, 1956, just days before the Olympics' Opening Ceremony, Soviet troops and tanks entered Budapest, Hungary, and violently suppressed the political freedoms sought by protesters. The Hungarian delegation, however, arrived successfully in Australia.

László had one of the most memorable achievements in Melbourne. Fighting in the light-middleweight division, he became the first Olympic boxer to win three consecutive gold medals, defeating José Torres of the United States. Only Teófilo Stevenson and Félix Félix, both from Cuba, have repeated this success. In addition to his three Olympic successes, László's amateur career included two European Championship gold medals, in 1949 and 1951.

Continuing the Story
In 1957, after considerable pressure from Hungarian boxing authorities, the thirty-one-year-old László was given permission by the communist Hungarian government to box professionally. He became the first Iron Curtain boxer to receive this privilege. Subsequently, he fought in thirty-two professional fights. He never lost a professional bout and was European middleweight champion from 1962 until his retirement, forced by the Hungarian government, in 1965.

From 1969 to 1992, he was the head coach of the Hungarian national boxing team and supervised one Olympic champion, in 1972; one world champion, in 1991; and eight European gold medalists. In 1993, he retired; he trained and coached young

Olympic Career

Date	Location	Loser	Result
Aug. 7-13, 1948	London, England	J. A. Wright	Points decision
July 19-Aug. 3, 1952	Helsinki, Finland	Theunis Van Schalkwyk	3d-round knockout
Nov. 22-Dec. 8, 1956	Melbourne, Australia	José Torees	Points decision

Professional Career

1957-64	Took part in 29 title fights: 27 wins, 2 draws
1962-65	European Middleweight Champion: 300 career wins; 12 losses

boxers privately until 1998. He was featured in two films: *Heavy Gloves* (1958) and *Valley of Slaps* (1980).

László defeated Spider Webbs, Tiger Jones, Randy Sandy, Lou Perry, and Chris Christensen. Three different world champions—Paul Pender, Joey Giardello, and Dick Tiger—could have battled the Hungarian but chose not to. In his relatively short career, László may have earned more than $150,000, a fortune in terms of a communist economic culture. In Hungary the press gave László the monikers "Masterful Magyar," the "Little Powerhouse," and the "Babe Ruth of Hungary." In 2001, Lazlo was inducted into the International Boxing Hall Of Fame. He died in 2003.

Summary

A good case can be make for László Papp as Hungary's greatest boxer. Out of a total of 312 fights he lost only 12. Arguably, his career reached its peak during his professional fighting years. Between 1957 and 1964, he fought in 29 title fights, winning 27 and drawing 2. Although he never took part in a world title fight, László's glorious victory over José Torres at Melbourne is noteworthy, for, later, Torres became a world champion. László followed up his professional boxing career with many years of service as a boxing coach and trainer.

Scott A. G. M. Crawford

Additional Sources

Findling, John E., and Kimberly D. Pelle, eds. *Historical Dictionary of the Modern Olympic Movement.* Westport, Conn.: Greenwood Press, 2004.

Greenspan, Bud. *One Hundred Greatest Moments in Olympic History.* Los Angeles: General, 1995.

The Olympics: Athens to Athens 1896-2004. London: Weidenfeld & Nicolson, 2004.

Wallechinsky, David, and Jaime Loucky. *The Complete Book of the Olympics: 2008 Edition.* London: Aurum Press, 2008.

Floyd Patterson

Born: January 4, 1935
    Waco, North Carolina
Died: May 11, 2006
    New Paltz, New York
Also known as: The Gentleman of Boxing; the Rabbit

Early Life

Born on January 4, 1935, in Waco, North Carolina, Floyd Patterson was the third of nine sons in a family of thirteen. In 1936, the family moved to the Bedford-Stuyvesant section of Brooklyn, New York, in an attempt to escape the misery of rural poverty.

The Pattersons found life in the ghetto a difficult struggle. Floyd, who started running with street gangs, stole things he felt his family needed, such as dresses for his mother and milk for the family. One day in 1945, a police officer caught him stealing a case of soda. The judge, after consulting with his mother, placed him in the Wiltwyck School for Boys in Esopus, New York.

Floyd loved the green, sprawling countryside surrounding Wiltwyck. He rode horses, studied nature, and acquired a fondness for snakes. He also met a gentle teacher named Vivian Costen, who helped him overcome his extreme shyness and lack of confidence. Walter Johnson, Wiltwyck's sports director, introduced Floyd to boxing. Together, the two teachers changed the young boy's life forever.

When Floyd returned to New York, he enrolled at Public School 614, a special facility for children who needed additional assistance. There he met Charles Schwerfel, one of the school's patrons, who employed Floyd in his Gramercy Park Hotel and persuaded him to try boxing as a professional career. Schwerfel and Frank LaVelle, a U.S. Customs employee who trained young boxers, induced Floyd to make the short walk up the steps to Gus D'Amato's gymnasium.

The Road to Excellence

D'Amato served as a father figure to Floyd during the early days when the young man amused boxing experts by jumping around the ring like "a cricket on a hot skillet." Where others saw awkwardness, D'Amato saw a brilliant quickness that enabled Floyd, at the age of fifteen, to capture the New York City Golden Gloves title in the 147-pound category.

As Floyd grew, so did his credentials. At the age of seventeen, he won a gold medal at the Olympics in Helsinki, Finland, by devastating four opponents in less than eighteen minutes of fighting. Following the Olympics, Floyd turned professional, winning his first thirteen bouts before losing a controversial decision to former light heavyweight champion Joey Maxim. A second streak of eighteen victories culminated with his fifth-round knockout of Archie Moore on November 30, 1956. At the age of twenty-one, Floyd be-

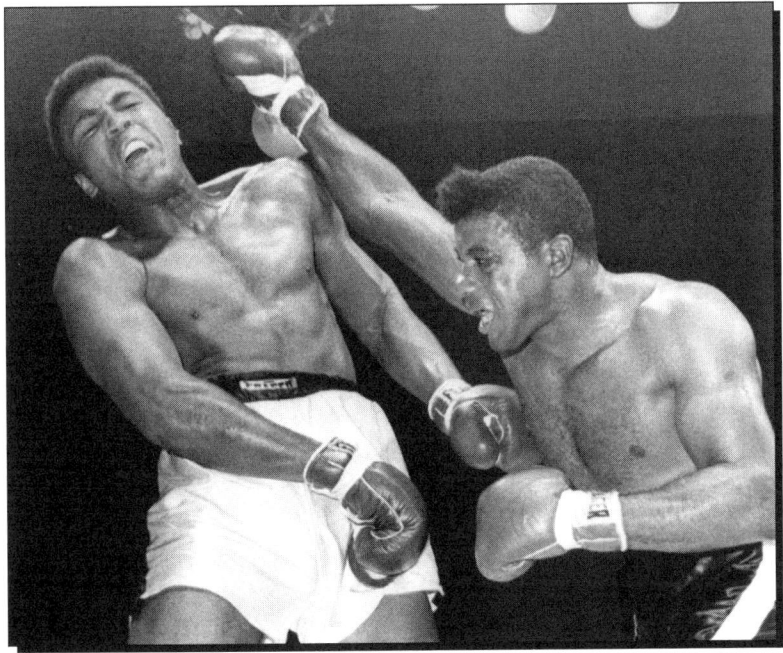

Floyd Patterson throws a punch at Cassius Clay in 1965. (AP/Wide World Photos)

Recognized World Heavyweight Championships

Date	Location	Loser	Result
Nov. 30, 1956	Chicago, Ill.	Archie Moore	5th-round knockout
July 29, 1957	New York, N.Y.	Tommy Jackson	10th-round technical knockout
Aug. 22, 1957	Seattle, Wash.	Pete Rademacher	6th-round knockout
Aug. 18, 1958	Los Angeles, Calif.	Roy Harris	13th-round technical knockout
May 1, 1959	Indianapolis, Ind.	Brian London	11th-round knockout
June 26, 1959	New York, N.Y.	Floyd Patterson (Ingemar Johansson, winner)	3d-round technical knockout
June 20, 1960	New York, N.Y.	Ingemar Johansson	5th-round knockout
Mar. 13, 1961	Miami Beach, Fla.	Ingemar Johansson	6th-round knockout
Dec. 4, 1961	Toronto, Canada	Tom McNeeley	4th-round knockout
Sept. 25, 1962	Chicago, Ill.	Floyd Patterson (Sonny Liston, winner)	1st-round knockout
July 22, 1963	Las Vegas, Nev.	Floyd Patterson (Sonny Liston, winner)	1st-round knockout
Nov. 22, 1965	Las Vegas, Nev.	Floyd Patterson (Muhammad Ali, winner)	12th-round technical knockout
Aug. 14, 1968	Stockholm, Sweden	Floyd Patterson (Jimmy Ellis, winner)	15th-round referee's decision

came the youngest heavyweight champion in boxing history to that time.

The Emerging Champion

Throughout his career, Floyd struggled to overcome some severe psychological handicaps. The insecure new champion suffered from low self-esteem. Too embarrassed to ride in parades or accept other honors befitting the heavyweight champion, Floyd found it difficult to defend himself against critics who mocked his "glass chin" and suggested he had had no difficult opponents. Successful defenses against questionable opponents like Pete Rademacher, Roy Harris, and Brian London seemed to prove the critics' case. Then, on June 26, 1959, when Ingemar Johansson knocked Floyd down seven times in three rounds, taking his title away, his career seemed to be over.

Floyd defied his critics. Bitterly ashamed over losing the crown, he went into seclusion for a year before returning to the ring against Johansson on June 20, 1960. In that fight, Floyd vindicated himself by knocking out the Swede with a vicious left hook. The first fighter ever to regain the heavyweight championship, Floyd enjoyed his finest hour.

Floyd began a second championship reign. After knocking out Johansson a second time and crushing Tom McNeeley, he came up against a massive ex-convict named Charles "Sonny" Liston. Liston, who outweighed Floyd by nearly 20 pounds, took the crown in a first-round knockout on September 25, 1962. Adding insult to injury, Liston duplicated this feat in a July 22, 1963, rematch.

Two consecutive one-round knockouts would have finished most fighters, but not Floyd. Rather than quitting, he staged yet another comeback, defeating five consecutive opponents, including the highly ranked Eddie Machen, before losing a twelve-round bid to regain the championship against Muhammad Ali on November 22, 1965.

Statistics

Bouts, 64

Knockouts, 40

Bouts won by decision, 15

Knockouts by opponents, 5

Bouts lost by decision, 3

Draws, 1

Honors and Awards

1950	New York City Golden Gloves Champion
1952	National Amateur Athletic Union middleweight champion
	Gold medal, U.S. Olympic Boxing
1956, 1960	*Ring* magazine Merit Award
	Edward J. Neil Trophy
1976	Inducted into *Ring* magazine Boxing Hall of Fame
1987	Inducted into U.S. Olympic Hall of Fame
1991	Inducted into International Boxing Hall of Fame

Continuing the Story

Floyd's durability during his post-championship career amazed his critics. He fought another seven years, beating reputable contenders like Oscar Bonavena, and nearly won the crown a third time on August 14, 1968, when ring officials gave Jimmy Ellis the World Boxing Association title in a controversial fifteen-round decision. Nine consecutive victories between 1968 and 1972 produced a second bout with Ali. It would be Floyd's last fight.

The two world champions met in New York on September 20, 1972. Unlike the first fight, the second was vicious as Ali mercilessly pummeled a thirty-seven-year-old Floyd. Finally, the referee stopped the fight at the end of the seventh round. Afterward, Floyd announced his retirement.

The years after Floyd's retirement were good ones. He devoted much time to teaching young men how to box in his Huguenot Boxing Club in New Paltz, New York. He lived on a thirty-five-acre farm that reminded him of the rural bliss he first encountered at Wiltwyck. Floyd overcame his emotional problems. "I have a wonderful family," he stated. "I am a happy man." In 2006, he died at home after battling prostate cancer and Alzheimer's disease.

Summary

Shy and insecure, Floyd Patterson turned away from childhood behaviors that pointed to a life of crime. A kindhearted teacher and a fatherly boxing manager turned his life in a positive direction. Floyd was not the greatest heavyweight champion in the world, but he may have been the most durable.

J. Christopher Schnell

Additional Sources

Liebling, A. J. *The Sweet Science.* Reprint. New York: North Point, 2004.

Mullan, Harry, and Bob Mee. *The Ultimate Encyclopedia of Boxing.* London: Carlton, 2007.

Newcombe, Jack. *Floyd Patterson, Heavyweight King.* New York: Bartholomew House, 1961.

Patterson, Floyd, and Bert Randolph Sugar. *The International Boxing Hall of Fame's Basic Boxing Skills: A Step-by-Step Illustrated Introduction to the Sweet Science.* New York: Skyhorse, 2007.

Remnick, David. *Life Stories: Profiles from The New Yorker.* New York: Random House, 2000.

Schulman, Arlene. *The Prize Fighters: An Intimate Look at Champions and Contenders.* New York: Lyons and Burford, 1994.

Willie Pep

Born: September 19, 1922
Middletown, Connecticut
Died: November 23, 2006
Rocky Hill, Connecticut
Also known as: Guglielmo Papaleo (birth name); the Will o' the Wisp; Willie the Wisp

Early life

Willie Pep was born Guglielmo Papaleo in Middletown, Connecticut, on September 19, 1922. He left high school at the age of sixteen to pursue boxing. During his amateur career, he won two Connecticut state titles: the flyweight, in 1938, and the bantamweight, in 1939. By this time, he had changed his name to Willie Pep. Many Italian fighters of the time, including heavyweight champion Rocky Marciano, did this to make their names more familiar to fans and reporters. Willie lost only three times as an amateur, once to Ray Robinson. Willie left the amateur ranks with a record of 62-3.

The Road to excellence

In 1940, at the age of seventeen, Willie turned professional and won his first 62 bouts. On July 3, 1940, in Hartford, Connecticut, he faced James McGovern in his first professional fight; he won a 4-round decision. Willie continued to win. He defeated notable contenders, including Joey Archibald and Pedro Hernandez, by decision.

On November 20, 1942, in New York City, Willie won a 15-round decision over Chalky Wright for the New York State featherweight championship. He defended that title three times: against Sal Bartolo, in Boston, Massachusetts, in June, 1943; against Wright, in New York City, in September, 1944; and against Phil Terranova, in New York City, in February, 1945. He won all these fights with 15-round decisions. During this time, he also suffered his first defeat, losing to lightweight champion Sammy Angott in New York on March 19, 1943, in a nontitle bout. Willie won his next 73 bouts. While Willie held the New York state title, the United States became involved in World War II. Willie served in both the Navy and the Army and was discharged in January, 1944. In May, 1946, Willie's professional boxing record stood at 97-1-1, with 30 knockouts.

The Emerging Champion

On May 27, 1946, in New York City, Willie faced National Boxing Association featherweight champion Bartolo for the undisputed featherweight title. Willie won this fight in the twelfth round with a rare knockout. Willie continued fighting in both title and nontitle bouts. On July 25, 1946, an apocryphal tale emerged from Willie's fight with Jackie Graves in Minneapolis, Minnesota. According to the story, Willie won a round without throwing a punch. He used evasive tactics to make Graves miss wildly throughout the round and compelled the judges to score it in his favor. Some have doubted this story, saying Willie threw not a few but many punches in that round.

Willie's career nearly ended on January 8, 1947, when he was involved in an airplane crash in Millville, New Jersey. The crash killed some passengers on board. Many suspected that, with a broken back and leg, Willie would never fight again. However, he surprised the boxing world, making a re-

Statistics

Bouts, 241

Knockouts, 65

Bouts won by decision, 164

Knockouts by opponents, 6

Bouts lost by decision, 5

Draws, 1

Milestones and Awards

1942-48, 1949-50	World Featherweight Champion
1963	Inducted into the *Ring* magazine Boxing Hall of Fame
1977	Inducted into the National Italian American Sports Hall of Fame
1990	Inducted into the International Boxing Hall of Fame
2002	Ranked sixth best fighter from the previous eighty years (*Ring* magazine)

covery and defeating Victor Flores only five months later. However, many felt that Willie lost something physically as a result of the plane crash. He made two defenses of his title. He defeated Jock Leslie by twelfth-round knockout in Flint, Michigan, in August, 1947; then, he beat Humberto Sierra by a tenth-round knockout in Miami, Florida, in February, 1948.

Continuing the story

In October, 1948, Willie began a four-fight series that defined his career. These fights were against Sandy Saddler. In their first bout, held in October, 1948, in New York's Madison Square Garden, Willie was defeated for the first time in six years, losing his title. Saddler had a three-inch height advantage over Willie and was able to hamper the smooth flowing defense of the Will 'o the Wisp. He knocked Willie down twice in the third round and knocked him out in the fourth. In February, 1949, in the rematch, also held in Madison Square Garden, Willie, cut on both eyes, survived near knockdowns in the tenth and fourteenth rounds to win a decision, regaining his title. *Ring* magazine declared this bout "the fight of the year."

After successful title defenses against Eddie Compo, Charley Riley, and the French fighter Ray Famechon, Willie fought Saddler a third time. In September, 1950, at Yankee Stadium, Willie was knocked down in the third round but was ahead on the judges' scorecards after the seventh, when he had to concede the fight with a dislocated shoulder. A year later, Willie met Saddler for the last time, losing by technical knockout in the ninth round when he quit because of a closed right eye. This fight, refereed by Ray Miller, was marred by dirty tactics committed by both Willie and Saddler, prompting the New York State Athletic Commission to suspend both fighters.

After his seven-month suspension, Willie continued fighting until 1959 and fought again briefly in 1965 and 1966. He never again challenged for the world title. However, in September, 1958, he was leading featherweight champion Hogan Bassey after 8 rounds of a 10-round fight before getting knocked out.

Summary

Willie is remembered by many as one of the greatest fighters of all time. His strength was in his defense; he had an ability to hit and move away from his opponents before they could hit back. In 1990, he became a charter member of the International Boxing Hall of Fame in Canastota, New York. With 229 victories in his career, he set the record for most wins of any world champion. Willie held the New York world featherweight title from 1942 to 1946 and the featherweight world championship from 1946 to 1948 and from 1949 to 1950.

Brett Conway

Additional Sources

Hauser, Thomas, and Stephen Brunt. *The Italian Stallions: Heroes of Boxing's Glory Days.* Toronto: Sport Media, 2003.

Heinz, W. C. *Once They Heard the Cheers.* Garden City, N.Y.: Doubleday, 1979.

Heller, Peter. *In This Corner . . . ! Forty World Champions Tell Their Stories.* New York: Simon and Schuster, 1973.

Sugar, Bert Randolph. *Boxing's Greatest Fighters.* Guilford, Conn.: Lyons Press, 2006.

Sugar Ray Robinson

Born: May 3, 1921
    Ailey, Georgia
Died: April 12, 1989
    Culver City, California
Also known as: Ray Robinson; Walker Smith, Jr. (given name)

Early Life
On May 3, 1921, Sugar Ray Robinson was born Walker Smith, Jr., to Walker and Marie Smith. When, as a fifteen-year-old flyweight, he needed an Amateur Athletic Union card to qualify for his first match, Walker, Jr., used the card of a retired amateur boxer. From then on, he fought under the name on that card, Ray Robinson. Later, after a sportswriter called him "Sugar Ray," he adopted that as his legal name.

Young Walker frequently visited Detroit's Brewster Center Gymnasium to watch the workouts of Joe Barrow, another amateur, later known as Joe Louis. Louis and Robinson remained lifelong friends. In 1932, Walker moved to New York City with his mother and two sisters. Walker helped out by doing odd jobs, including dancing on sidewalks and selling Harlem River driftwood. He left DeWitt Clinton High after only three years, changed his name, and became a boxer.

The Road to Excellence
His manager, then and throughout his career, was George Gainford. By 1940, Ray Robinson had won all eighty-five of his amateur bouts and earned the Golden Gloves featherweight (1939) and lightweight (1940) titles. It seemed that he could not be beaten. Ray's amateur experience gave him a confident, even cocky, attitude. These amateur bouts were a sensible, gradual preparation for his first professional fight in October, 1940, at the age of nineteen. In that debut, Ray knocked out Joe Eschevarria in two rounds at Madison Square Garden.

Sugar Ray later told how, on that October night, watching tough Fritzie Zivic defeat Henry Armstrong, he vowed to avenge his onetime idol. He fulfilled this promise, first by a decision and, in 1942, by a tenth-round knockout.

The Emerging Champion
Sugar Ray won his first forty fights, thirty-two by knockout. His record was 123-1 from 1940 through 1951. His only loss came in 1943, by a decision to a heavier Jake LaMotta.

World War II affected the lives of all Americans, including Sugar Ray's. He was drafted into the Army in March of 1943. After basic training, he was promoted to sergeant and assigned to Joe Louis's boxing group. He spent his two-year tour of duty giving boxing exhibitions at military bases and hospitals.

Sugar Ray married Edna Mae Holly in 1943. The marriage was his second and produced a son, Ray, Jr. In 1965, he married his third wife, Millie.

Sugar Ray Robinson, who was the middleweight champion five times in the 1950's. (Library of Congress)

Recognized World Welterweight Championships

Date	Location	Loser	Result
Dec. 20, 1946	New York, N.Y.	Tommy Bell	15th-round decision
June 24, 1947	Cleveland, Ohio	Jimmy Doyle	8th-round knockout
Dec. 19, 1947	Detroit, Mich.	Chuck Taylor	6th-round knockout
June 28, 1948	Chicago, Ill.	Bernard Docusen	15th-round decision
July 11, 1949	Philadelphia, Pa.	Kid Gavilan	15th-round decision
Aug. 9, 1950	Jersey City, N.J.	Charley Fusari	15th-round decision

Recognized World Middleweight Championships

Date	Location	Loser	Result
June 5, 1950	Philadelphia, Pa.	Robert Villemain	15th-round decision
Aug. 25, 1950	Scranton, Pa.	Jose Basora	1st-round knockout
Oct. 28, 1950	Philadelphia, Pa.	Carl (Bobo) Olson	12th-round knockout
Feb. 14, 1951	Chicago, Ill.	Jake LaMotta	13th-round technical knockout
July 10, 1951	London, England	Sugar Ray Robinson (Randy Turpin, winner)	15th-round decision
Sept. 12, 1951	New York, N.Y.	Randy Turpin	10th-round technical knockout
Mar. 13, 1952	San Francisco, Calif.	Carl (Bobo) Olson	15th-round decision
Apr. 16, 1952	Chicago, Ill.	Rocky Graziano	3d-round knockout
Dec. 9, 1955	Los Angeles, Calif.	Carl (Bobo) Olson	4th-round knockout
May 18, 1956	Los Angeles, Calif.	Carl (Bobo) Olson	4th-round knockout
Jan. 2, 1957	New York, N.Y.	Sugar Ray Robinson (Gene Fullmer, winner)	15th-round decision
May 1, 1957	Chicago, Ill.	Gene Fullmer	5th-round knockout
Sept. 23, 1957	New York, N.Y.	Sugar Ray Robinson (Carmen Basilio, winner)	15th-round decision
Mar. 25, 1958	Chicago, Ill.	Carmen Basilio	15th-round decision
Jan. 22, 1960	Boston, Mass.	Sugar Ray Robinson (Paul Pender, winner)	15th-round decision
June 10, 1960	Boston, Mass.	Sugar Ray Robinson (Paul Pender, winner)	15th-round decision

Recognized World Light Heavyweight Championship

Date	Location	Loser	Result
June 25, 1952	New York, N.Y.	Sugar Ray Robinson (Joey Maxim, winner)	14th-round knockout

During his prime, Sugar Ray may have been the greatest boxer of all time. Veteran ring broadcaster Don Dunphy rates him in the top four, with Rocky Marciano, Joe Louis, and Muhammad Ali. Sugar Ray was extremely fast, with great timing and balance, which enabled him to throw every type of punch known to boxing with optimum leverage. In addition, Sugar Ray was a serious student of the science of boxing.

Upon the retirement of welterweight champion Marty Servo, Sugar Ray won that title in a fifteen-round decision over Tommy Bell at Madison Square Garden in December, 1946. Sugar Ray defended his title five times in four years. In 1947, a victory over Jimmy Doyle in Cleveland proved extremely unfortunate: Doyle died the next day. Sugar Ray contributed $4,000 of his $5,000 purse to Doyle's family.

Among Sugar Ray's other unsuccessful challengers were Kid Gavilan (1949) and Charley Fusari (1950). Sugar Ray contributed his entire purse from this last fight to the Damon Runyon Cancer Fund. Over the years, Sugar Ray frequently donated his winnings to worthy causes. In 1950, he was awarded the Edward J. Neil Trophy, for the year's outstanding boxer, by the New York Boxing Writers Association.

In December, 1950, Sugar Ray toured Europe as a middleweight, winning five bouts in five weeks, four of them against European champions or former champions. Sugar Ray became Europe's boxing idol after this incredible achievement.

Back in the United States, Sugar Ray challenged Jake LaMotta for his middleweight crown on February 14, 1951. Sugar Ray had won three of their four previous bouts; LaMotta was the only man who had bested Sugar Ray in the ring. Weighing in at 155 pounds, Sugar Ray captured the championship from a bloodied but still standing LaMotta in the thirteenth round.

Continuing the Story

Thirty years old and entering a heavier boxing class, Sugar Ray moved into troubles in the ring. In

> ## Statistics
>
> Bouts, 202
> Knockouts, 110
> Bouts won by decision, 65
> Knockouts by opponents, 1
> Bouts lost by decision, 18
> Draws, 6
> No contests, 2
>
> ## Records
>
> Only professional boxer to win, and then recapture, the world championship title five times at the same weight classification
>
> ## Honors and Awards
>
> | | |
> |---|---|
> | 1939 | New York Golden Gloves featherweight champion |
> | 1939-40 | Inter-City Golden Gloves lightweight champion, New York versus Chicago |
> | 1940 | New York Golden Gloves lightweight champion |
> | 1942, 1951 | *Ring* magazine Merit Award |
> | 1950 | Edward J. Neil Trophy |
> | 1967 | Inducted into *Ring* magazine Boxing Hall of Fame |
> | 1975 | Inducted into Black Athletes Hall of Fame |
> | 1990 | Inducted into International Boxing Hall of Fame |

July, 1951, he lost his crown to English boxer Randy Turpin on points—only his second loss. He regained the championship in September. Bleeding from a head butt in the tenth round, Sugar Ray launched a furious attack to win by a technical knockout.

In April, 1952, Ray won a savage match over Rocky Graziano. In June of that year, his bid for Joey Maxim's light heavyweight title ended in a bizarre "knockout," the only one of Ray's career. The 104-degree heat had forced referee Ruby Goldstein to retire in the tenth round. Insurmountably ahead on points, with Maxim merely covering up and holding, Sugar Ray collapsed in his corner after the thirteenth round.

Sugar Ray retired after the Maxim fight to try his hand as a song-and-dance nightclub act. He returned to the ring in 1955, regaining the middleweight title by defeating Bobo Olson. In 1957, he lost the title to Gene Fullmer, again regained it, and lost it to Carmen Basilio, then took it back the next year. The Basilio bouts, both fifteen-round split decisions, were among Sugar Ray's toughest. By the time of his final retirement in 1965, Sugar Ray's record stood at 175 wins, 110 knockouts, and six draws. Most of his nineteen losses came while he was in his forties.

Throughout his career, Sugar Ray was a generous philanthropist. He gave tens of thousands of dollars to veterans' organizations, cancer and infantile paralysis research, the B'nai B'rith, and needy friends. He was the founder of the Sugar Ray Youth Foundation. Sugar Ray died on April 12, 1989, in Culver City, California.

Summary

Sugar Ray Robinson was welterweight champion from 1946 to 1951. He relinquished that title because he moved up to the middleweight division, whose crown he won five times between 1951 and 1960. In 1967, he was inducted into the *Ring* magazine Boxing Hall of Fame. After retiring, he devoted his life to helping children through his Los Angeles-based youth foundation, which continued to flourish under the care of his wife, Millie, after he died in 1989.

Daniel C. Scavone

Additional Sources

Blewett, Bert. *The A-Z of World Boxing: An Authoritative and Entertaining Compendium of the Fight Game from Its Origins to the Present Day.* Rev. ed. Parkwest, N.Y.: Robson Books, 2002.

Boyd, Herb, and Ray Robinson. *Pound for Pound: A Biography of Sugar Ray Robinson.* New York: Amistad, 2006.

Heller, Peter. *In This Corner . . . ! Forty World Champions Tell Their Stories.* 2d ed. New York: Da Capo Press, 1994.

Robinson, Sugar Ray, and Dave Anderson. *Sugar Ray: The Sugar Ray Robinson Story.* London: Robson, 1992.

Schiffman, Sheldon M. *Sugar Ray Robinson: Beyond the Boxer.* Nashville, Tenn.: Express Media, 2004.

Shropshire, Kenneth L. *Being Sugar Ray: The Life of Sugar Ray Robinson, America's Greatest Boxer and First Celebrity Athlete.* New York: BasicCivitas, 2007.

Sugar, Bert Randolph. *Boxing's Greatest Fighters.* Guilford, Conn.: Lyons Press, 2006.

Sandy Saddler

Born: June 23, 1926
  Boston, Massachusetts
Died: September 18, 2001
  Bronx, New York
Also known as: Joseph Saddler (full name)

Early Life
Sandy Saddler was born in Boston, Massachusetts, of parents from the West Indies. He grew up in New York City, beginning his boxing career as an amateur at the Police Athletic League. He had about 50 amateur fights and lost only three or four. In 1944, at the age of seventeen, he turned professional. He won his first fight but was knocked out in his second, the only knockout he suffered in his professional career.

The Road to Excellence
Sandy had 94 professional fights before he was given a shot at the featherweight title. He was known for a rough style of fighting; he used his gloves, his thumbs, his elbows, his knees, and whatever else he could to wear down his opponents. Because of this style of fighting, many considered him a dirty fighter instead of a great one. Sandy, a tall featherweight, had excellent movement in the ring and was known for having a precise jab, one that never compromised his balance. He also had one of the best right hands in boxing history.

In 1945, Sandy won all 24 of his bouts, 14 by knockout. In 1946, he lost a decision to Phil Terranova, the National Boxing Association featherweight champion, in a nontitle bout. On May 2, 1947, he knocked out Joe Brown, who later became a great lightweight champion. He then drew with later champion Jimmy Carter. On October 29, 1948, Sandy finally got his chance to fight for the featherweight title. He faced champion Willie Pep, who was making the fourth defense of his undisputed featherweight title and came into the fight with an impressive record of 134-1-1. That night, in Madison Square Garden, Sandy knocked Pep down twice in the third round and then finished him off in the fourth, winning the featherweight title.

The Emerging Champion
Sandy and Pep had 3 more fights, completing a 4-fight series that cemented each fighter's legacy. On February 11, 1949, Sandy faced Pep again, but this time, Sandy was the champion. The fight set an indoor attendance record of 19,097, and Pep fought what experts believe was the fight of his life; he outpointed Sandy for the world title. During the fight, Sandy cut Pep on both eyes and nearly knocked him down in the tenth and fourteenth rounds. Before fighting a third time, Sandy stayed busy. He won a decision over Harold Dade, the former bantamweight champion. He stopped later lightweight champion Paddy DeMarco in 9 rounds. On December 6, 1949, in Cleveland, Ohio, he won the lightly regarded super-featherweight

Sandy Saddler. (Hulton Archive/Getty Images)

championship when he defeated Cuban Orlando Zulueta in 10 rounds, becoming the first boxer to hold the super-featherweight title since 1935. He defended this title twice. He stopped Mexican Lauro Salas in 9 rounds in Cleveland. He then traveled to Havana, Cuba, and defeated Diego Sosa in 2 rounds.

Continuing the Story

Pep and Sandy had their third fight on September 8, 1950, at Yankee Stadium. In a dirty fight, Sandy forced Pep to retire after 7 rounds because of a dislocated shoulder. Sandy had knocked down Pep in the third round but was losing on the judges' cards at the time of the stoppage. Before their fourth fight, Sandy lost two decisions to DeMarco. However, between those fights, he knocked out Salas. On September 26, 1951, Sandy forced Pep to retire after 8 rounds. In a foul-filled fight that referee Ray Miller had trouble controlling, Pep's right eye was closed, which caused him to quit. The New York State Athletic Commission suspended both Sandy and Pep.

Sandy lost his next three nontitle bouts and did not get a chance to defend his featherweight title until 1955. He spent 1952 and 1953 in the Army. In 1954, he went to Paris, France, and knocked out Ray Famechon. In 1955, he defeated Teddy Davis in a 15-round decision, maintaining his title. He then defended his title for the last time when he knocked out Gabriel "Flash" Elorde from the Philippines in 13 rounds. Sandy's last fight was on April 14, 1956, a nontitle match that he lost to Larry Boardman. In 1956, Sandy damaged an eye in a taxicab accident; he was forced to retire in January, 1957. He finished with 103 knockouts, more than any other featherweight in history and in the top ten of all-time knockouts. Sandy worked as a trainer in the National Maritime Union Gymnasium of New York, where he coached sailors. He also trained professional boxers, including heavyweight champion George Foreman.

Summary

At 5 feet 8 inches, Sandy Saddler was tall for a featherweight and had a great knockout punch. *Ring* magazine ranked him fifth among power punchers. He was also known for using dirty tactics inside, which were plied successfully in three of his four fights against Pep. He finished with a career record of 144-16-2. He was featherweight champion from 1948 to 1949 and from 1950 to 1957. He was also junior lightweight champion from 1949 to 1951. Sandy felt he never got the respect he deserved, the kind of praise given to his rival Pep, because of racism in the United States.

Brett Conway

Statistics

Bouts, 162
Knockouts, 103
Bouts won by decision, 41
Knockouts by opponents, 1
Bouts lost by decision, 15

Milestones and Awards

Ranked fifth greatest puncher ever (*Ring* magazine)
Most career knockouts by a featherweight (103)
Inducted into *Ring* magazine Boxing Hall of Fame (1971)
Inducted into International Boxing Hall of Fame (1990)
Named second best featherweight of the twentieth century by the Associated Press
World Featherweight Champion (1948-49, 1950-57)

Additional Sources

Heller, Peter. *In this Corner . . . ! Forty World Champions Tell Their Stories.* New York: Simon and Schuster, 1973.

Pep, Willie, with Robert Sacchi. *Friday's Heroes: Willie Pep Remembers.* Bloomington, Ind.: Authorhouse, 2007.

Sugar, Bert Randolph. *Boxing's Greatest Fighters.* Guilford, Conn.: Lyons Press, 2006.

Félix Savón

Born: September 22, 1967
San Vicente, Cuba
Also known as: Félix Savó Fabre (full name)

Early Life

Félix Savón was born in San Vicente, Cuba, just eleven miles from the United States Navy base at Guantanamo. The son of peasants who later divorced, he grew up with few luxuries.

Félix began competing in sports at an early age, running track with his four sisters. In the fall of 1981 his sister Maure was accepted to a prestigious sports school in Guantanamo. Though Félix also wanted to attend, there were no spots open there for boys. Remaining at home, he participated in both track and rowing. By midterm in 1981, several boys had left the school, creating the opening Félix needed. The boxing coach came to Félix's house, offering him entry to the school. Félix was happy to compete in any sport, and boxing was chosen for him.

Weeks later, when he returned home for a visit, his mother saw that his hands were bruised and swollen. She wanted to pull him out of the school and told him that he would not be welcome to return home if he continued boxing. Félix tried to reassure her and eventually returned to school. Some months later his father also tried to get him to leave school. Officials told his father that Félix could leave only if his mother insisted, since he was living with her. His mother did not insist, and Félix was able to stay. That year he won a gold medal in the 1981 school games.

The Road to Excellence

In 1983 and 1984, Félix began to assert his dominance in Cuban boxing when he was twice awarded the Cuban Junior National Championship. By 1986, he was known outside Cuba. That year the nineteen-year-old dominated the heavyweight division and won the world championship crown. He followed up those wins with gold medals at the Pan-Am and World Cup Championships in 1987.

Félix's constant training and rigorous regimen pointed him toward the 1988 Olympics, where he was predicted to be the heavyweight champion. At 6 feet 4 inches and 201 pounds, he seemed assured of

Félix Savón at the Pan American games in 1996. (AP/Wide World Photos)

the title. Cuba, however, chose to boycott the Olympics that year, denying Félix his chance at a gold medal. He later had the chance to prove himself when he beat U.S. gold medalist Ray Mercer in a dual meet in Atlantic City, New Jersey. He may not have won the gold for his country, but he did prove that he was the heavyweight champion.

Many thought that twenty-two-year-old Félix should turn professional, but he refused. Although he made only 120 pesos per month boxing, supplemented by an additional 140 doing odd jobs at the sports school, he insisted that he boxed because he loved the sport and wanted to represent his country, not because he was interested in making money.

Between the 1988 and the 1992 Olympics, Félix added to his heavyweight titles, winning the world championships in both 1989 and 1991. In 1990, he won at the Goodwill Games and the World Championships Challenge. In 1991, he added a second Pan-American Games to his list of victories.

The Emerging Champion
At twenty-four, Félix had his first chance to win Olympic gold at the Games in Barcelona. In his early rounds he often appeared awkward, and he struggled in his quarterfinal round with American Danell Nicholson. By the third round it looked as if Félix would be eliminated until suddenly he landed a series of blows. He was unable to finish Nicholson but prevailed on points, winning 13 to 11. He had no problem in his final match, defeating Nigeria's David Izonritei 14 to 1. Félix emerged undefeated and won the gold medal.

Again he received offers to turn professional, and again he ignored them. Instead, he returned to Cuba to resume his training. The years following the 1992 Olympics were more of the same for Félix. Among his many victories were the 1993 World Amateur Boxing Championships, the 1994 World Goodwill Games, the 1995 Pan-American Games, and the 1995 World Amateur Boxing Championships. His trip to Atlanta for the 1996 Olympics added another gold medal to his many wins. With two Olympic gold medals, he was chasing his fellow countryman Teófilo Stevenson's three straight Olympic gold medals.

In 1997 and 1998, Félix proved to be the undisputed champion by again winning the World Amateur Boxing Championships and the Goodwill Games. In 1999, for the first time, Félix began showing his age but nevertheless brought home the silver medal from the 1999 World Amateur Boxing Championships.

Continuing the Story
Despite the defeat, Félix focused all of his attention on the 2000 Olympics in Sydney, Australia. He hoped to be able to tie Stevenson's record of three Olympic gold medals. His quarterfinal match was greatly anticipated. Félix was pitted against defending world champion Michael Bennett of the United States. The anticipation did not match the fight, however, and Félix won easily. The fight was called three seconds before the end of the third round because Félix was already winning by 15 points. He also won his semifinal match but received a cut under his left eye.

In the final match, he struggled against Russian Sultanhmed Ibzagimov. With only 14 seconds left in the fight, a blow from his opponent reopened the cut under Félix's eye. The referee stopped the fight in order to examine Félix. After the referee allowed the fight to continue, Félix evaded the Russian until the final bell was rung. He won, receiving a 20 to 12 judgment.

Félix's wife and five children, including his twin daughters, watched him on television, as did the rest of Cuba. In Sydney he tied Stevenson's record with his own three consecutive gold-medal wins. If

Major Championships

Year	Competition	Place
1985	World Junior Championships	1st
1986	World Championships	1st
1987	Pan-American Games	1st
	World Championships	1st
1989	World Championships	1st
1990	World Goodwill Games	1st
1991	Pan-American Games	1st
	World Championships	1st
1992	Olympic Games	Gold
1993	World Championships	1st
1994	World Goodwill Games	1st
1995	Pan-American Games	1st
	World Championships	1st
1996	Olympic Games	Gold
1997	World Championships	1st
1998	World Goodwill Games	1st
1999	World Championships	2d
2000	Olympic Games	Gold

Cuba had not boycotted the 1988 games, Félix could possibly have surpassed his idol by winning four gold medals. Félix retired after the 2000 Olympics.

Summary

During his impoverished childhood, Félix Savón had no idea that he would become a treasure in his Cuban homeland. Though not a polished fighter, he was powerful and driven. Throughout his career he refused offers to turn professional, once saying,

> I do not like professional boxing. There is a tremendous difference between Olympic-style and professional boxing. In the professional ranks the athlete is not protected at all, they don't take care of him at all, and of course the main interest is earning money. It's a dirty sport. In Olympic-style boxing, the amateur sport is clean and it's truly something that is good for the athlete.

With that attitude, he established himself as a heavyweight icon both inside and outside Cuba.

Deborah Service

Additional Sources

Blaudschun, Mark. "Félix's Superiority Shines Through in Bennett Battle." *Boston Globe*, September 27, 2000, p. G5.

Padgett, Tim, and Dolly Mascarenas. "Félix Félix." *Time* 156, no. 11 (September 11, 2000): 84.

Somrack, Daniel. *Cuban Legends of Boxing*. Guilford, Conn.: The Globe Pequot Press, 2006.

Max Schmeling

Born: September 28, 1905
Klein Luckow, Uckermark, Germany
Died: February 2, 2005
Hollenstedt, Germany
Also known as: Maximilian Adolph Otto Siegfried Schmeling (full name); Black Uhlan of the Rhine

German heavyweight Max Schmeling, who had a heavily publicized rivalry with Joe Louis in the 1930's. (Courtesy of Amateur Athletic Foundation of Los Angeles)

Early Life

Maximilian Adolph Otto Siegfried Schmeling was born September 28, 1905, in Klein Luckow, Uckermark, Germany, about seventy miles northwest of Berlin. His father was a pilot with a major steamship line and, soon after Max was born, moved his family to Hamburg, Germany's largest port city.

Max was nine when World War I broke out in 1914. His father lost his job; the family suffered greatly, often coming close to starving because of the blockade of the city. Thirteen years old when the war ended in 1918, Max had to find work because there was no money to continue his education.

As far back as he could remember, Max had wanted to be a boxer. At the time he was born, boxing was prohibited in Germany, but Max's father often talked about it and told his son that the English were the pioneers in the sport, having invented the rules. Therefore, in 1922, Max decided to leave Hamburg. With no money and trusting luck, he managed to get to Düsseldorf in the German Rhineland, then under English occupation.

The Road to Excellence

According to Max, luck and hard work enabled him to become a champion. He had no training in boxing, but he had a strong body, a good mind, and great enthusiasm. Max persuaded a merchant who was also a boxing enthusiast to give him a room and money to train. Beginning in 1924, Max devoted his life to boxing. Jack Dempsey, the American champion, whom Max resembled, became Max's model. Max managed to see several films of Dempsey and carefully studied his techniques. Dempsey visited Germany in 1924, and Max managed to spar with him, an experience he never forgot.

Max's promoter went bankrupt in 1926, and Max lost all his savings. By chance, he met Max Machon, a boxing manager from Berlin, who told Max that only in the capital could he make a name for himself in boxing. When he arrived in Berlin, Max did not even have

Recognized World Heavyweight Championships

Date	Location	Opponent	Result
June 12, 1930	New York, N.Y.	Jack Sharkey	4th-round win by foul
July 3, 1931	Cleveland, Ohio	Young Stribling	15th-round technical knockout
June 21, 1932	Long Island City, N.Y.	Max Schmeling (Jack Sharkey, winner)	15th-round split decision
June 22, 1938	New York, N.Y.	Max Schmeling (Joe Louis, winner)	1st-round knockout

enough money for car fare. Luck came his way again when he met Arthur von Bülow, the editor of the magazine *Boxsport*, who agreed to pay for the young man's continued training.

The Emerging Champion

Machon joined Max in Berlin, and together, Machon and von Bülow changed Max's life. After training up to fourteen hours a day, Max knocked out Max Diechmann on August 24, 1926, to become Germany's light-heavyweight champion. Max became the German heavyweight champion in 1928.

Because he had earned enough money, Max invited his widowed mother to live with him. Max also worked on improving his mind. Berlin was the cultural capital of Europe at the time, and Max managed to meet leading writers and artists who liked the attractive young boxer. Although Max learned from them, his boxing career always came first. He was in bed by ten o'clock every night; he never touched alcohol, tobacco, or other drugs.

Statistics

Bouts, 70
Knockouts, 38
Bouts won by decision, 15
Bouts won by fouls, 3
Knockouts by opponents, 5
Bouts lost by decision, 5
Draws, 4

Milestones

Awarded the Golden Ribbon of the German Sports Press Society
Named an honorary citizen of Los Angeles

Honors and Awards

1930   *Ring* magazine Merit Award
1970   Inducted into *Ring* magazine Boxing Hall of Fame

Although well known in Europe, Max knew that he would have to go to the United States to make money. He had studied American boxing techniques and knew them to be more brutal and dangerous than European methods, but he was prepared to take the risk.

Max, together with von Bülow and Machon, arrived in New York in 1930, but he could find no one to arrange the kind of match he wanted until he met Joe Jacobs, a fast-talking, streetwise native New Yorker who agreed to become his American manager. Jacobs arranged a match with Jack Sharkey, the American champion. Before any match, Max always tried to learn as much as possible about his opponent. He knew Sharkey had bad nerves and would do rash things. Max won the match on a disqualification to become the world champion, but it was a crown without real meaning. Max truly won the world championship when he knocked out Young Stribling in 1931, in Cleveland, Ohio.

Continuing the Story

In 1932, Max lost the heavyweight crown to Sharkey on points. Many, including Jacobs, disputed the decision, but Max accepted it.

Back in Germany in 1933, Max married the film actress Anny Ondra. Although nonpolitical, Max was disturbed by the Nazi takeover and the violent anti-Semitism of the regime. Unlike many of his artist friends, however, Max decided to stay in Germany.

In 1936, Max returned to the United States and reached the high point of his boxing career. On June 19, he defeated Joe Louis, who became world heavyweight champion the following year and is considered perhaps the greatest boxer at his weight in ring history. As with Sharkey, Max said his victory was the result of his having studied Louis's boxing techniques.

Max was embarrassed when the Nazis attempted to turn his victory into proof of black inferiority.

On June 22, 1938, the rematch between Max and Louis, held before seventy thousand spectators in Yankee Stadium in New York, was billed as the greatest event in boxing history. Grossing more than a million dollars, a huge sum during the Depression, it was both racially and politically motivated. The Nazis were so hated that Max had to be escorted to the ring under guard.

Determined to defend both the United States and his race, Louis attacked Max with unrelenting fury, knocking him out within 2 minutes and 4 seconds of the first round. Max was seriously injured from the bout and was never again the same fighter, although he won the European heavyweight boxing championship in 1939.

Max was drafted into the German army and served as a parachutist. After Germany's defeat in 1945, Max's home and property were confiscated. Although more than forty years old, he attempted a boxing comeback, without success, but managed to set himself up in business. Outgoing and friendly, the former heavyweight champion remained a popular and respected figure with both Germans and Americans.

Summary

Max Schmeling's long and distinguished career in boxing was proof that intelligence and a sense of fair play are as essential as a strong body to becoming a success. Max helped to raise boxing from a brutal, often illegal pastime to a respected sport. Some boxing experts rank Max Schmeling among the top ten heavyweight fighters in modern ring history.

Nis Petersen

Additional Sources

Erenberg, Lewis A. *The Greatest Fight of Our Generation: Louis Versus Schmeling.* New York: Oxford University Press, 2006.

Margolick, David. *Beyond Glory: Max Schmeling Versus Joe Louis and a World on the Brink.* London: Bloomsbury, 2006.

Myler, Patrick. *Ring of Hate: Joe Louis Versus Max Schmeling—The Fight of the Century.* New York: Arcade, 2006.

Schmeling, Max, and George B. von der Lippe. *Max Schmeling: An Autobiography.* Chicago, Ill.: Bonus Books, 1998.

Earnie Shavers

Born: August 31, 1945
Garland, Alabama
Also known as: Earnie Dee Shaver (birth name); the Acorn; Black Destroyer

Early Life

Earnie Shavers was born Earnie Dee Shaver in Garland, Alabama, on August 31, 1945. He was the fifth of ten children born to Curtis and Willie Belle Shaver. During Earnie's early years, his family lived a life of hard work and poverty in the pre-civil rights era South. The house where Earnie lived had no running water, electricity, or telephone, and he and his five brothers slept together in a single room. When he was five years old, he began picking cotton to help support his family. His mother, a deeply religious woman, was the force that kept the family together during these difficult times.

In 1950, an event occurred that brought a new direction to the life of the Shaver family. Earnie's father had purchased a mule from a white man and had been slowly paying back the debt he owed, but the bad cotton harvest meant he could not make the final two payments. When the white man came and tried to take back the mule, Earnie's father argued with him, a thing a black man was not permitted to do in the South at that time. That night the Ku Klux Klan came looking for Earnie's father, and he had to run for his life. He left Alabama and went north, taking refuge with a relative in Newton Falls, Ohio. He found work there and eventually sent money back to Alabama so that his family could join him. The family moved north in December of 1950.

The Road to Excellence

Life in Ohio marked a considerable improvement for the Shaver family. Among other things, the children gained an opportunity for a better education. Earnie attended the local elementary school, where he was encouraged in his studies. Later he got involved in athletics, and in his senior year at Newton Falls High School, he performed well in both football and track.

In 1963, after graduating from high school, Earnie found employment in a local factory, got married to a girl he had known in high school, and soon had two children to support. During this time, he became acquainted with a local gangster and began to get involved in criminal activities. In the back of his mind, however, he harbored a dream of becoming a professional athlete. In 1967, inspired by a local boxer named Richard Austin, Earnie traveled to Youngstown, Ohio, and visited the boxing gym where Austin trained. There, during a sparring session, he displayed the tremendous punching power that marked his career as a professional boxer.

The Emerging Champion

Between 1967 and 1969, Earnie, using the last name Shavers, pursued an amateur boxing career, beginning at the local Golden Gloves level and culminating in the national Amateur Athletic Union heavyweight title in 1969. Following this latter achievement, in November of 1969, he turned professional, signing with a management team that included Major League Baseball pitching star Dean Chance. From 1969 to 1972, Earnie compiled an amazing record of 44 wins and only 2 losses, with 43 of his victories coming by knockout. By the beginning of 1973, he was ranked tenth in the heavyweight division by the World Boxing Association.

Earnie's first fight of that year was against title contender Jimmy Young, over whom he scored a third-round knockout. After this victory he signed a management contract with the well-known boxing promoter Don King. Under King's guidance, Earnie participated in the fights that marked the

---

Statistics

Bouts, 89
Knockouts, 68
Bouts won by decision, 6
Knockouts by opponents, 7
Bouts lost by decision, 7

Honors and Awards

1969	Amateur Athletic Union heavyweight champion
1970-73	Won thirty-three consecutive fights

peak years of his career. Following temporary derailments when he was knocked out by Jerry Quarry, in December of 1973, and by heavy-hitting contender Ron Lyle, in September of 1975, he finally fought for the heavyweight title in September of 1977, losing a 15-round decision to the Muhammad Ali. In the Ali fight, Earnie hurt the champion badly in the second round, and, after the fight, Ali spoke of the tremendous power of Earnie's punches.

Continuing the Story
Following the title challenge against Ali, Earnie continued to fight and hold his own against the best fighters of the era. He fought twice with heavyweight Larry Holmes: He lost a 12-round decision in a World Boxing Council (WBC) title-elimination bout in 1978 and an eleventh-round technical knockout in a WBC heavyweight title fight two years later. In the second Holmes fight, Earnie knocked the champion down in the seventh round with a punch that had Holmes out cold for most of the count before he somehow managed to regain his feet. He also scored a first-round technical knockout over former champion Ken Norton. He continued to fight on a regular basis until 1983 and attempted brief comebacks in 1987 and 1995.

Summary
Earnie Shavers's significance as a boxer is twofold: He held a place in the heavyweight division during an era of great heavyweight fighters, and he was one of the hardest punchers in the history of the division. Earnie fought during an era that produced such heavyweight greats as Muhammad Ali, Larry Holmes, Ken Norton, Jerry Quarry, Ron Lyle, and Jimmy Young, and although he never won the heavyweight title, he fought all the greats on mostly even terms. His record of 74 victories, with 67 knockouts, and only 14 losses and 1 draw, attests to both his skill level and his devastating punching power.

Scott Wright

Additional Sources
Nack, William. "Pilgrimage to Mecca." *Sports Illustrated* 51, no. 14 (October 1, 1979).

Sharnik, Morton. "Importance of Being Earnie, Act I." *Sports Illustrated* 47, no. 11 (September 12, 1977).

Shavers, Earnie, Mike Fitzgerald, and Marshall Terrill. *Earnie Shavers: Welcome to the Big Time.* Champaign, Ill.: Sports, 2002.

Wiley, Ralph. "The Sum of the Month Club." *Sports Illustrated* 57, no. 4 (July 26, 1982).

Teófilo Stevenson

Born: March 29, 1952
Puerto Padre, Las Tunas, Cuba
Also known as: Teófilo Stevenson Lawrence (full name)

Early Life
The life of Teófilo Stevenson is not well known outside his native Cuba. He was born March 29, 1952, in Puerto Padre, Las Tunas, Cuba, an island only ninety miles from the United States but much more distant in way of life. When he was born, Cuba was a place where Americans went for their vacations. Life in Cuba changed seven years later, when Fidel Castro overthrew the government and communism was implemented.

Under a different political system, life did not become any easier. Teófilo and his family continued to live a peasant life. They did, however, obey a government ruling that mandated a participation in sports by the youth of the nation. Cuba had a long history of success in boxing. Two former world champions were national heroes in the years before Castro. Kid Chocolate was champion in the 1930's, and Kid Gavilan was world-famous twenty years later.

The Road to Excellence
When Teófilo was still in high school, his body was filling out. He weighed nearly 200 pounds by the time he was seventeen. He had the opportunity to participate in baseball, the national sport, or the one-on-one competition of boxing.

The Cuban government established schools to teach boxing. By 1970, Teófilo was learning his trade and winning three-round bouts against opponents throughout Cuba. Even though amateur bouts last only three three-minute rounds, Teófilo learned how difficult training was. As he trained, he had to box at full speed for three rounds, moving every second of the three minutes.

The Cuban government wanted its athletes to meet and defeat the best in the rest of the world. Every four years, the Pan-American Games are held. They are similar to the Olympics, with all the nations in North and South America taking part. At these games, the nearly 6-foot 6-inch future champion met different opponents who tested his ability. In 1971, Teófilo progressed all the way to the champion-

Cuba's Olympic champion Teófilo Stevenson. (Focus on Sport/Getty Images)

ship bout before losing to the American Duane Bobick.

The Emerging Champion

Defeat discourages some people, but Teófilo learned from this loss. In the Cuban style of boxing, the fighter stood tall and jabbed straight with the left hand. Teófilo had long arms and landed his jab easily. He also developed a right hand that was thrown straight and with power.

The boxing world soon learned how powerful Teófilo had become as a puncher. One year after losing to Bobick, Teófilo was in Munich, Germany, representing Cuba in the Olympic super heavyweight division. In the quarterfinals, Teófilo once again met Bobick. In round three, a series of hard blows closed Bobick's left eye, and he was put down for the full count. Teófilo went on to win the gold medal.

Cuba had its third world champion, and heavyweights are popular all over the world. In most countries, an Olympic champion becomes a professional. After Teófilo won the Olympic title, many promoters and managers from outside Cuba offered the champion almost $2 million to become a professional. Teófilo's reply was: "I believe in the revolution. I don't believe in professionalism." His ambition was to win three Olympic gold medals.

For two years after the 1972 Olympics, Teófilo fought throughout the world. In 1974, he fought and won the second most important amateur honor, the Amateur World heavyweight championship. More pressure was put on him to become a professional, but he wanted to win more amateur championships. In 1975, he won the Pan-American Games title that he failed to win in 1971.

The stage was set for the 1976 Olympics in Montreal. One of his opponents on the way to the finals was John Tate from the United States. Tate was knocked out in less than two minutes. Only two years after he was knocked out by Teófilo, Tate won the professional world heavyweight championship.

New contenders kept coming along to challenge the aging Teófilo. In 1978, he retained his World Amateur Boxing Championship, and the following year, he won a second Pan-American Games championship.

Continuing the Story

At the end of the 1970's, Teófilo had achieved all of his goals except for winning his third straight Olympic gold medal. That had been his stated goal since Munich in 1972. Controversy surrounded the 1980 Games held in Moscow. Many nations refused to take part because of the Soviet invasion of Afghanistan. In the final bout, Teófilo won a unanimous decision over the Soviet champion, Pyotr Zaev.

This Olympic title put him in a class with only one other three-time Olympic boxing champion, the legendary Hungarian László Papp—Félix Savón, another Cuban boxer, duplicated this feat in 2000. Papp, like Teófilo, came from a communist country and was not allowed to become a professional until he was more than thirty. Teófilo continued to compete in international bouts but was losing to young boxers he would have defeated a few years before.

There was a chance he could try for a fourth Olympic title in 1984. Once again, politics took control of sports. This time, Cuba refused to take part in the 1984 Games in Los Angeles.

A near-fatal accident closed out the active boxing career of Teófilo. A stove in his home exploded, and he suffered serious burns over much of his body. Reports out of Cuba about his condition were limited because of the government's control of the press. Eventually, he recovered from his burns.

Teófilo went on to teach and train the future amateur champions of his country. Much changed in the world after he was champion. He, however, continued to live in one of the most controlled nations in the world. By Cuban standards, he has lived a comfortable life. Moreover, he has what no government can either give or take away: the love and respect of his fellow Cubans.

Records

One of only two boxers to capture three Olympic gold medals
One of only two boxers to capture three Amateur World Championships

Honors, Awards, and Milestones

1972	World Trophy
1972, 1976, 1980	Gold medal, U.S. Olympic Boxing
1974, 1978, 1986	Amateur World heavyweight champion
1975, 1979	Gold medal, Pan-American Games

Summary

As a boxer, Teófilo Stevenson was feared for his accurate left jab, his overall hand speed, and his powerful right hand. As a citizen of Cuba, he was always loyal to the ideals of his nation. Teófilo's boxing career was a case of both what was and what might have been. In the world of amateur boxing, his name stands at the top. He was successful in world competition for a full decade. What might have been had he turned professional is something that will never be known. What is known is that he met and defeated many boxers who later became successful professionals.

Bruce Gordon

Additional Sources

Duncan, John. *In the Red Corner: A Journey into Cuban Boxing*. London: Yellow Jersey, 2001.

Mullan, Harry, and Bob Mee. *The Ultimate Encyclopedia of Boxing*. London: Carlton, 2007.

The Olympics: Athens to Athens 1896-2004. London: Weidenfeld & Nicolson, 2004.

Schulman, Arlene. *The Prize Fighters: An Intimate Look at Champions and Contenders*. New York: Lyons and Burford, 1994.

Somrack, Daniel. *Cuban Legends of Boxing*. Guilford, Conn.: The Globe Pequot Press, 2006.

Dick Tiger

Born: August 14, 1929
   Amaigbo, Orlu, Nigeria
Died: December 14, 1971
   Aba, Nigeria
Also known as: Richard Ihetu (birth name)

Early Life

Richard Ihetu, later to gain fame as Dick Tiger, was born on August 14, 1929, in Amaigbo, Orlu, Nigeria. With his four brothers and two sisters, he helped his parents work the farmland that gave them their meager existence.

The family moved to the capital city of Lagos when Dick was a teenager. As a young boy, he was taught to be polite and respectful. He always avoided fighting of any kind, but the English soldiers stationed in Lagos promoted boxing. Soon they were teaching the strong, growing boy the basic skills of the sport. By the time he was eighteen, Dick had reached the physical size and weight he would be for the rest of his life. He stood 5 feet 8 inches and weighed a solid 160 pounds. He became a professional boxer in his early twenties and fought sixteen times in nearly four years in his homeland. Dick earned only two hundred dollars for all these bouts.

The Road to Excellence

In 1955, he was already mature as a fighter. At twenty-six years of age, he went to London, England, for a chance at gaining world recognition and to earn a better living. He had to work a ten-hour-a-day factory job to pay for his lodging and training expenses. Success was not immediate, as he lost four straight bouts in England. He was seriously considering giving up and going back home to Nigeria when, at last, he won a fight with a dramatic one-round knockout, and his spirits were lifted. Until this time, he had no manager to help guide his career. Hogan Kid Bassey, a fellow Nigerian and featherweight world champion, introduced him to Jersey Jones and Jimmy August. They wanted to manage a champion as much as Dick wanted to be one.

Just twenty-one months after his first victory in England, Dick became a champion for the first time. He scored a nine-round knockout over Pat McAtee to win the British Empire middleweight title. This victory encouraged Dick's managers to take him to the United States in the summer of 1959. Dick's managers had a policy of never selecting easy opponents. Over a period of nine months, Dick fought eight times and won five times. He made his first visit to Canada in June, 1959, and surprisingly lost his Empire title. Less than six months later, however, he won back the title.

Dick Tiger in 1957. (Hulton Archive/Getty Images)

Recognized World Middleweight Championships

Date	Location	Loser	Result
Oct. 23, 1962	San Francisco, Calif.	Gene Fullmer	15th-round decision
Feb. 23, 1963	Las Vegas, Nev.	(Gene Fullmer, opponent)	15th-round draw
Aug. 10, 1963	Ibadan, Nigeria	Gene Fullmer	7th-round technical knockout
Dec. 7, 1963	Atlantic City, N.J.	Dick Tiger (Joey Giardello, winner)	15th-round decision
Oct. 21, 1965	New York, N.Y.	Joey Giardello	15th-round decision
Apr. 25, 1966	New York, N.Y.	Dick Tiger (Emile Griffith, winner)	15th-round decision

Recognized World Light Heavyweight Championships

Date	Location	Loser	Result
Dec. 16, 1966	New York, N.Y.	José Torres	15th-round decision
May 16, 1967	New York, N.Y.	José Torres	15th-round decision
Nov. 17, 1967	Las Vegas, Nev.	Roger Rouse	12th-round technical knockout
May 24, 1968	New York, N.Y.	Dick Tiger (Bob Foster, winner)	4th-round knockout

The Emerging Champion

Dick had a chance to gain the biggest prize of all, a world championship. To achieve that meant fighting one of the most rugged champions of the past fifty years, Gene Fullmer. Fighting the best people available was not common boxing practice, but Dick always believed in giving his best against the best.

On October 23, 1962, in San Francisco, California, the thirty-three-year-old Nigerian became world middleweight champion after fifteen hard-fought rounds. A crowning point in Dick's career came ten months later, when Dick returned to his native Nigeria to defend his title against Fullmer. Before his home folks, he won by stopping the American in seven rounds.

Eventually, Joey Giardello, a boxer from Philadelphia, took the title from Dick with a fifteen-round decision. Dick was thirty-four years of age, which is considered old for a fighter. Dick, however, was always well-conditioned, having led a life free from drinking and smoking. He surprised many people by winning the championship back from Giardello nearly two years later.

Just before turning thirty-seven, he lost his title for the last time by a decision to the legendary Emile Griffith. This seemed like a logical time to retire, but Dick had a wife and four children to support and needed to earn more money for the present as well as for the future.

Continuing the Story

A year after losing his middleweight championship, Dick added some extra weight to fight at the 175-pound light heavyweight level. Champion José Torres thought he would have an easy defense of his title against the aging Nigerian. On December 16, 1966, the fight was held in the famed Madison Square Garden in New York City. Dick surprised both Torres and the world by winning a fifteen-round decision. To prove the win was not just a stroke of luck, he fought Torres a second time and won again.

Following a knockout victory over Roger Rouse in Las Vegas, Nevada, Dick defended his title against Bob Foster, one of the hardest punchers of any weight division. Dick was thirty-eight years old and long past the time when boxers have retired. In round four, a big left hook put Dick down and out.

Dick continued to fight for two more years. His last professional bout was against his old foe Grif-

Statistics

Bouts, 81
Knockouts, 26
Bouts won by decision, 35
Knockouts by opponents, 2
Bouts lost by decision, 15
Draws, 3

Honors and Awards

1962, 1965	*Ring* magazine Merit Award
1962, 1966	Edward J. Neil Trophy
1974	Inducted into *Ring* magazine Boxing Hall of Fame
1991	Inducted into International Boxing Hall of Fame

fifth, when Dick was forty-one. When his ring battles were over, Dick returned to live in his native land, where, in the Nigerian-Biafra War, he lost much of the wealth he had earned in the ring.

Fate dealt Dick one last blow: He was diagnosed as having pancreatic cancer. The beloved hero of Nigeria died when he was only forty-two years of age.

Summary

Fans today may not remember the man who held two universally recognized championships. Dick Tiger was not a flamboyant athlete like many featured in the media today, but a quiet, unassuming man who was always gentle in manner. When he died, American writer and artist Ted Carroll summed him up in one simple sentence: "He was that rare individual whose abilities in his chosen profession matched his qualities as a man."

Bruce Gordon

Additional Sources

Ifaturoti, Damola. *Dick Tiger: The Life and Times of Africa's Most Accomplished World Boxing Champion.* Princeton, N.J.: Sungai Books, 2002.

Makinde, Adeyinka. *Dick Tiger: The Life and Times of a Boxing Immortal.* Tarentum, Pa.: Word Association, 2004.

Mee, Bob. *Boxing: Heroes and Champions.* Edison, N.J.: Chartwell Books, 1997.

Walsh, Peter. *Men of Steel: The Lives and Times of Boxing's Middleweight Champions.* London: Robson, 1993.

Félix Trinidad

Born: January 10, 1973
Fajardo, Puerto Rico
Also known as: Félix Juan Trinidad García (full name); Tito; Félix Trinidad, Jr.

Early Life
Félix "Tito" Juan Trinidad García was born in Puerto Rico on January 10, 1973, to Irma Garcia and Félix, Sr. At the age of twelve, Félix was introduced to boxing by his father, who had been a featherweight champion in 1979. Young Félix's talents were immediately recognized. With the guidance of his father, in a short time, he won five Puerto Rican national amateur championships and had an amateur career record of 51-6; twelve of the wins came by knockout. In all his efforts, he was supported by his three sisters, two brothers, and additional family members.

While Félix's amateur victories were impressive, his father was concerned that he had not developed the punching power needed to compete as a professional. The young athlete grew in strength and size until, in 1990, his punching power was equal to his boxing prowess, and he entered the professional arena.

The Road to Excellence
Félix's first ten professional bouts showcased his skills as a slugger. He defeated nine of the ten opponents by knockout. In his first thirty-six matches he achieved thirty victories by knockout, earning him the highest knockout percentage of any boxer in history.

Key elements in Félix's success were determination and the ability to overcome adversity. In the fourth round of a 1991 bout with Jake Rodriquez, Félix injured his left hand. In spite of excruciating pain, he continued to fight for six rounds, winning the bout by unanimous decision. The following year in Paris, France, he fought Argentina's Alberto Cortez. Cortez was a formidable opponent and knocked Félix down in the second round, the first knockdown of his professional career. Thinking he would end the bout in the third round, Cortez was surprised when Félix unleashed a barrage of punches that prompted the referee to stop the fight, declaring Félix the winner.

The Emerging Champion
In June of 1993, Félix fought two-time world champion Maurice Blocker for the International Boxing Federation (IBF) welterweight title. The match was short: Félix defeated his opponent in the second round, establishing his reputation as a champion with the prowess of a skillful boxer and a powerful knockout punch. In the same year, he successfully defended his title against the number-one contenders Luis Garcia and Anthony Stephens.

In 1994, Félix established himself as one of the best. On January 29 of that year, he fought and defeated Héctor "Macho" Camacho, an international favorite. After an eight-month break from boxing,

Félix Trinidad delivering a left cross to the head of Roy Jones, Jr. (Brendan McDermid/Reuters/Landov)

Recognized World Welterweight Championships

Date	Opponent	Result
June 19, 1993	Maurice Blocker	Knockout
Aug. 6, 1993	Luis Garcia	Knockout
Oct. 23, 1993	Anthony Stephens	Knockout
Jan. 29, 1994	Héctor Camacho	Win
Sept. 17, 1994	Luis Ramon Campas	Knockout
Dec. 10, 1994	Oba Carr	Knockout
Apr. 8, 1995	Roger Turner	Knockout
Nov. 18, 1995	Larry Barnes	Knockout
Feb. 10, 1996	Rodney Moore	Knockout
May 18, 1996	Freddie Pendleton	Knockout
Sept. 7, 1996	Ray Lovato	Knockout
Jan. 11, 1997	Kevin Lueshing	Knockout
Apr. 3, 1998	Mahenge Zulu	Knockout
Feb. 20, 1999	Pernell Whitaker	Win
May 29, 1999	Hugo Pineda	Knockout
Sept. 18, 1999	Oscar De La Hoya	Win

Recognized World Light-middleweight Championships

Date	Opponent	Result
Mar. 3, 2000	David Reid	Win
July 22, 2000	Mamadou Thiam	Knockout
Dec. 2, 2000	Fernando Vargas	Technical knockout

Recognized World Middleweight Championships

Date	Opponent	Result
May 12, 2001	William Joppy	Technical knockout
Sept. 29, 2001	Bernard Hopkins	Technical knockout (loss)

Félix returned to the ring to fight Luis Ramón "Yory Boy" Campas, who delighted the crowd and stunned Félix with a second-round knockdown. Campas's moment of glory was short-lived, however, as Félix returned in the fourth round to score a decisive victory over his opponent. In December, Félix was knocked down in the second round again as he faced Oba "Motor-City" Carr. Again, Félix rallied and scored an eighth-round technical knockout (TKO).

In 1995, Félix faced Roger "Stingray" Turner, the number-nine contender for the title. This time, the second round belonged to Félix; he delivered a left hook that ended the fight by TKO. By 1996, Félix had become a headliner, attracting large crowds and defeating both Rodney Moore and Freddie Pendleton.

Félix's first victory of 1997 was in a match against Kevin Lueshing. Once again, however, the second round proved unlucky for Félix, and Lueshing knocked Félix to the canvas. As in the past, Félix asserted his control in the third round and scored a TKO, winning his thirty-first match. In the summer of 1997, Félix moved up to the super-welterweight division to defeat Troy Waters at Madison Square Garden.

Continuing the Story

On April 3, 1998, more than twelve thousand fans filled the stands at the Coliseo de Ruben Rodriguez when Félix returned to Puerto Rico to defend his welterweight title against Zaire's Mahenge Zulu. The fight lasted four rounds before Zulu was defeated by TKO. In 1999, Félix returned to Madison Square Garden to defend his title against six-time world champion Pernell "Sweet Pea" Whitaker. After twelve rounds of fighting, the judges declared Félix the victor.

Attention turned to a bout between Félix and Oscar De La Hoya. However, Félix had to defeat Colombia's Hugo Pineda. Félix defended his title at the Roberto Clemente Coliseo before a crowd of eight thousand. He achieved victory in the fourth round and looked ahead to the De La Hoya fight.

The highly anticipated bout with De La Hoya took place on September 18, 1999. The two fighters, in spite of their physical similarities, were different. While De La Hoya was a matinee idol, with a large following and numerous endorsements, and had become a familiar face on television and in magazines, Félix was an island favorite who could boast of a large and enthusiastic following from the Puerto Rican community. Both fighters had earned reputations as hard hitters and knowledgeable boxers.

The fight lasted for twelve rounds, ending in a close but unchallenged victory for Félix and making him both the IBF and the World Boxing Council welterweight champion. On March 3, 2000, Félix, the double champion, continued to astound boxing fans in a bout with David Reid. He earned another victory and added the World Boxing Association (WBA) super-welterweight championship to his list of achievements. A bout with Fernando Vargas on December 2, 2000, made Félix the IBF titleholder and the undisputed king of the 154-pound division. *Ring* magazine named Félix the fighter of the year for 2000.

> **Statistics**
>
> Bouts, 45
> Knockouts, 35
> Bouts won by decision, 7
> Knockouts by opponents, 1
> Bouts lost by decision, 2

On May 12, 2001, as part of an effort to unify the WBA middleweight crown, Félix defeated William Joppy in the first round. Later that year, at Madison Square Garden, he lost a championship fight to Bernard Hopkins when Félix, Sr., threw in the towel, and the referee stopped the match in the twelfth round. Félix fought once more before he retired following a May, 2002, fourth-round victory over former middleweight champion Hacine Cherifi.

After a twenty-nine-month retirement, Félix won against Ricardo Mayorga before one of his worst performances in a May, 2005, loss to Ronald Wright in Las Vegas. Wright pounded Félix with a right jab, and Félix could not get inside to use his power. In frustration, he struck Wright below the belt and lost a point in the ninth round for doing so. Always one of boxing's biggest draws, Félix took home $8 million for the fight. On May 16, 2005, he announced his second retirement at the urging of his father but, like many fighters, he found putting down the gloves difficult and missed the feeling of a big win.

On January 19, 2008, Félix returned to the ring but lost a unanimous decision to legendary boxer Roy Jones, Jr. Félix's record dropped to 42 wins (35 by knockout) and 3 losses (1 by knockout). Félix contemplated another fight, perhaps at the welterweight level.

Summary

Félix Trinidad became a beloved Puerto Rican icon who mastered the skill of boxing and defeated the best opponents the sport had to offer. His many titles are testament to his hard work and natural talent. Eventually, he will take a place in the International Boxing Hall of Fame.

Don Evans, updated by Caryn E. Neumann

Additional Sources

Hoffer, Richard. "Class Dismissed." *Sports Illustrated*, September 27, 1999, 56.

Nack, William. "Star Power." *Sports Illustrated*, February 19, 1996, 30.

"Oscar vs. Félix." *Sports Illustrated*, September 20, 1999, 29.

Schulberg, Budd. *Ringside: A Treasury of Boxing Reportage.* Chicago: Ivan R. Dee, 2006.

"The Upper Hand." *Sports Illustrated*, March 13, 2000, 52.

Gene Tunney

Born: May 25, 1897
New York, New York
Died: November 7, 1978
Greenwich, Connecticut
Also known as: James Joseph Tunney (full name); the Fighting Marine

Early Life

Gene Tunney's background was unusual for a boxer. He was born on May 25, 1897, in Greenwich Village in New York City, of Irish descent. He graduated from parochial school in 1911 and from La Salle Academy in 1915. His educational level exceeded that of many other boxers, and his interest in learning never left him. After his schooling ended, he worked for the Ocean Steamship Company of New York as a clerk. When the United States entered World War I in 1917, Gene enlisted in the Marine Corps and went to France with the American Expeditionary Force (AEF). In 1919, he won the light-heavyweight championship of the AEF.

The Road to Excellence

After Gene's discharge from the Marines, he decided to become a professional boxer. The choice was unusual for someone of his educational background, but he had proved his talent in the Marines and believed that he had a chance to become a success.

Gene had to overcome a major obstacle: He was not an extremely powerful puncher like his greatest rival, Jack Dempsey. Fighting skill did not come naturally to Gene, and his achievements were the result of hard work and study. His style emphasized correct technique rather than slugging away at the opponent. He rarely made a mistake in the ring and, although through experience he developed a strong knockout punch, he often won his matches by outscoring his opponents.

Gene's methodical approach went even further. He carefully studied other boxers, learning their strengths and weaknesses and continually adding to his store of techniques. He also scouted his opponents and was thoroughly familiar with the styles of the men he fought. Gene's careful preparation paid off, and he became a successful light heavyweight. He won the U.S. light-heavyweight championship in 1922 and lost only one match in his career in that division.

The Emerging Champion

Gene's one loss was to Harry Greb, one of the toughest light heavyweights of all time and probably the dirtiest of all major fighters. Greb had amazing endurance and was able to withstand Gene's punches while dishing out a continual assortment of low blows and punches to the back of the neck. One of Greb's favorite techniques was a head butt, delivered when the fighters were clinched. He never let up and gave Gene a severe beating.

Heavyweight champion Gene Tunney, who won eighty of his eighty-six fights. (Courtesy of Amateur Athletic Foundation of Los Angeles)

Statistics

Bouts, 77
Knockouts, 43
Bouts won by decision, 21
Bouts won by fouls, 1
Bouts lost by decision, 2
Draws, 1
No decisions, 8
No contests, 1

Honors and Awards

1928	*Ring* magazine Merit Award
1941	Walker Memorial Award
1954	Inducted into *Ring* magazine Boxing Hall of Fame
1990	Inducted into International Boxing Hall of Fame

Gene took the loss in stride and continued with his program of boxing study and rigorous training. He refused to let the setback interfere with his career and, in 1923, defeated Greb to regain the light-heavyweight title. In 1924, he defeated Georges Carpentier, the most popular fighter in France.

Gene then entered the heavyweight division, where he faced his supreme challenge. The world heavyweight champion was Jack Dempsey, considered by most boxing authorities as one of the greatest fighters of all time. He was also one of the hardest punchers in the history of boxing, and few opponents remained standing after Dempsey had rushed at them with a rain of blows. Gene followed his usual plan. He made a careful study of Dempsey and decided to try to outbox the fierce champion. Gene's plan proved a success in the match, held in Philadelphia on September 23, 1926. His steady jabs wore out Dempsey, and he did not succumb to the temptation to abandon science and become involved in a slugfest. To do so with Dempsey would have been fatal. At the end of the tenth round, Dempsey was out on his feet and Gene won a unanimous decision. He had won the title by defeating a boxing legend.

Continuing the Story

Many boxing fans dismissed Gene's victory as a fluke. Dempsey had not trained much for the bout and had been upset and distracted because of legal disputes with his former manager Jack Kearns. Like Gene, Dempsey was a man of great fortitude, and he was determined to regain his title.

Gene had to face another problem. His scientific style and refusal to slug toe-to-toe with opponents were not popular with the fans. Even worse for his popularity, Jack Dempsey was extremely well liked, and Gene's victory won him few new friends.

Gene was undaunted and once more followed his characteristic methods of careful training and preparation for the return match with Dempsey. The bout, this time held in Chicago, took place on September 22, 1927, one year after Gene had won the title.

Gene's methods at first proved highly successful. Even against a much better trained Dempsey, Gene's boxing skill put him well ahead until the seventh round, when Dempsey sprang at Tunney with one of his famed charges, backed him into a corner, and knocked him down.

Instead of retreating to a neutral corner, as the rules of the match required, Dempsey stood over his opponent for several seconds. Exactly how long he did this has been much disputed, but it was at least four seconds before the referee began his count. Gene was able to get up before the count reached ten. By the next round, he was ready to resume his former tactics, and he continued to outscore Dempsey until the end of the match. He was awarded a unanimous decision. The "long count" made this match one of the most controversial bouts in the history of heavyweight fighting.

After defeating Tom Heeney in 1928, Gene retired from boxing. He served as a corporate director for a number of businesses and banks and was chairperson of the board of the American Distilling Company. His business career was inter-

Recognized World Heavyweight Championships

Date	Location	Opponent	Result
Sept. 23, 1926	Philadelphia, Pa.	Jack Dempsey	10th-round unanimous decision
Sept. 22, 1927	Chicago, Ill.	Jack Dempsey	10th-round unanimous decision
July 26, 1928	New York, N.Y.	Tom Heeney	11th-round technical knockout

rupted by World War II, in which he served as director of physical fitness for the United States Navy. He died in 1978.

Summary

Gene Tunney illustrated the virtue of careful preparation. Although not the most naturally gifted heavyweight boxer of his era, he was one of the most intelligent. He made boxing into a genuine science and planned his bouts with the skill of a general going into battle. His technique enabled him to conquer one of the most powerful of all heavyweight boxers.

Bill Delaney

Additional Sources

Cavanaugh, Jack, and Gene Tunney. *Tunney: Boxing's Brainiest Champ and His Upset of the Great Jack Dempsey.* New York: Random House, 2006.

Evans, Gavin. *Kings of the Ring: The History of Heavyweight Boxing.* London: Weidenfeld & Nicolson, 2005.

Evensen, Bruce J. *When Dempsey Fought Tunney: Heroes, Hokum, and Storytelling in the Jazz Age.* Knoxville: University of Tennessee Press, 1996.

Jarrett, John. *Gene Tunney: The Golden Guy Who Licked Jack Dempsey Twice.* London: Robson, 2003.

Van Every, Edward. *The Life of Gene Tunney: The Fighting Marine.* New York: Dell, 1926.

Mike Tyson

Born: June 30, 1966
Brooklyn, New York
Also known as: Michael Gerard Tyson (full name); Iron Mike; Kid Dynamite

Early Life
Michael Gerard Tyson was born on June 30, 1966, in a rough section of Brooklyn, New York. He was the youngest of three children and never knew his father. Growing up in the Brownsville slums, he seemed destined to live a life of poverty and crime. Mike spent much of his boyhood in a gang, vandalizing his neighborhood. On the verge of becoming a serious criminal, Mike was sent to a reformatory school in upstate New York. Even that school could not handle Mike's violent temperament, and he was sent to another school reserved for the most difficult students. A counselor saw Mike's athletic potential and began to teach him boxing fundamentals. The discipline of the sport helped to reform Mike, and his school performance improved.

Mike Tyson knocking out Trevor Berbick to become the heavyweight champion in 1986. (AFP/Getty Images)

The Road to Excellence
The counselor introduced Mike to Gus D'Amato, a famous fight trainer and manager. Although D'Amato was seventy years old and Mike only thirteen, the trainer eventually became Mike's legal guardian. As Mike grew, D'Amato taught the younger fighter the skills and philosophies that took him to the top of the heavyweight boxing world.

In 1981 and 1982, Mike won the boxing Junior Olympiad championship. He also won the national Golden Gloves heavyweight championship in 1984. In March, 1985, Mike turned professional, winning his first bout by a knockout. His amazing succession of victories quickly gained the attention of the entire sporting world. Within twenty months, he won twenty-five fights, twenty-three by knockout.

As his opponents fell, Mike's stature rose. He gained nicknames like "Kid Dynamite" and "Iron Mike." Many experts saw the brash young fighter as the savior of a dull and listless division. Not since the days of Muhammad Ali had a heavyweight generated such interest.

The Emerging Champion
As Mike came onto the boxing scene, the heavyweight division was in disarray. The three boxing commissions, the International Boxing Federation (IBF), the World Boxing Association (WBA), and the World Boxing Council (WBC), each had a different champion. Many experts considered Mike the boxer most likely to unify the three titles.

Mike began his quest to unify the three belts by challenging Trevor Berbick for the WBC title. Mike beat Berbick by a knockout in the second round. On that day, November 22, 1986, Mike became the youngest heavyweight champion ever, at twenty years, five months. Four months later, on March 7, 1987, Mike beat James Smith for the WBA crown.

Tony Tucker, the IBF champion, was the last person standing between Mike and the undisputed heavyweight title. Tucker also proved to be Mike's toughest opponent. On August 1, 1987, the two fighters went the full twelve rounds in a close contest, which Mike won by unanimous decision.

Mike became the toast of the sports scene. The fighter's youth, charisma, and seeming invincibility vaulted him to worldwide popularity. He was also one of the world's richest athletes, having earned more than $60 million by 1989.

Continuing the Story

As Mike's fame spread, so did the reports on his background and personal life. Mike fueled a flood of stories with his whirlwind romance and sudden marriage to actress Robin Givens on February 7, 1988. The following eight months were among the most turbulent in Mike's life; divorce papers were filed on October 8, 1988.

In spite of a trying personal life, Mike continued his dominance in the ring. He reigned as the heavyweight champion for three years, with ten title defenses. Then, on February 10, 1990, Mike met lightly regarded James "Buster" Douglas, in Tokyo, Japan. Oddsmakers had refused to make odds on the fight because few people expected Douglas to last past the first round. Douglas, however, shocked the sports world with one of the most stunning upsets in boxing history.

Douglas controlled the fight until Mike knocked him down late in the eighth round, but Douglas came back strong, knocking out Mike in the tenth round. Undaunted, Mike was determined to regain his crown. Within one year of his defeat, Mike fought twice more, winning both bouts by knockouts. Before Mike could get a rematch, Douglas lost the title in a bout with Evander Holyfield in October, 1990.

In the months that followed, many people in the boxing world predicted that Mike would soon regain the heavyweight crown. His fearsome power and aggressive attitude restored him as a top contender. Mike won a twelfth-round unanimous decision over Donovan "Razor" Ruddock on June 28, 1990.

Then, Mike was accused of raping a contestant in the Miss Black America Pageant in an Indianapolis, Indiana, hotel room on the morning of July 19, 1991. In the aftermath, he became the target of two civil lawsuits alleging sexual harassment. Mike was formally indicted by a Marion County, Indiana, grand jury on October 10, 1991, and charged with rape.

In the interim, a world championship match with Holyfield, scheduled for November 8, was postponed after Mike injured his ribs during a training session. On February 10, 1992, Mike was

Recognized World Heavyweight Championships

Date	Location	Loser	Result
Nov. 22, 1986	Las Vegas, Nev.	Trevor Berbick	2d-round technical knockout
Mar. 7, 1987	Las Vegas, Nev.	James Smith	12th-round unanimous decision
May 30, 1987	Las Vegas, Nev.	Pinklon Thomas	6th-round technical knockout
Aug. 1, 1987	Las Vegas, Nev.	Tony Tucker	12th-round unanimous decision
Oct. 16, 1987	Atlantic City, N.J.	Tyrell Biggs	7th-round technical knockout
Jan. 22, 1988	Atlantic City, N.J.	Larry Holmes	4th-round technical knockout
Mar. 20, 1988	Tokyo, Japan	Tony Tubbs	2d-round knockout
June 27, 1988	Atlantic City, N.J.	Michael Spinks	1st-round knockout
Feb. 25, 1989	Las Vegas, Nev.	Frank Bruno	5th-round technical knockout
July 21, 1989	Atlantic City, N.J.	Carl Williams	1st-round technical knockout
Feb. 10, 1990	Tokyo, Japan	Mike Tyson (Buster Douglas, winner)	10th-round knockout
Mar. 16, 1996	Las Vegas, Nev.	Frank Bruno	3d-round knockout
Sept. 7, 1996	Las Vegas, Nev.	Bruce Seldon	1st-round knockout
Nov. 9, 1996	Las Vegas, Nev.	Mike Tyson (Evander Holyfield, winner)	11th-round technical knockout
June 28, 1997	Las Vegas, Nev.	Mike Tyson (Evander Holyfield, winner)	3d-round disqualification
June 8, 2002	Memphis, Tenn.	Mike Tyson (Lennox Lewis, winner)	8th-round knockout

Statistics

Bouts, 58

Knockouts, 44

Bouts won by decision, 6

Knockouts by opponents, 5

Records

Captured his first world heavyweight title at 20 years, 145 days of age—the youngest world heavyweight champion in professional boxing history

Honors and Awards

1981-82	Junior Olympiad Champion
1983-84	U.S. Junior Champion
1983	National Golden Gloves silver medalist
	U.S. Champion (versus the Federal Republic of Germany)
1984	U.S. Olympic Trials silver medalist
	National Golden Gloves heavyweight champion
1986, 1988	*Ring* magazine Merit Award
1988	WBC Boxer of the Year

convicted and spent the next three years in prison. He was released on March 25, 1995, and was fighting again five months later. In 1996, he won the WBA heavyweight title after knocking out Frank Bruno in the third round. He added the WBC title in September of the same year when he destroyed Bruce Seldon with a knockout in the first round.

On November 9, 1996, Mike faced Holyfield, his first real challenge since returning to boxing. Mike's considerable punching power and the intimidation that he inspired in his opponents were not enough to get him past Holyfield, who won by technical knockout in the eleventh round of one of the most exciting heavyweight title fights in boxing history. Soon after, talk began circulating about a rematch.

The rematch took place on June 28, 1997. In one of the most bizarre fights ever, an outmatched Mike was disqualified in the third round for biting off a portion of Holyfield's right ear and spitting it onto the mat. Mike claimed that he was retaliating for Holyfield's head-butting. Two days later, the Nevada State Athletic Commission revoked Mike's boxing license and fined him $3 million.

After a year of numerous legal problems outside boxing, Mike had his license reinstated in October, 1998. In February, 1999, Mike went to prison for nine months for assaulting two motorists following a traffic accident. Upon his release, he fought Orlin Norris on October 23, 1999. The match ended with a no-contest ruling following Mike throwing a left hook after the bell sounded to end the first round. Norris could not continue. Mike's increasingly erratic behavior made it apparent that he had lost his focus on boxing.

Mike fought three times in 2000, winning each bout by knockout and continuing his effort to regain a heavyweight title. However, the last match, on October 20, against Andrew Golota, was later declared a no contest after Mike tested positive for marijuana after the fight. Though he continued to win, he had Holyfield and Lennox Lewis standing between him and a heavyweight championship.

A fight between Mike and Lewis had long been anticipated. In 2000, Mike had famously warned Lewis that "I want to eat your heart. I want to eat your children." At a January, 2002, press conference, a brawl erupted among the boxers and their respective entourages. On June 8, 2002, in Memphis, Tennessee, Mike fought Lewis in a bout to unify the heavyweight titles of the International Boxing Organization (IBO), IBF, and WBC. He was knocked out in the eighth round.

In August, 2003, after earning about $400 million in boxing, Mike filed for bankruptcy with $34 million in debts. He scheduled several bouts to pay off his debts, including matches against British boxer Danny Williams and journeyman Kevin McBride. On July 30, 2004, Williams knocked out Mike in the fourth round. Approximately a year later, on June 11, 2005, Mike quit before the start of the seventh round against McBride. Stating he had lost interest in boxing, Mike announced his retirement. In fifty-eight professional fights, he had 50 wins (44 by knockouts) and 6 losses (5 by knockouts).

Summary

Mike Tyson became a boxing legend. Raised in the worst slums of New York, he emerged from his harsh environment with the determination to succeed. With the aid of his supportive trainer, Mike stormed to the top of the boxing world, becoming the most exciting champion since his idol, Muhammad Ali. As Mike's career progressed, each bout added an intriguing chapter to the story. Though fans and critics deplored much of his behavior in and out of the ring, few deny the dominance he experienced in the early years.

William B. Roy, updated by Caryn E. Neumann

Additional Sources

Cashmore, Ellis. *Tyson: Nature of the Beast.* New York: Polity, 2005.

Heller, Peter. *Bad Intentions: The Mike Tyson Story.* New York: Da Capo Press, 1995.

Hoffer, Richard. *A Savage Business: The Comeback and Comedown of Mike Tyson.* New York: Simon & Schuster, 1998.

Layden, Joe. *The Last Great Fight: The Extraordinary Tale of Two Men and How One Fight Changed Their Lives Forever.* New York: St. Martin's Press, 2007.

O'Connor, Daniel. *Iron Mike: A Mike Tyson Reader.* New York: Da Capo Press, 2002.

Torres, Jose. *Fire and Fear: The Inside Story of Mike Tyson.* New York: Times Books, 1989.

Soccer

Freddy Adu

Born: June 2, 1989
Tema, Ghana
Also known as: Fredua Koranteng Adu (full name)

Early Life

On June 2, 1989, Fredua "Freddy" Koranteng Adu was born in Tema, Ghana, a West African town best known for fishing and soccer. When Freddy was two years old, his uncle in the United States sent him a soccer ball. By the time he was six, Freddy was playing pickup games with older boys, who taught him to be tough. In 1997, when Freddy was eight years old, his parents, Maxwell and Emelia, won an immigration lottery and moved the family to the United States. The family settled in Potomac, Maryland, but was soon abandoned by Freddy's father; Freddy's mother had to work long hours to support Freddy and his younger brother, Fro. Emelia, Freddy, and his brother became U.S. citizens in 2003.

The Road To Excellence

Freddy attended the Heights School in Potomac. He excelled in his academic studies but had never played organized soccer before coming to the United States. When he was in fourth grade, a friend invited him to play for the soccer team after he noticed Freddy's ball-dribbling skills. Soon, Freddy's natural ability and soccer talent captured the attention of soccer coaches in the area, and Freddy was asked to join the Potomac soccer team, the Cougars.

When Freddy was ten, he was invited to play in a tournament with the U.S. Olympic Development Program under-fourteen (U-14) team. He was the youngest member of the team. Traveling to Italy, he made soccer history when he scored more points than any other player and was named most valuable player. His remarkable accomplishments for his age captured the attention of European soccer clubs and athletic company marketing executives. Freddy received offers from corporations, which entailed lucrative product endorsement contracts, and from European soccer teams. However, Freddy's mother kept him grounded, refusing all offers and insisting education came first. Freddy's superior, innate talent resulted in much speculation and questions about the accuracy of his age.

In 2001, at twelve years old, Freddy was invited to train at the prestigious IMG Academies in their soccer development program located in Bradenton, Florida. Freddy became the youngest player on the American U-17 men's national team and, over the next two years, scored 57 goals in eighty-seven games. He helped his team qualify for the 2003 FIFA World Youth Championship Tournament, scoring 4 goals over two games and helping his team to win the tournament.

Besides his outstanding soccer skills, Freddy

Freddy Adu warming up with the U.S. team before a 2008 game against Mexico. (Bob Levey/Getty Images)

excelled at basketball and in his academic studies, skipping the seventh grade and completing four years of high school in two. In his first art contest, in fifth grade, he won top prize in the county.

The Emerging Champion

In January, 2004, Freddy was the first player selected in the Major League Soccer (MLS) draft. At the age of fourteen, Freddy signed with the MLS team D.C. United. He became the youngest and highest-paid player in American professional soccer. He also signed an endorsement deal with the athletic-shoe manufacturer Nike. During his career with D.C. United, playing in midfield and forward positions, Freddy accumulated 11 goals and 17 assists over eighty-seven games. He helped D.C. United win the 2004 MLS Championship Cup and was named an MLS all-star in 2004 and 2006. His 17 career assists tied him for eighth all-time in the team's history.

Although Freddy excelled at soccer, playing in many championship and MLS games, he was still a teenager and often acted as such. Occasional arguments with his coaches sometimes resulted in his suspension or expulsion from a game or team. At the end of the 2006 season, he was traded to Real Salt Lake, the MLS team in Utah, and reunited with his former Maryland coach John Ellinger. Freddy played with Real Salt Lake for one year, accruing one goal and two assists in eleven games. His lackluster year with the Real Salt Lake City team cast doubt upon his abilities as he started to mature and reached the age of eighteen, when he was eligible to obtain coveted European soccer-club work permits and offers.

MLS Statistics

Season	GP	GS	Min.	G	Ast.	Pts.
2004	30	14	1,440	5	3	13
2005	25	16	1,487	4	6	14
2006	32	29	2,521	2	8	12
2007	11	10	899	1	2	4
Career	98	69	6,347	12	19	43

Notes: GP = games played; GS = games started; Min. = minutes played; G = goals; Ast. = assists; Pts. = points

Milestones

Went professional at age fourteen (2003)

Youngest player in MLS history

Youngest professional player in U.S. team sports in more than one hundred years

Youngest player to score a goal in MLS history (April 17, 2004)

Youngest player on U.S. team (2006)

Captain of the U.S. Under-20 men's team (2007)

Member of 2008 U.S. Olympic team

Continuing the Story

In December of 2006, Freddy trained with players from Manchester United's youth academy. In 2007, Freddy received an offer from Benfica, in Lisbon, Portugal, and MLS agreed to transfer him to the European team. The move to a European soccer club was one for which Freddy hoped and worked. He made his first appearance with the team on August 14, 2007, but had limited playing time afterward. In his first year with Benfica, he scored 5 goals but had no assists. Freddy had to prove himself all over again as an aggressive and talented player in the more competitive arena of European soccer. In July, 2008, he moved from Benfica to Monaco.

Summary

Freddy Adu set milestones in professional American soccer as the youngest player in MLS history. He continued to be a talented soccer player and emerging superstar, one who the MLS hoped would increase fan interest in soccer in the United States. Besides soccer, Freddy used his fame to bring attention to the plight of hunger in the world as a spokesperson for the United Nations World Food Program. He was also involved with the America SCORES and NikeGO after-school programs.

Alice C. Richer

Additional Sources

LaCanfora, Jason. "My Career Hasn't Really Started Yet." *Sports Illustrated*, September 24, 2007.

The Lincoln Library of Sports Champions. 7th ed. Cleveland: Lincoln Library, 2004.

Murcia, Rebecca Thatcher. *Freddy Adu: Young Soccer Super Star.* Hockessin, Del.: Mitchell Lane, 2005.

Wahl, Grant. "Freddy Adu: At Thirteen, America's Greatest Soccer Prodigy Has the World at His Feet." *Sports Illustrated*, March 3, 2003.

Michelle Akers

Born: February 1, 1966
Santa Clara, California

Early Life
The daughter of Robert and Anne Akers, Michelle Akers was born on February 1, 1966, in Santa Clara, California. She grew up in a Seattle, Washington, suburb. Michelle described herself as a stereotypical tomboy interested in sports, who wanted to play for the Pittsburgh Steelers and was told by her first-grade teacher that girls could not play football. Her mother signed up eight-year-old Michelle for a soccer team. Intensely competitive, Michelle wanted to quit because her team frequently lost. Eventually, she began to enjoy playing soccer and even dreamed of becoming a professional player in Europe.

After her parents' divorce, Michelle reacted to the situation by engaging in irresponsible behavior. She confided her feelings of self-loathing to her soccer coach, Mr. Kovats, who persuaded her to become a Christian. She later called this experience the turning point in her life. Michelle played soccer for Seattle's Shorecrest High School and was named an all-American three times. After graduating in 1984, she enrolled at the University of Central Florida on a soccer scholarship.

The Road to Excellence
Michelle excelled during her collegiate soccer career and held the school's record for career goals and assists. She joined the United States Soccer Federation (USSF) national team in 1985, taking off a year from college to travel to Europe for international competitions. In Italy, on August 21, 1985, her first international game ended in a 2-2 tie with Denmark, and Michelle scored the team's first goal. Michelle was selected to the National Collegiate Athletic Association all-American first team four times between 1984 and 1988. After earning a bachelor's degree in liberal studies and health in 1989, Michelle began playing soccer professionally in Europe.

In April, 1990, Michelle married Roby Stahl, a former soccer professional, and divided her time between their Florida home and Sweden, where Tyreso, her club team, was based. In 1990, 1991, and 1992 she was named the USSF female athlete of the year. In 1991, she played in the first Women's World Cup, in China. The Golden Boot winner, she was the top scorer, with 10 goals in six games. Michelle, who had scored the first goal, also scored the tie-breaking goal

Michelle Akers celebrating Team USA's victory in the 1999 Women's World Cup. (Tom Hauck/Getty Images)

Major Championships

Year	Competition	Place
1991	FIFA World Cup	1st
1995	FIFA World Cup	3d
1996	Olympic Games	Gold
1998	Goodwill Games	1st
1999	FIFA World Cup	1st

three minutes prior to the conclusion of the final match, and the team beat Norway 2-1. This was the first world championship won by an American soccer team. Considered the best soccer player in the world, Michelle was also the first female player paid to endorse shoes.

The Emerging Champion

Michelle played two additional seasons with Tyreso, in 1992 and 1994. In 1992, she had 43 goals and became the leading scorer of all the Swedish professional players, male or female. She also played for the U.S. national team. During a 1993 Olympic Sports Festival match at San Antonio, Texas, she collapsed. Physicians diagnosed her as suffering from chronic fatigue and immune dysfunction syndrome (CFIDS). Exhausted and enduring pain, Michelle still insisted on playing soccer for the national team. She divorced her husband in January, 1995.

Later that year, Michelle was injured in the first game of the 1995 Women's World Cup in Sweden. She was able to play in the semifinal match versus Norway, which the United States lost, finishing the tournament in third place. Michelle struggled to minimize the agonizing symptoms of CFIDS by following a diet free of sugar and dairy products, taking vitamin supplements, undergoing physical therapy, and renewing her spirituality. She testified to Congress about the effects of CFIDS in May, 1996. Michelle also underwent approximately one dozen knee surgeries and sought treatment for a broken cheekbone, a dislocated shoulder, and several concussions.

With her teammates, Michelle prepared for the 1996 Atlanta Olympic Games, the first Olympiad to feature medal competition for women's soccer. Sustained by intravenous treatments, she played in all five games for the United States and scored an essential goal against Norway in the semifinal. Michelle won a gold medal when the American team defeated China 2-1.

Continuing the Story

At the 1999 Women's World Cup, Michelle, sapped of energy because of CFIDS, accidentally ran into Briana Scurry, the goalkeeper, and suffered a head injury. Michelle was carried from the field and connected to intravenous tubing in the training room. Realizing that the American team had won, Michelle insisted on removing her tubes to join her teammates on the field.

Although she anticipated playing in the 2000 Sydney, Australia, Olympics, on August 24, 2000, Michelle announced her retirement from international competition because she had reinjured her shoulder during a match against Russia, in which she scored her last international goal.

The last member of the original U.S. national team to retire, Michelle played in a total of 153 international games and scored 105 goals, making her one of only five American women to score more than 100 international goals. At the time of her retirement, she also held the Women's World Cup record for goals with a total of 12.

Michelle's other milestones included American records for most goals during in one game (5) and the most goals during one season (39). In December, 2000, FIFA named her the woman footballer of the century. After her retirement from international play, Michelle wanted to play in the Women's United Soccer Association professional league but gave up that plan because of her slow recuperation from her shoulder injury. Instead, she turned her attention to raising a family and running a farm near Orlando, Florida, that cares for rescued horses. She also wrote several books and continued to promote the game of soccer.

Summary

In 2002, two years after Michelle Akers's retirement from playing, she and China's Sun Wen shared FIFA's woman player of the century honor. Significant because she was a pioneering female soccer athlete, Michelle is universally regarded as one of the most outstanding international soccer players of either gender. In fact, in 2004, she and former teammate Mia Hamm were the only women among the 125 players that FIFA named to its centennial list of the great living soccer players.

At the time of her retirement, Michelle was considered one of the greatest women's soccer players because of her athleticism, public promotion of soccer, and alliance with the national team since its creation in 1985. Tony DiCicco, the 1999 American Women's World Cup coach, stated that Michelle was the player who legitimized women's soccer as a sport.

Teammates, coaches, and fans admired Michelle for her work ethic, commitment, and perseverance. She was described as a powerful, swift, and intimidating player who recognized risks necessary to succeed on the field. Sometimes called a phenomenon, Michelle foreshadowed younger soccer stars such as Hamm.

Elizabeth D. Schafer, updated by the Editors

Additional Sources

Akers, Michelle, and Gregg Lewis. *The Game and the Glory: An Autobiography.* Grand Rapids, Mich.: Zondervan, 2000.

Akers, Michelle, and Tim Nash. *Standing Fast: Battles of a Champion.* Burlington, N.C.: JTC Sports, 1997.

Akers, Michelle, and Judy Nelson. *Face to Face with Michelle Akers.* Bloomington, Ind.: Integrated Resources, 1996.

Hunt, Chris. *The Complete Book of Soccer.* Buffalo, N.Y.: Firefly Books, 2006.

O'Reilly, Jean, and Susan K. Cahn, eds. *Women and Sports in the United States: A Documentary Reader.* Boston: Northeastern University Press, 2007.

Radnedge, Keir, and Gary Lineker. *The Ultimate Encyclopedia of Soccer: The Definitive Illustrated Guide to World Soccer.* London: Carlton Books, 2004.

Rasmussen, R. Kent. "Women's World Cup of Soccer Draws Unprecedented Attention." In *Great Events: 1900-2001.* Vol. 8. Pasadena, Calif.: Salem Press, 2002.

Honors, Awards, and Milestones

Year	Honor
1984, 1986-88	NCAA first team All-American
1985	ESPN Athlete of the Year
1988	Hermann Trophy, presented by UCF to the school's best female soccer player
1989	U.S. Olympic Committee Female Soccer Player of the Year
1990, 1992, 1999	U.S. Soccer Federation Female Player of the Year
1991	USOC Athlete of the Year
	FIFA Golden Boot for scoring the most goals
	FIFA Silver Ball Award
1992	Canon Shot Award
1994	Distinguished Alumnus Award by UCF
1995	UCF Alumni Association created the Michelle Akers Award
1996	Gold medal, Olympic Games
1998	FIFA Merit of Honor Award
	Inducted into UCF Hall of Fame
1999	FIFA Bronze Ball Award
	Confederation of North, Central American, and Caribbean Association Football Century Player of the Year
2000	*Sports Illustrated* Sportswomen of the Year, with teammates
	FIFA Woman Footballer of the Century
	Soccer America College Team of the Century
2001	National Soccer Hall of Fame Medal of Honor
2002	FIFA Woman Player of the Century (award shared with China's Sun Wen)
2004	Named to the FIFA 100 (one of two women to receive honor)
	Inducted into U.S. National Soccer Hall of Fame

Roberto Baggio

Born: February 18, 1967
 Caldogno, Italy
Also known as: Roby; the Divine Ponytail

Early Life

Roberto Baggio was born to Fiorindo and Matilda Baggio on February 18, 1967, in Caldogno, Italy. Roberto has seven siblings: four sisters and three brothers. His father was a store owner, and his mother was a housekeeper. As his mother had eight children with which to contend, Roberto had plenty of freedom as a child. Rather than focusing on schoolwork, young Roberto spent his days motorcycle riding and playing soccer.

Roberto played for his local youth club. After witnessing Roberto score 6 goals in one game, the coach of the professional team in Vicenza, Italy, persuaded Roberto to sign with the team. Thus, in 1982, Roberto began his professional football career with Serie C1 Vicenza. He spent three years playing for Vicenza before the Serie A club Fiorentina signed him in 1985. With Vicenza, Roberto honed his skills; with Fiorentina, he began to build his legend as Italy's greatest soccer player.

The Road to Excellence

Roberto played in his first Serie A game with Fiorentina on September 21, 1986. However, he did not score his first Serie A goal until May 10, 1987, against Napoli. Though it took some time, the goal was the first of many. In 1990, after five years in Fiorentina, where he built a reputation as one of the world's best ball handlers and strikers, Roberto was sold to the more powerful Juventus club for 25 billion Italian lira (the equivalent of $19 million). This transfer fee was a record at the time. Roberto was so beloved in Fiorentina that riots broke out after the news of his trade to Juventus. Fifty people were injured. Roberto's response to his fans: "I was compelled to accept the transfer."

During the 1990's, playing with Juventus and with the Italian national team, Roberto solidified his reputation as one of the world's best soccer players. In Roberto's first five years with Juventus, he scored 78 goals in 141 matches. This number was even more impressive considering the Italian Serie A league is known for intense defensive squads.

The Emerging Champion

In 1993, Roberto had his greatest year in the Italian Serie A league. That season, he led Juventus to the Union of European Football Associations (UEFA) Cup Championship, was named European player of the year, and was also named

Roberto Baggio handling the ball for Italy in a game against Brazil.
(Bob Thomas/Getty Images)

FIFA world player of the year. The following year, Roberto led Juventus to the Serie A and Coppa Italia Championships. At this point, the consensus was that Roberto, "The Divine Ponytail," was the greatest soccer star in the world.

On the world's greatest soccer stage, the World Cup, Roberto had some of his greatest moments and by far the worst moment of his football career. Roberto was the first Italian player to play in three World Cups—1990, 1994, and 1998. During that span he amassed 9 goals. However, by many, he will forever be remembered for one penalty kick. In 1994, Italy was playing Brazil for the World Cup Championship. Roberto was at the height of his career. The match came down to penalty kicks, and, needing to make a goal to keep Italy alive, Roberto struck a ball that sailed high. Brazil had won the World Cup. This is the prevailing image many have of Roberto.

Continuing the Story

However, those who followed his career knew Roberto to be one of the all-time greats. His numbers are astounding, with 218 goals in his career. He made 76 out of 91 penalty tries, which is the best of all time in Italy. He scored 27 goals in fifty-six games for his national team. He also tied for the most goals by an Italian in a World Cup competition with 9.

In 1996, Roberto was transferred to AC Milan. He helped the club win the *scudetto*, or Italian championship. Roberto was the first to win consecutive championships while playing for two different clubs; he had won with Juventus in 1995. In

Professional Statistics

Season	Team	Games Played	Goals
1982-83	Vicenza	1	0
1983-84	Vicenza	6	1
1984-85	Vicenza	29	12
1985-86	Fiorentina	0	0
1986-87	Fiorentina	5	1
1987-88	Fiorentina	27	6
1988-89	Fiorentina	30	15
1989-90	Fiorentina	32	17
1990-91	Juventus	33	14
1991-92	Juventus	32	18
1992-93	Juventus	27	21
1993-94	Juventus	32	17
1994-95	Juventus	17	8
1995-96	Milan	28	7
1996-97	Milan	23	5
1997-98	Bologna	30	22
1998-99	Inter Milan	23	5
1999-00	Inter Milan	18	4
2000-01	Brescia	25	10
2001-02	Brescia	12	11
2002-03	Brescia	32	12
2003-04	Brescia	26	12
Totals		**488**	**218**

1997, Roberto transferred to the Bologna club and scored a personal best 22 goals. He played for several other teams, before retiring as a member of the Brescia club in 2004.

Summary

Roberto Baggio was the first player in more than fifty years to score more than 200 professional goals. FIFA placed Roberto on its all-time team. Along with all of his other honors, he was also voted the world's most loved player in 2001.

Theodore Shields

Honors and Awards

1990	Under-23 European Soccer Player of the Year
1990-91	UEFA Cup Winners' Cup top scorer
1993	European Player of the Year (Ballon d'Or)
	FIFA International Player of the Year
2000	Azzuri Team of the Century
2002	FIFA "Dream Team"
2004	Pelé's FIFA 100
	Giuseppe Prisco Award

Additional Sources

Goldblatt, David. *The Ball Is Round: A Global History of Soccer*. New York: Riverhead Books, 2008.

McCarthy, Patrick. "Sport and Society in Italy Today." *Journal of Modern Italian Studies* 5, no. 3 (2001).

Oller, Jan Paul. *The Cup of Death: Soccer-USA 1994*. Bloomington, Ind.: 1stBooks Library, 2000.

Alan Ball

Born: May 12, 1945
        Farnworth, Lancashire, England
Died: April 24, 2007
        Warsash, Hampshire, England
Also known as: Alan James Ball, Jr. (full name)

Early Life

Alan James Ball, Jr., was born on May 12, 1945, in Farnworth, Lancashire, England, a town situated in the hotbed of English soccer, between the rival cities of Liverpool and Manchester. Therefore, Alan was surrounded by soccer from the moment he was born. His father was involved in professional soccer, first as a player and then as a manager. Alan's father instilled a passionate enthusiasm for soccer in his young son, coaching and teaching him the skills of the game. The hours of practice paid off. Despite his small stature, Alan dominated school games with his tireless running and commitment. His red hair also made him stand out from the crowd. Alan was soon recognized as an outstanding young player who was earmarked for stardom in professional soccer.

The Road to Excellence

Predictably, Alan was scouted by many professional teams. He chose to sign as an apprentice professional for Blackpool, which was then in the First Division. Alan learned quickly, and in May of 1962, he was offered a full professional contract, which he signed. He made his debut for Blackpool during the 1962-1963 campaign; however, it was not until the following season that he established himself as a first-team regular. He started out playing right-winger for Blackpool, a position once occupied by the legendary Stanley Matthews. Soon Alan's terrier-like qualities were acknowledged by the Blackpool management, and he was moved to a deeper and more involved position in midfield.

In the more central midfield role the young dynamo was able to utilize his skill, tenacity, and fierce competitive spirit more effectively. During the 1963-1964 season, Alan played thirty-one games for Blackpool and scored 13 goals. Even as a teenager standing only 5 feet 6 inches tall and weighing little more than 140 pounds, Alan succeeded against the best in the profession.

Alan Ball passing the ball to an Everton teammate. (Popperfoto/Getty Images)

In the next few seasons, Alan established himself as one of the game's premier young players. His great promise was recognized by Alf Ramsey, the England soccer manager, who chose Alan for the England under-21 team that played Wales in 1965. Alan excelled when representing his country. Soon after his under-21 debut, he was chosen to represent the full international team. Alan's first senior outing was a grueling 1-1 draw against Yugoslavia in Belgrade. The game was played on his twentieth birthday.

The Emerging Champion

Alan had matured very quickly into an outstanding midfield player. He was very much in the forefront of Alf Ramsey's thinking. The England manager was looking to build a team to win the World Cup, which was to be held in England in the summer of 1966. Ramsey saw Alan's nonstop running and enthusiasm as providing the midfield "engine room" for his team.

Following his England debut, Alan was selected for ten of the fourteen international matches played in preparation for the World Cup tournament. England's World Cup campaign proved successful, and on July 30, 1966, Alan took the field at London's Wembley Stadium for the World Cup Final.

Many people questioned Ramsey's decision to select the Blackpool youngster ahead of more experienced players. The World Cup Final, played in front of more than ninety thousand fans, provided Alan with the perfect stage for proving that Ramsey had been correct in picking him. Alan was the star of the battle against West Germany. With his socks rolled down to his ankles, Alan covered every inch of the Wembley turf. His brilliant midfield play was a vital part of England's epic 4-2 overtime victory. Alan's fighting spirit made him a national hero overnight.

Continuing the Story

After the World Cup, Alan was a much sought after player. Less than a month after England's victory, he was transferred from Blackpool to Everton for $110,000. This was the first six-figure transfer fee paid between two English clubs. After five successful years at Everton, Alan was breaking records again. This time a British record fee of $210,000 was paid by Arsenal for his services. While at Arsenal, Alan played his last game for England. In all, Alan played seventy-two games for his country, scoring eight goals. Over a ten-year period, Alan's outstanding play made him a vital part of the England team.

In 1976, at the age of thirty-one, Alan dropped into the English Second Division by joining Southampton. He had an immediate impact on the team, which gained promotion to the First Division in his first season.

In the course of his career, Alan acquired a great knowledge of the game. He wanted to use his understanding of soccer, coupled with his passion for the game, in a managerial capacity once his playing days were over. Alan rejoined Blackpool, his first club, as player-manager in May, 1980, after a brief stay in the North American Soccer League with the Vancouver Whitecaps. His first managerial term was not a happy experience. Alan found it difficult to work with players who had neither his ability nor his commitment to the game, and after a few unhappy months he finished the 1980-1981 season back at Southampton.

In May, 1984, following brief spells as a player for Southampton and the Bristol Rovers, Alan reentered soccer management when he was appointed manager of Second Division Portsmouth. His second spell at the helm of a soccer club was much more successful. Within three seasons, he had built a team that won promotion to the First Division. In 1989, Alan left Portsmouth under controversial circumstances. Inevitably, however, anyone of his ability and expertise would not be without a job for long. Soon after leaving Portsmouth, he was appointed the manager of Stoke City. He managed throughout the 1990's, with four different English clubs: Exeter City, Southampton, Manchester City, and a second stint at Portsmouth.

Alan's last years were a combination of triumph

Career Highlights

72 international appearances for England
8 international goals

Honors, Awards, and Milestones

1966	World Cup champion
2000	Made Member of Order of the British Empire
2004	Inducted into English Football Hall of Fame

and tragedy. In 2000, he was given the Member of the Order of the British Empire (MBE) award. Three years later he was inducted into the English Football Hall of Fame. In 2004, he wrote a best-selling autobiography. However, he suffered through the cancer-related death of his wife and his daughter's cancer diagnosis. Alan himself died of a heart attack in April, 2007. Soon after his death, the Alan Ball Memorial Cup, a soccer match featuring English and international players, was played in his honor; all proceeds went to charity.

Summary

A glance at Alan Ball's career suggests that everything fell easily into place for the son of a former professional soccer player. However, Alan's success was built upon sheer hard work and determination. These qualities enabled the red-haired wonder to become one of England's finest midfield players.

David L. Andrews

Additional Sources

Ball, Alan. *It's All About a Ball: An Autobiography*. London: W. H. Allan, 1978.

Ball, Alan, and James Mossop. *Playing Extra Time*. London: Pan, 2005.

LaBlanc, Michael L., and Richard Henshaw. *The World Encyclopedia of Soccer*. Detroit: Gale Research, 1994.

Gordon Banks

Born: December 30, 1937
Sheffield, South Yorkshire, England

Early Life

Gordon Banks was born on December 30, 1937, in the city of Sheffield, South Yorkshire, England. He came from a working-class family in which money was scarce. At fifteen, he left school and went to work in a coal mine. Life was very difficult for Gordon as a youngster. All that kept him going during long, grueling hours in the mine were his dreams of becoming a goalkeeper. Gordon was fortunate, because he possessed some of the attributes needed to be a goalkeeper: He was agile and had great leaping ability. Like many working boys, Gordon lived for Saturday's games. He played goal for a local team called Millspaugh. After he had established himself on the Millspaugh team, his consistently outstanding displays brought him to the attention of scouts from professional clubs.

The Road to Excellence

Chesterfield, of the Third Division, showed the greatest interest in Gordon. The club eventually offered him a contract, and he signed a part-time professional contract in September, 1955. Gordon's dream of becoming a professional soccer player was becoming a reality. Despite his new contract with Chesterfield, he still had a lot to learn to become a professional. He took every advantage of the opportunity he had been given and worked tirelessly to improve his game.

Progress came quickly, and Gordon was soon starring for Chesterfield's youth and reserve teams. However, a required stint in the national service briefly interrupted his professional career. Luckily, while in the British army, Gordon found time to play for his regimental team. This kept him sharp and alert and reminded the scouts in the professional game that he was a talented prospect. Chesterfield still kept an interest in Gordon, and when he left the army, the team offered him a full professional contract.

The 1958-1959 season was Gordon's only one on Chesterfield's first team. His amazing agility and leaping ability made it clear that he was destined for better things. After playing only twenty-three games for Chesterfield, Gordon signed with Leicester City in May, 1959. Leicester, a First Division club, took a gamble on the young, gangly, promising, but inexperienced goalkeeper.

The Emerging Champion

At Chesterfield, Gordon was the automatic choice as the starting goalkeeper. Joining Leicester meant that he had to compete for the starting spot. Gordon rose to the challenge admirably, and within a few months he had established himself as the first-team keeper. Leicester's gamble paid off. The seven years Gordon spent at Leicester were successful for him and the club. Gordon's commanding presence had a large bearing on Leicester's two Football Association (FA) Cup Final appearances and the team's League Cup victory.

Sooner or later, Gordon was bound to gain international recognition, and in April, 1963, he was selected for the England team to play against Scotland. Playing for his country inspired Gordon to even greater levels of achievement. He pushed himself through hours of fitness training and goalkeeping practices, with the single-minded aim of becoming the best goalkeeper in England. By the time of the 1966 World Cup, Gordon had achieved his goal: He was the best in England. Moreover, his controlled and composed performances helped England win the tournament and demonstrated that he was in fact the best goalkeeper in the world.

Career Highlights

73 international appearances for England

Honors, Awards, and Milestones

1964	English League Cup champion
1966	World Cup champion
1970	Order of the British Empire
1972	English Footballer of the Year
2002	Inducted into English Football Hall of Fame

Continuing the Story

In April, 1967, Gordon moved to the Stoke City team after the Leicester management decided that Peter Shilton was a more-than-adequate replacement for its twenty-nine-year-old England international. The trauma of dismissal from Leicester motivated Gordon to sustain his brilliance. For six years following England's World Cup triumph, Gordon maintained the high standards he had set. Indeed, it was in this period that he reached his peak as a goalkeeper.

Gordon won 36 more England caps in his time with Stoke. His most memorable performance came in a game against Brazil, played during the 1970 World Cup in Mexico. One save in that game assured Gordon of soccer immortality. In the tenth minute of the game, Pelé, the Brazilian superstar, leapt like a salmon to head a cross downward toward the corner of the net. Pelé was already shouting "Goal!" Miraculously, Gordon sprang across the goal and somehow managed to push the ball over the bar. Pelé said later the save was the greatest he had ever seen. To many observers, Gordon's great save seemed an act of instinctive genius. In reality it was years of dedicated training that allowed Gordon to be able to make such saves.

Another highlight for Gordon occurred in 1972, when Stoke City beat Chelsea in the League Cup Final. The year also marked the end of Gordon's playing career. In October, 1972, Gordon lost the sight in his right eye following a horrific car crash. After attempting a comeback, Gordon finally admitted defeat. He announced his retirement from the game in the summer of 1973.

Soccer had lost one of its greatest players through a tragic twist of fate. Although he was unable to continue playing, Gordon did not leave the game completely. He ventured briefly into management and passed on his incredible expertise and knowledge of the game to numerous professional goalkeepers. Gordon received numerous accolades for his performance on the pitch. Pelé named him one of the top 125 soccer players of all time, and the International Federation of Football History & Statistics (IFFHS) ranked him second behind Lev Yashin as the greatest goalie of the twentieth century. In 2002, he was inducted into the English Football Hall of Fame.

Summary

Gordon Banks was arguably the best goalkeeper the world has ever seen. His greatest attribute was an ability to make even the most incredible save look simple. He was naturally gifted, and it seemed as though everything came easily to him. Only through total commitment and dedication, however, was Gordon able to make the most of his natural talents and become the best in the world.

David L. Andrews

Additional Sources

Banks, Gordon. *Banks of England*. London: A. Barker, 1980.

_____. *Banksy: My Autobiography*. London: Michael Joseph, 2002.

Mullan, Don. *Gordon Banks: A Hero Who Could Fly*. Dublin: A Little Book Company, 2006.

Franz Beckenbauer

Born: September 11, 1945
Munich, West Germany (now in Germany)
Also known as: The Kaiser

Early Life
Franz Beckenbauer was born in the district of Giesing, in the city of Munich in West Germany (now Germany), on September 11, 1945. As a young boy growing up in post-World War II West Germany, young Franz dreamed of playing professional soccer. He started his soccer career with the Munich 60 Club, where he played from 1954 to 1958. The team was located in Giesing, so Franz was able to play on the same team as many of his boyhood friends.

The Road to Excellence
Franz had planned to play for the professional club 1860 Munich, but a fight between him and its star player prevented this. Franz signed with Bayern Munich, the club with which he played for the majority of his career. In 1964, at the age of nineteen, Franz was named to Bayern Munich's first-division team in his first year of eligibility. The promotion, which was similar to a baseball player getting promoted from the minor to major leagues, was an impressive feat for a player of his age. Franz was about to emerge into the international soccer arena.

The Emerging Champion
Only four weeks after starting his career in the German first division, in Stockholm, Franz made his debut with the German national team in an important World Cup qualification game against the Swedish team. Franz began a career that kept him on the German national team for twenty years. During the 1966 World Cup, Franz was employed at an offensive position in midfield, although he had played only defense for Bayern Munich. With Franz stabilizing the middle of the field, West Germany advanced to the final game of the World Cup before losing to host England in a dramatic overtime game. Franz's outstanding performance in the 1966 tournament caused the German press and populace to label the twenty-one-year-old "the Kaiser," or the king, of soccer.

In his second World Cup competition, in Mexico in 1970, Franz again played midfield, even though he wanted to play his more familiar defender's role. Characteristically, Franz placed the success of his team before his own wishes, and West Germany reached the semifinals of the tournament before losing to Italy.

After the 1970 World Cup tournament, Franz's

West Germany's Franz Beckenbauer dribbling against England in the 1966 World Cup. (Popperfoto/Getty Images)

patience and sacrifice were rewarded. West Germany's national team coach, Helmut Schoen, finally put Franz in his accustomed defender position. The move enabled Franz to reach his full potential for the German national team.

Franz revolutionized the position often called "sweeper." Before Franz's time, the sweeper played behind the defenders but in front of the goalkeeper, acting as a last zone of defense on the field. Franz, however, added an incredible offensive dimension to the position. He became the playmaker on the field. With his accurate, precise passing, he utilized all nine offensive players.

With Franz as sweeper and captain of the national squad, the 1970's were known as the golden years of German soccer. In 1974, Bayern Munich won the European Cup and the West German team won the World Cup. Bayern Munich repeated as European Cup winners in 1975 and 1976, and Franz received European soccer's highest individual honor when he was selected as European player of the year in both 1972 and 1976.

Continuing the Story

In 1977, at the age of thirty-two, Franz surprised the soccer world when he signed to play with the New York Cosmos of the North American Soccer League (NASL). Franz explained that his superstar status in Germany had taken such a toll on him personally that he needed the anonymity of American soccer. His three marriages and other aspects of his personal life were well publicized in the German media. In the United States, Franz led the Cosmos to three league championships and was a vital contributor to the short-lived success of NASL.

Despite his NASL achievements, Franz wanted to end his soccer career in the German first division, so he signed with the Hamburg SV team for the 1981 and 1982 seasons. In 1982, Franz led Hamburg to the league championship but injuries plagued him, and he was forced to retire from active play after the season. His retirement as a player did not mean the end of his relationship with German soccer, though. Soon after his playing days ended, Franz was named coach of the West German national team. In 1986, he led the team to a second-place finish in the World Cup tournament in Mexico.

In 1990, Franz reached the pinnacle of success for a "total" soccer player. When West Germany de-

Career Highlights

103 international appearances for West Germany
14 international goals

Honors, Awards, and Milestones

1972, 1976	European Player of the Year (Ballon d'Or)
1974	World Cup champion as player
1974-76	European Cup champion
1977	NASL Most Valuable Player
1977-78, 1980	NASL champion
1990	World Cup champion as coach
1998	Inducted into National Soccer Hall of Fame
	Inducted into International Football Hall of Champions
2006	FIFA World Cup chief organizer
2007	Received the International Federation of Football History & Statistics' (IFFHS's) Universal Genius of World Football award

feated Argentina in the World Cup Final, Franz became only the second person ever to win the World Cup as both a player and a coach. Following his success at the World Cup, Franz accepted a coaching position with Olympique de Marseilles. In 1994, he returned to Bayern Munich as a coach, leading them to the Bundesliga title. Later, he became the club president. Franz remained president of Bayern until 1998, when he left to become vice president of the German Football Association.

In 2004, the Union of European Football Associations Golden Jubilee Poll voted Franz the second best European player of the previous fifty years. Franz launched a successful campaign to make Germany the host for the 2006 World Cup. In 2006, Franz served as president of the organizing committee for the World Cup, a demanding position which required Franz to oversee a tournament of 194 national soccer teams. Franz was praised for the meticulous and professional planning he brought to this task. The successful operation of the World Cup tournament was seen as a personal triumph for Franz.

Summary

Franz Beckenbauer was possibly the most successful player in German soccer history. He added an attacking dimension to the position of sweeper, introducing a new weapon to soccer offense. He was the first man to be a player, a captain, and a coach on World Cup championship teams. As a player, he was noted for both his elegance and precision. With more than one hundred international game appearances, he truly deserved the title of the "Kaiser" of German soccer.

Leonard K. Lucenko, updated by Howard Bromberg

Additional Sources

Bauer, Gerhard. *New Soccer Techniques, Tactics, and Teamwork.* New York: Chrysalis, 2003.

Hahn, James, and Lynn Hahn. *Franz Beckenbauer: Soccer Superstar.* St. Paul, Minn.: EMCParadigm, 1978.

Hesse-Lichtenberger, Ulrich. *Tor! The Story of German Football.* London: WSC Books, 2003.

Kissinger, Henry. "Franz Beckenbauer." *Time* 167, no. 19 (May 8, 2006): 115.

LaBlanc, Michael L., and Richard Henshaw. *The World Encyclopedia of Soccer.* Detroit: Gale Research, 1994.

MacDonald, Tom. *The World Encyclopedia of Soccer: A Complete Guide to the Beautiful Game.* London: Arness, 2005.

Radnedge, Keir. *Fifty Years of the European Cup and Champions League: Featuring Interviews with Sir Bobby Robson, Alfredo di Stefano, Eusébio, Franz Beckenbauer, Ian Rush, Paolo Maldini, Zinedine Zidane.* London: Carlton, 2007.

David Beckham

Born: May 2, 1975
Leytonstone, England
Also known as: David Robert Joseph Beckham (full name)

Early Life

David Beckham's story was one of "rags to riches." Born in Leytonstone, near London, England, he grew up in the working-class London suburb of Chinford. His father, Ted, was a gas-fitter who played soccer with amateur teams in his neighborhood. His mother, Sandra, was a beautician. David had an older sister, Lynne, three years his senior and a younger sister, Joanne, five years his junior. The family had a considerable struggle financially as David was growing up.

British star David Beckham, playing for the Los Angeles Galaxy. (Jeff Vinnick/Getty Images)

David's father rooted for the Manchester United soccer team, and soon David shared this enthusiasm. David, not yet in his teens, declared that he wanted to play for Manchester United when he was old enough. David's father encouraged his ambitions, playing soccer with him almost daily. He soon quit playing for the local team with which he was associated so that he could devote himself totally to coaching David, whose interests in art, bicycling, and roller skating were eclipsed by his devotion to soccer.

The Road to Excellence

By the time he was seven, David was a team member of the Ridgeway Rovers. Among the smallest players on the team, he knew that if he were knocked down, he had to get up and continue playing. The Rovers coaches demanded strict obedience and attention to the game. If players intended to be in the team's games, they had to attend all practice sessions. A single absence eliminated them from the week's game.

The Emerging Champion

When he was ten, David attended the Bobby Charlton Soccer School for a week and liked the competition with players from around the world. The following summer, he attended the camp for a second session, performing well enough to win the skills contest, which earned him two weeks' attendance at a soccer camp in Barcelona, Spain. Already, scouts from Manchester United, who had become aware of his exceptional ability, began courting David. When he was thirteen, he accepted an offer from Manchester United. Too young to qualify as a professional player, he spent two years on Manchester United's developmental team, going frequently to Manchester for training.

When David became a member of Manchester United's youth team two years later, he was too young to have his own apartment, so he boarded with a family in Manchester. In 1992, he played in his first Manchester United game, entering as a substitute player. The team lent David to the Preston North End team in 1994-1995, and he played impressively. In 1995, several United players moved to other leagues, so David and other rookies replaced them.

Continuing the Story

During his time with Manchester United, David scored an impressive 61 goals. In 1997, he started dating Victoria "Posh" Adams, a singer with the Spice Girls. On July 4, 1999, the two were married in a wedding that attracted international attention, cost nearly $1 million, and employed a staff of 437 persons.

Clearly a world-class player, in 2003, David, following a disagreement with United's manager Alex Ferguson, was traded to Spain's Real Madrid soccer team for an unprecedented 24.5 million Euros. In 2006, David earned over $27 million. As excessive as his remuneration seemed to many of his critics, Real Madrid's investment in him was thought to have increased the club's revenues by more than $500 million in the four years he played for the club.

In 2007, David signed a contract with the Los Angeles Galaxy of Major League Soccer (MLS). It was expected that his association with the team would stimulate interest in soccer in the United States, where the game is eclipsed in popularity by football, basketball, and baseball. The Galaxy committed to paying David $32.5 million over a five-year period. During this time, endorsements and merchandise fees were expected to bring David more than $200 million.

In July, 2007, David, his wife, and their three children relocated to Beverly Hills, moving into a thirteen-thousand-square-foot mansion for which they paid $12 million. In the Los Angeles Galaxy game against the Wellington Phoenix team in New Zealand, David made an impressive beginning with his new team. He played for a full ninety minutes although he was contractually obligated to play for only fifty-five. Besides setting up three goals, he scored from the penalty spot, winning the game for Los Angeles. In April, 2008, David scored his first MLS goal in a victory over the San Jose Earthquakes, and on May 2, 2008, he had his first multiple-goal game, scoring twice, versus Real Salt Lake. After the MLS season ended, the Galaxy lent David to AC Milan in Italy. He played so well for Milan through their 2008-2009 season that the team negotiated with the Galaxy to buy his contract.

Summary

During the 1990's and 2000's, few soccer players could match David Beckham in skill and international popularity. From 2000 to 2006, David served as captain of the English national team. While he was with Manchester United, the team won

Professional Statistics

Season	Team	Games	Goals
1994-95	Manchester United	4	0
1995-96	Manchester United	33	7
1996-97	Manchester United	36	7
1997-98	Manchester United	37	9
1998-99	Manchester United	35	6
1999-00	Manchester United	31	6
2000-01	Manchester United	31	9
2001-02	Manchester United	28	11
2002-03	Manchester United	31	6
2003-04	Real Madrid	32	3
2004-05	Real Madrid	29	4
2005-06	Real Madrid	33	3
2006-07	Real Madrid	22	3
2007	Los Angeles Galaxy	5	0
2008	Los Angeles Galaxy	18	5
Totals		**405**	**79**

Honors, Awards, and Milestones

1996, 1999	FA Cup winner (with Manchester United)
1996-97, 1999-2001, 2003	Premier League champion (with Manchester United)
1997	Professional Footballers' Association young player of the year
	Sir Matt Busby Award
1998	FIFA World Cup all-star
	FIFA World Player of the Year
1999	UEFA Club Player of the Year
	UEFA Champions League winner (with Manchester United)
2001	BBC sports personality of the year
2003	Order of the British Empire (officer)
2004	ESPY Award: best male soccer player
2007	Primera División champion (with Real Madrid)
2008	ESPY Award: best MLS player

six Premier League Cups. In 2007, he helped Real Madrid to a Primera División championship. He was committed to the Los Angeles Galaxy until 2012.

R. Baird Shuman

Additional Sources

Beckham, David, and Tom Watt. *Beckham: Both Feet on the Ground.* New York: HarperCollins, 2003.

Carlin, John. *White Angels: Beckham, Real Madrid, and the New Football: The Inside Story.* New York: Bloomsbury, 2004.

Roza, Greg. *David Beckham: Soccer Superstar.* New York: Rosen, 2006.

Watson, Galadriel Findlay. *David Beckham.* Calgary, Alta.: Weigl, 2007.

Wheeler, Jill C. *Awesome Athletes: David Beckham.* Edina, Minnesota: Abdo, 2007.

George Best

Born: May 22, 1946
Belfast, Northern Ireland
Died: November 25, 2005
London, England

Early Life
George Best was born on May 22, 1946, in Belfast, the main city of Northern Ireland. His background was typical of soccer's blue-collar origins and social status in Europe. To many youngsters growing up in the economically depressed industrial hinterlands of the British Isles, soccer offered a means of escape. George had numerous examples of boys with origins even less promising than his own on which to base his own dreams of stardom in England. George played schoolboy soccer for the local Creggagh Boys' Club, where his talent came to the attention of Bob Bishop, the legendary and influential Manchester United scout. Bishop was instrumental in signing fifteen-year-old George to what, in the early-to-mid-1960's, was the most glamorous soccer club in England, Manchester United.

The Road to Excellence
George's inclusion in United's first team created an immediate impact. His slight build and flowing long, black hair caused controversy. Some thought that the looks of "swinging London" had invaded the conservative domain of soccer. George's skill soon silenced the critics. Despite his youth and small size, George managed to mesmerize his more experienced opponents. He possessed uncanny control of the ball and had the body control to go with it. Though George lacked the prowess in the air of his teammate Denis Law, he compensated by beating defenders with speed and dexterity of foot. Like Law, George was gifted with a sense of improvisation, finding ways to score goals from the most slender of opportunities. He could distribute the ball as expertly as he could complete a sequence with a goal. His shot on goal was typically well placed rather than fast or explosive. He brought all these skills with him from Belfast. With the surge of interest that soccer received from England's victory in the 1966 World Cup, George's name was on everybody's lips. He was one of the few players of his day in England whom people not otherwise interested in soccer went to a game to see. During his rise to stardom, George also had to learn to temper his on-field behavior. He was often accused of taunting opponents by the way he went past them; however, he was often expected to

Manchester United player George Best attempting to head the ball. (Bob Thomas/Getty Images)

Career Highlights

34 international appearances for Northern Ireland
9 international goals

Honors, Awards, and Milestones

1963	English Football Association Cup champion
1965, 1967	English League champion
1968	European Cup champion
	European Player of the Year (Ballon d'Or)
	English Footballer of the Year
2001	Awarded honorary doctorate by the Queen's University of Belfast
2002	Made Freeman of Castlereagh, Northern Ireland
	Inducted into English Football Hall of Fame
2006	Received Professional Footballers' Association (PFA) Special Merit Award

tolerate persistent and brutal fouling as if it were a natural part of the game. He may also have had problems adjusting to English life and handling stardom while still a teenager.

The Emerging Champion

George won a Football Association Cup Medal and a Football League Championship Medal with Manchester United. His most memorable performance for the club, however, came in the European Champions Cup Final at Wembley Stadium, London, in 1968. United beat Benfica of Lisbon, 4-1, in overtime, with George scoring two goals. In 1968, he was named both English footballer of the year and European player of the year. Although he continued to play well for a number of years after this triumph, his inspirational moments became progressively fewer and farther apart.

George's increasing lack of interest in soccer and his increasing lack of respect for his skills was reflected in his international career. He played 34 times for Northern Ireland, a modest total of appearances in view of his ability to change the course of a game with just a simple body feint. Even more disappointing was his meager total of nine goals in international games.

Continuing the Story

Distracted by the fame and fortune that his gifts had earned for him, George grew erratic on the field and in the clubhouse. In 1973, he left Manchester United and signed with the Los Angeles Aztecs of the North American Soccer League (NASL). With the decline of the NASL, George moved from club to club among the lower divisions of the English League. He played subsequently for Motherwell and Hibernian in Scotland and for Cork Celtic in the League of Ireland before retiring from competitive soccer.

After retiring, George was an occasional soccer commentator for Sky Sports. Near the end of his life, he returned to soccer as a youth coach. On November 25, 2005, George died from an alcohol-related illness. Though he was often criticized for his behavior while under the influence of alcohol, upon word of his death, the citizens of England and Northern Ireland greatly mourned the loss. More than 100,000 people lined the streets to glimpse his funeral procession.

Summary

George Best did for soccer in England what the Beatles did for pop music: He made it socially acceptable to the middle class. For that reason alone, his is a memorable image from a memorable time. His cultural significance should not be emphasized at the cost of overlooking his soccer skills, however. George was arguably the greatest soccer player ever to come out of Ireland and one of the most entertaining European players of his time—when he wanted to be. His grace on the ball and alertness off it, his impudent flicks and bursts of speed, his ability to dribble, and his overall self-confidence were among the most obvious of his fabulous gifts.

George O'Brien

Additional Sources

Best, Barbara. *Our George: A Family Memoir of George Best.* London: Macmillan, 2007.

Best, George, and Roy Collins. *Blessed: The Autobiography.* London: Ebury, 2002.

Martin, Ivan. *George Best: The Legend in Pictures.* Belfast: Appletree Press, 2006.

Meek, David. *George Best: Tribute to a Legend.* London: Weidenfeld & Nicolson, 2005.

Smith, Bernie, and Maureen Hunt. *George Best: A Celebration.* London: John Blake, 2007.

Williams, Richard. *George Best: A Life in the News, from the Pages of the "Guardian" and the "Observer."* London: Aurum, 2006.

Danny Blanchflower

Born: February 10, 1926
Belfast, Northern Ireland
Died: December 9, 1993
London, England
Also known as: Robert Dennis Blanchflower (full name)

Early Life
Robert Dennis Blanchflower—nicknamed "Danny"—was born in Belfast, Northern Ireland, on February 10, 1926. A love of soccer ran in his family. Danny's mother, Selina, played inside right for the Belfast ladies' soccer team, and Danny practiced soccer by dribbling a tennis ball with his brother Jackie on their morning newspaper delivery route. Jackie, too, was destined to become a professional soccer player of distinction.

When Danny was fourteen, he bought a set of soccer jerseys and started a team called Bloomfield United, only to lose his place on his own team when the older boys in the neighborhood became interested. After he left high school, Danny became an apprentice electrician and played soccer as an amateur for the Irish club Glentoran. In 1944, during World War II, he volunteered for the Royal Air Force (RAF). The RAF sent him to St. Andrews University in Scotland for training as an electrical engineer.

The Road to Excellence
As a teenager, Danny idolized his fellow Irishman Peter Doherty, of Manchester City and Derby County fame, who was one of the greatest soccer players Ireland produced. Danny modeled his own game on the example set by Doherty, of whom he later said, "He was the great North Star that twinkled brightly in the heavens, promising untold glory, beckoning me to follow, and always showing the way." Danny admired Doherty for his brilliant, constructive, precise play and his inspiring personality—the qualities for which Danny himself was soon to be admired.

Immediately after World War II, Danny returned to Northern Ireland, where he signed with Glentoran as a professional. He soon made his mark; he was only twenty-one when the Irish League selected him to play as an inside forward against the English League in 1947.

Ambitious and self-confident, Danny quickly realized that playing for Glentoran in the small Irish League could never take him to the top of his cho-

Danny Blanchflower entering the pitch for a Tottenham Hotspurs game in 1960. (Hulton Archive/Getty Images)

sen profession. To establish himself, he had to take the route that many famous Irish soccer players had taken before him—to England. In 1948, when the Barnsley Football Club, in the northern English county of Yorkshire, showed an interest in him, he eagerly seized the opportunity. Leaving Glentoran, he was set to play in what was then the most skilled and demanding soccer league in the world.

The Emerging Champion

Within a year of arriving at Barnsley, Danny made his first appearance for Northern Ireland, in a match against Wales. In 1951, he was transferred to Aston Villa, one of England's leading soccer clubs. Three years later he was on the move again, this time to Tottenham Hotspur, known as "Spurs." The London club paid a fee of £30,000 for Danny, which was then a record fee for a halfback. Danny had always wanted to play for a London team. Within a year he was captain of the team, as well as an established Irish international.

Danny was an attacking wing-half. Many times when the Spurs' defense was under heavy pressure, Danny changed the direction or pace of the game suddenly. Then, with a deft and always accurate pass, he set up an opportunity for his forwards. Danny was always cool under pressure and was rarely forced into making a hurried or imprecise clearance. Always eager for the ball, he loved to take charge of a game.

Arthur Rowe, the Spurs' manager, decided to build his successful team around Danny's commanding skills. This made the Spurs an exciting team to watch, because Danny was an unorthodox player. He could improvise and was often unpredictable. He had the ability to adapt to whatever the situation demanded, and this, together with his strong personality, made him an ideal team captain.

Continuing the Story

The small country of Northern Ireland was not accustomed to much soccer success, but under Danny's leadership the Northern Irish international team had some of its finest moments. In 1957, for example, Northern Ireland defeated England 3-2 in London. The victory was the first for Northern Ireland against England in twenty-seven years, and Danny was mobbed by delighted supporters as he left the field. The victory enabled Northern Ireland to share the four-nation British Championship for the 1957-1958 season. The Northern Irish success continued with Danny leading his team to the quarterfinals of the World Cup competition in Sweden in 1958, a feat that no Northern Irish team had equaled before. In 1958, Danny was also elected English footballer of the year.

Danny's career also had setbacks. In 1956, after a quarrel with the manager, Danny was dropped from the Spurs' first team. He promptly resigned the captaincy. In the 1958-1959 season he was omitted from the team again. After a three-month absence he made a triumphant return. As captain of the team, he masterminded Tottenham's dazzling 6-0 victory over Leicester City, scoring the fifth goal.

One of Danny's greatest triumphs came in the 1961 season. He captained Tottenham as it became the first team in the twentieth century to win the "Double"—the Football Association Cup and the Football League championship—in the same season. This won him another English footballer of the year award; he is one of the few players to have won the award twice.

Danny's reputation for responsibility and fair play was enhanced by an incident in Belfast in 1957. A match between Northern Ireland and Italy had turned sour, and at the end of the game the crowd attacked the Italian players. Danny took charge of the situation, instructing each Northern Irish player to protect one of the Italians. This ensured that all the Italians left the field safely.

When he retired in 1964, Danny had made 337 first-team appearances for Tottenham Hotspur and scored 15 goals. He had also played fifty-six

---

Career Highlights

56 international appearances for Northern Ireland

Honors, Awards, and Milestones

1958, 1961	English Footballer of the Year
1961	English League champion
1961-62	English Football Association Cup champion
1998	English Football League One Hundred Legends
2003	Inducted into English Football Hall of Fame

times for Northern Ireland, a record at the time. After his retirement he became a soccer journalist and television commentator. Danny died in 1993. He was inducted into the English Football Hall of Fame a decade after his death.

Summary

For a dozen years, Danny Blanchflower's skill and flair made an unforgettable impact on British soccer. Without Danny, Tottenham Hotspur might never have become the brilliant team it was in the early 1960's. Not only did Danny win virtually every honor in the game, but his lively personality and Irish wit also made him a well-known and entertaining public figure.

Bryan Aubrey

Additional Sources

Bowler, Dave. *Danny Blanchflower: A Biography of a Visionary*. London: Gollancz, 1997.

Galvin, Robert, and Mark Bushell. *Football's Greatest Heroes: The National Football Museum's Hall of Fame*. London: Robson, 2005.

Hunt, Chris. *The Complete Book of Soccer*. Buffalo, N.Y.: Firefly Books, 2006.

Billy Bremner

Born: December 9, 1942
 Stirling, Scotland
Died: December 7, 1997
 Doncaster, England
Also known as: William John Bremner (full name); Chalky

Early Life
William John "Billy" Bremner was born on December 9, 1942, in Stirling, Scotland, a city about halfway between Edinburgh and Glasgow. Billy was an only child, and his father worked in a shop selling newspapers. Life was not easy for Billy; he grew up in a tough district of Stirling. At an early point, he showed the determination never to give up.

The Road to Excellence
Billy had great soccer ability even in elementary school. He played for St. Mary's Primary School on the under-eleven-year-old team when he was only nine years old. At St. Modan's Secondary School, known locally as a soccer powerhouse, the thirteen-year-old Billy began playing for an under-twenty-one-year-old team, Gowan Hill. He was always small, and at that age he was playing against grown men nearly twice his size. In his last year in school, Billy was selected to play four times for the Scottish Boys' team. This gave him the chance to be seen by scouts from several clubs. He tried out with Chelsea and Arsenal, both leading clubs of the day, before signing with Leeds United in December, 1959.

Like all young apprentices, Billy had glamourless tasks to perform before he got the chance to play for the first team. Apprentices are prospects that teams expect to become excellent players, but while in the learning stages, they are assigned such chores as picking up litter after matches and cleaning first-team players' shoes. In January, 1960, Billy made his first appearance for Leeds and showed his enormous determination to win. Sometimes this spirit went too far, however, and Billy was often ejected, fined, or suspended for losing his temper on the field. Billy's hair color, like his temperament, was fiery, and his complexion was pale; this gained him the nickname "Chalky." Off the field, though, Billy was a caring person who collected money for needy friends and staff at Leeds. In 1963, Billy married his childhood sweetheart, Vicky, and the couple later had three children, Billy, Donna, and Amanda.

The Emerging Champion
In 1964, Billy helped his team to win the English Second Division Championship and gain promotion to the First Division. Between 1965 and 1974, Leeds was consistently at or near the top of English and European soccer. During this era, Billy was the captain of Leeds United, and the team's success was due in large part to Billy's determined and demanding leadership.

Leeds lost so many finals between 1965 and 1967 that some people said that the team was unable to

Billy Bremner of Leeds United kneeling and covered in mud during a game with Derby County in 1972. (Popperfoto/Getty Images)

win. Though Leeds was otherwise highly successful, the team's losses in several championship games led to much criticism from fans. All that changed between the years 1968 and 1974, when, under Billy's captaincy, Leeds won the Union of European Football Associations (UEFA) Cup, the League Cup, the First Division Championship, and the Football Association (FA) Cup. In 1970, Leeds came close to winning the unique treble of League, FA, and European cups, but the team was runner-up in all three. Billy's contribution to Leeds's success was recognized when he was chosen as the footballer of the year in England.

In addition to his place with Leeds, Billy was selected to play for the full international Scottish team, and three years later, in 1968, he was appointed its captain. In 1974, Billy captained Scotland to the World Cup group finals, against all predictions. Pelé, the great Brazilian player, called Billy one of the best players in the world. In 1975, Billy was banned permanently from the Scottish team after he was reportedly involved in a fight following Scotland's game in Denmark. The ban was removed in 1977, but it was too late for Billy. While at Leeds, he appeared fifty-four times for his country, a team record. At the time of the ban, he was one appearance short of the Scottish record.

Billy and the Leeds manager Don Revie had a good relationship on and off the field. The relationship was one of the most perfect manager-captain partnerships ever. A testimonial match, in which the gate receipts are given to the player, held for Billy in 1974, raised £37,000 (nearly $75,000), a club record. Eventually, however, even Billy began to slow down, and in September, 1976, he was transferred to Hull City, a smaller club.

Continuing the Story

Billy played for Hull City for two years. Then he went to the Doncaster Rovers of the fourth division. He played a handful of games for them and was managing the team by the end of 1978. Two years later, he nearly had to play professionally again when his team was hit by the flu. Typical of Billy's tenacious attitude, he thought of coming out of retirement for his team to have enough players. He led Doncaster to promotion to the Third Division twice before he was asked to manage his old club, Leeds United, in October, 1985. In 1987,

Career Highlights

54 international appearances for Scotland

Honors, Awards, and Milestones

1968	English League Cup champion
1968, 1971	UEFA Cup champion
1969, 1974	English League champion
1970	English Footballer of the Year
1972	English Football Association Cup champion
1998	English Football League One Hundred Legends
1999	Statue erected at Leeds United Stadium
2004	Inducted into English Football Hall of Fame
	Inducted into Scottish Football Hall of Fame

he steered Leeds into the semifinals of the FA Cup competition, and the team narrowly missed earning a coveted promotion from the Second Division into the First Division. Despite this success, Billy was dismissed as Leeds manager in September, 1988, and he returned to manage the Doncaster Rovers in 1989.

In 1997, Billy died of a heart attack. He was posthumously honored with numerous awards including induction into both the English Football Hall of Fame and the Scottish Football Hall of Fame. He was voted the greatest player in Leeds United history and, in fact, a statue of Billy was erected outside the Leeds United home field.

Summary

The 5-foot 5-inch, 150-pound midfielder was a human dynamo. Billy Bremner's gritty performances, tough tackling, and flippant in-game comments made him unpopular with opposing teams and led to many ejections, fines, and suspensions. Nevertheless, he also led by his example of enthusiasm, drive, and determination.

Shirley H. M. Reekie

Additional Sources

Bale, Bernard. *Bremner! The Legend of Billy Bremner.* London: Chameleon, 1999.

Bremner, Billy. *Billy Bremner's Book of Soccer.* London: Pelham, 1974.

Galvin, Robert, and Mark Bushell. *Football's Greatest Heroes: The National Football Museum's Hall of Fame.* London: Robson, 2005.

Hunt, Chris. *The Complete Book of Soccer.* Buffalo, N.Y.: Firefly Books, 2006.

Fabio Cannavaro

Born: September 13, 1973
Naples, Italy
Also known as: Fabio Mamerto Cannavaro (full name)

Early Life

Fabio Cannavaro was born in Naples, Italy, on September 13, 1973. He grew up in a crowded and poor neighborhood, the second of three children born to Gelsomina and Pasquale Cannavaro. His father played soccer at the semiprofessional level, and his younger brother, Paolo, later became a professional soccer player. While playing as a junior for the local team Bagnoli, Fabio was spotted by scouts from Napoli and joined the club as a youth player. At the time, Napoli was enjoying the most successful period in its history. Led by the brilliant Argentinean Diego Maradona, the club won the Italian Serie A league title in 1986-1987 and 1989-1990, as well as the Union of European Football Associations (UEFA) Cup in 1988-1989 and two Italian Cups. Fabio was once asked to mark Maradona in a practice game and played so fiercely that coaches warned him to ease off. Fabio's illustrious opponent was apparently impressed by what he saw.

The Road to Excellence

By the time that Fabio made his first-team debut for Napoli in March, 1993, Maradona had left and the club was struggling both on and off the pitch. In 1995, financial constraints forced Napoli to sell Fabio, its promising young defender, to Parma. As part of a strong defense that also included goalkeeper Gianluigi Buffon and Frenchman Lillian Thuram, Fabio played a decisive role in Parma's emergence as one of Italy's leading teams during the latter half of the 1990's. While the league title remained elusive, Parma won the UEFA Cup and the Italian Cup twice during Fabio's seven years with the team.

In 1997, when Fabio made his debut for the senior Italian team against Northern Ireland, his defensive qualities were recognized at the highest level. This was a natural progression, given that Fabio had already won two European championships with the Italian under-twenty-one team in 1994 and 1996. He played his first international tournament for Italy at the 1998 World Cup in France, where the *Azzurri* ("blues") lost in the quarter-finals to the hosts in a penalty shoot-out. Fabio then excelled alongside Lazio's Alessandro Nesta on the team that reached the final of the 2000 European

Italian team player Fabio Cannavaro in 2008. (AP/Wide World Photos)

Championships in Belgium and the Netherlands. The Italians led France 1-0 in the last moments of the game. However, the French scored a late equalizer and went on to win 2-1 in extra time.

The Emerging Champion

In 2002, after seven years and more than two hundred games, Fabio left Parma for Inter Milan. He spent two somewhat frustrating years there. Despite heavy financial investment, the team failed to win anything, and Fabio spent much of his second season on the sidelines because of a fractured tibia. In 2004, he moved again, this time joining the "old lady" of Italian soccer, Juventus. Reunited with his ex-Parma teammates Buffon and Thuram, Fabio helped "Juve" to win the Serie A title in both 2004-2005 and 2005-2006. He won the award for best defender in Italian soccer in 2005, having finished runner-up three times during his time at Parma.

However, an investigation into match fixing in Italian soccer games—the so-called *Calciopoli* scandal—concluded that several teams, including Juventus, had attempted to influence games by selecting preferred referees for their games. Although no Juventus players were implicated—the general manager Luciano Moggi was the culprit—the Italian Football Federation stripped Juventus of its two most recent league titles and relegated the club to the second division (Serie B) in July, 2006.

Against this backdrop of crisis, Fabio captained the Italian team at the 2006 World Cup Final in Germany. In addition to the *Calciopoli* scandal, shortly before their quarterfinal match against Ukraine, the players learned that the former Juventus and Italy player Gianluca Pessotto had apparently tried to commit suicide. The incident drew the scrutinized squad even closer together. Italy won that game 3-0, before defeating the hosts Germany in the semifinal. In the final against France, in Berlin, Fabio led Italy to victory on penalties after the game had finished 1-1. Italy's defense conceded only two goals in seven games. Many observers felt that Fabio was the tournament's best player, though the official award went to France's Zinedine Zidane.

Continuing the Story

Juventus's relegation to Serie B, coupled with a two-year ban from all European competition, broke up the team that dominated Italian soccer between 2004 and 2006. In July, 2006, Fabio moved to the Spanish team Real Madrid. Though Fabio had some difficulties adjusting to the heavier attacking style of football played in Spain, his debut season ended in triumph, with Real Madrid winning the league title for the thirtieth time. That season, he also won the 2006 International Federation of Association Football (FIFA) world player of the year award and the European footballer of the year award, the first defender to attain the honor since the German Franz Beckenbauer in 1972.

Summary

Fabio Cannavaro was one of the finest defenders in world soccer during the 1990's and 2000's. Though relatively small for a center back, at just over 5 feet 7 inches, Fabio rarely seemed to be at a disadvantage against even the strongest, most skillful forwards because of his speed, anticipation, and aerial ability. Fabio was also disciplined. During the 2006 World Cup Final, he did not receive a single yellow card in seven games. In 2008, with his career entering its final stages, he still played regularly for Real Madrid and remained the captain of the Italian team. In a culture that is proud of the art of strong defensive play, Fabio occupied a prominent place among the great defenders in Italian soccer history.

Alan McDougall

Honors and Awards

2005-06	Serie A Defender of the Year
2006	FIFA World Player of the Year
	European Player of the Year (Ballon d'Or)
	World Soccer Player of the Year
	World Cup Silver Ball Award
	World Cup team of the tournament
	Serie A Player of the Year
	Italian Player of the Year

Additional Sources

Agnew, Paddy. *Forza Italia: The Fall and Rise of Italian Football*. London: Ebury Press, 2007.

Foot, John. *Calcio: A History of Italian Football*. London: Harper Perennial, 2007.

Hawkey, Ian. "The Big Interview: Fabio Cannavaro." *The Sunday Times* (London), September 17, 2006.

Eric Cantona

Born: May 24, 1966
Marseille, France

Also known as: Eric Daniel Pierre Cantona (full name); Eric the King

Early Life

Eric Cantona, who became one of Europe's most successful and most controversial soccer players, was born on May 24, 1966, in Marseille, in the southern part of France. One of three children of Albert and Leonor Cantona, Eric had an unexceptional childhood. He once said that he was average in everything. His assessment, however, did not apply to soccer. Eric possessed obvious physical talents on the soccer field, and he first joined the Club des Caillols, a neighborhood soccer club in Marseille, with friends of his age. Beginning in the youngest age-group soccer league, he was an enthusiastic and dependable player. He was first noticed for his ability when he turned fourteen and was briefly considered for the OGC Nice soccer club. Recognizing that his natural talents needed the refinements of systematic training, in July, 1981, he joined a soccer training club in Auxerre, near Paris. There, the head coach, Guy Roux, honed Eric's skills for the next two years on the youth team. Eric played his first adult match in November, 1983, against Nancy. His potential for greatness as a professional player had to be deferred, however, as Eric performed one year of required military service.

The Road to Excellence

Eric signed his first professional contract in 1986. For the next two years, his rough-and-tumble style brought him great success. In 1988, he and his team won the junior championship. However, Eric was often overly aggressive: He punched teammates, tackled opponents, and increasingly used vulgar language. In August, 1988, expecting to be selected for the France national team after winning the junior championship, he was extremely colorful in expressing to the media his thoughts about Henri Michel, who was in charge of the selection. Eric failed to make the team. The result of Eric's outburst was a year-long suspension from the national team. His contract was then sold by Auxerre to the Olympic Club of Marseille, where he received a substantial 22-million-francs contract with the first division soccer league of his native town. In the forty-eight games he played for Marseille from 1988 until 1991, he scored 15 goals. Still, his volatile temper ostracized teammates and coaches. Constantly in conflict with head coach Gerard Gili, Eric was eventually suspended from the team and loaned to Bordeaux, where he played for six months, scoring 6 goals in eleven matches. From there, he traveled to Montpellier and again did

Manchester United forward Eric Cantona in 1994. (Mike Hewitt/Getty Images)

Honors, Awards, and Milestones

1992	English Football League champion (with Leeds)
1993-94, 1996-97	Premier League Champion (with Manchester United)
1993-96	Captain of the French national soccer team
1994	Professional Footballers Association Player of the Year
1996	Football Writers Association Player of the Year
1996-97	Captain of Manchester United
1998	English Football League One Hundred Legends
2002	Inducted into English Football Hall of Fame

well, scoring 13 goals in thirty-nine games and helping the team win its first French Cup. Eric continued to fight with his teammates and opponents; no one seemed to escape his aggression. He verbally attacked Gerard Gili's successor, Franz Beckenbauer, a famous German soccer player. When the Marseille chairman, Bernard Tapie, became the focus of Eric's ire, not even gratitude for the part he played in winning the French title could salvage the unruly player's position. Transferred to Nîmes, Eric continued his aggressive style. Again, his season was marked by disciplinary actions, resulting in months of suspension. In December, 1991, Eric had become exasperated by these disciplinary actions and decided to retire from soccer at the age of twenty-five.

The Emerging Champion

Two of Eric's fans, Michel Platini, who was in charge of selecting the French national soccer team, and Gérard Houllier, technical manager of the French national soccer team, persuaded Eric to restart his career in England, arguing that doing so would provide the vehicle to allow him to participate in the 1992 European Championships. In February, 1992, Eric signed with Leeds and helped the team win the England Championship, scoring 9 goals in twenty-eight games. In November, 1992, Leeds traded Eric to Manchester United. While becoming a star in England, Eric was named captain of the French soccer team. However, his personal style was not well suited to a leadership position, and the French team was repeatedly defeated, leading to Eric's removal. As a player in England, though, his success continued. In 1994, he was named player of the year, after scoring 18 goals in thirty-four games.

Continuing the Story

Eric's soccer career with Manchester United was punctuated by brilliant if aggressive play on the field and colorful verbal battles off it. By 1997, he had grown weary of the controversies and sanctions. Attracted to other pursuits, he decided to retire from the sport. Painting had been his hobby since he was a child, and acting had always interested him. After his retirement, he acted in more than a dozen movies and started directing as well. He kept his ties with the world of soccer: He coached and became captain of the French national beach soccer team. He married Isabelle Ferrer, with whom he had two children, in 1987. Their marriage ended in divorce. In June, 2007, he married actress Rachida Brakni.

Summary

Eric Cantona's career, which lasted only fifteen years, was punctuated by exceptional victories, lengthy suspensions, world-class achievements, and major failures. He became the first foreign-born soccer player to be inducted in the English Football Hall of Fame and was listed as one of the English Football League One Hundred Legends.

Denyse Lemaire and David Kasserman

Additional Sources

Bryson, Kit. *The Meaning of Cantona: Meditations on Life, Art and Perfectly Weighted Balls.* Edinburgh, Scotland: Mainstream, 1997.

Cantona, Eric. *The Complete Cantona.* London: Headline Books, 1997.

Cantona, Eric, and Alex Fynn. *Cantona on Cantona.* London: Andre Deutsch, 1996.

Goldblatt, David. *The Ball Is Round: A Global History of Soccer.* New York: Riverhead Books, 2006.

Roberto Carlos

Born: April 10, 1973
 Garça, state of São Paulo, Brazil
Also known as: Roberto Carlos da Silva Rocha (full name)

Early Life
Roberto Carlos da Silva Rocha, better known as simply Roberto Carlos, was born in the town of Garça in São Paulo, Brazil, on April 10, 1973. Roberto was born on a coffee farm and given his first soccer ball at the age of three. By the time he was eight years old, he was already playing men's soccer on his father's team. In 1981, when his family moved to Cordeirópolis, in the state of São Paulo, Roberto was invited to join the city team Jogo Abertos do Interior.

The Road to Excellence
Unlike many of his Brazilian counterparts, Roberto was not a prodigy. His stardom came after years of toiling in relative obscurity. In 1993, at the age of twenty, he signed his first professional contract with the Brazilian league team of Palmeiras. After Roberto had several strong seasons with Palmeiras, the European leagues took notice of him. In 1995, he was signed by Serie A Italian team Internazionale Milano.

Roberto spent only one season with Internazionale Milano, but the experience gave him a taste of the tough, defensive European-style soccer, which strengthened his game. The following season, Roberto signed with perennial Spanish powerhouse Real Madrid. He played for Real Madrid for eleven years, the bulk of his career.

The Emerging Champion
In his eleven seasons with Real Madrid, Roberto scored 47 goals in 370 games. His goal total was an incredibly high number considering he played a defensive position. Many of these goals were the result of free kicks, an aspect of his game that became a staple for both Real Madrid and the Brazilian national team. Roberto made some of the most amazing free kicks in history. In fact, in 1997, he made what became known as the "free kick of the century." Playing for Brazil against France, Roberto lined up 40 yards out on the right side of the goal. When the ball left his foot it appeared to be heading for the corner flag. However, Roberto created such spin with his left foot that the ball bent back and clipped the post while heading into the upper left corner of the goal. French goalkeeper Fabien Barthez scarcely moved.

During Roberto's eleven-year stay at Real Madrid, the team had enormous success. It won the Spanish League, La Liga, four times—in 1996-1997, 2000-2001, 2002-2003, and 2006-2007—and

Roberto Carlos keeping his eye on the soccer ball during the quarterfinals of the 2006 World Cup. (AFP/Getty Images)

the Spanish Super Cup three times—in 1997, 2001, and 2003. In addition, Real Madrid won the Union of European Football Associations (UEFA) Champions League in 1997-1998, 1999-2000, and 2001-2002; the European Super Cup in 2002; and the International Cup in 1998 and 2002.

In addition to his amazing free kicks, Roberto became known as one of the world's greatest defenders. In fact, during his stint with Real Madrid, many experts considered him one of the best defenders in the world. In 1997, many believed that he should have been given the Golden Ball Award as FIFA's world player of the year. Instead, it went to his Brazilian teammate Ronaldo. However, the following year, Roberto was awarded the EFE Trophy, given by the Spanish news agency to the best Ibero-American soccer player. In addition to his time with Real Madrid, Roberto played for the Brazilian national team in 1998, 2002, and 2006; the team won the World Cup in 2002. In 125 games for Brazil, Roberto scored 19 goals, a tremendously high number for a defender.

Continuing the Story

During the 2006-2007 season with Real Madrid, Roberto's increasingly poor performances began to draw the ire of fans and coaches alike. At the age of thirty-four, he no longer seemed able to dominate on the defensive end in the manner that he once could. Following a poor 2006-2007 season with Real Madrid, Roberto transferred to the Turkish team Fenerbahce. He said he wished to finish out his playing career with this team, and he hoped to play in the World Cup in 2010.

Summary

Roberto Carlos's career can be judged in many ways. He was one of the most magnificent free kickers of his era. For a decade he was viewed by most experts and fans as the greatest defender on the planet. Furthermore, Pelé listed him as one of the 125 greatest living soccer players.

Theodore Shields

Additional Sources

Goldblatt, David. *The Ball Is Round: A Global History of Soccer.* New York: Riverhead Books, 2008.

Hunt, Chris. *The Complete Book of Soccer.* Buffalo, N.Y.: Firefly Books, 2006.

Soccer Stars. Chicago: Triumph Books, 2007.

Honors, Awards, and Milestones

1996	Bronze medal, Olympic Games
1997	FIFA runner-up for best player in the world
1998	EFE Trophy
2001-03	UEFA Champions League best defender
2002	World Cup winner with Brazilian team
2004	Pelé's top 125 greatest living soccer players

Bobby Charlton

Born: October 11, 1937
Ashington, Northumberland, England
Also known as: Robert Charlton (full name); Sir Robert Charlton

Early Life

Robert "Bobby" Charlton was born in Ashington, a bleak mining village in northeast England, on October 11, 1937. His father was a miner. Soccer had run in the family for four generations. Bobby's great-grandfather had six sons and five daughters, and they all played soccer. Bobby's uncle was Jackie Milburn, a famous Newcastle United and England star, and four of Bobby's other uncles played professionally for Football League clubs. Bobby's mother, Elizabeth, loved soccer and encouraged Bobby and his elder brother Jack, who also became a star player, in their early efforts. She even coached Bobby and improved his sprinting ability. However, Bobby's soccer skills came naturally to him. Even as a thin nine-year-old, he was easily able to weave his way past boys five years his senior. He was soon captain of his secondary school soccer team.

The Road to Excellence

At secondary school, Bobby owed a great deal to the encouragement he received from Norman McGuiness, his sports master. McGuiness later commented that Bobby was so naturally talented he needed little coaching, and McGuiness was determined that Bobby should play for the England schoolboy team. This dream came true in 1953, when Bobby played for England in a schoolboys' international. He scored 2 goals.

Bobby was also indebted to Stuart Hemingway, the headmaster of Bedlington Grammar School, which Bobby began attending when he was eleven. Impressed by Bobby's potential, Hemingway wrote to Matt Busby, the manager of Manchester United, one of the most famous soccer clubs in the land. Bobby was fifteen years old at the time, and eighteen professional soccer clubs were interested in signing him. His brother Jack had already joined Leeds United. Bobby, however, chose Manchester United, and he left Ashington for Manchester in July, 1953. Two years later he signed as a professional. Joe Armstrong, Manchester United's chief coach, predicted that Bobby would play for England before he was twenty-one.

Bobby made his first appearance for the Manchester United first team against Arsenal in 1956. He had just celebrated his nineteenth birthday. More celebrations followed when Bobby scored two goals in United's victory. During his first season of top-class soccer, Bobby scored 10 goals in fourteen games, and he was considered to be a player to watch.

Bobby Charlton. (Hulton Archive/Getty Images)

The Emerging Champion

In the mid-1950's, Busby was developing a fine group of young players, and Manchester United was becoming one of the great teams in English soccer history. The players were known as the "Busby Babes," and Bobby was one of them. Tragedy struck in February, 1958. Manchester United was returning from a European match when the team plane crashed on a runway at Munich, West Germany. Eight players were killed, but Bobby escaped with only minor injuries.

When Bobby returned to the rebuilt team in March, he was no longer a junior player. Even though he was only twenty, he was able to carry great responsibility, and his explosive shooting power won many games for his team. He also fulfilled Armstrong's prediction that he would play for England before he was twenty-one, scoring a brilliant goal in England's 4-0 victory over Scotland.

In spite of this success, Bobby was passed over for the England team that played in Sweden in the World Cup tournament of 1958. Although everyone agreed that Bobby was a soccer genius, his critics said that he was erratic and did not work hard enough. By the following year, however, he had forced his way back onto the England team. By then, Bobby was playing at outside-left rather than inside-forward, and his speed and powerful shot, with either foot, could be devastating. He was one of England's outstanding players in the 1962 World Cup in Chile.

Continuing the Story

When Sir Alf Ramsey became the England team manager in 1962, he decided to build the England team around Bobby. Developing a new tactical formation that virtually eliminated wingers, Ramsey played Bobby as a deep-lying center-forward. From this position, Bobby was able to utilize his newly developed passing abilities. He specialized in long, sweeping cross-field passes that could alter the pace and direction of a game. In addition, he was always dangerous when he set off on a powerful run from a deep position. Often he covered 20 or 30 yards before unleashing an unstoppable shot from the edge of the penalty area. His game became far more consistent than before, and he rarely had a bad match.

Career Highlights

106 international appearances for England
49 international goals (English record)

Honors, Awards, and Milestones

1957, 1965, 1967	English League champion
1963	English Football Association Cup champion
1966	World Cup champion
	European Player of the Year (Ballon d'Or)
	English Footballer of the Year
1968	European Cup champion
1969	Order of the British Empire
1974	English Professional Football Association Merit Award
	Commander of the British Empire
1994	Knighted by Queen Elizabeth II
2002	Inducted into first class of International Football Hall of Champions

He also won a reputation for sportsmanship—he never lost his temper or argued with referees.

Bobby's greatest moments came in 1966, when England won the World Cup. He scored a typically spectacular goal against Mexico, and two more against Portugal in the semifinals. After England's success, Bobby was probably the most popular player in the country, and he was greatly admired all over the world. Along with Denis Law and George Best, Bobby was part of the brilliant Manchester United forward line of the 1960's that helped Manchester to win the Football League championship twice. He was captain of the Manchester United team from 1968 to 1973.

Another great moment for Bobby came in 1968: He scored 2 goals in the European Cup final, steering Manchester United to a 4-1 victory over the Portuguese team, Benfica. Bobby made 106 appearances for England in all and scored 49 international goals, an English record. In 1969, in recognition of his services to soccer, he was awarded the Order of the British Empire (OBE), and in 1974, he received the Commander of the British Empire (CBE) award. In 1994, Bobby was knighted by Queen Elizabeth II.

Bobby finished his career as player-manager for Preston North End. He later became a director of Manchester United and organized schools for the training of young players. He was also an integral participant in England's successful bid to host the 2012 Olympics and was elected to the English Football Hall of Fame as a member of its first class in 2002.

Summary

Bobby Charlton was one of those rare players who could win a game in a few moments of supreme skill. His exciting style of play made the crowds roar with anticipation whenever he received the ball. When the film of the 1966 World Cup Final was released in England, Bobby's magnificent goal against Mexico still brought audiences to their feet, even though everyone knew it was coming. Bobby's unflappable temperament and his loyalty to his club made him a great ambassador for the game.

Bryan Aubrey

Additional Sources

Charlton, Bobby. *My Manchester United Years: The Autobiography.* London: Headline, 2007.

Charlton, Bobby, and Melvyn Bragg. *The Rules of Association Football, 1863.* Oxford: Bodleian Library, 2006.

Galvin, Robert, and Mark Bushell. *Football's Greatest Heroes: The National Football Museum's Hall of Fame.* London: Robson, 2005.

Murphy, Alex, and Andrew Endlar. *The Official Illustrated History of Manchester United: All New—The Full Story and Complete record, 1878-2006.* London: Orion, 2006.

Jack Charlton

Born: May 8, 1935
Ashington, Northumberland, England
Also known as: John Charlton (full name); Giraffe

Early Life
John "Jack" Charlton was born in Ashington, Northumberland, in the northeast of England on May 8, 1935. The large town nearest to Ashington is Newcastle-upon-Tyne. Newcastle is not only the capital of the distinctive Tyneside region but also home to Newcastle United, one of the most prominent soccer teams in England during Jack's formative years. Newcastle United's success undoubtedly influenced young Jack's commitment to soccer, particularly since he was a nephew of the star of the Newcastle team, the legendary forward Jackie Milburn.

The Road to Excellence
Like most soccer players of his generation, Jack began his soccer career by playing for amateur local teams. In 1951, he signed with the Leeds United amateurs, another typical step on the road to a soccer career in England. Football League clubs such as Leeds United have, in effect, their own farm systems: teams that compete at lower levels of competition than the first team does.

In 1952, having proved himself at the amateur level, Jack signed as a professional with Leeds United, and he stayed with the club throughout his playing career. In all, Jack made 773 appearances for Leeds, a club record. The fact that he stayed at Leeds is worth underlining, since Jack's career spanned the period when fees for transfers—or cash trades—skyrocketed.

The Emerging Champion
Through most of Jack's career at Leeds, the club was a rather ordinary member of the Football League. Jack's gangly physique and strength as a header of the ball enabled him to retain his position of center-half, anchoring the defense. In particular, Jack became known for occupying a position on the opposition's goal line during corner kicks. His ability in the air eventually earned for him the nickname "Giraffe."

Although Jack had proved to be a thoroughly reliable professional and had adapted to the tactical revolution that took place in English soccer in the early 1960's, his career did not blossom fully until twelve years after he had become a professional. One reason for his somewhat slow development was that much of his playing time was spent in the Football League second division. Division numbers are intended to suggest level of player ability: Leeds United was promoted to the more competitive first division in 1964. Jack's breakthrough came when he was picked to play for England's international team against Scotland in 1965. In that game Jack and his brother Bobby, the renowned Manchester United forward, became the first two brothers to play for England in the twentieth century. Jack made the most of the opportunity to play internationally and quickly became the defensive mainstay of the English team that won the World Cup in 1966. In 1967, Jack was named English footballer of the year.

Jack Charlton. (Bob Thomas/Getty Images)

> **Career Highlights**
>
> 35 international appearances for England
>
> **Honors, Awards, and Milestones**
>
> | | |
> |---|---|
> | 1966 | World Cup champion |
> | 1967 | English Footballer of the Year |
> | 1968 | English League Cup champion |
> | 1968, 1971 | UEFA Cup champion |
> | 1969 | English League champion |
> | 1972 | English Football Association Cup champion |
> | 1974 | English Football League Manager of the Year |
> | | Order of the British Empire |
> | 2005 | Inducted into English Football Hall of Fame |

At about the same time, Manager Don Revie was beginning to make his mark at Leeds United. Under his direction, Leeds became the dominant team in English soccer in the late 1960's and early 1970's. Although the Leeds team won fewer championships than expected, it compiled a record of consistency that was virtually unprecedented. In addition to winning the Football League Championship in 1969 and the Football Association Cup in 1972, the team met with considerable international success, winning what is now known as the Union of European Football Associations (UEFA) Cup in 1968 and 1971.

Jack's career as a player for England continued to flourish until the World Cup competition in Mexico in 1970. He played his last international game in that tournament, having been "capped" thirty-five times for his country. A "cap" refers to the piece of ceremonial headgear awarded international players upon their selection for the national team. Jack retired in 1973 after playing professionally for twenty years, during which time he became a model of tenacity and tactical shrewdness, making up for deficiencies in speed and ball control with an almost legendary work ethic.

Continuing the Story

Jack continued to work in soccer after his retirement. He was manager of Middlesborough from 1973 to 1977 and, in his first season, led the team back to the first division. He was named manager of the year in 1974 and spent another successful term as manager of the Sheffield Wednesday club from 1977 to 1983. He also made a less productive managerial contribution at Newcastle United in 1983-1984.

In February, 1986, Jack was the surprise choice to manage the Republic of Ireland national team. He performed this task with outstanding success, leading the team to the finals of the 1988 European Championships and to the 1990 World Cup Group Finals. In the 1994 World Cup, Ireland was the only representative from the British Isles. Though they were defeated by Holland, Ireland defeated the eventual runner-up team, Italy, 1-0.

Jack's managerial style was reflected in the uncompromising, unfashionable, economical, defense-minded play of the Irish team. In the rare moments when he was not engaged in soccer, Jack indulged in his hobbies of shooting and fishing.

Summary

Though Jack Charlton was by no means a naturally gifted athlete, his career was a classic example of how determination, dedication, and intelligence can enable a player to reach the highest levels of competition. His contribution to English national life was rewarded by enrollment in the Order of the British Empire by Queen Elizabeth II in 1974. For his contribution to soccer, Jack was inducted into the English Football Hall of Fame in 2005.

George O'Brien

Additional Sources

Charlton, Jack, and Peter Byrne. *Jack Charlton: The Autobiography.* New York: Partridge Press, 1996.

Galvin, Robert, and Mark Bushell. *Football's Greatest Heroes: The National Football Museum's Hall of Fame.* London: Robson, 2005.

Hunt, Chris. *The Complete Book of Soccer.* Buffalo, N.Y.: Firefly Books, 2006.

McKinstry, Leo. *Jack and Bobby.* London: Collins-Willow, 2003.

Brandi Chastain

Born: July 21, 1968
   San Jose, California
Also known as: Brandi Denise Chastain (full name)

Early Life
While growing up in Northern California, Brandi Chastain learned to love the game of soccer at an early age. She said that by the time she was six years old she knew this was the sport for her. Her grandfather helped encourage her love of the game by offering an incentive for every goal she kicked and a bigger one for each assist she made. Thanks to his emphasis of assists over goals, Brandi learned the importance of teamwork.

Brandi's parents, Roger and Lark, were among her biggest fans and supporters. She also loved to play all kinds of games with her younger brother. At the age of eight Brandi joined her first team, the Quakettes, and never looked back.

The Road to Excellence
Brandi played soccer for Archbishop Mitty High School in San Jose, winning three state championships. From the ages of twelve to sixteen she played for the Horizons, a team coached by her father. She also was noticed by the U.S. Olympic development group and played for her state team before moving on to a regional squad and then a national under-sixteen team. She excelled at soccer and her academics, receiving scholarship offers from a number of colleges and universities, including women's soccer power the University of North Carolina. She chose to stay close to home and play for University of California in Berkeley, just up the eastern shore of San Francisco Bay.

The Emerging Champion
In 1986, Brandi began her college career in spectacular fashion and was named *Soccer America*'s freshman player of the year. However, she was injured during the 1987 and 1988 seasons. After recovering from her injuries, she transferred to Santa Clara University, which was even nearer than Berkeley to her hometown of San Jose. There, she graduated in 1990 with a degree in television and communications. While at Santa Clara, she also led the Broncos to two final four appearances in the National Collegiate Athletic Association's women's

Brandi Chastain in celebration after helping Team USA win the final match of the 1999 Women's World Cup with a penalty kick. (AP/Wide World Photos)

World Cup Statistics

Season	Record	GP	G	Ast.	Pts.
1991	6-0-0	2	0	1	1
1999	5-0-1	6	1	2	4
2003	5-1-0	1	0	0	0
Totals	16-1-1	9	1	3	5

Notes: GP = games played; G = goals; Ast. = assists; Pts. = points

Olympic Statistics

Year	Record	GP	G	Ast.	Pts.
1996	4-0-1	5	0	0	0
2000	4-1-1	5	1	0	2
2004	5-0-1	3	0	0	0
Totals	13-1-3	13	1	0	2

Notes: GP = games played; G = goals; Ast. = assists; Pts. = points

soccer tournament. In 1989, she was named a member of the college all-Far West team. The following season, in 1990, she was part of the all-American first team, and the International Soccer Association of America named her national player of the year.

Brandi began playing for the U.S. national team in 1991, seeing action in two games. In between her many travels with the national team, Brandi worked as an assistant coach for the Santa Clara women's soccer team. Eventually, because of her traveling, she gave up the full-time position to serve as a volunteer.

In 1996, Brandi was a member of the gold-medal-winning Olympic team. When she joined the national team she was not a striker but a defender. In 1998, the team won the gold medal at the Goodwill Games; in 1999, it won the Women's World Cup title. The latter victory brought much recognition to the team and women's sports in general, as millions watched the games and cheered the team to victory.

Brandi's name became a household word when her picture appeared on the cover of all the major sports magazines following the victory. In fact, she was the first person to appear on the covers of *Sports Illustrated*, *Time*, and *Newsweek* all at the same time. Her picture, as she removed her shirt in triumph, celebrating in her sports bra, became a symbol of the growing recognition of female athletes as strong, feminine, independent women. That single picture propelled Brandi and women's soccer to the forefront of the sporting world in 1999. The national team won a silver medal in the 2000 Olympics in Sydney, Australia.

Continuing the Story

In addition to winning many championships with the national team, Brandi played professionally in Japan for Skiroke Serena. She was selected as the team's most valuable player. While she enjoyed that experience, she would have preferred to play in her own country. This opportunity came in the spring of 2001, with the creation of a new professional women's soccer league. Once again, Brandi returned to her hometown, this time to join the San Jose CyberRays, for whom she played until the league folded in 2003. Meanwhile, she continued to play on the U.S. women's national team. In 2004, she helped lead the team to its second Olympic gold medal, at Athens. At the end of that year, she retired from playing.

While still in her playing career, Brandi also became a motivational speaker. The winning penalty kick she had scored during the 1999 Women's World Cup made her one of the most famous athletes in the United States, ensuring her popularity on the lecture circuit. While traveling across the country, she spoke at schools, colleges, and other community centers. She also endorsed numerous products and became a leading spokesperson for soccer. She and her husband, Jerry Smith, continued to work with the Santa Clara University women's soccer team. Smith was the head coach, and Brandi was his assistant. Not by coincidence, when the two young British soccer players (played by Keira Knightley and Parminder Nagra) in the 2002 film *Bend It Like Beckham* go to the United States on

Honors, Awards, and Milestones

1986	*Soccer America* freshman player of the year
1990	NCAA first team All-American
	ISAA Player of the Year
1991, 1999	Women's World Cup champion, with American team
1996	Gold medal, Olympic Games
2000	Silver medal, Olympic Games
2004	Gold medal, Olympic Games

soccer scholarships, they attend Santa Clara University.

Summary

Brandi Chastain brought much attention to the sport of women's soccer. Her excellence on the field was an inspiration to young women everywhere. The image of her taking off her shirt remains a strong statement of the power and confidence of female athletes.

Leslie Heaphy, updated by the Editors

Additional Sources

Chastain, Brandi. *It's Not About the Bra: Play Hard, Play Fair, and Put the Fun Back into Competitive Sports.* San Francisco: Collins, 2004.

Crothers, Tim. "Spectacular Takeoff." *Sports Illustrated* 93 (July 3, 2000): 64.

Goldblatt, David. *The Ball Is Round: A Global History of Soccer.* New York: Riverhead Books, 2008.

Hunt, Chris. *The Complete Book of Soccer.* Buffalo, N.Y.: Firefly Books, 2006.

O'Reilly, Jean, and Susan K. Cahn, eds. *Women and Sports in the United States: A Documentary Reader.* Boston: Northeastern University Press, 2007.

Radnedge, Keir, and Gary Lineker. *The Ultimate Encyclopedia of Soccer: The Definitive Illustrated Guide to World Soccer.* London: Carlton Books, 2004.

Rasmussen, R. Kent. "Women's World Cup of Soccer Draws Unprecedented Attention." In *Great Events: 1900-2001.* Vol. 8. Pasadena, Calif.: Salem Press, 2002.

Johan Cruyff

Born: April 25, 1947
Amsterdam, the Netherlands
Also known as: Hendrik Johannes Cruijff (birth name); Johan Cruijff; Flying Dutchman; Golden Dutchman

Early Life
Johan Cruyff was born on April 25, 1947, in Amsterdam, in the Netherlands. Growing up in Holland, Johan had an interesting choice of winter sports—ice-skating, field hockey, and soccer. In all these sports, Holland enjoyed a degree of international success. However, fate determined that soccer would attract Johan. Because Johan's father, a grocer, was deceased, Johan's mother had to find work, and she found employment as a cleaning lady in the Ajax Stadium in Amsterdam. The stadium was the home of a professional soccer team called Ajax.

The Road to Excellence
European soccer is based on a vast grassroots movement, drawing its players from the immediate community and utilizing the talents of very young players. Johan trained and practiced diligently from the age of four. He knew that to be accepted as a soccer apprentice took a degree of good fortune and an enormous amount of hard work.

At the age of ten, Johan was selected to be a member of the elite Ajax Juniors after a grueling process that eliminated two hundred other hopeful players. Rinus Michels, a famous Dutch coach, later said of Johan that even "as a baby he was an exceptional player." In addition to his skill and deftness, Johan had remarkable physical strength and stamina for his size. At fifteen years of age, he was only 5 feet 3 inches tall and weighed just 115 pounds.

The Emerging Champion
In 1965, when Johan joined the senior Ajax team as a forward, the team had been continually finishing in the lower half of its league. Johan proved to be a dynamo. He scored goals, led by example, and was an inspiring player.

Johan followed up three consecutive Dutch player of the year awards with two European player of the year awards in 1971 and 1973. He starred for Ajax and the Dutch national team, and although Holland lost the World Cup Final to West Germany

Dutch player Johan Cruyff dribbling the ball under pressure from a West German defender in the World Cup in 1974. (AFP/Getty Images)

> **Career Highlights**
>
> 48 international appearances and 33 goals for Holland
>
> **Honors, Awards, and Milestones**
>
> | | |
> |---|---|
> | 1966-68, 1970, 1972-73, 1982-84 | Dutch League champion |
> | 1967-69 | Dutch Player of the Year |
> | 1971-73 | European Cup champion |
> | 1971, 1973-74 | European Player of the Year (Ballon d'Or) |
> | 1974 | World Cup Most Valuable Player |
> | 1979 | NASL Player of the Year |
> | 1986 | *World Soccer* Manager of the Year |
> | 1998 | Inducted into International Football Hall of Champions |

in 1974, he was voted the tournament's most valuable player.

One year earlier, in 1973, Johan had left Ajax to join El Club de Futbol de Barcelona in Spain. Sporting superstars are frequently motivated by complex reasons for switching clubs. Among Johan's reasons for leaving Holland was that he wanted to join his former coach, Rinus Michels; he also was unhappy with Holland's 80 percent level of income tax for people earning what he did. Barcelona paid Ajax the sum of $2,250,000 for Johan, which was the highest transfer sum in soccer history up to that time.

In the 1970's, European professional soccer clubs were willing to invest huge amounts of money in attempts to create championship teams. In his first year with Barcelona, Johan was paid a basic sum of $10,000 a month, and once incentives, bonuses, and endorsements were added to that, it was not surprising that the Spanish press came to name Johan not the "Flying Dutchman" but the "Golden Dutchman."

Perhaps Johan's greatest asset was his ability to motivate and transform his teammates. Just as he had with Ajax in 1965, he turned a losing team into an incredible power that won or drew its next twenty-six games. At the end of the season, Barcelona was the Spanish League champion, and Johan was on his way to becoming a major Spanish folk hero.

Johan's inspiring leadership continued into 1974, with Barcelona winning the Spanish League title again. In 1976 and 1977, Barcelona was runner-up. Sadly, the pressure of public celebrity took its toll on Johan and his family. In June, 1978, he announced his retirement. He commented bleakly that "even if you go to the toilet, somebody's marking you."

Happily, Johan's retirement was short-lived. He decided to play some exhibition games for the New York Cosmos of the North American Soccer League (NASL), who had done a brilliant job of resurrecting the career of the Brazilian star Pelé. However, the chance to play again under Michels took Johan to the NASL's Los Angeles Aztecs. In July of 1979, Johan signed a two-year contract with the Aztecs worth, in total, more than $2 million.

Although he was thirty-two years of age, Johan proved that he still possessed magical skills. Players in the NASL were awed by Johan's ability to beat defender after defender. Just as with Ajax and Barcelona, Johan was such a dangerous threat that opposing teams had to devise two-player formations to defend against the Dutchman.

Continuing the Story

In 1979, Johan was the NASL's player of the year, but he never really enjoyed playing with the Aztecs because the team played some of its games indoors on artificial turf. Johan negotiated a sizable contract with the NASL's Washington Diplomats and announced that "real" soccer should be played on proper grass. The Diplomats had a natural grass soccer field. In 1980, Johan played in Washington, but he left near the start of the 1981 season. He transferred to the Levante club in Spain.

One goal that is still talked about took place on August 16, 1981. Johan, playing for the Diplomats and surrounded by three defenders, banged in a goal from 40 yards out against the Toronto Blizzard.

At the end of 1981, Johan re-signed with Ajax of Amsterdam. Many soccer players stay in the game into their late thirties with skills and speed that erode and then evaporate. That was not the case with Johan. Although his blinding pace and acceleration were diminished, his artistry and technical ability remained untarnished. He took Ajax to two championship titles, and then, as a swan song, joined Feyenoord—another Dutch professional soccer team—and guided the team to a league championship. In 1985, Johan was appointed as Ajax's technical director, and one year later he was named European manager of the year.

Later, Johan replaced Terry Venables as the coach of Barcelona, and in 1989, he led the team to the European Cup Winners' Cup. In 1992, he added the European Cup championship to his list of accomplishments, helping Barcelona step out of the shadow of national rival Real Madrid. By 1994, he had won four successive Spanish Championships. In 1996, however, he was replaced after two disappointing seasons. During his tenure with Barcelona, he won eleven trophies in eight years, successfully making the transition from player to coach.

Johan has won numerous accolades, including the Royal Netherlands Football Association's (KNVB) golden player award, which, in 2003, designated Johan as the most outstanding Dutch player in the last fifty years. In 2006, Johan received the lifetime achievement award at the Laureus World Sports Awards.

Summary

Johan Cruyff was the world's top player through much of the 1970's, and some experts rank him with Pelé among soccer's all-time greats. Like the Brazilian superstar, Johan turned his teams into winners wherever he played.

Scott A. G. M. Crawford

Additional Sources

Barend, Frits, and Henk van Dorp. *Ajax, Barcelona, Cruyff: The ABC of an Obstinate Maestro.* London: Bloomsbury, 1998.

Hunt, Chris. *The Complete Book of Soccer.* Buffalo, N.Y.: Firefly Books, 2006.

Janssen, Roel. "Hail Number Fourteen." *Europe* 367 (1997).

LaBlanc, Michael L., and Richard Henshaw. *The World Encyclopedia of Soccer.* Detroit: Gale Research, 1994.

Landon Donovan

Born: March 4, 1982
Ontario, California
Also known as: Landon Timothy Donovan (full name); LD; Lanny; Landycakes; Lando; Primadonovan

Early Life
Landon Donovan was born in Ontario, California, on March 4, 1982. He and his twin sister, Tristan, and older brother, Josh, were raised by their single mother, Donna, in Redlands, California. As a struggling single-parent family, the Donovans often felt ostracized. Landon's older brother taught Landon the basics of soccer. When Landon was five years old, he played in his first organized game in a league with six- and seven-year-olds. He scored 7 goals.

The Road to Excellence
By the time Landon was a freshman in high school, he had become a star. During that first high school season, Landon was named league most valuable player. As a sophomore, Landon transferred high schools and played in only ten games. He scored 16 goals and had 12 assists. In 1997, he also began playing for the U.S. national under-seventeen team. During his first season of international competition, Landon was the team's leader in both goals, with 23, and assists, with 13. He was named an all-American by the National Soccer Coaches of America.

While he could not devote himself to his high school team as a sophomore, Landon still managed to score 15 goals and rack up 19 assists in a short season. Following the season, he was named to the 1999 *Parade* magazine high school all-American team. As Landon continued his exploits on the international level, many hailed him as the best prospect in the history of American soccer. With lofty expectations, Landon was soon approached by international teams. In 1998, the German squad Bayer Leverkusen began courting Landon. The change would be enormous, but Landon and his father, who had recently reentered his life, both felt that playing in Europe was best for the development of Landon's game.

The Emerging Champion
In the spring of 1999, Landon left the United States to play for Bayer Leverkusen. The team signed the seventeen-year-old to a four-year contract worth $400,000. Then, Landon signed a more lucrative deal with Nike. Though Landon

Los Angeles Galaxy forward Landon Donovan surveying the field in a game against the Columbus Crew in 2008. (Greg Bartram/MLS/Getty Images)

MLS Statistics

Season	GP	GS	Min.	G	Ast.	Pts.
2001	22	17	1,666	7	10	24
2002	20	18	1,681	7	3	17
2003	22	21	1,882	12	6	30
2004	23	22	2,018	6	10	22
2005	22	20	1,887	12	10	34
2006	24	24	2,147	12	8	32
2007	25	24	2,191	8	13	29
2008	24	22	2,046	19	9	47
Totals	182	168	15,518	83	69	235

Notes: GP = games played; GS = games started; Min. = minutes played; G = goals; Ast. = assists; Pts. = points

learned much about the technical aspects of soccer, he was not happy in Germany. In 2001, he was loaned to the San Jose Sharks of Major League Soccer (MLS) and returned to the United States. In his first season in MLS, Landon led the Sharks to the MLS Championship. He played four seasons in MLS and was named U.S. soccer athlete of the year in 2003. Then, in 2004, Landon returned to Germany a more accomplished and confident player.

Landon's second stay in Germany did not turn out much better than his first. He did not receive many starts and soon desired to return to the United States. This time, Landon returned home to play for the Los Angeles Galaxy. Over the subsequent years, he became the second all-time leading playoff scorer in MLS history. In 2007, he was teamed with international superstar David Beckham. After that, the two formed a potent offensive duo. In 2008, the Galaxy lent Landon to Bayern Munich.

While Landon accomplished much in MLS, he might best known for his play for the U.S. national team. He was named best young player for the 2002 World Cup. After his performance at the prestigious event, many predicted an even better showing for the U.S. team in the 2006 World Cup. However, the Americans did not advance from group competition, and Landon took much of the blame. Nonetheless, Landon is considered among the greatest all-time American soccer players. In addition to his three MLS Championship Cups and numerous player of the year awards, Landon became the national team's leader in both all-time goals, with 36, and assists, with 23.

Continuing the Story

Landon planned to play in the 2010 World Cup in South Africa. At that time, Landon would be twenty-eight and in the prime of his career, providing the United States with perhaps its best chance at World Cup glory. Landon was a part of the original group of players involved in "Project 2010." The goal of the project was to bring a World Cup Championship to the United States by 2010. As a member of the Galaxy, Donovan continued to excite his hometown crowd. As a member of the U.S. national team, he impressed the international community and was considered perhaps the greatest player in American soccer history.

Summary

Landon Donovan is the all-time leading scorer for the U.S. men's national soccer team. From his hometown of Redlands, California, he became a nationally recognized player in high school. Afterward, he played in Europe to hone his skills. However, he did not become a dominant player until he returned to the United States to play in MLS. Many consider Landon to be the best soccer player in both MLS and U.S. history.

Theodore Shields

Additional Sources

Buckley, James. *Landon Donovan*. Chanhassen, Minn.: Child's World, 2007.

"Donovan Returns to MLS to Play for Galaxy." *USA Today*, March 31, 2005.

Murcia, Rebecca Thatcher. *Landon Donovan: World Class Soccer Star*. Hockessin, Del.: Mitchell Lane, 2005.

"U.S. World Cup Hopes Lie at Donovan's Talented Feet." *The New York Times*, May 13, 2006.

Honors and Awards

1999	Under-17 World Championship golden ball award
2001	MLS all-star game most valuable player
2002-04, 2007-08	Honda Player of the Year
2002, 2003, 2005	CONCACAF Gold Cup Best XI
2003	MLS Best XI
	MLS Cup Most Valuable Player
2003, 2004	U.S. Soccer Player of the Year
2005	MLS all-time Best XI
2005-08	Los Angeles Galaxy Golden Boot
2008	MLS Golden Boot

Eusébio

Born: January 25, 1942
Lourenço Marques, Portuguese East Africa (now Mozambique)
Also known as: Eusébio da Silva Ferreira; the Black Pearl; the Black Panther

Early Life
Eusébio da Silva Ferreira was born on January 25, 1942, in Lourenço Marques, Mozambique, which was then known as Portuguese East Africa. Eusébio was born in a squalid section of Lourenço Marques and lived his early life in shanty houses. School had little to offer the young Eusébio. He spent most of his time in the streets playing soccer barefoot with other poor boys. No one could have imagined that the little street urchin would one day become one of the most famous soccer players in the world.

The Road to Excellence
The young Eusébio made a considerable impact as a soccer player, and he became well known in the area in which he lived. He was strong, fast, skillful, and courageous. People began talking about the young boy with such prodigious talent. At fifteen, Eusébio was signed by Sporting Clube de Lourenço Marques, the leading club in the city. The club decided to take a gamble on the untried but talented youngster. Becoming a professional soccer player transformed Eusébio's life. As a signing bonus, he was given a new pair of soccer boots; he wept when he received them. They were the first boots he had ever owned.

Eusébio may have been inexperienced, but he quickly made an impact as a professional. In his three years with Sporting Clube he scored 55 goals, and his dazzling exploits on the field came to the attention of the soccer-playing world. In 1960, the Brazilian manager, José Bauer, came to Mozambique to see how good Eusébio was. He was extremely impressed. Bauer was convinced that Eusébio could have an impact upon world soccer. In the early 1960's, Mozambique was still a part of Portuguese East Africa, and Bauer was convinced that Eusébio should go to Portugal to play. In 1960, Bauer contacted Bela Guttmann, the manager of Benfica, Portugal's leading club, and told him what great potential Eusébio had. Bauer recommended that Benfica sign the African prodigy. Guttman took Bauer's advice and arranged for Eusébio to travel to Portugal. Eusébio arrived amid great secrecy. However, he had to wait until 1961 for his registration to clear before he made his debut for Benfica.

The Emerging Champion
Eusébio played his first game for Benfica in a club tournament in Paris. In that competition he came up against Pelé, who was already established as one of the best players in the world. Eusébio rose to the challenge and proved to be Pelé's equal, and they both became the stars of the tournament. Eusébio even managed to score three goals against Santos, Pelé's team.

Even though Benfica had just won the European Cup, Eusébio settled into the team quickly. His dynamic displays at center forward led to his selection to the Portuguese national team within months of his debut for Benfica. Already Eusébio was dominating Portuguese football, and he continued to do so throughout his fourteen-year career with Benfica. With Eusébio at the helm, Benfica dominated Portuguese league and cup competitions and performed heroically in Europe, retaining the European Cup in 1962 and finishing as runner-up in 1963, 1965, and 1968. In the 1962 final, Eusébio inspired his team to a 5-3 win against mighty Real Madrid. On that night, Eusébio could proudly claim to be the king of European soccer. In 1965, Eusébio's coronation was confirmed when he was chosen European player of the year. He certainly deserved his nickname of the "Black Pearl."

Continuing the Story
The 1966 World Cup tournament, played in England, provided Eusébio with the most memorable moments of his career. He scored the most goals in the competition, with 9 in six games. Almost single-handedly, he took Portugal to a third-place finish in the tournament.

In the quarterfinal game, Portugal was down 3-0 to North Korea, the surprise team of the tournament. Staring defeat in the face, Eusébio took over, scoring four goals and setting up the fifth for a grateful teammate. In Portugal's 5-3 win, Eusébio had engineered one of the most remarkable comebacks in soccer history. The incredible victory against North Korea set up a semifinal meeting against England, the home nation. In front of a huge crowd that was willing England to victory, Eusébio played his heart out. Although he scored another goal, Eusébio could not prevent England, the eventual tournament winner, from progressing into the final; England won the riveting game 2-1. Still, Eusébio's individual displays against North Korea and England demonstrated that he was one of the most exciting players in the world.

By 1966, nobody doubted Eusébio's ability. The Brazilian team Vasco de Gama even offered Benfica $500,000 for Eusébio's services. Vasco de Gama thought that Eusébio was the only player in the world who could provide a counter-attraction to the great Pelé, most likely a correct assumption. The major part of Eusébio's career was spent at Benfica, where he led the club to ten league championships and five cup wins in his fourteen seasons. During this time, he was the leading scorer in Portugal on nine occasions, and he also managed to play a record seventy-seven games for Portugal's national team. Like any outstanding goal scorer, Eusébio received some brutal treatment from opposing defenders. The battering finally took its toll, and at the end of the 1975 season, Eusébio left Benfica to play in the United States. In the less physical world of the North American Soccer League, he again demonstrated the skills that had thrilled European crowds for a decade and a half.

Career Highlights

77 international appearances for Portugal
46 international goals

Honors, Awards, and Milestones

1962	European Cup champion
1963-65, 1967-69, 1971-73	Portuguese League Champion
1965	European Player of the Year (Ballon d'Or)
1966	World Cup high scorer (9 goals)
1998	Inducted into International Football Hall of Champions

Summary

Eusébio went from abject poverty to world fame and fortune. From the time he left Africa, Eusébio was constantly expected to prove himself. He hurdled every challenge that confronted him, and his fast, skillful, and determined play brought him the goals and the acclaim he richly deserved.

David L. Andrews

Additional Sources

Hunt, Chris. *The Complete Book of Soccer.* Buffalo, N.Y.: Firefly Books, 2006.

Radnedge, Keir. *Fifty Years of the European Cup and Champions League.* London: Carlton, 2007.

Radnedge, Keir, and Gary Lineker. *The Ultimate Encyclopedia of Soccer: The Definitive Illustrated Guide to World Soccer.* London: Carlton Books, 2004.

Julie Foudy

Born: January 23, 1971
  San Diego, California
Also known as: Julie Maurine Foudy (full name)

Early Life

Julie Maurine Foudy was born and raised in San Diego, California. Her parents, Judy and Jim Foudy, had four children, of whom Julie was the youngest. Julie enjoyed activities like swimming, boogie boarding in the Pacific Ocean, and playing softball on a team coached by her father. Julie began playing soccer at the age of six during recess, and her involvement in competitive soccer began as she got older. In the seventh grade, she was a member of a club team that traveled to Oslo, Norway, to compete in the Oslo Cup. Shortly after that, Julie got involved in the Olympic Development Program, which introduced her to the U.S. women's national team.

The Road to Excellence

Julie attended Mission Viejo High School in Southern California, where she was a two-time first-team all-American. She was honored as the player of the year for Southern California three straight years, in 1987, 1988, and 1989. Her senior year in high school, she was also named the *Los Angeles Times* soccer player of the decade. Julie played her first game for the U.S. national team in 1988, at the age of seventeen, and her first international game for the United States in a match against France in Rimini, Italy, on July 29, 1988. In 1989, she began her four-year soccer career at Stanford University. In the same year, Julie was named the *Soccer America* freshman of the year and selected to the National Soccer Coaches Association of America (NSCAA) all-American team. She was also named the 1989 Stanford University freshman athlete of the year. Julie was named to the NSCAA all-American team not only in her freshman season but also for the additional three years that she played college soccer. In 1991 and 1992, she was a finalist for the Hermann Trophy, which recognizes the nation's top women's collegiate soccer player. She finished her career at Stanford with 52 goals, 32 assists, and 136 points and was honored as the team's most valuable player for three consecutive years, in 1989, 1990, and 1991. In 1993, she graduated from Stanford with a degree in sociology.

The Emerging Champion

In 1991, Julie scored her first goal as a member of the U.S. national team and helped to capture the world championship. She started as an attacking midfielder on the 1991 team, and she played as a defensive midfielder on the 1995 and 1996 national teams, showing her ability to contribute in a variety of ways on the field. Julie's capacity for leadership earned her the title of captain of the U.S. national teams in the 2000 and 2004 Olympic Games, World Cup qualifying in 2002, and the 2003 World Cup. During her career as a midfielder, she col-

Julie Foudy celebrating after scoring a goal against Russia in 2000. (AP/Wide World Photos)

Honors, Awards, and Milestones

1989-93	NSCAA All-American
1991, 1999	World Cup champion
1996, 2004	Gold medal, Olympic Games
1997	FIFA Fair Play Award
2000	Silver medal, Olympic Games
2000-04	U.S. team captain
2007	Inducted into National Soccer Hall of Fame

lected 271 "caps," or international games played, making her the third most capped player in world soccer history at the time. Another historical title Julie held was the most national team appearances: She played in 231 games as a member of the U.S. squad. This achievement placed her at number three among men and women in the category.

Julie was a member of the U.S. teams that won the Women's World Cup in 1991 and 1999 and the Olympic gold medal in 1996 and 2004. During the 1996 Olympic Games, she played every minute of the five U.S. matches. She was also a part of the 2000 U.S. team that won the silver medal in the Olympic Games. Julie played in twenty-four World Cup games, twelve World Cup qualifiers, and sixteen Olympic matches. She was a member of U.S. teams at the 1991, 1995, 1999, and 2003 Women's World Cups and the 1996, 2000, and 2004 Olympics. In those four Women's World Cups and three Olympic Games, she played every one of the thirty U.S. games.

Continuing the Story

In addition to her role with the national team, in 1994, Julie played for the Tyreso Football Club in Sweden with several of her U.S. teammates. She played for the Sacramento Storm, which won the 1993 and 1995 California State Amateur championships. She also played one season in the United Soccer Leagues W-League and one season in the Japanese professional league. From 2001 to 2003, Julie played for the San Diego Spirit in the Women's United Soccer Association (WUSA) and was a second-team all-star in each of those three seasons. She played fifty-nine WUSA regular-season games and one WUSA playoff game. She was a founding member of the league and later became heavily involved in efforts to revive professional soccer for women. In 2004, Julie played her final game as a member of the U.S. national team against Mexico in Carson, California. She concluded her international career with 21 international goals and 114 international appearances.

Julie became a political activist, advocating for women's rights, rights for children, and fair labor. She served as the president of the Women's Sports Foundation, a charitable educational non-profit organization dedicated to advancing the lives of girls through sports. She was the first American and woman to win the FIFA Fair Play Award, which acknowledged her 1997 advocacy of ending child labor. In addition, Julie was a strong proponent of Title IX equality, trying to ensure equal opportunities for young girls. She and her husband, Ian Sawyers, created the Julie Foudy Sports Leadership Academy, an organization that teaches girls how to be leaders on the field and in life through soccer. Julie embraced her status as an athlete to influence decision making surrounding issues important to her.

Summary

In 2007, Julie was inducted into the National Soccer Hall of Fame along with teammate Mia Hamm. After her retirement from playing soccer, she served as a broadcaster for not only soccer but also women's basketball. Her desire to succeed and her passion for making a difference in the lives of young people made her stand out and reflected her on-field success.

Deborah Stroman

Additional Sources

Christopher, Matt. *On the Field with . . . Julie Foudy*. Boston: Little, Brown, 2000.

Savage, Jeff. *Julie Foudy: Soccer Superstar*. Minneapolis: Lerner, 1999.

Simon, Rita James. *Sporting Equality: Title IX Thirty Years Later*. New Brunswick, N.J.: Transaction, 2005.

Garrincha

Born: October 28, 1933
Pau Grande, Brazil
Died: January 20, 1983
Rio de Janeiro, Brazil
Also known as: Manuel Francisco dos Santos (full name)

Early Life

Manuel Francisco dos Santos was born in 1933, in Pau Grande, Brazil. Like many Brazilian soccer stars, Manuel came from humble beginnings. He was reared in a poor village in the suburbs of Rio de Janeiro, and he was captivated by soccer from an early age. Manuel was a sickly child. He was nearly killed by polio. The disease distorted his right leg—even after surgery his leg was permanently crooked. As a result of his disability, Manuel was nicknamed "Garrincha," a Portuguese expression that means "little bird." The problems he faced in his early life would have proved insurmountable to many people, yet Garrincha was determined to become a great soccer player. In fact, many people believe that his abnormal right leg encouraged him to develop skills that were beyond the range of other players.

Brazilian forward Garrincha stealing the ball from an English defender during a World Cup game. (Popperfoto/Getty Images)

The Road to Excellence

As a youth, Garrincha had little time for formal education. All he wanted to do was play soccer. The hours he spent playing with a ball had a great effect on his overall health. As he grew older and played more, his body became stronger. Garrincha also developed an individual and distinctive style of play; he was skillful and fast, a great dribbler of the ball. Garrincha was a natural winger.

Even though his attributes marked him as an obvious winger, he joined his local team, Pau Grande, as an inside left when he was fourteen. He was soon converted to the wing. The chirpy youngster became a favorite on the team, as much for his personality as for his play on the field. Even in his early career Garrincha showed the flashes of brilliance for which he later became world-famous. His play, however, was often marred by long periods of inactivity, when he would simply drift out of the game. He was always a demanding player to coach.

Garrincha served his soccer apprenticeship at Pau Grande, and, by 1953, he decided to try out for a better club. He chose Botafogo, the biggest club in Rio de Janeiro. Garrincha had a trial with Botafogo and impressed the club's management sufficiently for them to offer him a contract. Unlike many young players, Garrincha did not have to serve time on Botafogo's reserve teams. The club coach realized that Garrincha had an immense amount of potential and, from the start, wanted to play this exciting young talent on the first team.

The Emerging Champion

At Botafogo, Garrincha blossomed. With better players around him, he was able to use his individual skills more effectively. In the next few years, Garrincha taunted and mesmerized opponents and charmed crowds throughout Brazil. In 1954, he was selected for the prestigious Rio select team, and, in 1957, he made his full international debut for Brazil.

Garrincha's first match in the famous yellow and blue of Brazil was not a happy experience. He found getting into the flow of the game difficult, and as a result of his below-par performance, he was dropped for the next game. With the World Cup looming in Sweden, in 1958, Garrincha was on the fringes of the national side. On his return to Botafogo, he regained his confidence and convinced the Brazilian coach, Vincente Feola, that he could not be overlooked. Although Garrincha was selected to travel to Sweden, he began the tournament as a reserve. Following a lackluster performance against England, a group of Brazilian players went to Feola to plead for Garrincha to be in the starting lineup for the final group game against Russia. Garrincha was inconsistent, but he did possess a spark of individual genius that could ignite any team.

Feola eventually relented and picked Garrincha for the Russia game. Garrincha's performance in Brazil's 2-0 victory set the whole soccer world abuzz. The lightning-quick and impudently skillful Brazilian marvel became the talk of the World Cup. After beating Wales, Brazil progressed to the semifinal stage against France. In a one-sided encounter the Brazilians, led by Didi, Pelé, and Garrincha, trounced the French 5-2. The final of the 1958 World Cup proved to be an intriguing duel between Sweden, the home nation, and the talented Brazilians. Garrincha was the instrumental figure in Brazil's 5-2 victory. His swerving run set up the first two Brazilian goals, and his play was breathtaking throughout the game. The "little bird" was on top of the world.

Continuing the Story

Garrincha returned from Sweden a national hero, but he did not rest on his laurels. He led Botafogo to three Brazilian championships between 1957 and 1962, and continued to shine among the numerous stars of Brazilian soccer. Garrincha was at his peak in the 1962 Chile World Cup. He almost single-handedly beat England in the quarterfinals with two stunning goals. He then repeated the performance in the semifinal against Chile. He was irrepressible; when he was at his best no defender in the world could guard him.

Garrincha's dazzling display against Chile was spoiled by his ejection late in the game, when he retaliated after receiving yet another painful kick. Additionally, he was struck by a bottle as he walked back to the dressing room and required stitches for a nasty head wound. After Garrincha's dismissal from the game, he should have missed the final against Czechoslovakia. However, the soccer authorities backed down, and Garrincha was allowed to parade his dazzling array of skills in the 3-1 victory in which Brazil retained its world crown. Following the 1962 World Cup, injury problems began to hamper Garrincha's career. Doctors discovered that his knee joints were rapidly wearing away, and that caused him to lose some of his electric speed. In 1966, he was transferred to Corinthians, another Brazilian club. Despite a few flashes of his old brilliance in the 1966 World Cup in England, Garrincha realized that his best days were past. He spent the remainder of his career playing for a succession of clubs before finally retiring from soccer in 1972. Beset by financial, marital, and substance abuse problems in the years following his retirement, Garrincha died in 1983.

Summary

As a soccer player, Garrincha was unique. He captivated crowds around the world with his great individualism. Garrincha had an instinctive and natural ability that stood out in an era of great players. After polio threatened to end his life, Garrincha was even more determined to excel.

David L. Andrews

Additional Sources

Castro, Ruy. *Garrincha: The Triumph and Tragedy of Brazil's Forgotten Footballing Hero.* London: Yellow Jersey, 2005.

"Garrincha." *Soccer Digest* 21, no. 6 (1999).

Hunt, Chris. *The Complete Book of Soccer.* Buffalo, N.Y.: Firefly Books, 2006.

LaBlanc, Michael L., and Richard Henshaw. *The World Encyclopedia of Soccer.* Detroit: Gale Research, 1994.

Career Highlights

51 international appearances for Brazil

Honors, Awards, and Milestones

1958, 1962	World Cup Champion
1961-62	Brazilian League Champion
1999	Inducted into International Football Hall of Champions

Steven Gerrard

Born: May 30, 1980
    Whiston, Merseyside, England
Also known as: Steven George Gerrard (full name)

Early Life

Steven George Gerrard was born in Whiston, a suburb of Liverpool, England, on May 30, 1980. He grew up on the Bluebell council estate in Huyton, about five miles east of the city center. A boyhood fan of the Liverpool soccer team, Steven was first spotted by scouts from the club at the age of nine, while playing for a local team, the Whiston Juniors. In 1994, he joined Liverpool as a youth player and signed his first professional contract three years later. Although Steven's talent was obvious, he was not a child prodigy like his friend and contemporary Michael Owen. Steven never played for the England Schoolboys team. Growth spurts restricted the number of games that he played in his later teenage years.

The Road to Excellence

In November, 1998, at the age of eighteen, Steven made his Liverpool debut coming on as a substitute in a league game against Blackburn. His versatility, athleticism, and skill were obvious, and he became a first-team regular during the 1999-2000 season. In December, 1999, Steven scored his first Liverpool goal in a 4-1 victory over Sheffield. In May, 2000, he made his English national team debut against Ukraine and played a small role in England's disappointing campaign at that summer's European Championships in Belgium and the Netherlands. Persistent back problems threatened Steven's career at the time, curtailing his ability to play a full season. These problems were not resolved overnight and forced Steven to miss the 2002 World Cup Final in Japan and Korea in order to undergo a groin operation. Subsequently, his body held up much more reliably to the demands of professional soccer.

The Emerging Champion

Steven's breakthrough season came in 2000-2001, when Liverpool won a "treble" of cup competitions. Steven was an integral part of the team coached by Frenchman Gérard Houllier, which played in a counter-attacking style heavily dependent on Steven's midfield drive and Michael

Steven Gerrard. (Gareth Copley/PA Photos/Landov)

Owen's pace and goal-scoring instincts. Steven made fifty appearances that season, scoring ten goals, including one in the Union of European Football Associations (UEFA) Cup final, a 5-4 triumph over the Spanish side Alavés. He was also voted young player of the year by his peers from the Professional Footballers' Association.

The following season, Steven helped Liverpool to finish second in the league and scored his first goal for England in its 5-1 victory against Germany in a World Cup qualifying game in Munich. His form during the early part of the 2002-2003 season was patchy, but he recovered to score the opening goal in Liverpool's 2-0 victory over Manchester United in the League Cup final in February, 2003. At the start of the 2003-2004 season, Steven replaced Sami Hyypiä as Liverpool captain, becoming the first local player to take the job since Phil Thompson more than twenty years earlier.

Continuing the Story

Although Steven played well in his first season as captain, the team did not perform to expectations, finishing fourth in the league and winning no trophies. Houllier was fired at the end of the season, and media speculation that summer—when Steven played for England at the European Championships in Portugal—suggested that Steven might seek a transfer. However, Liverpool appointed the Spaniard Rafael Benítez as its new coach and Steven decided to stay. In domestic competition, Benítez's first season was modest: Liverpool finished fifth in the league, was defeated in the League Cup final by Chelsea, and lost embarrassingly to Burnley in the Football Association (FA) Cup.

Honors and Awards

Year	Award
2001	Professional Footballers' Association Young Player of the Year
2001, 2003-04, 2006	Premier League player of the month (March, March, December, April)
2001, 2006	Liverpool FC fans' player of the year
2005	UEFA Champions League Most Valuable Player
2006	Professional Footballers' Association Player of the Year
2007	Order of the British Empire (MBE)
	English national football team player of the year

Professional Statistics

Season	Team	Games Played	Goals
1998-99	Liverpool	11	0
1999-00	Liverpool	28	1
2000-01	Liverpool	33	7
2001-02	Liverpool	28	3
2002-03	Liverpool	34	5
2003-04	Liverpool	34	4
2004-05	Liverpool	30	7
2005-06	Liverpool	32	10
2006-07	Liverpool	36	7
2007-08	Liverpool	34	11
Totals		300	55

In European soccer's elite competition, the Champions League, the story was different. Steven ensured that Liverpool made early progress, scoring the decisive goal in a 3-1 victory over Olympiakos. To many people's surprise, Liverpool reached the final, defeating Juventus and Chelsea en route. The final, in Istanbul, Turkey, against Italian team AC Milan was arguably the greatest match in Liverpool club history. Losing 3-0 at halftime, Liverpool scored 3 goals in six second-half minutes to tie the game. Steven scored the first—a powerful header. Liverpool then crowned its astonishing comeback by winning the match in a penalty shoot-out.

Following a second successive summer of transfer speculation, Steven decided to commit fully to Liverpool. The results were immediate. Steven enjoyed his best season in 2005-2006, scoring 23 goals from midfield in fifty-three league and nonleague games. The season culminated in another dramatic performance, this time against West Ham United in the FA Cup final. With Liverpool trailing 3-2 with just seconds to go, Steven scored a superb long-range goal—his second of the game—to send the game into extra time. Liverpool then won the cup in a penalty shootout, with Steven scoring one of the penalties.

Summary

Steven Gerrard captained Liverpool to a second Champions League final in three years in May, 2007, where the team lost 2-1 to AC Milan. When available for selection, Steven remained one of the first names on every England team sheet and was appointed captain of the national team by Coach Fabio Capello. Steven was widely recognized as one of the finest midfielders in the world: supremely fit, defensively able, a persistent attacking threat, and a leader by example. Steven's big-game mentality was illustrated by the fact that he was the first Englishman to score in each of the Champions League, UEFA Cup, FA Cup, and League Cup finals. Steven will be recognized as one of the greatest players in Liverpool's history.

Alan McDougall

Additional Sources

Balague, Guillaume. *A Season on the Brink: A Portrait of Rafael Benitez's Liverpool.* London: Orion, 2006.

Gerrard, Steven, and Henry Winter. *My Autobiography.* London: Bantam Books, 2006.

Williams, John, and Steven Hopkins. *The Miracle of Istanbul: Liverpool FC from Paisley to Benitez.* Edinburgh: Mainstream, 2005.

Johnny Giles

Born: June 11, 1940
Dublin, Ireland
Also known as: Michael John Giles (full name); John Giles

Early Life
Johnny Giles was born on June 11, 1940, in Dublin, Ireland. While he was growing up, the controlling body of Irish national games, the Gaelic Athletic Association, exercised a ban on what it described as "foreign" games. Soccer came under this ban. The effect was that anybody who played soccer could not play the national games of hurling and Gaelic football. The ban was rigorously enforced, despite the fact that Dublin was a city with a rich soccer tradition. To play soccer, therefore, was an open act of rebellion against prevailing cultural attitudes. Another effect of the ban was an absence of soccer at the school level. In addition, the game's organizational structure at the crucial youth level was limited. Johnny played in schoolboy leagues for the Stella Maris club, a recreational institution. He graduated to the most celebrated of all Irish amateur soccer teams, Home Farm, which, over the years, has been a breeding ground for soccer excellence.

The Road to Excellence
Support for soccer in Ireland was insignificant during Johnny's boyhood. As a result, domestic opportunities to earn a living from playing the game were virtually nonexistent. Even the best players with the top Irish clubs could only afford to be semiprofessionals. As in many other areas of Irish life, lack of opportunity meant talent often left the country. Johnny's development proved no exception to this general rule. In 1957, he signed as a professional with the English club Manchester United.

In the late 1950's, Manchester United was struggling to rebuild in the aftermath of the traumatic Munich air crash that had decimated the fabulous team of the mid-1950's. Johnny played at outside right for Matt Busby, United's legendary manager, and was a key contributor to the team's successful comeback. The high point of this process was the winning of the Football Association Cup in 1963.

The Emerging Champion
At the end of the successful 1963 season Johnny was transferred to Leeds United. This team was on the verge of becoming one of the most dominant in English soccer history. Johnny played a crucial role in its success. Under the intense managerial style of Don Revie, Leeds perfected the 4-2-4 formation, then relatively new to English soccer. Johnny combined memorably with Scottish international star Billy Bremner to control the midfield. The aim was to establish the tempo of the game, holding the ball until it could be effectively and accurately released to open forwards. Johnny's ability to win the ball from opponents, to screen it protectively, and to deliver it with pinpoint accuracy was one of the primary sources of Leeds's remarkable consistency in both the two English championships and in European club competition.

Johnny won an English League Division II Championship Medal with Leeds in 1964, a League Championship Medal in 1969, a Football Association Cup Winners' Medal in 1972, and medals from 1968 and 1971 triumphs in the competition now known as the Union of European Football Associations (UEFA) Cup. Despite his slender build, Johnny proved adept at defending both the ball and himself, and his sense of timing compensated well for a basic lack of speed.

Johnny also had an illustrious international career for the Republic of Ireland. His first appearance for the national team was in 1959, against Sweden. He represented his country a total of fifty-nine times. At that time, the national team was overshadowed by the success of the other Irish international team, Northern Ireland. As a result, Johnny's skillful blend of defensive maneuvering and accurate passing did not earn the full international respect it deserved.

Continuing the Story
In 1975, Johnny left Leeds to become player-manager with West Bromwich Albion, a First Division team in the English midlands. Two years later, he returned to Dublin to accept a similar position with the premier Irish soccer club of the time, the

> **Career Highlights**
>
> 59 international appearances for Ireland
>
> **Honors, Awards, and Milestones**
>
> 1963, 1972 English Football Association Cup champion
> 1968, 1971 UEFA Cup champion
> 1969 English League champion

Shamrock Rovers. Johnny's attempt to develop a youth program to develop Irish players for soccer in Ireland foundered from lack of support, but he guided the Shamrock Rovers to success on the playing field.

Still committed to soccer's development, Johnny went to play in the North American Soccer League (NASL) for the Vancouver Whitecaps near the end of his career. The style of soccer favored by the NASL did not appeal to him, however, and after a brief return engagement with West Bromwich Albion, Johnny retired from professional soccer in 1980. He then worked in Dublin as a soccer columnist and soccer television analyst.

Johnny's later career was also distinguished by his management of the Republic of Ireland national team, a position he held for thirty-seven games from 1973 to 1980. This was a period in which the Ireland team had some players of genuine European quality. In particular, Johnny was fortunate to have midfielder Liam Brady, through whose gifts many of Johnny's tactical insights were realized. Under Johnny's direction, Irish international soccer gained an invaluable measure of respect from its European opposition and a crucial foundation of self-respect, upon which future success under Jack Charlton's management was established. Johnny's contribution to Ireland's soccer development is sometimes underrated because of his teams' inconsistent performances, particularly away from home.

Summary

Johnny Giles was an indispensable member of one of the great English soccer machines of the postwar period. His ball control, sense of timing, and competitiveness made him a consummate team player, and his soccer intelligence, accuracy in passing, and sense of open space made him a midfield player of genuine vision.

George O'Brien

Additional Sources

Galvin, Robert, and Mark Bushell. *Football's Greatest Heroes: The National Football Museum's Hall of Fame.* London: Robson, 2005.

Hunt, Chris. *The Complete Book of Soccer.* Buffalo, N.Y.: Firefly Books, 2006.

LaBlanc, Michael L., and Richard Henshaw. *The World Encyclopedia of Soccer.* Detroit: Gale Research, 1994.

Radnedge, Keir. *The Complete Encyclopedia of Soccer.* London: Carlton, 2006.

Mia Hamm

Born: March 17, 1972
   Selma, Alabama
Also known as: Mariel Margaret Hamm (full name)

Early Life

The daughter of William and Stephanie Hamm, Mariel Margaret Hamm was born on March 17, 1972, in Selma, Alabama, where her father, a United States Air Force officer, was stationed. Nicknamed Mia in honor of a ballerina whom her mother admired, she ironically disliked dancing lessons; she enjoyed playing ball with her five siblings and friends instead. Her older brother, Garrett, an orphaned Thai American whom the Hamms had adopted, was a talented athlete who encouraged Mia's involvement in sports by choosing her to play on his teams for neighborhood games.

Mia moved with her family to several U.S. Air Force bases in Europe and the United States. Sports helped her to adjust to new surroundings and befriend people despite her tendency to be shy. Her father became interested in soccer when the family lived in Italy. Garrett was also a soccer enthusiast. Although Mia enjoyed playing a variety of sports, she focused on soccer because she liked that game best. Joining peewee leagues, Mia was often the only girl playing in games. She gradually developed skills, confidence, and self-discipline, becoming her teams' leading scorer.

The Road to Excellence

As a teenager, Mia played soccer for Notre Dame High School in Wichita Falls, Texas, and quickly attracted attention because of her extraordinary talent, agility, and speed. Coach John Cossaboon asked Mia to join the Olympic development team he was organizing. He also invited Anson Dorrance, the University of North Carolina's women's soccer coach and U.S. national team coach, to watch Mia play. Awestruck by Mia's superb performance, Dorrance recognized Mia's potential and recruited her for the national team.

At the age of fifteen, Mia was the youngest member in the team's history. Her first international match was against China on August 3, 1987. She graduated from Lake Braddock High School at Burke, Virginia, in 1989. She scored her first international goal on July 25, 1990, against Norway.

Playing for Dorrance at the University of North Carolina, Mia dominated women's college soccer. During her col-

Mia Hamm and a Swedish defender competing for the ball during a game at the 1996 Olympic Games in Atlanta, Georgia. (AP/Wide World Photos)

legiate career, she played in seventy consecutive victorious games, which led to four National Collegiate Athletic Association (NCAA) Championships. The North Carolina team lost only one game while Mia was a member. She was designated a first-team all-American and Atlantic Coast Conference player of the year four times each and was twice chosen as the women's college soccer player of the year. During her senior year in 1992, she recorded 32 goals and 33 assists during NCAA competition. Her NCAA career total of 103 goals, 72 assists, and 278 points set a record. She was the first soccer player selected as the best female college athlete in the United States.

The Emerging Champion

Taking a year off from her college playing in 1991, Mia became a world-renowned soccer player. In 1991, she accompanied Dorrance and the national team to China, where the United States won the first Women's World Cup; Mia scored 2 goals. Her college number, 19, was retired when she graduated with a political science degree in 1994. She married classmate Christian Corry, a military helicopter pilot. The couple divorced in 2001.

Mia scored 2 goals during the five games of the second Women's World Cup, in 1995, in which the United States placed third. She was named most valuable player and played the position of goalkeeper when goalie Briana Scurry was ejected from the match. Despite suffering from a sprained ankle, Mia played in the championship match at the 1996 Atlanta Olympics, winning a gold medal when the United States defeated China 2-1.

Because of limited television coverage, the victorious gold medal winners received minimal national attention. Mia, however, was noted as a role model for aspiring athletes. The press praised her athleticism and humility. Mia received accolades and endorsements not often granted to female sports figures. In 1997, she was declared the best female soccer player and also was designated the most popular female athlete. She was the first person, woman or man, named the U.S. soccer athlete of the year for three consecutive years (1994-1996). In 1996, Garrett Hamm died of aplastic anemia, a rare blood disorder. Mia asked corporate sports giant Nike to place Garrett's initials on her signature shoes and hosted the Garrett Games, benefit soccer matches to raise research money.

Major Championships

Year	Competition	Place
1987	Olympic Festival	Silver
1989	Olympic Festival	Gold
	NCAA Championships	1st
1990	NCAA Championships	1st
	Olympic Festival	Gold
1991	Women's World Cup	1st
1992	NCAA Championships	1st
1993	NCAA Championships	1st
	World University Games	Silver
1996	Olympic Games	Gold
1999	Women's World Cup	1st
2000	Olympic Games	Silver
2003	WUSA Founder's Cup	1st
	FIFA World Cup	3d
2004	Olympic Games	Gold

Continuing the Story

Mia scored her one hundredth goal at the U.S. Cup in Rochester, New York, on September 18, 1998. During a match against Brazil on May 22, 1999, she set the world record for goals scored in international play when she kicked in her 108th. At the 1999 Women's World Cup, Mia played adeptly, scoring against Denmark within seventeen minutes, resulting in the 3-0 American victory. Her second goal occurred during the match with Nigeria. She persevered with the U.S. team to defeat China in the championship game after a two-hour, scoreless stalemate and penalty kickoff.

One year after the World Cup, Mia endured a scoring slump but managed to kick her 121st international goal during the 2000 Gold Cup semifinals. She traveled to the Sydney, Australia, Olympic Games in September, 2000. Mia scored the game-winning goal against the Brazilian team to qualify for the final match against Norway. In the final, she kicked the ball to teammate Tiffeny Milbrett, who scored a goal with only fifteen seconds remaining in the game, tying the score and forcing overtime. However, the Norwegians won 3-2.

In February, 2000, Mia was one of the soccer stars who helped establish the Women's United Soccer Association (WUSA), the world's first women's professional soccer league. The season began in April, 2001, with franchises in Atlanta, Boston, North Carolina, New York, Philadelphia, San Diego, the San Francisco Bay Area, and Washington, D.C. Mia joined the Washington Freedom team. In 2001 and 2002, the International Federation of Association Football (FIFA) named her women's world player of the year. The Freedom won the Founder's Cup Championships in 2002 and 2003, but in September, 2003, WUSA suspended operations.

At the 2004 Olympics in Athens, Greece, Mia won a gold medal with the American team. Afterward, she went on a ten-game farewell tour with the women's national team. On December 8, 2004, in Carson, California, after a game with Mexico, Mia retired from soccer. In March, 2007, she gave birth to twin daughters. She had married baseball star Nomar Garciaparra in 2003.

Summary

Mia Hamm was a pioneer in promoting women's sports worldwide. In 1999, she established the Mia Hamm Foundation with two objectives: to endow medical research and efforts to treat people with bone marrow diseases like her brother's and to fund women's athletics.

Mia's achievements inspired girls to participate in sports, specifically soccer, and enhanced opportunities for women athletes. When she retired in 2004, Mia had scored 158 goals, the world record for international competition, and she was credited as the world's best all-around woman soccer player. She was U.S. Soccer's female athlete of the year for five consecutive years (1994-1998), and she won two Women's World Cups and two Olympic gold medals.

Considered the first woman team-sport superstar, Mia became an icon. In 1997, she was one of *People* magazine's "Fifty Most Beautiful People"; in September, 2003, she appeared on the cover of *Sports Illustrated*. She was also the first soccer player elected to carry the American flag for Olympic Closing Ceremonies. She and her teammates appeared in the HBO documentary *Dare to Dream: The Story of the U.S. Women's Soccer Team* (2005). In 2007, she was elected to the U.S. National Soccer Hall of Fame. In January, 2008, a new league, Women's Professional Soccer, revealed its logo, which used Mia's silhouette.

Elizabeth D. Schafer, updated by Alice Myers

Additional Sources

Christopher, Matt. *On the Field with . . . Mia Hamm.* Boston: Little, Brown, 2005.

Fisher, David. *Mia Hamm.* Kansas City, Mo.: Andrews McMeel, 2000.

Hamm, Mia, with Aaron Heifetz. *Go for the Goal: A Champion's Guide to Winning in Soccer and Life.* New York: HarperCollins, 2000.

Longman, Jere. *The Girls of Summer: The U.S. Women's Soccer Team and How It Changed the World.* New York: HarperCollins, 2001.

Schnakenberg, Robert. *Mia Hamm.* Philadelphia: Chelsea House, 2003.

Smith, Gary. "The Secret Life of Mia Hamm." *Sports Illustrated* 99, no. 12 (September 22, 2003): 58.

Honors and Awards

Year	Award
1989-90	NCAA All-Tournament Team
1989-90, 1992-93	ACC Player of the Year
	First Team All-American
1991, 1993	Missouri Athletic Club Award
	Hermann Award
1992	NCAA tournament most valuable player, offensive
1993	NCAA tournament most valuable player
1994	Most valuable player of the Chiquita Cup
	Jersey number retired by University of North Carolina
1994-98	U.S. Soccer Federation Female Athlete of the Year
1995	Honda-Broderick Award for U.S. most outstanding female collegiate athlete for the year
1997	Women's Sports Foundation Athlete of the Year
1998-99	ESPY Female Athlete of the Year
1999	ESPY Soccer Player of the Year
	Sports Illustrated Sportswomen of the Year, with teammates
2001-02	FIFA World Player of the Year
2007	Inducted into National Soccer Hall of Fame
2008	Inducted into Texas Sports Hall of Fame

April Heinrichs

Born: February 27, 1964
Denver, Colorado

Early Life
April Heinrichs, the youngest of five daughters, first played soccer at the age of six in a recreational league in Littleton, Colorado. She wore a reversible T-shirt and red stirrup socks, and she stuffed *Reader's Digest* magazines in her socks for shin guards. Her parents often found her asleep in her bed with cleats still on her feet. Because of her abilities, April usually played in an older age group; she enjoyed the challenge. Her parents were constantly positive, encouraging her athletic endeavors without pressuring her. Throughout her high school years, April played soccer on a club team; she was also a talented basketball player.

After graduating from high school, April accepted a basketball scholarship at Mesa College, a National Collegiate Athletic Association (NCAA) Division II school, in Grand Junction, Colorado. In the fall of 1982, while April was at Mesa College, she traveled with her club soccer team to Brown University to participate in a club tournament. A club coach from Virginia took notice of April and informed coaches Anson Dorrance, at the University of North Carolina (UNC), and Jim Rudy, at the University of Central Florida, of her talent. In turn, both coaches contacted April, and shortly, she made the decision to leave Mesa College and transfer to UNC.

The Road to Excellence
April attended UNC from 1983 to 1986. During this time, the team participated in four consecutive NCAA Championship games and won titles in 1983, 1984, and 1986. April received many college accolades, including Intercollegiate Soccer Association of America national player of the year in 1984 and 1986; all-American in 1984, 1985, and 1986; and third-team all-American in 1983. Furthermore, she made the NCAA all-tournament team from 1983 to 1986, was named the most valuable player for the 1984 tournament, and was designated the most valuable offensive player of the tournament in 1985 and 1986. By the end of her college career, April had compiled 87 goals and 51 assists—a total that only Mia Hamm, Tiffeny Milbrett, and Danielle Fotopoulos have broken. The UNC team had an 85-3-2 record over the course of the four years that April played. She was the first women's soccer player at UNC to have her uniform number retired. She graduated with a degree in television and film.

Because of her reputation for skillfulness and mental toughness, April was named to the U.S. national team. The first time the national team played abroad in 1985, April was injured and missed the opportunity to participate. By 1986, she returned to cocaptain the team with Emily Pickering and traveled to Italy, demonstrating her special talents. She was scouted by Italian club team owners, and she and Megan McCarthy were signed to play in the Italian Professional League.

The Emerging Champion
Having played at UNC and on the U.S. national team, April had a chance to compare her abilities with other top-level women players. She realized she had the talent to compete with these women. April continued her play in an internationally competitive league in Italy, where she was a popular figure. The attention she received was challenging because April was reserved and shy. Even so, because of her intensity and work ethic on the field, April emerged as a team leader and a role model. She played in the Italian Professional League with Prato and Juventus, each for one year.

April continued to play on the U.S. national team through 1992. She consistently demonstrated her strong leadership abilities on and off the field. In addition, her exceptional skillfulness and tactical awareness were reflected in the success of the national team. April and teammates Michelle Akers and Carin Jennings were referred to as the "triple-edged sword" because of their complimentary abilities that often overwhelmed opponents. April was named the U.S. Soccer Federation player of the year in 1986 and 1989. In 1991, at the first ever Women's World Cup, April helped the U.S. team beat China in the final. Upon her retirement from

Honors, Awards, and Milestones

1983-84, 1986	NCAA champion
1986, 1989	U.S. Soccer Female Athlete of the Year
1990	*Soccer America* Female Player of the 1980's
1991	World Cup champion
1995	Atlantic Coast Conference Coach of the Year
1998	Inducted into National Soccer Hall of Fame
2000-05	Coach, U.S. women's national team
2001	National Soccer Coaches Association of America Women's Committee Award of Excellence

the national team, April had accrued 38 goals in forty-seven games. Because of a congenital knee condition and the long layoff between World Cup tournaments, April retired as a player.

Continuing the Story

During her years playing on the national team, April gained valuable coaching experience. Upon graduation from UNC, she served as an assistant coach at The College of William and Mary and was the head coach at Princeton University in 1990, the University of Maryland from 1991 to 1996, the University of Virginia from 1996 to 1999, and the University of California at Irvine in 2006. She was named the Atlantic Coast Conference coach of the year in 1995. Her overall college coaching record was 119-86-16.

April became a full-time assistant coach with the U.S. national team in January, 1995. She assisted the team at the 1995 Women's World Cup in Sweden and the 1996 Olympic Games, at which the team won a gold medal. Soon afterward, she left this position to become the head coach of the under-sixteen national team. April was named the U.S. national team head coach on January 18, 2000. During her tenure, from 2000 to 2004, April had a coaching record of 87-17-20 with a .782 winning percentage. The team won a silver medal at the 2000 Olympic Games in Australia and a gold medal at the 2004 Olympic Games in Greece. At the 2003 World Cup, the United States team finished in third place.

Summary

April Heinrichs was one of the first widely recognized women's soccer players and coaches in the United States and the world. Despite limited organized soccer leagues in her youth and poor funding with the U.S. national team, April still emerged with great technical and tactical abilities. Named the female player of the 1980's by *Soccer America*, awarded the National Soccer Coaches Association of America Women's Committee Award of Excellence, and as the first woman to be inducted into the National Soccer Hall of Fame in Oneonta, New York, April is a legend in women's athletics and the soccer world.

Shawn Ladda

Additional Sources

Fair, Lorrie, and Mark Gola. *Fair Game: A Complete Book of Soccer for Women.* Chicago: Contemporary Books, 2003.

Smith, Lissa, ed. *Nike Is a Goddess: The History of Women in Sports.* New York: Grove Atlantic, 2001.

Thierry Henry

Born: August 17, 1977
Les Ulis, Essonne, France
Also known as: Thierry Daniel Henry (full name); Henry

Early Life

Thierry Daniel Henry, known in soccer circles as simply Henry, was born on August 17, 1977, in the Parisian suburb of Les Ulis, Essonne. His father, Antoine, was born on Désirade Island in Guadeloupe, while his mother, Maryse, was born in Martinique. Thierry grew up in the tough, heavily urbanized district of Les Ulis, which did not have good soccer facilities. The local club team scouted Thierry when he was as young as seven years old. In 1990, when Thierry was only thirteen years old, an AS Monaco scout came to watch him play with his club team. In the game, Thierry scored all 6 goals in a 6-0 romp. The scout, Arnold Catalano, asked Thierry to join AS Monaco immediately as a youth player. In 1994, at the age of sixteen, Thierry signed a professional contract with AS Monaco and made his debut as a professional soccer player.

The Road to Excellence

During Thierry's first full season with AS Monaco, he scored 3 goals in eighteen games. Soon, he was scoring more often. In 1996, he was named French young footballer of the year; the following season, he helped his club AS Monaco win the Ligue 1 title. The following season, he led Monaco to the Union of European Football Associations (UEFA) Champions League semifinal and set a French record by scoring 7 goals in the competition. In 1998, he played in his first FIFA World Cup and helped lead France to its first World Cup Championship.

In 1999, after five impressive seasons with AS Monaco, Thierry left to play for Juventes of the Italian Serie A league for a reported £10.5 million (approximately $18 million). Thierry was not happy with Juventes and made only sixteen appearances with the club. His international fame was to be found elsewhere.

Thierry Henry leaping to connect with the ball in a 2008 game between France and Italy. (Phil Cole/Getty Images)

The Emerging Champion

In late 1999, after a short stay with Juventes, Thierry transferred to the British club Arsenal for another reported £10.5 million. In his first season with Arsenal, he scored 26 goals and helped lead the club to the UEFA Champions Cup Finals. Then, in 2000, he led the French national team to the UEFA EURO 2000 Championship. France's national soccer team had reached its peak thanks in large part to Thierry. During the 2000-2001 season with Arsenal, Thierry became the team's top scorer. Success came for both the team and Thierry. That season, Arsenal finally overtook Manchester United and Liverpool to win the league title and defeated Chelsea, 2-0, to capture the Football Association

Challenge Cup (FA Cup) title. At this point, with 32 goals, Thierry was not only the top scorer on his team but also the top scorer in the league.

Over the next few years, Thierry's success continued. After leading Arsenal to another FA Cup Championship in the 2002-2003 season, Thierry was named the players' player of the year and Football Writers Association player of the year. Perhaps more significantly, Thierry began to be noticed on an international level. In 2003 and 2004, he was runner-up for the FIFA world player of the year. In 2005-2006, Thierry became the top goal scorer in Arsenal history and was named the Football Writers Association player of the year for the third time.

Continuing the Story

In 2007, Thierry was unexpectedly transferred to FC Barcelona of the Spanish League for the sum of £24 million (approximately $41 million). Reportedly, FC Barcelona agreed to pay Thierry £6.8 million (approximately $12 million) per year over four years. In his first season with FC Barcelona, Thierry was the club's top scorer with 19 goals. However, the team failed to win a championship, and Thierry's future with the club was in question. At the age of thirty-one, Thierry still had some soccer to play. So, while his status at Arsenal and as a French national player was secured, his legend was not complete.

Honors and Awards

Year	Award
1998	French Legion of Honor
2000, 2003-06	French player of the year
2001-02, 2003-06	Premier League top scorer
2002-03, 2003-04	Professional Footballers' Association players' player of the year
2002-04, 2005-06	Football Writers Association player of the year
2003	Confederations Cup golden ball
2003, 2006	Onze d'Or Award
2004	Pelé's FIFA 100
2004-05	European golden boot

Summary

In July, 2008, Arsenal fans named Thierry Henry the clubs' greatest player of all time. He became an international icon, doing commercials with golfer Tiger Woods and tennis player Roger Federer. Thierry became one of the world's most famous athletes.

Theodore Shields

Additional Sources

Derbyshire, Oliver. *Thierry Henry: The Biography—The Amazing Life of the Greatest Footballer on Earth.* London: John Blake, 2006.

Goldblatt, David. *The Ball Is Round: A Global History of Soccer.* New York: Riverhead Books, 2008.

O'Connell, Michael. *Thierry Henry.* London: Artnik, 2006.

Geoff Hurst

Born: December 8, 1941
Ashton-under-Lyne, England
Also known as: Sir Geoffrey Charles Hurst (full name); Geoffrey Charles Hurst (birth name)
Other major sport: Cricket

Early Life

Geoffrey Charles Hurst was born on December 8, 1941, in Ashton-under-Lyne, England. Soccer ran in his family. Geoff's father had for many years played as a halfback for Oldham Athletic, a Lancashire club in the lower divisions of the Football League. His father exerted a strong influence on Geoff's early years, but as a schoolboy Geoff found that soccer was not the only sport at which he could excel. He also had considerable talent for cricket, and in his teenage years it seemed as if cricket would win his full allegiance. He even moved away from home in order to join Essex County Cricket Club, where many world-class cricketers had made their reputations. Geoff's love of soccer, however, and his determination to make the grade as a professional remained.

The Road to Excellence

While he lived in Essex, Geoff was not far from the First Division London soccer club West Ham United, which soon became interested in the strongly built, energetic youngster. Hurst signed as a professional with West Ham in April, 1959, when he was seventeen years old. At this stage of Geoff's career he was a wing-half, and his solid play soon earned him a number of first team appearances. However, West Ham was well supplied with quality wing-halves, and Geoff's performance was not consistently strong enough to guarantee for him a regular place on the team.

The keys to Geoff's later success were his dogged persistence and his willingness to learn from the West Ham, and later England, manager Ron Greenwood, who was known for the intelligence and subtlety of his coaching and for his tactical knowledge. Greenwood saw the potential in Geoff and resisted an attempt by the West Ham club directors to sell him to a Second Division team. Under Greenwood's guidance, Geoff looked set for a modestly successful career. No one, however, could have predicted the spectacular course that it was soon to take.

The Emerging Champion

The crucial moment came when Greenwood decided that Geoff should switch position, from wing-half to striker. The move was an immediate success. Geoff discovered that he had the qualities a top-class striker needed. He was strong and fearless and was a very hard worker. He could score goals with his powerful shot from either foot, or with a skillful flick of the head.

During West Ham's success in the mid-1960's, Geoff played a key part. In 1965, he was on the

England's Geoff Hurst celebrating his goal against Argentina in the 1966 World Cup. (Popperfoto/Getty Images)

Career Highlights

49 international appearances for England
24 international goals

Honors, Awards, and Milestones

1964	English Football Association Cup champion
1965	European Cup Winners' Cup champion
1966	World Cup champion

team that won the European Cup Winners' Cup, when West Ham defeated the German team, Munich 1860, in the final at Wembley Stadium in London. Geoff was an ideal teammate for the other West Ham stars of the 1960's. Bobby Moore, who was the England team captain, used Geoff's tall figure as a target in his clearances from the defense, and rarely would Geoff let him down. Geoff could control a ball quickly, and he was hard to distract when he sensed a chance for a goal.

With another West Ham and England star, Martin Peters, Geoff perfected the near-post ball. Peters would cross the ball with pinpoint accuracy from the wing, and Geoff would be waiting at the near goalpost to knock the ball in the net with his head. The move worked like a dream, and Geoff started to score goals regularly—one every two games, on average. By 1965, with the 1966 World Cup competition coming up, he was a serious contender for a place on the England team.

Continuing the Story

Geoff made his first appearance for England against West Germany in February, 1966. He then played in a crucial match later in the year. England was playing Argentina in a World Cup quarterfinal in London. With thirteen minutes to go, the score was 0-0. Then Peters collected the ball on the wing, crossed into the goalmouth, and Geoff, with a tremendous leap, headed the ball home. The near-post maneuver had worked again, and Geoff's superb goal had won the match for England. However, that was nothing compared to what was to come.

In the World Cup Final, England played West Germany. After the Germans had taken an early lead, Geoff equalized for England with a fine header. After ninety minutes of play, the score was tied at 2 goals each. The tension was unbearable as the game went into overtime. Twenty minutes from the end, Geoff unleashed a tremendous right-foot shot to put England ahead. Then, in the final minute, he raced onto a pass from Bobby Moore, outstripped a disorganized German defense, and crashed an unstoppable left-foot shot past goalkeeper Tilkowski. England had won the World Cup for the first time, and Geoff was the first player ever to score 3 goals in a World Cup Final. He became a national hero overnight.

Over the next nine years, Geoff continued his goal-scoring exploits. He was known as a deadly taker of penalty kicks and as an unselfish player who worked to provide goal-scoring opportunities for his teammates as well as for himself. Geoff represented England again in the World Cup in Mexico in 1970. He scored the winning goal against Romania, but he could not prevent England from losing in the quarterfinals to West Germany. Geoff played forty-nine times for England during his career, scoring twenty-four goals.

In 1972, Geoff was transferred from West Ham to Stoke City, for which he scored 30 goals in three seasons. In 1976, Geoff moved to the Seattle Sounders of the newly formed North American Soccer League. After Geoff's playing career was over in the late 1970's, he returned to England and became an assistant to his old mentor Ron Greenwood, who had become the England manager. Geoff later became manager of Telford United and Chelsea.

Summary

Geoff Hurst's strength, perseverance, and shooting power made him one of the outstanding strikers in English soccer during the 1960's and 1970's. His magnificent achievements in international competition, especially in the 1966 World Cup Final, made him a household name throughout the soccer world. He was knighted in 1998.

Bryan Aubrey

Additional Sources

Galvin, Robert, and Mark Bushell. *Football's Greatest Heroes: The National Football Museum's Hall of Fame.* London: Robson, 2005.

Hunt, Chris. *The Complete Book of Soccer.* Buffalo, N.Y.: Firefly Books, 2006.

Hurst, Geoff. *World Champions.* London: Headline, 2006.

Hurst, Geoff, and Michael Hart. *1966 and All That: My Autobiography.* London: Headline, 2006.

Pat Jennings

Born: June 12, 1945
Newry, County Down, Northern Ireland
Also known as: Patrick Anthony Jennings (full name)

Early Life

Patrick Anthony Jennings was born on June 12, 1945, in Newry, a working-class town in Northern Ireland near the Mourne Mountains. Pat's father was a lumberjack who worked in the mountains. Even though he earned a steady income, the family had to work together to make ends meet. With eight children—seven boys and one girl—in the family, Pat and his brothers took on odd jobs during the summers. They took any work they could find, from gathering kindling wood to collecting empty lemonade bottles, to earn the odd penny. In their spare time, they played soccer. At the age of fifteen, Pat left school to find a full-time job. He worked alongside his father cutting and loading lumber, but a bright career as a professional soccer player started soon thereafter.

Goalie Pat Jennings in 1982. (Bob Thomas/Getty Images)

The Road to Excellence

Pat's first organized soccer experience came at the age of eleven, when he played on a team for boys under nineteen. As the goalkeeper, he led the team to the league championship game. Despite his success preceding the final, Pat was left out of the starting eleven for the game because his coaches feared that he was too small to play in such an important match. They wanted a bigger boy in the goal to ensure victory. Though disappointed, Pat was not discouraged. His passion for the game was too strong.

The next season the league disbanded, and five years passed before Pat again played organized soccer. In the meantime, he and his brothers played early-morning backyard matches before school started, sometimes with nothing more than a tennis ball. After school they had matches with their friends wherever they could find an open patch of ground. During school hours, Pat played Gaelic football, a game that can best be described as a cross between soccer and rugby.

Pat was sixteen when he returned to organized soccer. One of his older brothers was playing on a local junior team that needed a goalkeeper, and Pat was asked to join. Pat made an immediate impact on the team, which won the Irish Junior Cup. Though he had been with the team for only six months, people around the country already knew of Pat Jennings. Soon after winning the Junior Cup, Pat was chosen to play for Northern Ireland's under-twenty-three national team. He led them to the finals of the European Youth Championship. They lost to England, but Pat stood out. He gained confidence by learning that he could compete with the best youth players in the world. Pat's whole life changed after that.

The Emerging Champion

After only a few days back in Ireland, Pat signed a professional contract to play in England with the Watford Football Club. When Pat joined Watford he was seventeen years old, and they were a club struggling at the bottom of the Third Division standings. Pat was a bright spot on the team. His first two appearances were shutouts. His sure hands, steady demeanor, and confidence were already evident. His contribution to the team was so great that by the end of his first full season, Watford was only one point shy of earning promotion to the Second Division.

Pat was an innovative player. His command of the penalty area separated him from other goalkeepers. Where most goalkeepers in his day came no farther than six yards off their line to protect the goal, Pat covered the entire penalty area, sometimes coming fifteen yards to catch high crossing passes under challenge. Pat attributed that skill—and his trademark style of catching crosses one-handed—to his Gaelic football days.

By the end of 1964, after Pat's only full season with Watford, some of the biggest clubs in England started to take notice of him. The next year, he signed with Tottenham Hotspur, at the time one of the top teams in Great Britain. Only two years before, the team had won a rare double—League Championship and English Football Association (EFA) Cup titles in the same season—but had won no championships since. Tottenham looked to the young Irish goalkeeper to help bring another title.

It took some time for Pat to adjust to the higher level, so for a short while he played with Tottenham's reserve team to gain experience. The next season, 1967, after earning his place on the first team, he led the "Spurs" to the EFA Cup title. That same year, he achieved something extraordinary for a goalkeeper when he scored a goal by punting a ball the length of the field and bouncing it over the opposing goalkeeper's head.

From 1971 to 1973, Pat led the Spurs to three more cup titles: The League Cup in 1971, the Union of European Football Associations (UEFA) Cup in 1972, and another League Cup in 1973. The year Tottenham won its second League Cup, Pat was recognized as England's footballer of the year. In 1977, though, Tottenham fell upon hard times, and Pat, who was then thirty-two, became the scapegoat. At the start of the 1978 season, he was sold to a new team, the Arsenal Football Club.

Continuing the Story

To Arsenal, Pat brought the same sort of success that Tottenham had enjoyed during the earlier

Career Highlights

119 international appearances for Northern Ireland

Honors, Awards, and Milestones

1967, 1979	English Football Association Cup champion
1971, 1973	English League Cup champion
1972	UEFA Cup champion
1973	English Footballer of the Year
1976	English Professional Football Association player of the year

part of the decade. From 1978 through 1980, Arsenal appeared in the EFA Cup final game. The team won the Cup in 1979. While Pat was establishing himself as one of the premier goalkeepers in Britain playing for Tottenham and Arsenal, he was doing the same thing on the international level with Northern Ireland. At the age of twenty-nine, he earned his fiftieth full cap playing for Northern Ireland. Twelve years later, when he retired from the game, he had represented his country 119 times. On top of that, he had more than one thousand professional matches to his credit. Pat capped his career by leading Northern Ireland to consecutive World Cup appearances in 1982 and 1986. In 1986, he was the oldest player in the tournament, at forty-one. He was inducted into the English Football Hall of Fame in 2003.

Summary

Pat Jennings was a gifted athlete who excelled as a goalkeeper. He possessed a competitive spirit that drove him to be the best. He had a passion for the game that was unconquerable. Though he experienced setbacks, he met success at every level. With a career that lasted more than twenty years, Pat is considered one of the true legends in the soccer world.

Mark A. Newman

Additional Sources

Hunt, Chris. *The Complete Book of Soccer.* Buffalo, N.Y.: Firefly Books, 2006.

Radnedge, Keir, and Gary Lineker. *The Ultimate Encyclopedia of Soccer: The Definitive Illustrated Guide to World Soccer.* London: Carlton Books, 2004.

Wolff, Alexander. "Peacefully Done." *Sports Illustrated* 79, no. 22 (1993).

Cobi Jones

Born: June 16, 1970
Detroit, Michigan
Also known as: Cobi N'Gai Jones (full name)

Early Life

Cobi N'Gai Jones was born in Detroit, Michigan, on June 16, 1970, but moved with his family to Westlake Village, California, when he was young. The youngest of four boys born to Freeman and Mada Jones, Cobi grew up as a typical Southern California child, enjoying the sun and playing several different sports. He was, by his own admission, a shy boy who liked to keep to himself. However, he began to express himself on the soccer field, becoming a star player as a youth. His talent continued to shine at Westlake High School, where he joined future U.S. national teammate Eric Wynalda on one of the top prep squads. Despite his early success, Cobi never thought he had a future in soccer.

The Road to Excellence

In 1988, Cobi was invited to join the soccer team at the University of California, Los Angeles (UCLA) at a "walk on." Since he was not given an athletic scholarship, he had to gain admission to the institution on his own academic merit. Nonetheless, Cobi earned a starting position on the team after only a few games of his freshman season. He finished the year as UCLA's top freshman scorer, with 4 goals and 7 assists.

Though only 5 feet 7 inches tall, Cobi had blazing speed and great agility. As an attacking midfielder, he could roam the central part of the field while taking off on quick forays down the sidelines, feeding the ball to goal scorers. By this time, he had also adopted his famous dreadlocks hairstyle, a look that made him instantly recognizable in the coming years. UCLA won the National Collegiate Athletic Association championship in 1990. The next year, Cobi earned all-American honors. He finished his college career with 37 assists, second on the all-time UCLA list.

Cobi's speed, determination, and overall exciting play grabbed the attention of U.S. national team coaches. His first big break came when he was selected for the U.S. team at the Pan American Games in 1991. Cobi made the most of his chance, tallying a goal and an assist against Canada. The U.S. team went on to win the gold medal. That opportunity led to a shot at the U.S. Olympic team in 1992. Although he was cut twice before making the final squad, Cobi played in all three games at the Summer Olympics in Barcelona.

The Emerging Champion

Cobi made his debut with the U.S. national team on September 3, 1992, in a match against Canada. The next month, the United States played in the Confederations Cup in Saudi Arabia. There were rumors that Cobi was going to be cut for expressing his opinion about how the team played. In a game against the Ivory Coast, however, Cobi excelled,

Cobi Jones dribbling in a game against Cuba in 2002. (Jeff Gross/Getty Images)

scoring 1 goal and assisting on 2 others as the Americans beat the African champions 5-2. From then on, the California player was an indelible feature of the national team.

After decades of relegation to the lower tiers of international soccer, the United States was considered a dangerous team by the early 1990's. Cobi and other young players were at the core of this renaissance. In 1993, Cobi led the national team in appearances, with thirty, and tied for the team lead in assists. In 1994, the World Cup, soccer's most prized championship, was played in the United States. Cobi played in all four games, including a win over heavily favored Colombia in his hometown of Los Angeles.

Soon after the World Cup, Cobi signed with Coventry City of the English Premiere League. After one year, he moved on to Vasco da Gama in the Brazilian league. Cobi always seemed to save his best performances for the U.S. team, however. He scored the game-winning goal against Nigeria in the 1995 U.S. Cup. Later that year, the United States advanced to the semifinals of the Copa America. Cobi notched an assist on one of his patented end-line crosses when the United States beat Argentina 3-0.

Continuing the Story

In 1996, the United States got its own soccer showcase when Major League Soccer (MLS) kicked off its first season. Cobi was assigned to the Los Angeles Galaxy. He did not disappoint his hometown fans, scoring the Galaxy's first-ever goal on opening day. He had always been one of the fastest players in the world, but his ballhandling and defensive skills had often been scrutinized. In MLS, he began to hone his talent to a higher level of technical and tactical sophistication. He racked up 7 goals that first season, including the first 3-goal game of his career. Cobi was named to the Western Conference all-star team, and the Galaxy advanced all the way to the MLS Championship Cup Finals.

Although his club duties kept him busy during the MLS season, Cobi continued to star for the U.S. team. On February 10, 1998, he earned his one hundredth cap, denoting an appearance for the national team, in the CONCACAF Gold Cup semifinal against Brazil. Cobi became the youngest man in the world to reach this milestone. Fittingly, the game was played in Los Angeles, where the United States won a historic victory, avenging its loss in the 1994 World Cup. However, the United States did not fare well in the 1998 World Cup, losing three consecutive matches. Cobi's play was one of the bright spots, though, further enhancing his international reputation.

Back home with the Galaxy, Cobi turned in his best season in 1998. During that year, he was named MLS player of the month for March. The 19 goals he scored that season were more than double those of his next-best seasons and accounted for more than one-quarter of his MLS career total of 70. In one game against New England, he posted only the third 8-point game in MLS history, scoring 3 goals and assisting on 2 others. He finished the season as the league's second-highest goal scorer and was the top vote getter on the all-star team. He capped the year by winning the U.S. Soccer male athlete of the year award.

Cobi spent his entire professional playing career with the Los Angeles Galaxy, for which he played more than three hundred games and scored 70 goals. After the 2006 season, he considered retiring but decided to stay with the Galaxy after the team acquired the English star David Beckham. During his final season, he played in twenty-five games and scored 4 goals.

In October, 2007, at the age

MLS Statistics

Year	GP	GS	Min.	G	Ast.	Pts.
1996	28	27	2,375	7	4	18
1997	26	25	2,228	7	9	23
1998	24	24	2,136	19	13	51
1999	28	28	2,488	8	8	24
2000	25	25	2,291	7	6	20
2001	22	22	1,890	6	10	22
2002	19	18	1,638	3	13	19
2003	28	28	2,574	2	8	12
2004	23	20	1,751	0	5	5
2005	31	27	2,397	3	6	12
2006	27	18	1,710	4	4	12
2007	25	19	1,679	4	5	13
Totals	306	281	25,157	70	91	231

Notes: GP = games played; GS = games started; Min. = minutes played; G = goals; Ast. = assists; Pts. = points

of thirty-seven, Cobi played his final game for the Galaxy and officially retired. Afterward, the team made his jersey number, 13, the first in MLS history to be retired. Less than a month later, Cobi was hired as an assistant coach. During the 2008 season, the Galaxy got off to a poor start. In August, the team fired Coach Ruud Guillit, and Cobi suddenly found himself interim head coach. His tenure as head coach lasted only one week, however, as the team soon brought in former U.S. national team coach Bruce Arena to head the team, and Cobi returned to his role as an assistant coach.

In addition to his place as one of the most popular American soccer players on the field, Cobi also found celebrity on the screen. In 2002, he had a brief stint cohosting the sports-video show *Sweat* on television. The following year, 2003, he had a small part in the comedy film *Just for Kicks*, in which he plays a delivery man who happens to look exactly like Cobi. He has also frequently appeared as himself on both documentary and comedy television shows, including *Beverly Hills, 90210*; *Arli$$*; and *Player$*.

Summary

At the time of his retirement, Cobi Jones ranked as one of the longest-tenured and most popular players in MLS history. He also was the all-time leader in appearances for the U.S. men's national team with 164. His speedy runs down the wing, dreadlocks flapping in the wind, had been a fixture of American soccer for many years. Although initially known for his quickness, he developed into a first-class midfielder through diligence and hard work. A former coach said of him, "He's made the most of the talent he has by sheer will and intelligence." His long and brilliant service for the U.S. national team helped make Cobi one of the most beloved and famous players the United States ever produced.

John Slocum, updated by the Editors

Additional Sources

Goldblatt, David. *The Ball Is Round: A Global History of Soccer*. New York: Riverhead Books, 2008.

Hunt, Chris. *The Complete Book of Soccer*. Buffalo, N.Y.: Firefly Books, 2006.

Jones, Cobi, and Andrew Gutelle. *Cobi Jones' Soccer Games*. New York: Workman, 1998.

Kirkpatrick, Rob. *Cobi Jones: Soccer Star*. New York: PowerKids Press, 2000.

Radnedge, Keir, and Gary Lineker. *The Ultimate Encyclopedia of Soccer: The Definitive Illustrated Guide to World Soccer*. London: Carlton Books, 2004.

Wyllie, John Philip. "Keeping up with Jones." *Soccer Digest* 23 (October, 2000): 20.

Kevin Keegan

Born: February 14, 1951
Armthorpe, Doncaster, South Yorkshire, England
Also known as: Joseph Kevin Keegan (full name)

Early Life

Joseph Kevin Keegan was born on February 14, 1951, in the village of Armthorpe near the industrial city of Doncaster, South Yorkshire, England. He was the second of Joseph and Doris Keegan's three children and was educated at local Catholic schools. Kevin left school at fifteen and got a job in the stores of a local brass factory; he played soccer for the factory team. Early in 1968, just before his seventeenth birthday, he signed as an apprentice for a local Football League club, Scunthorpe United, and appeared in his first Football League game for Scunthorpe the following season.

The Road to Excellence

In contrast to the many Scottish and Irish players in the Football League, English players usually begin their careers with teams that are not in the top division. Kevin's career followed the basic pattern of professional development. Scunthorpe United was not a very successful club. Kevin played there for three seasons, refusing to be discouraged by his surroundings and showing his commitment to the game. It took some strength of character to accept his unglamorous beginnings, and this strength was an immense resource when he moved to First (later called Premier) Division soccer.

Teams in the lower divisions of the Football League often feature former stars who are on the wane. Their presence gives games at the lower level an additional competitive edge and provides younger players with necessary on-the-job training. Kevin's immediate success at the highest level of club competition showed how much he had learned from playing with and against old-timers. For all of his experience, however, Kevin's short stature and light frame kept him waiting for the chance to break into the big time. However, the wait was worth it.

The Emerging Champion

In 1971, Kevin was transferred for a modest sum to Liverpool, a team that, under the management of the legendary Bill Shankly, was about to eclipse Leed United as the dominant First Division team in England and become one of the most powerful clubs in Europe. Like many of the major soccer clubs in England, Liverpool is not simply a sports

Kevin Keegan of England. (Bob Thomas/Getty Images)

organization but a cultural phenomenon. Its success on the field over the years has produced a core of die-hard fans. These fans' loyalty has an almost tribal intensity that reaches its height in the two yearly games against Liverpool's crosstown rival, Everton. Kevin adapted to the large crowds and passionate support so well that he was nicknamed "The King of the Kop." The Kop is the name of the terraces where the home fans are loudest at Anfield, Liverpool's ground. The name comes from Spion Kop, a notorious battle in the Boer War—which gives some idea of the frenzy to be found there.

In the mid-1970's, Kevin won the highest awards of English and European soccer. Liverpool triumphed in the English League Championship in 1973 and 1976 and in the more glamorous Football Association Cup competition of 1974. European success came in the Union of European Football Associations (UEFA) Cup competitions of 1973 and 1976 and in the more prestigious European Champions Cup of 1977. The championship game of this competition against the powerful German Club Bayern Munich was arguably Kevin's finest for Liverpool. The performance ended his career for that club on a high note. During his years at Liverpool, Kevin played in 321 games and scored 100 goals.

In 1977, Kevin signed with Hamburg SV of the German Bundesliga for half a million pounds—then a record amount of money for an English player. Unlike many English players who go abroad, he adapted successfully to a different system of play and way of life. In both 1978 and 1979, he was elected European player of the year, the highest individual honor in European soccer. In 1980, he returned to England to play for Southampton in the First Division.

Kevin also had a successful international career playing for England. Between 1973 and 1982, he played sixty-three games for England, scoring twenty-one goals and frequently captaining the team. England's national team did not perform especially well during Kevin's career, however. For Liverpool and Hamburg, in particular, Kevin's speed, skill, courage, and vision made him one of the most exciting players of his generation.

Continuing the Story

Kevin spent two years at Southampton, playing in sixty-eight games and scoring 37 goals. He then

Career Highlights

63 international appearances for England
21 international goals

Honors, Awards, and Milestones

1972, 1976-77	English League champion
1973, 1976	UEFA Cup champion
1974	Football Association Cup champion
1976, 1982	English Footballer of the Year
1977	European Champions Cup champion
1978-79	European player of the year
1979	German League champion
1982	Order of the British Empire
1992-93	Division One manager of the season
2002	Inducted into English Football Hall of Fame

moved to Newcastle United, one of several well-known English clubs experiencing hard times in the Second Division of the league. Clearly, he was no longer quite so speedy and quick-witted. The injuries that had blighted his international career were becoming more frequent and more difficult to heal. He played two seasons with Newcastle before announcing his retirement on his birthday in 1984.

In 1982, Kevin was awarded the Order of the British Empire—one of England's national honors—for his popularity and sportsmanship. The award's official citation recognized his services to soccer. As a player, Kevin was a media favorite, always courteous and available for interviews. In 1979, his book *Playing Against the World* enhanced his media presence, and he went on to become a television commentator during coverage of important international games. His career in retirement showed the ease with which athletes can become show-business stars.

In 1992, Kevin returned to Newcastle United as club manager; he was responsible for both the financial and coaching aspects of the team. Kevin was an immediate success at Newcastle. In his first full season, the club won a place in the prestigious Premier Division.

After finishing as runner-up to Manchester United in the Premier Division in 1996, Kevin resigned as manager in 1997 and joined the Fulham club as chief operating officer and, later, coach. In 1999, he was named the new coach of the England team and secured a spot in the Euro 2000 finals with a qualifying win over Poland and a victory over Scotland in the playoffs. However, England was eventually eliminated at the group stage. After another disappointing elimination, this time in the 2000 World Cup qualifier against Germany, Kevin resigned as England's head coach.

In 2001, Kevin became the manager for Manchester City, a position he held until 2005. He was inducted into the English Football Hall of Fame in 2002.

Summary

Kevin Keegan was a deceptively powerful and tenacious player. His quickness, inventiveness, and hard work helped make English club soccer an international force in the 1970's.

George O'Brien

Additional Sources

Hunt, Chris. *The Complete Book of Soccer.* Buffalo, N.Y.: Firefly Books, 2006.

Keegan, Kevin. *Kevin Keegan: My Autobiography.* London: Warner, 1998.

Radnedge, Keir, and Gary Lineker. *The Ultimate Encyclopedia of Soccer: The Definitive Illustrated Guide to World Soccer.* London: Carlton Books, 2004.

Alexi Lalas

Born: June 1, 1970
Birmingham, Michigan
Also known as: Panayotis Alexander Lalas (full name)

Early Life

Panayotis Alexander Lalas, better known as Alexi Lalas, was born in Birmingham, Michigan, on June 1, 1970. Alexi's father was a college professor and director of Greece's national observatory, and his mother was a writer and poet. By most accounts, Alexi started playing soccer at the age of ten or eleven. By the time he reached high school, he was one of the top players in Michigan. After his senior year, he was named the top prep player in the state. Along with soccer, Alexi excelled on the ice. He led his team to the state hockey championship his senior year at Cranbrook-Kingswood Preparatory School.

The Road to Excellence

Following high school, Alexi attended Rutgers University in New Jersey on a soccer scholarship.

American Alexi Lalas getting in between the ball and a Swedish player in 1995. (AP/Wide World Photos)

He played on the Rutgers soccer team from 1988 to 1991. While at Rutgers, he became one of the top defensive players in the nation. Following the 1989 and 1990 seasons, he was named a third-team all-American. After the 1991 season, he made first-team all-American and was the recipient of the Herman Trophy, an award presented each year by the Missouri Athletic Club to the nation's top collegiate male and female soccer players. In addition, in the National Collegiate Athletic Association Men's Soccer Championship, Alexi led the Scarlet Knights to the semifinals in 1989 and to the championship game in 1990. Alexi also continued to play hockey while at Rutgers and led his team in scoring during the 1990 season. Also in 1990, he began his long run as a member of the U.S. national team.

The Emerging Champion

Between 1991 and 1998, Alexi had ninety-six caps, or games played, with the U.S. national team. While he played in numerous games for the United States between 1991 and 1993, he did not become a full-time starting defender for the team until early 1994. Later in the same year, Alexi made his mark in American soccer history and on the world. In the 1994 FIFA World Cup, Alexi performed brilliantly. He played every minute of the four U.S. World Cup games and was named an honorable-mention all-star for the tournament. Off the field, he was a rock guitarist with long, wild, red hair and a goatee. Fans all over the world were taken with his flamboyant personality and playing style.

Following the 1994 Olympics, Alexi became the first American player in the modern era to play in the Italian Serie A league. In 1995 and 1996, he played for the Padova squad before returning to the United States to play in the fledgling Major League Soccer (MLS). When the league formed, the MLS

National Team Statistics

Season	GP	G	Ast.	Pts.
1991	2	0	2	2
1993	25	4	3	11
1994	22	1	1	3
1995	12	2	0	4
1996	14	0	4	4
1997	14	2	0	4
1998	4	1	0	2
Totals	96	10	10	29

Notes: GP = games played; G = goals; Ast. = assists; Pts. = points

MLS Statistics

Season	GP	GS	Min.	G	Ast.	Pts.
1996	25	25	2,218	1	1	3
1997	30	29	2,607	2	3	7
1998	25	25	2,250	2	0	4
1999	30	30	2,700	4	1	9
2001	11	9	764	2	2	6
2002	26	26	2,364	4	4	12
2003	22	19	1,760	1	1	3
Totals	169	163	14,663	16	12	44

Notes: GP = games played; GS = games started; Min. = minutes played; G = goals; Ast. = assists; Pts. = points

tried to distribute high-profile players evenly among the teams, and Alexi was placed with the New England Revolution. After two relatively quiet years with the Revolution, he was traded to the New York/New Jersey MetroStars in 1998 and then the Kansas City Wizards in 1999. However, when he was traded to the Los Angeles Galaxy, he finally made his mark in the MLS. He played for the Galaxy from 2001 to 2004. In 2002, he led the team to the MLS Championship Cup and was named to the MLS Best XI. He retired permanently from MLS on January 12, 2004.

Continuing the Story

Following his playing career, Alexi became involved in MLS management. As one of the main faces of soccer in the United States, he would have had a positive influence on any MLS organization. He became the general manager of the San Jose Earthquakes. Soon thereafter, in 2005, he was transferred within the Anschutz Entertainment Group (AEG) and become president of the MetroStars. In this capacity, he was a key figure in the franchise's transition after Anschutz sold the team to Red Bull. The team's name changed to Red Bull New York. In August of 2006, Alexi left New York to become general manager of the Galaxy. In August, 2008, he was released from his position.

In addition to his athletic prowess, Alexi was also an accomplished musician. He played guitar and sang for his band the Gypsies. In 1998, the band opened for Hootie and the Blowfish during the latter's European tour. That same year, Alexi also did solo work, releasing an album called *Ginger* on CMC International records. His music has been described as melodic hard rock, and he built a small but loyal following, particularly among soccer fans.

Summary

Alexi Lalas's significance cannot be measured by the same standards used to evaluate offensive-minded soccer players. Alexi was a defender, so his numbers, such as goals scored and assists, were not as impressive as those of many of his contemporaries. However, in the 1990's, he meant more to American soccer than perhaps any other player. In the 1994 FIFA World Cup, Alexi was the outspoken leader of the first competitive U.S. team in decades. In that role, he inspired a generation of young American players.

Theodore Shields

Additional Sources

Kirkpatrick, Rob. *Alexi Lalas, Soccer Sensation*. New York: PowerKids Press, 2002.

Lalas, Alexi, and Thomas Lee Wright. *Kickin' Balls: The Alexi Lalas Story*. New York: Simon & Schuster, 1996.

Honors, Awards, and Milestones

1988	Michigan's top prep player
1989-90	Third-team all-American
1990	Runner-up, NCAA Men's Soccer Championship (with Rutgers University)
1991	First-team all-American
	Hermann Trophy
1994	Honorable-mention all-star, World Cup
	First modern-era American player in Serie A (Italy)
1995	U.S. Soccer athlete of the year
2002	MLS Championship Cup (with Los Angeles Galaxy)
	MLS Best XI

Denis Law

Born: February 24, 1940
Aberdeen, Scotland

Early Life

Denis Law was born in the fishing port of Aberdeen, Scotland on February 24, 1940. Denis's background is typical of many gifted Scottish soccer players who eventually play professionally in England. He grew up in impoverished circumstances. When his career was at its zenith, it was said that his ball-control skills came from playing on poorly paved laneways with a ball made of a stocking stuffed with newspaper and held together with string.

In 1957, just out of school, Denis signed as a professional with Huddersfield Town, an English First Division club. At that time, Huddersfield was managed by the legendary Bill Shankly, also a Scot, who later became the manager who molded Liverpool into the dominant force in English soccer in the 1970's.

Denis's appearance caught fans' attention even more than his skill. He wore spectacles and looked physically ill-suited for a career in professional soccer. In the words of one noted commentator, "he looked more like a coat-hanger than a footballer." Appearances proved to be deceptive.

The Road to Excellence

In 1960, Denis was transferred from Huddersfield Town to the First Division club, Manchester City. The fee of £100,000 was enormous for the time. A year later, however, Denis made an even more spectacular move. He signed with an Italian club, Torino. This move, though unusual, was not unique. English soccer players, desiring to break free of the restrictive wage structure and repressive regimes of clubs at home, aspired to the lives of superstars in the Italian First Division. Others to make the transition included Denis's gifted contemporary Jimmy Greaves.

Life in physical Italian soccer was difficult, and life as a highly paid performer in the glare of the Italian media was even more difficult. Denis fared better than many of the other British players of his generation who went to Italy. After two hard years, however, he returned to England. Manchester United, his old club's crosstown rival, paid Torino what was then a record fee to acquire him—£116,000.

The Emerging Champion

To the fans who flocked to Manchester United's ground, Old Trafford, only one phrase described Denis: They called him "The King." In his ten years with United he scored 171 goals. Still, it was not merely his accuracy as a striker that was revered. Despite his frail physical makeup, Denis was a daredevil. His ability to head the ball was astounding, given his relatively short stature. He unflinchingly took on defenders much more physically powerful. Above all, perhaps, he was an extremely witty and resourceful player. The quickness with which he could assess and seize an opportunity was phenomenal. He also possessed close ball control, one of the gifts for which Scottish forwards are particularly renowned. This control, together with superb acceleration over short distances, enabled him to run rings around the opposition. As his tally of goals in a perpetually defensive-minded league shows, he was a deadly finisher. In 1964, he was voted European player of the year.

While with Manchester United, Denis won a Football Association Cup Winners' Medal and a Football League Championship Medal. However, injury kept him from playing in Manchester United's triumph

---

Career Highlights

55 international appearances for Scotland
30 international goals

Honors, Awards, and Milestones

1963	English Football Association Cup champion
1963, 1965, 1967	English League champion
1964	European player of the year
1975	English Professional Football Association Merit Award
2002	Inducted into English Football Hall of Fame

in the European Champions' Cup at Wembley Stadium, London, in 1968.

Denis also had a highly successful career playing for Scotland's national team. Although Scotland had had plenty of players with wonderful individual gifts, the national team's international record was not what it should have been. Thanks, in part, to Denis's efforts near the end of his career, Scotland made it to the World Cup group finals in Germany in 1974. In all, Denis appeared fifty-five times for his country and scored 30 goals, a Scottish record he shares with Kenny Dalglish.

Continuing the Story

In 1973, Denis returned to his old club, Manchester City, on a "free transfer"—in other words, no money changed hands. When such a trade is made, the player's career is usually assumed to be over. Ironically, one of Denis's most memorable contributions to Manchester City during his second stint with the team was in the 1973-1974 season when he scored the goal that relegated Manchester United to Division II the following year.

Despite his remarkable durability, injuries took their cumulative toll on Denis, and he retired in 1974. He became a commentator on live soccer broadcasts on British Broadcasting Corporation (BBC) radio, where his bubbly and enthusiastic interjections were a pleasing reminder of his playing style. In 2002, he was inducted into the English Football Hall of Fame.

Summary

One of the first Scottish superstars to ignite the postwar English soccer scene, Denis Law was memorable for his flair and daring. His ability to weave through a posse of defenders before teeing up the ball for teammate Bobby Charlton's thunderous shot remains a vivid image of his great years with Manchester United. His intuitive sense of space, the opportunism and quick-wittedness that earned for him so many critical goals, and his uncanny gift for field awareness were evidence of his rare feel for the game. These gifts, together with his all-out physical daring, made him one of those players in whom the combination of skill and commitment produced an athletic genius.

George O'Brien

Additional Sources

Hughes, Brian. *The King: Denis Law, Hero of the Stretford End*. Manchester: Empire, 2003.

Law, Denis. *The King*. London: Bantam, 2004.

Law, Denis, Pat Crerand, and Michael Leitch. *United: The Legendary Years, 1958-1968*. London: Virgin, 1997.

Kristine Lilly

Born: July 22, 1971
New York, New York
Also known as: Kristine Marie Lilly (full name)

Early Life

Kristine Marie Lilly was born to Teresa and Stephen Lilly in New York on July 22, 1971. She grew up in Wilton, Connecticut, and played soccer from second grade to eighth grade on a local boys' team. She also used to practice with her older brother and his friends at the Lilly home.

Kristine was captain of Wilton High School's girls' soccer team during her junior and senior years. She also played second base on the varsity softball team and guard on the girls' basketball squad. Her high school soccer team won the state title in her freshman, sophomore, and senior years. Through those years, she played well enough to be invited to a position on the national team, and on August 3, 1987, having just turned sixteen, Kristine made her first U.S. team appearance in Tianjin, China. The U.S. team won 2-0.

The Road to Excellence

There was a good deal of overlap between Kristine's college and national-team appearances. Anson Dorrance was her coach with the University of North Carolina (UNC) Tar Heels as well as for the national team, which won the United States its first world championship. Her college teammate Mia Hamm was also a valuable member of the national team, who had joined at the same time.

In December, 1991, Kristine was awarded the Hermann Trophy, given to the nation's top male and female college soccer players. Also in 1991, she won the Missouri Athletic Club player of the year award, the Adidas/Intercollegiate Soccer Association player of the year award, and the Honda national player of the year award. In 1993, she won the U.S. Soccer female athlete of the year award. She became famous for her mastery of the deceptive "fake strike" technique.

Kristine played on four national championship teams at UNC. She graduated from the university in December, 1993, with a degree in radio, television, and motion picture production. Not surprisingly, she was a college all-American four times, making her the first woman ever to be an all-American four years in a row. When she finished her college playing career, she had a record of 78 goals and

American Kristine Lilly passing to teammates up the field in a 2006 game against Australia. (Keizo Mori/UPI/Landov)

41 assists. In 1994, the university retired her jersey number 15.

In 1994, Kristine played for the Tyreso Football Club in Sweden, along with several of her U.S. teammates—Michelle Akers, Julie Foudy, and Mary Harvey. In 1995, she joined a mostly male professional team, the Washington Warthogs, of the Continental Indoor Soccer League, and was the only woman player in the entire league at that time. She felt that playing against men helped her to develop more mental and physical quickness, in order to compensate for male advantages in strength.

The Emerging Champion

Kristine was dubbed the "Queen of Caps," which refers to the English practice of giving caps to athletes who represent their nations in international games. In May, 1998, in Kobe, Japan, Kristine set a world record for women by playing in her 152d international game, breaking the mark that had been set by Heidi Stoere of Norway. The following January, she earned her 165th cap to pass the all-time men's record. She eventually earned more than 300 caps—a number that had once been thought unreachable.

Meanwhile, although Kristine traditionally played the left side of midfield, U.S. coach Tony DiCicco moved her to the position of forward, which had been her position on the University of North Carolina team. Also in 1998, she was a member of the gold-medal-winning U.S. team at the Goodwill Games.

In 1999, Kristine made one of the crucial saves that helped the United States defeat China in the Women's World Cup Final in Pasadena, California. She was named most spectacular player of that game, which the United States won, 5-4. In the tournament leading up the final, she played in every minute of every U.S. game. From January to July, 1999, Kristine kept an online World Cup diary on the CNN/*Sports Illustrated* Web site, with a form for sending questions or comments to her.

Continuing the Story

The success of the United States in the 1999 Women's World Cup elevated women's soccer to an unprecedented status of popularity. In February, 2000, major U.S. media companies, women soccer stars, and individual investors formed the Women's United Soccer Association, the top women's professional soccer league, which combined the best American and international players. With franchises in Atlanta, Boston, New York, Philadelphia, San Diego, the San Francisco Bay Area, and Washington, D.C., the new league's inaugural season started in April, 2001. Kristine was one of the founding soccer players for this new league and appeared on the Boston Breakers. The new women's league lasted only three seasons, during which Kristine played in fifty-nine games for the Breakers, scored 14 goals, and provided 27 assists. In 2005, Kristine returned to Sweden, where she joined the KIF Örebro club.

Through these years, Kristine continue to win distinction with the U.S. national team. In September, 2000, the U.S. team won the silver medal at the Olympics in Sydney, Australia. The final

National Team Statistics

Season	GP	GS	Min.	G	Ast.	Pts.
1987	7	7	600	1	0	2
1988	8	7	640	0	2	2
1990	6	6	444	1	3	5
1991	27	26	2,156	7	12	26
1993	16	15	1,305	9	2	20
1994	13	13	1,170	7	4	18
1995	21	20	1,755	12	2	26
1996	23	23	2,003	8	6	22
1997	18	18	1,588	7	9	23
1998	24	24	1,920	8	11	27
1999	28	27	2,395	20	7	47
2000	34	30	2,666	6	5	17
2001	3	2	217	0	0	0
2002	16	16	1,291	3	9	15
2003	19	18	1,407	3	3	9
2004	28	28	2,451	8	8	24
2005	8	8	684	4	3	11
2006	20	19	1,723	13	7	33
2007	21	20	1,771	12	5	29
2008	2	0	73	0	0	0
Totals	342	327	28,259	129	98	356

Notes: GP = games played; GS = games started; Min. = minutes played; G = goals; Ast. = assists; Pts. = points

> **Honors, Awards, and Milestones**
>
> | | |
> |---|---|
> | 1991 | Hermann Trophy |
> | | Missouri Athletic Club player of the year |
> | 1991, 1999 | Women's World Cup champion, with American team |
> | 1993, 2006-07 | U.S. Soccer's female player of the year |
> | 1996, 2004 | Gold medal, Olympic Games |
> | 2000 | Silver medal, Olympic Games |
> | | *Soccer America* college team of the century |
> | 2004-08 | Captain, U.S. national soccer team |
> | 2006 | Appeared in 300th international game |
> | | Runner-up for the FIFA women's world player of the year |
> | 2007 | Oldest woman to score a goal in the World Cup |

game, which went into overtime, resulted in a 3-2 loss to Norway. Four years later, Kristine was again on the U.S. team, which won a gold medal at the Athens Olympic Games. However, she was on maternity leave from the team when it won another gold medal at the 2008 Games in Beijing, China.

Meanwhile, Kristine played in two more World Cup competitions, in 2003 and 2007. Several major players retired from international competition at the end of 2004, but Kristine stayed on the team and earned new distinctions. In 2006, she finished second in the world, behind Brazil's Marta, in voting for FIFA women's soccer player of the year. At the same time, she was named U.S. Soccer's female athlete of the year for a second-consecutive year. She had another strong season in 2007. In 2008, she announced she would play for the Women's Professional Soccer team in Boston.

Summary

Kristine Lilly has one of the most extraordinary records of championships in sports history. After leading her high school team to three consecutive state championships, she led her university team to four consecutive national championships. At the same time, she began a career on the U.S. national team that lasted twenty years through 2007 and won her shares in two Olympic gold medals and two World Cup championships. By 2007, she had played in 342 international games, scored 129 goals, and had 98 assists. Kristine played soccer in countries all over the world, including Australia, Bulgaria, Cyprus, Denmark, Haiti, Japan, Sweden, Taiwan, and Trinidad and Tobago. Each summer, the internationally famous soccer star runs the Kristine Lilly Soccer Academy in Wilton, where the entry sign says, "Welcome to Wilton—Hometown of Kristine Lilly."

Alice Myers, updated by the Editors

Additional Sources

Goldblatt, David. *The Ball Is Round: A Global History of Soccer.* New York: Riverhead Books, 2008.

Hunt, Chris. *The Complete Book of Soccer.* Buffalo, N.Y.: Firefly Books, 2006.

Longman, Jere. *The Girls of Summer: The U.S. Women's Soccer Team and How It Changed the World.* New York: HarperCollins, 2000.

Miller, Marla. *All-American Girls: The U.S. Women's National Soccer Team.* New York: Pocket Books, 1999.

Pellerud, Even, with Sam Kucey. *Coaching and Leadership in Women's Soccer.* Spring City, Pa.: Reedswain, 2005.

Radnedge, Keir, and Gary Lineker. *The Ultimate Encyclopedia of Soccer: The Definitive Illustrated Guide to World Soccer.* London: Carlton Books, 2004.

Rasmussen, R. Kent. "Women's World Cup of Soccer Draws Unprecedented Attention." In *Great Events: 1900-2001.* Vol. 8. Pasadena, Calif.: Salem Press, 2002.

Gary Lineker

Born: November 30, 1960
 Leicester, England
Also known as: Gary Winston Lineker (full name)

Early Life

Gary Winston Lineker was born on November 30, 1960, in Leicester, England, a city about one hundred miles north of the capital, London. His father, Barry Lineker, was a market trader, running the well-established family fruit and vegetable stall in Leicester.

Gary's father was an average soccer player, but his grandfather had played soccer for a county schoolboy team and for top army teams. When Gary was still a toddler, his father and grandfather kicked soccer balls to him. The grandson had inherited the grandfather's special ability: He could use both feet equally well.

The Road to Excellence

In elementary school, Gary and his brother, Wayne, helped their school win a local trophy. Gary next attended the City of Leicester Boys' Grammar School, a college preparatory school, where he especially liked math and sports. He did well both academically and athletically. He passed tough examinations in six subjects at the age of sixteen and became his school's 400-meter sprint champion.

In 1976, Gary left school, and he was good enough in sports to be offered opportunities in both cricket and soccer. He became an apprentice soccer player with Leicester City, his local club. Perhaps because Gary was so small—5 feet 6 inches and less than 125 pounds—Leicester was the only soccer club to offer him a chance.

On January 1, 1979, Gary started playing for Leicester; he scored his first goal three months later. He was often mentioned in the newspapers because he averaged 1 goal every two games. In 1984, he began playing for England's national team, when he came on as a substitute. In 1985,

England's Gary Lineker battling a player from Paraguay during the 1986 World Cup in Mexico. (Bob Thomas/Getty Images)

he scored in the first match in which he started for England.

In June, 1985, Gary achieved star status when he was transferred to a top club, Everton, for £800,000 (approximately $1.6 million), the highest fee Everton had ever paid for a player. Everton paid so much for Gary because he was quick, with excellent timing and balance. He also had a reputation as a likable, levelheaded player, with a great sense of humor.

The Emerging Champion

Gary continued his fantastic scoring rate at Everton, scoring 40 goals in fifty-seven games. He was the top scorer in the entire English League.

The year 1986 was hectic but successful for Gary. He was selected footballer of the year by two sports organizations. In June, he was bought by Barcelona, a top team in the Spanish Soccer League, for £2.2 million (approximately $4.4 million). Gary wanted to play in international club competition, from which English clubs were banned because of crowd rowdiness.

In 1986, Gary played for England in the World Cup in Mexico and was the tournament's top scorer, with six goals. Just before leaving for Barcelona in July, Gary married his girlfriend of seven years.

Life in Barcelona had its ups and downs for Gary. First, he had to learn a new language, Spanish, to understand what his teammates were saying. Within two years, he was asked to comment about soccer on Spanish television, and did so, in fluent Spanish. On the field, Gary was told to play a wing position, when he was really a center-forward. He accepted the role without complaint but believed that he his ability could have been better utilized. Nevertheless, in 1989, Gary won a European Cup Winners' Cup Medal with Barcelona and scored the winning goal from his new position.

Gary had a good reputation to go with his skill on the field. He was a sporting competitor who had never even been cautioned by a referee, let alone ejected, in his entire career. Additionally, he was recognized as an excellent thinker and speaker on soccer. He also had one ritual: Because of his poor blood circulation, he liked to have a long, hot bath before a game.

Gary was also talented in three other sports, each very different from soccer. He was a good snooker player, he continued to play some cricket, and he had a golf handicap of only fourteen.

Continuing the Story

Although Gary had adapted well to Spain, he was happy to return to play in England in June, 1989, when he was transferred to Tottenham Hotspur, a top London club, for £1.1 million (approximately $2.2 million). The excitement this caused was illustrated by the fact that within two days of Gary's transfer more than £100,000 worth of season tickets were sold.

In most of the world, a soccer player receives a percentage of his transfer fee. Gary could have made more money by agreeing to be transferred to a French or Italian club, but he wanted to return to England.

In the 1990 World Cup in Italy, Gary was instrumental in England's unexpected trip to the semifinals. He scored a total of four goals in the tournament. He also was named the captain of England in 1990. In 1991, Gary won an FA Cup Championship with Hotspur and raised his international goal total to 48, just one behind Bobby Charlton's England record of 49. In 1992, Gary moved to Japan to assist in the launch of the new J-League. While he was playing with Grampus Eight in Japan, a series of foot injuries hampered his debut. Gary announced his retirement in 1994.

Gary was also successful in off-the-field business. He signed several deals with equipment manufacturers to endorse their products. Companies

Career Highlights

80 international appearances for England

48 international goals

Honors, Awards, and Milestones

1986	World Cup high scorer (6 goals)
	English Footballer of the Year
	English Professional Football Association player of the year
1989	European Cup Winners' Cup champion
1991	FA Cup Championship
1992	Gordon Strachan Football Writers' Association Footballer of the Year
2002, 2004	Received RTS Television Sport Award: Best Sports Presenter

were eager to have such a pleasant, articulate person to help sell their merchandise. He also became a successful newspaper columnist and radio announcer.

Summary

Other English players with an average of a goal in every two games are Bobby Charlton and Geoff Hurst. Gary Lineker was the only player to achieve that feat during the 1990's. He brought intense excitement to every game in which he played, and his patience with the press, his modesty, and his cleancut image on and off the field have made him one of the most remarkable and popular players ever.

Shirley H. M. Reekie

Additional Sources

Galvin, Robert, and Mark Bushell. *Football's Greatest Heroes: The National Football Museum's Hall of Fame.* London: Robson, 2005.

Lineker, Gary. *The Definitive Guide to the World Cup with Gary Lineker.* London: EMP Sport, 2006.

_____. *Gary Lineker's Definitive Guide to Euro Championship 2000.* London: EMP Sport, 2000.

_____. *Soccer.* New York: Dorling Kindersley, 2000.

Lineker, Gary, and Stan Hey. *Gary Lineker's Golden Boots: The World Cup's Greatest Strikers, 1930-1998.* London: Hodder & Stoughton, 1998.

Radnedge, Keir, and Gary Lineker. *The Ultimate Encyclopedia of Soccer: The Definitive Illustrated Guide to World Soccer.* London: Carlton Books, 2004.

Diego Maradona

Born: October 30, 1960
Buenos Aires, Argentina
Also known as: Diego Armando Maradona (full name)

Early Life

Diego Armando Maradona was born on October 30, 1960, to a poor family in a suburb of Buenos Aires, Argentina. At his birth, the midwife said to his mother that there was no need to worry—her son was all muscles. Diego had eight brothers and sisters. Like many other poor children in South America, the children spent much of their time playing soccer with a makeshift ball in the back streets. Diego's remarkable talent marked him from an early age. In later years he said he had two reasons to make money in soccer: The first was to earn enough so that his father would not have to work hard; the second was to buy a pair of trousers of his own.

The Road to Excellence

With the exception of Pelé, perhaps no soccer player ever showed as much natural talent as Diego. By the time Diego was fifteen, the Argentine national team coach Cesar Menotti said, he already had first-class technique. Diego was already an excellent soccer player before he started serious training. Still, several years passed before he reached true greatness.

The coach of Argentine Juniors, a local team, first spotted Diego's talents when Diego was thirteen. Diego's ball control amazed everyone who saw him. Though Diego was short—he grew to only 5 feet 6 inches as an adult—he was stocky and immensely fast. By the age of sixteen he was playing professionally. At seventeen he made his international debut for Argentina. To Diego's annoyance, however, Menotti left him off the Argentina squad for the 1978 World Cup, which Argentina won.

Over the next few years, Diego's honors accumulated. In 1979 and 1980, he was the top marksman in the Argentine league. In 1979 and 1980, he was named South American player of the year. In 1981, his new team, Boca Juniors, won the Argen-

Diego Maradona of Argentina during the 1986 World Cup. (Bob Thomas/Getty Images)

tine League Championship. Still, experts believed that Diego was not achieving his true potential. They complained that in a team game he played as an individualist.

The 1982 World Cup confirmed the critics' suspicions. A poor Argentine team was defeated early by Brazil, and Diego was ejected for kicking an opposing player. The same year he transferred to the Barcelona team in Spain for a fee of $10 million. His two years there, before a transfer to the Napoli club in Italy, were unhappy ones. Injury and illness prevented him from showing his best form.

The Emerging Champion

Not until the World Cup in 1986 did Diego finally emerge as the truly great player people had always said he could become. He had gradually matured as a person and a player, and he had learned to handle the adulation that had received since his midteens. On the soccer field he still showed fantastic individual touches, but he became a team player.

In 1983, Argentina appointed a new national coach, Carlos Bilardo, who immediately flew to Europe to meet with Diego. Bilardo told Diego that he would have to follow his orders at all times. Eventually Bilardo grew to have such confidence in Diego that he made him captain of the Argentina team.

Before the 1986 World Cup Final, two players were most often mentioned as the greatest soccer players in the world: Diego and Michel Platini of France. Many, including Pelé, believed that Platini, with his accurate passing and great team play, had the edge. In addition, the teams on which Platini played usually won.

By the competition's end, Diego was undisputedly number one. Reporters said that some of his five goals would be talked about for fifty years. To score his second goal against England in the World Cup quarterfinal, he collected the ball on the halfway line and beat three opponents and the goalkeeper before placing the ball in the back of the net. Two more goals followed in the semifinal versus Belgium. In the final, Diego set up all three Argentine goals as his team beat West Germany and became the world champion.

Continuing the Story

Diego's success continued with the Napoli club, which won the Italian League championship in 1986-1987 and again in 1989-1990. In between, Napoli collected the Union of European Football Associations (UEFA) Cup, winning a competition held among some of the greatest teams in Europe.

No longer could anyone say that Diego did not play with successful teams or that he could not blend his talent with a team's overall strategy. Moreover, he still had uncanny ball control with his left foot. It seemed as though no space was too small for him to beat an opponent. Rival teams assigned two players to mark Diego, and he still won games by setting up goals for his teammates. Though Diego disliked training, he was always fit for important matches. Sometimes, as in 1989, he gained weight, but when he needed to lose it, he did. Though he was officially a striker, he roamed over soccer fields, always in the thick of the action. People talked about his goals as miracles, goals only he could have scored.

By the late 1980's, Diego was probably the most famous sportsman in the world outside the United States. Wherever soccer was played, Diego was recognized as its most talented exponent. By the time of the 1990 World Cup, Argentina had lost many of its best players. Sometimes three opponents would mark Diego, and when he would beat them he would be fouled. Troubled by a foot injury, Diego failed to score in any match. Nevertheless, his team reached the final game before losing to West Germany. Such was Diego's popularity with Neapolitan fans that when Argentina played Italy in Naples some cheered for Argentina against their own country.

Diego's career was interrupted in 1991, however, when he was arrested by police in Buenos Aires for drug possession. The result was a fifteen-month suspension from Italian and world competition, effectively marking the beginning of the end of his career. Following his reinstatement, he tried to revive his career in Seville and later with Argentina. He returned to World Cup competition in

Honors, Awards, and Milestones

1979-80	South American player of the year
1981	Argentine League champion
1986	World Cup champion
	World Cup most valuable player (Golden Ball)
1987, 1990	Italian League champion
1989	UEFA Cup champion

1994 but was banished when he tested positive for cocaine use. Diego finished his career with the Boca Juniors and formally retired in 1997. In 2005, he became the vice president of Boca Juniors, a position he held for one year. He has written a best-selling autobiography and was briefly the host of an Argentine talk show entitled *La Noche del 10*.

Summary

Diego Maradona's achievements rank him with the greatest soccer players of all time: Pelé, Alfredo di Stefano, Franz Beckenbauer, and Johan Cruyff. The ball control of Diego's left foot, his explosive speed, his passing ability, and his team leadership made him a unique player with an instantly recognizable style. His amazing skills brought him fame and wealth; sadly, they brought him troubles as well.

Philip Magnier

Additional Sources

Burns, Jimmy. *Hand of God: The Life of Diego Maradona*. Guilford, Conn.: Lyons Press, 2003.

Ludden, John. *Once upon a Time in Naples*. Manchester: Parrs Wood, 2005.

Maradona, Diego, Daniel Arcucci, and Ernesto Cherquis Bialo. *El Diego*. London: Yellow Jersey, 2005.

Maradona, Diego, Daniel Arcucci, Ernesto Cherquis Bialo, and Marcela Mora y Araujo. *Maradona: The Autobiography of Soccer's Greatest and Most Controversial Star*. New York: Skyhorse, 2007.

Marta

Born: February 19, 1986
Dois Riachos, Alagoas, Brazil
Also known as: Marta Vieira da Silva (full name); Pele with Skirts

Early Life

Marta Vieira da Silva was born into poverty on February 19, 1986, in Dois Riachos, a backwater village in Brazil's Alagoas state. The daughter of Aldário, a barber who left the family when Marta was an infant, and Tereza da Silva, she grew up with three siblings: José, Valdir, and Angela.

Marta became a soccer fan at an early age in a country fanatical about the sport and one that has produced legions of international stars. Marta, too, dreamed of playing soccer professionally. However, since females in Brazilian society are discouraged from participating in the sport, and were prohibited by law from playing it until 1979, she had to play with boys or older males who verbally abused her. The only reason they allowed her to play at all was that she was a striker with uncanny dribbling and shooting skills.

The Road to Excellence

After fighting for the right to play, at twelve, Marta was permitted to join an all-male regional team. After leading the team to two consecutive championships, she was subsequently banned from playing. When Marta was fourteen, a scout from Rio de Janeiro—where women's teams existed—suggested she come to the big city to try out. Traveling more than 1,000 miles by bus, she arrived in Rio. Although she was only 5 feet 2 inches and a slender 105 pounds, she so impressed Vasco da Gama that she was immediately made a part of the major women's team.

Playing with Vasco from 2000 to 2002, Marta lived with family friends in Rio and received expense money. In 2002, she played in the FIFA Under-Nineteen (U-19) Women's Global World Championship in Canada. Afterward, she played with Santa Cruz for a season in 2002-2003. At age seventeen, she helped Brazil capture gold at the 2003 Pan-American Games and played at the 2003 Women's World Cup. Marta's performance was impressive enough to earn a call from the manager of a Swedish professional team, Umeå IK. As soon as she turned eighteen in 2004, Marta signed a contract to play in Sweden. She participated at the 2004 FIFA U-19 Women's World Championship in Thailand, where she received the Adidas golden ball award as best player. Also selected for the Brazilian national women's team at the 2004 Athens Olympics, Marta starred, as Brazil won a silver medal, losing to the United States in the final.

The Emerging Champion

The first Brazilian woman to play professionally in Europe, and the highest-paid female player, with a

Marta skipping past a defender toward the ball at the 2007 Women's World Cup in China. (Paul Gilham/Getty Images)

salary of $80,000, Marta was an instant success. She led Umeå IK to the Union of European Football Associations (UEFA) Cup finals her first season, scoring 22 goals. She scored 21 goals in each of the following two years to lead an undefeated Umeå IK team to the Swedish league championships in 2005 and 2006. For her performance in 2006, Marta was selected as FIFA women's world player of the year. In 2006, she was the first female athlete inducted into the Brazilian sports hall of fame.

Marta learned to speak Swedish and became one of the most popular players in the league and one of the world's best-known female soccer stars. She was such a sensation that Swedish television produced a documentary about her, entitled *Marta, Pele's Cousin.*

In 2007, Marta again shone on the international stage. Playing for Brazil at the Pan-American Games in Rio de Janeiro, she was the top scorer with 12 goals, as her team won the gold medal. At the 2007 Women's World Cup in China, she scored 7 goals, earning the Adidas golden boot award as top scorer and the Adidas golden ball award as best player. That same year, Marta inspired Umeå IK, after three consecutive years as runner-up, to capture the Swedish Cup. For the second year in a row, FIFA named Marta women's world player of the year.

Continuing the Story

In 2008, Marta signed a one-year contract with Umeå IK, for approximately $165,000. Playing for Brazil at the 2008 Beijing Olympics, she performed admirably as the team won its second consecutive silver medal, again losing to the United States in the finals.

In September, 2008, Marta and some of her Brazilian teammates were selected in an international draft to play in the new edition of the Women's Professional Soccer League, which debuted in 2009.

Honors, Awards, and Milestones

2004	FIFA Under-19 women's world championship Golden Ball
	Under-20 World Cup golden ball
2004-06	Swedish women's soccer league top scorer
2004, 2008	Silver medal, Olympic Games
2005	Runner-up FIFA women's international soccer player of the year
2006-07	FIFA women's international soccer player of the year
2007	Women's World Cup golden ball
	Women's World Cup golden boot
	Gold medal, Pan-American Games
	Swedish women's soccer league best forward of the year

Many expected the league to flourish. The new league had support from Major League Soccer and benefited from the incredible growth of the sport in the United States, where more than 3 million players were registered with the American Youth Soccer Association. Marta became the center forward for the Los Angeles franchise.

Summary

Considered the best women's soccer player of her generation, Marta Vieira da Silva—known simply as Marta—had to fight for the right to play in her native Brazil. By the time she was in her early twenties, she had accomplished much in soccer. A two-time Olympic silver medalist, a member of two gold-medal-winning Pan-American teams, and twice the FIFA women's world player of the year, Marta inspired female athletes in Brazil and around the world to play soccer through her determination.

Jack Ewing

Additional Sources

Bellos, Alex. *Futebol: Soccer, the Brazilian Way*. New York: Bloomsbury USA, 2003.

Kucey, Sam. *Even Pellerud on Coaching and Leadership in Women's Soccer*. Spring City, Pa.: Reedswain, 2005.

Stewart, Barbara. *Women's Soccer: The Passionate Game*. Vancouver, B.C.: Greystone Books, 2004.

Stanley Matthews

Born: February 1, 1915
Hanley, Stoke-on-Trent, Staffordshire, England
Died: February 23, 2000
Newcastle-under-Lyme, Staffordshire, England
Also known as: Sir Stanley Matthews

Early Life
Stanley Matthews was born in Hanley, in the English Midlands, on February 1, 1915. His father, Jack Matthews, a barber and a professional boxer, was known as "The Fighting Barber of Hanley." Jack Matthews instilled in his son a habit of rigorous self-discipline. He trained Stanley as a sprinter, and, at the age of six, Stanley competed in a 100-yard race at nearby Stoke-on-Trent. Every morning Stanley was expected to rise at six o'clock and exercise with his father and two brothers.

Stanley Matthews in 1951. (AP/Wide World Photos)

Stanley always wanted to be a professional soccer player. He practiced endlessly, either dribbling a rubber ball on his own or joining in games with his school friends wherever they could find a suitable place—in streets or on strips of wasteland. Stanley's father, on the other hand, wanted him to become a boxer. Nevertheless, he agreed to support his son's soccer ambitions if Stanley was selected for the England schoolboy side before he left school.

The Road to Excellence
Stanley met his father's condition. When he was thirteen he was selected to play for England against Wales in a schoolboy international game. He played well in what was for him the unusual position of outside right. To his bitter disappointment, however, he was not selected for the following international game against Scotland. Stanley remembered the advice of his father, who had told him never to take anything for granted in life; this helped him to recover his spirits.

Stanley later attributed much of his success to the training and upbringing he had received from his father. Jack Matthews warned his son not to get a swollen head over some early praise he had received in the newspapers. Jack Matthews watched all Stanley's early matches, offering constructive advice and criticism after each game. The level-headed, self-disciplined attitude that Stanley's father instilled in his son helped Stanley cope with the adulation he later received.

In 1930, at the age of fifteen, Stanley began work as an office boy with the Stoke City Football Club. He also played more than twenty games for the Stoke City reserve team before signing as a professional when he was seventeen. By 1933, he was playing regularly on the Stoke first team. The following year, Stanley played his first match for England's national team, against Wales at Cardiff, and scored a goal in England's victory.

The Emerging Champion
During the 1930's, Stanley established himself as a favorite of the Stoke City and England fans. He was

destined to become one of the greatest soccer players of all time.

Playing at outside right, Stanley was a superb dribbler of the ball. His balance was perfect, and no one could match his speed over the first ten yards. Time after time, Stanley would dribble the ball, at a leisurely pace, up to the opposing fullback. Then he would sway in one direction, getting the fullback off balance, and then sway back in the other direction, eluding the despairing lunge of his opponent. At that point Stanley would take off at top speed down the wing, leaving the unfortunate defender either flat on his back or trailing hopelessly behind. Stanley often beat two or three defenders in this way before crossing the ball into the goal area. His crosses were so accurate that they usually landed within a yard of a teammate.

One sign of Stanley's extraordinary reputation came in 1938, when he requested a transfer from Stoke City. Three thousand people attended a public meeting to protest. Leaflets circulated throughout the town saying "Stanley Matthews Must Not Go." Stanley agreed to stay on, and he remained with Stoke for another eight years before he was transferred to Blackpool in 1946.

Continuing the Story

By the 1940's, Stanley had become a soccer legend. In those days, before matches were televised, people would travel hundreds of miles just to see him play. His presence on the field lent a kind of magic to the atmosphere. He was like a miracle worker, and opposing defenses were often driven to panic as soon as he got the ball. The wizard of English soccer was held in awe by fans the world over.

Perhaps Stanley's finest match came in 1953, when he played for Blackpool in the Football Association Cup final against the Bolton Wanderers. With twenty minutes of the game remaining, Bolton had a 3-1 lead. Then Stanley turned on his deadly skill. After one long run down the wing that left several defenders beaten, Stanley crossed the ball and Stan Mortensen scored for Blackpool. With Stanley creating havoc every time he got the ball, Bolton struggled to hold on to its lead. A goal from a free kick tied the score, and thirty seconds from the end Stanley set off on another incredible run. Two defenders were left sprawling before Stanley made a perfect pass to his colleague Bill Perry, who scored the winning goal. The match became known as the "Matthews Final."

Stanley's sportsmanship was also legendary. He was a modest man, and he always remained calm and dignified on the field. He never retaliated, even when he was badly fouled by his opponents.

Stanley's remarkable physical fitness enabled him to continue playing long after other players of his age had retired. In 1957, he was past the age of forty when he played for England for the fifty-fourth time. In 1965, he became the oldest player ever to appear in a Football League match.

After Stanley's retirement, he became the first soccer player to be knighted, by Queen Elizabeth II, for his services to professional soccer. For a brief period he became manager of Port Vale. He died in 2000 and was inducted into the English Football Hall of Fame in 2002.

Summary

Many soccer experts regard Sir Stanley Matthews as the greatest soccer player of all time. His astonishing ball control and body swerve mesmerized defenders, and his speed left them floundering. In a playing career that spanned thirty-five years, he consistently brought to English soccer a level of artistry that it has rarely seen, before or since.

Bryan Aubrey

Additional Sources

Matthews, Stanley. *The Way It Was: My Autobiography*. London: Headline, 2000.

Miller, David. *Stanley Matthews: The Authorized Biography*. London: Pavilion, 1989.

Career Highlights

54 international appearances for England
11 international goals

Honors, Awards, and Milestones

1948, 1963	English Footballer of the Year
1953	English Football Association Cup champion
1956	European player of the year (Ballon d'Or)
1957	Commander of the British Empire
1965	Knighted by Queen Elizabeth II
1987	English Professional Football Association Merit Award
1992	Awarded FIFA Gold Merit Order
	Inducted into International Football Hall of Champions
2002	Inducted into English Football Hall of Fame

Bobby Moore

Born: April 12, 1941
Barking, borough of London, Essex, England
Died: February 24, 1993
London, England
Also known as: Robert Frederick Chelsea Moore (full name)

Early Life
Robert Frederick Chelsea Moore was born on April 12, 1941, in Barking, borough of London, Essex, England, in close proximity to Dagenham, the hometown of his future manager, Alf Ramsey. Bobby had a happy childhood; his parents, Robert and Doris Moore, never had a lot of money, but they made sure that they gave their only child every support and encouragement. From an early age, Bobby dreamed of playing soccer for England. When Bobby played for Barking Primary School, no one could have imagined that the dreams of the little blond boy would one day come true.

The Road to Excellence
Although Bobby was a good schoolboy soccer player, he was by no means exceptional. Consequently, it was something of a surprise that West Ham United, the local professional team, offered him a chance to play for its schoolboy team. As a schoolboy, Bobby showed more promise at cricket than at soccer. He even captained the South of England Schools' cricket team. Soccer, however, captured Bobby's imagination. He was determined to make the grade.

At West Ham, Bobby's keen positional play impressed his coaches. He was not the quickest or most mobile player, but his ability to read the game enabled him to avoid potentially dangerous situations that might have exposed his limitations.

Bobby played as a central defender for West Ham's reserve teams, and his intelligent play helped him progress toward a spot on the first team. He was even selected to play for the England Youth team. In June, 1958, Bobby signed as a professional. Three months later, at the age of seventeen, he made his professional debut for West Ham in a game against Manchester United.

In the 1960-1961 season, Bobby established himself on the West Ham first team. Through sheer hard work, he had become a superb tackler. His tackling skill allowed him to steal the ball from opponents and then use the ball constructively in attack. By his twenty-first birthday, Bobby was already one of the most accomplished defenders in the English game.

Bobby Moore. (Hulton Archive/Getty Images)

244

> **Career Highlights**
>
> 108 international appearances for England
>
> **Honors, Awards, and Milestones**
>
> | | |
> |---|---|
> | 1964 | English Football Association Cup champion |
> | | English Footballer of the Year |
> | 1965 | European Cup Winners' Cup champion |
> | 1966 | World Cup champion |
> | | World Cup Player of the Tournament |
> | | British Broadcasting Corporation Sports Personality of the Year |
> | 1967 | Order of the British Empire |
> | 1999 | Inducted into International Football Hall of Champions |
> | 2002 | Inducted into English Football Hall of Fame |
> | 2003 | Chosen as UEFA's Golden Player of England |
> | 2007 | Statue erected at Wembley Stadium |

The Emerging Champion

Bobby's stylish and creative defensive play guaranteed his selection for England's national team. In May, 1962, he won his first cap—an appearance on the national team. International soccer posed no problems for Bobby, and he immediately starred in the England defense. Bobby's rapid rise to the top was completed in May, 1963. An injury to the England captain, Jimmy Armfield, meant that at the tender age of twenty-two Bobby captained his country in a full international match against Czechoslovakia.

Bobby also found success at the club level. He was the captain of victorious West Ham teams in the 1964 Football Association and 1965 European Cup Winners' Cup finals. Both these games were played at Wembley Stadium, the home of the England international team. Also at Wembley, Bobby was to experience the greatest triumph of his career.

In 1964, national team manager Alf Ramsey chose Bobby to lead England in the 1966 World Cup tournament, which was to be held in England. Although Bobby was quiet and reclusive in his private life, on the soccer field he was a dominating character. He constantly made himself available to receive the ball, and he acted with a calm authority at all times. These qualities made him a natural leader.

England's blond captain guided the team to the World Cup Final against West Germany. Perhaps Bobby's most valuable contribution during the tournament was the quick free kick he took to set up Geoff Hurst's equalizing goal. This intelligent play paved the way for England's 4-2 victory over the West Germans.

On July 30, 1966, Bobby climbed the stairs to the Wembley Royal Box and joyfully accepted the World Cup Winners' Trophy from Queen Elizabeth II. Later he was voted player of the tournament by the sportswriters at the World Cup. England and Bobby were on top of the world.

Continuing the Story

In 1967, Bobby received the Order of the British Empire in recognition of his invaluable contribution to England's World Cup victory; he was still only twenty-five. The England captain was at his peak between 1966 and 1970, and he continued to star for both England and West Ham.

The 1970 World Cup, played in Mexico, provided Bobby with a further opportunity to display his immense talents. In a qualifying-round game against Brazil, he played one of his best-ever games. That performance prompted the Brazilian star Pelé to describe Bobby as the finest defender in the world. Ultimately, the Mexico tournament proved to be a disappointment for the England team and for Bobby. The team lost a heartbreaking quarter-final game against an avenging West German team, and Bobby's participation was clouded by personal problems even before the tournament began. Bobby was accused, wrongly, of stealing a bracelet from a shop in Colombia. The affair was blown up into an international incident. Throughout the affair, to his credit, Bobby conducted himself with the same calm integrity that he showed on the playing field.

After the 1970 World Cup, Bobby entered the twilight of his career. In 1973, he played for England for the last time. That game against Italy was Bobby's 108th international appearance, at the time, a world record.

In March, 1974, Bobby finally left West Ham and dropped down to the weaker Second Division to join Fulham. He joined forces with his old England colleague Alan Mullery. These two seasoned professionals led Fulham to a miraculous appearance in the 1975 Football Association Cup Final. However, the dream ended at Wembley as Fulham was beaten by, of all teams, West Ham.

In 1976, Bobby retired. He had brief spells as the

manager of nonleague Oxford City and the professional club Southend United. Perhaps because of his reserved personality, Bobby did not relish the challenge of soccer management. After leaving soccer, Bobby wrote for national newspapers and helped to run a chain of pubs.

He died in 1993 and was honored with numerous posthumous awards. In 2003, the Union of European Football Associations (UEFA) designated Bobby as England's "Golden Player," as the country's greatest player of the past fifty years. In 2007, outside of Wembley Stadium, a statue of Bobby was unveiled.

Summary

Bobby Moore became a great player because he was dedicated and determined to get to the top. From an early age he identified his strengths and weaknesses and worked to perfect his game accordingly. As a youngster, Bobby had always dreamed of playing for England. In the end, his career surpassed even his wildest dreams.

David L. Andrews

Additional Sources

Daniels, Phil. *Moore than a Legend: From Barking to Bogota—A Fascinating New Insight into the Real Bobby Moore from Those Who Knew Him Best.* Romford, Greater London, England: Goal!, 1997.

Lewis, Richard. *England's Eastenders: From Bobby Moore to David Beckham, a Breeding Ground for Brilliance.* Edinburgh: Mainstream, 2002.

Moore, Bobby. *My Soccer Story.* London: St. Paul, 1967.

Moore, Tina. *Bobby Moore: By the Person Who Knew Him Best.* London: HarperSport, 2006.

Powell, Jeff. *Bobby Moore: The Life and Times of a Sporting Hero.* London: Robson, 2002.

Gerd Müller

Born: November 11, 1945
Nödlingen, Bavaria, Germany
Also known as: Gerdhard Müller (full name); Der Bomber

Early Life

Gerdhard Müller was born in Nödlingen, Bavaria, Germany, on November 11, 1945. World War II had ended only three months earlier, and Europe was at peace for the first time in six years. Still, times were difficult for Germany, which had to rebuild itself after the ravages of war. Gerd's early life reflected the harshness of the times. His father died when Gerd was a young boy, and he had to leave school at the age of fifteen. He became an apprentice weaver.

Gerd was born with soccer "in his blood," but as soon as he was old enough to kick a ball in earnest, he discovered that Zinzen possessed no properly marked soccer fields. For years, he and his school friends would improvise with hats and coats for goalposts and anything they could find for a soccer ball.

The Road to Excellence

Even though Gerd had no proper playing facilities, his talent shone through. When he was seventeen, he arranged to have a trial with TSV Nördlingen, the soccer club nearest to his home. Traveling the seven miles home by bus after the trial, he felt triumphant. The Nördlingen coaching staff had been impressed by his skills and had offered him a contract.

Gerd's first match for Nördlingen was the first time he had played on a properly marked-out field. He had to wear borrowed soccer shoes, because he possessed none of his own, but that did not put him off his game, and he scored 2 goals. Over the next two seasons, he scored a total of 46 goals for Nördlingen. Many clubs became interested in signing him, but some decided that Gerd lacked the speed and all-around mobility to effectively challenge the best defenses. Gerd was small for a striker—he stood only 5 feet 8 inches tall—and, at the time, he was also overweight. His teammates at Nördlingen nicknamed him "Dicker" (Fatty).

Wilhelm Neudecker, the president of the Bayern Munich soccer club, was impressed by Gerd's goal-scoring abilities, however. In 1964, he persuaded the Bayern coach, Tchik Cajkovski, to sign him, even though Cajkovski was not enthusiastic. Cajkovski regarded Gerd as "a bear amongst racehorses." Gerd soon proved him wrong, scoring 2 goals in his debut for Bayern's senior team and a total of 35 goals in his first season. His performance helped Bayern win promotion to West Germany's highest league, the Bundesliga.

The Emerging Champion

In 1966-1967, Gerd shared top scoring honors in the Bundesliga, with 28 goals. He also won a West German Cup Winners' Medal and made his first appearance for West Germany's national team. Gerd was on the way to becoming one of the most lethal strikers in the history of the game. He had lost weight and sharpened his reflexes. He excelled in the penalty area and was adept at turning half-chances into goals. He could score goals with either foot and from almost

Gerd Müller kicking the ball in a 1974 game. (AFP/Getty Images)

247

Career Highlights

63 international appearances for West Germany
68 international goals
14 World Cup goals (all-time record)

Honors, Awards, and Milestones

1966-67, 1971	West German Cup champion
1967, 1969	West German player of the year
1967, 1974-76	European Cup champion
1969, 1972-74	West German League champion
1970	European player of the year (Ballon d'Or)
	World Cup high scorer (10 goals)
1972	European Championship champion
1974	World Cup champion
1998	Inducted into International Football Hall of Champions

impossible angles. After receiving the ball, he could pivot and turn in a moment, in either direction, leaving opposing defenders beaten. His skills were the result of endless practice. In training sessions, Gerd arrived an hour earlier and left an hour later than the other players in order to perfect his goal-scoring skills.

Gerd's years of playing produced a steady stream of successes. In 1967, he won another West German Cup Winners' Medal and a European Cup Winners' Medal. In the semifinal of the latter competition, he scored 4 goals against the Belgian team Standard Liege. He also scored 4 goals for West Germany in a 6-0 win against Albania. By 1969, Gerd was playing regularly for his country. In the same year, Bayern Munich won the Bundesliga title for the first time in its history. The team's success was due in large measure to Gerd's goal-scoring exploits. He was the league's top scorer with 30 goals and gained the nickname "Der Bomber."

In the 1970 World Cup in Mexico, Gerd was the tournament's leading scorer, with 10 goals. These included the winning goal against England in the quarterfinal and two goals against Italy in the semifinal, which West Germany lost 4-3. Then at the top of his profession, Gerd was voted European player of the year.

Continuing the Story

In 1972, Gerd scored twice for West Germany in that team's 3-0 European Championship final victory over the Soviet Union, a prelude to three years of amazing success for Der Bomber. From 1972 to 1974, Bayern Munich won the Bundesliga championship each year, and Gerd was the leading goal scorer in the Bundesliga in each of those years, with 40, 36, and 30 goals.

One of Gerd's greatest triumphs came in the 1974 World Cup Final in West Germany. He achieved every player's dream by scoring the winning goal, against Holland. Just before halftime, Gerd collected a pass from his teammate Rainer Bonhof inside the penalty area. The pass had arrived behind Gerd, but he controlled the ball, turned quickly, and shot past the Dutch goalkeeper, Jan Jongbloed, almost in one movement.

For the last five years of his career with Bayern Munich, Gerd was involved in a dispute with West Germany's soccer administrators and did not play for his country again. His international record, however, speaks for itself: He scored 68 goals in 63 matches for West Germany, a feat that few players from any country can match. He also scored 365 goals in 427 Bundesliga games, and more than 600 goals in all competitions.

In 1979, Gerd moved to the United States, where he played for the Fort Lauderdale Strikers in the North American Soccer League. In 1981, he left Florida and retired to Munich. He continued to watch his old team play, as well as to contribute a soccer column to a European newspaper. He eventually returned to Bayern Munich as a coach.

Summary

Gerd Müller was the most successful striker in West German soccer history and one of the deadliest goal scorers ever. He seemed to possess a "sixth sense" for positioning, particularly in the penalty area; whenever he had the ball, there was danger for the opposing defense. Gerd played a large part in making West Germany the outstanding national team in the world in the early and mid-1970's.

Bryan Aubrey

Additional Sources

Hunt, Chris. *The Complete Book of Soccer.* Buffalo, N.Y.: Firefly Books, 2006.

Radnedge, Keir, and Gary Lineker. *The Ultimate Encyclopedia of Soccer: The Definitive Illustrated Guide to World Soccer.* London: Carlton Books, 2004.

Michael Owen

Born: December 14, 1979
Chester, England
Also known as: Michael James Owen (full name)

Early Life
Michael James Owen was born in Chester, England, on December 14, 1979. He grew up a few miles across the border in Hawarden, Wales, the fourth of five children in a supportive and loving family. His father, Terry, had been a professional soccer player and traveled to watch the young Michael in every game that he played. That Michael would follow in his father's footsteps became evident quickly. By the age of ten, he had broken a local schoolboy goal-scoring record previously held by another of Chester's famous sporting sons, the legendary former Liverpool striker Ian Rush.

The Road to Excellence
These precocious feats set the tone for Michael's career in junior soccer. At the age of eleven, he was already training informally with one of the country's biggest clubs, Liverpool. At fourteen he was selected to spend two years at Lilleshall, an elite youth soccer center run by the English Football Association (FA). During this period, Michael played with distinction for England at both under-fifteen (U-15) and U-16 levels. In December, 1996, after leaving Lilleshall, he signed a professional contract with Liverpool.

In May, 1997, Michael made his first-team debut, coming on as a substitute and, characteristically, scoring a goal in a 2-1 defeat at Wimbledon. During the following season, with star striker Robbie Fowler frequently injured, Michael played regularly on the talented but underachieving Liverpool team. Michael finished his first full campaign with 18 league goals. In February, 1998, he became the youngest player to be selected for the senior England team and, in May, the youngest player ever to score for England. Both records were broken by Wayne Rooney.

The Emerging Champion
Michael was selected by Coach Glenn Hoddle for the England squad that traveled to France for the 1998 World Cup. He did not begin the tournament in the lineup but made an immediate impact when he entered as a substitute in the second group game, against Romania, scoring the equalizing goal. Although England lost the game, 2-1, Michael's place on the team was secured. After winning its final group match, England faced Argentina in the second round. The game, which England eventually lost on penalty kicks after a 2-2 tie, was famous for David Beckham's red card and

Michael Owen of Newcastle United. (John Walton/PA Photos/Landov)

Michael's brilliant goal, in which he slalomed past several Argentine defenders at lightning pace before driving the ball into the top right-hand corner of the net to put England ahead 2-1. The goal was one of the tournament's iconic moments and announced Michael's arrival on the international stage at the age of just eighteen.

The following season, 1998-1999, Michael scored 23 goals for Liverpool in league and cup games but seriously damaged his hamstring against Leeds in April, 1999—the first sign of the injury problems that increasingly disrupted his career. After a disappointing experience with England at the 2000 European Championships, in 2000-2001, he enjoyed the best season of his career. Under Coach Gérard Houllier, Liverpool won a trifecta of cup competitions, including the FA Cup, which Michael won almost singlehandedly for his team, scoring two late goals to hand Arsenal a 2-1 defeat in the final. In September, 2001, in Munich, Michael's fine year continued when he scored a "hat trick," three goals, for England in a 5-1 victory against Germany during a World Cup qualifying game. In December, he was named European footballer of the year, becoming just the fourth Englishman—and the first Liverpool player—to win this prestigious award.

Honors and Awards

1998	Professional Footballers' Association young player of the year
	BBC sports personality of the year
	Carling Premiership player of the year
1998-99	Premier League most goals (shared)
1998, 2002, 2006	British World Cup team
2001	*World Soccer* player of the year
	European player of the year (Ballon d'Or)

Continuing the Story

After the high points of 2001, Michael's career entered a less certain phase. He continued to perform well for England, scoring important goals in the 2002 World Cup in Japan and Korea—where England lost to Brazil in the quarterfinals—and the 2004 European Championships in Portugal—where England was eliminated by the hosts, also in the quarterfinals. With 40 goals in eighty-eight games, he ranked as the fourth-highest goal scorer in national team history, closing in steadily on Bobby Charlton's all-time record of 49.

Michael was still scoring goals regularly for Liverpool. However, the club was unable to challenge Manchester United and Arsenal for the league title. In May, 2004, Houllier was fired and replaced by the Spaniard Rafael Benítez. After 158 goals in 267 games, Michael decided to leave his boyhood club, joining Real Madrid that August. His subsequent struggle to secure a regular place in the first team at Real Madrid had less to do with his form than with the *Galáctico* ("star") system, which ensured that the most highly marketable players, such as David Beckham, Zinedine Zidane, and Raúl, were never dropped. Michael scored an impressive 16 goals in forty-one appearances for Real Madrid, many of which were as a second-half substitute. As the 2006 World Cup approached, however, he decided to leave Real Madrid, signing with Newcastle United in August, 2005.

Michael's career at Newcastle was severely hampered by injury. In December, 2005, he broke a bone in his foot and returned to action only shortly before the end of the season. At the 2006 World Cup in Germany, he looked sluggish in England's opening two games and suffered anterior cruciate ligament damage in his team's final group game with Sweden. In April, 2007, after his return to fitness, further injury problems ensured that Michael's on-field contributions to a struggling team were sporadic.

Professional Statistics

Season	Team	Games Played	Goals
1996-97	Liverpool	2	1
1997-98	Liverpool	36	18
1998-99	Liverpool	30	18
1999-00	Liverpool	27	11
2000-01	Liverpool	28	16
2001-02	Liverpool	29	19
2002-03	Liverpool	35	19
2003-04	Liverpool	29	16
2004-05	Real Madrid	36	13
2005-06	Newcastle United	11	7
2006-07	Newcastle United	3	0
2007-08	Newcastle United	29	11
Totals		295	149

Summary

Michael Owen is one of the finest goal scorers in English soccer history. In the latter years of his career, injuries blunted his sharpness, taking away the explosive pace that defined the joyous early stages of his career. However, he improved other aspects of his play by way of compensation, becoming a more complete—if perhaps less exciting—center forward. Throughout the ups and downs, Michael scored goals consistently, proving on innumerable occasions to be a big-match player. In 2008, at twenty-eight years old, he was young enough to add further successes to what had already been an outstanding career.

Alan McDougall

Additional Sources

Derbyshire, Oliver. *Michael Owen: The Biography*. London: John Blake, 2007.

Owen, Michael, and Paul Hayward. *Off the Record: My Autobiography*. London: Collins Willow, 2004.

Williams, John. *Into the Red: Liverpool FC and the Transformation of English Football*. Edinburgh: Mainstream, 2002.

Cindy Parlow

Born: May 8, 1978
Memphis, Tennessee
Also known as: Cynthia Marie Parlow (full name); CP

Early Life
Cynthia "Cindy" Marie Parlow, born on May 8, 1978, in Memphis, Tennessee, was an example of a true scholar-athlete. As a youngster, she played soccer against her three brothers and soon began to excel at the sport. With a fiery competitive nature, Cindy sought to be the best player in her school. She accomplished all of her goals in sports and academics, becoming the 1994 Tennessee High School player of the year and a two-time all-American at Germantown High School. She was named the most valuable player in state and regional tournaments and received all-region and all-state selections.

Cindy had the ability to play offense and defense; she scored 105 goals and was an assist leader with 83. Cindy was also a good basketball player: She won the most valuable player award her freshman season but chose to focus on soccer for the remainder of her high school career. She competed not only for her high school team but also for the area soccer program. She joined the Memphis Football Club and helped the team win state championships from 1990 to 1995. The latter year, she was second in the nation at the under-seventeen (U-17) level. In 1992 and 1995, her teams won the regional championships. In addition, she was an excellent student: She held a 4.0 grade point average and ranked in the top 5 percent in her class. Her intelligence and drive motivated her to complete high school in three years.

Cindy decided to attend the University of North Carolina at Chapel Hill (UNC), where the women's soccer program was well respected. She majored in nutrition and continued her excellence in the classroom and on the field.

The Road to Excellence
Life as a student-athlete was exciting for Cindy. With her unique talent and determination, she made an immediate impact on the program. She hustled at all times and became a four-time all-American. In her first year, she was named the Atlantic Coast Conference (ACC) rookie of the year and the 1995 *Soccer America* freshman of the year. The UNC teams continued to excel and Cindy was a part of National Collegiate Athletic Association women's soccer championship teams in 1996, 1997, and 1998. In the latter year, she led her team to an undefeated regular season and scored 21 goals and made 11 assists. Her positive response to

Cindy Parlow celebrating Team USA's victory over Brazil in the 1999 Women's World Cup. (Jed Jacobsohn/Getty Images)

UNC coaching and the display of leadership twice earned her the Hermann Trophy as the outstanding female collegiate soccer player, in 1997 and 1998, and the ACC female athlete of the year in 1999. At the end of her UNC career, she had 68 goals and 53 assists. On teams that had numerous stars, Cindy stood out among the best. She was a leader on a team that was recognized as a collection of the greatest soccer players in the country.

Honors, Awards, and Milestones

1996	*Soccer News* college athlete of the year
1996, 2004	Gold medal, Olympic Games
1997-98	Hermann Trophy
1999	Atlantic Coast Conference female athlete of the year
	World Cup champion
2000	Silver medal, Olympic Games

The Emerging Champion

In March, 1995, Cindy was invited to play forward for the U.S. women's national team and scored her first goal in January of 1996, against the team's rival, Russia. Cindy was the youngest player on the team but showed no fear of competition. Her dexterity with the ball and leadership skills were apparent. Since she was still enrolled at UNC, she played in only thirteen games for the U.S. team. However, she did win the gold medal with the team that participated in the Goodwill Games. She also played for the U.S. U-21 team at the Nordic Cup. Cindy enjoyed the international competition and became a fixture on the U.S. team. She scored two goals and started all six games for the United States during the 1999 World Cup, which the team won. She was also a member of the 1996, 2000, and 2004 Olympic teams, as well as the 2003 Women's World Cup team.

Continuing the Story

Suffering from post-concussion syndrome and having no more to prove as a professional soccer player, Cindy retired from international competition on July 30, 2006. Her mark on the game had been established, and many of her records endured. She made 158 appearances on the U.S. women's national team and scored 75 goals, which, at the time of her retirement, ranked in the top ten all time. A creative scorer, in 2000, Cindy made four "hat tricks"—scoring three goals in a game—one short of the U.S. record for a calendar year. Furthermore, she became one of only two U.S. players to ever score three "hat tricks" in two consecutive games.

Residing in Chapel Hill with her husband, Cindy remained active with soccer-related programs. She cofounded the Women's United Soccer Association and played for the Atlanta Beat, helping her team reach the playoffs in each of the league's three seasons of operation, 2001 to 2003.

Summary

Cindy Parlow made a tremendous impression on the world of international and intercollegiate women's soccer. She was the youngest player ever to win both an Olympic gold medal and a Women's World Cup title. Young girls who play soccer sought to emulate Cindy's style and passion on the field. Her numerous accomplishments were acknowledged in her hometown of Memphis: A street was renamed Cindy Parlow Drive to recognize her success.

Deborah Stroman

Additional Sources

Fair, Lorrie, and Mark Gola. *Fair Game: A Complete Book of Soccer for Women.* New York: McGraw-Hill, 2003.

Wahl, Grant. "Dateline: Greensboro, N.C." *Sports Illustrated* 87, no. 24 (December 15, 1997): 34.

Pelé

Born: October 23, 1940
Três Corações, Minas Gerais, Brazil
Also known as: Edson Arantes do Nascimento (full name)

Early Life

Edson Arantes do Nascimento, "Pelé," was born on October 23, 1940, in the small town of Três Corações in the state of Minas Gerais in Brazil. Life in Três Corações was not easy for young Edson. The house in which he grew up was part of a row of dwellings that was built with used bricks and held together with cracked plaster and peeling paint.

Edson's father, João Ramos do Nascimento, "Dondinho," was an excellent professional soccer player. Dondinho had the misfortune of playing for a small club in a small town, but his love for the game was not diminished by his meager earnings or by a career-ending knee injury. With the approval of Dondinho, young Edson spent practically all his free time playing soccer, sometimes substituting grapefruits or balls of socks for soccer balls.

The Road to Excellence

When Edson was about eight years old, he was given the nickname "Pelé"; he does not know what the name means or who gave it to him. Edson at first resented the name and was in numerous fights to try to stop young boys from calling him Pelé. The name stuck, however, and for the rest of his career Edson Arantes do Nascimento was known to the world as Pelé.

Pelé's first real team was the juvenile team of the Bauru Athletic Club (BAC). Young Pelé, thirteen at the time, considered playing for BAC one of the greatest thrills of his life. He saw it as a stepping-stone to a future as a professional soccer player. While Pelé had a great deal of raw talent, the legendary Brazilian superstar Waldemar de Brito, Pelé's first real coach, disciplined Pelé and stressed

Brazil's legendary forward Pelé executing a "bicycle kick" in 1960. (AP/Wide World Photos)

Career Highlights

Led Brazil to three World Cup championships
12 World Cup goals
108 international appearances for Brazil
90 international goals

Honors, Awards, and Milestones

1958-62, 1964-65, 1967-69, 1973		Brazilian League champion
	1962-63	Copa Libertadores champion
		Intercontinental Cup champion
	1973	South American player of the year
	1975	Inducted into Black Athletes Hall of Fame
	1976	NASL most valuable player
	1977-78	NASL champion
	1998	Inducted into International Football Hall of Champions
	1999	International Olympic Committee Athlete of the Century
		UNICEF Football Player of the Century
	2000	FIFA Footballer of the Century
		Laureus World Sports Awards lifetime achievement award
	2005	BBC Sports Personality of the Year lifetime achievement award

to him the need to perfect his fundamental skills. De Brito taught Pelé the famous "bicycle kick" that Pelé later used to score countless goals.

The Emerging Champion

In 1958, at the age of seventeen, Pelé reached soccer stardom; he was chosen to play on the Brazilian national soccer team in the World Cup competition in Sweden, where the world soccer community first saw the emergence of the man who would become the king of soccer. Pelé scored six goals in the tournament, including two in Brazil's 5-2 victory over Sweden in the final game. Thanks largely to the exploits of Pelé, Brazil was the world soccer champion.

After 1958, Pelé's life was changed forever. He played for Santos of São Paulo, Brazil's most respected club team. During this period Pelé met Rosmeri, who later became his wife.

By the 1962 World Cup tournament, Pelé was fast becoming a superstar. Brazil won the World Cup again in 1962; however, Pelé missed most of the action because of a badly bruised groin muscle.

Pelé continued playing for Santos, scoring goal after goal with artistic beauty. By the 1966 World Cup in England, Pelé seemed up to the challenge of making Brazil the first team to win the World Cup three times. Pelé was fouled almost every time he touched the ball, and injuries caused him to miss almost the entire tournament. Brazil was eliminated before reaching the quarterfinals.

In 1969, while playing for Santos, Pelé scored his 1,000th goal in his 909th game. Many soccer fans thought the 1,000-goal plateau could never be reached, and Pelé's feat brought him adulation from fans all over the world. His magic name created sellouts wherever he played in international competition.

With the 1,000-goal milestone behind him, Pelé concentrated on a more important pursuit—a 1970 World Cup victory in Mexico. Before the tournament started, Pelé had his doubts about playing. He had suffered serious injuries in both the 1962 and 1966 World Cups, and his thirty-year-old body had seen enough rough action. However, Pelé looked at the big picture—he would play one last tournament for Brazil and try to win an unprecedented third World Cup.

Pelé was in top form in Mexico in 1970. He led Brazil to a 4-1 final-game victory over Italy, and Brazil won its third World Cup title. Pelé's efforts enabled Brazil to claim the title of the first three-time world champion.

Continuing the Story

Pelé played for Santos for four more years, retiring on October 2, 1974, in Rio de Janeiro. In a tender moment, Pelé honored the fans who had supported him for so long by waving good-bye. It seemed that Pelé would no longer be around.

However, Pelé was not through yet. In June, 1975, at New York's famous 21 Club, he signed a three-year contract with the New York Cosmos of the North American Soccer League (NASL). Both the Cosmos and Pelé hoped to cultivate U.S. interest in the world's most popular sport. With the help of Pelé, soccer in the United States began to flourish. In 1978, Pelé led the Cosmos to an NASL championship and, for a brief while, put soccer in the American sports limelight. Following his retirement from soccer, Pelé served as Brazil's minister for sport and an international ambassador for soccer. Thirty years after his retirement, he remained one of the most revered and recognizable figures in international soccer.

Summary

Pelé is widely recognized as soccer's greatest player ever. His tremendous individual skills made him the world's most popular player at the same time as he led his country's team to unprecedented international success. Later he helped to bring credibility to American soccer, another in a long line of achievements by soccer's brightest star.

Leonard K. Lucenko

Additional Sources

Clifford, Simon. *Play the Brazilian Way: The Secret Skills of the World's Greatest Footballers.* London: Boxtree, 1999.

Harris, Harry. *Pelé: His Life and Times.* New York: Parkwest, 2002.

Pelé, Orlando Duarte, Alex Bellos, and Daniel Hahn. *Pelé: The Autobiography.* London: Simon & Schuster, 2006.

Pelé, and Robert L. Fish. *Pelé, My Life and the Beautiful Game.* New York: Skyhorse, 2007.

Viner, Brian. *Ali, Pelé, Lillee, and Me: A Personal Odyssey Through the Sporting Seventies.* London: Pocket, 2007.

Michel Platini

Born: June 21, 1955
   Joeuf, France
Also known as: Michel François Platini (full name)

Early Life
Michel François Platini was born on June 21, 1955, in Joeuf, France. His family was of Italian ancestry. The Platinis were a soccer family, and Michel seemed born to play the game. His father, Aldo Platini, was coach of the Nancy soccer club, which played not far from the family home in northeastern France. Michel's father encouraged Michel's early love of soccer, and Michel had undeniable skills from the beginning. His athletic ability helped him to deal with the teasing of his school friends, who found the quiet and self-conscious boy an easy target for their boisterous humor.

The Road to Excellence
After Michel graduated from high school, his only desire was to become a professional soccer player. Not surprisingly, given his father's position, Nancy became interested in him. Michel signed as a professional player for Nancy in 1973. At the age of eighteen, he achieved his ambition of playing in the premier soccer league in France.

Early in his career, Michel could not decide whether he preferred to play as a midfielder or as a striker. As a striker he could easily win glory by scoring goals, but playing in midfield gave him the opportunity to think creatively about the pattern of play and create goal-scoring chances for his teammates.

During the 1970's, Michel became a familiar figure in the soccer stadiums of France. He could always be spotted easily because of his unusual habit of wearing his shirt outside his shorts. More important, Michel could often be seen scoring goals—in the seven years he played for Nancy, he scored 98 times. He also began to build a reputation as an expert taker of free kicks, able to swerve and dip his shots to deceive opposing defenses. It took him many months of constant practice, staying behind after the other players had gone, to perfect this art.

Michel Platini leaving his feet to reach the soccer ball in 1986. (George Gobet/AFP/Getty Images)

The Emerging Champion
In 1976, Michel first played for France's national team, against Czechoslovakia, scoring a goal in a 2-2 draw. He was also a member of the French Olympic team that played in Montreal that year.

In 1978, he helped Nancy win the French Cup, scoring the winning goal against Nice in the final match. Despite his youth, Michel was already earning praise as one of the best players in Europe.

Career Highlights

72 international appearances for France
41 international goals

Honors, Awards, and Milestones

1976	French Olympic team member
1976-77	French Football player of the year
1978	French League Cup champion
1981	French League champion
1983	Italian League Cup champion
1983-85	Italian League high scorer
	European player of the year (Ballon d'Or)
1984	European Super Cup champion
	European Cup Winners' Cup champion
	European Championship champion
1984, 1986	Italian League champion
1985	European Cup champion
	Intercontinental Cup (Toyota Cup) champion
1988	Officer of Legion of Honor
1998	Inducted into International Football Hall of Champions
2007	Elected president of Union of European Football Associations (UEFA)

Later that year, he played for France in the World Cup group finals in Argentina. Michel left Nancy and joined St. Étienne in 1979. He helped his new club to victory in the French championship in 1981, and he was twice on the losing side in the French Cup final.

France had rarely achieved much soccer success on the international level, but the emergence of Michel as a masterful player coincided with one of the most successful periods the French team had ever enjoyed. In 1982, captained by Michel, France reached the semifinals of the World Cup in Spain before losing to West Germany in an exciting game. Michel scored a goal in that match and was one of the stars of the tournament. Two years later he captained France as it won the European Football Championship. The performance was one of Michel's finest. He scored 9 goals in only five games, including the winning goal—scored from a free kick—against Spain in the final match.

In the meantime, in 1982, Michel had been transferred from St. Étienne to the Italian club Juventus. Settling down immediately, he became the leading goal scorer in the Italian League the following year. He was soon idolized by the Italian fans.

What made Michel a great player was the precision of his game. His tactical skills were outstanding. When he received the ball in midfield, he assessed the situation rapidly, carried the move forward, and then released the ball with absolute accuracy to the player who was in the best position to continue. He was equally skilled in creating an opportunity for himself. He did all this with an economy of energy, as if he knew instinctively the best and quickest route to the opponent's goal.

Continuing the Story

Michel's success with Juventus was virtually unbroken. He helped the team win the Italian League championship in 1984 and 1986. Juventus reached the final of the European Cup in 1983 and won the trophy in 1985, with Michel scoring the winning goal against Liverpool from a penalty kick. Juventus went on to win the Intercontinental Cup in December, 1985, in Tokyo, Japan. That year, Michel was named European player of the year for the third successive time.

During his career Michel had to overcome many injuries, including a twice-broken ankle, a fractured vertebra, a kneecap injury, two concussions, a pelvic injury, and a joint inflammation that took a year to heal. This last injury hampered his performance in the World Cup finals in Mexico in 1986. It did not stop him, however, from scoring a fine goal that helped to defeat Brazil in the quarterfinals before France was eliminated in the semifinals by West Germany.

After the 1986 World Cup finals, Michel announced his retirement. Two years later, he became coach of the French national team and faced the task of creating a team as successful as the ones on which he had played. Although France failed to qualify for the World Cup finals in 1990, Michel built an attractive, attacking team that won seven of its eight games during the 1989-1990 season. Michel left the French national team following their 1992 European Championship victory but was called upon to help organize the 1998 World Cup tournament with France as the host country. Michel worked with great success as copresident of the French organizing committee. The victory by the French team in the 1998 World Cup was a personal triumph for Michel. He continued to contribute his talent to world soccer as an administrator and expert. He served as vice president of the French Football Federation. In 2007, he was elected president of the Union of European Football Associations.

Summary

Michel Platini was one of the greatest soccer players of the 1980's. Pelé, probably the greatest player of all time, said Michel was the best, most complete player in the world. Diego Maradona, perhaps Pelé's only equal in soccer ability, described Michel as a phenomenon. Michel's consistent and majestic skills in midfield and as a striker brought unprecedented success to his club and his country. His success as a soccer executive added to his legacy.

Bryan Aubrey, updated by Howard Bromberg

Additional Sources

Goldblatt, David. *The Ball Is Round: A Global History of Soccer.* New York: Riverhead Books, 2006.

Hunt, Chris. *The Complete Book of Soccer.* Buffalo, N.Y.: Firefly Books, 2006.

"Michel Platini." *Soccer Digest* 21, no. 5 (1999).

Radnedge, Keir, and Gary Lineker. *The Ultimate Encyclopedia of Soccer: The Definitive Illustrated Guide to World Soccer.* London: Carlton Books, 2004.

Ferenc Puskás

Born: April 2, 1927
Kispest, Hungary
Died: November 17, 2006
Budapest, Hungary
Also known as: Ferenc Puskás Biró (full name); Ferenc Purczeld Biró (birth name)

Early Life

Ferenc Puskás was born on April 2, 1927, in Kispest, Hungary. Soccer ran in his family: Ferenc's father played for Kispest's professional team. Ferenc, like most youngsters in soccer-mad Hungary, learned to control a soccer ball almost from the time he could walk. His father encouraged him, even though he was poor and could afford to buy only one pair of soccer boots for his two sons. Ferenc shared the boots with his elder brother.

Ferenc's next-door neighbor was a boy named Jozsef Bozsik whose passion for soccer was as great as Ferenc's. Boznik and Ferenc became best friends, developing their soccer skills together in the streets of Kispest, kicking at anything that was kickable. They lived near Kispest's soccer ground and sometimes had the use of a field adjoining the first team's pitch. At the age of ten, Ferenc and Jozsef played together for Kispest's juvenile team.

The Road to Excellence

Soccer in Hungary was not disrupted by World War II. In 1943, at the age of sixteen, Ferenc made his first appearance as inside forward on Kispest's senior team. Bozsik soon joined him as a wing-half, and the two became regular members of the team.

Ferenc's father was still a major influence on him, but although he was a soccer coach, he did not try to teach Ferenc or fill his mind with technical advice. He thought his son should be free to develop his own style, and Ferenc was grateful for this wise advice. Ferenc needed little coaching, and he complemented his natural skill with hard work. After training, he remained behind for hours, kicking balls against a brick wall and learning to control the ball from all angles. His astonishing ball control became a hallmark of his play. Ferenc also developed shooting power in his left foot that made him famous. Many times, he scored goals from a distance of twenty yards or more.

The Emerging Champion

In 1945, at the age of eighteen, Ferenc appeared in his first international game. Playing at inside-left, he scored Hungary's first goal in a 5-2 win over Austria. After World War II, soccer in Hungary was reorganized. In 1949, Kispest became the official army soccer club and was renamed Honved. The club supplied several players to the Hungarian national team, which quickly became one of the greatest soccer teams in the world. Along with his childhood friend Bozsik, Ferenc was one of the stars of the "Magnificent Magyars," as they became known. He had risen through the ranks of the Hungarian army and became known as the "galloping major."

One of Ferenc's greatest moments came in 1953, when Hungary became the first team from outside the British Isles to defeat England on English soil. Ferenc, the captain of the Hungarian team, scored twice in Hungary's sensational 6-3 victory. The following year, in Budapest, he scored two goals in the rematch with England, which Hungary won 7-1.

In 1954, Hungary had been unbeaten for four years and was the favorite to win the World Cup. Ferenc, however, was injured and missed the quarter- and semifinals. Although he played in the final

Career Highlights

84 international appearances for Hungary
4 international appearances for Spain
85 international goals for Hungary

Honors, Awards, and Milestones

1950	Central European Cup champion
1950, 1952, 1954-55	Hungarian League champion
1958	Spanish League champion
1958-60	European Cup champion
1960	Intercontinental Cup champion
1998	Inducted into International Football Hall of Champions

against West Germany, he was probably not fully fit. However, he still managed to score Hungary's first goal with his legendary left foot, and he nearly saved the game for Hungary in the last minute, when he scored a goal that was negated by an offsides penalty. Germany won 3-2; Hungary suffered its first defeat in thirty-two matches. Hungary did not lose again for two years.

In 1956, Ferenc was on tour with Honved when the Hungarian Revolution broke out. He decided not to return to his homeland. In his eleven-year international career, he had played eighty-four games for Hungary and scored 85 goals—a remarkable record.

Continuing the Story

After the revolution, Ferenc decided to live in Vienna, Austria. His soccer career appeared to be over. However, he was about to embark on another golden period. In 1957, he joined the Spanish club Real Madrid, which was the finest professional team in the world at the time. Many said that Ferenc, at thirty, was past his best, but he proved them wrong. Making up in guile what he might have lost in speed, he finished his first season as the leading goal scorer in the Spanish Soccer League. Over the next decade, he formed a formidable partnership with Alfredo di Stefano, another of the great forwards of the era.

In 1960, Ferenc scored four goals in a twenty-seven-minute period as Real Madrid raced to a 7-3 victory over Eintracht Frankfurt in the European Cup Final. In 1962, Ferenc became the first man to score hat tricks in two European Cup Finals, but his three goals were not enough to save Real Madrid from a 5-3 defeat by Benfica.

Ferenc became a dual Hungarian-Spanish citizen and played for Spain in the 1962 World Cup in Chile. In 1967, at the age of forty, he was still donning the famous all-white Real Madrid uniform.

After he retired from playing, Ferenc coached soccer all over the globe, in Egypt, Paraguay, Saudi Arabia, Greece—where he helped the Panathinaikos Club to the European Cup Final in 1971—and Australia. In 1993, at the age of sixty-six, he was granted a pardon by the Hungarian government and became a coach for the Hungarian Football Federation. He remained active in the soccer community until 2000, when he was diagnosed with Alzheimer's disease. He died in 2006.

Summary

Ferenc Puskás ranks among soccer's immortals. Those who were privileged to watch him play, or who played against him, never forgot the experience. "Nobody had a left foot like him," said Jackie Sewell, who played in the famous game between England and Hungary in 1953. Ferenc's devastating goal-scoring skill and his ability to do almost magical things with the ball were key factors in enabling Ferenc's Hungarian national and Real Madrid teams to become two of the greatest in soccer history.

Bryan Aubrey

Additional Sources

Cantor, Andrés, and Daniel Arcucci. *Goooal! A Celebration of Soccer.* New York: Simon & Schuster, 1996.

Hunt, Chris. *The Complete Book of Soccer.* Buffalo, N.Y.: Firefly Books, 2006.

Puskás, Ferenc. *Ferenc Puskás: Captain of Hungary.* Stroud, Gloucestershire, England: Stadia, 2007.

Puskás, Ferenc, Klara Jamrich, and Rogan P. Taylor. *Puskás on Puskás: The Life and Times of a Footballing Legend.* London: Robson, 1998.

Tab Ramos

Born: September 21, 1966
  Montevideo, Uruguay
Also known as: Tabaré Ricardo Ramos Ricciardi (full name)

Early Life
Born the son of professional Uruguayan soccer player Julien Ramos, Tab Ramos left Uruguay with his family when he was eleven years old. He moved to Kearney, New Jersey, where he continued to develop his soccer talent. He did not speak English but made friends because of his abilities with the soccer ball. However, his father prioritized school over soccer. He was once kept from playing soccer for receiving a poor midterm grade. The young Tab learned his lesson and never let his grades slip again. In high school, he played for St. Benedict's Preparatory School. He also played on a club team with future U.S. teammates John Harkes and Tony Meola. He was a soccer star for his high school team and scored 161 goals during his time at St. Benedict's, a state record. During his senior year as a high school student, he was named the 1983 *Parade* magazine player of the year.

The Road to Excellence
Tab chose to attend North Carolina State University instead of playing for the New York Cosmos, a team in the North American Soccer League. This turned out to be a good decision as the league folded the next year. While at North Carolina State, Tab was an all-Atlantic Coast Conference (ACC) athlete each of his four years and an all-American athlete for three years. He tied for the title of leading scorer in the ACC during his fourth year of college. During his time at North Carolina State, Tab met his wife Amy, who also played soccer at the university.

While playing for North Carolina State, Tab gained recognition nationally. In the summer of 1988, he left school during his third year to play for the U.S. Olympic team, which won a bronze medal. He left school again to sign with the U.S. men's national team. Tab did not receive his undergraduate degree until 2000.

In 1989, Tab earned his first interna-

Uruguayan American Tab Ramos. (Shaun Botterill/Getty Images)

MLS Statistics

Season	GP	Min.	G	Ast.	Pts.
1996	25	2,158	3	10	16
1997	13	1,006	2	4	8
1998	17	1,455	1	5	7
1999	5	347	0	3	3
2000	20	1,660	2	6	10
2001	18	1,459	0	5	5
2002	14	926	0	3	3
Totals	112	9,011	8	36	52

Notes: GP = games played; GS = games started; Min. = minutes played; G = goals; Ast. = assists; Pts. = points

U.S. National Team Statistics

Season	GP	GS	Min.	G	Ast.	Pts.
1988	2	2	180	0	0	0
1989	9	9	781	2	3	7
1990	17	17	1,530	0	3	3
1992	6	6	525	1	1	3
1993	9	9	802	0	3	3
1994	7	6	514	0	1	1
1995	8	2	350	1	2	4
1996	12	12	1,006	1	1	3
1997	3	3	270	1	0	2
1998	5	3	209	1	0	2
2000	3	1	139	1	0	2
Totals	81	70	6,306	8	14	30

Notes: GP = games played; GS = games started; Min. = minutes played; G = goals; Ast.= assists; Pts.= points

tional "cap" playing for the U.S. national team against the Guatemalan national team. His skill with the ball was remarkable, and he was an offensive threat as a midfielder. He scored his first international goal against Costa Rica two weeks later.

The Emerging Champion

Despite his size, 5 feet 6 inches and 140 pounds, Tab had an amazing first step and speed that made him difficult to mark. His skill and comfort with the ball were praised by many soccer experts, including Bruce Arena, the U.S. team's coach from 1998 to 2006. Tab played in three World Cup Tournaments for the United States as a midfielder. He started playing for the U.S. national team in 1989 and, over the next six years, was loaned to Mexican and Spanish professional teams to help develop U.S. players internationally. In Spain, Tab played for Unió Esportiva Figueres and, later, Real Betis Balompié, where he continued to excel as a player.

In 1990, prior to playing in Europe, Tab played in his first World Cup. While the U.S. team did not advance into the round of sixteen, Tab stood out as an adroit and integral player for the team. During the 1994 World Cup, hosted in the United States, the U.S. team made it into the second round, where they were beaten by World Cup winner, Brazil. Tab started in every game for the United States in the 1994 World Cup until he fractured his skull during the game against Brazil. Tab played an even larger role in the 1998 World Cup, scoring versus Costa Rica to qualify the U.S. team for the tournament. While the U.S. team did not advance as far in 1998 as it had in 1994, Tab was a key reason the U.S. team returned to the tournament for a third consecutive appearance. Tab completed his national team World Cup play with 87 caps and 8 goals.

Continuing the Story

In 1995, Tab Ramos was the first player to sign with the New Jersey MetroStars in the newly formed Major League Soccer (MLS) league. He played with the MetroStars for seven years and retired in 2002. During that time, he battled with injuries, thus limiting his influence in MLS. He had 36 assists and 8 goals during his career with the MetroStars. He was an MLS all-star in 1996, 1998, and 1999 and scored the first goal in an MLS all-star game.

In 2000, Tab completed his requirements for a degree in literature and foreign language from North Carolina State. He lived, with his wife and two children, and worked in New Jersey. He remained an active member in the world of soccer. Tab helped young people develop their soccer skills as president and founder of the Tab Ramos Soccer Programs, the New Jersey Soccer Academy, and the Tab Ramos GOAL! Foundation, and as a partner in the Tab Ramos Sports Programs. He was

Honors and Awards

1983	*Parade* national high school player of the year
1990	United States Soccer Federation athlete of the year
1990, 1994, 1998	U.S. World Cup team
1994	CONCACAF player of the year
1996, 1998-99	MLS all-star
2005	Inducted into National Soccer Hall of Fame

also on the board of directors for the New Jersey Sports Hall of Fame. Since St. Benedict's Preparatory School was so influential in his career development, he maintained ties with his high school. In fact, he announced his retirement from MLS in the conference room of this high school that developed a number of influential American soccer players. In 2005, Tab Ramos was elected into the National Soccer Hall of Fame in Oneota, New York.

Summary
Tab Ramos was the first athlete to sign with MLS. He was also among three of the first U.S. players to play in three World Cups. He continued to influence soccer in the United States through his soccer training center.

Russell Medbery

Additional Sources
Caligiuri, Paul, and Dan Herbst. *High-Performance Soccer.* Champaign, Ill.: Human Kinetics, 1997.

Reyna, Claudio, and Mike Woitalla. *More than Goals: The Journey from Backyard Games to World Cup Competition.* Champaign, Ill.: Human Kinetics, 2004.

Wahl, Grant. "U.S. Tribute to Tab Is Overdue." *Sports Illustrated* 94, no. 19 (May 7, 2001): 89.

Alf Ramsey

Born: January 22, 1920
 Dagenham, Essex, England
Died: April 28, 1999
 Ipswich, Suffolk, England
Also known as: Alfred Ernest Ramsey (full name); Sir Alfred Ernest Ramsey; the General

Early Life

Alfred Ernest Ramsey was born on January 22, 1920, in Dagenham, England. He spent his formative years in this East London suburb, an area that has produced many great soccer players over the years. Alf was the son of a hay and straw merchant. His origins were modest and humble, if not impoverished. Alf was brought up in a conventional household that stressed the importance of hard work and integrity. Much of Alf's early life was rather dull, as his family had little money to spare on toys and entertainment. The only thing that really caught Alf's imagination was soccer.

The Road to Excellence

Alf spent hour after hour practicing his soccer skills. This dedication paid dividends, as Alf became a noted schoolboy soccer player. Portsmouth was the first league club to show an interest in him. After Alf signed as an amateur player with Portsmouth, however, World War II intervened, and Alf's career ground to a temporary halt.

With the resumption of a full English Football League program in 1946, Alf signed a professional contract with Southampton. Alf worked hard at his game while at Southampton, and he was rewarded for his efforts with selection to England's national team in 1948.

In May, 1949, Alf was transferred from Southampton to Tottenham Hotspur. Alf's career was strengthened at Tottenham, primarily because of the influence of Arthur Rowe, the Tottenham manager. Rowe was renowned for his tactical innovations, and he developed a push-and-run strategy that relied upon quick and accurate passing and constant running into support positions. Alf's precise passing skills and endless stamina were well suited to Tottenham's energetic style of play.

Playing at right back, Alf was a key figure in Tottenham's successes in the early 1950's. His outstanding play and calm authority made him an obvious choice for the Tottenham captaincy, and in this capacity, he lived up to his nickname of "The General."

During this period, Alf played in twenty-eight consecutive international matches for England. That brought him into contact with Walter Winterbottom, England's manager. Winterbottom was a great proponent of coaching in an era in which coaching was largely frowned upon. Alf learned and built upon his innovative ideas.

Alf Ramsey of Tottenham Hotspur kicking the ball with a flourish. (Hulton Archive/Getty Images)

The Emerging Champion

Alf had a successful playing career, but it was as a manager that he achieved greatness. In August, 1955, Ipswich Town gave Alf his first opportunity to manage a soccer club. Alf was immediately successful. In his seven seasons at Ipswich, Alf transformed a lowly club into the best team in England. A Third Division team in 1955, Ipswich Town won the Football League Championship in 1962. Alf worked the Ipswich miracle by gaining the respect and loyalty of his players. His managerial strength lay in an ability to make even modest players believe that they could compete and win against the best in the game.

England's professional Football Association (FA) took great notice of the developments at Ipswich. When Walter Winterbottom resigned as England's manager, the association turned to Alf, who took charge of the national team in October, 1962.

Despite mixed results in the early phase of his reign as England's new manager, Alf was quietly confident in his own ability and that of his players. During the summer of 1963, in an uncharacteristic display of emotion, Alf shocked the soccer world by stating that "England will win the World Cup in 1966."

In the next three years, Alf built a strong squad. He instilled a great sense of team spirit in his players, which was reflected in their play on the field. Alf's England teams sacrificed individual flair and brilliance in favor of a more balanced team effort.

The 1966 World Cup was held in England; therefore, the home country was one of the pretournament favorites. After some disappointing performances, however, many critics dismissed England's chances. Alf remained loyal to his players and was always confident that they would win the World Cup.

England began the tournament in a goal-less draw against Uruguay. Subsequent victories against Mexico and France ensured that England would progress to the quarterfinal stage of the competition. In the quarterfinals, England beat the hard-tackling Argentine team. A battling semifinal victory against Portugal took England to the World Cup Final.

Alf guided his team shrewdly throughout the tournament, and the performances steadily improved. In the final match, England faced West Germany to decide the champions of the world. In an open and adventurous game, England triumphed 4-2 in overtime. The prophecy Alf had made three years earlier had come true.

Continuing the Story

Following England's historic victory, Alf became a national hero. In recognition of his services to English soccer, he received a knighthood. Having guided his country to the World Cup, Alf was adamant that England should not rest on its laurels. Alf immediately set about building a team to defend the World Cup trophy in Mexico in 1970.

By 1970, Alf had molded an even stronger squad than the one which had been so successful in 1966. In Mexico, England played with the commitment and character that typified Alf's teams. However, the magic could not be repeated, and West Germany avenged its defeat of four years earlier by beating England 3-2 at the quarterfinal stage.

Between 1970 and 1974, England's performances grew steadily worse. A large part of the problem lay with Alf's continued loyalty to the aging stars who had served him so well in the past. After England's failure to qualify for the 1974 World Cup, there were increasing calls for Alf to resign. Finally, in April, 1974, Alf was dismissed by the Football Association. Alf was disillusioned by his firing. Following a brief stay at Birmingham City, he turned his back on soccer and immersed himself in developing his business interests. Alf died in 1999; in 2002, he was inducted into the English Football Hall of Fame.

Summary

Alf Ramsey holds a unique place in English soccer history. His calm authority, integrity, and loyalty played a crucial part in England's 1966 World Cup triumph. Certainly, Alf did not deserve the shabby

---

Career Highlights

32 international appearances for England

Honors, Awards, and Milestones

1951	English Football League champion
1966	World Cup champion (as manager)
	Knighted by Queen Elizabeth II
1986	English Professional Football Association Merit Award
2002	Inducted into English Football Hall of Fame

treatment he received from the soccer authorities, and his self-imposed exile robbed the soccer world of one of its most knowledgeable and respected leaders.

David L. Andrews

Additional Sources

Bowler, Dave. *Winning Isn't Everything . . .: A Biography of Sir Alf Ramsey.* London: Orion Books, 1999.

Galvin, Robert, and Mark Bushell. *Football's Greatest Heroes: The National Football Museum's Hall of Fame.* London: Robson, 2005.

McKinstry, Leo. *Sir Alf: A Major Reappraisal of the Life and Times of England's Greatest Football Manager.* London: HarperSport, 2007.

Marquis, Max. *Sir Alf Ramsey: Anatomy of a Football Manager.* London: Barker, 1970.

Ramsey, Alfred. *Talking Football.* London: Stanley Paul, 1952.

Ramsey, Alfred, and Kenneth Wheeler. *Soccer: The British Way.* London: Sportman's Book Club, 1965.

"Sir Alfred Ramsey." *The Economist* 351 (May 8, 1999): 1.

Rivaldo

Born: April 19, 1972
Paulista, near Recife, Pernambuco, Brazil
Also known as: Rivaldo Vitor Borba Ferreira Victor (full name)

Early Life

Rivaldo was born Rivaldo Vitor Borba Ferreira Victor on April 19, 1972, in Paulista, near the port city of Recife, capital of the state of Pernambuco, Brazil. The son of Romildo and Marlucia, he grew up in dire poverty, with two older brothers and two younger sisters, near the beaches of Brazil's Atlantic coast. Always hungry, he became bowlegged and lost many of his teeth as a youngster because of malnutrition. Later, he had to be fitted with dentures. During the day, Rivaldo was sent to meet incoming ocean liners, where he sold trinkets and souvenirs to tourists. In the evenings, he played soccer with his brothers and friends on the beach. He hoped that he or one of his brothers would become skilled enough to earn a living as a professional soccer player and help lift the family out of the slums.

The Road to Excellence

In 1988, at the age of sixteen, Rivaldo had become good enough to sign his first professional contract with youth club Paulista. The following year, his father died in an automobile accident.

A tall, slender youth positioned as an attacking midfielder, Rivaldo bounced among a number of Brazilian teams. He slowly moved up to stiffer competition as his reputation as a playmaker and scorer grew. In 1991, he left Paulista to play for Santa Cruz. In 1992-1993, he was with São Paulo, and the following year, he signed with SC Corinthians, one of the most popular teams in Brazil's top soccer division. That same year, Rivaldo first appeared on the Brazilian national team and scored the only goal in an exhibition match against Mexico.

In 1994, Rivaldo switched teams again, moving to SE Palmeiras, one of Brazil's best clubs. He helped Palmeiras win its second consecutive league championship and was awarded the silver ball, as the best player at his position, in two consecutive seasons. In his final year with the club, Rivaldo was chosen for the bronze-medal-winning Brazilian national team at the 1996 Olympics.

The Emerging Champion

In 1996, Rivaldo and his Palmeiras teammate Amaral signed with the Parma soccer team in Italy. However, a contract dispute led Rivaldo to depart Italy for Spain, where he signed with Deportivo la Coruña, a top professional club. During his single season with Deportivo, Rivaldo tallied 21 goals in forty-one games to finish among the league's top-

Rivaldo pointing skyward after scoring a goal for his Greek club team. (Yiorgos Karahalis/Reuters/Landov)

ten scorers. After the season, his contract was transferred to FC Barcelona for approximately $26 million.

Rivaldo stayed with Barcelona for five years, from 1997 to 2002. In his first season, he recorded 19 goals in thirty-four games, leading the club to a league championship and King's Cup. In 1998, with Rivaldo making sensational bicycle kicks, Barcelona again took the Cup. That same year, Rivaldo was a member of the Brazilian national team at the World Cup and scored 3 goals as the team took second place, losing to France in the finals.

In 1999, Rivaldo continued as a top scorer with Barcelona. Among other honors, he was selected as Spanish League player of the year, FIFA world player of the year, European player of the year, and *World Soccer* player of the year. He also joined the Brazilian team for the 1999 Copa América, becoming the tournament's top scorer and most valuable player, as Brazil took the title.

In 2002, while again playing a superior brand of football for Barcelona, Rivaldo starred for Brazil at the World Cup. He scored in five consecutive matches and set up teammate Ronaldo for goals in the victorious final against Germany. For his performance, Rivaldo was declared a World Cup all-star.

Continuing the Story

After the 2002 Spanish season, Rivaldo left the Barcelona club, with which he had scored 90 goals in 160 games—to sign with AC Milan in the Italy's top professional league. Because of injuries, he played few games, though the team finished as champions of the Union of European Football Associations (UEFA) League and took the Coppa Italia and the European Super Cup. After a single season, Rivaldo went back to Brazil to play briefly with Cruzeiro in Belo Horizonte. In 2004, he returned to Europe and, after a bidding war between British and Greek teams, signed with Olympiacos FC in the Greek Super League.

In three years with Olympiacos, from 2004 to 2007, Rivaldo was in his usual solid form. He led the team to three consecutive league championships, helped Olympiacos take consecutive Greek Cups in 2005 and 2006, and earned honors as best foreign player in 2006 and 2007.

In 2007, after scoring 43 goals in eighty-one league and cup games with Olympiacos, Rivaldo moved on to the Super League rival AEK Athens FC. After a single successful season, in late 2008, he signed a two-year contract for more than 10 million Euros to play with FC Bunyodkor in Uzbekistan.

Summary

One of the world's greatest soccer players in the 1990's and 2000's, Rivaldo overcame extreme poverty and malnutrition to become an international star. Playing for a series of teams in his native Brazil as well as professional clubs in Spain, Italy, Greece, and Uzbekistan, Rivaldo wowed fans with graceful ballhandling capabilities and sensational scoring

Professional Statistics

Season	Team	Games Played	Goals
1991	Santa Cruz	0	0
1992	Mogi Mrim	27	9
1993	Corinthians	19	11
1994	Palmeiras	29	13
1994	Corinthians	22	6
1995	Palmeiras	45	17
1996	Palmeiras	30	23
1996-97	Deportivo La Coruña	41	21
1997-98	FC Barcelona	34	19
1998-99	FC Barcelona	37	24
1999-00	FC Barcelona	31	12
2000-01	FC Barcelona	35	23
2001-02	FC Barcelona	20	8
2002-03	Milan	22	5
2003-04	Milan	0	0
2004	Cruzeiro	0	0
2004-05	Olympiacos	23	12
2005-06	Olympiacos	22	7
2006-07	Olympiakos	25	17
2007-08	AEK Athens	29	8
Totals		491	235

Honors, Awards, and Milestones

1993-94	Brazilian golden ball
1996	Bronze medal, Olympic Games
1998, 2002	World Cup all-star
1999	FIFA world player of the year
	European soccer player of the year
	World Soccer player of the year
	Onze Mondial European soccer player of the year
	Most goals, Copa América
	Most valuable player, Copa América
	Spanish League player of the year
2000	Most goals: UEFA Champions League
2006-07	Best foreign player: Greek Super League

abilities. More than just a talented scorer, Rivaldo demonstrated he was a team player as well. He led both the Brazilian national team and a number of his professional clubs to the heights of competition and, in the process, became a highly sought-after and well-compensated player. Rivaldo's late father, who never doubted that one of his three sons would become a soccer great, would have been proud of Rivaldo's achievements.

Jack Ewing

Additional Sources

Foer, Franklin. *How Soccer Explains the World: An Unlikely Theory of Globalization.* New York: HarperCollins, 2004.

Goldblatt, David. *The Ball Is Round: A Global History of Soccer.* New York: Riverhead Trade, 2008.

Hornby, Hugh. *Soccer.* New York: Dorling Kindersley, 2005.

Radnedge, Keir. *The Complete Encyclopedia of Soccer.* London: Carlton, 2002.

Romário

Born: January 29, 1966
Rio de Janeiro, Brazil
Also known as: Romário de Souza Faria (full name); O Baixinho (Portuguese for the Little One)

Early Life

Romário de Souza Faria was born on January 29, 1966, in Rio de Janeiro, Brazil. Living on the outskirts of Rio in a favela, or slum district, he learned to play soccer as a child. Although Romário was small for his age and struggled with asthma, his father recognized his talent as a soccer player. Encouraged by his father to work hard, Romário became skilled enough to join the small Brazilian soccer team Olaria in 1982. At the age of nineteen, Romário entered the professional world of soccer when he signed with the Brazilian team Vasco Da Gama.

The Road to Excellence

Many soccer experts underestimated Romário as a player because of his small stature. However, rival players soon learned that he was tough, quick, and intuitive on the soccer field with an uncanny ability to "charm" the soccer ball into the net. From 1985 to 1988, he won two Brazilian State Championships and scored 73 goals over 113 game appearances. In 1988, he transferred to the Dutch team PSV Eindhoven and scored 98 goals in 109 games. In the same year, while a member of the Brazilian national team, he won an Olympic silver medal and was a top scorer with 7 goals. He was an integral part of PSV Eindhoven's Dutch championships in 1989, 1991, and 1992 and in the Dutch Cup wins in 1989 and 1990. In 1989 and 1990, he was the Dutch league's top goal scorer.

The Emerging Champion

In 1993, Romário moved to the Spanish team FC Barcelona and scored 34 goals over forty-six games. In 1994, he was the top goal scorer for the Spanish league, Primera División. In 1994, Romário was a member of the Brazilian national team in the World Cup, playing in all seven games. The team won the World Cup, Brazil's first title in twenty-four years, with Romário scoring five goals. Romário was voted the most outstanding player of the tournament. In the same year, he was voted the FIFA world player of the year. He was a hero in Brazil and solidified his reputation as one of the greatest soccer players in the world.

In 1995, Romário went to the Brazilian team Flamengo, playing with the club for two seasons and scoring 31 goals over forty-six games.

Romário at the 1994 World Cup. (Bob Thomas/Getty Images)

From 1996 to 1998, he played with the Spanish team Valencia, scoring 5 goals in eleven games and missing the World Cup because of injuries. In 1999, he returned to Flamengo and scored 26 goals in thirty-nine games. The following year, he returned to Vasco da Gama. During the two years he played with the team, he accrued 41 goals and helped the team win the Mercosur Cup and the Brazilian league championship.

From 2002 to 2004, Romário played with the Rio de Janeiro team Fluminense. In 2003, he was loaned to the Saudi Arabian team Al Saad. During this time, he scored 35 goals in a combined sixty-six games with the two teams. Romário was well known for ignoring team discipline and arguing with his coaches, and a conflict between him and the Fluminense coach led to his release from the team. He returned to Vasco da Gama in 2005.

Continuing the Story

In 2005, at the age of thirty-nine, Romário scored 22 goals during the Brazilian championship games, making him the top goal scorer of the championship. He also played in the FIFA Beach Soccer World Cup Final. In 2006, in a surprising move, Romário joined the United Soccer Leagues team Miami FC, a second-tier U.S. soccer club which developed players for Major League Soccer. After four months, he returned again to Vasco da Gama as a player and coach, recording his unofficial one-thousandth goal on May 20, 2007.

On December 21, 2007, Romário was suspended for 120 days for failing a drug test. After a game in October, he tested positive for the banned substance finasteride, a masking agent of anabolic steroids. Romário claimed he was using an anti-balding medication which contained finasteride and had been unaware the drug was present in the preparation. He denied enhancing his performance on the soccer field. On February 14, 2008,

Honors, Awards, and Milestones

1986-87, 1996-2000	Most goals: Rio de Janeiro League
1988	Silver medal, Olympic Games
	Most goals: Olympic Games
1989-92	Most goals: Dutch League
1989, 1990	Most goals: Dutch Cup
1990, 1993	Most goals: UEFA Champions League
1994	Most goals: Spanish League
	EFE Trophy
	World Cup golden ball
	Onze Mondial European soccer player of the year
	FIFA world player of the year
1997	Most goals: Confederations Cup
1998-99	Most goals: Brazilian Cup
2000	Brazilian golden ball
	South American soccer player of the year
	El Pais best player
2001, 2005	Most goals: Brazilian League

Brazil's Superior Tribunal of Sports Justice acquitted him of this doping charge. In February, 2008, after a coaching disagreement with Vasco da Gama club president Eurico Miranda, Romário announced his retirement effective March 30, 2008. He planned to remain involved in soccer by promoting the 2014 World Cup.

Summary

Romário is still considered one of Brazil's most famous and intuitive soccer forwards ever. Known for his temperamental behavior and sudden bursts of speed on the soccer field, he was the second highest goal scorer in soccer history, surpassed only by Pelé, who scored 1,281 goals.

Alice C. Richer

Additional Sources

Di Peco, Vittoria. *The Story of Romário.* Richmond Hill, Ont.: V. Casonato, 1993.

Hunt, Chris. *The Complete Book of Soccer.* New York: Firefly Books, 2008.

Radnedge, Keir. *The Ultimate Encyclopedia of Soccer: The Definitive Illustrated Guide to World Soccer.* London: Carlton Books, 2004.

Ronaldinho

Born: March 21, 1980
  Porto Alegre, Brazil
Also known as: Ronaldo de Assis Moreira (full name); Ronaldinho Gaucho

Early Life

Few celebrity athletes are known by their nicknames only. However, Ronaldinho, born Ronaldo de Assis Moreira and also known as Ronaldinho Gaucho, is one of the few. The nickname Ronaldinho means "little Ronaldo" and differentiated him from Ronaldo Luiz Nazário de Lima, who is also from Brazil. Ronaldinho grew up in a family of five. He had an older brother, Roberto, who also played professional soccer before injuries forced retirement. Ronaldinho also had an older sister, Deisi. His family was close and was brought even closer with the death of his father, João, when Ronaldinho was eight. His family was involved with Ronaldinho's professional activities.

The Road to Excellence

From a young age, Ronaldinho loved soccer. He started playing futsal and beach soccer. Both of these sports require incredible and quick ball-control skill, a trademark of Ronaldinho's professional career. Ronaldinho began dazzling audiences as early as age thirteen, when he scored 23 goals in one game.

By age seventeen, Ronaldinho was already becoming well known for his brilliant ball handling and dynamic goal scoring. He was part of the winning under-seventeen (U-17) Brazilian national soccer team. During the FIFA U-17 World Championship in Egypt, Ronaldinho was the leading scorer.

At eighteen, Ronaldinho signed with a Brazilian professional team and played five games before moving on to bigger opportunities with the Brazilian national team. At that point, he already had the trademark long curly hair and crooked-toothed smile that made him popular with the media. In his first year with the national team, he continued to develop his reputation as an offensive threat when he scored against Venezuela. He was the top scorer in the Confederations Cup, even though his team lost in the finals.

The Emerging Champion

When he played, Ronaldinho exhibited a sheer joy that was visible on his face. The soccer ball seemed to be an extension of his body. This passion for the game helped Ronaldinho win the respect of fans all over the world. He joined his first European professional team, Paris St. Germain, after his success in 2001 international play. During the 2002 World Cup, he scored brilliantly against England in the

Ronaldinho taking a penalty kick at the 2008 Olympic Games in Beijing, China. (Alvin Chan/Reuters/Landov)

Professional Statistics

Season	Team	Games Played	Goals
1998-98	Grêmio	48	7
1999-99	Grêmio	47	22
2000-00	Grêmio	15	8
2001-02	Paris St-Germain	28	9
2002-03	Paris St-Germain	27	8
2003-04	FC Barcelona	32	15
2004-05	FC Barcelona	35	9
2005-06	FC Barcelona	29	17
2006-07	FC Barcelona	32	21
2007-08	FC Barcelona	17	8
Totals		310	124

quarterfinals, helping to bring Brazil to another World Cup championship.

Following some challenges and negotiations with Paris St. Germain and Manchester United, Ronaldinho moved to Spain to play for FC Barcelona. In Barcelona, his uncanny ball control thrilled crowds and helped bring his team to decisive victories and a second-place finish during his first year with the team. Ronaldinho's ability to feint and dance around a ball and then explode with speed toward the goal was unparalleled. He had the ability to maintain possession of the ball in the air, juggling around three or more defenders. This type of skill, coupled with his ability to produce goals, made him an exciting draw for Barcelona fans.

During his second season with Barcelona, Ronaldinho helped lead the team to the top of its league, beating longtime rivals Real Madrid. By 2006, he had received formal recognition as one of the best players in the world. He was named world soccer player of the year and FIFA world player of the year in 2004 and 2005 and Fédération International de Footballeurs Professionels (FIFPro) world player of the year in 2005 and 2006.

Continuing the Story

The humble Ronaldinho often seemed uncomfortable with comparisons to the game's greatest players. However, his accomplishments on the field put him in elite soccer company. He played as an attacking midfielder or striker, depending whether he was with the Brazilian national team or FC Barcelona. While playing for Barcelona, Ronaldinho was usually covered by at least two defensive players.

In the 2006 World Cup in Germany, Brazil was a favorite to win. However, Ronaldinho and the rest of the Brazilian team did not do as well as anticipated. There were rumors that Ronaldinho neglected his soccer duties to carouse late at night with a French model; however, these allegations were denied by Ronaldinho. Regardless of the reasons, the brilliant footballer slumped in subsequent professional competition. In 2008, he was traded from FC Barcelona to AC Milan.

Summary

Ronaldinho was recognized by FIFA as the best player in the world for three years. His scoring ability and flair with the ball made him one of the great soccer players of all time. Though modest, Ronaldinho was recognized as one of Brazil's greats, alongside Pelé and Ronaldo.

Russell Medbery

Additional Sources

O'Connell, Michael. *Ronaldinho*. London: Artnik, 2005.

Soutar, Jethro. *Ronaldinho: Football's Flamboyant Maestro*. London: Robson, 2007.

Honors, Awards, and Milestones

1999	Most goals: Confederations Cup
	Confederations Cup golden ball
2002	World Cup all-star
2004	Pelé's FIFA 100
	EFE Trophy
2004-05	FIFA world player of the year
2004, 2006	Spanish League best foreign player
2005	European soccer player of the year
2005-06	FIFPro world player of the year
	UEFA club soccer player of the year

Ronaldo

Born: September 18, 1976
 Rio de Janeiro, Brazil
Also known as: Ronaldo Luiz Nazário de Lima
 (full name); the Phenomenon; Little Buddha

Early Life

Ronaldo Luiz Nazário de Lima was born in Rio de Janeiro, Brazil, on September 18, 1976. His neighborhood, Bento Ribeiro, was notorious for its high rate of crimes, especially homicides, due to drug trafficking. On Ronaldo's birth certificate his father registered the date as September 22. Ronaldo, therefore, celebrates his birthday on both the real and the official dates. His father abandoned the family because he abused alcohol and other substances, but Ronaldo had the saving good fortune of his mother and an older brother and sister to look out for him.

The Road to Excellence

Like millions of young Brazilians, Ronaldo learned soccer with his neighborhood companions, playing barefoot on side streets and vacant lots. A withdrawn boy with protruding teeth, Ronaldo found in soccer a world he could dominate. In endlessly kicking and running with his first soccer ball, and playing daily, he forged his singular skill for commanding a ball. Having developed powerful, muscular legs, he joined a local soccer team when he was nine years old. At the age of eleven, he scored more than 150 goals in one season.

At thirteen, Ronaldo was invited to test for the Flamengo soccer team, its red and black colors nationally recognized. However, he could not join Flamengo because the team would not pay his bus fare to attend training sessions. Nonetheless, in 1990, he began playing with a Second Division Rio team, São Cristóvão, which provided a house for his family near its headquarters. Ronaldo discontinued his education before graduation.

The Emerging Champion

While playing for São Cristóvão, Ronaldo encountered fortune and fame. In fifty-four games over two seasons, he made 36 goals. Ronaldo, a frontline striker, had stunning speed and accuracy. Scouted by agents Reinaldo Pitta and Alexandre Martins, Ronaldo entered a ten-year contract with them. The agents gained extraordinary control over his career. Since Ronaldo was a minor, his father signed the contract, not really understanding its contents.

In 1993, Ronaldo joined the Cruzeiro soccer team, in Belo Horizonte, northwest of Rio. The value of his transfer was $30,000, and his monthly salary, $5,000.

Ronaldo scoring on a penalty shot against the Netherlands at the 1998 World Cup. (AP/Wide World Photos)

In the 1993-1994 season, in sixty matches, Ronaldo netted an extraordinary 58 goals.

Continuing the Story

In 1994, Ronaldo became a world star. He was only seventeen. At the beginning of the year, he emerged internationally, on the team playing against Argentina. Though he did not play, he was on the Brazil World Cup team, which won for a record-breaking fourth time. More significantly, Ronaldo's agents decided to improve his appearance and thereby his marketability. He got braces for his teeth, reducing their protrusion. He had his head shaved, which made him look more aggressive and macho.

The "new" Ronaldo became a European player. By the end of 1994, he joined the PSD Eindhoven team in the Netherlands. In fifty-six matches over two seasons he made 55 goals, becoming the top scorer in the league, while his team won the Dutch Cup. Ronaldo, the former slum boy, gained a seasonal salary of $1 million.

Ronaldo dazzled his growing fans with his extraordinary speed and dominance and his ability to manipulate the ball equally with his right and left feet while advancing with sudden speed. At over 6 feet tall and weighing 180 pounds, he was much larger than most Brazilians, adding intimidating size to frightening speed.

Traded in 1996 to the Spanish FC Barcelona team for $20 million, Ronaldo obtained a salary of $1.5 million dollars per season. In a season of thirty-seven games, he made 34 goals. With his easy smile and shaved head, he was named "Little Buddha." In 1997, he was traded to Inter Milan, in Italy, for $30 million. His salary surpassed $5 million per season.

The most traumatic year in Ronaldo's career was 1998. He was the key member of the Brazil team that went to Paris to play in the World Cup. Brazilian fans expected a fifth championship. Ronaldo was deeply affected by the pressure of this sentiment.

While still on the Eindhoven team, Ronaldo had suffered a knee injury. The pain from the injury reappeared during the playoffs and remained for the World Cup. He received medical treatment that affected his attention and control. Besides his physical pain, he endured severe psychological tensions. His teammates were divided and antagonistic. He and his fiancé quarreled. In the final game, France, a team of little reputation, defeated the world-renowned Brazilian team by a score of 3-0. Shamed and humiliated, the Brazilians returned home, receiving the country's vehement wrath, which fell particularly on Ronaldo. No one knew the background events that had shadowed Ronaldo's performance.

The following year, Ronaldo married Milene Domingues and returned to play for Internazioniale. He led his team to a Copa América victory. His knee was injured at the end of the year, and he was not able to return as an impact player until the World Cup in 2002, where he led the Brazilian national team to its fifth World Cup title. Ronaldo scored 2 goals in the final game and 8 goals in the tournament. His skill and scoring ability made him a popular player with international fans. Following this victory, Ronaldo signed with the Spanish team Real Madrid and scored 21 goals in his first thirty games.

Honors, Awards, and Milestones

Year	Award
1991	Conmebol U-16
1994	World Cup champion
1995	Top scorer in the Dutch league
1996	Dutch Cup
	Bronze medal, Olympic Games
1996-97	Top scorer in Spanish league
1996-97, 2002	*World Soccer* player of the year
1997	Spanish Cup
	Cup Winners Cup
	Copa América winner
	European golden boot
1997-98, 2002	Continental Cup championship
1997, 2002	FIFA best player of the year
	Best European Footballer
1998	FIFA best player of the year
	UEFA Cup
	Best Striker and Footballer of World Cup France
1998, 2002	Best Player of Italy
	Best Foreign Player of Italy
	World Cup all-star team
1999	Copa América winner; Golden Boot Award of the tournament
	Selected as one of the best players in the 1990's by various media
2002	World Cup golden boot
	World Cup silver ball
	Intercontinental Cup most valuable player
	BBC Sports Personality of the Year: Overseas Personality
2003-04	Top scorer in Spanish league
2006	All-Time World Cup Goalscorer (15)
	World Cup bronze boot

In 2006, in Germany, Ronaldo played in his fourth World Cup. He scored 3 goals during the tournament, giving him an amazing total of 15 World Cup goals. Despite criticism for his lack of conditioning, Ronaldo was an effective scorer for Brazil. Afterward, he signed with AC Milan, where he suffered another injury at the beginning of 2008.

Summary

When barely out of his teens, Ronaldo already was described as a Brazilian star comparable to the great Pelé. Ronaldo joined the pantheon of players Brazil has so richly generated. His most prominent skills throughout his career were his speed and agility and his stunning accuracy with the ball.

Edward A. Riedinger, updated by Russell Medbery

Additional Sources

Clarkson, Wensley. *Ronaldo! King of the World.* London: Blake, 2002.

_____. *Ronaldo! Twenty-one Years of Genius and Ninety Minutes That Shook the World.* London: Blake, 1998.

Mosley, James. *Ronaldo: The Journey of a Genius.* Edinburgh: Mainstream, 2006.

Orr, Tamra. *Ronaldo.* Hockessin, Del.: Mitchell Lane, 2007.

Paddock, Mark. *Ronaldo.* Toronto: Firefly Books, 1999.

Rushin, Steve. "Joy to the World." *Sports Illustrated* 88 (June 15, 1998): 112-117.

Kyle Rote, Jr.

Born: December 25, 1950
Dallas, Texas

Early Life
Kyle Rote, Jr., was born on Christmas Day, 1950, in Dallas, Texas, to Kyle and Betty Rote. In 1950, Kyle's father, the premier college football player in the United States, was drafted in the first round by the New York Giants of the National Football League (NFL), after a stellar college career at Southern Methodist University.

Kyle, Jr., learned early the advantages and disadvantages of having a celebrity father. Traveling with his parents during the fall and returning to Dallas in the off-season, Kyle got an up-close view of what life was like in the world of professional sports.

Kyle Rote, Jr., who was one of the top players in the North American Soccer League in the 1970's. (Courtesy of Kyle Rote, Jr.)

While his father starred as a sticky-fingered pass receiver for the New York Giants in a game known in the United States as football, Kyle found himself drawn to the game known to the world at large as "football" but to Americans as soccer.

The Road to Excellence
Kyle, Sr., could punt and kick with the best of them, but Kyle, Jr., would someday do even more amazing things with his feet—and his head. Fully expecting to follow in his dad's footsteps as a football player, Kyle entered eagerly into youth football. Kyle used his natural abilities and father's counsel to excel in football, the sport often called a "religion" in Texas, even at the schoolboy level. By the time he was in high school, he was seeking a spring and summer sport to help him with football conditioning.

Kyle turned to soccer, believing that the combination of foot, body, eye, hand, and head coordination required for the sport would make him a better football player. Soon he was wondering if he might choose a different course for his life than his father had.

However, Kyle had some barriers to overcome. He had begun playing soccer only in his teens. A game that had been played for nearly 150 years but had only recently become a scholastic sport in Dallas offered challenges to a young man used to using his hands for any game involving a ball. In addition, football was still at the center of Kyle's athletic interests. Kyle found it difficult to be a Texan and say that he really preferred a "foreign" game like soccer. Soon, however, Kyle was thinking of football as conditioning for soccer.

Fortunately for Kyle, Dallas was one of the few U.S. cities that had taken seriously the goal of developing world-class soccer players so that an American team could compete successfully in international competition. The time was right for Kyle to pursue his dream, and he received an accelerated education in the sport.

The Emerging Champion
Kyle's high school, Highland Park, had produced more than its share of professional football players,

including the immortal Doak Walker and Bobby Layne, NFL hall of famers. Kyle Rote, Jr., became Highland Park High School's first professional soccer player. He emerged as a premier scoring forward among U.S. high school athletes.

The route to his remarkable success, however, would be somewhat circular. In 1969, Kyle enrolled at Oklahoma State University (OSU) on a football scholarship, but he was torn between his love for soccer and his desire to continue the glorious Rote legacy in football.

Finally, Kyle made his decision. He transferred to the little-known University of the South, an Episcopal school in Sewanee, Tennessee. This institution offered Kyle something that OSU could not: a first-class soccer program and a chance for Kyle to study and express his Christian faith.

Kyle never led his college team to a national soccer championship, but he played so well in his three years at the University of the South that he attracted the attention of scouts for the North American Soccer League (NASL). At that time, the recently formed NASL was in search of American stars to draw fans to the game so popular elsewhere.

Kyle was a natural choice, and in 1972 the Dallas Tornado team made him its first-round draft choice. Just as his father had been called upon to bring football into the hearts and minds of the American sports fan, Kyle, Jr., was asked to draw the attention not only of fans but also of younger athletes who might be smitten with the game he had come to love.

Continuing the Story

In his first game as a professional, Kyle started for Dallas and scored a goal. He led the NASL in scoring his rookie season with 30 points, including 10 goals and 10 assists, in a sport not known for its high scoring. The NASL credited scorers with two points for each goal and one point for each assist. For his achievements, Kyle won NASL rookie of the year honors.

Kyle quickly established his reputation as a striker on the Tornado, the player counted on for the deft pass, the timely steal, or the crucial goal when a game was on the line. Because soccer is a game of feet, mind, and eyes, it requires of its stars heightened peripheral vision and balletic finesse, not the bulky or muscular prowess of the pro football player. Kyle was perfect for the sport.

Kyle played for his hometown Dallas Tornado for five seasons before he was traded to the Houston Hurricane in 1978. He scored only 6 points for Houston and then retired as a player from the struggling league, which folded a few seasons later. When he left the NASL, he was Dallas's all-time leading scorer with 42 regular-season goals.

Kyle was an all-around athlete, and he earned additional fame when, in 1974, 1976, and 1977, he won three American Broadcasting Company (ABC) *Superstars* competitions—a series of diverse events in which athletes from many different sports competed for prize money. After his professional soccer playing career was over, Kyle moved into sports broadcasting, covering both college football and soccer. He returned briefly to the world of professional soccer as a coach for the Memphis Americans in the Major Indoor Soccer League in the 1983-1984 season. After that, he has remained an ambassador for soccer. Kyle also enjoyed a successful career as a motivational speaker, sports agent, and author of several books on soccer.

Summary

Kyle Rote, Jr., was a pioneer in a sport struggling to become popular among North American fans and athletes. On his own terms, Kyle excelled in professional sports with the same flair, discipline, and success as his father. He will always be remembered as a fine example of a young athlete determined to excel despite the odds against him, playing a sport virtually ignored in his native country but loved throughout the world.

Bruce L. Edwards

Honors and Awards

1973	NASL rookie of the year
	NASL high scorer
1974	U.S. National Team member
1974, 1976-77	ABC-TV *Superstars* competition champion

Additional Sources

Dolan, Edward, and Richard B. Lyttle. *Kyle Rote, Jr.: American-Born Soccer Star.* Garden City, N.Y.: Doubleday, 1979.

Rote, Kyle, Jr. *Kyle Rote, Jr.'s Complete Book of Soccer.* New York: Simon & Schuster, 1988.

Rote, Kyle, Jr., and Ronald Patterson. *Beyond the Goal.* Waco, Tex.: Word Books, 1975.

Rote, Kyle, Jr., and Donn Risolo. *Wilson Guide to Soccer.* St. Paul, Minn.: Publication Partners, 1995.

Karl-Heinz Rummenigge

Born: September 25, 1955
Lippstadt, West Germany
Also known as: Kalle Rummenigge (full name); Red Cheeks

Early Life

Karl-Heinz Rummenigge was born in Lippstadt, West Germany, on September 25, 1955. Unlike many of his contemporaries, Karl was not blessed with amazing athletic ability. He achieved greatness in sport through hard work. Reflecting on his youth in Lippstadt, Karl remarked that nothing was ever handed to him. As a young, up-and-coming soccer player, Karl had to start from the bottom, sitting on the substitutes' bench and carrying suitcases to the team bus. A shy, soft-spoken man, Karl was given the nickname "Red Cheeks" because he always blushed when interviewed by reporters or reprimanded by coaches.

The Road to Excellence

In 1975, at the age of twenty, Karl was signed by Bayern Munich, a German first-division club. Bayern Munich was then the top team in Europe, having won the European Cup, the highest championship in European soccer, in 1974. Karl's promotion to such a successful team at so young an age showed how highly Bayern Munich's management thought of his potential, but Karl did not crack the team's starting lineup right away. Instead, Karl carried the legendary Franz Beckenbauer's bags, and he saw hardly any playing time as Bayern Munich repeated as European Cup champions in 1975 and 1976.

Karl's lack of playing time did not discourage him, though. With the assistance of trainer Dettman Cramer, Karl worked diligently on all aspects of his game. Cramer transformed Karl into a dribbling and offensive wizard who was West Germany's dominant player in the 1980's.

Karl's strength was his ball control. He learned to keep the ball as close to his foot as possible, lulling his opponents into submission. Once this occurred, Karl unleashed a thundering shot with his right foot.

The Emerging Champion

With his tireless, unselfish work ethic, Karl led West Germany to the European Championship in 1980 and Bayern Munich to the German Championship in 1980 and 1981. Karl's dynamic offensive abilities led to his selection as European player of the year in 1980 and 1981. Karl played in three World Cups in his career, leading West Germany to second-place finishes in both 1982 and 1986.

Perhaps the finest moments of Karl's career came in the 1982 World Cup semifinal game between West Germany and France. Karl, the West German team captain, had suffered a hamstring injury in an earlier round of the tournament, and without him the West Germans had struggled to

Karl-Heinz Rummenigge at the 1982 World Cup in Spain. (Bob Thomas/Getty Images)

> **Career Highlights**
>
> 95 international appearances for West Germany
>
> **Honors, Awards, and Milestones**
>
> | | |
> |---|---|
> | 1975-76 | European Cup champion |
> | 1980 | European Championship champion |
> | 1980-81 | German League champion |
> | | European player of the year (Ballon d'Or) |
> | 1982, 1984 | German League Cup champion |

reach the semifinals. West Germany's semifinal opponent was France, led by Michel Platini. With Karl watching from the sidelines, the two teams battled to a 1-1 tie at the end of regulation time, and World Cup rules required the teams to play two 15-minute overtime periods.

In the first overtime, the French scored a quick goal to take a 2-1 lead. With his team on the brink of elimination, Karl, still slowed by his injury, went into the game. After another French goal made the score 3-1, with West Germany hanging by a thread, Karl went to work. With time running out in the first overtime period, Karl displayed the ballhandling skills that had made him famous. He took the ball wide to the left side of the field and closed on the French goal, scoring to narrow the French lead to 3-2. Inspired by its injured captain's efforts, the West German team dominated the second overtime period, tying the French at 3-3 and then defeating them on penalty kicks to gain a berth in the championship game. Although the West Germans lost in the finals to Italy, Karl had shown the world that, even when injured, he was among the game's most exciting players.

Karl also gained fame as one of soccer's most gentlemanly players. Throughout his career, he was continually fouled and hacked; opponents would do almost anything to get the ball away from him. Even so, Karl never lashed out at his opponents or fouled them back, and he became as respected for his temperament as for his athletic skills.

Continuing the Story

In 1980 and 1981, Karl was the top goal scorer in the German league. In 1984, he was transferred to Inter Milan of the Italian league for a sum of ten million deutsche marks. In the Italian league, Karl's soccer career was reborn. Playing in Italy allowed him to take on an added role as a world ambassador of soccer. He spent countless off-the-field hours devoting time to various charitable organizations. Karl matured in Italy. He was a star who was willing to listen and learn, and who was also to be found laughing with fans. A hard worker on the field, Karl was also an exceptional person off the field.

Summary

After his retirement from competition, Karl-Heinz Rummenigge traveled all over the world and presented soccer clinics to players and coaches. His appearance at the National Soccer Coaches Association of America drew more than two thousand coaches, all of whom were eager to learn from a man famous as a superb player, a dedicated worker, and a true gentleman.

Leonard K. Lucenko

Additional Sources

Hesse-Lichtenberger, Ulrich. *Tor! The Story of German Football.* London: When Saturday Comes Books, 2003.

Radnedge, Keir, and Gary Lineker. *The Ultimate Encyclopedia of Soccer: The Definitive Illustrated Guide to World Soccer.* London: Carlton Books, 2004.

Witzig, Richard. *The Global Art of Soccer.* New Orleans, La.: CusiBoy, 2006.

Hugo Sánchez

Born: July 11, 1958
    Mexico City, Mexico
Also known as: Hugo Sánchez Márquez (full name); Hugol; Pentapichichi

Early Life

Hugo Sánchez Márquez was born on July 11, 1958, in Mexico's capital city. His father was Héctor Sánchez, who had won fame playing professional soccer in Mexico. Hugo wanted to follow in his father's footsteps and began playing soccer at an early age. An older sister, Olympic gymnast Herlinda Sánchez Márquez, taught Hugo a few moves that increased his flexibility and agility. By his teens, Hugo had become highly skilled in his chosen sport.

At the age of seventeen, Hugo was selected to play for the Mexican national team. He participated at the 1975 Pan-American Games and at the 1976 Summer Olympics. By the time he was eighteen, he had more than eighty international caps, and he signed a contract with the Universidad Nacional Autónoma de México (UNAM) Pumas, a professional team that represented Mexico's national university. At the same time, he enrolled at the university to study for a degree in dentistry.

The Road to Excellence

In Hugo's first year with the team, the Pumas won the championship of the Primera División of the Mexican football league. By 1978, he was the league's top scorer, with 20 goals. The following year UNAM, which played in the fall, winter, and spring, agreed to a player exchange for the summer season with the North American Soccer League (NASL). Hugo was loaned to the San Diego Sockers. Playing as a scoring forward or "striker," Hugo became a dominant force for the Sockers, and averaged nearly 1 goal per game in both 1979 and 1980.

The rest of the year, Hugo continued to star for the Pumas. In five seasons, he tallied 99 goals, tying for the league's top scoring honors in 1980, his final year with the team. That year, thanks to Hugo's talents, the Pumas won a second league title and also captured the Confederation of the North, Central American, and Caribbean Association Football (CONCACAF) Champions Cup.

Hugo's prowess in Mexico had not gone unnoticed in Europe. In 1981, Arsenal, a powerful team in England's Premier League, offered him a con-

Mexico's Hugo Sánchez pushing the ball forward against West Germany at the 1986 World Cup. (AFP/Getty Images)

tract, but he signed instead with Atlético Madrid, in Spain's top professional league, commonly known as La Liga. For a time, Hugo floundered while adapting to the more precise and controlled European style of soccer. He soon began to hit his stride, however.

The Emerging Champion
By the 1984-1985 La Liga season, Hugo was scoring regularly. He impressed spectators with spectacular windmill kicks and his unique goal-scoring celebration: a series of backward somersaults. Hugo led Atlético Madrid to a second-place finish in the league; helped the team capture the Copa del Rey (King's Cup) and the Super Copa championships; and won the Pichichi Trophy, awarded to the league's top goal scorer.

The following season, Hugo signed with Real Madrid. Playing on a team laden with soccer stars—including José Antonio Camacho, Rafael Gordillo, and Jorge Valdano—Hugo was a standout. He inspired Real Madrid to five consecutive league titles, a Union of European Football Associations Cup in 1986, and the Copa del Rey in 1989. Hugo, scoring at least 27 goals per season from 1986 to 1990, racked up 207 goals in 283 games, and booted 38 goals in 1989-1990 to tie the single-season record. For his achievements, he was awarded four consecutive Pichichi trophies and the European golden boot award as Europe's top scorer.

During the same period, Hugo also played for the Mexican national team but did not fare as well. Though Hugo scored 29 goals in sixty matches, the Mexican team was in disarray—it did not participate in the 1982 and 1990 World Cups. Furthermore, Hugo, always volatile, often feuded with the Mexican Football Federation. Thus, soccer fans of his native country did not have the opportunity to witness Hugo's heroics during his prime playing years. In the three World Cups in which he participated, he scored just 1 goal.

Continuing the Story
As he aged, and as his career wound down, Hugo returned to Mexico for a season. Afterward, he played for clubs in Spain and Austria and with the Dallas Burn in Major League Soccer. In 1997, nearing the age of forty, he finished his playing career on the Atlético Celaya team in Guanajuato, Mexico.

In retirement, Hugo returned to his profession as a dentist. By 2000, he was back on the soccer pitch as head coach of the UNAM Pumas. Though he led the Pumas to two consecutive Mexican league championships, the team performed poorly in tournaments, and Hugo resigned after the 2005 season. He briefly coached Necaxa before his selection as the head coach of the Mexican national team in 2006.

Hugo's tenure as the Mexican team's coach was marked by contrasts: stunning victories and disappointing defeats. In the 2007 CONCACAF Gold Cup, Mexico lost to the United States. The team rebounded with triumphs against Venezuela, Paraguay, and Ecuador but lost again to the United States. In the Confederación Sudamericana de Fútbal (South American Football Confederation) competition for the Copa América, Mexico upset world champion Brazil but finished in third place. In World Cup preliminaries, Mexico tied with teams from Australia and Finland and lost to Ecuador. In qualifying for the 2008 Olympics, Mexico tied Canada, lost to Guatemala, and was eliminated. In March, 2008, Hugo was fired.

Hugo married Isabel Martín and settled in Mexico City. He has a grown son, Hugo Sánchez Portugal—who played soccer before becoming a sports commentator—and a daughter from a previous marriage.

Summary
Hugo Sánchez was one of Mexico's best soccer players and the best Mexican import to ever play in Europe. A prolific scorer with a colorful personal-

Honors, Awards, and Milestones

Year	Achievement
1978	Most goals: Mexican League
1985-88, 1990	Most goals: Spanish League
1987, 1990	Spanish League best foreign player
1989-90	European golden boot
2000	International Federation of Football History and Statistics best Mexican soccer player of the twentieth century
	International Federation of Football History and Statistics best North America and Central America soccer player of the twentieth century
2004	Pelé's FIFA 100
2006-08	Head coach, Mexico's national soccer team

ity, a devastating windmill kick, and crowd-pleasing performances, Hugo played at a high level of proficiency on the international stage for more than twenty years. He led virtually every team for which he played to new heights while garnering many individual trophies. In 1999, he was voted among the top fifty soccer players of the twentieth century and the best ever from the CONCACAF region.

Jack Ewing

Additional Sources

Cresswell, Peterjohn, and Simon Evans. *The Rough Guide to European Football: A Fans' Handbook.* London: Rough Guides, 2000.

Galeano, Eduardo. *Soccer in Sun and Shadow.* London: Verso, 2003.

Goldblatt, David. *The Ball Is Round: A Global History of Soccer.* New York: Riverhead Trade, 2008.

Briana Scurry

Born: September 7, 1971
Minneapolis, Minnesota

Early Life

The youngest of nine children born to Earnest and Robbie Scurry, Briana Scurry grew up in Dayton, Minnesota, a predominantly white suburb of Minneapolis. The Scurry family was one of the few African American families to live in the small, farming community of two thousand people.

As a child, Briana was soft-spoken. One of her hobbies was painting model airplanes. In junior high and high school, she had aspirations of becoming a lawyer.

During her school years, Briana enjoyed playing many sports including basketball, softball, floor hockey, karate, football, and soccer. She began her soccer career while she was in the fourth grade. Throughout her youth she played for the Minneapolis Kickers. She continued in sports through high school and was named an all-state power forward in basketball and an all-American soccer player. In 1989, her high school soccer team won the Minnesota state championship, and Briana was named the state's top athlete.

The Road to Excellence

From Minnesota, Briana traveled east to attend the University of Massachusetts, where she became a goalkeeper on the women's soccer team. Her coach, whom she credited with molding her as a goalkeeper, was Jim Rudy. Briana played for Massachusetts from 1990 to 1993. In 1992, she participated in the Boston soccer-fest all-star tournament. There she received the notice of the U.S. women's soccer coach, Anson Dorrance, and the goalkeeper coach, Tony DiCicco. In 1993, Massachusetts lost, 4-1, to the University of North Carolina—which was coached by Dorrance—in the National Collegiate Athletic Association Division I final.

At Massachusetts, Briana compiled a record of 37 shutouts in 65 starts. Her goals against average was only 0.56—less than one goal per game. After finishing her college career, she was invited to participate in the national team's camp.

The Emerging Champion

In 1993, Briana was named starting goalkeeper for the U.S. national team as it prepared to qualify for the second Women's World Cup competition. Her debut came in a game against Portugal on March 16, 1994. The final score was 5-0—the first of many shutouts for Briana. In 1995, Briana started five of six games in the Women's World Cup. The U.S. team finished third. In 1996, Briana started every game for the U.S. national team during the Olympics in Atlanta, Georgia. When the U.S. team won the gold medal, Briana followed through on a promise and ran naked through the streets to celebrate.

Goalie Briana Scurry preparing for the 2004 Olympic Games in Athens, Greece. (Scott Barbour/Getty Images)

World Cup Statistics

Year	Record	GP	GAA	ShO
1995	3-1-1	5	0.81	2
1999	5-0-1	6	0.50	4
2003	5-1-0	6	0.83	3
2007	1-1-0	2	2.50	0
Totals	14-3-2	19	0.89	9

Notes: GP = games played; GAA = goals against average; ShO = shutouts

Continuing the Story

In 1999, the Women's World Cup soccer tournament reached unprecedented levels of popularity when it was played in the United States for the first time. A three-week, sixteen-team, thirty-two-match tournament, it drew huge crowds and large television audiences. On July 10, 1999, when the U.S. team met China at the Rose Bowl in Pasadena, California, the game set a world record for women's sporting events, with more than 90,000 people—including U.S. president Bill Clinton—in attendance. Forty million television viewers tuned in to see the most-watched soccer match in the history of American television.

The World Cup Final offered 90 minutes of regulation play and two 15-minute extra-time periods without any scoring in what proved to be a fierce defensive struggle in which expert goalkeeping on both sides played a decisive role. The game was finally decided on penalty kicks, with the two teams alternating as each took five shots on the opposing keeper. Stopping a penalty kick is one of the toughest challenges in sports. Consequently, penalty-kick shootouts are usually decided by misses, not by makes.

After the United States and China had both made their first two penalty kicks, Briana blocked China's third kick, by Liu Ying. A few minutes later, the fifth American kicker, Brandi Chastain, made a penalty kick that gave the United States a 5-4 advantage and a victory in the game. Briana's stop was afterward regarded as the biggest during the entire World Cup competition.

In 2000, after the success of the World Cup season, the U.S. team undertook a twelve-match "victory tour" to raise awareness of women's soccer and

National Team Statistics

Year	Record	GP	GAA	ShO
1994	11-1-0	12	0.43	7
1995	11-2-2	15	0.74	9
1996	15-1-1	17	0.66	8
1997	10-1-0	11	0.69	7
1998	15-1-2	18	0.50	12
1999	17-2-1	20	0.66	11
2000	0-0-3	3	1.19	0
2002	7-0-0	8	0.25	3
2003	14-1-0	16	0.61	7
2004	23-1-4	28	0.68	15
2006	3-0-0	3	n/a	1
2007	3-1-0	4	0.80	2
Totals	129-11-13	155	0.65	82

Notes: GP = games played; GAA = goals against average; ShO = shutouts; n/a = not available. Note that Scurry did not play for the national team in 2001 and 2005.

Olympic Games Statistics

Year	Record	GP	GAA	ShO
1996	4-0-1	5	0.60	2
2000	0-0-0	0	—	—
Totals	4-0-1	5	0.60	2

Notes: GP = games played; GAA = goals against average; ShO = shutouts

boost interest in a women's professional league to begin play in 2001. As expected, the victory tour had record attendance. Furthermore, the U.S. team captured the silver medal in the 2000 Olympics in Sydney. In those Games, Briana played backup goalkeeper, after suffering shin injuries that caused her to miss four months of play earlier in the year. She was replaced on the U.S. team by Siri Mullinax.

After the Women's United Soccer Association formed in 2001, Briana spent three seasons as starting goalkeeper for the Atlanta Beat. The collapse of the league in 2003 was a big disappointment, but Briana's career was not over. The following year, she and the core of the 1993 Women's World Cup championship team won the gold medal in women's soccer at the Athens Olympics. In the final game against a talented Brazilian team, Briana made save after remarkable save to help lead the United States to a 2-1 victory.

Over the next several years, as Briana moved into her late thirties, Hope Solo gradually took over as the principal goalkeeper on the U.S. national team. Although Briana's playing time was severely reduced, she remained an important member of the team because of her experience and inspirational leadership. When the United States entered the 2007 World Cup competition in China, Solo defended the goal in every game until the team reached a semifinal match against Brazil. Although Solo had compiled a string of shutouts leading into that game, Coach Greg Ryan decided to start Briana in goal—apparently because of her past successes against the Brazilians. The result was a disaster that altered the lives of several people involved.

The skilled and speedy Brazilians beat the United States 4-0. Afterward, Solo publicly criticized both the U.S. coach and Briana, claiming that she would have stopped the goals that Briana had allowed. For her outburst, Solo was suspended from the team, and Briana played goal in the third-place game against Norway, which the United States won 4-1. Afterward, Ryan was dismissed as coach, even though he had lost only one of more than fifty games during his tenure as head coach.

During the year following the 2007 World Cup competition, Briana again demonstrated the sportsmanship and class that had made her one of the most important members of the national team by forgiving Solo for her behavior and helping to welcome her back to the national team. Meanwhile, Briana continued to train and prepare for the 2008 Olympic Games in China. She was disappointed not to be chosen for the team, but the contributions she had made in helping to heal past wounds and bring the team together paid dividends, as the American women won their second-consecutive gold medal.

Summary

Briana Scurry began playing soccer as a young girl in Minnesota. From there, she went on to become a strong goalkeeper for her university's soccer team.

Honors, Awards, and Milestones

1989	Minnesota State Soccer Champions, Anoka High School
	Minnesota's Top Athlete
1992	Boston Soccer-Fest all-star team
1995	3d place, U.S. Women's World Cup Soccer Team
1996, 2004	Gold medal, Olympic Games
1999	1st place, U.S. Women's World Cup Soccer Team
2000	Silver medal, Olympic Games

After she finished college she was recruited as goalkeeper for the U.S. women's soccer team and was hailed as the hero of the seminal 1999 Women's World Cup, the series which drew the most widespread attention to women's soccer of any games to date. A multiple Olympic medalist, Briana was widely recognized as an ultimate team-first player and courageous role model for all athletes.

Betsy L. Nichols, updated by the Editors

Additional Sources

Bamberger, Michael. "Dream Come True." *Sports Illustrated* 91, no. 24 (December 20, 1999): 46-60.

Caparez, Dean. "Akers and Scurry Take Out Brazil." *Soccer America* 54, no. 28 (July 19, 1999): 8-9.

Christopher, Matt. *In the Goal with Briana Scurry*. Boston: Little, Brown, 2000.

Goldblatt, David. *The Ball Is Round: A Global History of Soccer*. New York: Riverhead Books, 2008.

Hunt, Chris. *The Complete Book of Soccer*. Buffalo, N.Y.: Firefly Books, 2006.

Luder, Bob. "Life in the Whirlwind of Celebrity." *Soccer America* 54, no. 42 (October 25, 1999): 27.

Radnedge, Keir, and Gary Lineker. *The Ultimate Encyclopedia of Soccer: The Definitive Illustrated Guide to World Soccer*. London: Carlton Books, 2004.

Rasmussen, R. Kent. "Women's World Cup of Soccer Draws Unprecedented Attention." In *Great Events: 1900-2001*. Vol. 8. Pasadena, Calif.: Salem Press, 2002.

Peter Shilton

Born: September 18, 1949
Leicester, England
Also known as: Peter Leslie Shilton (full name)

Early Life

Peter Leslie Shilton was born on September 18, 1949, in Leicester, a large city in central England. Peter's father was a greengrocer, and the Shilton family lived in a house with a garden where Peter set up a makeshift soccer goal between two trees. When financial problems forced the Shilton family to sell the house and move, Peter took his practicing out into the street, where over and over he tossed a soccer ball high in the air and then sprang up to catch it with his arms extended.

When Peter was young, for some reason, he was convinced that he would be a dwarf, so he hung from the banisters with his mother clutching his ankles so that he did not fall. Later, Peter confessed: "I pulled and pulled on my arms and legs every day. Crazy, I know, but I did grow eventually, and that was all I was worried about."

By the time he was twelve, Peter spent hours at a time organizing his soccer-playing friends to give him a barrage of shots. On every occasion he checked the angle, the speed, and the trajectory of the ball. He had fun, but his primary target was to become a good goalkeeper.

The Road to Excellence

In 1966, Peter began his professional career with Leicester City, a successful team that had appeared in the English League Cup Final in 1964 and 1965. Peter's position, goalkeeper, was filled on the Leicester squad by Gordon Banks, a star of the English national team and the top goalkeeper in English soccer. Peter impressed the Leicester management so strongly, though, that in 1967 the team released Banks and installed seventeen-year-old Peter in his place. Peter played for Leicester until 1974, helping the team to an English second-division championship in 1971 and appearing in 286 games. In 1974, Peter was transferred to the Stoke City club, where he made 110 appearances in goal. In 1977, he moved to the Nottingham Forest team.

At Nottingham Forest Peter enjoyed his greatest professional success. In his first season there, he led the club to the English Football League championship and then to victory in the European Cup, the most prestigious professional championship in European soccer. In the final game against FC Malmö of Sweden, Peter did not allow a goal, and Nottingham eked out a 1-0 win. In recognition of his accomplishments, Peter was chosen as player of the year by the English Professional Football Association.

The next year, Nottingham repeated its extraordinary success, winning the English League title again and then defending its European Cup championship. Once again, Peter's goalkeeping was a key element in the team's success, as Nottingham defeated Germany's SV Hamburg club 1-0 to retain its place as the top club in Europe.

Peter Shilton blocking a shot on goal. (Arthur Jones/Getty Images)

The Emerging Champion

Although Peter's professional career was impressive, his greatest accomplishments came on another level altogether. Most European countries have dozens of professional soccer teams and hundreds of players competing on the club level. Only the best of these players are selected to play for each country's national team and represent their country in international competitions such as the World Cup; selection to a national squad is an honor much like selection to an all-star team in baseball or basketball.

In 1971, at the age of twenty-one, Peter took over from Banks as the English national team's goalkeeper. Few players are able to maintain such a level of excellence for more than a few years; even such greats as Pelé of Brazil and Johan Cruyff of Holland, who played nearly into their forties, starred in their last few seasons on the club, not the national, level. Peter, though, was still a contender for the position of England's national goalkeeper as he neared his fortieth birthday.

Peter's extraordinary longevity as a world-class player was in large part a result of a rigorous training program. In 1988, one British sportswriter observed: "No one who has watched Shilton's rigorously punishing schedule in training will be surprised by the longevity of his career. In a ceaseless pursuit of perfection he stretches himself to the point of exhaustion."

Though outstandingly talented, he never prepared merely to rely on his natural ability and instinctive reactions. In 1988, at the age of thirty-nine, Peter was again named as England's number-one goalkeeper, and he announced that his crowning ambition was to represent England in the 1990 World Cup competition in Italy.

Continuing the Story

In 1990, Peter's dream came true. Peter was the first player past the age of forty to compete in a World Cup since Dino Zoff had played in goal for Italy in 1982. During the competition, Peter broke the all-time record of 119 international appearances held by Pat Jennings of Northern Ireland. Although England was eliminated in a tense semifinal game with West Germany, Peter could console himself with his record-breaking total of 125 international appearances. On his return to England, Peter announced his retirement from the national team, saying "I always wanted to finish at the top."

In 1991, Peter received the Order of the British Empire (OBE) for his contributions to English sport. In 2002, he was inducted into the English Football Hall of Fame.

Summary

Retirement is never an easy step for an elite athlete to take. Peter Shilton handled his retirement as well as he handled all the shots on goal he had faced in 125 appearances for England. Peter showed style, good sense, and excellent timing.

Scott A. G. M. Crawford

Additional Sources

Galvin, Robert, and Mark Bushell. *Football's Greatest Heroes: The National Football Museum's Hall of Fame.* London: Robson, 2005.

Shilton, Peter. *Goalkeeping in Action.* London: Stanley Paul, 1988.

_____. *Peter Shilton: The Autobiography.* London: Orion, 2005.

_____. *Shilton on Goalkeeping.* London: Headline, 1992.

Tomas, Jason, and Peter Shilton. *Peter Shilton, the Magnificent Obsession.* Kingswood, Tadworth, England: World's Work, 1982.

Career Highlights

Most international appearances for England, 125
Most Football League appearances, 1,005

Honors, Awards, and Milestones

1971	English Second Division champion
1978	English Professional Football Association player of the year
1978-79	English League Cup champion
1979-80	European Cup champion
1990	English Professional Football Association Merit Award
1991	Order of the British Empire
2002	Inducted into English Football Hall of Fame

Sissi

Born: June 2, 1967
Esplanada, Bahia, Brazil
Also known as: Sisleide do Amor Lima (full name)

Early Life

Sisleide do Amor Lima, or Sissi (pronounced "see-SEE"), was born on June 2, 1967, in Esplanada, Bahia, Brazil. One of seven children of a road-construction worker and his wife, Sissi grew up in Salvador, in northern Brazil. She became intensely interested in soccer at an early age, and even before she had a ball, she and her playmates practiced in the streets, using oranges, rolled up socks, and other substitutes.

Soccer is one of the most popular pastimes in Brazil, but the neighborhood boys sometimes excluded Sissi from street games on the basis of her gender. She was undaunted, however; she kept practicing, even tearing the heads from her dolls to use for soccer balls. Her parents finally bought her a ball, a rare possession among the children of her neighborhood, so the boys let her play with them. Many noticed her skills as a player. By the age of fourteen, she had joined Flamengo of Feira de Santana, a professional soccer team, and moved away from her parents' home.

The Road to Excellence

In 1985, four years after her professional debut, Sissi signed with another team and moved to Salvador. From 1989 to 1996, she focused on indoor soccer and played for the Corinthians, Bordon, Marvel, Eurosport, and Sapesp. She resumed playing field soccer with Saad of Campinas and eventually transferred to Palmeiras.

In 1988, Sissi joined the Brazilian national team. As she rose in fame, she acquired the shortened version of her name. In many ways, Sissi's career paralleled the acceptance of women's soccer, both within Brazil and internationally. Just as she was gaining national recognition, FIFA, soccer's international governing body, decided to organize a world championship series for women.

The first Women's World Cup was held in 1991, hosted by China; the second was held in 1995, hosted by Sweden. Although the Brazilian team finished ninth in both tournaments, it captured the enthusiasm of the Brazilian public, which had been focused largely on the male athletes until that time. In 1995, Sissi, who had been playing as a midfielder for the São Paulo women's team, was chosen for Brazil's South American championship team.

The Emerging Champion

After Brazil improved its status in women's soccer by winning

Sissi of Brazil kicking the ball past a German defender at the Olympic Games in 2000. (AP/Wide World Photos)

Honors, Awards, and Milestones

1995, 1998	South American soccer champion, with Brazilian team
1996	Bronze medal, Brazilian Olympic team
1999	MasterCard all-star team
	Adidas Golden Shoe, for top scorer of Women's World Cup (with Sun Wen)
	Silver Ball (Women's World Cup second-most valuable player)
2000	Brazilian Olympic team member
2001	Women's United Soccer Association (WUSA) first team
2002	WUSA Humanitarian of the Year Award
2002-03	WUSA first team
2005	Women's Premier Soccer League (WPSL) most valuable player
2008	FIFA ambassador

the bronze medal in the 1996 Olympics, Sissi began to attract international attention. In the Games, she had scored Brazil's goal in a 1-1 draw against Germany, thus allowing Brazil to advance to the semifinals and to the bronze. She played in every one of the Olympic matches. In 1998, Sissi again represented Brazil on its South American championship team and played brilliantly.

Although Sissi missed the U.S. Women's Cup in 1998 because of a knee injury, she became an international star at the 1999 Women's World Cup, hosted by the United States. She began the tournament with a hat trick, scoring 3 goals, in a 7-1 win over Mexico. Then, she scored both of the goals in a victory over Italy. In the quarterfinal meeting with Nigeria, the game went into 14 minutes of overtime, after Brazil lost its 3-0 lead. About 25 yards away from the Nigerian goal, Sissi took a free kick with her left foot and put the ball inside the left goalpost. With Sissi's dramatic kick, Brazil won 4-3 and advanced to the semifinal.

At the 1999 World Cup, Sissi tied Sun Wen of China as the highest scorer in the tournament, with a total of 7 goals and 3 assists. Brazil finished in third place, and the soccer-loving Brazilians were ecstatic. Sissi's coach, Wilson Oliveira Rica, hailed her as "the queen of soccer."

Continuing the Story

On the basis of her stellar performance in the World Cup, Sissi was selected by the FIFA technical study group as one of the sixteen members of the MasterCard all-star team of the 1999 FIFA Women's World Cup. On behalf of the all-stars, MasterCard donated $16,000 to FIFA's charity, the SOS Children's Villages, which provides homes for disadvantaged children around the world. The MasterCard all-star-team program, which was created in 1991, recognizes and honors top soccer players in this way. Sissi and Sun were awarded the Adidas Golden Shoe as the joint top scorers, and their trophies were presented at the FIFA world player of the year gala in Brussels, Belgium, on January 24, 2000.

On June 27, 2000, before 16,386 fans at the Foxboro Stadium in Massachusetts, Sissi played for Brazil in a game against the United States. The scoreless game was decided by a coin toss, but the fans were excited by the closely matched players. The event helped build interest in the forthcoming professional league, the Women's United Soccer Association (WUSA), which combined the best American and international players.

Meanwhile, Sissi continued to gain valuable experience, playing for Brazil in the 2000 Olympics in Sydney, Australia. Although Germany defeated Brazil 2-0 for the bronze medal, Sissi was recognized as one of the best players in the world. A month after the Olympics, she was selected for participation in the WUSA program to place foreign players in the league. On October 30, 2000, she and her Brazilian national teammate Katia, a forward, were assigned to one of the new WUSA teams, the Bay Area CyberRays, based in San Jose, California.

Sissi's success continued with the CyberRays, where she was teamed with rival Brandi Chastain. Sissi admitted to admiring Chastain and enjoyed playing with her. She said that learning English was more difficult than learning to play with all of her teammates. The CyberRays, with all of their talent, became a dominant team and won the inaugural WUSA Founders Cup Championship.

Because of lack of revenue, the WUSA folded after only three years of operation. This development did not affect Sissi adversely. She changed her focus and began putting her energies into other endeavors. Staying with her first love of soccer, Sissi became the head women's soccer coach at Las Positas College in Livermore, California. In addition, she coached at Clayton Valley High School in Concord, California.

Sissi also devoted time to charities. Her focus was the Contra Costa County adoptions and homeland unit. Through this organization, she helped people both adopt and foster children. Ever the role model, Sissi adopted two children, a girl and a boy.

Summary

Sissi helped to expand the Brazilian passion for soccer to include women players. Through talent and determination, she became one of the greatest women soccer players in the world. Her influence permeated women's soccer as many on the 2007 Brazilian team credited Sissi as an inspiration. Her reach went beyond soccer as she involved herself with charities.

Alice Myers, updated by P. Huston Ladner

Additional Sources

"Catch the Foreign Stars." *Sports Illustrated* 92, no. 25 (June 19, 2000): 69.

Rutledge, Rachel. *The Best of the Best in Soccer.* Brookfield, Conn.: Millbrook Press, 1999.

Stewart, Barbara, and Helen Stoumbos. *Women's Soccer: The Passionate Game.* Vancouver, B.C.: Greystone Books, 2003.

Alfredo di Stefano

Born: July 4, 1926
Buenos Aires, Argentina
Also known as: Alfredo di Stefano Laulhé (full name)

Early Life
Alfredo di Stefano Laulhé was born on July 4, 1926, in Buenos Aires, Argentina. His parents were both of Italian descent, and his father had played professional soccer. Alfredo was born and raised in a working-class section of Buenos Aires. Like most Argentine boys he loved playing soccer, and he spent hours with a ball at his feet, practicing and perfecting his skills. In addition to soccer, he enjoyed running in cross-country races. These trials of strength and endurance greatly enhanced Alfredo's stamina, which was always a trademark of his soccer game.

The Road to Excellence
As Alfredo entered his teens, it became increasingly obvious that he was going to be an outstanding soccer player. Not only did he possess the intricate skills necessary for good ball control and distribution, but also he had great strength, which meant he was able to use his talent even in the most physically demanding games.

Much to the delight of his family, in 1942, Alfredo was signed by River Plate, a famous club from Buenos Aires. After a two-year apprenticeship in which he further developed his all-around skills, Alfredo made his debut for the River Plate first team in 1944.

At the time, Alfredo could not establish himself on the River Plate team, although he was recognized as a tremendous prospect. In order for Alfredo to gain regular first-team experience, he was loaned to the Huracan club for a year in 1945. With Huracan his career really took off. Alfredo scored 50 goals in sixty-six games and returned to River Plate with even greater feats expected of him.

Alfredo lived up to his billing. He displaced the legendary center-forward Adolfo Pedernera on the River Plate team and established himself as the most consistent goal scorer in Argentine soccer. Alfredo's performances were so outstanding that it was just a matter of time before he was selected for the Argentine national team. Consequently, in 1947, he played the first of his seven games for the blue and white of Argentina.

The Emerging Champion
By his early twenties, Alfredo had established himself as one of the brightest young stars of South American soccer. However, he was soon tempted to leave his native country. The Colombian soccer league had broken away from the international governing body of soccer and was offering huge salaries. In 1949, Alfredo joined the mass exodus of Argentine soccer stars when he joined the Colombian club Millonarios de Bogota.

With Millonarios, Alfredo played on a team almost exclusively made up of fellow Argentineans. In Colombia, he matured into a superlative player and dominated the league. In his four years at Millonarios, he made 292 appearances and scored a staggering 259 goals. Alfredo led the team to two league titles and was even chosen on four occasions for the Colombian national team.

Alfredo was the most influential player in all of South America. His incredible exploits soon came to the envious attention of Santiago Bernabeu, the owner of the Spanish soccer team Real Madrid. When Alfredo eventually signed with Real Madrid in 1953, Bernabeu stated that the "White Arrow" had transformed the face of European soccer with one stroke of his pen.

As the Real Madrid captain, Alfredo helped the club achieve successes that even its most loyal sup-

---

Career Highlights

European Cup all-time leading scorer (49 goals)
42 international appearances for Argentina, Colombia, and Spain

Honors, Awards, and Milestones

1956-60	European Cup champion
1957, 1959	European player of the year (Ballon d'Or)
1960	Intercontinental Cup champion

porter would have thought impossible. With Alfredo playing as a deep-lying center-forward, Real Madrid won the European Cup five consecutive times beginning in 1956. Alfredo was at the heart of these triumphs, which established Real Madrid as one of the greatest soccer teams of all time. He was a dominant captain who led by example; he could dribble, tackle, head, and pass the ball. His tactical awareness was superb, and he had a tenacious attitude on the field. All in all, Alfredo was a complete player.

Alfredo's greatest triumph came in the 1960 European Cup Final. Playing in Glasgow in front of 135,000 fans, Alfredo inspired Real to a 7-3 victory over the West German club Eintracht Frankfurt. In one of the most breathtaking displays ever, Alfredo scored a hat trick—3 goals in one game—and mesmerized the crowd with his never-ending stamina and superb skills.

Continuing the Story

Between 1953 and 1964, Alfredo played 624 times for Real and scored 405 goals. He was even selected for the Spanish national team after he became a Spanish citizen. He played thirty-one games for his adopted country and scored 23 goals.

Despite Alfredo's great ability, there was a price to pay for such single-minded commitment to winning. Alfredo was never hesitant about criticizing mistakes made by inferior teammates. On the soccer field Alfredo had to be the leader, and everyone else had to follow him. Inevitably, this caused conflict with some of the other great players on the Real team. Didí, the brilliant Brazilian, and Raymond Kopa, the French superstar, were forced to leave Real Madrid in order to escape Alfredo's domineering personality.

Having led Real Madrid for more than a decade, in 1964, Alfredo moved to Español, where he spent the last two seasons of his illustrious career. After scoring 19 goals in eighty-one games for Español, Alfredo, nearing forty, retired as a player in 1966.

Alfredo moved into soccer coaching and management. He enjoyed relatively successful spells in Argentina, Spain, and Portugal. At one time, he was even in charge of his beloved Real Madrid. However, Alfredo's managerial career never approached the kind of success he achieved as a player. His uncompromising attitude, as well as a tendency to expect too much from those less gifted than himself, often made Alfredo unpopular with his playing staff. Frequently, as a manager, Alfredo had difficulty motivating players as he had done when he was orchestrating the team as a player.

Summary

Alfredo di Stefano was one of the greats of soccer. His technical brilliance and endless stamina distanced him from all but the best. What made Alfredo different from many gifted players was his single-minded attitude toward winning. He was determined to succeed, and this total commitment was communicated to his teammates. Not only was Alfredo one of the best players ever to play the game, but he also inspired his Real Madrid players to become one of the best club teams of all time.

David L. Andrews

Additional Sources

Ball, Phil. *Morbo: The Story of Spanish Football.* London: When Saturday Comes Books, 2003.

Radnedge, Keir. *Fifty Years of the European Cup and Champions League: Featuring Interviews with Sir Bobby Robson, Alfredo di Stefano, Eusébio, Franz Beckenbauer, Ian Rush, Paolo Maldini, Zinedine Zidane.* London: Carlton, 2007.

Witzig, Richard. *The Global Art of Soccer.* New Orleans, La.: CusiBoy, 2006.

Sun Wen

Born: April 6, 1973
Shanghai, China

Early Life
Sun Wen was born on April 6, 1973, in Shanghai, China. When she was a child, it was not culturally popular or acceptable for a girl to play soccer or any team sport. However, her father, Sun Zhong Gao, encouraged her to start playing soccer when she was ten years old. An avid soccer fan and recreational player himself, Wen's father took Wen to try out for a local soccer team at a children's sports center in Shanghai. At the age of thirteen, Wen began standard training.

China's Sun Wen advancing the ball at the Women's World Cup in 2003. (Jeff Gross/Getty Images)

The Road to Excellence
While involved in regular soccer training, Wen continued her studies and earned a degree in languages, specializing in Mandarin. In 1990, she made her first international appearance and quickly earned a reputation as a gifted forward who could create scoring opportunities, both for herself and for her teammates.

The Emerging Champion
Wen scored twice in China's semifinal game at the 1995 FIFA Women's World Cup. In the 1996 Olympics, she helped China earn the silver medal. She scored her team's only goal in the 2-1 loss to the host Americans. In the first half of that game, she received a pass from Zhou Hua and sent the ball over and past the American goalie, Briana Scurry.

Continuing the Story
Wen scored 2 goals in the first six minutes of the game against Taiwan in the semifinals of the tenth Asian Games, the tournament that qualified China to play in the 1999 FIFA Women's World Cup. During this World Cup, held in the United States in June and July, 1999, Wen emerged as the individual most highly rated by 150 accredited journal' She won the Adidas Golden Ball Award as th player and shared the Adidas Golden Shoe joint top scorer with Brazilian Sissi. In in with the press in 1999, Wen spoke of h some of which had been published in n She was also featured in advertisemen' can television.

In February, 2000, major Americ panies, women soccer stars, and ind formed the Women's United S (WUSA), the world's first wo soccer league. In the meantim distinguish herself in the 2000 she was injured during a ga 2000 Summer Olympics i scored 4 goals and won the

On November 29, 2 World Cup Chinese soc Ailing, goalkeeper Ga

Major Championships

Year	Competition	Place
1991	Women's World Cup	5th
1992	Olympic Games	Gold
1993	World Championships	1st
1994	World Goodwill Games	1st
1995	Women's World Cup	4th
1996	Olympic Games	Silver
1998	Goodwill Games	2d
	Asian Games	1st
1999	Women's World Cup	2d
	Chinese Women's Super Cup with Shanghai team	1st
2003	Women's World Cup	5th
2006	Asian Football Confederation (AFC) Women's Championship	1st

Lirong and Fan Yunjie—signed with the WUSA. With franchises in Atlanta, Boston, North Carolina, New York, Philadelphia, San Diego, the San Francisco Bay Area, and Washington, D.C., the league's inaugural season began in April, 2001. Wen joined the Atlanta Beat. In 2002, FIFA presented its woman player of the century award to Wen and American Michelle Akers.

In September, 2003, WUSA suspended operations, and Wen retired from soccer. She studied international relations at the prestigious Fudan University in her hometown of Shanghai. She also worked as a journalist. On December 15, 2005, she returned to play soccer with the Chinese women's team. In 2006, after the team won the Asian Football Confederation women's championship, Wen retired again, because of knee injuries.

Summary

With her excellence in soccer, Sun Wen contributed to increasing national popular support for the sport in China, where she attained legendary status and fame. Through her interest in popular culture and her awe-inspiring athletic skill, she made substantial contributions to international goodwill. She was actively involved in four Olympics. She competed in the 1996 and 2000 Games. Wen was part of the torch relay for the 2004 Athens Olympics, and she reported on the Games for a Shanghai newspaper. After her retirement from the Chinese national team, she worked with the International Olympic Committee. During the 2008 Beijing Olympics, she was part of the Shanghai local organization committee, which assisted FIFA. In May, 2008, Wen was the first to carry the torch in its relay in Shanghai. She also served as a soccer technical official at the Beijing Olympics.

Alice Myers

Additional Sources

Jiang Xueqin. "Olympics: China, Ahead of the Field." *Asiaweek*, September 6, 2000, 1.

Springer, Shira. "China's Winning Ways: National Women's Soccer Team Follows an Unforgiving Daily Schedule in Pursuit of First World Cup Title." *Boston Globe*, July 4, 1999.

Stewart, Barbara. *Women's Soccer: The Passionate Game*. Vancouver, B.C.: Greystone Books, 2004.

"Sun Wen." *Current Biography* 62, no. 4 (April, 2001): 79-83.

Williams, Jean. *A Beautiful Game: International Perspectives on Women's Football*. New York: Berg, 2007.

Zagoria, Adam. "Summer Job, with Benefits: Chinese Players Sign on to the WUSA for Good Money, Less Intense Training, and Oh, Yes, Fast Food." *Sports Illustrated Women* 4, no. 3 (May 1, 2002): 26.

Marco van Basten

Born: October 31, 1964
Utrecht, the Netherlands
Also known as: Marcel van Basten (full name)

Early Life

Marco van Basten was born on October 31, 1964, in the historic city of Utrecht in the Netherlands. As a boy, Marco excelled in most sports and wanted to become a famous gymnast. He never even dreamed of playing professional soccer. Even as a youngster, he revealed the confidence and ambition that later put him ahead of the competition. He once wrote on his school desk, "There's nobody better than me, apart from me."

The Road to Excellence

Marco's enjoyment of soccer led him to join the Dutch amateur soccer club Elinwijk. He still had little thought of making a living from the game, but this changed when his soccer skills, which were startlingly mature for a sixteen-year-old, came to the attention Ajax, a Dutch soccer club. At the time, Ajax, the foremost club in Holland, boasted the great Johan Cruyff as its star player. In 1981, Marco joined Ajax and made his first team debut that same year at the age of seventeen, when he came on late in a game as a substitute for Cruyff. In the light of later events, the moment was highly symbolic, for Marco was soon known as the "second Cruyff."

From the beginning of his career, Marco showed an almost uncanny ability to score goals from his position of center forward. Cruyff, though, saw in the young Marco more than merely a powerful and graceful goal scorer. He noticed that Marco had the same leadership qualities that he had possessed at a young age, and he took Ajax's new star under his wing. Marco remained grateful to Cruyff, his first mentor, whom he regarded as one of the finest soccer coaches in the world. Under Cruyff's guidance, Marco's ambitions were concentrated entirely on soccer. All thoughts of becoming a gymnast vanished.

The Emerging Champion

In 1983, Marco came to the attention of soccer fans throughout the world with his fine performances for his country in the World Youth Cup Finals in Mexico. For his club team Ajax, he was scoring goals at a prolific rate, almost one a game. Marco's all-around skill impressed people most; his game seemed to have no weak spots. He was fast, equally effective with left or right foot, good in the air, strong, and exciting to watch. Marco thrilled the fans; in addition to his all-around skills, he was a daring player, prepared to take risks and attempt the unexpected. "You mustn't be afraid to fall on your face," he once said. "If you don't dare to make mistakes, you'll never shine."

In 1986, Marco's fifth year with Ajax, Marco became team captain at the age of twenty-two. In that year, he also won the prestigious golden boot award

Marco van Basten traps the ball at the 1990 World Cup. (Bob Thomas/Getty Images)

for his feat of scoring 37 goals in twenty-six games during the 1985-1986 season. He followed this up with 31 goals the next season, when he led his team to victory in the European Cup Winners' Cup competition, scoring the winning goal against Locomotive Leipzig in the final.

The soccer world lay at Marco's feet. Many of Europe's top clubs attempted to sign him away from Ajax. In 1987, he was transferred to the Italian team Milan for a fee of $2.2 million. Milan beat out competition from Italy's Roma, Spain's Barcelona, and Germany's Werder Bremen to win Marco's services. At Milan, Marco joined up with another Dutchman, Ruud Gullit, who was also one of the finest players in Europe. The two formed a brilliantly effective partnership.

Continuing the Story

Marco was ready for his greatest achievements for both his club and his country, but one of his finest moments was preceded by a setback. During the European Championships finals in 1988, he was named only as a substitute in Holland's opening game against the Soviet Union. He was disappointed, but Cruyff told him to be patient. In the next game, Marco was included in the team from the outset, and he scored all 3 goals in Holland's 3-0 defeat of England. He scored again in the semifinal against West Germany. In the final, Marco scored a brilliant goal from a seemingly impossible angle, and this helped Holland to a 2-0 win over the Soviet Union. Marco said later he could hardly believe that he had scored such an extraordinary goal and would never be able to repeat it.

Marco also helped Milan to become what many experts regarded as the best club in the world. In the 1988-1989 season, he was Milan's top scorer. The following season, he was top scorer in the Italian League with 19 goals. He also scored twice in Milan's 4-0 win over Steaua Bucharest in the final of the European Champions Cup. The following year, in the same competition, he won another winner's medal after Milan's 1-0 win over Portugal's Benfica. Marco was top scorer in the Italian League again in 1991-1992 with 25 goals, and he would have repeated in 1992-1993 had it not been for an injury that kept him out of action for several months.

Marco's career had its disappointments. He did not reach his true form during the World Cup in Italy in 1990, and Holland was quickly eliminated. Nor did he excel during the 1992 European Championships, missing a penalty kick in the semifinals against Denmark. However, Marco's ambition and determination always enabled him to recover from setbacks. During the early 1990's, soccer fans throughout the world were increasingly of the opinion that Marco had overtaken Argentina's Diego Maradona as the world's greatest soccer player.

In 1993, Marco suffered severe ankle injuries that required surgery. After two years of rehabilitation in an effort to regain his form, he announced his retirement in 1995. After his retirement, Marco entered the coaching ranks, eventually taking over the Dutch national team in 2004. In 2008, he became the coach for Ajax, his former team.

Summary

Marco van Basten's stature in the soccer world stems from the fact that he was consistently one of the best players on the best team in the best league in the world. According to no less an authority than Cruyff, Marco's talent, skill, and unforgettable goals made him the world's greatest striker of his time.

Bryan Aubrey

Additional Sources

Hunt, Chris. *The Complete Book of Soccer.* Buffalo, N.Y.: Firefly Books, 2006.

Radnedge, Keir, and Gary Lineker. *The Ultimate Encyclopedia of Soccer: The Definitive Illustrated Guide to World Soccer.* London: Carlton Books, 2004.

Career Highlights

58 international appearances for Holland
24 international goals

Honors, Awards, and Milestones

1986	Golden Boot Award
1988	Italian Super Cup champion
1988-89, 1992-94	European player of the year (Ballon d'Or)
1989-90, 1994	European Super Cup champion
	European Cup champion
1989, 1992-93	Italian League champion
1990	World Club Cup champion
1992	World player of the year

Abby Wambach

Born: June 2, 1980
Pittsford, New York

Early Life

Abby Wambach grew up in the great soccer area of Rochester, New York, the youngest of seven children; she had four older brothers. She started playing the game of soccer at the age of four years old. Because she showed her talent early, she was encouraged to participate in the boys' league rather than the girls' league. Abby played both soccer and basketball at Our Lady of Mercy High School but chose to focus on soccer in college. She was named the 1997 high school soccer player of the year.

The Road to Excellence

Abby earned a scholarship at the University of Florida and played there from 1998 to 2001. She was a four-year selection to the all-American team and Southeastern Conference player of the year twice. In her senior year, her college team made it to the semifinals of the 2001 National Collegiate Athletic Association tournament. In addition, she set records for goals, with 96; assists, with 49; points, with 241; game-winning goals, with 24; and the number of 3-goal games, with 10. Her senior year, Abby was a finalist for the Hermann Trophy, honoring the best college soccer player, and the Missouri Athletic Club player of the year award.

After graduation in 2001, under-twenty-one national team coach Jerry Smith told Abby she had the abilities to make the national team with hard work and determination. She made the national team that year and played her first games at the Nike U.S. Women's Cup. In 2002, Abby was chosen second overall in the Women's United Soccer Association (WUSA) draft by the Washington Freedom. Abby was honored with the rookie of the year selection. In 2003, the franchise won the league championship, the Founders Cup. The combination of Abby and Mia Hamm was too powerful for the teams in the WUSA. The players combined for 66 points. Abby had 33 points, including 13 goals and 7 assists.

The Emerging Champion

April Heinrichs, the U.S. national team coach, recognized the great combination of Hamm and Abby during the 2003 WUSA season. As a result, Abby started all five 2003 World Cup games. She was the leading scorer for the U.S. team with 3 goals, one of which was the game win-

Abby Wambach celebrating after scoring for Team USA in a 2007 Women's World Cup game. (Alvin Chan/Reuters/Landov)

ner against Norway in the tournament's quarter-finals. In the 2004 Olympic Games held in Athens, Greece, Abby was the leading scorer for the U.S. team with 4 goals. She scored the winning goal in the gold-medal game versus Brazil. For her efforts in 2003 and 2004, Abby was the named the 2004 U.S. player of the year.

In 2007, just prior to the World Cup, Abby finished fourth in the voting for FIFA women's world player of the year. She was a dominant force at the 2007 World Cup held in China. The team came in third place, and, individually, Abby scored the second most goals in the tournament. Abby led the U.S. team with 17 goals during the calendar year. The number of matches it took her to reach 50 goals was second only to Michelle Akers. In addition, as of 2008, Abby had 86 goals in 105 international contests.

Continuing the Story

As the team prepared for the 2008 Olympic Games in Beijing, China, Abby continued to be a force on the national level. After the 2007 World Cup, controversy arose over decisions made by Coach Greg Ryan. As a result, his contract was not renewed. A new era for U.S. women's soccer began with the appointment of national team coach Pia Sundhage, considered to be one of the best coaches in the world. Preparing for the Olympics at the Algarve Cup in Portugal, the U.S. Team beat China 4-0, the largest margin ever for the U.S. team over China. Abby scored one of the goals and continued to be a goal leader for the U.S. Team. However, she broke her left leg in the final pre-Olympics game and did not play at all in Beijing, where the U.S. team won another gold medal.

Summary

Abby Wambach was considered to be one of the most dangerous strikers in the world. She grew up as a talented soccer and basketball athlete. She earned all-American honors as a college soccer player at the University of Florida. Upon graduation, she was drafted in the WUSA Professional Women's Soccer League, playing for the Washington Freedom alongside Mia Hamm. At the 2007 Women's World Cup in China, Abby's performance was dominant, drawing comparisons to Akers's contribution in the 1991 Women's World Cup.

Shawn Ladda

Additional Sources

Bechtel, Mark. "The Mouth That Scored." *Sports Illustrated* 107, no. 13 (October 1, 2007): 64.

Orr, Tamra. *No Hands Allowed: Abby Wambach*. Hockessin, Del.: Mitchell Lane, 2008.

Shea, Therese. *Soccer Stars*. New York: Children's Press, 2007.

WUSA Statistics

Year	GP	GS	Min.	G	Ast.	Pts.
2002	19	19	1,689	10	10	30
2003	18	18	1,620	13	7	33
Totals	37	37	3,309	23	17	63

Notes: GP = games played; GS = games started; Min. = minutes played; G = goals; Ast. = assists; Pts. = points

National Team Statistics

Year	GP	GS	Min.	G	Ast.	Pts.
2001	1	0	15	0	0	0
2002	7	4	355	5	4	14
2003	14	9	867	9	0	18
2004	33	26	2,309	31	13	75
2005	8	8	659	4	5	13
2006	21	20	1,848	17	8	42
2007	21	20	1,717	20	4	44
2008	20	19	1,642	13	9	35
Totals	125	106	9,412	99	43	241

Notes: GP = games played; GS = games started; Min. = minutes played; G = goals; Ast. = assists; Pts. = points

Billy Wright

Born: February 6, 1924
Ironbridge, England
Died: September 3, 1994
London, England
Also known as: William Ambrose Wright (full name); the Ironbridge Rocket

Early Life
William Ambrose Wright was born on February 6, 1924, in Ironbridge in the English Midlands, twenty miles from Wolverhampton. As a schoolboy, he was a fan of the London soccer team Arsenal, the leading English team in the 1930's.

Billy always wanted to become a professional soccer player, even though he was slightly built and did not excel at the game. However, Norman Simpson, his sports master at Madely Senior School, took note of his potential. In 1937, when Billy was only thirteen, Simpson wrote to the famous Wolverhampton Wanderers Football Club, nicknamed the "Wolves," to ask if Wright could be given a job on the grounds staff. Billy's father, a worker at the local iron foundry, would have preferred Billy to have joined Aston Villa, another famous Midlands club. Billy's mother, however, was happy with the choice of the Wolves, and as soon as Billy had completed his schooling, he set off for Wolverhampton.

The Road to Excellence
At Wolverhampton, Billy came under the influence of the team manager Major Frank Buckley, a stern disciplinarian who put Billy to work doing routine chores. Billy respected Buckley and was bitterly disappointed the next year when Buckley told him he was too small to make the grade as a player and that Buckley was sending him home. Nevertheless, Buckley reversed his decision when the groundsman told him how hardworking and useful Billy was.

By 1939, Billy had played center-forward for the Wolves' "B" team and had made his first-team debut at outside-right. He signed as a professional at the age of seventeen in 1941. After this he settled down as a halfback, the position he was to occupy for the rest of his career.

In the early stages of Billy's career he was indebted to Frank Broome, one of his colleagues on the Wolves team. Broome was a seasoned international forward who taught Billy how to place passes and take up the correct position.

In May, 1942, Billy suffered the worst setback of his career when he broke his ankle during the semifinal of the League War Cup. The injury was bad, and Buckley and the medical specialists feared it would finish Billy's career—almost before it had begun. Billy remained determined during his recovery, however, and several months later he returned to the Wolves as fit as ever.

The Emerging Champion
In 1947, Billy made his first appearance for England's national team against Belgium at Wembley Stadium in London. Soon Billy was captaining the Wolves team, and in 1949, he led them to victory in the Football Association Cup final against Leicester City. In the same year, he became captain of England.

Billy's game was outstanding for its consistency. He rarely had a bad match. He was fast and had strong tackling ability. Former England manager Ron Greenwood said that Billy was one of the best ball winners of his era. However, if Billy were beaten in a tackle, he was extremely quick to recover. He was also formidable in the air, since he was usually able to outjump opposing forwards, most of whom were several inches taller than Billy, who stood 5 feet 8 inches.

Billy was a steady and determined player rather than a flamboyant one. He was not an individualist but a team player whose style could be integrated easily into that of the rest of the team. He was not known for his forays upfield to support the attack but for solid defensive work. Reluctant to take risks, he put safety first.

As Billy's skills and reputation grew, he learned a great deal from Stan Cullis, who took over from Buckley as the Wolves' manager in 1949. Cullis was a former center-half for the Wolves and for England, and he gave Billy the benefit of his knowledge about tactics and captaincy.

> **Career Highlights**
>
> 90 times national team captain (world record)
> 105 international appearances for England
>
> **Honors, Awards, and Milestones**
>
> | | |
> |---|---|
> | 1949 | English Football Association Cup champion |
> | 1952 | English Footballer of the Year |
> | 1954, 1958-59 | English League champion |
> | 1959 | Commander of the British Empire |
> | 2002 | Inducted into English Football Hall of Fame |

Continuing the Story

In 1952, Billy won the English footballer of the year award, a prelude to seven years of almost unbroken success. The Wolves became one of the glamour teams of the 1950's, and Billy captained them to League championships in 1954, 1958, and 1959. He also helped the Wolves to some famous victories over some of the best European teams, including Moscow Spartak, Honved of Hungary, and Spain's Real Madrid.

From 1951 to 1959, Billy played 70 consecutive matches for England, a record. He was also the first man to play one hundred times for England, most of them as captain. Billy represented England in three World Cup competitions: in Brazil in 1950, Switzerland in 1954, and Sweden in 1958. During the World Cup in 1954, he switched positions from wing-half to center-half, and it is generally thought that this move extended his playing career. Playing in the center of the field meant that he did not have to cover as much ground as he had done at wing-half.

Billy was renowned for his sportsmanship and sense of fair play. He rarely showed anger, and he never argued with a referee over a decision. His loyalty to his club and his country won for him the respect and admiration of the British public. Even when he was well into his thirties, he retained his boyish enthusiasm for the game. Many younger players were thankful for his kindness in helping them through their first big matches.

In 1959, Billy retired from the game and was made a Commander of the British Empire (C.B.E.) by Queen Elizabeth II. The award honored his outstanding contribution to English soccer.

For a brief period in the mid-1960's, Billy served as the manager of the Arsenal Football Club in London. He did not achieve the same success as a manager that he had as a player. Some years later, he became a successful television executive. In 2002, he was inducted posthumously into the English Football Hall of Fame.

Summary

Billy Wright was one of the finest and most popular players England has produced. An honest and straightforward man, both on the field and off, he was dedicated to his craft. His skill and reliability made him the defensive rock around which the Wolves and England built their teams in the 1950's.

Bryan Aubrey

Additional Sources

Cox, Richard William, Dave Russell, and Wray Vamplew. *Encyclopedia of British Football*. Portland, Oreg.: F. Cass, 2002.

Douglas, Geoffrey. *The Game of Their Lives*. New York: HarperCollins, 2005.

Giller, Norman. *Billy Wright: A Hero for All Seasons*. London: Robson, 2002.

Wright, Billy. *Captain of England*. London: Stanley Paul, 1950.

_____. *Football Is My Passport*. London: Stanley Paul, 1957.

Eric Wynalda

Born: June 9, 1969
Fullerton, California

Early Life

Eric Wynalda was born on June 9, 1969, in Fullerton, California. He grew up in Westlake Village, California, and excelled at soccer at an early age. In fact, one season in children's soccer, Eric scored more goals than the entire rest of the division in which his team played. During high school, Eric continued to excel. Playing at Westlake Village High School, Eric was elected three times to California's all-state high school team.

After high school, Eric chose to attend and play soccer at San Diego State University. During his three seasons with San Diego State, he amassed 34 goals and 25 assists. In Eric's freshman season, the team advanced to the NCAA men's soccer championship game. However, it lost to Clemson University and did not return to the championship game during Eric's tenure.

The Road to Excellence

Following Eric's junior year at San Diego State University, Eric chose to sign a professional contract with the United States Soccer Federation (USSF). At this time, in 1990, Eric had the dubious honor as the first U.S. soccer player to get a red card in World Cup play. He finished his first year with the U.S. national team with 5 goals in eighteen games. Soon after the World Cup, Eric was loaned by the USSF to play for the San Francisco Bay Blackhawks. During his time with the Blackhawks, Eric was focused mostly on playing with the U.S. national team. However, in 1992, that ended when he was dismissed from the team for elbowing a teammate in the face. Eric's temper always put a strain on his career, and it continued to do so. Soon after his dismissal from the U.S. national team, Eric was kicked off the Blackhawks for constantly arguing with the coach, Laurie Calloway.

With no interest coming from any team in the United States, Eric decided to play in Europe. He made his desires known, and in August of 1992, the USSF loaned him to the Bundesliga club Saarbrücken in Germany for $45,000. In playing for Saarbrücken, Eric became the first American-born player to ever play in Germany's top league. He scored 8 goals in the first part of the season, prompting Saarbrücken to purchase Eric's $405,000 contract. During the 1993-1994 season, Eric scored 12 goals, and his contract was purchased by the Ger-

Eric Wynalda playing in a 1993 game for Team USA. (David Leah/Allsport/Getty Images)

man club VFL Bochum for $850,000. Eric did not fare as well with Bochum and was openly criticized by his coach. He was suspended from the team and was without a home in the soccer world once again.

The Emerging Champion

In 1996, Eric left Germany and returned to the United States, signing with fledgling Major League Soccer (MLS). To ensure balance, MLS evenly distributed star players throughout the organization. The league sent Eric to the San Jose Clash, and on April 6, 1996, Eric scored the first goal in MLS history. After a stellar 1996 season, Eric was named U.S. soccer athlete of the year. For the remainder of his MLS career, he moved from team to team and constantly battled injuries.

While Eric's starring role in MLS was relatively short-lived, Eric was a mainstay on the U.S. national soccer team. He played in his first national-team game in Costa Rica in 1990. He earned a red card at the 1990 World Cup. The 1994 World Cup was immensely important to U.S. soccer. The world soccer community had scoffed when the United States was chosen to host the World Cup. The sport was, in fact, not nearly as popular among adults in the United States as it was with people in the rest of the world. However, both the U.S. team and the nation as whole impressed the international community. The 1994 World Cup set records for total and average attendance. Eric scored on a free kick to tie Switzerland in an opening-round game, and the U.S. team advanced to the knockout round for the first time since World War II.

Honors, Awards, and Milestones

1992, 1996	U.S. Soccer Athlete of the Year
1996	Scored first goal ever in Major League Soccer history
2000	Honda U.S. soccer player of the 1990's
2004	Inducted into National Soccer Hall of Fame

Continuing the Story

In 1998, Eric became one of four U.S. players in history to play in three World Cups. However, after the success of 1994, the 1998 World Cup was a great disappointment for the U.S. team. It did not win a game and finished thirty-second out of thirty-two teams. The performance was a great setback that ushered in a new generation of American players. However, Eric and his generation of American soccer players had helped renew interest in the sport in the United States.

Summary

Eric Wynalda was one of four Americans to play in three World Cups. He also scored the first goal in MLS history. Until his record was broken by Landon Donovan, he was the U.S. national team's all-time leader in goals scored, with 33. In 2004, he was elected to the National Soccer Hall of Fame.

Theodore Shields

MLS Statistics

Season	GP	GS	Min.	G	Ast.	Pts.
1996	27	26	2,326	10	13	33
1997	14	9	923	5	11	21
1998	16	16	1,424	6	5	17
1999	6	6	487	2	1	5
2000	11	6	653	1	2	4
2001	24	13	1,349	10	5	25
Totals	**98**	**76**	**7,162**	**34**	**37**	**105**

Notes: GP = games played; GS = games started; Min. = minutes played; G = goals; Ast. = assists; Pts. = points

Additional Sources

Bamberger, Michael. "High and Mighty: Eric Wynalda, Top Scorer for the U.S. Team, Has Toned Down His Act but Raised His Game." *Sports Illustrated* 85, no. 22 (1996): 50.

Barron, David. "Wynalda Weighs in on MLS Cup Matchup." *Houston Chronicle*, November 10, 2006, p. 2.

Marchand, Andrew. "Five Questions for Eric Wynalda." *New York Post*, July 7, 2006, p. 58.

Lev Yashin

Born: October 22, 1929
Moscow, Soviet Union (now in Russia)
Died: March 20, 1990
Moscow, Soviet Union (now in Russia)
Also known as: Lev Ivanovich Yashin (full name); Black Panther; Octopus

Early Life

Lev Ivanovich Yashin was born in Moscow, Soviet Union (now in Russia), on October 22, 1929. His parents were factory workers, and the family lived in an older-style wooden communal apartment building on the outskirts of the city.

During the 1930's, life in Moscow was difficult. Most people were poor, and many were persecuted by the Soviet government. One of the few pleasant distractions from such concerns was participation in sports. Lev began his sports career by playing hockey with friends on a frozen pond near his home. From an early age, he earned a reputation as an uncanny goalkeeper. Working with limited equipment—often no mask, no body padding, and no glove—Lev did whatever he had to do to stop the puck from getting past him. He was of ordinary size, but with long legs and arms, and he was extremely wiry and quick. Because it seemed that he could always get an arm out to intercept any shot at the goal, his friends began to call him "Octopus."

The Road to Excellence

The distractive powers of sport proved even more important in Lev's life during World War II. In late 1941, Nazi armies had almost reached Moscow. They were repelled only by the most concerted effort, involving not only the military, in which Lev was still too young to serve, but also the civilian population of the city. Lev's parents were heroically engaged in the effort. Lev spent all his nonschool time playing on hockey teams sponsored by the Communist Youth Organization in order to entertain the struggling populace. In the summer, Lev and his friends turned their athletic skills to soccer, the sport in which Lev achieved lasting renown. By the time the war ended, Lev had become one of the most highly regarded goalkeepers in the Moscow youth leagues.

When Lev finished high school in 1946, he went to work in the factories, as his parents had before him. He stayed active in soccer, however, by playing with a number of Moscow soccer clubs. He then played on a Soviet army team while completing his two-year military service obligation. Returning to civilian life in 1950, Lev was accepted as a backup goalkeeper for Dynamo, one of Moscow's most popular world-class soccer teams. The remainder of Lev's career was associated with this great team.

In 1954, Dynamo's regular goalkeeper became ill, and Lev was called upon to play in important games. His performance assured his permanence in the position. His athletic dives to stop opposing kicks thrilled the huge crowds that attended Dynamo's games versus Moscow rivals Torpedo and Spartak and teams from other cities. In the next two years, no team scored more than 2 goals in a

Soviet goalkeeper Lev Yashin making a diving save during a World Cup semifinal game against West Germany in 1966. (Hulton Archive/Getty Images)

Career Highlights

78 international appearances for the Soviet Union

Honors, Awards, and Milestones

1954-55, 1957, 1959, 1963	Soviet League champion
1956	Gold medal, Olympic Games
1960	European Championship champion
1960, 1965-66	Soviet goalkeeper of the year
1963	European player of the year (Ballon d'Or)
1998	Inducted into International Football Hall of Champions

game against Lev's defense, and Dynamo was the national champion in 1954 and 1955. Lev's popularity soared, as did his standard of living in Soviet society. He was chosen to represent his country in the 1956 Olympic Games in Melbourne, Australia, and thanks largely to his sparkling defense, his team was victorious.

The Emerging Champion

In 1956, Soviet premier Nikita Khrushchev initiated a thaw in the restrictions on art, dance, music, and literature, a development that occasioned much hope among the Soviet people. With such a spirit of hope, Lev became a member of the Communist Party in 1957. Possibly, party membership played a role in his selection for the Soviet Union's World Cup team in 1958 and for the Soviet team that won the first European Championship in 1960. Lev's play in these tournaments was extraordinary, establishing him internationally as soccer's leading goalkeeper.

In the remaining years of the 1960's, Lev was active on two more Soviet Olympic teams—1960 in Rome and 1964 in Tokyo—and on two more World Cup teams. With the exception of a disconcertingly mediocre series of games in South America during the 1962 World Cup competition, Lev was continually remarkable in defense of the goal. Soccer analysts attributed his success to his amazingly quick reactions and his fine sense of anticipation, but Lev often said he was simply willing to sacrifice more of himself physically than others were in order to stop the ball.

Despite such sacrifice, Lev was rarely injured. Perhaps his luck was attributable to his schedule of almost constant play: daily practice, weekly games with Dynamo, and seventy-eight games with the Soviet national team. In 1963, he was the first goalkeeper named European player of the year and received soccer's coveted Ballon d'Or Award.

Continuing the Story

As he approached forty years of age, Lev gradually began to coach more than play with Dynamo. He also served as adviser to the Soviet national team. In 1972, he announced his official retirement as a soccer player. In that year, he graduated from the prestigious Moscow Higher Party School, a leadership training institution of the Communist Party's Central Committee. He became an administrator of the Dynamo team and a member of the Soviet Union's State Council on Physical Culture and Sports. In his eighteen years in this capacity, he was central in the Soviet Union's eventual formal recognition of the professional status of its athletes.

Before his death of stomach cancer on March 20, 1990, he approved a measure to give state pensions to world-class athletes whose competitive youth deprived them of other life skills in a society that gave them little reward except renown.

In June of 1990, two months after Lev's death in Moscow, the yearly Lev Yashin Invitational Soccer Tournament was instituted in his honor in Anchorage, Alaska. In 2003, the International Federation of Association Football (FIFA) named Lev the top goalkeeper of the twentieth century.

Summary

Lev Yashin's remarkable goalkeeping career helped change popular opinion about the importance of a goalie, making the goalkeeping position central to a team's success. Fans of soccer all over the world still recognize a "Yashin style" of play for goalkeepers. After his days as a player were over, Lev continued to devote his life to the advancement of sport.

Lee B. Croft

Additional Sources

Galeano, Eduardo H. *Soccer in Sun and Shadow.* Rev. ed. New York: Verso, 2003.

Hunt, Chris. *The Complete Book of Soccer.* Buffalo, N.Y.: Firefly Books, 2006.

Radnedge, Keir, and Gary Lineker. *The Ultimate Encyclopedia of Soccer: The Definitive Illustrated Guide to World Soccer.* London: Carlton Books, 2004.

Zinedine Zidane

Born: June 23, 1972
    Marseille, France
Also known as: Zinedine Yazid Zidane (full name); Zizou

Early Life

Zinedine Zidane was born June 23, 1972, in Marseille, a city on France's southern coast. Located across the Mediterranean Sea from Algeria, Marseille is home to many people of North African ancestry. Born to Algerian parents and raised without luxuries, Zinedine was much like other boys in his neighborhood. When it came to playing soccer, however, Zinedine distinguished himself.

Zinedine first played soccer in a plaza outside his house, developing his skills with his older brothers. At the age of nine, Zinedine joined his first organized team, soon winning the captain's armband. Two years later, he joined a more prestigious team, Septèmes-les-Vallons, where his skillful play earned him an invitation to try out for a regional team. While Zinedine was showcasing his skills for this team, a scout for the Cannes team of the French second division noticed him. Zinedine was fourteen, and joining Cannes meant moving to a city two hours from Marseille. Determined to become a professional soccer player, Zinedine joined Cannes in July, 1986.

The Road to Excellence

As did most European soccer clubs, Cannes fielded both a youth and a senior team. Arriving at Cannes, Zinedine joined the youth team, where he remained the following two years. However, the youth and senior teams trained together, allowing Zinedine to learn from senior players. On May 20, 1989, shortly before he turned seventeen years of age, Zinedine made his senior debut, coming on against Nantes in a first division game. He played one other senior match in the 1988-1989 season but none the following year. In the 1990-1991 season, Zinedine started regularly for the senior team, and on February 10, 1991, he scored his first professional goal. The 1991-1992 season was Zinedine's last for Cannes. In June, 1992, he was sold to Bordeaux for 3.5 million francs, approximately $700,000.

At Bordeaux, Zinedine developed into one of France's top players. In his first season, he scored 10 goals, which turned out to be the highest total of his career. Following his second season, he was named French young footballer of the year. In 1994, Zinedine made his debut for the French national team. Entering in the sixty-third minute of a match against the Czech Republic, he scored twice

French player Zinedine Zidane handling the ball in a World Cup contest in 1998. (Popperfoto/Getty Images)

in 2 minutes, earning France a 2-2 draw. Following his sensational debut, Zinedine was a player of international renown.

The Emerging Champion

In May, 1996, Zinedine was sold to Juventus, one of Italy's top teams. The transfer fee was 35 million francs, about $7 million, ten times what Bordeaux had paid Cannes. While at Juventus, Zinedine won two Italian championships and many important tournaments. At the end of 1997, he finished third in the voting for the Ballon d'Or, the award given to Europe's top soccer player. From 1996 to 2001, a magisterial Zinedine dominated Italy's Serie A. However, his greatest triumphs occurred in international matches.

The 1998 World Cup was held in France. Having helped his team into the final, Zinedine scored twice against Brazil, heading both goals. Emmanuel Petit added a third goal to give France a 3-0 victory. Following the tournament, Zinedine was a national hero, not just because he had helped France win the World Cup, but also because he symbolized a new, multicultural France. In 1998, Zinedine was named a knight of the French Legion of Honor, one of France's highest honors. He was also voted French footballer of the year, European footballer of the year, and FIFA world player of the year.

In 2000, France won the European Championship, soccer's second most important tournament. The victory represented the first time since 1974 that a nation had been simultaneously world and European champion. In July, 2001, Zinedine's status as the world's best player was confirmed when Real Madrid acquired him from Juventus for 76 million euros, approximately $66 million. The transfer fee was the largest ever paid.

Professional Statistics

Season	Team	Games Played	Goals
1989	Cannes	2	0
1990	Cannes	0	0
1991	Cannes	28	1
1992	Cannes	31	5
1993	Bordeaux	35	10
1994	Bordeaux	34	6
1995	Bordeaux	37	6
1996	Bordeaux	34	6
1997	Juventus	29	5
1998	Juventus	32	7
1999	Juventus	25	2
2000	Juventus	32	3
2001	Juventus	33	6
2002	Real Madrid	31	7
2003	Real Madrid	33	9
2004	Real Madrid	33	6
2005	Real Madrid	29	6
2006	Real Madrid	29	9
Totals		507	94

Honors, Awards, and Milestones

1994	French youth soccer player of the year
1997, 2001	Italian League best foreign soccer player of the year
1998	European soccer player of the year
	French Legion of Honor
1998, 2000, 2001	*Onze Mondial* European soccer player of the year
1998, 2000, 2003	FIFA world player of the year
1998, 2006	World Cup all-star
2000	UEFA European Championship player of the tournament
2001-03	UEFA Best XI
2002	UEFA Champions League most valuable player
2006	World Cup golden ball

Continuing the Story

In signing with Real Madrid, Zinedine joined Luis Figo, Raúl, and Roberto Carlos as *Galácticos* in Real Madrid's constellation of stars. Zinedine's first season at Real Madrid was his best. Having twice lost with Juventus in the Champions League final, Zinedine helped Real Madrid to win the 2002 final, lashing a miracle volley to beat Bayer Leverkusen 2-1. Less satisfying was Zinedine's 2002 World Cup. After injuring himself five days before the tournament began, he watched France lose its first two games. Finally able to play against Denmark, Zinedine was ineffective. France lost 2-0, exiting the tournament without having scored a goal.

In 2004, France again crashed out of an important tournament, losing to Greece in the quarterfinals of the European Championship. Six weeks later, Zinedine announced his retirement from international soccer, citing age and fatigue. He was thirty-two years old.

Zinedine's retirement from international soccer lasted one year. In August, 2005, concerned that France was in danger of missing the 2006 World Cup, Zinedine rejoined the team. Inspired by Zinedine's return, France qualified for the World Cup in Germany. On July 9, 2006, in extra-time of the World Cup Final, Zinedine was given a red card for headbutting Italian defender Marco Materazzi. The score at the time was 1-1, both Zinedine and Materazzi having scored. The match ended with Italy winning on penalty kicks, and Zinedine's ejection arguably cost his team the tournament.

Summary

Zinedine Zidane was one of the best players of his generation and one of the top players of all time. Zinedine's success was attributable to his ability to control the ball. Whether dribbling through a tangle of defenders, passing to a teammate on the opposite side the field, or shooting at the goal from a difficult angle, Zinedine guided the ball with uncanny precision. As a soccer player, Zinedine will be remembered for his wondrous feats, not his 2006 moment of madness. Zinedine was also important for the role he played in unifying a multicultural French population. An iconic figure on France's most successful team, Zinedine embodied all that France had gained through acceptance of diversity.

Matt Brillinger

Additional Sources

Ballard, John. *The Dictionary of World Football.* London: Boxtree, 1999.

Collie, Ashley Jude. *World of Soccer: A Complete Guide to the World's Most Popular Sport.* New York: Rosen, 2002.

Radhesh, V. K. S. *2002 World Cup Football Super Stars.* Anna Nagar, India: Sura Books, 2003.

Steve Zungul

Born: July 28, 1954
Split, Dalmatia, Yugoslavia (now in Croatia)
Also known as: Slaviša Žungu (full name); Lord of All Indoors; Mr. Inside

Early Life

Slaviša "Steve" Žungu was born on July 28, 1954, in the coastal city of Split in Dalmatia, Yugoslavia (now in Croatia). His father was a semiretired army instructor who was also a commercial fisherman. Steve's talent for soccer was evident when he was very young, and when he was eleven, a document was forged to give his age as fifteen so he could play in a youth tournament.

Sometimes Steve fished with his father on the Adriatic Sea from midnight until five in the morning. At school in the mornings he learned auto mechanics, but nothing replaced his love of soccer, to which he devoted his afternoons and evenings. When he was fifteen, he ran away from home to play in a soccer match. He was gone for a week, to the anger of his family. His mother locked him in his room and told him that there would be no more soccer, but he climbed down two stories on a rope and went to practice.

The Road to Excellence

When Steve was seventeen, he was signed by Hajduk Split, a team in Yugoslavia's first division. Yugoslavia was the only Eastern European country that permitted professional soccer, and Steve was soon making his mark in the game. He scored 250 goals in 350 games with Hajduk Split, helping them to three league championships in six years. In 1978, he was named by *France Football* magazine as one of the six best forwards in Europe. At the time, he was also the leading scorer for the Yugoslav national team.

In 1978, Steve was due to report for eighteen months of military service. He decided to leave Hajduk Split and travel to the United States. There he met Don Popovic, who was coach of the New York Arrows in the Major Indoor Soccer League (MISL), which was about to commence its first season. Popovic was also a Yugoslav and a former Hajduk Split player, and he offered Steve a chance to play in a few exhibition games. Steve jumped at the opportunity and quickly made an impact in a new type of soccer, very different from the outdoor game to which he was accustomed. The exhibition games led to a longer stay, and at the end of the 1978-1979 season, Steve had scored 43 goals in eighteen games. He was only two goals short of the league's scoring championship.

The Emerging Champion

Steve's phenomenal goal-scoring feats helped the Arrows to dominate MISL in its early years. Steve led the team to four successive championships, in 1979, 1980, 1981, and 1982. He became MISL's all-time leading scorer, with 419 goals and 222 assists. On one occasion he scored three times in 37 seconds. In 1980, he won the league's triple crown for most goals, assists, and points. He did it again in 1981-1982 and 1984-1985.

In addition to his immense natural ability, Steve owed his success to his constant practice and his will to win. He once told a reporter,

> I hate to lose; I hate to be beaten at anything. How I score goals I cannot tell you; it happens in a dream. It comes from God. But why is easy—I will not lose. It hurts me physically to be defeated.

Steve was a hard competitor; he knew that he might get rough treatment from the opposition, but when felled he simply got up and continued the game. In his goal scoring, he was just as lethal with either foot, and his positioning was almost perfect, which enabled him to take advantage of rebounds. Steve was a thinker, too. He once said to a young player that when a game was over it was not only the body but also the brain that should be tired.

Steve owed a lot of his success to Popovic, whom Steve regarded as the best coach in the game. The two outspoken men had a stormy relationship, but each had confidence in the other.

Steve loved his new home of New York, and the Arrows' fans took him to their hearts. He was known admiringly as the "Lord of All Indoors" and was once described as the Pelé of indoor soccer. "ZSHUN-gul, ZSHUN-gul" the crowd chanted when the Arrows needed a goal. The team strategy was simple: Get the ball to Steve and let him finish off the move with a goal.

During his years with the Arrows, Steve became a celebrity around New York. Some of the publicity concentrated on his fondness for fast cars and the New York nightlife. On the soccer field, however, he earned his glory.

Continuing the Story

In 1983, Steve was traded to the Golden Bay Earthquakes of the North American Soccer League (NASL). The move gave Steve a chance to play outdoor soccer for the first time in nearly five years. After a few months at Golden Bay, he teamed up again with Popovic, who was hired as coach.

The Golden Bay franchise soon folded, though, so Steve took his talents to the San Diego Sockers, one of the most formidable teams in the MISL. He made a typically dramatic impact, scoring five times in his first match in a 10-2 victory. He also helped the Sockers to the MISL championship in 1985.

After that success, Steve was traded to the Tacoma Stars, where he won his sixth MISL scoring title, in 1986. In 1988, Steve was back with San Diego, helping the team to win the championship for a record fifth time in 1989. The win was Steve's seventh championship. After helping the Sockers to repeat the feat in 1989-1990—although he played in only sixteen games—Steve announced his retirement. He retired with 652 goals in the MISL, a record at the time.

Career Highlights

MISL all-time high scorer (652 goals, 1,123 points)

Honors, Awards, and Milestones

1971, 1974-75	Yugoslavian League champion
1972-77	Yugoslavian League Cup champion
1975	Yugoslavian League Cup most valuable player
1979-82, 1985, 1986	MISL most valuable player
1979-82, 1985, 1989-90	MISL champion
1980, 1982, 1985	MISL Playoff most valuable player
	MISL Triple Crown winner
1984	NASL most valuable player

Summary

Steve Zungul was the most successful and celebrated player in the history of the MISL. His goal-scoring was prolific: He rarely missed a chance, and he had an almost uncanny knack of knowing in advance where the ball would be. "He's the Nureyev of soccer," said one soccer coach, referring to the great Russian ballet dancer. Like Rudolf Nureyev, Steve was a supreme artist in his chosen profession.

Bryan Aubrey

Additional Sources

Allaway, Roger, Colin Jose, and David Litterer. *The Encyclopedia of American Soccer History.* Lanham, Md.: Scarecrow Press, 2001.

"Faces of the World Cup." *The San Diego Union-Tribune*, May 30, 2002, p. D6.

Graham, Glenn P. "MISL at a Glance." *The Baltimore Sun*, October 4, 2002, p. D5.

Jose, Colin. *North American Soccer League Encyclopedia.* Haworth, N.J.: St. Johann Press, 2003.

Resources

Bibliography

Boxing

Blewett, Bert. *The A-Z of World Boxing: An Authoritative and Entertaining Compendium of the Fight Game from Its Origins to the Present Day.* Rev. ed. Parkwest, N.Y.: Robson Books, 2002.

Boddy, Kasia. *Boxing: A Cultural History.* London: Reaktion Books, 2008.

Bodner, Allen. *When Boxing Was a Jewish Sport.* Westport, Conn.: Praeger, 1997.

Dahlberg, Tim. *Fight Town: Las Vegas, the Boxing Capital of the World.* Las Vegas, Nev.: Stephens Press, 2007.

Dempsey, Jack, and Frank G. Menke. *How to Fight Tough.* Boulder, Colo.: Paladin Press, 2002.

Dumas, Andy. *Fit to Fight: Get in the Best Shape of Your Life with the Workouts of Professional Boxers.* New York: Skyhorse, 2008.

Duncan, John. *In the Red Corner: A Journey into Cuban Boxing.* London: Yellow Jersey, 2001.

Evans, Gavin. *Kings of the Ring: The History of Heavyweight Boxing.* London: Weidenfeld & Nicolson, 2005.

Evensen, Bruce J. *When Dempsey Fought Tunney: Heroes, Hokum, and Storytelling in the Jazz Age.* Knoxville: University of Tennessee Press, 1996.

Finger, David E. *Rocky Lives! Heavyweight Boxing Upsets of the 1990's.* Dulles, Va.: Potomac Books, 2006.

Fleischer, Nat, and Sam Andre. *An Illustrated History of Boxing.* 6th ed. New York: Citadel Press, 2001.

Hauser, Thomas. *Chaos, Courage, Corruption, and Glory: A Year in Boxing.* Toronto: Sport Classic Books, 2005.

———. *The View from Ringside: Inside the Tumultuous World of Boxing.* Toronto: SportClassic Books, 2004.

Hauser, Thomas, and Stephen Brunt. *The Italian Stallions: Heroes of Boxing's Glory Days.* Toronto: Sport Media, 2003.

Heller, Peter. *In This Corner . . . ! Forty-two World Champions Tell Their Stories.* 2d ed. New York: Da Capo Press, 1994.

Hietala, Thomas R. *The Fight of the Century: Jack Johnson, Joe Louis, and the Struggle for Racial Equality.* Armonk, N.Y.: M. E. Sharpe, 2004.

Hudson, David L., Jr., and Mike H. Fitzgerald, Jr. *Boxing's Most Wanted: The Top Ten Book of Champs, Chumps, and Punch-Drunk Palookas.* Washington, D.C.: Brassey's, 2004.

Kimball, George. *Leonard, Hagler, Hearns, Durán, and the Last Great Era of Boxing.* Ithaca, N.Y.: McBooks Press, 2008.

Liebling, A. J. *The Sweet Science.* Reprint. New York: North Point Press, 2004.

McIlvanney, Hugh. *The Hardest Game: McIlvanney on Boxing.* Chicago: Contemporary Books, 2001.

Mee, Bob. *Boxing: Heroes and Champions.* Edison, N.J.: Chartwell Books, 1997.

Mercante, Arthur, and Phil Guarnieri. *Inside the Ropes.* Ithaca, N.Y.: McBooks Press, 2006.

Montoya, Delilah, María Teresa Márquez, and C. Ondine Chavoya. *Women Boxers: The New Warriors.* Houston, Tex.: Arte Público Press, 2006.

Mullan, Harry. *Boxing: The Complete Illustrated Guide.* London: Carlton Books, 2003.

Mullan, Harry, and Bob Mee. *The Ultimate Encyclopedia of Boxing.* Rev. ed. London: Carlton, 2008.

Myler, Patrick. *A Century of Boxing Greats: Inside the Ring with the Hundred Best Fighters.* London: Robson Books, 1999.

Myler, Thomas. *The Sweet Science Goes Sour: How Scandal Brought Boxing to Its Knees.* Vancouver, B.C.: Greystone Books, 2006.

Patterson, Floyd, and Bert Randolph Sugar. *The International Boxing Hall of Fame's Basic Boxing Skills: A Step-by-Step Illustrated Introduction to the Sweet Science.* New York: Skyhorse, 2007.

Roberts, James, and Alexander Skutt. *The Boxing Register: International Boxing Hall of Fame Official Record Book.* Ithaca, N.Y.: McBooks Press, 2006.

Schulberg, Budd. *Ringside: A Treasury of Boxing Reportage.* Chicago: Ivan R. Dee, 2006.

———. *Sparring with Hemingway: And Other Legends of the Fight Game.* Chicago: Ivan R. Dee, 1995.

Schulman, Arlene. *The Prize Fighters: An Intimate Look at Champions and Contenders.* New York: Lyons and Burford, 1994.

Sekules, Kate. *The Boxer's Heart: How I Fell in Love with the Ring.* New York: Villard, 2000.

Silverman, Jeff, ed. *The Greatest Boxing Stories Ever Told: Thirty-six Incredible Tales from the Ring.* Guilford, Conn.: Globe Pequot Press, 2004.

Smith, Kevin. *Boston's Boxing Heritage: Prizefighting from 1882 to 1955.* Charleston, S.C.: Arcadia, 2002.

Somrack, Daniel. *Cuban Legends of Boxing.* Guilford, Conn.: The Globe Pequot Press, 2006.

Sugar, Bert Randolph. *Boxing's Greatest Fighters.* Guilford, Conn.: Lyons Press, 2006.

Suster, Gerald. *Lightning Strikes: The Lives and Times of Boxing's Lightweight Heroes.* London: Robson Books, 1994.

Todd, Gary. *Workouts from Boxing's Greatest Champs: Get in Shape with Muhammad Ali, Fernando Vargas, Roy Jones, Jr., and Other Legends.* Berkeley, Calif.: Ulysses Press, 2004.

Walsh, Peter. *Men of Steel: The Lives and Times of Boxing's Middleweight Champions.* London: Robson, 1993.

Soccer

Agnew, Paddy. *Forza Italia: The Fall and Rise of Italian Football.* London: Ebury Press, 2007.

Allaway, Roger, Colin Jose, and David Litterer. *The Encyclopedia of American Soccer History.* Lanham, Md.: Scarecrow Press, 2001.

Ball, Alan, and James Mossop. *Playing Extra Time.* London: Pan, 2005.

Ball, Phil. *Morbo: The Story of Spanish Football.* London: When Saturday Comes Books, 2003.

Ballard, John. *The Dictionary of World Football.* London: Boxtree, 1999.

Bauer, Gerhard. *New Soccer Techniques, Tactics, and Teamwork.* New York: Chrysalis, 2003.

Bellos, Alex. *Futebol: The Brazilian Way of Life.* New York: Bloomsbury USA, 2002.

Bremner, Billy. *Billy Bremner's Book of Soccer.* London: Pelham, 1974.

Caligiuri, Paul, and Dan Herbst. *High-Performance Soccer.* Champaign, Ill.: Human Kinetics, 1997.

Cantor, Andrés, and Daniel Arcucci. *Goooal! A Celebration of Soccer.* New York: Simon & Schuster, 1996.

Charlton, Bobby, and Melvyn Bragg. *The Rules of Association Football, 1863.* Oxford: Bodleian Library, 2006.

Clifford, Simon. *Play the Brazilian Way: The Secret Skills of the World's Greatest Footballers.* London: Boxtree, 1999.

Collie, Ashley Jude. *World of Soccer: A Complete Guide to the World's Most Popular Sport.* New York: Rosen, 2002.

Cox, Richard William, Dave Russell, and Wray Vamplew. *Encyclopedia of British Football.* Portland, Oreg.: F. Cass, 2002.

Cresswell, Peterjohn, and Simon Evans. *The Rough Guide to European Football: A Fans' Handbook.* London: Rough Guides, 2000.

Douglas, Geoffrey. *The Game of Their Lives.* New York: HarperCollins, 2005.

Fair, Lorrie, and Mark Gola. *Fair Game: A Complete Book of Soccer for Women.* Chicago: Contemporary Books, 2003.

Foer, Franklin. *How Soccer Explains the World: An Unlikely Theory of Globalization.* New York: HarperCollins, 2004.

Foot, John. *Calcio: A History of Italian Football.* London: Harper Perennial, 2007.

Galeano, Eduardo H. *Soccer in Sun and Shadow.* Rev. ed. New York: Verso, 2003.

Galvin, Robert, and Mark Bushell. *Football's Greatest Heroes: The National Football Museum's Hall of Fame.* London: Robson, 2005.

Goldblatt, David. *The Ball Is Round: A Global History of Soccer.* New York: Riverhead Books, 2008.

Hamm, Mia, with Aaron Heifetz. *Go for the Goal: A Champion's Guide to Winning in Soccer and Life.* New York: HarperCollins, 2000.

Hesse-Lichtenberger, Ulrich. *Tor! The Story of German Football.* London: When Saturday Comes Books, 2003.

Hornby, Hugh. *Soccer.* New York: Dorling Kindersley, 2005.

Hunt, Chris. *The Complete Book of Soccer.* New York: Firefly Books, 2008.

Hurst, Geoff. *World Champions.* London: Headline, 2006.

Jose, Colin. *North American Soccer League Encyclopedia.* Haworth, N.J.: St. Johann Press, 2003.

Kucey, Sam. *Even Pellerud on Coaching and Leadership in Women's Soccer.* Spring City, Pa.: Reedswain, 2005.

LaBlanc, Michael L., and Richard Henshaw. *The World Encyclopedia of Soccer.* Detroit: Gale Research, 1994.

Lineker, Gary. *The Definitive Guide to the World Cup with Gary Lineker.* London: EMP Sport, 2006.

_____. *Soccer.* New York: Dorling Kindersley, 2000.

Lineker, Gary, and Stan Hey. *Gary Lineker's Golden*

Boots: The World Cup's Greatest Strikers, 1930-1998. London: Hodder & Stoughton, 1998.

Longman, Jere. *The Girls of Summer: The U.S. Women's Soccer Team and How It Changed the World.* New York: HarperCollins, 2000.

Ludden, John. *Once upon a Time in Naples.* Manchester: Parrs Wood, 2005.

MacDonald, Tom. *The World Encyclopedia of Soccer: A Complete Guide to the Beautiful Game.* London: Arness, 2005.

Miller, Marla. *All-American Girls: The U.S. Women's National Soccer Team.* New York: Pocket Books, 1999.

Murphy, Alex, and Andrew Endlar. *The Official Illustrated History of Manchester United: All New—The Full Story and Complete Record, 1878-2006.* London: Orion, 2006.

Oller, Jan Paul. *The Cup of Death: Soccer-USA 1994.* Bloomington, Ind.: 1stBooks Library, 2000.

Page, Jason. *Ball Games: Soccer, Table Tennis, Handball, Hockey, Badminton, and Lots, Lots More.* Minneapolis: Lerner Sports, 2000.

Pellerud, Even, with Sam Kucey. *Coaching and Leadership in Women's Soccer.* Spring City, Pa.: Reedswain, 2005.

Radhesh, V. K. S. *2002 World Cup Football Super Stars.* Anna Nagar, India: Sura Books, 2003.

Radnedge, Keir. *The Complete Encyclopedia of Soccer.* Rev. ed. London: Carlton, 2007.

———. *Fifty Years of the European Cup and Champions League: Featuring Interviews with Sir Bobby Robson, Alfredo di Stefano, Eusébio, Franz Beckenbauer, Ian Rush, Paolo Maldini, Zinedine Zidane.* London: Carlton, 2007.

Ramsey, Alfred, and Kenneth Wheeler. *Soccer: The British Way.* London: Sportman's Book Club, 1965.

Reyna, Claudio, and Mike Woitalla. *More than Goals: The Journey from Backyard Games to World Cup Competition.* Champaign, Ill.: Human Kinetics, 2004.

Rote, Kyle, Jr. *Kyle Rote, Jr.'s Complete Book of Soccer.* New York: Simon & Schuster, 1988.

Rote, Kyle, Jr., and Ronald Patterson. *Beyond the Goal.* Waco, Tex.: Word Books, 1975.

Rote, Kyle, Jr., and Donn Risolo. *Wilson Guide to Soccer.* St. Paul, Minn.: Publication Partners, 1995.

Rutledge, Rachel. *The Best of the Best in Soccer.* Brookfield, Conn.: Millbrook Press, 1999.

Schoff, Jill Potvin. *Women's Soccer Scrapbook: The Ultimate Insider's Guide.* New York: Somerville House, 2000.

Shilton, Peter. *Goalkeeping in Action.* London: Stanley Paul, 1988.

Stewart, Barbara. *Women's Soccer: The Passionate Game.* Vancouver, B.C.: Greystone Books, 2004.

Stewart, Mark. *Soccer: A History of the World's Most Popular Game.* New York: Franklin Watts, 1998.

Williams, Jean. *A Beautiful Game: International Perspectives on Women's Football.* New York: Berg, 2007.

Williams, John, and Steven Hopkins. *The Miracle of Istanbul: Liverpool FC from Paisley to Benitez.* Edinburgh: Mainstream, 2005.

Witzig, Richard. *The Global Art of Soccer.* New Orleans, La.: CusiBoy, 2006.

Boxing and Soccer Resources on the World Wide Web

Sports sites on the World Wide Web offer rich sources of information on athletes, teams, leagues, and the various sports themselves. Through careful searching, one can find up-to-date news on almost every sport; schedules; detailed statistics; sports; biographies of athletes; histories of teams, leagues, and individual sports; and much more. Since the previous edition of *Great Athletes* was published in 2001, both the number and quality of sports Web sites offering unrestricted access have increased significantly, making it easier than ever before to find information. However, while finding information on the Web has grown easier, evaluating the reliability of the information one finds may be growing harder.

The vast majority of sports Web sites are maintained by fans and bloggers whose objectivity and accuracy can be difficult to judge. Even articles on sites such as Wikipedia may present problems. Wikipedia articles are often detailed, up to date, and accurate, but they are not fully vetted and can be altered at any time by any user. Search engines such as Google and Yahoo! are efficient tools for finding information on athletes quickly, but if they are used carelessly, they may direct users to unreliable sites. For this reason, it is generally wise to begin any Web search with a list of Web sites that are proven to be reliable.

The purpose of this list is to help guide readers to the best Web sources for boxing and soccer and to call attention to the variety of sites available online. Preference has been given to sites maintained by professional sports organizations, reputable news services, online magazines, halls of fame, and television networks, as well as other sites that provide accurate and unbiased information. However, a few blog sites are included to ensure coverage of subjects not well covered elsewhere, such as Asian boxing.

Most of the sites listed here can be found quickly by entering their names into an online search engine. If that approach does not work, one can simply type a URL (uniform resource locator) into the address line of a Web browser. Note that it is usually unnecessary to enter "http://" and that many sites can be found through more than a single URL. As still more sites are certain to emerge, it is advisable to use text searches to find new sites. Also, look for links to other sites on the pages that you visit.

Every site listed here was inspected and found to be working in January, 2009. Many of these sites offer links to merchandisers, but every effort has been made to avoid sites that serve primarily as sites for vendors and sports handicappers. URLs often change; if a link fails to work, search the name of the Web site with a standard Web search engine such as Google or Yahoo!

General Sites

AllSports
http://www.allsports.com

Broadcast Sports
http://www.broadcastsports.com

Cable News Network (CNN)/Sports Illustrated (SI)
http://sportsillustrated.cnn.com

Canadian Broadcasting Corporation (CBC) Sports
http://cbc.ca/sports

CBS SportsLine
http://cbs.sportsline.com

College Sports Information Directors of America (CoSIDA)
http://www.cosida.com

ESPN
http://espn.go.com

Excite: Sports
http://sports.excite.com

Express Sport Live (European Sporting News)
http://www.sportslive.net

FOXSports
http://www.foxsports.com

Home Box Office (HBO) Sports
http://www.hbo.com/realsports

International Association for Sports Information
http://www.iasi.org/home.html

MSNBC Sports
http://nbcsports.msnbc.com

New England Sports Network
http://www.nesn.com

One on One Sports
http://www.1on1sports.com

PioneerPlanet: Sports
http://www.pioneerplanet.com/sports

Real Fans Sports Network
http://www.realfans.com

Sport Science
http://www.exploratorium.edu/sports

The Sporting Life
http://www.sporting-life.com

SportingNews.com
http://www.sportingnews.com

Sports Illustrated **(magazine)**
http://www.pathfinder.com/si

Sports Network
http://www.sportsnetwork.com/home.asp

Sports Schedules as You Like 'Em
http://www.cs.rochester.edu/u/ferguson/schedules

SportsFan Radio Network
http://www.sportsfanradio.com

SportsFeed (news)
http://www.sportsfeed.com

SportsLine USA
http://www.sportsline.com

Turner Network Television (TNT) Sports
http://tnt.turner.com/sports

USA Network Sports
http://www.usanetwork.com/sports

USA Today-Sports
http://www.usatoday.com

Women's Sports Information
http://www.womenssportsinformation.com

World Wide Web Virtual Library: Sports
http://www.sportsvl.com

Yahoo! Sports
http://dir.yahoo.com/recreation/sports

Boxing

Boxing Canada: The Canadian Amateur Boxing Association
http://www.boxing.ca

Boxing in Asia
http://asianboxing.blogspot.com

Boxing News
http://www.boxingscene.com

Boxing Talk
http://www.boxingtalk.com

Canadian Boxing Federation (CBF)
http://www.canadianboxing.com

European Boxing Association (EBA)
http://www.europeboxing.com

Femboxer.com
http://femboxer.com

Fighters.com News
http://www.fighters.com

Home Box Office (HBO) Boxing
http://www.hbo.com/boxing

International Boxing Hall of Fame (IBHOF)
http://www.ibhof.com

USA Boxing
http://usaboxing.org

World Boxing Association (WBA)
http://www.wbaonline.com

World Boxing Council (WBC)
http://www.wbcboxing.com

Soccer

American Youth Soccer Organization (AYSO)
http://soccer.org/home.aspx

Ballparks
http://www.ballparks.com

Confederation of North, Central America and Caribbean Association Football
http://www.concacaf.com

ESPNSoccernet
http://soccernet.espn.go.com

International Federation of Association Football (FIFA)
http://www.fifa.com

Internet Soccer Fans Association (ISFA)
http://www.isfa.com

Major League Soccer (MLS)
http://www.mlsnet.com

MaxPreps: America's Source for High School Sports
http://www.maxpreps.com/national/home.aspx

Soccer America (magazine)
http://www.socceramerica.com

Soccer Times
http://www.soccertimes.com

World Cup Soccer
http://www.fifa.com/worldcup

Glossary

Boxing

AIBA. *See* Association Internationale de Boxe Amateur.

amateur: Boxer who competes for honors, rather than money, and who does not attain professional status. Olympic boxers must maintain their amateur status.

Association Internationale de Boxe Amateur (AIBA): Governing body of amateur boxing events.

bantamweight: Weight classification for boxers between 112 and 118 pounds.

bare-knuckle boxing: Original boxing format, in which boxers do not wear protective gloves.

below the belt: Area beneath the boxer's waistline that is illegal to punch.

belt: Award given to the champion in each weight division by each sanctioning body.

bob and weave: Defensive strategy in which a boxer moves from side to side to avoid an opponent's punches.

body punch: Boxing punch delivered to the side of the body below the rib cage.

bout: Boxing match. In modern competitions, most bouts contain from three to twelve rounds. Each round is three minutes long, with a one-minute rest period in between rounds. How many rounds a bout lasts depends on the weight classification and whether the match is amateur or professional.

boxing: Sport in which two fighters use their fists, covered with padded gloves, to engage in close-range combat.

canvas: Floor of the boxing ring.

combination: Flurry of different punches thrown rapidly and successively, usually as part of a practiced plan of attack during a boxing match.

corner man: Boxer's assistant who gives advice throughout the fight and in between rounds and can also perform minor medical duties, such as stopping cuts from bleeding.

count: Number of seconds called off by a referee over a fallen boxer. After the count begins, boxers have ten seconds to get back on their feet or their opponents are declared the winners by knockouts.

counterpunch: To answer or respond immediately to an opponent's lead punch or jab with a punch or a jab during a boxing match.

cross: Strong punch delivered with the boxer's lead hand.

decision: Result of a fight given after both fighters have completed the prescribed number of rounds with neither knocking out the other.

draw: Fight resulting in a tie based on the scorecards of the ringside judges.

featherweight: Weight classification for 126-pound boxers.

fix: Situation occurring when the results of a fight have been illegally predetermined.

flyweight: Weight classification for boxers between 108 and 112 pounds.

going the distance: Situation in which both boxers complete the scheduled number of rounds in their bout, with neither knocking out the other.

Golden Gloves: Nationwide series of amateur boxing elimination tournaments. Regional champions are qualified to compete for the title in their respective weight classifications at the annual Golden Gloves National Championship Tournament.

haymaker: Seldom used and unorthodox punch in which the boxer winds up and punches with maximum force in an attempt to knock out an opponent. Boxers attempting to deliver haymakers usually expose themselves dangerously to counterpunches.

headgear: Protective equipment worn over the head and face by amateur and women fighters; required of all boxers in the Olympics.

heavyweight: Weight classification in professional boxing for athletes weighing more than 190 pounds. In amateur boxing, the maximum is 200 pounds. *See also* super heavyweight.

hook: Punch delivered close to the opponent's body in which a boxer extends an arm from a bent-elbow position.

IBF. *See* International Boxing Federation.

International Boxing Association (AIBA). *See* Association Internationale de Boxe Amateur.

International Boxing Federation (IBF): Body

321

founded in 1983 as one of the four official sanctioned boxing organizations.

jab: Type of boxing punch that is a sharp, rapid snap of the arm, and which is thrown a short distance, often directly at the head or face.

knockdown: Situation occurring when a boxer falls to the canvas after sustaining a hit.

knockout: Victory scored by a boxer who is able to render an opponent unconscious or otherwise unable to continue the match. Following knockdowns, fallen boxers have ten seconds to get back on their feet or their fights are declared over. *See also* technical knockout.

light flyweight: Weight classification for boxers with a weight limit of 108 pounds.

light heavyweight: Weight classification in professional boxing with a 175-pound maximum. In amateur boxing, the maximum is 178 pounds.

lightweight: Weight classification in professional boxing with a 135-pound maximum. In amateur boxing, the maximum is 132 pounds.

majority decision: Victory scored by a boxer when two of three ring officials declare the boxer the winner, while the third official declares the bout a draw. *See also* split decision.

manager: Professional boxer's representative responsible for the scheduling and promotion of the client's matches.

mandatory eight-count: Boxing rule specifying that once a knockdown occurs, the referee's count must automatically reach eight before the match can resume, if indeed it can resume. This count is used to allow fallen boxers a few extra seconds to regain their composure before continuing their fights.

middleweight: Weight classification in professional boxing with a 160-pound limit. In amateur boxing, the limit is 165 pounds.

neutral corner: One of the two corners in a boxing ring not occupied by either boxer. A boxer who knocks down an opponent is required to retreat to one of the neutral corners.

no decision: Fight result made by the referee if it is determined one of the boxers has suffered a significant injury from an accidental foul and is unable to proceed.

on the ropes: Expression that literally means a boxer has been punched against the ropes of the ring and figuratively indicates a boxer is about to lose the fight.

one-two punch: Two punches thrown in quick succession.

points: Scores awarded by boxing judges for punches landed accurately to different areas of the body.

pound for pound: Expression used to compare boxers within different weight classifications based on their records, physical characteristics, and other attributes. A flyweight boxer could never defeat a fit heavyweight boxer because of the differences in their sizes and punching strength, but the flyweight might be considered better, "pound for pound."

punch: General term for any moment a boxer's fist connects with the opponent's body or face.

punch drunk: Colloquial term for *dementia pugilistica*, a deteriorating neurological condition brought about by multiple punches to the head over an extended period of time.

purse: Money earned by both boxers for participating in a professional fight.

referee's decision: Victory scored by a boxer who has been declared the winner by the referee while the two ring judges have each declared a draw.

ring: Enclosed area in which a fight occurs.

rope-a-dope: Technique popularized by Muhammad Ali in which a boxer rests against the ropes, covers up with hands and arms, and allows the other boxer to punch until tiring.

round: Three-minute periods into which boxing matches, or bouts, are divided. One-minute rest periods separate each round. The number of rounds in a match depends on whether the event is amateur or professional.

saved by the bell: Term originating during the late nineteenth century, when boxers knocked to the floor were saved from being counted out by the sounding of the bell ending the rounds. In modern boxing, boxers knocked down can be counted out even after the round ends. The expression has found its way in general usage as a term for a last-second reprieve from an undesired event, such as being called upon to answer a question in a classroom.

sparring: Practice boxing session.

split decision: Victory scored by a boxer after two of three ring officials declare the boxer the winner while the third official declares the boxer's opponent the winner. *See also* majority decision.

super heavyweight: Weight classification in Olympic (amateur) boxing for athletes weighing more than 200 pounds.

technical knockout (TKO): Victory scored by a boxer after the referee stops the match because the other boxer cannot continue fighting or can no longer put up a defense, or because the other boxer has indicated a desire to stop the fight.

throw in the towel: Action of a corner man undertaken when he believes that a boxer is taking a dangerous and potentially life-threatening beating. The expression has found its way in general usage as a term for giving up in any endeavor.

TKO. *See* technical knockout.

unanimous decision: Victory scored by a boxer whom both ring judges and the referee declare the winner when no knockout occurs.

uppercut: Punch thrown from below the shoulder and within close proximity to the opponent with the jaw as the target for the punch.

WBA. *See* World Boxing Association.

WBC. *See* World Boxing Council.

WBF. *See* World Boxing Foundation.

welterweight: Weight classification for boxers between 140 and 147 pounds.

World Boxing Association (WBA): Oldest of the sanctioning bodies of boxing.

World Boxing Council (WBC): Boxing organization founded in 1963 in an attempt to place agreed-upon international standards on the sport.

World Boxing Foundation (WBF): One of the sanctioning bodies of boxing; formerly the World Boxing Federation.

Soccer

advantage: Situation occurring when members of the team controlling the ball outnumber their opposition when they go on the attack.

all-American: Nationwide honor awarded yearly to the best high school and college soccer players. All-American honors are awarded by a variety of organizations and publications, and their prestige varies.

American Youth Soccer Organization (AYSO): Primary youth soccer association in the United States.

assist: Pass completed to a teammate who scores a goal almost immediately.

association football: Term by which most of the world knows "soccer," which derives from the word "association." Association football arose in England, where its name distinguished it from rugby football. A game in which two teams attempt to advance, without using hands or arms, a round ball along a rectangular field.

attacker: General term for the player with possession of the ball.

attacking midfielder: Midfielder who plays directly behind the forwards and facilitates the offense by passing the ball to the forwards near the opposition's goal.

attacking team: Team with possession of the ball.

AYSO. *See* American Youth Soccer Organization.

back: Alternative term for a defender.

banana kick: Kick that curves in the air used to circumvent a goalkeeper or defender.

bicycle kick: Spectacular soccer maneuver that involves falling backward, to an almost upside-down vertical position, while using an overhead scissors-like leg motion to kick the ball.

break. *See* advantage.

breakaway: Situation occurring when an offensive player is able to take the ball past the defenders with a clear path to the goal.

Bundesliga: Germany's primary professional soccer league.

cap: Unofficial honor awarded to soccer players representing their countries in international games. The number of "caps" a player earns represents the number of international matches in which the player has appeared.

carrying the ball: Foul in which the goalkeeper takes four or more steps while still in possession of the ball.

center: Type of pass in which a player kicks the ball from the edge to the middle of the field.

center circle: Central area of the field demarcated by a circle with a 10-yard radius. Kickoffs made at the start of each half and after each score are made from the center spot in the middle of the circle.

Champions League: Also known as the UEFA Champions League. An annual competition that pits the top soccer teams in Europe against each other.

chest trap: Technique to control the ball while it is in the air by using the chest to block it.

chip pass: Quick pass kicked over a defender's head to a nearby teammate.

chip shot: Kick lobbed in the air in an attempt to get it over the goalkeeper's head and under the goalpost.

clear: Situation occurring when the defensive team kicks the ball away from its own goal.

CONCACAF. *See* Confederation of North, Central American and Caribbean Association Football.

Confederation of North, Central American and Caribbean Association Football (CONCACAF): Organization that oversees World Cup qualifying games between teams from the Americas.

Confederations Cup: Soccer tournament held every four years featuring teams from each regional confederation, the reigning World Cup champion, and the host county.

Copa Libertadores: Yearly international soccer tournament among the champions and runners-up from leagues in South American countries to determine the best South American club team.

corner arc: Marking at each of the four corners on the field from which a corner kick is taken.

corner kick: Restart in a soccer game in which the attacking team is awarded a free kick from the corner of the field on the opposing team's goal line after the opposing team touches a ball that goes out of play over the goal line. *See also* free kick; penalty kick.

cross. *See* center.

defenders: Players without possession of the ball.

direct free kick. *See* free kick.

dribble: Advancing of the ball with the feet, which are generally used to tap it in a left-right alternation.

drop kick: Situation occurring when goalkeepers transfer the ball from their hands to their feet and then kick it off the ground.

end line: Boundary line extending from sideline to sideline at each end of the field. Also known as goal line.

European Cup: Yearly and prestigious international men's tournament between the national soccer champions from all European countries.

extra time: Term generally used in international soccer for overtime periods used to settle games that finish in ties in regulation time. In major international competitions, extra time consists of two full 15-minute periods, with teams switching the goals they defend between periods. When games finish in ties after extra time, they are usually settled by penalty kicks.

FA. *See* Football Association.

Fédération Internationale de Football Association (FIFA): Soccer's international governing body, which sponsors such events as the World Cup.

field. *See* pitch.

FIFA: Acronym for the French form of International Federation of Football Association, the world governing body of soccer.

football: International term for the game that Americans call soccer. *See* association football.

Football Association (FA): Soccer's governing body in England.

forwards: Players whose primary responsibility is scoring.

foul: Infraction resulting in a free kick for the opposing team.

free kick: Restart in a game when one team is allowed to kick the ball into play, without obstruction from the opposing team, after the other team commits a foul on the field. A direct free kick, which is awarded for certain kinds of major fouls, may be kicked directly into the opposing goal for a score. An indirect free kick, which is awarded for certain technical fouls, must touch another player (of either team) before entering a goal to score. *See also* corner kick; penalty kick.

goal: Upright frame, enclosed in the back by a net, through which the ball must pass for the attacking team to score. The standard goal is eight feet high and twenty-four feet wide. "Goal" is also the term used for the score itself. Goals are scored only when the entire ball enters the goal after passing over the entire width of the goal line. In contrast to American football, "breaking the plane" of the goal line is insufficient to make a score.

goal area: Lined area directly in front of each goal and inside the penalty area on a soccer field; the area is twenty yards wide and six yards deep. Its sole purpose is to delimit the area from which a goal kick may be made. *See also* penalty area.

goal kick: Restart in soccer in which the defending team puts the ball back into play after it goes over any part of the goal line, but not inside the goal, when the attacking team is last to touch it. Any defending player may take the kick, which must be made from within the goal area and must clear the penalty area.

goal line. *See* end line.

goalkeeper: Player who is accorded special privileges while protecting the team's goal. Goalkeepers wear jerseys of colors different from those of other players so they can be readily identified. In contrast to all other players, goalkeepers can handle the ball with their hands—but only within their own penalty areas. They can also go anywhere on the field and do anything that any other player is permitted to do. Also known as keeper throughout most of the world but popularly called "goalie" in the United States.

goalposts: Vertical posts that constitute the outside boundaries of a goal. They stand 24 feet apart.

halfbacks. *See* midfielders.

halftime: Designated intermission at the midpoint of a game.

halfway line: Line dividing a soccer field into two equal halves. When kickoffs are taken to start or restart play, all players must begin on their own side of the halfway line. The line is also important in making offsides calls, as players can be in offside positions only on their opponents' side of the line.

hand ball: Illegal play resulting in a free kick, occurring when any player, other than a goalkeeper within the penalty area, intentionally touches the ball with any part of an arm or hand.

hat trick: Three goals in one game scored by the same player. The term was originally applied to the feat of scoring three consecutive, unanswered goals.

header: Ball propelled when deliberately struck by the head of a player. Often used for scoring attempts, headers are almost always made with the forehead and are especially effective on crossing passes near the goal.

heading: Using the head to shoot a soccer ball toward the goal, pass the ball to a teammate, or clear the ball away from one's own goal. Heading is generally done from a spot just above the forehead.

in play: Condition of a ball that remains inside the field's boundaries when an official has not called a stoppage. In contrast to many other ball sports, the ball is considered to be in play in soccer so long as some part of it is not beyond the outside edge of the touchlines or goal lines, even if the bottom of the ball touches the ground beyond one of those lines. Likewise, goals are scored only when the entire ball passes over the entire width of the goal line within the goal itself.

indirect free kick. *See* free kick.

injury time: Additional time at the end of a period based on time lost during the period because of players' injuries.

keeper. *See* goalkeeper.

kickoff: Forward pass made from the field's center spot to begin a game or half or to restart a game after a score. As in American football, the team that scores kicks off. In contrast to American football, the kicking team's principal objective is to retain control of the ball, not to deliver it to the opposing team.

Major League Soccer (MLS): Primary soccer league in the United States.

man-to-man: Common defensive strategy in which each defender guards a specific forward from the opposing team.

match: Official name for a soccer game.

midfielders: Players who play behind the forwards and in front of the defenders. Usually the players who run the greatest distance in games, midfielders facilitate scoring and assist on defense.

MLS. *See* Major League Soccer.

NASL. *See* North American Soccer League.

National Collegiate Athletic Association (NCAA): Major governing body for collegiate sports, including soccer, in the United States.

North American Soccer League (NASL): Soccer league that operated in the United States from 1967 until 1985 and enjoyed its greatest popularity during the 1970's. The league featured numerous international stars, including Brazilian icon Pelé, Germany's Franz Beckenbauer, and the Netherlands' Johann Cruyff.

offsides: Moment when one or more attacking players advance too far upfield. Players can be offsides only when they are in the opponents' half of the field and when fewer than two opposing players are closer to the goal line than they are. Being in an offside position can be a violation of the rules only at the moment the attacking team attempts a pass or scoring play that involves an offside player. Hence, referees should signal offside violations only at the moment when the attacking team passes or shoots the ball, and only when they judge offside players to be gaining an advantage from their offsides position.

overtime. *See* extra time.

penalty area: Demarcated part of a soccer field directly in front of each goal, measuring forty-four yards in width and eighteen yards in depth. The area delimits the space within which goalkeepers can handle the ball with their hands. Defensive fouls within the penalty area that would result in direct free kicks for similar fouls made outside the penalty area result in penalty kicks for the attacking teams. Attacking teams cannot take direct free kicks within an opposing team's penalty area, but they can take indirect free kicks there. Defending teams can take both kinds of free kicks from within their own penalty areas. *See also* goal area.

penalty kick: Free kick awarded to a soccer team when the opposing team commits a major foul within its own penalty area. All players but the defending goalkeeper and the designated kicker must be outside the penalty area when the referee signals for the kick to be made. The ball is placed on the marked "penalty spot," twelve yards in front of the goal line, which the goalkeeper's feet must be touching at the moment the ball is kicked. Any player on the attacking team may take a penalty kick, regardless of who has been fouled. *See also* corner kick; free kick.

pitch: British term for a soccer playing field. The dimensions of a field's penalty areas, goal areas, and center circle are fixed, but the outside dimensions of FIFA-sanctioned fields are not. Fields must be between 100 and 150 yards in length, be between 50 and 100 yards in width, and be longer than they are wide.

play on: Expression used by referees, in words or by hand gestures, to indicate that a game should not be stopped because of a perceived penalty.

Premier League: Top professional soccer league in England.

Primera División: Top professional soccer league in Spain. Also known as La Liga.

red card: Card shown by the referee to a player who commits excessive violence or multiple infractions, representing an ejection from the match; two yellow cards result in a red card.

save: Movement by a goalkeeper to stop a shot from scoring.

scissors volley: Acrobatic soccer maneuver that involves leaning backward and throwing both feet high into the air to kick a ball passing over the player's body, which assumes a nearly horizontal position, with a scissors-like leg motion. Made famous by the legendary Brazilian player Pelé, this rarely seen technique is used mostly for shots close to the goal.

Serie A: Top professional soccer league in Italy.

shot: Ball kicked or headed toward the opponent's goal for the purpose of scoring.

side tackle: Technique used by a defender to strip the ball from the attacker by tapping the ball away with a foot.

slide tackle: Technique in which a defender slides feet-first to dislodge the ball from an opponent's attempt to dribble it.

soccer: Term derived from "association football" that is used in the United States for a sport known to most of the rest of the world as "football." *See* association football.

striker: Offensive soccer player who occupies the central forward position and who has a major responsibility to score goals.

sweeper: Defensive soccer player who is free to roam in front of or behind a team's rear defensive line.

tackling: Maneuver used to dislodge the ball from the attacker. In contrast to American football, soccer players "tackle" the ball, not an opposing player.

throw-in: Sideline play in which a player uses two hands to hurl the ball onto the field to restart the game after an out-of-bounds play. Throw-ins are taken only from touchlines along the sides of the field. When the ball goes out of bounds over the goal line, the game is restarted by either a goal kick or a corner kick, depending on which team last touched the ball.

touchlines: Side lines that run the length of the outside boundaries of soccer and rugby fields.

UEFA. *See* Union of European Football Associations.

Union of European Football Associations (UEFA): Governing body for European soccer, founded in 1954. One of six confederations that sends teams to the World Cup.

World Cup: Almost certainly the single most popular one-sport competition in the world, soccer's World Cup tournament features the best teams from thirty-two countries, selected during two-year-long elimination tournaments within the regional associations recognized by the International Federation of Football Association (FIFA). The World Cup in men's soccer began in Uruguay in 1930 and has been held every four years—except during World War II. Competition in the women's World Cup began in 1991.

yellow card: Card given to a player for an excessive foul or unsportsmanlike conduct. Two yellow cards earn a red card, which results in expulsion from the game.

zone: Defense strategy in which players cover a specific area of the field as opposed to covering a specific player.

Christopher Rager

Boxers Time Line

Birthdate	Boxer	Birthplace
March 31, 1878	Jack Johnson	Galveston, Texas
March 4, 1883	Sam Langford	Weymouth Falls, Nova Scotia, Canada
September 14, 1886	Stanley Ketchel	Grand Rapids, Michigan
June 24, 1895	Jack Dempsey	Manassa, Colorado
April 7, 1896	Benny Leonard	New York, New York
April 26, 1897	Eddie Eagan	Denver, Colorado
May 25, 1897	Gene Tunney	New York, New York
September 28, 1905	Max Schmeling	Klein Luckow, Uckermark, Germany
February 11, 1909	Max Baer	Omaha, Nebraska
December 12, 1912	Henry Armstrong	Columbus, Mississippi
December 13, 1913(?)	Archie Moore	Benoit, Mississippi
May 13, 1914	Joe Louis	Near Lafayette, Alabama
October 8, 1917	Billy Conn	Pittsburgh, Pennsylvania
January 1, 1919	Rocky Graziano	New York, New York
May 3, 1921	Sugar Ray Robinson	Ailey, Georgia
July 10, 1921	Jake LaMotta	New York, New York
September 19, 1922	Willie Pep	Middletown, Connecticut
September 1, 1923	Rocky Marciano	Brockton, Massachusetts
March 25, 1926	László Papp	Budapest, Hungary
June 23, 1926	Sandy Saddler	Boston, Massachusetts
August 14, 1929	Dick Tiger	Amaigbo, Orlu, Nigeria
May 8, 1932(?)	Sonny Liston	Sand Slough, Arkansas
January 4, 1935	Floyd Patterson	Waco, North Carolina
December 15, 1938	Bob Foster	Albuquerque, New Mexico
January 17, 1942	Muhammad Ali	Louisville, Kentucky
January 12, 1944	Joe Frazier	Beaufort, South Carolina
August 31, 1945	Earnie Shavers	Garland, Alabama
January 10, 1949	George Foreman	Marshall, Texas
November 3, 1949	Larry Holmes	Cuthbert, Georgia
June 16, 1951	Roberto Durán	Guararé, Panama
March 29, 1952	Teófilo Stevenson	Puerto Padre, Las Tunas, Cuba
April 19, 1952	Alexis Arguello	Managua, Nicaragua
May 23, 1954	Marvin Hagler	Newark, New Jersey
May 17, 1956	Sugar Ray Leonard	Wilmington, North Carolina
October 18, 1958	Thomas Hearns	Memphis, Tennessee
July 12, 1962	Julio César Chávez	Ciudad Obregón, Mexico
October 19, 1962	Evander Holyfield	Atmore, Alabama
January 15, 1965	Bernard Hopkins	Philadelphia, Pennsylvania
September 2, 1965	Lennox Lewis	London, England
June 30, 1966	Mike Tyson	Brooklyn, New York
August 10, 1967	Riddick Bowe	Brooklyn, New York
September 22, 1967	Félix Savón	San Vicente, Cuba

Boxers Time Line

Birthdate	Boxer	Birthplace
June 12, 1968	Christy Martin	Bluefield, West Virginia
January 16, 1969	Roy Jones, Jr.	Pensacola, Florida
September 7, 1971	Shane Mosley	Lynwood, California
January 10, 1973	Félix Trinidad	Fajardo, Puerto Rico
February 4, 1973	Oscar De La Hoya	Los Angeles, California
February 24, 1977	Floyd Mayweather, Jr.	Grand Rapids, Michigan
December 31, 1977	Laila Ali	Miami Beach, Florida
December 17, 1978	Manny Pacquiao	Kibawe Bukidnon, Mindanao, Philippines

Soccer Players Time Line

Birthdate	Player	Birthplace
February 1, 1915	Sir Stanley Matthews	Hanley, Stoke-on-Trent, England
January 22, 1920	Alf Ramsey	Dagenham, Essex, England
February 6, 1924	Billy Wright	Ironbridge, England
February 10, 1926	Danny Blanchflower	Belfast, Northern Ireland
July 4, 1926	Alfredo di Stefano	Buenos Aires, Argentina
April 2, 1927	Ferenc Puskás	Kispest, Hungary
October 22, 1929	Lev Yashin	Moscow, Russia
October 28, 1933	Garrincha	Pau Grande, Brazil
May 8, 1935	Jack Charlton	Ashington, England
October 11, 1937	Bobby Charlton	Ashington, England
December 30, 1937	Gordon Banks	Sheffield, South Yorkshire, England
February 24, 1940	Denis Law	Aberdeen, Scotland
June 11, 1940	Johnny Giles	Dublin, Ireland
October 23, 1940	Pelé	Três Corações, Minas Gerais, Brazil
April 12, 1941	Bobby Moore	Barking, England
December 8, 1941	Geoff Hurst	Ashton-under-Lyne, England
January 25, 1942	Eusébio	Lourenço Marques, Mozambique
December 9, 1942	Billy Bremner	Stirling, Scotland
May 12, 1945	Alan Ball	Farnworth, Lancashire, England
June 12, 1945	Pat Jennings	Newry, Northern Ireland
September 11, 1945	Franz Beckenbauer	Munich, West Germany
November 11, 1945	Gerd Müller	Nödlingen, Germany
May 22, 1946	George Best	Belfast, Northern Ireland
April 25, 1947	Johan Cruyff	Amsterdam, the Netherlands
September 18, 1949	Peter Shilton	Leicester, England
December 25, 1950	Kyle Rote, Jr.	Dallas, Texas
February 14, 1951	Kevin Keegan	Armthorpe, England
July 28, 1954	Steve Zungul	Split, Yugoslavia (now in Croatia)
June 21, 1955	Michel Platini	Joeuf, France
September 25, 1955	Karl-Heinz Rummenigge	Lippstadt, West Germany
July 11, 1958	Hugo Sánchez	Mexico City, Mexico
October 30, 1960	Diego Maradona	Buenos Aires, Argentina
November 30, 1960	Gary Lineker	Leicester, England
February 27, 1964	April Heinrichs	Denver, Colorado
October 31, 1964	Marco van Basten	Utrecht, Netherlands
January 29, 1966	Romário	Rio de Janeiro, Brazil
February 1, 1966	Michelle Akers	Santa Clara, California
May 24, 1966	Eric Cantona	Marseille, France
September 21, 1966	Tab Ramos	Montevideo, Uruguay
February 18, 1967	Roberto Baggio	Caldogno, Italy
June 2, 1967	Sissi	Esplanada, Bahia, Brazil
July 21, 1968	Brandi Chastain	San Jose, California

Soccer Players Time Line

Birthdate	Player	Birthplace
June 9, 1969	Eric Wynalda	Fullerton, California
June 1, 1970	Alexi Lalas	Birmingham, Michigan
June 16, 1970	Cobi Jones	Detroit, Michigan
January 23, 1971	Julie Foudy	San Diego, California
July 22, 1971	Kristine Lilly	New York, New York
September 7, 1971	Briana Scurry	Minneapolis, Minnesota
March 17, 1972	Mia Hamm	Selma, Alabama
April 19, 1972	Rivaldo	Paulista, Brazil
June 23, 1972	Zinedine Zidane	Marseille, France
April 6, 1973	Sun Wen	Shanghai, China
April 10, 1973	Roberto Carlos	Garça, Brazil
September 13, 1973	Fabio Cannavaro	Naples, Italy
May 2, 1975	David Beckham	Leytonstone, England
September 18, 1976	Ronaldo	Rio de Janeiro, Brazil
August 17, 1977	Thierry Henry	Les Ulis, Esonne, France
May 8, 1978	Cindy Parlow	Memphis, Tennessee
December 14, 1979	Michael Owen	Chester, England
March 21, 1980	Ronaldinho	Porto Alegre, Brazil
May 30, 1980	Steven Gerrard	Whiston, Merseyside, England
June 2, 1980	Abby Wambach	Pittsford, New York
March 4, 1982	Landon Donovan	Ontario, California
February 19, 1986	Marta	Dois Riachos, Alagoas, Brazil
June 2, 1989	Freddy Adu	Tema, Ghana

All-Time Great Boxers

International Boxing Hall of Fame

Established in 1989, the International Boxing Hall of Fame is headquartered in Canastota, New York. The organization uses a panel of Boxing Writers' Association members and boxing historians to select inductees, who must be retired from competitive boxing for five years. Inductees are divided among four categories. Three of these categories are for boxers, and the fourth, designated "Non-participants," encompasses managers, trainers, referees, writers, and others who are enshrined for reasons other than actual boxing. The "Pioneers" category includes boxers from the nineteenth century and earlier; "Old Timers" are early twentieth century boxers; and the "Modern Era" category includes late twentieth century and early twenty-first century boxers.

Only inductees from the latter two categories are listed here. Their years of induction are given in parentheses.

Modern Era

Muhammad Ali (1990)
Sammy Angott (1998)
Fred Apostoli (2003)
Alexis Arguello (1992)
Henry Armstrong (1990)
Carmen Basilio (1990)
Wilfred Benitez (1996)
Nino Benvenuti (1992)
Jackie (Kid) Berg (1994)
Jimmy Bivins (1999)
Joe Brown (1996)
Ken Buchanan (2000)
Charley Burley (1992)
Orlando Canizales (2009)
Miguel Canto (1998)
Michael Carbajal (2006)
Jimmy Carter (2000)
Marcel Cerdan (1991)
Antonio Cervantes (1998)
Bobby Chacon (2005)
Jeff Chandler (2000)
Ezzard Charles (1990)
Curtis Cokes (2003)
Billy Conn (1990)
Pipino Cuevas (2002)
Roberto Durán (2007)
Flash Elorde (1993)
Jeff Fenech (2002)
George Foreman (2003)
Bob Foster (1990)
Joe Frazier (1990)
Gene Fullmer (1991)
Khaosai Galaxy (1999)
Victor Galindez (2002)
Kid Gavilan (1990)
Joey Giardello (1993)
Wilfredo Gómez (1995)
Humberto Gonzalez (2006)
Billy Graham (1992)
Rocky Graziano (1991)
Emile Griffith (1990)
Marvin Hagler (1993)
Masahiko (Fighting) Harada (1995)
Larry Holmes (2008)
Beau Jack (1991)
Lew Jenkins (1999)
Eder Jofre (1992)
Ingemar Johansson (2002)
Harold Johnson (1993)
Ismael Laguna (2001)
Jake LaMotta (1990)
Sugar Ray Leonard (1997)
Lennox Lewis (2009)
Sonny Liston (1991)
Nicolino Locche (2003)
Duilio Loi (2005)
Ricardo Lopez (2007)
Joe Louis (1990)
Mike McCallum (2003)
Barry McGuigan (2005)
Rocky Marciano (1990)
Joey Maxim (1994)
Brian Mitchell (2009)
Bob Montgomery (1995)
Carlos Monzon (1990)
Archie Moore (1990)
Matthew Saad Muhammad (1998)
Jose Napoles (1990)
Azumah Nelson (2004)
Terry Norris (2005)
Ken Norton (1992)
Ruben Olivares (1991)
Carl (Bobo) Olson (2000)
Carlos Ortiz (1991)
Manuel Ortiz (1996)
Carlos Palomino (2004)
László Papp (2001)
Willie Pastrano (2001)
Floyd Patterson (1991)
Eusebio Pedroza (1999)
Willie Pep (1990)
Pascual Pérez (1995)
Eddie Perkins (2008)
Aaron Pryor (1996)
Dwight Muhammad Qawi (2004)
Sugar Ramos (2001)
Sugar Ray Robinson (1990)
Luis Rodriguez (1997)
Edwin Rosario (2006)
Sandy Saddler (1990)
Vicente Saldivar (1999)
Salvador Sanchez (1991)
Max Schmeling (1992)
Michael Spinks (1994)
Dick Tiger (1991)

Jose Torres (1997)
Randy Turpin (2001)
Jersey Joe Walcott (1990)
Pernell Whitaker (2007)
Holman Williams (2008)
Ike Williams (1990)
Chalky Wright (1997)
Tony Zale (1991)
Daniel Zaragoza (2004)
Carlos Zarate (1994)
Fritzie Zivic (1993)

Old Timers

Lou Ambers (1992)
Baby Arizmendi (2004)
Abe Attell (1990)
Max Baer (1995)
Jimmy Barry (2000)
Benny Bass (2002)
Battling Battalino (2003)
Paul Berlenbach (2001)
James J. Braddock (2001)
Jack Britton (1990)
Lou Brouillard (2006)
Panama Al Brown (1992)
Tommy Burns (1996)
Tony Canzoneri (1990)
Georges Carpentier (1991)
Kid Chocolate (1994)
Joe Choynski (1998)
James J. Corbett (1990)
Young Corbett III (2004)
Johnny Coulon (1999)
Eugene Criqui (2005)
Les Darcy (1993)
Jack Delaney (1996)
Jack Dempsey (1990)
Jack (Nonpareil) Dempsey (1992)
Jack Dillon (1995)

Jim Driscoll (1990)
George Dixon (1990)
Johnny Dundee (1991)
Sixto Escobar (2002)
Jackie Fields (2004)
Bob Fitzsimmons (1990)
Tiger Flowers (1993)
Joe Gans (1990)
Frankie Genaro (1998)
Mike Gibbons (1992)
Tommy Gibbons (1993)
George Godfrey (2007)
Harry Greb (1990)
Young Griffo (1991)
Harry Harris (2002)
Len Harvey (2008)
Pete Herman (1997)
Peter Jackson (1990)
Joe Jeannette (1997)
James J. Jeffries (1990)
Jack Johnson (1990)
Gorilla Jones (2009)
Louis (Kid) Kaplan (2003)
Stanley Ketchel (1990)
Dixie Kid (2002)
Johnny Kilbane (1995)
Frank Klaus (2008)
Fidel LaBarba (1996)
Sam Langford (1990)
George (Kid) Lavigne (1998)
Benny Leonard (1990)
Battling Levinsky (2000)
Harry Lewis (2008)
John Henry Lewis (1994)
Ted (Kid) Lewis (1992)
Tommy Loughran (1991)
Benny Lynch (1998)
Joe Lynch (2005)
Jack McAuliffe (1995)
Charles (Kid) McCoy (1991)
Packey McFarland (1992)

Terry McGovern (1990)
Jimmy McLarnin (1991)
Sam McVey (1999)
Sammy Mandell (1998)
Freddie Miller (1997)
Charley Mitchell (2002)
Pedro Montañez (2007)
Owen Moran (2002)
Battling Nelson (1992)
Kid Norfolk (2007)
Philadelphia Jack O'Brien (1994)
Billy Papke (2001)
Billy Petrolle (2000)
Willie Ritchie (2004)
Maxie Rosenbloom (1993)
Barney Ross (1990)
Tommy Ryan (1991)
Jack Sharkey (1994)
Tom Sharkey (2003)
Jimmy Slattery (2006)
Mysterious Billy Smith (2009)
Billy Soose (2009)
Freddie Steele (1999)
Young Stribling (1996)
Charles (Bud) Taylor (2005)
Lew Tendler (1999)
Marcel Thil (2005)
Gene Tunney (1990)
Pancho Villa (1994)
Barbados Joe Walcott (1991)
Mickey Walker (1990)
Freddie Welsh (1997)
Jimmy Wilde (1990)
Jess Willard (2003)
Kid Williams (1996)
Harry Wills (1992)
Ad Wolgast (2000)
Midget Wolgast (2001)
Teddy Yarosz (2006)

Ring *Magazine Eighty Best Fighters*

In 2002, *Ring* magazine celebrated its eightieth anniversary by ranking the eighty best fighters of the previous eight decades, as selected by its own writers. These rankings pay no attention to weight divisions, but many of these boxers fought in more than one division.

1. Sugar Ray Robinson
2. Henry Armstrong
3. Muhammad Ali
4. Joe Louis
5. Roberto Durán
6. Willie Pep
7. Harry Greb
8. Benny Leonard
9. Sugar Ray Leonard
10. Pernell Whitaker
11. Carlos Monzon
12. Rocky Marciano
13. Ezzard Charles
14. Archie Moore
15. Sandy Saddler
16. Jack Dempsey
17. Marvin Hagler
18. Julio Cesar Chavez
19. Eder Jofre
20. Alexis Arguello
21. Barney Ross
22. Evander Holyfield
23. Ike Williams
24. Salvador Sanchez
25. George Foreman
26. Kid Gavilan
27. Larry Holmes
28. Mickey Walker
29. Ruben Olivares
30. Gene Tunney
31. Dick Tiger
32. Fighting Harada
33. Emile Griffith
34. Tony Canzoneri
35. Aaron Pryor
36. Pascual Perez
37. Miguel Canto
38. Manuel Ortiz
39. Charley Burley
40. Carmen Basilio
41. Michael Spinks
42. Joe Frazier
43. Khaosai Galaxy
44. Roy Jones, Jr.
45. Tiger Flowers
46. Panama Al Brown
47. Kid Chocolate
48. Joe Brown
49. Tommy Loughran
50. Bernard Hopkins
51. Felix Trinidad
52. Jake LaMotta
53. Lennox Lewis
54. Wilfredo Gomez
55. Bob Foster
56. Jose Napoles
57. Billy Conn
58. Jimmy McLarnin
59. Pancho Villa
60. Carlos Ortiz
61. Bob Montgomery
62. Freddie Miller
63. Benny Lynch
64. Beau Jack
65. Azumah Nelson
66. Eusebio Pedroza
67. Thomas Hearns
68. Wilfred Benitez
69. Antonio Cervantes
70. Ricardo Lopez
71. Sonny Liston
72. Mike Tyson
73. Vicente Saldivar
74. Gene Fullmer
75. Oscar De La Hoya
76. Carlos Zarate
77. Marcel Cerdan
78. Flash Elorde
79. Mike McCallum
80. Harold Johnson

Ring *Magazine Fighters of the Year*

Founded in 1922 as a boxing and wrestling publication, *Ring* magazine soon focused only on boxing and developed into both an important source of news and an influential voice in professional boxing. Since 1928, its writers have annually awarded a medal to at least one boxer whom they have regarded as the previous year's most outstanding fighter, based on criteria related to the boxer's skill, good sportsmanship, and public image.

1928 Gene Tunney
1929 Tommy Loughran
1930 Max Schmeling
1931 Tommy Loughran
1932 Jack Sharkey
1933 (no award)
1934 Tony Canzoneri and Barney Ross
1935 Barney Ross
1936 Joe Louis
1937 Henry Armstrong
1938 Joe Louis
1939 Joe Louis
1940 Billy Conn
1941 Joe Louis
1942 Sugar Ray Robinson
1943 Fred Apostoli
1944 Beau Jack
1945 Willie Pep
1946 Tony Zale
1947 Gus Lesnevich
1948 Ike Williams
1949 Ezzard Charles
1950 Ezzard Charles
1951 Sugar Ray Robinson
1952 Rocky Marciano
1953 Bobo Olson
1954 Rocky Marciano
1955 Rocky Marciano
1956 Floyd Patterson
1957 Carmen Basilio
1958 Ingemar Johansson
1959 Ingemar Johansson
1960 Floyd Patterson
1961 Joe Brown
1962 Dick Tiger
1963 Cassius Clay
1964 Emile Griffith
1965 Dick Tiger
1966 (no award)
1967 Joe Frazier
1968 Nino Benvenuti
1969 Jose Napoles
1970 Joe Frazier
1971 Joe Frazier
1972 Muhammad Ali and Carlos Monzon
1973 George Foreman
1974 Muhammad Ali
1975 Muhammad Ali
1976 George Foreman
1977 Carlos Zarate
1978 Muhammad Ali
1979 Sugar Ray Leonard
1980 Thomas Hearns
1981 Sugar Ray Leonard and Salvador Sanchez
1982 Larry Holmes
1983 Marvin Hagler
1984 Thomas Hearns
1985 Marvin Hagler and Donald Curry
1986 Mike Tyson
1987 Evander Holyfield
1988 Mike Tyson
1989 Pernell Whitaker
1990 Julio César Chávez
1991 James Toney
1992 Riddick Bowe
1993 Michael Carbajal
1994 Roy Jones, Jr.
1995 Oscar De La Hoya
1996 Evander Holyfield
1997 Evander Holyfield
1998 Floyd Mayweather, Jr.
1999 Paulie Ayala
2000 Félix Trinidad
2001 Bernard Hopkins
2002 Vernon Forrest
2003 James Toney
2004 Glen Johnson
2005 Ricky Hatton
2006 Manny Pacquiao
2007 Floyd Mayweather, Jr.
2008 Manny Pacquiao

ESPN Fifty Greatest Boxers of All Time

In 2007, ESPN selected fifty boxers as the greatest of all time for a special television series. Among the criteria for selection were the quality of the fighters' in-ring performances, the fighters' tangible achievements, their dominance over periods of time, and the attention they brought to the boxing profession.

Rank	Boxer	Weight divisions	Career	W-L-D	KO's
1	Sugar Ray Robinson	welterweight, middleweight	1940-1965	175-19-6	109
2	Muhammad Ali	heavyweight	1960-1981	56-5-0	37
3	Henry Armstrong	featherweight, lightweight, welterweight	1932-1945	151-21-9	101
4	Joe Louis	heavyweight	1934-1951	68-3-0	54
5	Willie Pep	featherweight	1940-1966	230-11-1	65
6	Roberto Durán	lightweight, welterweight, jr. middleweight, middleweight	1968-2001	103-16-0	70
7	Benny Leonard	lightweight	1911-1932	85-5-1	69
8	Jack Johnson	heavyweight	1897-1928	77-13-14	48
9	Jack Dempsey	heavyweight	1914-1927	61-6-8	50
10	Sam Langford	lightweight, welterweight, middleweight, heavyweight	1902-1926	167-38-37	117
11	Joe Gans	lightweight	1891-1909	120-8-9	85
12	Sugar Ray Leonard	welterweight, jr. middleweight, middleweight, sup. middleweight, lt. heavyweight	1977-1997	36-3-1	25
13	Harry Greb	middleweight	1913-1926	105-8-3	48
14	Rocky Marciano	heavyweight	1947-1956	49-0-0	43
15	Jimmy Wilde	flyweight	1910-1923	131-3-2	99
16	Gene Tunney	heavyweight	1915-1928	61-1-1	45
17	Mickey Walker	welterweight, middleweight, lt. heavyweight, heavyweight	1919-1935	93-19-4	60
18	Archie Moore	lt. heavyweight, heavyweight	1935-1963	183-24-10	131
19	Stanley Ketchel	middleweight, heavyweight	1903-1910	52-4-4	49
20	George Foreman	heavyweight	1969-1997	76-5-0	68

Rank	Boxer	Weight divisions	Career	W-L-D	KO's
21	Tony Canzoneri	bantamweight, featherweight, lightweight, jr. welterweight	1925-1939	137-24-10	44
22	Barney Ross	lightweight, jr. welterweight, welterweight	1929-1938	72-4-3	22
23	Jimmy McLarnin	Flyweight, lightweight, welterweight	1923-1936	62-11-3	20
24	Julio César Chávez	sup. featherweight, lightweight, jr. welterweight, welterweight	1980-2005	108-6-2	87
25	Marcel Cerdan	middleweight	1934-1949	106-4-0	61
26	Joe Frazier	heavyweight	1965-1981	32-4-1	27
27	Ezzard Charles	middleweight, lt. heavyweight, heavyweight	1940-1959	96-25-1	58
28	Jake LaMotta	middleweight	1941-1954	83-19-4	30
29	Sandy Saddler	featherweight, jr. lightweight	1944-1957	144-16-2	103
30	Terry McGovern	bantamweight, featherweight	1897-1908	60-4-4	42
31	Billy Conn	middleweight, lt. heavyweight, heavyweight	1935-1948	63-12-1	14
32	Jose Napoles	welterweight, middleweight	1958-1975	77-7-0	54
33	Ruben Olivares	bantamweight, featherweight	1965-1988	88-13-3	78
34	Emile Griffith	welterweight, jr. middleweight, middleweight	1958-1977	85-24-2	23
35	Marvin Hagler	middleweight	1973-1987	62-3-2	57
36	Eder Jofre	bantamweight, featherweight	1957-1976	72-2-4	50
37	Thomas Hearns	welterweight, jr. middleweight, middleweight, sup. middleweight, lt. heavyweight, cruiserweight	1977-2006	61-5-1	48
38	Larry Holmes	heavyweight	1973-2002	69-6-0	44

Rank	Boxer	Weight divisions	Career	W-L-D	KO's
39	Oscar De La Hoya	jr. lightweight, lightweight, jr. welterweight, welterweight, jr. middleweight, middleweight	1992-	38-5-0	32
40	Evander Holyfield	cruiserweight, heavyweight	1984-	41-8-2	26
41	Ted "Kid" Lewis	featherweight, welterweight, middleweight, lt. heavyweight, heavyweight	1909-1929	173-30-14	71
42	Alexis Arguello	featherweight, jr. lightweight, lightweight, jr. welterweight	1968-1995	80-8-0	64
43	Marco Antonio Barrera	jr. featherweight, featherweight, jr. lightweight	1989-	63-5-0	42
44	Pernell Whitaker	lightweight, jr. welterweight, welterweight	1984-2001	40-4-1	17
45	Carlos Monzon	middleweight	1963-1977	87-3-9	59
46	Roy Jones, Jr.	middleweight, sup. middleweight, lt. heavyweight, heavyweight	1989-	50-4-0	38
47	Bernard Hopkins	middleweight, lt. heavyweight	1988-	47-4-1	32
48	Floyd Mayweather, Jr.	jr. lightweight, lightweight, jr. welterweight, welterweight, jr. middleweight	1996-	38-0-0	24
49	Erik Morales	sup. bantamweight, featherweight, jr. lightweight	1993-	48-5-0	34
50	Mike Tyson	heavyweight	1985-2005	50-6-0	44

Multidivision Boxing Champions

Between 1892, the beginning of the modern era of boxing, and 2009, only twenty boxers won world titles in three or more recognized weight divisions. Almost two-thirds of their titles came after 1980, during a time when the numbers of both weight divisions and title-awarding governing bodies were proliferating. Among these twenty multidivision champions, only Henry Armstrong held titles in three different divisions simultaneously.

Five Divisions
Sugar Ray Leonard: 1979, welterweight; 1981, junior middleweight; 1987, middleweight; 1988, super middleweight; 1988, light heavyweight

Four Divisions
Oscar De La Hoya: 1994, lightweight; 1996, junior welterweight; 1997, welterweight; 2001, junior middleweight

Roberto Durán: 1972, lightweight; 1980, welterweight; 1983, junior middleweight; 1989, middleweight

Thomas Hearns: 1980, welterweight; 1982, junior middleweight; 1987, middleweight; 1987 and 1991, light heavyweight

Pernell Whitaker: 1989, lightweight; 1992, junior welterweight; 1993, welterweight; 1995, junior middleweight

Three Divisions
Alexis Arguello: 1974, featherweight; 1978, junior lightweight; 1981, lightweight

Henry Armstrong: 1937, featherweight; 1938, lightweight; 1938, welterweight

Iran Barkley: 1988, middleweight; 1992, light heavyweight; 1992, super middleweight

Wilfred Benitez: 1976, junior welterweight; 1979, welterweight; 1981, junior middleweight

Tony Canzoneri: 1928, featherweight; 1930, lightweight; 1931 and 1933, junior welterweight

Julio César Chávez: 1984, junior lightweight; 1987, lightweight; 1989, junior welterweight

Jeff Fenech: 1985, bantamweight; 1987, junior featherweight; 1988, featherweight

Bob Fitzsimmons: 1891, middleweight; 1897, heavyweight; 1903, light heavyweight

Wilfredo Gomez: 1977, junior lightweight; 1984, featherweight; 1985, junior featherweight

Emile Griffith: 1961 and 1963, welterweight; 1962, junior middleweight; 1966, middleweight

Roy Jones, Jr.: 1993, middleweight; 1994, super middleweight; 1996, light heavyweight

Mike McCallum: 1984, junior middleweight; 1989, middleweight; 1994, light heavyweight

Terry McGovern: 1899, bantamweight; 1900, featherweight; 1900, lightweight

Barney Ross: 1933, lightweight; 1933, junior welterweight; 1934 and 1935, welterweight

Wilfredo Vazquez: 1987, bantamweight; 1992, junior featherweight; 1996, featherweight

All-Time Great Soccer Players

International Football Hall of Champions

Despite the international popularity of soccer, the game has yet to establish a permanent hall of fame. In 1998, the Fédération Internationale de Football Association (FIFA), soccer's international governing body, launched an ambitious project to be called the International Football Hall of Champions. After inducting two groups of players, the hall suspended inductions. These fourteen players, listed with their countries and dates of induction, are the only members enshrined in the hall.

Franz Beckenbauer, Germany (1998)
Sir Bobby Charlton, England (1998)
Johan Cruyff, Netherlands (1998)
Alfredo Di Stéfano, Argentina/Colombia/Spain (1998)
Eusébio, Mozambique/Portugal (1998)
Just Fontaine, Morocco/France (1999)
Garrincha, Brazil (1999)
Sir Stanley Matthews, England (1998)
Bobby Moore, England (1999)
Gerd Müller, Germany (1999)
Pelé, Brazil (1998)
Michel Platini, France (1998)
Ferenc Puskás, Hungary (1998)
Lev Yashin, Russia/Soviet Union (1998)

The FIFA 100

To celebrate its approaching centennial in 2004, the governing body of international soccer, the Fédération Internationale de Football Association (FIFA), asked the legendary Brazilian soccer star Pelé to create a list of the fifty greatest active players and the fifty greatest retired soccer players who were still living. Although the unranked list that Pelé created contained names of 125 professional players, seventy-seven of whom were retired and forty-eight of whom were then active, the list is nevertheless known as the "FIFA 100" because it commemorates FIFA's one-hundredth anniversary.

Only two players on Pelé's list are women—forward Mia Hamm and midfielder Michelle Akers, both of whom are also the only Americans on the list. Players are listed here by their primary positions. Names of those who were retired in 2004 are asterisked (*).

Forwards
Roberto Baggio, Italy
Marco van Basten,* Netherlands
Gabriel Batistuta, Argentina
Dennis Bergkamp, Netherlands
Giampiero Boniperti,* Italy
Emilio Butragueño,* Spain
Eric Cantona,* France
Hernan Crespo, Argentina
Johan Cruijff,* Netherlands
Teófilo Cubillas,* Peru
Kenny Dalglish,* Scotland
El Hadji Diouf, Senegal
Eusébio,* Portugal
Just Fontaine,* France
Enzo Francescoli,* Uruguay
Mia Hamm,* United States
Thierry Henry, France
Kevin Keegan,* England
Mario Kempes,* Argentina
Jürgen Klinsmann,* Germany
Patrick Kluivert, Netherlands
Brian Laudrup,* Denmark
Gary Lineker,* England
Diego Maradona,* Argentina
Roger Milla,* Cameroon
Gerd Müller,* Germany
Ruud van Nistelrooy, Netherlands
Michael Owen, England
Jean-Pierre Papin,* France
Abedi Pele,* Ghana
Pelé,* Brazil
Alessandro Del Piero, Italy
Robert Pires, France
Ferenc Puskás,* Hungary
Raúl, Spain
Rob Rensenbrink,* Netherlands
Romário, Brazil
Romerito,* Paraguay
Ronaldo, Brazil
Paolo Rossi,* Italy
Karl-Heinz Rummenigge,* Germany
Hugo Sánchez,* Mexico
Javier Saviola, Argentina
Uwe Seeler,* Germany
Alan Shearer, England
Andriy Shevchenko, Ukraine
Omar Sivori,* Argentina
Alfredo di Stéfano,* Argentina
Hristo Stoichkov,* Bulgaria
Davor Šuker,* Croatia
Francesco Totti, Italy
David Trezeguet, France
Christian Vieri, Italy
George Weah,* Liberia
Iván Zamorano,* Chile

Midfielders
Michelle Akers,* United States
Michael Ballack, Germany
David Beckham, England
Emre Belözoğlu, Turkey
George Best,* Northern Ireland
Zbigniew Boniek,* Poland
Paul Breitner,* Germany
Jan Ceulemans,* Belgium
Bobby Charlton,* England
Rui Costa, Portugal
Edgar Davids, Netherlands
Didier Deschamps,* France
Franky van der Elst,* Belgium
Luis Enrique, Spain
Falcão,* Brazil
Luís Figo, Portugal
Ruud Gullit,* Netherlands
Gheorghe Hagi,* Romania
Júnior,* Brazil
Roy Keane, Ireland
René van de Kerkhof,* Netherlands
Willy van de Kerkhof,* Netherlands
Raymond Kopa,* France
Michael Laudrup,* Denmark
Josef Masopust,* Czech Republic
Lothar Matthäus,* Germany
Hidetoshi Nakata, Japan
Pavel Nedvěd, Czech Republic
Johan Neeskens,* Netherlands
Jay-Jay Okocha, Nigeria
Michel Platini,* France
Frank Rijkaard,* Netherlands
Rivaldo, Brazil
Rivelino,* Brazil
Gianni Rivera,* Italy
Ronaldinho, Brazil (also forward)
Clarence Seedorf, Netherlands
Sócrates,* Brazil
Carlos Valderrama,* Colombia

Juan Sebastián Verón, Argentina
Patrick Vieira, France
Zico,* Brazil (also forward)
Zinedine Zidane, France

Defenders
Carlos Alberto,* Brazil
Franco Baresi,* Italy
Franz Beckenbauer,* Germany (sweeper)
Giuseppe Bergomi,* Italy
Hong Myung-Bo, Korea Republic
Cafu, Brazil
Roberto Carlos, Brazil
Marcel Desailly, France
Giacinto Facchetti,* Italy
Elías Figueroa,* Chile
Paolo Maldini, Italy
Alessandro Nesta, Italy
Daniel Passarella,* Argentina
Djalma Santos,* Brazil
Nílton Santos,* Brazil
Lilian Thuram, France
Marius Trésor,* France
Javier Zanetti, Argentina (also midfielder)

Goalkeepers
Gordon Banks,* England
Gianluigi Buffon, Italy
Rinat Dasayev,* Russia
Oliver Kahn, Germany
Sepp Maier,* Germany
Jean-Marie Pfaff,* Belgium
Rüştü Reçber, Turkey
Peter Schmeichel,* Denmark
Dino Zoff,* Italy

World Soccer Magazine *100 Greatest Twentieth Century Players*

In 1999, the English publication *World Soccer Magazine* published this list of the one hundred greatest soccer players of the twentieth century, as chosen in a reader poll.

1. Pelé, Brazil
2. Diego Maradona, Argentina
3. Johan Cruyff, Netherlands
4. Franz Beckenbauer, Germany
5. Michel Platini, France
6. Alfredo di Stéfano, Argentina
7. Ferenc Puskás, Hungary
8. George Best, Northern Ireland
9. Marco van Basten, Netherlands
10. Eusébio, Portugal
11. Lev Yashin, Russia
12. Bobby Charlton, England
13. Ronaldo, Brazil
14. Bobby Moore, England
15. Gerd Müller, Germany
16. Roberto Baggio, Italy
17. Stanley Matthews, England
18. Zico, Brazil
19. Franco Baresi, Italy
20. Garrincha, Brazil
21. Paolo Maldini, Italy
22. Kenny Dalglish, Scotland
23. Gabriel Batistuta, Argentina
24. Eric Cantona, France
25. Gheorghe Hagi, Romania
26. Romário, Brazil
27. Jairzinho, Brazil
28. Zinedine Zidane, France
29. Ruud Gullit, Netherlands
30. John Charles, Wales
31. Lothar Matthäus, Germany
32. Gordon Banks, England
33. Jürgen Klinsmann, Germany
34. Dennis Bergkamp, Netherlands
35. Karl-Heinz Rummenigge, Germany
36. Gary Lineker, England
37. Giuseppe Meazza, Italy
38. Rivelino, Brazil
39. Didi, Brazil
40. Ian Rush, Wales
41. Peter Schmeichel, Denmark
42. Paolo Rossi, Italy
43. George Weah, Liberia
44. Michael Owen, England
45. Just Fontaine, France
46. Duncan Edwards, England
47. Dino Zoff, Italy
48. Hristo Stoichkov, Bulgaria
49. David Beckham, England
50. Tom Finney, England
51. Rivaldo, Brazil
52. Claudio Caniggia, Argentina
53. Tostão, Brazil
54. Frank Rijkaard, Netherlands
55. José Luis Chilavert, Paraguay
56. Kevin Keegan, England
57. Paul Gascoigne, England
58. Roger Milla, Cameroon
59. Michael Laudrup, Denmark
60. Andriy Shevchenko, Ukraine
61. David Ginola, France
62. Glenn Hoddle, England
63. Sócrates, Brazil
64. Roberto Carlos, Brazil
65. Alan Shearer, England
66. Daniel Passarella, Argentina
67. Davor Šuker, Croatia
68. Dixie Dean, England
69. Sándor Kocsis, Hungary
70. Juan Alberto Schiaffino, Uruguay
71. Christian Vieri, Italy
72. Mario Kempes, Argentina
73. Johan Neeskens, Netherlands
74. Luigi Riva, Italy
75. José Nasazzi, Uruguay
76. Günter Netzer, Germany
77. Alessandro Del Piero, Italy
78. Carlos Valderrama, Colombia
79. Ricardo Zamora, Spain
80. Enzo Francescoli, Uruguay

81. Edgar Davids, Netherlands
82. Francisco Gento, Spain
83. Jim Baxter, Scotland
84. Falcão, Brazil
85. Ryan Giggs, Wales
86. Sepp Maier, Germany
87. Zbigniew Boniek, Poland
88. Pat Jennings, Northern Ireland
89. György Sárosi, Hungary
90. Giacinto Facchetti, Italy
91. Alan Hansen, Scotland
92. Raymond Kopa, France
93. Bryan Robson, England
94. Matthias Sammer, Germany
95. Ladislav Kubala, Hungary
96. Neville Southall, Wales
97. Gérson, Brazil
98. Paulo Futre, Portugal
99. Preben Elkjær, Denmark
100. Bebeto, Brazil

FIFA World Players of the Year

In 1991, the Fédération Internationale de Football Association (FIFA) began honoring the top male soccer players in the world by having the coaches and captains of international teams elect the best player of each year. In 2001, a second annual award was begun for women players. Because of the voting system, the men's awards have tended heavily to favor players in the European leagues.

Year	Player	Nationality	Club
Men			
1991	Lothar Matthäus	Germany	Internazionale
1992	Marco van Basten	Netherlands	Milan
1993	Roberto Baggio	Italy	Juventus
1994	Romário	Brazil	Barcelona
1995	George Weah	Liberia	Milan
1996	Ronaldo	Brazil	Barcelona
1997	Ronaldo	Brazil	Internazionale
1998	Zinedine Zidane	France	Juventus
1999	Rivaldo	Brazil	Barcelona
2000	Zinedine Zidane	France	Juventus
2001	Luís Figo	Portugal	Real Madrid
2002	Ronaldo	Brazil	Real Madrid
2003	Zinedine Zidane	France	Real Madrid
2004	Ronaldinho	Brazil	Barcelona
2005	Ronaldinho	Brazil	Barcelona
2006	Fabio Cannavaro	Italy	Real Madrid
2007	Kaká	Brazil	Milan
2008	Cristiano Ronaldo	Portugal	Manchester United
Women			
2001	Mia Hamm	United States	Washington Freedom
2002	Mia Hamm	United States	Washington Freedom
2003	Birgit Prinz	Germany	FFC Frankfurt
2004	Birgit Prinz	Germany	FFC Frankfurt
2005	Birgit Prinz	Germany	FFC Frankfurt
2006	Marta	Brazil	Umeå IK
2007	Marta	Brazil	Umeå IK
2008	Marta	Brazil	Umeå IK

World Soccer Magazine *World Players of the Year*

Issued in England, *World Soccer Magazine* is a leading publication covering international soccer. Since 1982, its editors have annually named one world player of the year.

Year	Player	Nationality	Club
1982	Paolo Rossi	Italy	Juventus
1983	Zico	Brazil	Udinese
1984	Michel Platini	France	Juventus
1985	Michel Platini	France	Juventus
1986	Diego Maradona	Argentina	Napoli
1987	Ruud Gullit	Netherlands	A.C. Milan
1988	Marco van Basten	Netherlands	A.C. Milan
1989	Ruud Gullit	Netherlands	A.C. Milan
1990	Lothar Matthäus	Germany	Internazionale
1991	Jean-Pierre Papin	France	Olympique Marseille
1992	Marco van Basten	Netherlands	A.C. Milan
1993	Roberto Baggio	Italy	Juventus
1994	Paolo Maldini	Italy	A.C. Milan
1995	Gianluca Vialli	Italy	Juventus
1996	Ronaldo	Brazil	FC Barcelona
1997	Ronaldo	Brazil	FC Barcelona and Internazionale
1998	Zinedine Zidane	France	Juventus
1999	Rivaldo	Brazil	FC Barcelona
2000	Luís Figo	Portugal	FC Barcelona and Real Madrid
2001	Michael Owen	England	Liverpool FC
2002	Ronaldo	Brazil	Internazionale and Real Madrid
2003	Pavel Nedvcd	Czech Republic	Juventus
2004	Ronaldinho	Brazil	FC Barcelona
2005	Ronaldinho	Brazil	FC Barcelona
2006	Fabio Cannavaro	Italy	Juventus and Real Madrid
2007	Kaká	Brazil	A.C. Milan
2008	Cristiano Ronaldo	Portugal	Manchester United

Indexes

Name Index

Adu, Freddy, 155
Akers, Michelle, 157
Ali, Laila, 3
Ali, Muhammad, 6
Arguello, Alexis, 10
Armstrong, Henry, 13

Baer, Max, 16
Baggio, Roberto, 160
Ball, Alan, 162
Banks, Gordon, 165
Beckenbauer, Franz, 167
Beckham, David, 170
Best, George, 173
Blanchflower, Danny, 175
Bowe, Riddick, 19
Bremner, Billy, 178

Cannavaro, Fabio, 180
Cantona, Eric, 182
Carlos, Roberto, 184
Charlton, Bobby, 186
Charlton, Jack, 189
Chastain, Brandi, 191
Chávez, Julio César, 22
Conn, Billy, 26
Cruyff, Johan, 194

De La Hoya, Oscar, 29
Dempsey, Jack, 33
Donovan, Landon, 197
Durán, Roberto, 36

Eagan, Eddie, 40
Eusébio, 199

Foreman, George, 42
Foster, Bob, 45
Foudy, Julie, 201
Frazier, Joe, 48

Garrincha, 203
Gerrard, Steven, 205
Giles, Johnny, 208
Graziano, Rocky, 51

Hagler, Marvin, 53
Hamm, Mia, 210
Hearns, Thomas, 56
Heinrichs, April, 213
Henry, Thierry, 215
Holmes, Larry, 59
Holyfield, Evander, 62
Hopkins, Bernard, 66
Hurst, Geoff, 217

Jennings, Pat, 219
Johnson, Jack, 69
Jones, Cobi, 221
Jones, Roy, Jr., 72

Keegan, Kevin, 224
Ketchel, Stanley, 75
Klitschko, Vitali, 78
Klitschko, Vladimir, 78

Lalas, Alexi, 227
LaMotta, Jake, 81
Langford, Sam, 84
Law, Denis, 229
Leonard, Benny, 86
Leonard, Sugar Ray, 88
Lewis, Lennox, 91
Lilly, Kristine, 231
Lineker, Gary, 234
Liston, Sonny, 94
Louis, Joe, 96

Maradona, Diego, 237
Marciano, Rocky, 99
Marta, 240
Martin, Christy, 102
Matthews, Stanley, 242
Mayweather, Floyd, Jr., 105
Moore, Archie, 108
Moore, Bobby, 244
Mosley, Shane, 111
Müller, Gerd, 247

Owen, Michael, 249

Pacquiao, Manny, 114
Papp, László, 117
Parlow, Cindy, 252
Patterson, Floyd, 119
Pelé, 254
Pep, Willie, 122
Platini, Michel, 257
Puskás, Ferenc, 260

Ramos, Tab, 262
Ramsey, Alf, 265
Rivaldo, 268
Robinson, Sugar Ray, 124
Romário, 271
Ronaldinho, 273
Ronaldo, 275
Rote, Kyle, Jr., 278
Rummenigge, Karl-Heinz, 280

Saddler, Sandy, 127
Sánchez, Hugo, 282
Savón, Félix, 129
Schmeling, Max, 132
Scurry, Briana, 285
Shavers, Earnie, 135
Shilton, Peter, 288
Sissi, 290
Stefano, Alfredo di, 293
Stevenson, Teófilo, 137
Sun Wen, 295

Tiger, Dick, 140
Trinidad, Félix, 143
Tunney, Gene, 146
Tyson, Mike, 149

Van Basten, Marco, 297

Wambach, Abby, 299
Wright, Billy, 301
Wynalda, Eric, 303

Yashin, Lev, 305

Zidane, Zinedine, 307
Zungul, Steve, 310

Country Index

ARGENTINA
   Diego Maradona, 237
   Alfredo di Stefano, 293

BRAZIL
   Roberto Carlos, 184
   Garrincha, 203
   Marta, 240
   Pelé, 254
   Rivaldo, 268
   Romário, 271
   Ronaldinho, 273
   Ronaldo, 275
   Sissi, 290

CANADA
   Lennox Lewis, 91

CHINA
   Sun Wen, 295

CROATIA
   Steve Zungul, 310

CUBA
   Félix Savón, 129
   Teófilo Stevenson, 137

ENGLAND
   Alan Ball, 162
   Gordon Banks, 165
   David Beckham, 170
   Bobby Charlton, 186
   Jack Charlton, 189
   Steven Gerrard, 205
   Geoff Hurst, 217
   Kevin Keegan, 224
   Lennox Lewis, 91
   Gary Lineker, 234
   Stanley Matthews, 242
   Bobby Moore, 244
   Michael Owen, 249
   Alf Ramsey, 265
   Peter Shilton, 288
   Billy Wright, 301

FRANCE
   Eric Cantona, 182
   Thierry Henry, 215
   Michel Platini, 257
   Zinedine Zidane, 307

GERMANY
   Franz Beckenbauer, 167
   Gerd Müller, 247
   Karl-Heinz Rummenigge, 280
   Max Schmeling, 132

GHANA
   Freddy Adu, 155

HUNGARY
   László Papp, 117
   Ferenc Puskás, 260

IRELAND
   Johnny Giles, 208

ITALY
   Roberto Baggio, 160
   Fabio Cannavaro, 180

KYRGYZSTAN
   Vitali Klitschko, 78
   Vladimir Klitschko, 78

MEXICO
   Julio César Chávez, 22
   Hugo Sánchez, 282

MOZAMBIQUE
   Eusébio, 199

NETHERLANDS
   Johan Cruyff, 194
   Marco van Basten, 297

NICARAGUA
   Alexis Arguello, 10

NIGERIA
   Dick Tiger, 140

NORTHERN IRELAND
   George Best, 173
   Danny Blanchflower, 175
   Pat Jennings, 219

PANAMA
   Roberto Durán, 36

PHILIPPINES
   Manny Pacquiao, 114

PORTUGAL
   Eusébio, 199

PUERTO RICO
   Félix Trinidad, 143

SCOTLAND
   Billy Bremner, 178
   Denis Law, 229

SOVIET UNION
   Lev Yashin, 305

UNITED STATES
   Freddy Adu, 155
   Michelle Akers, 157
   Laila Ali, 3
   Muhammad Ali, 6
   Alexis Arguello, 10
   Henry Armstrong, 13
   Max Baer, 16
   Riddick Bowe, 19
   Brandi Chastain, 191
   Billy Conn, 26
   Oscar De La Hoya, 29
   Jack Dempsey, 33
   Landon Donovan, 197
   Eddie Eagan, 40
   George Foreman, 42
   Bob Foster, 45
   Julie Foudy, 201

Joe Frazier, 48
Rocky Graziano, 51
Marvin Hagler, 53
Mia Hamm, 210
Thomas Hearns, 56
April Heinrichs, 213
Larry Holmes, 59
Evander Holyfield, 62
Bernard Hopkins, 66
Jack Johnson, 69
Cobi Jones, 221
Roy Jones, Jr., 72
Stanley Ketchel, 75
Alexi Lalas, 227
Jake LaMotta, 81
Sam Langford, 84
Benny Leonard, 86
Sugar Ray Leonard, 88
Kristine Lilly, 231
Sonny Liston, 94
Joe Louis, 96
Rocky Marciano, 99
Christy Martin, 102
Floyd Mayweather, Jr., 105
Archie Moore, 108
Shane Mosley, 111
Cindy Parlow, 252
Floyd Patterson, 119
Willie Pep, 122
Sugar Ray Robinson, 124
Kyle Rote, Jr., 278
Sandy Saddler, 127
Briana Scurry, 285
Earnie Shavers, 135
Gene Tunney, 146
Mike Tyson, 149
Abby Wambach, 299
Eric Wynalda, 303

URUGUAY
    Tab Ramos, 262

YUGOSLAVIA
    Steve Zungul, 310

Boxers by Weight Divisions

FEATHERWEIGHTS
- Alexis Arguello, 10
- Henry Armstrong, 13
- Manny Pacquiao, 114
- Willie Pep, 122
- Sugar Ray Robinson, 124
- Sandy Saddler, 127

FLYWEIGHTS
- Manny Pacquiao, 114

HEAVYWEIGHTS
- Muhammad Ali, 6
- Max Baer, 16
- Riddick Bowe, 19
- Billy Conn, 26
- Jack Dempsey, 33
- Eddie Eagan, 40
- George Foreman, 42
- Bob Foster, 45
- Joe Frazier, 48
- Larry Holmes, 59
- Evander Holyfield, 62
- Jack Johnson, 69
- Roy Jones, Jr., 72
- Vitali Klitschko, 78
- Vladimir Klitschko, 78
- Sam Langford, 84
- Lennox Lewis, 91
- Sonny Liston, 94
- Joe Louis, 96
- Rocky Marciano, 99
- Floyd Patterson, 119
- Félix Savón, 129
- Max Schmeling, 132
- Earnie Shavers, 135
- Teófilo Stevenson, 137
- Gene Tunney, 146
- Mike Tyson, 149

JUNIOR LIGHTWEIGHTS
- Alexis Arguello, 10
- Oscar De La Hoya, 29
- Floyd Mayweather, Jr., 105

JUNIOR MIDDLEWEIGHTS
- Oscar De La Hoya, 29
- Floyd Mayweather, Jr., 105

JUNIOR WELTERWEIGHTS
- Alexis Arguello, 10
- Julio César Chávez, 22
- Oscar De La Hoya, 29

LIGHT HEAVYWEIGHTS
- Laila Ali, 3
- Muhammad Ali, 6
- Billy Conn, 26
- Eddie Eagan, 40
- Bob Foster, 45
- Thomas Hearns, 56
- Evander Holyfield, 62
- Bernard Hopkins, 66
- Roy Jones, Jr., 72
- Jake LaMotta, 81
- Sugar Ray Leonard, 88
- Archie Moore, 108
- Floyd Patterson, 119
- Sugar Ray Robinson, 124
- Max Schmeling, 132
- Dick Tiger, 140
- Gene Tunney, 146

LIGHT MIDDLEWEIGHTS
- Roy Jones, Jr., 72
- László Papp, 117

LIGHT WELTERWEIGHTS
- Floyd Mayweather, Jr., 105

LIGHTWEIGHTS
- Alexis Arguello, 10
- Henry Armstrong, 13
- Julio César Chávez, 22
- Billy Conn, 26
- Oscar De La Hoya, 29
- Roberto Durán, 36
- Benny Leonard, 86
- Christy Martin, 102
- Floyd Mayweather, Jr., 105

Shane Mosley, 111
Manny Pacquiao, 114
Sugar Ray Robinson, 124

MIDDLEWEIGHTS
- Laila Ali, 3
- Billy Conn, 26
- Oscar De La Hoya, 29
- Eddie Eagan, 40
- Rocky Graziano, 51
- Marvin Hagler, 53
- Thomas Hearns, 56
- Bernard Hopkins, 66
- Roy Jones, Jr., 72
- Stanley Ketchel, 75
- Jake LaMotta, 81
- Sugar Ray Leonard, 88
- Shane Mosley, 111
- László Papp, 117
- Floyd Patterson, 119
- Sugar Ray Robinson, 124
- Dick Tiger, 140
- Félix Trinidad, 143

SUPER BANTAMWEIGHTS
- Manny Pacquiao, 114

SUPER FEATHERWEIGHTS
- Julio César Chávez, 22
- Manny Pacquiao, 114

SUPER HEAVYWEIGHTS
- Teófilo Stevenson, 137

SUPER LIGHTWEIGHTS
- Julio César Chávez, 22

SUPER MIDDLEWEIGHTS
- Laila Ali, 3
- Roberto Durán, 36
- Thomas Hearns, 56
- Roy Jones, Jr., 72
- Sugar Ray Leonard, 88

WELTERWEIGHTS
    Henry Armstrong, 13
    Julio César Chávez, 22
    Billy Conn, 26
    Oscar De La Hoya, 29
    Roberto Durán, 36
    Rocky Graziano, 51
    Thomas Hearns, 56
    Sugar Ray Leonard, 88
    Floyd Mayweather, Jr., 105
    Shane Mosley, 111
    Sugar Ray Robinson, 124
    Félix Trinidad, 143

Soccer Position Index

DEFENDERS
- Franz Beckenbauer, 167
- Fabio Cannavaro, 180
- Roberto Carlos, 184
- Jack Charlton, 189
- Brandi Chastain, 191
- Alexi Lalas, 227
- Bobby Moore, 244
- Alf Ramsey, 265

FORWARDS
- Freddy Adu, 155
- Michelle Akers, 157
- Roberto Baggio, 160
- George Best, 173
- Eric Cantona, 182
- Bobby Charlton, 186
- Johan Cruyff, 194
- Landon Donovan, 197
- Eusébio, 199
- Garrincha, 203
- Mia Hamm, 210
- Thierry Henry, 215
- Geoff Hurst, 217
- Kevin Keegan, 224
- Denis Law, 229
- Kristine Lilly, 231
- Gary Lineker, 234
- Diego Maradona, 237
- Marta, 240
- Gerd Müller, 247
- Michael Owen, 249
- Cindy Parlow, 252
- Pelé, 254
- Ferenc Puskás, 260
- Romário, 271
- Ronaldinho, 273
- Ronaldo, 275
- Kyle Rote, Jr., 278
- Karl-Heinz Rummenigge, 280
- Hugo Sánchez, 282
- Alfredo di Stefano, 293
- Sun Wen, 295
- Marco van Basten, 297
- Abby Wambach, 299
- Eric Wynalda, 303
- Steve Zungul, 310

GOALKEEPERS
- Gordon Banks, 165
- Pat Jennings, 219
- Briana Scurry, 285
- Peter Shilton, 288
- Lev Yashin, 305

MIDFIELDERS
- Freddy Adu, 155
- Michelle Akers, 157
- Alan Ball, 162
- David Beckham, 170
- Danny Blanchflower, 175
- Billy Bremner, 178
- Bobby Charlton, 186
- Brandi Chastain, 191
- Johan Cruyff, 194
- Julie Foudy, 201
- Steven Gerrard, 205
- Johnny Giles, 208
- Cobi Jones, 221
- Kristine Lilly, 231
- Diego Maradona, 237
- Stanley Matthews, 242
- Michel Platini, 257
- Tab Ramos, 262
- Rivaldo, 268
- Ronaldinho, 273
- Sissi, 290
- Billy Wright, 301
- Zinedine Zidane, 307